Contents

PART III
Policy and administration   303

Figures

Tables

Boxes

Contributors

John Coakley is Associate Professor of Politics at University College Dublin and Director of the Institute for British–Irish Studies. He has edited *The Social Origins of Nationalist Movements* (1992); *Changing Shades of Orange and Green: Redefining the Union and the Nation in Contemporary Ireland* (2002); *The Territorial Management of Ethnic Conflict* (2nd edn, 2003); and *From Political Violence to Negotiated Settlement: The Winding Path to Peace in Twentieth-century Ireland* (with Maurice Bric, 2004).

Neil Collins is Professor and Head of the Department of Government at University College Cork. His current research interests are in political corruption, clientelism and e-politics. He recently co-edited, with Terry Cradden, *Political Issues in Ireland Today* (2004).

Eileen Connolly is Lecturer in Politics in the School of Law and Government in Dublin City University. Her recent publications include articles in the *European Journal of Women's Studies* and in *Irish Studies in International Affairs*. Her research interests include gender and the state and gender in international relations and ideational theory.

Robert Elgie is Paddy Moriarty Professor of Government and International Studies in the School of Law and Government at Dublin City University. Among his publications are *Semi-Presidentialism in Europe* (1999) and *Divided Government in Comparative Perspective* (2001), both as editor. He is currently working on a research project on the parliamentary activity of the head of government in Ireland, 1922–2003. The project, conducted in collaboration with John Stapleton at the University of Limerick, is funded by the Irish Research Council for the Humanities and Social Sciences.

Peter Fitzgerald is currently completing a PhD on political leadership in Dublin City University. His research interests include political parties, political leadership and political marketing. His most recent publication is a study of the 2002 Irish Labour Party leadership election for the *British Elections and Parties Review*.

Michael Gallagher is Associate Professor in the Department of Political Science, Trinity College, University of Dublin. His research interests include electoral systems and political parties. He is co-author of *Representative Government in Modern Europe* (3rd edn, 2001) and *Days of Blue Loyalty: The Politics of Membership of the Fine Gael Party* (2002), and co-editor of *How Ireland Voted 2002* (2003), *The Referendum Experience in Europe* (1996) and *Candidate Selection in Comparative Perspective* (1988).

Yvonne Galligan is a Reader in Politics and Director of the Centre for Advancement of Women in Politics at Queen's University Belfast. A Trinity College PhD (1995), her primary research interests are in comparative gender politics, comparative public policy and the Irish political system. She has written widely in these areas and her publications include *The Development of Mechanisms to Monitor Gender Equality in Ireland* (2001), *Contesting Politics: Women in Ireland, North and South* (co-editor, 1999) and *Women and Politics in Contemporary Ireland* (1998).

Tom Garvin is Professor and Head of the Department of Politics at University College Dublin. He has published extensively on Irish politics and is author of *The Evolution of Irish Nationalist Politics* (1981), *Nationalist Revolutionaries in Ireland 1858–1928* (1987), *1922: The Birth of Irish Democracy* (1996), *Mythical Thinking in Political Life* (2001) and *Preventing the Future: Politics, Education and Development in Ireland, 1937–1967* (2004).

Lee Komito is a Senior Lecturer in Library and Information Studies at University College Dublin. He is author of *The Information Revolution and Ireland: Prospects and Challenges*, as well as articles on clientelism, social and political impact of new information technologies and ethnographic studies of information systems and work practices. He is currently researching governance, new technologies, political participation and communities.

Brigid Laffan is Jean Monnet Professor of European Politics, University College Dublin and Research Director, Dublin European Institute, University College Dublin. She is academic co-ordinator of an EU-funded Fifth Framework Programme entitled 'Organising for Enlargement'. She has published widely on European integration and on Ireland's relations with the EU in the *Journal of Common Market Studies* and in the *European Journal of Public Policy*. She co-authored, with Rory O'Donnell and Michael Smith, *Europe's Experimental Union: Re-thinking Integration* (1999).

Michael Laver is Professor of Political Science at Trinity College, University of Dublin. He is author of a range of books and articles on the politics of party competition in different contexts, including *Playing Politics: The Nightmare Continues* (1997), *Private Desires, Political Action* (1997) and *Representative Government in Modern Europe* (2001), and he has edited *Estimating the Policy Positions of Political Actors* (2001).

Peter Mair is Professor of Comparative Politics at Leiden University. He has published extensively in the area of comparative politics. He is co-author of *Identity, Competition and Electoral Availability* (1990), which was awarded the Stein Rokkan Prize in Comparative Social Research, and of *Representative Government in Modern Europe* (2001), author of *Party System Change* (1997) and co-editor of *The Enlarged European Union* (2002).

Michael Marsh is Associate Professor of Politics at Trinity College, University of Dublin. He is author of a wide variety of articles on parties and electoral behaviour. He has co-edited *Candidate Selection in Comparative Perspective* (1988), *How Ireland Voted 1997* (1999) and *How Ireland Voted 2002* (2003) and is co-author of *Days of Blue Loyalty* (2002).

Gary Murphy is Senior Lecturer in Government in the School of Law and Government at Dublin City University. He has published widely on interest groups and their relationship with the state in a number of journals and texts and is currently engaged in research on the relationship between political elites and the citizenry in terms of democratic account-ability. He is the author of *Economic Realignment and the Politics of EEC Entry in Ireland* (2003) and is currently co-editor of *Irish Political Studies*.

Aodh Quinlivan is Lecturer in Politics in the Department of Government at University College Cork, and he worked earlier in Cork County Council. He is a specialist in local government studies and in reform of the public sector. He has just finished a major review of the Association of Municipal Authorities of Ireland.

Richard Sinnott is Director of the Public Opinion and Political Behaviour Research Programme at the Institute for the Study of Social Change, University College Dublin. His publications include *Irish Voters Decide* (1995), *People and Parliament in the European Union* (co-author, 1998), *Public Opinion and Internationalized Governance* (co-editor, 1995) and articles on Irish and European public opinion and political behaviour. He is co-director (with Michael Marsh) of the 2002 Irish National Election Study.

Ben Tonra is Jean Monnet Professor of European Foreign, Security and Defence Policy at University College Dublin where he is also Senior Lecturer and Academic Director of the Dublin European Institute.

Liam Weeks is a PhD student at the Department of Political Science, Trinity College, University of Dublin. He has published on Irish politics in the journals *Irish Political Studies* and *Representation*, and in the books *How Ireland Voted 2002* (2003) and *Elections in Europe* (forthcoming). He is completing a thesis on the significance of independent politicians in Ireland, and is a recipient of a Government of Ireland Scholarship from the Irish Research Council for the Humanities and Social Sciences.

Foreword

Tom Garvin

Politics in the Republic of Ireland now enters its fourth edition, much revised, expanded and reorganised so as to be a very different book than its first edition, published in 1992. That edition was the creation of the Political Studies Association of Ireland, founded in 1982 as a result of an earlier Dublin-centred 'workshop' initiative in 1976 by a group of youngish academic political scientists from University College Dublin, Trinity College, University of Dublin and Queen's University Belfast. Since the mid-1970s, Irish political science in both Northern Ireland and the Republic of Ireland has developed enormously, and what was the activity of a handful of pioneers led by Basil Chubb, Brian Farrell, Con O'Leary and John Whyte in the 1960s has become the concern of dozens of scholars from all over Ireland and, increasingly, of political scientists and colleagues in cognate disciplines across the English-speaking world, mainland Europe and Japan. Links with allied subjects such as history, sociology, economics and anthropology have become increasingly important.

The book reflects the continuing growth of Irish political science as an academic profession, and can be seen as being driven by the same perceptions as its predecessors: the need for an up-to-date and comprehensive textbook embodying the latest insights and approaches to the study of Irish politics. Greater emphasis is being given to the actual processes of central and local government. The latter area has traditionally been a somewhat murky one, as Irish local government has been something of an academic orphan for some time, due in part to the difficulty in collecting data and also to the apparent weakness of Irish local representative institutions. The growing perceived significance of local government is generated by a greater perception than hitherto of its importance in the planning process and its many opportunities for corruption, features not sufficiently adverted to in earlier writings. Relationships with Northern Ireland, fraught for decades, are in the process of being transformed, as are Dublin–London relationships.

As with the third edition, the fourth edition reflects the increasing liveliness of modern Irish political life. The last decade of the twentieth century was a period of extraordinary political upheaval and cultural transformation. A series of huge scandals in church and state has conclusively shattered the old informal alliance of the two that existed in the Republic since the foundation of independent Ireland in 1922. Growing secularisation has resulted in the fading of clerical authority, much as growing levels of political information have demonstrated that many of our political leaders have feet of clay. The European Union has become a huge factor in Irish political development. The doubling of the Gross National Product per head that has occurred since 1987 has resulted in an inrush of immigrants, mostly younger people of Irish origin or immediate descent, but also significant numbers of Europeans, Americans, Asians and Africans. Religious variety has increased, numbers of Muslims in particular increasing as they have elsewhere in the European Union. Demands for pluralism have been linked with pressure for the establishment of legally enforceable rights for women, Travellers, gay people, single parents, non-marital children and racial and religious minorities. These demands and pressures have met with less resistance than formerly and have scored some signal successes. The old consensual, Catholic, semi-agrarian and monistic white Ireland of a generation ago has almost disappeared.

Economic growth has been associated with a parallel transformation of the younger generation into a highly trained, better educated and independent minded workforce. The end of emigration and the return of many migrants have had a profound, if not precisely measurable, cultural impact as skills and experience acquired elsewhere, whether in the United States, Europe or the Third World, inform Irish workplace practice and Irish political attitudes. Greater cosmopolitanism and better education have brought greater confidence. Simple success also has bred a self-assurance that was very often lacking in earlier generations. The Irish political system, which in part engineered this vast sea change, is now under pressure from that very transformation to reform itself and be capable of governing a twenty-first-century first world country in a rational and enlightened way. As this book shows, its record is a mixed one but a hopeful one. Ireland, and even the Republic of Ireland, cannot be described as an uneventful place any more.

University College Dublin
March 2004

Preface

The first edition of *Politics in the Republic of Ireland* was published in 1992, and since that time the book has been extensively used as a textbook on Irish Politics courses in universities and colleges in Ireland and elsewhere. It is worth quoting from the preface to the first edition to remind new readers of the thinking behind the original venture:

> The aim throughout has been to produce a book that combined real substance and a readable style. It is aimed particularly at undergraduates at third-level institutions, but we hope that it will also meet the needs of the wider public interested in the politics and government of Ireland. In addition, since no country's politics can be understood in isolation, the authors have written their chapters with a comparative (especially a western European) dimension very much in mind. The venerable generalisation that 'Ireland is different', so there is no need to make the effort to compare its politics with those of other countries, is no longer adequate. It is a well-worn observation that Ireland has become a more outward-looking country since the 1950s, and its academic community has not been unaffected by this development. *Politics in the Republic of Ireland* is among the fruits of these broader horizons.

Evidently this formula found favour with readers, so a second edition was produced in 1993, a third followed in 1999, and the appearance of this edition reflects continued demand for a comprehensive textbook on Irish politics.

When a book runs into a fourth edition, it is tempting to reflect that it has proved itself to be a successful product and to conclude that it requires only minor tinkering to retain its position in the market. However, authors and editors have resisted any such temptation, and we have been determined to ensure that the fourth edition of *Politics in the Republic of Ireland* is as fresh as the first edition was in 1992. Multi-edition textbooks run the risk of acquiring a patchwork character, with up-to-date facts and figures slotted somewhat uncomfortably into a framework that was appropriate a decade or two ago when the authors were younger and more enthusiastic. We have been determined not to see *Politics in the Republic of Ireland* suffer this fate of death by a thousand updates, and any reader who chooses to compare the fourth edition with its precursors will immediately notice the extent of the changes. Even if the authors are older than they were in 1992, they have retained their enthusiasm for their subjects.

This edition contains four completely new chapters. Recent developments in electoral law have provided a wealth of fascinating material on the operation of Ireland's political parties, and these are examined extensively in Chapter 6. The establishment of a survey-based Irish election study in 2002 has given us unprecedented insights into the behaviour of Irish voters, a subject that is explored in Chapter 7. The topic of multi-level governance, together with some of the associated implications (such as, perhaps, greater potential for corruption), is tackled in Chapter 14. And, for the first time, *Politics in the Republic of Ireland* explores the Northern Ireland dimension to 'southern' politics, which is analysed in Chapter 15.

Needless to say, each of the remaining chapters has been thoroughly revised, not merely by being updated but, where appropriate, by being re-organised and generally refreshed. A number of new contributors have been recruited as authors or co-authors, and they have been as patient and (ultimately) cooperative as the *in situ* contributors in dealing with the editors' persistent requests for rewriting, amendments, clarifications, reconsiderations and, most painful of all, deletions.

As with previous editions, a number of people have helped by giving their comments on individual chapters or in other ways, and we should like to thank particularly John Garry, Gerard Hogan, Mamiek Marsudi and Krzysztof Trebunia-Tutka, along with many others who in various ways have facilitated the publication of this book. Feedback from student users at a variety of institutions has been helpful in suggesting ideas to strengthen the book. In addition, we are very pleased that Tom Garvin, now the doyen of Irish political science, has agreed to contribute a Foreword. We are also glad that this edition, like its predecessor, is being co-published by Routledge and PSAI Press. The latter is the publishing arm of the Political Studies Association of Ireland, the body that draws together and represents those engaged in the professional study of politics in and of Ireland.

We should also like to thank Routledge's editorial team of Craig Fowlie (and his predecessor Mark Kavanagh), Belinda Dearbergh and Laura Sacha for their expeditious shepherding of the typescript towards publication. Our hope is that this fourth edition of *Politics in the Republic of Ireland* will contribute to a fuller understanding of the endlessly fascinating Irish political process.

John Coakley and Michael Gallagher
Dublin, July 2004

Glossary

Áras an Uachtaráin (*aw*-rus un *ook*-ta-rawn)   Residence of the President

ard-fheis (ord-*esh*)   national convention [of a political party]

Bunreacht na hÉireann (*bun*-rokt ne *hay*run)   constitution of Ireland

Cathaoirleach (ka-*heer*-luck)   chairman [of the Senate]

Ceann Comhairle (kyon *kohr*-le)   speaker or chairperson [of the Dáil]

Clann na Poblachta (clon ne *pub*-lak-ta)   'party of the republic' [party name, 1946–65]

Clann na Talmhan (clon ne *tal*-oon)   'party of the land' [party name, 1939–65]

comhairle ceantair (*koh*-er-le *kyon*-ter)   district council [in Fianna Fáil]

comhairle dáilcheantair (*koh*-er-le *dawl*-kyon-ter)   constituency council [in Fianna Fáil]

cumann (*kum*-man)   branch [of a political party or other organisation]; plural **cumainn**

Cumann na nGaedheal (*kum*-man ne *ngale*)   'party of the Irish' [party name, 1923–33]

Dáil Éireann (dawl *ay*-run)   national assembly of Ireland; plural **Dála**

Éire (*ay*-reh)   Ireland

Fianna Fáil (*fee*-an-a *fawl*)   'soldiers of Ireland' [party name]

Fine Gael (*fin*-a *gale*)   'Irish race' [party name]

Gaeltacht (*gale*-tuckt)   Irish-speaking districts

garda [síochána] (*gawr*-da shee-*kaw*-ne)   [civic] guard, policeman; plural **gardaí**

Oireachtas (*ih*-rock-tus)   parliament

Saorstát Éireann (*sayr*-stawt *ay*-run)   Irish Free State

Seanad Éireann (*sha*-nad *ay*-run)   senate of Ireland

Sinn Féin (shin *fayn*)   'ourselves' [party name]

Tánaiste (*taw*-nish-deh)   deputy prime minister

Taoiseach (*tee*-shuck)   prime minister; plural **Taoisigh**

Teachta Dála (*tak*-tuh *dawl*-uh)   Dáil deputy, TD

Uachtarán (*ook*-ta-rawn)   president

Note

A number of the party names in the Glossary have a range of alternative translations; see John Coakley, 'The significance of names: the evolution of Irish party labels', *Études Irlandaises*, 5, 1980: 171–81. The pronunciation system indicated above is approximate only, and follows in part that in Howard Penniman and Brian Farrell (eds), *Ireland at the Polls: a Study of Four General Elections* (Durham, NC: Duke University Press, 1987): 265–6. Italics indicate stressed syllables.

Acronyms

AIM	Action, Information, Motivation
AMS	additional member system (type of electoral system)
C&AG	Comptroller and Auditor General
CEO	Chief Executive Officer
CRG	Constitution Review Group
DFI	Disability Federation of Ireland
EU	European Union
FF	Fianna Fáil
FG	Fine Gael
IBEC	Irish Business and Employers Confederation
ICTU	Irish Congress of Trade Unions
IFA	Irish Farmers' Association
INOU	Irish National Organisation of the Unemployed
IRA	Irish Republican Army
IRB	Irish Republican Brotherhood
MP	Member of Parliament
MSP	Member of Scottish Parliament
NDP	National Development Plan
NEAP	National Employment Action Plan
NESC	National Economic and Social Council
NSSB	National Social Service Board
NWCI	National Women's Council of Ireland
PCW	Programme for Competitiveness and Work
PDs	Progressive Democrats
PESP	Programme for Economic and Social Progress
PNR	Programme for National Recovery
PPF	Programme for Prosperity and Fairness
PR	proportional representation
RTÉ	Radio Telefís Éireann
SDLP	Social Democratic and Labour Party (Northern Ireland)
SF	Sinn Féin
SMI	Strategic Management Initiative
STV	single transferable vote
TD	Teachta Dála (member of the Dáil)
UN	United Nations

Part I

The context of Irish politics

1   The foundations of statehood

John Coakley

Writing recently about the evolution of Irish democracy over the past two centuries, one observer aptly identified two major landmarks in the country's constitutional development: its incorporation in a union with Great Britain in 1800 and its membership of the European Union in the late twentieth century (Girvin, 2002). These two developments indeed symbolise two important and inter-related features of Ireland's relationship with its neighbours. Pre-independence Ireland was dominated by one of these relationships, which cast a heavy shadow on the post-1922 period; but as the twenty-first century began the second acquired increased prominence.

Our concern in this book is not primarily, however, to explore Ireland's external relationships (though these are analysed in Chapters 15 and 16); rather, we focus on the political evolution of the state itself. As in the case of other states, it is impossible to grasp the contemporary position without an understanding of the past. Although political histories of Ireland often start at 1922 and conventional wisdom stresses the 'new era' that then began, significant elements of continuity underlay the sharp political break that took place at the time that the state was founded. Before looking at the establishment of the state itself and at subsequent developments, then, we must examine the legacy of the old regime.

In the first section of this chapter, we look at institutional developments and political processes of the pre-independence period that were to prove of enduring significance in Irish political life. Many of these are rather different from the political events that were seen as important at the time, and that form the subject matter of conventional historical studies (for more general histories of the period see Lyons, 1973; Foster, 1988; Jackson, 1999; Townshend, 1999). The second section discusses the political background to the establishment of the independent Irish state. We move on in the third section to examine the political themes of the post-independence period, linking them with earlier developments.

The legacy of British rule

The apparatus of the modern state first developed in Ireland under the tutelage of the English monarchy. Prior to this, Gaelic Irish society, though attaining a high degree of cultural, artistic and literary development in the early medieval period, had shown few signs of following the path of contemporary European political development. The Norman invasions that began in 1169 and the establishment of the Lordship of Ireland that followed (with the Norman King of England exercising the functions of Lord of Ireland) marked the beginning of rudimentary statehood. Although Norman or English control was little more than nominal for several centuries, the vigorous Tudor dynasty subjugated the island in the sixteenth century, a process whose beginning was marked by the promotion in 1541 of the Lord of Ireland to the status of King. The Kingdom of Ireland continued thereafter to have its own political institutions, though a much more profound degree of British influence followed the passing of the Act of Union in 1800, which created a new state, the United Kingdom of Great Britain and Ireland (UK). The story of Irish resistance to these processes is well known, and does not require re-telling here. Our focus is instead on the relatively neglected issue of pre-1922 state building.

In looking at the legacy of this system of government to independent Ireland, we may identify three areas in which spillover effects were important. First, at the *constitutional* level, certain roles and offices that had evolved over the centuries provided an important stepping stone for the builders of the new state. Second, at the *administrative* level, the development of a large civil service bequeathed to the new state a body of trained professional staff. Third, at the *political* level, a set of traditions and practices had been established in the decades before 1922 that greatly reduced the learning curve for those involved in the construction of independent Ireland.

The constitution of the old regime

In an era when travel was slow, difficult and dangerous, it was neither sensible nor practical for expanding dynasties to seek to govern all of their territories from a fixed centre or capital. In common with the peripheral areas of other medieval states, then, Norman Ireland acquired a set of political institutions that were gradually to evolve into modern ones. The hub around which political life revolved, at least in theory, was the King's personal representative in Ireland, an officer to whom the term 'Lord Lieutenant' was eventually applied. The Lord Lieutenant was advised on everyday affairs of government by a 'Privy Council' made up of his chief officials, and on longer-term matters by a 'Great Council' or Parliament that met irregularly.

The evolution of the Irish Parliament followed a path similar to that of the English Parliament (see Farrell, 1973; Johnston-Liik, 2002). It first met in

Castledermot, Co. Kildare, in 1264, and for the next four centuries it continued to assemble from time to time in various Irish towns, with Dublin increasingly becoming dominant. By 1692 it had acquired the shape that it was to retain up to 1800, resembling closely its British counterpart. Its House of Commons consisted of 300 members (two each from 32 counties, from 117 cities, towns or boroughs and from Trinity College, Dublin), and its House of Lords of a small but variable number: archbishops and bishops of the established (Protestant) Church of Ireland and lay members of the Irish peerage.

By accepting the Act of Union of 1800, this parliament voted itself out of existence, opting instead for a merged or 'united' parliament for all of Great Britain and Ireland. In the new House of Commons there were to be 100 Irish MPs (about 15 per cent of the total), while the House of Lords would receive 32 additional members: the Irish peerage would elect 28 of its number for life, and four members of the Irish Protestant episcopate would sit in the House of Lords in rotation.

Although the legislative branch of government thus disappeared completely from Ireland, the executive branch did not. Throughout the entire period of the union (1800–1922), the existence of a 'Government of Ireland' was recognised – a critical weakness in the scheme for Irish integration with Britain (Ward, 1994: 30–8). The Lord Lieutenant, as representative of the sovereign, was formal head of this government. This post was always filled by a leading nobleman who, in addition to his governmental functions, was 'the embodiment of the "dignified" aspects of the state, the official leader of Irish social life' (McDowell, 1964: 52). He left the actual day-to-day running of the process of government, however, to his principal assistant, the Chief Secretary. This official had responsibility for the management of Irish affairs in the House of Commons and, although he was not always a member of the cabinet, he was at least a prominent member of the governing party. Over the decades, effective power passed from the Lord Lieutenant to the Chief Secretary, following the pattern of a similar shift in power in Britain from the King to the prime minister. (Significantly, the Lord Lieutenant's official residence, the Viceregal Lodge in the Phoenix Park, has now become the President's residence, Áras an Uachtaráin, while the Chief Secretary's Office in Dublin Castle went on to become the core of the Department of the Taoiseach.)

Even after the union, Ireland remained constitutionally distinct from the rest of the UK. Although all legislation was now enacted through the UK parliament, in many policy areas (including education, agriculture, land reform, policing, health and local government) separate legislation was enacted for the different components of the United Kingdom. For example, the parliament of 1880–5 passed 71 acts whose application was exclusively Irish (out of a total of 422 acts, the rest being 'English', 'Scottish', 'United Kingdom' or other). Electoral reforms illustrate the extent to which Ireland was treated in a distinctive way even in the matter of representation at

Westminster: it was only in 1884 that a uniform electoral law was adopted for all parts of the UK.

The question of electoral reform indeed has a central place in the process of constitutional evolution. It has been assumed since the late nineteenth century that democratic elections have four characteristics, and these are frequently written into modern constitutions: voting is *direct*, the process is *secret*, all votes are of *equal* weight and suffrage is *universal*. Elections to the old Irish House of Commons and to its post-union successor always operated on the basis of direct voting: electors selected their members of parliament without the intervention of any intermediate electoral college, so the first of the four conditions was met.

The second condition was met rather later. Traditionally, voting was open: a public poll was conducted at a central place in the constituency, and voters declared publicly the names of the candidates for whom they wished their votes to be recorded. This obviously permitted intimidation by opinion leaders such as landlords and clergy, but the Ballot Act (1872) abruptly and permanently changed these practices: in future voting was to be carried out by secret ballot, except in the case of illiterates and other incapacitated persons.

Third, in the old Irish House of Commons voters' voices were of unequal weight; large counties (such as Cork) and small boroughs (such as Tulsk, Bannow and Ardfert) were all represented by two MPs each, with complete disregard for their greatly varying populations. This position was rectified in three principal stages. In 1800 the smaller boroughs were abolished; in 1885 all seats were redistributed to conform more closely to the distribution of the population; and in 1922 the new constitution prescribed that the ratio of deputies to population would be the same across the country.

Fourth, although in many countries extension of the right to vote was characterised by a number of major reforms and the proportion enfranchised increased in stages, the process in Ireland was more complex. This may be seen in Box 1.1. The most sweeping early changes were the extension of the right to vote to Catholics (1793) and the abolition of the county 'forty-shilling freehold' (1829), one greatly extending, the other greatly reducing the electorate. The reforms of 1832, 1850 and 1868 (unlike the English reforms of 1832 and 1867) were rather less traumatic. The major reforms were those of 1884, associated with the birth of modern politics in Ireland, 1918, linked with another episode of electoral revolution, and 1923, which completed the process (for an illustration of the impact of these reforms on the proportion of the population entitled to vote, see Figure 1.1 and discussion below).

Emergence of state bureaucracy

Underneath the political superstructure of the Irish government, the modern Irish civil service developed gradually. It consisted of a number of

---

Box 1.1 Extension of voting rights, 1793–1973

Act	*Major effect*
Catholic Relief Act, 1793	Extension of vote to Catholics
Parliamentary Elections (Ireland) Act, 1829	Raising of county qualification from £2 to £10
Representation of the People (Ireland) Act, 1832	Extension of county and borough franchise
Representation of the People (Ireland) Act, 1850	Extension of county franchise
Representation of the People (Ireland) Act, 1868	Extension of borough franchise
Representation of the People Act, 1884	Uniform householder and lodger franchise
Representation of the People Act, 1918	Universal male and limited female suffrage
Electoral Act, 1923	Universal suffrage
Electoral (Amendment) Act, 1973	Reduction of voting age from 21 to 18

---

departments, offices and other bodies employing considerable numbers of officials and established from time to time as the need was seen to arise. Formal control of these bodies was normally collegial rather than individual: they were directed by 'boards' or 'commissions' or groups of 'commissioners', generally overseen by the Chief Secretary. The extent of the Chief Secretary's influence was not uniform; it was decisive in the case of the Local Government Board (founded in 1872), for instance, but indirect in the case of others, such as the Board of National Education (1831). There were 29 of these bodies by 1911, employing a staff of 4,000 (see Box 1.2).

In addition to these 'Irish' departments answerable to the Chief Secretary, a number of departments of the 'Imperial' civil service also had branches in Ireland. These were controlled ultimately by the relevant British cabinet ministers, and in some cases employed very large staffs in Ireland. The pre-union Post Office (1785) was merged with its British counterpart (1831), and underwent rapid expansion in the late nineteenth century. The old Irish revenue boards also survived the union, but were merged with their British counterparts following the Anglo-Irish customs amalgamation of 1823; they also developed considerable staffs (see Meghen, 1962; McDowell 1964). By 1911 these bodies, 11 in all, had some 23,000 employees in Ireland, of whom 20,000 worked in the Post Office.

***Box 1.2* Civil service continuity, 1914–24**

Board/agency in 1914	*Location in 1924 (department)*
United Kingdom government departments in Ireland	
Revenue Commissioners	Department of Finance
Registrar of Friendly Societies	
Ordnance Survey	
Ministry of Transport	Department of Industry and
Board of Trade	Commerce
Post Office	Department of Posts and Telegraphs
Irish government departments	
General Prisons Board (1877)	Department of Justice
Public Record Office (1867)	
Registry of Deeds (1708)	
Commissioners of National Education (1831)	Department of Education
Board of Intermediate Education (1878)	
Local Government Board (1872)	Department of Local
Registrar General's Office (1844)	Government and Public Health
Department of Agriculture and Technical Instruction (1899)	Department of Lands and Agriculture
Land Commission (1881)	
Congested Districts Board (1891)	
Fisheries branches of Department of Agriculture and Congested Districts Board	Department of Fisheries

Note

A considerable number of additional boards and agencies have been omitted from this list. Two new departments, Defence and External Affairs, were created ab initio in 1922. The Attorney General's office was based on the offices of the former Attorney General and Solicitor General of Ireland, and also incorporated other offices. The Department of the President of the Executive Council was in effect based on the office of Chief Secretary of Ireland.

By the beginning of the twentieth century, then, Ireland already had a very sizeable civil service, with more than 27,000 employees spread over 29 Irish and 11 UK departments. In addition, there were large field staffs in certain other areas: two police forces, the Dublin Metropolitan Police (1787) with about 1,200 and the Royal Irish Constabulary (1836) with about 10,700, and the body of national teachers, numbering some 15,600. Together, these amounted in 1911–13 to about 55,000 state employees, not including the large numbers of army and naval personnel stationed in Ireland.

Finally, it is necessary to consider the system of local government. In urban areas this had consisted of 68 cities, towns and boroughs whose local administrations survived the Act of Union, each governed by a council or corporation headed by a mayor, 'sovereign', 'portreeve' or 'provost'. Although some of these bodies were open to limited forms of election, most were not; a report in 1835 showed that most were oligarchic and self-perpetuating, that almost all were exclusively Protestant, and that only one (Tuam) had a Catholic majority. Comprehensive reform took place with the Municipal Corporations (Ireland) Act, 1840, which abolished all of these bodies and replaced those in the ten largest cities by corporations elected on a limited franchise. A second set of urban elective bodies was set up under acts of 1828 and 1854: towns with a certain minimum population were to be allowed to elect Town Commissioners to make provision for lighting of streets, paving and other local infrastructural purposes.

In rural areas the principal authority was the county grand jury, made up of large property owners selected by the county sheriff (an official appointed, in turn, by the Lord Lieutenant) and responsible for most of the activities that we associate with county councils today. As public intervention grew in the nineteenth century, however, most notably in the areas of poor relief and health, responsibilities were delegated to other bodies. In 1838 the country was divided into 130 Poor Law Unions, each governed by a Board of 'Guardians', of whom some were elected and some held office ex officio. The 'union workhouses' through which they administered poor relief continue to form a prominent feature of the local urban landscape (though they have been converted to serve a variety of other uses today); the dispensaries through which they attended to public health survive to the present; and the rating system by which they were funded formed a lasting basis for local taxation, though much of it was dismantled in the 1970s.

The final stage in the modernisation of the local government system came with the Local Government (Ireland) Act, 1898. This drew up the basis of the system of local government that has survived with some changes to the present by transferring the administrative functions of the county grand juries to new, elected county councils (see Chapter 14). It also further democratised the franchise for elections to the Boards of Guardians of Poor Law Unions, and introduced a new, lower tier of local government, consisting of rural district councils (corresponding to the rural portions of poor law unions, except when these crossed county boundaries, in which case the portions of the unions in different counties became separate rural districts) and urban district councils in the larger towns; in the smaller towns, the Town Commissioners continued. The only significant change in this system before independence was the introduction of proportional representation in 1920 (see Roche, 1982).

The birth of modern party politics

Although the impression is sometimes given that modern forms of politics began in Ireland in 1922, or at the earliest with the foundation of Sinn Féin a few years before that, this is misleading. The reality is that modern party politics began in the 1880s, and had earlier roots. The growth of party politics in nineteenth-century Ireland indeed follows closely a pattern of evolution identified elsewhere (Sartori, 1976: 18–24). Three phases in this growth may be identified; the transition between them was marked by significant changes in levels of electoral mobilisation.

In the first phase, political life was dominated by *parliamentary parties*, defined as groups of MPs without any kind of regular electoral organisation to provide support at election time. In so far as parties existed before the 1830s, they fell into this category. These were not parties in any recognisably modern sense; instead, Irish MPs allied themselves after 1800 to one or other of the two great English groupings, the Tories and the Whigs. Already during this period, however, the linkage between the Tory Party and the Protestant establishment was beginning to find expression in geographical terms, as Tories achieved a much stronger position in the north than in the south. This may be seen in Appendix 2a, which summarises the results of the 31 elections that took place under the Act of Union (because of the large number of uncontested elections, we have to rely on distribution of seats rather than of votes for an indication of party strengths). This point emerges even more clearly from Table 1.1, which is based on this appendix: in the ten elections before 1832, Tories already controlled 74 per cent of the seats in the present territory of Northern Ireland, but only 45 per cent of those in the south.

In the second phase we see the appearance of *electoral parties*, consisting not merely of loosely linked sets of MPs but rather of groups standing for some more or less coherent policy positions and supported by constituency organisations that enjoyed a degree of continuity over time (see Hoppen, 1984). This phase began around 1830 and lasted for approximately five decades. It was characterised by the metamorphosis of the Whigs into the Liberal Party, which increasingly became the party of Catholic Ireland, and of the Tories into the Conservative Party, which quickly became the party of Protestants. The members of these parties in parliament were supported by organisations at constituency level. These support groups used such names as 'Independent Clubs' on the Liberal side and 'Constitutional Clubs' on

Table 1.1 Irish parliamentary representation, 1801–1918

Period (*Number of elections*)	*1801–31* *(10)*	*1832–80* *(12)*	*1885–1910* *(8)*	*1918* *(1)*
North				
Tories/Unionists	73.6	78.6	69.5	80.0
Whigs/Liberals	14.1	18.5	2.5	0.0
Nationalists, etc.	–	0.0	28.0	10.0
Others	12.3	2.9	0.0	10.0
(Number)	(220)	(276)	(200)	(30)
South				
Tories/Unionists	44.5	24.4	3.7	4.0
Whigs/Liberals	41.4	39.6	0.0	0.0
Nationalists, etc.	–	35.3	96.3	2.7
Others	14.1	0.7	0.0	93.3
(Number)	(780)	(980)	(624)	(75)
All Ireland				
Tories/Unionists	50.9	36.3	19.7	25.7
Whigs/Liberals	35.4	35.0	0.6	0.0
Nationalists, etc.	–	27.5	79.7	4.8
Others	13.7	1.2	0.0	69.5
(Number)	(1,000)	(1,256)	(824)	(105)

Source: Calculated from Appendix 2a.

Note
Party strengths are indicated as percentages of seats won. Before 1832 party affiliations are approximate only. 'Tories/Unionists' includes Liberal Unionists; 'Nationalists, etc.' includes independent nationalists; in 1918, 'Others' refers to Sinn Féin MPs. The north is defined as the present area of Northern Ireland, the south as the Republic. The number of MPs returned by constituencies in the north was 22, 23 and 25 in the first three periods; in the south it was 78 in the first and third periods and 82 in the second period, except for the last two elections, in 1874 and 1880, when the number was 80.

the Conservative side. From a comparative perspective, this was unusual in two respects. First, constituency organisations developed at a remarkably early stage in the Irish case. Second, the content of the Liberal–Conservative polarisation, with its sectarian overtones, contrasted sharply with the issues at stake behind similarly named instances of polarisation elsewhere in Europe, where constitutional issues (such as conflict between the monarchy and parliament) were to the fore. In particular, the association between Catholicism and liberalism appears anomalous in a European context where liberalism was associated with anticlericalism.

Given the fact that the electorate was restricted to the wealthy (who were disproportionately Protestant), Irish Conservatives, though reduced from their position of overall dominance (especially in the south, where they now controlled only 24 per cent of the seats), enjoyed solid support throughout most of this period. The relationship between the Liberals and the Catholic vote was, however, much less secure, and was open to challenge from parties representing specifically Irish interests. The most significant of these were O'Connell's Repeal Party in the 1830s and 1840s, the Independent Irish Party in the 1850s, the rather amorphous National Association in the 1860s and, most importantly, the Home Rule Party from 1874 onwards.

The third phase was marked by the birth of modern *mass parties*. These took the form of tightly disciplined parliamentary groups resting on the support of a permanent party secretariat and a well-oiled party machine: thousands of members were organised into branches at local level, with provision for constituency conventions to select candidates and for an annual conference to elect an executive and, at least in theory, to determine policy. This development took place first on the Catholic side, with the formation of the Irish National League (1882) as constituency organisation of the Home Rule or Nationalist Party. This was modelled on an earlier agrarian organisation, the Land League (1879); another organisational predecessor, the Home Rule League, founded in 1873, had followed the model of the electoral party. On the Protestant side a similar development took place in 1885 with the formation of the Irish Loyal Patriotic Union (from 1891, the Irish Unionist Alliance) to represent southern Unionists, and a range of similar organisations, eventually brought together under the Ulster Unionist Council in 1905, to represent northern Unionists. These parties were prototypes of the party organisations that appeared after 1922 in the south (see Chapters 5 and 6), and, indeed, the Ulster Unionist Council continues to the present to constitute the organisational apex of the Ulster Unionist Party in Northern Ireland.

The 1885 election marks the birth of modern Irish party politics. It was characterised by a strict polarisation between Protestant and Catholic Ireland, in which the Liberals were completely eliminated, being decisively defeated by the Nationalist Party in competing for Catholic votes. In the territory that was to become the Republic of Ireland, Nationalists won virtually all of the seats. In the north, a geographical balance between Nationalists and Unionists was established that was to persist to 1969, a phenomenon of electoral continuity without parallel in Europe (after 1969, the Nationalists were replaced by the Social Democratic and Labour Party and the Unionists were seriously challenged, most notably by the Democratic Unionist Party).

Nationalist domination of the south lasted for more than 30 years, for most of this period in single-party form (the most important exceptions were the deep divisions within the party in 1890–1900 precipitated by the issue of the leadership of Charles Stewart Parnell and the creation of a small breakaway party, largely confined to Co. Cork, by William O'Brien in 1910). The Irish National League indeed suffered serious consequences from the Parnellite split (the more electorally successful anti-Parnellites setting up their own rival Irish National Federation); but when the two wings of the party reunited in 1900 they adopted a new organisation, the United Irish League,

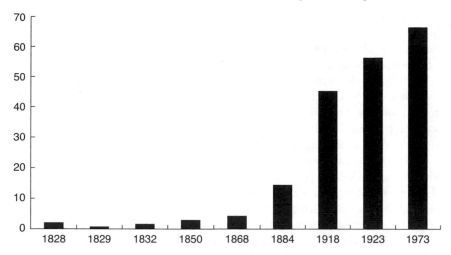

Figure 1.1 Electorate as percentage of population, 1828–1973

Source: Coakley, 1986.

Note: The data refer to all of Ireland up to 1918, but only to the south in 1923 and 1973.

as their constituency body. Nationalist Party dominance in the south was consolidated at local level by the 1898 reforms.

Two important points need to be made about the background to the emerging Irish party system. The first is the relationship between electoral reform and political mobilisation. The appearance of significant new political forces has often been associated with major waves of franchise extension; indeed, it is obvious that new groups that target unenfranchised sections of the population can win their electoral support only if these groups are actually given the vote. Franchise extension alone, however, does not necessarily bring about electoral mobilisation, as the Irish experience vividly illustrates. This may be seen by looking at political mobilisation in the context of changes in the proportion of the population actually entitled to vote, as summarised in Figure 1.1. Thus, the enormous expansion of voting strength that followed from the Catholic Relief Act of 1793 had a negligible political effect; instead, landowners simply had more voters to manage at election time. By contrast, the first appearance of modern electoral parties began in 1830, *after* the huge disenfranchisement of 1829 and before the reform of 1832. Again, the wave of electoral rebellion that began in the late 1870s and that marked the birth of modern mass politics took place a few years *before* the 1884 reform; it was to be seen vividly at the level not only of parliamentary but also of local elections (Feingold, 1975). The major reforms of 1884 and 1918 may, in fact, be seen as permitting the consummation of new voter–party alliances rather than as making the match in the first place. This political mobilisation was not confined to the electoral level;

it extended also to the formation of new organisations with mass membership in the economic, cultural, sporting and other domains, and to the growth of a more radical press (see Legg, 1998).

Second, divisions between the main Irish parties corresponded closely to social divisions. Irish political life was dominated by three principal relationships in the 120 years after the Act of Union came into effect: between Ireland and the United Kingdom, between Catholics and Protestants and between tenants and landlords. By the 1880s the two major parties had adopted fairly unambiguous positions on these issues: the Nationalist Party stood for Home Rule for Ireland, for defence of Catholic rights and for the principle of state intervention to promote the interests of tenant farmers. The Unionist Party adopted a contrary position on each of these issues. The two parties were supported by two clearly defined communities, the line of division coinciding with the religious cleavage. As an instance of early electoral mobilisation behind monolithic ethnic blocs, this development was without parallel in the Europe of the time (see Coakley, 2002, 2004).

The transition to independence

The Irish political agenda of the pre-independence period was dominated by the issue of Ireland's relationship with the United Kingdom, and election results made it clear that most voters endorsed the policy of 'Home Rule' or devolved government for Ireland. It was not, however, the constitutional nationalist movement but rather a more militant alternative that was responsible for the chain of events that led to the establishment of the new state. We must turn now to this more radical tradition and examine the British response to its demands and activities (for overviews of developments in this period, see Augusteijn, 2002; Costello, 2003).

1916 and the republican ideal

For an important section of Irish public opinion, the efforts of the Nationalist Party to win Home Rule for Ireland were not merely futile but rested on a flawed interpretation of the nature of Irish–British relations. This more radical strand shared with mainstream nationalism an interpretation of Irish history that cast the neighbouring island in a negative light: the British presence in Ireland was based on a process of conquest in which foul means had overshadowed fair ones; the lands of Irish Catholics had been confiscated and the Catholic religion had been suppressed; British trade policy had sought to stifle nascent Irish industrialisation in the eighteenth century; the Act of Union had been procured by bribery and corruption; and Britain's indifference to the terrible problems of Irish poverty had been highlighted most vividly in a failure to intervene effectively in the catastrophic famine of 1845–9, in the course of which a million people died and a million emigrated. While there was some substance to these charges, of greater importance than their objective truth or falsity is the fact that they were generally believed: there was a widespread acceptance among Irish Catholics of a version of Irish history that associated British rule with evil, and that largely ignored such material benefits as it had brought. This ideological package was disseminated in the oral tradition and in popular literature and, in a rather bizarre development, even through the national school system (a network of state elementary schools established in 1831) in the last two decades before 1922.

While Irish Catholic opinion in general drew the conclusion from this version of history that some form of self-government for Ireland was a necessary antidote, the more radical strand referred to above went further. Since British rule in Ireland had been achieved by military force, the argument ran, it could only be reversed by the same means: by armed rebellion, not by parliamentary or constitutional means. Furthermore, since Britain's presence in Ireland was seen as entirely illegitimate, the ultimate goal became a complete break and the establishment of a separate Irish republic. This perspective was reinforced by powerful cultural arguments: among other organisations, the Gaelic Athletic Association (1884) and the Gaelic League (1893) emphasised, respectively, the distinctiveness of Ireland's sporting traditions and its language, and sought to cultivate these to combat English influence.

The most obvious representative of political separatism was the Irish Republican Brotherhood (IRB), established in 1858 and committed to setting up an independent republic by force of arms. In this it followed a tradition of revolutionary activism that could be traced back to the Young Ireland movement that had attempted a rebellion in 1848; it also claimed the United Irishmen of the 1790s as its ancestors, even though their movement and their rebellion in 1798 were Protestant-led and were influenced by the values of French radical democracy, not Irish ethnic nationalism. Although the IRB's attempted insurrection in 1867 was a failure, it was not without sympathy in prominent places: many members and supporters of the parliamentary Nationalist Party may well have seen Home Rule as a half-way house to complete separation of Ireland from Great Britain, and MPs with IRB associations were occasionally elected. Nevertheless, extreme nationalist organisations were unable to challenge the electoral machine of the Nationalist Party. This is clear from the experience of Sinn Féin, a radical nationalist group founded in 1905 by a journalist, Arthur Griffith. Its object was to establish a separate Irish state linked to Great Britain only through a shared head of state, the King; but such electoral success as it enjoyed was confined to local level.

A spiral of paramilitary developments began in the years immediately before the First World War. The first stage was the formation in January 1913 of the Ulster Volunteers, organised by the political leaders of Ulster unionism and committed to opposing Home Rule for Ireland. In reaction to this, the Irish Volunteers were founded later in the same year to support Home Rule. But most volunteers abandoned the organisation on the outbreak of the First World War, forming a separate body and enlisting in large numbers in the British Army, in conformity with Nationalist Party policy. The remaining core group continued, and engaged in rebellion in Dublin in April 1916 (the Easter Rising) under IRB leadership, declaring Ireland to be an independent republic with the IRB Military Council as its provisional government. The rebellion was crushed within days and appears to have had little popular support, but the circumstances of the execution of its leaders and the harsh treatment of other suspects alienated public opinion. This alienation was reinforced by the government's threat to introduce conscription in 1918 and by a pan-European climate of political radicalism in the closing months of the war. The main beneficiary was Sinn Féin, reconstituted in 1917 as a broad nationalist front under the leadership of Eamon de Valera, the senior surviving commander of the 1916 rebels. Despite military defeat, the 1916 rebels were elevated to the pantheon of Irish nationalism, and Patrick Pearse and the other executed leaders were long to be regarded as the spiritual fathers of independent Ireland.

As Table 1.1 shows, Sinn Féin gained an overwhelming electoral victory in the 1918 general election, when it won 73 of Ireland's 105 seats. Although it is true that a significant number of voters supported the Nationalist Party, demoralisation within the party itself and the fact that the electoral system caused minorities to be under-represented left it with only two seats in the south and four in the north. Sinn Féin won almost all of the remaining seats in the south (see Coakley, 1994).

Hardly surprisingly, Sinn Féin took this result as a mandate to pursue its separatist policy (see Laffan, 1999). Its members refused to take their seats in the British Parliament, and instead established their own revolutionary assembly, Dáil Éireann, in January 1919 (see Farrell, 1994). The Dáil ratified the 1916 rebels' proclamation of Ireland as an independent republic, set up its own government under de Valera, and in 1919–21 accepted responsibility for a guerrilla war against the security forces fought by the Irish Republican Army (IRA), reconstituted from the Irish Volunteers (Hopkinson, 2002). These efforts were reinforced by an attempt, which inevitably had strictly limited success, to set up a separate state and to obtain international recognition for it, especially by bringing American pressure to bear on the British. The Dáil could not hope to control the official Irish government agencies, and its efforts to secure the running of its writ were restricted by the small size of its civil service, and by the fact that this could not operate openly. Nevertheless, after the local elections of 1920 it was able to detach the loyalty of most local authorities from the Local Government Board, and it enjoyed some success in establishing a network of local courts (see Garvin, 1996: 63–91).

From Home Rule to partition

One of the reasons advanced to explain the rapid electoral advances of the militants is the failure of the British to make sufficient concessions to constitutional nationalists. It is true that the British had belatedly brought forward Home Rule proposals for Ireland (O'Day, 1998). The first such bill had, however, been defeated in the House of Commons in 1886. A second Home Rule Bill was passed by the House of Commons but was blocked by the House of Lords in 1893. The third Home Rule Bill had to wait until the Nationalist Party again held the balance of power after the 1910 election. Introduced in 1912, it eventually became law in 1914, assisted by the transformation of the Lords' veto from an absolute into a suspensory one in 1911. This bill proposed to establish a bicameral parliament in Dublin that would legislate in areas of domestic concern (essentially, those covered by the 'Irish' government departments described above), with a separate Irish executive or cabinet. Ireland would continue to send MPs to Westminster, but their numbers would be greatly reduced.

The implementation of the Home Rule Act was postponed because of the outbreak of war but also for a more fundamental reason: opposition in Ulster. The Protestant population of Ireland did not share the view of Irish history described above, perceiving itself as being connected by a wide range of historical ties to Britain, from where the ancestors of many Irish Protestants had come as colonists in the seventeenth century. In addition to seeing the British link as a guarantee of civil and religious liberties in a Catholic island, many Protestants, especially in the north-east, regarded the Act of Union as having brought significant economic benefits and as having assisted the industrialisation of Belfast and its hinterland; these benefits, they believed, would be threatened by Irish autonomy (see Laffan, 1983; Fitzpatrick, 1998).

Determined political pressure and threatened paramilitary resistance in Ulster, together with support from within the British Conservative Party and the risk of an army mutiny, were sufficient to ensure that the terms of the Home Rule Act would have to be changed. The result was the partition of Ireland by the Government of Ireland Act, 1920. This broadly reproduced the 1914 Act but instead of concentrating power in a single capital it made provision for parallel institutions in Belfast (to govern six northeastern counties that contained 71 per cent of the Irish Protestant population) and Dublin (to govern the remaining 26 counties). The Act came into effect in 1921, and was successfully implemented in one of the new states that it created, Northern Ireland, where it formed the basic constitutional document until 1972.

Although the Act proved largely ineffective in the south, its provisions for the government of 'Southern Ireland' formed an important precedent for constitutional development, and indeed defined the framework for the pattern of parliamentary democracy that was to become so deeply ingrained in the new Irish state (see Chapter 8). Alongside the Irish government there was to be a parliament of two houses. The House of Commons was to consist of 128 members elected by proportional representation by means of the single transferable vote. The Senate was to consist of 64 members, of whom three were ex officio members (the Lord Chancellor and the Lord Mayors of Dublin and Cork), 17 were to be nominated by the Lord Lieutenant to represent commerce, labour and the scientific and learned professions, and 44 were to be elected by five other groups (the Catholic bishops were to elect four of their number, the Protestant bishops two, southern Irish peers 16, privy councillors eight and county councillors 14). In the first election to the House of Commons in 1921, Sinn Féin won 124 seats, all uncontested, and interpreted this election and that to the Northern Ireland House of Commons as elections to the 'second Dáil'. Since only four MPs turned up for the first meeting of the legally constituted house (all from Trinity College, Dublin) and two for the second, it adjourned *sine die*. Although attendance at the Senate was better (18 senators attended at least one of its two meetings) it suffered the same fate, and, in the absence of support from any significant group, the act ceased to have real effect in the south. With this disappeared the last remaining institutional links with Northern Ireland until the Good Friday Agreement of 1998 (see Chapter 15).

The Treaty and the new state

The deadlock between the Dáil and the British government was finally broken following the conclusion of a military truce in July 1921. In the subsequent negotiations between the two sides, a 'Treaty' was agreed in December 1921. This went much further than conceding Home Rule, but stopped well short of permitting complete separation. Instead, a state would be established that would be almost fully independent, but which would be a British dominion and would recognise the King as its head. There would be a representative of the Crown to stand in for the King in Ireland, and constitutional provision would be made for a parliamentary oath of allegiance to the constitution and fidelity to the King. Partition would remain, but the location of the boundary line would be determined by an intergovernmental commission. The British would also retain naval facilities in certain seaports. Since two of the six counties and other border areas had Catholic majorities, the Irish negotiators believed that this would result in a major revision of the line of the border, and that this in turn might undermine the viability of the northern state.

Although the Treaty was narrowly ratified by the Dáil in January 1922 by a majority of 64 to 57, the division that it generated was bitter and saw the resignation of de Valera as head of government and the departure of his anti-Treaty supporters from the Dáil. The constitutional position that followed was complex. First, the second Dáil continued to exist, though only pro-Treaty Sinn Féin members now attended. On 10 January 1922 Arthur

Griffith was elected President of the Dáil government in succession to de Valera and a new Dáil government was appointed; on Griffith's death on 12 August 1922 he was succeeded as President by William T. Cosgrave. Second, the Treaty made provision for a meeting of 'members of parliament elected for constituencies in Southern Ireland', who duly came together on 14 January for their one and only meeting; at this they formally approved the Treaty and elected a Provisional Government with Michael Collins, guiding force of the IRA campaign and head of the IRB, as its Chairman. On Collins's death on 22 August 1922 he was succeeded as Chairman by Cosgrave. Although Cosgrave's succession to both of these posts helped to disguise the anomalous existence of two governments, both pro-Treaty, with overlapping membership, this overlap was not complete. A general election took place in June 1922, and when the new (third) Dáil eventually met on 9 September 1922, again in the absence of the anti-Treaty deputies, it removed this anomaly by electing Cosgrave to the single post of President. The Dáil also approved the new constitution on 25 October 1922, and when this came into force Cosgrave became President of the Executive Council (yet another title for the prime minister) on 6 December 1922.

The consolidation of statehood

The new state, then, did not have a particularly easy birth. The remaining chapters in this volume look at the kinds of political structures and patterns of behaviour that have evolved in Ireland since independence. Since the authors have where appropriate set their examinations of contemporary politics in historical context, a detailed overview of post-1922 politics is not needed here (for general historical accounts, see Girvin, 1989; Lee, 1989; Keogh, 1994; Harkness, 1996; for the early decades of the new state, see Cronin and Regan, 2000). It is nevertheless necessary to review a number of themes that link contemporary politics with the events and institutions already discussed. First, the nature of the independence struggle left the new state with a series of challenges to its legitimacy. Second, a steady evolution took place in the content of political conflict. Third, however, the administrative structures inherited by the new state provided an important bedrock of stability.

Problems of legitimacy

The new Irish state was faced with a formidable challenge to its legitimacy (MacMillan, 1993: 165–85; Prager, 1986; Regan, 1999; Kissane, 2002). It would be forced to work within the framework of the Treaty while at the same time presenting itself as authentic heir to the republican tradition. This was reflected in the curious anomaly described above: the coexistence for several months in 1922 of a President of the Dáil Government (Griffith) and a Chairman of the Provisional Government (Collins). This was a deliberate attempt by the new regime to claim legitimacy in the eyes both of Irish republicans and British politicians and to fudge the essential incompatibility between these positions; but it also meant that the post-1922 President of the Executive Council could claim continuity with the republican tradition. Partial symbolic success in this is reflected in the fact that, to the present, each Dáil is numbered on the basis of a recognition of the Dáil of 1919 as the first one (the Dáil elected in 2002, for instance, was designated the 29th Dáil even in official circles, though it was only the 27th since the state came into existence in 1922).

This attempt to turn two ways at once presented the state with fundamental challenges from both directions. At one extreme, its birth upset those who remained loyal to the United Kingdom: the sizeable unionist population, which had wished to maintain the political integrity of the British Isles, and the significant population that had supported the Nationalist Party in the 1918 election and which would have been happy with devolved government for Ireland within the United Kingdom. Since the union appeared irretrievably dissolved, however, and the spectre of de Valera and the Republicans appeared to be the main alternative to the Free State, many former supporters of the Unionist and Nationalist parties switched to a position of neutrality towards (or even support for) the new regime.

At the other extreme, and with weightier political consequences, the new regime also offended those Republicans who took the view that the proclamation of a republic in 1916 and its confirmation by the Dáil in 1919 were irreversible. They regarded the Irish Free State as a hideously deformed alternative to 'the Republic', deficient not only because it represented a truncation of the 'national territory' but also because it retained important links of subordination to the United Kingdom, at least at a symbolic level. This issue split the IRA, whose pro-Treaty wing became the core of the new national army; it eventually spilled over into open armed conflict, during a civil war that lasted from June 1922 to May 1923 (see Garvin, 1996; Purdon, 2000). In the course of this, many hundreds died as a consequence of armed clashes, executions and assassinations. In the early stages of the civil war, the anti-Treaty Sinn Féin members sought to undermine the constitutional position of the pro-Treaty side. They asserted that the 1922 general election was not legitimate since the second Dáil (elected in 1921) had not dissolved itself, declared themselves to be the 'second Dáil' and met on 25 October 1922 to elect de Valera once more as 'President of the Republic'. Even after the civil war, this group (now known simply as Sinn Féin) continued to abstain from the Dáil. This fundamental challenge to a new state was not unique to Ireland: in the emerging post-war states of Finland, Estonia, Latvia and Lithuania similar civil wars were fought, though these had a more obviously social content, pitting left against right (see Coakley, 1987).

The building of the new state and its institutions was in the hands of a group of people who supported the political and economic status quo either through conviction or out of political realism. Their cornerstone was the constitution of 1922, which, ironically, they designed and amended in such a way that their rivals could dismantle it after 1932 (by extending the period during which the constitution could be amended by legislation from eight to 16 years, they in effect gave any subsequent parliamentary majority free rein to make fundamental changes; see Chapter 3). The core of the new political elite was made up of pro-Treaty members of Sinn Féin, who reorganised under the label Cumann na nGaedheal in 1923 (this had been the name of a precursor of the old Sinn Féin, organised by Arthur Griffith in 1900). Led by Cosgrave, its character was shaped by other strong political figures of a broadly conservative disposition, a conservatism that was reflected in a new, close relationship with the Catholic Church. Although the 1922 constitution was an entirely secular document, the new government quickly moved to show its deference to Catholic moral values. Thus divorce was prohibited, restrictions were placed on the sale of alcohol, and censorship of films and publications was greatly intensified. Yet other policy areas showed a willingness to innovate: state intervention in the energy production sector was represented by the initiation in 1925 of the Shannon hydroelectric scheme, for instance, and, in a rather different area, the new government sought vigorously to promote the Irish language.

Although Cumann na nGaedheal struggled to protect the autonomy of the new state and even to extend it within the Commonwealth, its conservatism in the constitutional arena and its increasingly unreserved defence of the Treaty had two kinds of consequence for political realignment in the 1920s. First, those who had accepted Collins's argument that the Treaty was 'a stepping stone to the Republic' became disillusioned, and broke with the party. This issue was used as a pretext in the 'Army Mutiny' of 1924, when a group of senior officers demanded action from the government to end partition (though other motivations arising from army demobilisation probably took precedence over this; see Lee, 1989: 96–105). Another division took place on the leaking of the report of the Boundary Commission in 1925 (set up under the terms of the Treaty, the commission recommended that only marginal changes be made to the line of the border). Second, however, former supporters of the now-defunct Nationalist and Unionist parties increasingly came to identify with Cumann na nGaedheal, especially after 1927. Many of the former had briefly given their support to a short-lived party, the National League, in 1927; the latter had either remained detached, voted for independent candidates, or, in the 1920s, supported two smaller parties, the Farmers' Party and the Business Men's Party.

One of the most significant developments in the normalisation of the new state occurred following a major split within Sinn Féin in 1926. Support for that party had been dropping off in the mid-1920s, as it continued its policy of abstention from the Dáil, and de Valera resolved on an alternative strategy. At the party's 1926 ard-fheis (convention), he proposed a resolution to the effect that, in the event of the removal of the oath of allegiance, abstention from the Dáil would become a matter 'not of principle but of policy'. The resolution was defeated, and de Valera and his supporters broke with Sinn Féin and shortly afterwards founded an alternative republican party, Fianna Fáil. The popularity of this move became obvious in June 1927, when a general election gave Fianna Fáil 44 seats, to Sinn Féin's five.

There were two further stages in this process of political normalisation. On 10 July 1927 a leading minister, Kevin O'Higgins, was assassinated. Among the measures adopted in response by the government was a bill requiring all future parliamentary candidates to declare that, if elected, they would take the oath of allegiance. This left abstentionist parties with a difficult choice: either to enter parliament or to be wiped out. Fianna Fáil decided on the former course, and de Valera and his supporters took the oath in August 1927 in what they described as an empty gesture. Ironically, by thus forcing Fianna Fáil into the Dáil, the government changed the balance of political forces there and, facing defeat, called a second general election in 1927 at which both Cumann na nGaedheal and Fianna Fáil gained, at the expense of smaller parties (see Appendices 2b and 2c).

The ultimate stage in political normalisation followed the next election, in 1932. Fianna Fáil became the largest party and, although it did not have an overall majority, it was able to form a government with Labour Party support. This peaceful transfer of power by the victors in the civil war to the vanquished was an important milestone in the consolidation of democracy in Ireland. Within a year, a new general election gave Fianna Fáil an overall majority, and it was to remain in power without interruption until 1948 (see Dunphy, 1995; for later developments within Fianna Fáil see Hannan and Gallagher, 1996).

The early years of the new Fianna Fáil government were characterised, not surprisingly, by vigorous moves to dismantle some of those elements in the constitution that Republicans found objectionable. Thus, the oath of allegiance, the right of appeal to the Privy Council in London (a limited but symbolically important restriction on the sovereignty of the Irish judicial system) and the Governor-General's right to veto legislation were abolished in 1933. Although these amendments were strongly opposed by the British on the grounds that they violated certain provisions of the Treaty, the context within which they took place had changed considerably since 1922. Imperial conferences in 1926 and 1930 moved towards giving Commonwealth states greater independence from London, culminating in the Statute of Westminster (1931), which authorised any Commonwealth state to amend or repeal British legislation that affected it.

The character of the constitution was even more fundamentally altered in 1936, when the Senate was abolished and the sudden abdication of King Edward VIII was used as an opportunity to remove almost all references to the Governor-General from the constitution. This left the way open for the adoption of a new constitution, which, although it stopped short of declaring Ireland a republic, made no mention of the Commonwealth and was intended to symbolise the completion of the process of Irish independence, at least for part of Ireland (see Chapter 3).

Opposition to a British role in Ireland also extended to the issue of 'land annuities', payments due to the British exchequer from Irish farmers as a consequence of loans taken by them to purchase their holdings under the provisions of the Land Acts of the pre-1922 period. On coming to power in 1932, de Valera simply retained these repayments for the Irish exchequer. An Anglo-Irish trade war followed, with each side imposing import duties on selected goods from the other; it was concluded by a trade agreement in 1938 and British acceptance of a one-off lump sum payment. The second issue was that of the naval facilities that the British had been allowed to retain under the terms of the Treaty. This issue was settled more amicably, also as part of the 1938 settlement: the British ceded control of the ports, thus laying the ground for the policy of neutrality that the Irish government was able to follow during the war.

As these changes proceeded, the original pro-Treaty forces found themselves increasingly impotent. The spectre of extreme republicanism raised by the Fianna Fáil victory in 1932 and the polarised climate of the 1930s formed the background for the formation of a fascist-type movement in Ireland. This was born as the Army Comrades' Association (1931), and was transformed in 1933 into the National Guard (popularly known as the Blueshirts), led by the former head of the police, General Eoin O'Duffy. The parallels with continental European fascist movements were close: the fascist salute, the wearing of a distinctive shirt as a uniform, anti-communist rhetoric and, most importantly, an authoritarian nationalist ideology that was suspicious of parliamentary government and sympathetic towards a reorganisation of the state along corporatist lines, where the primary divisions would not be between parties but rather between different socio-economic segments, such as agriculture, industry and the professions (see Manning, 1987; Bew *et al.*, 1989: 48–67; Cronin, 1997). This development was followed by a further realignment of anti-Fianna Fáil forces. In 1933 a demoralised Cumann na nGaedheal merged with the Blueshirts and another small party, the National Centre Party, to form the United Ireland Party, which quickly became better known by its Irish name, Fine Gael. Led initially by O'Duffy, the party came increasingly to resemble the old Cumann na nGaedheal party, especially after William Cosgrave replaced O'Duffy as leader in 1935. Fine Gael, however, was no match for Fianna Fáil in electoral terms, and its share of the vote dropped until 1948. Then, in an ironic development, its worst-ever electoral performance was followed by its entry into a coalition government; and, even more ironically, this government moved to break the last remaining links between Ireland and the Commonwealth, with the decision in 1948 to declare the state a republic (see Gallagher and Marsh, 2002).

By this stage, then, the anti-Treaty side had accommodated itself to post-Treaty realities, and the pro-Treaty side had actually declared the country a republic. While one might have expected this to copper-fasten the legitimacy of the state, a problem remained. The rump of Sinn Féin and the IRA that survived after 1926 remained adamant in their hostility to the state, which they continued to reject as an illegitimate, British-imposed institution. Instead they continued to give their allegiance to the 'Second Dáil', and then to the Army Council of the IRA, to which the remnants of the 'Second Dáil' transferred their authority in 1938. While this might appear to be of importance only in the world of myth, myths can be of powerful political significance. It is precisely in terms of this myth that the reborn IRA and Sinn Féin were able after 1970 to claim legitimacy for their struggle to oust the British from Northern Ireland (see Chapter 2 for a discussion of the concept of legitimacy).

Political issues in the new Ireland

The most visible political conflicts in the new Irish state have already been discussed above; during the 1920s and the 1930s these focused largely on constitutional matters, or on matters pertaining to Anglo-Irish relations. On these issues, the principal line of division was between the pro- and anti-Treaty splinters from Sinn Féin. Other political interests also sought, however, to force alternative issues onto the political agenda, and the proportional representation electoral system permitted them to gain significant Dáil representation (see Chapters 4 and 5; for an overview of the parties' electoral strengths, see Appendix 2b, and Sinnott, 1995; on the contemporary Irish political system, see Chubb, 1992; Hazelkorn and Murray, 1995; Dooney and O'Toole, 1998; Collins, 1999; Collins and Cradden, 2001; Taylor, 2002).

The most significant of these in the long term was the Labour Party, which had been conceived by the Irish Trades Union Congress in 1912 and was finally born in 1922 as a party committed to a moderate policy of defence of workers' rights. The party was marginalised by debates on the national question, on which it was unable to adopt a distinctive position, and moved quickly into the role that it has retained ever since: that of third party in a three-party system (see Gallagher 1982). In the absence also of a significant classical revolutionary left, the consistent weakness of Labour has been remarkable in a European context (see Chapter 5).

A second important issue was that of agriculture. In 1922 a Farmers' Party appeared, drawing its strength from the large farmers of the south and east. The Farmers' Party found it difficult to maintain an identity separate from that of Cumann na nGaedheal, and it faded away after 1927. A successor party with a similar support base, the National Centre Party (founded in 1932 as the National Farmers' and Ratepayers' League), was one of the parties that, as we have seen, merged to form Fine Gael. In 1939 a farmers' party of a rather different kind appeared. This was Clann na Talmhan, originating among the small farmers of the west. This party won significant support in the elections of the 1940s and even participated in two governments, but it was unable to prevent its voters from drifting back to the two large parties subsequently.

Three other types of political force also fought for Dáil seats. First, especially in the 1920s and the 1930s a considerable number of independent deputies represented diverse opinions, including those of former unionists and nationalists. Increasingly, however, the support base of deputies of this kind was mopped up by the larger parties. Second, former nationalists made a more determined attempt to re-group through the National League (founded in 1926), which won eight seats in the June 1927 general election. In fact, following Fianna Fáil's entry to the Dáil, the prospect of a minority Labour–National League coalition government, with Fianna Fáil support, appeared to be a realistic possibility. The calling of a snap second election in 1927 put paid to the prospects of this party, however; it lost all but two of its seats. Third, there have been dissident republican parties caused by divisions within Cumann na nGaedheal in the 1920s (the National Group in 1924 and Clann Éireann in 1925) and within Fianna Fáil in the 1970s (Aontacht Éireann in 1971 and, to the extent that it may be seen as a separate party, Independent Fianna Fáil in Donegal from 1973). By contrast to these small groups, another republican party, Clann na Poblachta, founded in 1946 by Seán McBride, a former IRA chief of staff, appeared destined for greater things (Rafter, 1996; McDermott, 1998). This party was able to capitalise on post-war disillusion with Fianna Fáil and win ten seats in the 1948 election. But following bitter internal disputes, most notably over the 'Mother and Child' scheme for the provision of comprehensive post-natal care in the social welfare system (on which the party's health minister, Noel Browne, had clashed with the Church), its support collapsed in the 1951 election and never subsequently recovered (for minor parties generally, see Gallagher, 1985: 93–120; Coakley, 1990).

It was, indeed, precisely the intervention of Clann na Poblachta in the 1948 general election that ushered in a new era in Irish politics. Fianna Fáil was unable to form a government after the election, and was replaced in office by a five-party coalition supported also by independent deputies, the first 'Inter-Party' government (McCullagh, 1998). In this Clann na Poblachta sat alongside its principal enemy, Fine Gael, together with Clann na Talmhan, Labour and the National Labour Party (a group of deputies that had broken with Labour and maintained a separate party in the years 1944–50). Headed by Fine Gael's John A. Costello, this coalition broke up in disarray in 1951, to be replaced by a Fianna Fáil government. Costello was nevertheless back in 1954, this time heading a three-party coalition of Fine Gael, Labour and Clann na Talmhan. Following the 1957 election, however, Fianna Fáil returned for a second 16-year period in office.

The fact that a single party was in power for this lengthy period disguises the extent of change that took place between 1957 and 1973. The period began under de Valera's leadership with a cabinet still made up largely of activists of the 1919–23 period; after a transition under Seán Lemass (1959–66), one of the youngest of those involved in the independence movement, it ended with a younger cabinet led by Jack Lynch and consisting of ministers without direct experience of the civil war (see Chapter 11 for an assessment of recent government leaders). The ghosts of the civil war were, however, disturbed by the outbreak of the Northern Ireland 'troubles' in 1969. In a dramatic incident in May 1970 that became known as the 'arms crisis', Lynch dismissed two ministers, Neil Blaney and Charles Haughey, for alleged involvement in the illegal purchase and supply of arms to Northern Ireland nationalists, and, in related developments, he accepted the resignations of two more. Together with the ensuing trial, this incident was to haunt Fianna Fáil for over two decades (see O'Brien, 2000).

Although the Northern Ireland problem thus ensured that certain traditional issues would remain on the agenda, the post-war period was in general characterised to an increasing extent by conflict over economic rather than constitutional matters. Protests over high rates of unemployment and inflation in the 1950s forced these issues into the political arena, though without translating them into votes for the left. The principal policy shifts were, indeed, a consequence of civil service decisions rather than of public debates; the outstanding example was the pursuit of foreign investment rather than reliance on traditional Sinn Féin-type policies of encouragement of indigenous industry (see Garvin, 2004). The most notable landmarks were the announcement of the first Programme for Economic Expansion (1958), the signing of the Anglo-Irish Free Trade Agreement (1965) and the decision to join the European Communities (1972).

The 16 unbroken years of Fianna Fáil rule that ended in 1973 were succeeded by 16 years of alternation between Fine Gael–Labour coalitions and single-party Fianna Fáil governments; the pattern was broken in 1989, when Fianna Fáil entered a coalition for the first time (for a list of governments, see Appendix 3c). Some election results of the period were decisive, such as that of 1977, in which Fianna Fáil emulated its 1938 performance by winning a majority not only of Dáil seats but also of popular votes (though ironically party leader Lynch's popularity ebbed quickly afterwards, and he was replaced in 1979 after an intense internal party campaign by Charles Haughey). All subsequent election results were less decisive, however, and brought a new element of unpredictability to electoral competition.

Although the old political issues continued on until the end of the century, new ones arose (see Crotty and Schmitt, 1998). In particular, moral issues acquired greater prominence. Despite the weakness of the secular tradition in Irish society, politicians were increasingly forced to take positions that might place them at odds with the Catholic Church. In the 1970s the sale of contraceptives was finally permitted; in the 1980s the issues of abortion and divorce found their way into the public forum, though in both cases referendum results came up with conservative verdicts. The 1990s witnessed more radical constitutional and legislative change. In 1993 the sale of contraceptives was further liberalised and homosexual activity was decriminalised. In 1995 a referendum narrowly approved a constitutional amendment removing the prohibition on divorce legislation, and the law was subsequently changed to permit dissolution of marriage on a relatively restricted basis. Finally, the abortion issue raised its head once more. In 1992 the Supreme Court ruled that abortion was permitted by the constitution under certain limited circumstances (see Box 3.2), and a proposed constitutional amendment later in the same year designed to negate this interpretation was defeated at a referendum. This stalemate has continued subsequently; no further liberalisation in the position has taken place, and an attempt to eliminate the current limited grounds for abortion was defeated at a referendum in 2002. These changes coincided with growing secularisation and an erosion in the moral influence of the Catholic Church (see Chapter 2), and with increasing prominence for the issue of women's rights and women's representation in the political domain (see Chapter 10; Galligan, 1998; Galligan *et al.*, 1999).

If changes reflecting the new secularism of Irish society were the most visible manifestations of the demise of certain values of the old Ireland, they were not the only ones. The changes described above were in part facilitated by a transformation in Irish social structure, itself a consequence of the unprecedented pace of economic growth and the development of levels of wealth undreamt of by earlier generations. Economic development was, in turn, a function of Ireland's changing relationship with Europe. Popular endorsement of the Single European Act, of the Maastricht Treaty and of the Amsterdam Treaty in 1987, 1992 and 1998 paved the way for Irish participation in a new, European state structure, and implied substantial Irish support for the restriction of formal Irish sovereignty (though not necessarily as a result of an extended debate on the issue). This trend appeared to have been halted in 2001, when voters narrowly rejected the Nice Treaty in a referendum; but the government pushed ahead with a second referendum on the same issue in 2002, this time deploying its resources in a more determined way and securing acceptance of the treaty. A sea-change appears also to have taken place in another aspect of traditional nationalist values: in 1998 voters supported by an overwhelming majority a proposal to drop the constitutional claim on Northern Ireland as part of the Good Friday Agreement of April 1998 (see Chapter 15). This was accompanied by an increasing level of southern Irish intervention in the affairs of Northern Ireland, even if this took place in the context of firm guarantees regarding the constitutional status of Northern Ireland as part of the United Kingdom.

All of these developments were reflected not only in policy changes within the traditional parties but also in the appearance of new parties. On the left, the Labour Party was challenged by a form of transformed republicanism. The remnants of the Sinn Féin movement that had survived the 1926 split had been reactivated in the 1950s and the 1960s; in 1970 this small party again split, with a more activist wing breaking away as 'Provisional Sinn

Féin' and becoming a major political force in Northern Ireland in the 1980s. The remaining 'official' Sinn Féin was gradually transformed into a radical left party of secular and, strangely, anti-nationalist orientation, and was renamed the Workers' Party in 1982. After steadily building up its Dáil strength to seven deputies in 1989, this party split in turn in 1992, six of its seven Dáil deputies breaking away to form a new party, Democratic Left. Following losses in the 1997 election, however, the party began to reconsider its position, and in January 1999 it merged with Labour. While this might have been expected to inoculate Labour against challenges from the left, its working class support has been increasingly attacked by the more radical (formerly 'Provisional') Sinn Féin.

On the right, a new liberal-type party, the Progressive Democrats, appeared in 1985. Although the immediate cause of the party's appearance was a deep division within Fianna Fáil on Northern Ireland policy and on the issue of Charles Haughey's leadership, the new party managed quickly to establish a distinctive niche for itself: conservative on economic policy, liberal on social policy and moderate on Northern Ireland. It became the first party to form a coalition with Fianna Fáil, after the 1989 election. Although this coalition collapsed in 1992, the party re-entered coalition with Fianna Fáil in 1997 and renewed this arrangement after the 2002 election.

The new flexibility within Fianna Fáil and its willingness to contemplate coalition marks a decisive shift in the dynamics of Irish party competition (see Chapter 5). Albert Reynolds, who succeeded Haughey as leader of Fianna Fáil in 1992, negotiated an historic coalition with the Labour Party in 1993. In an even more remarkable development, when this coalition collapsed in 1994 it was replaced, without a general election, by a 'rainbow coalition' of Fine Gael, Labour and Democratic Left led by Fine Gael's John Bruton. Under Bertie Ahern (who succeeded Reynolds as leader of Fianna Fáil in 1994), the strategy of openness regarding coalition possibilities has if anything been accentuated.

Although the more open attitudes to coalition formation and the new issues that have come to the fore in Irish politics echo those in continental Europe, the kind of political forces that we find elsewhere in Europe have been weak or absent, and the link between parties and particular social classes has been tenuous (see Chapter 7). In a political system dominated by two successors of a nationalist party and with only a weak Labour Party, there has been little room for the appearance of alternative political forces. It is true that farmers' parties have appeared from time to time, but these proved ephemeral. The most characteristically European phenomenon has been the Green Party, which has established a foothold for itself since 1989. At the opposite pole, the most distinctive phenomenon on the Irish electoral landscape has been the independent deputy; during the 1990s, indeed, it appeared as if independents were about to enjoy a new period of influence, as insecure governments turned to them for politically expensive support in time of need. Fragmentation increased further in 2002, as the three large parties and three smaller ones were joined in the Dáil by no fewer than 14 other deputies (independents or one-person parties); but the political arithmetic of the Dáil permitted the formation of a two-party coalition with a secure majority, reducing the influence of the smaller groups. At the same time, though, there is little evidence that the traditional role of the Dáil deputy that is so vividly illustrated by independents – one foot in the world of national policy making, the other in the parochial concerns of the constituency – has changed to any significant degree (see Chapter 9).

The administrative infrastructure

If the pattern of politics in post-1922 Ireland shows strands of continuity beneath seemingly dramatic political changes, stability is even more strikingly a characteristic of the administrative system that has lain underneath. As we have seen, the old regime had built up a formidable administrative infrastructure already before 1922, and this was to serve the new state well.

First, the central bureaucracy continued with little change. Officials transferred from the old regime constituted the core of the new civil service, which for many years consisted of about 20,000 employees. The small number of members of the old Dáil civil service (of whom 131 were transferred in 1922) made little impact on this, and the character of this body changed very slowly as new staff were recruited. Thus, in 1922 98.9 per cent of civil servants had been recruited under the old regime; by 1927–8 this figure had dropped to 64.3 per cent, and as late as 1934 a majority (50.1 per cent) of civil servants had been recruited to the pre-1922 service (calculated from Commission of Inquiry into the Civil Service, 1935: 3, 9, 138). The fact that so large a body of civil servants could adapt to working in an entirely different state structure owes much to the 'greening' of the Irish civil service that had been taking place steadily since the advent of open competition for recruitment to lower ranks of the civil service in 1876 and a deliberate policy of appointing or promoting nationalist-oriented civil servants to senior ranks from 1892 onwards, at least under Liberal administrations (McBride, 1991; see also O'Halpin, 1987).

The external staff associated with certain departments posed particular problems. Surprisingly, the Department of Education had little difficulty with its body of teachers and inspectors, even though these had been recruited and trained under the old regime. The shift towards ideals of Irish nationalism was not difficult for teachers, since they had allegedly been associated with such ideas even before 1922; the main problem lay in raising their proficiency in the Irish language to a level that would allow them to become effective agents in the state's language revival policy. Matters were different in the area of security. Although the Dublin Metropolitan Police continued until 1925, the more politicised, paramilitary Royal Irish Constabulary (RIC) was disbanded in the south and renamed the Royal Ulster

Constabulary (RUC) in the north. The new, unarmed Civic Guard (Garda Síochána) was launched as a freshly recruited force in 1922, though it used the administrative structures, buildings and other property of the RIC. It eventually settled into a force of more than 6,000. There was a similarly complete break in the military domain: the withdrawing British Army was replaced by an Irish Army built up around a nucleus of the pro-Treaty members of the IRA. It expanded rapidly in response to civil war needs, and by the end of March 1923 had some 50,000 soldiers. This number had dropped to 16,000 by the following year, and after 1926 further rapid reduction brought this figure to 6,700 by 1932. Apart from temporary expansion during the Second World War, the army was to remain at this size until the end of the 1960s. Then, following the outbreak of the Northern Ireland troubles and with increased crime in the south, the size of both the defence forces and the police was increased by about 50 per cent in the 1970s, though the role of the former continued to be defined in minimalist terms (see O'Halpin, 1996).

As to its structure, the new civil service was a rationalisation of the old one (for case studies of the departments of the Environment and of Finance, respectively, see Daly, 1997 and Fanning, 1978). The 29 'Irish' departments were reorganised into a smaller number of new departments; but in areas associated with 'imperial' departments, while the new state inherited thousands of civil servants, it had to create new structures on the British model (in foreign affairs, defence and finance, for instance). The formal organisation of the new system was defined in the Ministers and Secretaries Act, 1924; subsequent changes (such as the transfer of areas from one department to another, or the creation of new departments) were on a smaller scale, but their cumulative effect was to increase the number of departments under the control of individual ministers from 10 in 1922 to 15 by the end of the century. Of these, six core departments have continued with little change other than in name: those of the President of the Executive Council (renamed Taoiseach, 1937), Finance, External Affairs (renamed Foreign Affairs, 1971), Home Affairs (renamed Justice, 1924, and Justice, Equality and Law Reform, 1997), Defence, and Education (renamed Education and Science, 1997). The other four core departments of the early service (Local Government, Industry and Commerce, Posts and Telegraphs, and Agriculture) had been replaced by the end of the century by nine departments with rather unstable boundaries. These cover various areas of economic development and planning, management of the public sector, health and welfare, and culture and recreation (see listing of government departments in Appendix 4, and Chapter 12; for general evaluations of the public policy process, see Chapter 14; Dunne *et al.*, 2000; FitzGerald, 2002; Taylor, 2002; Adshead and Millar, 2003).

At the level of local government, continuity was even more obvious. The old system continued after 1922, still governed by the principles of the 1898

Act, with only incremental change. In terms of formal structures, the most significant changes were the abolition of poor law unions and their boards of guardians (1923) and of rural district councils (1925), and the transfer of their functions to county councils. This left the state with a system of local government sharply different from the European norm, where local government has traditionally been two-tiered: an upper level consisting of a small number of counties or provinces, modelled on the French *départements* and acting largely as agencies of the central government, and a lower level consisting of a very large number of communes or municipalities of greatly varying sizes, each one with a local council and considerable administrative powers. Especially after 1925, the latter level was largely missing from Ireland, and the main focus of local representative government was centred on county level. While a restructuring of local government was being discussed up to the early twenty-first century, only minor changes were actually implemented (see Chapter 14).

Post-independence governments have also been disposed to exercise central control to a much greater degree than their predecessors. This may be seen in the first place in a willingness to suspend local authorities and replace them by appointed commissioners (especially in earlier years, allegations of corruption against local authorities were often used as a justification for this). This was the fate of several councils in the 1920s (including those of the cities of Dublin and Cork); Dublin city council was again suspended in 1969. Second, from 1942 a system of 'county management', implemented earlier in the cities, gave considerable executive power at local level to an official appointed by the Local Appointments Commission, itself a central body. Third, the term of office of all councils was extended in 1953 from three to five years, but elections were regularly postponed by the government. Thus elections should have taken place every five years since 1965, but they were normally deferred for lengthy periods; instead of end-of-decade and mid-decade elections, they have taken place in 1967, 1974, 1979, 1985, 1991 and 1999. A constitutional change in 1999, however, was designed to ensure that deferrals of this kind will be much more difficult in future and the 2004 local elections took place as scheduled.

One of the most significant changes in the area of state intervention lay in the creation of 'state-sponsored bodies' to carry out a range of functions, many of them connected to economic development. The number of such bodies, over which government control has been only indirect, increased steadily from an initial four in 1927 to well over 100 by 1990. In part under the impact of European Union legislation designed to encourage competition, though, the partial dismantling of this semi-state sector commenced in the 1990s, as major public sector organisations began to be sold off to private investors. The most dramatic example was in the telecommunications sector. Part of the Department of Posts and Telegraphs was hived off in 1984 as a state-sponsored body, Telecom Éireann; in 1999 this was floated on the

stock exchange and passed into private ownership. Other large civil service
institutions have also moved half way in this direction; the postal services
part of the Department of Posts and Telegraphs, for example, was also given
the status of a state-sponsored body in 1984 as An Post, and the forestry
service, Coillte, was detached from the Department of Energy in 1989.
These and other state-sponsored bodies, such as the national airline Aer
Lingus (1936), the national airports authority Aer Rianta (1937) and the
Electricity Supply Board (1927), may well pass out of state ownership in the
coming years. Another area of intersection between the public and private
domains that generated great controversy related to serious allegations of
bribery, corruption and inappropriate links between politics and business
(see Chapter 14 and Collins and O'Shea, 2000).

Conclusion

It is obvious that the birth of the new Irish state marked a decisive shift in
Irish political development, but we should not ignore the extent to which its
political institutions built on pre-1922 roots. Although there was a sharp
break both in constitutional theory and at the level of the political elite,
narrowly defined, there was little change in much of the administrative
infrastructure. While local government was radically restructured, the civil
service, the judicial system and the educational system were merely over-
hauled; and all continued to be staffed by much the same personnel after
1922 as before.

   In this the Irish experience is not greatly different from that in other post-
revolutionary societies. Radical though some strands in the independence
movement may have been, it was the more cautious, conservative wing that
ultimately won power in the new state and shaped its character during the
early, formative years. While it is true that the context of politics was
redefined with the advent of independence in 1922, and that Fianna Fáil's
victory in 1932 led to further far-reaching changes, in the future it is likely
that the most profound changes in the character of Irish politics will be
incremental, as the freedom of action of the Irish political system is compro-
mised by its incorporation in a larger political entity. To recall the remark
at the beginning of this chapter about the two unions between which Irish
political development has been wedged, it might be observed that while the
very constitutional radicalism of the Act of Union of 1800 provoked almost
immediate political polarisation, leading ultimately to powerful anti-Union
sentiment, the institutional incrementalism of the European Union has so
far provided a less provocative and barely noticed model of effective political
integration.

References and further reading

Adshead, Maura and Michelle Millar, 2003. *Public Administration and Public Policy in Ireland: Theory and Methods*. London: Routledge.

Augusteijn, Joost (ed.), 2002. *The Irish Revolution, 1913–1923*. Basingstoke: Palgrave.

Bew, Paul, Ellen Hazelkorn and Henry Patterson, 1989. *The Dynamics of Irish Politics*. London: Lawrence and Wishart.

Chubb, Basil, 1992. *The Government and Politics of Ireland*, 3rd edn. London: Longman.

Coakley, John, 1986. 'The evolution of Irish party politics', in Brian Girvin and Roland Sturm (eds), *Politics and Society in Contemporary Ireland*. London: Gower, pp. 29–54.

Coakley, John, 1987. 'Political succession during the transition to independence: evidence from Europe', in Peter Calvert (ed.), *The Process of Political Succession*. London: Macmillan, pp. 161–70.

Coakley, John, 1990. 'Minor parties in Irish political life, 1922–1989', *Economic and Social Review* 21:3: 269–97.

Coakley, John, 1994. 'The election that made the First Dáil', in Brian Farrell (ed.), *The Creation of the Dáil*. Dublin: Blackwater Press, pp. 31–46.

Coakley, John, 2002. 'Religion, national identity and political change in modern Ireland', *Irish Political Studies* 17:1: 4–28.

Coakley, John, 2004. 'Critical elections and the prehistory of the Irish party system', in Tom Garvin, Maurice Manning and Richard Sinnott (eds), *Dissecting Irish Democracy: Essays in Honour of Brian Farrell*. Dublin: University College Dublin Press, pp. 134–59.

Collins, Neil (ed.), 1999. *Political Issues in Ireland Today*, 2nd edn. Manchester: Manchester University Press.

Collins, Neil and Mary O'Shea, 2000. *Understanding Corruption in Irish Politics*. Cork: Cork University Press.

Collins, Neil and Terry Cradden, 2001. *Irish Politics Today*, 4th edn. Manchester: Manchester University Press.

Commission of Inquiry into the Civil Service, 1935. *Final Report with Appendices*. Dublin: Stationery Office.

Costello, Francis J., 2003. *The Irish Revolution and its Aftermath, 1916–1923: Years of Revolt*. Dublin: Irish Academic Press.

Cronin, Mike, 1997. *The Blueshirts and Irish Politics*. Dublin: Four Courts Press.

Cronin, Mike and John M. Regan (eds), 2000. *Ireland: The Politics of Independence, 1922–49*. Basingstoke: Macmillan.

Crotty, William and David E. Schmitt (eds), 1998. *Ireland and the Politics of Change*. London: Longman.

Daly, Mary E., 1997. *The Buffer State: The Historical Roots of the Department of the Environment*. Dublin: Institute of Public Administration.

Dooney, Sean and John O'Toole, 1998. *Irish Government Today*, 2nd edn. Dublin: Gill and Macmillan.

Dunphy, Richard, 1995. *The Making of Fianna Fáil Power in Ireland, 1923–1948*. Oxford: Oxford University Press.

Dunne, Joseph, Attracta Ingram and Frank Litton (eds), 2000. *Questioning Ireland: Debates in Political Philosophy and Public Policy: Celebrating Fergal O'Connor OP, Teacher and Philosopher*. Dublin: Institute of Public Administration.

Fanning, Ronan, 1978. *The Irish Department of Finance, 1922–58*. Dublin: Institute of Public Administration.

Farrell, Brian (ed.), 1973. *The Irish Parliamentary Tradition*. Dublin: Gill and Macmillan.

Farrell, Brian (ed.), 1994. *The Creation of the Dáil*. Dublin: Blackwater Press.

Feingold, W. F., 1975. 'The tenants' movement to capture the Irish poor law boards, 1877–1886', *Albion* 7: 216–31.

FitzGerald, Garret, 2002. *Reflections on the Irish State*. Dublin: Irish Academic Press.

Fitzpatrick, David, 1998. *The Two Irelands 1912–1939*. Oxford: Oxford University Press.

Foster, Roy, 1988. *Modern Ireland 1600–1972*. London: Allen Lane.

Gallagher, Michael, 1982. *The Irish Labour Party in Transition 1957–82*. Manchester: Manchester University Press.

Gallagher, Michael, 1985. *Political Parties in the Republic of Ireland*. Dublin: Gill and Macmillan.

Gallagher, Michael and Michael Marsh, 2002. *Days of Blue Loyalty: The Politics of Membership of the Fine Gael Party*. Dublin: PSAI Press.

Galligan, Yvonne, 1998. *Women and Politics in Contemporary Ireland: From the Margins to the Mainstream*. London: Pinter.

Galligan, Yvonne, Eilís Ward and Rick Wilford (eds), 1999. *Contesting Politics: Women in Ireland North and South*. Boulder, CO: Westview; Limerick: PSAI Press.

Garvin, Tom, 1996. *1922: The Birth of Irish Democracy*. Dublin: Gill and Macmillan.

Garvin, Tom, 2004. *Preventing the Future: Politics, Education and Development in Ireland, 1937–1967*. Dublin: Gill and Macmillan.

Girvin, Brian, 1989. *Between Two Worlds: Politics and Economics in Independent Ireland*. Dublin: Gill and Macmillan.

Girvin, Brian, 2002. *From Union to Union: Nationalism, Democracy and Religion in Ireland*. Dublin: Gill and Macmillan.

Hannan, Philip and Jackie Gallagher (eds), 1996. *Taking the Long View: Seventy Years of Fianna Fáil*. Dublin: Blackwater Press.

Harkness, D. W., 1996. *Ireland in the Twentieth Century: Divided Island*. Basingstoke: Macmillan.

Hazelkorn, Ellen and Tony Murray, 1995. *A Guide to Irish Politics*. Dublin: Educational Company of Ireland.

Hopkinson, Michael, 2002. *The Irish War of Independence*. Dublin: Gill and Macmillan.

Hoppen, K. T., 1984. *Elections, Politics and Society in Ireland 1832–1885*. Oxford: Clarendon Press.

Jackson, Alvin, 1999. *Ireland 1798–1998: Politics and War*. Oxford: Blackwell.

Johnston-Liik, Edith Mary, 2002. *History of the Irish Parliament 1692–1800: Commons, Constituencies and Statutes*. 6 vols. Belfast: Ulster Historical Foundation.

Keogh, Dermot, 1994. *Twentieth Century Ireland: Nation and State*. Dublin: Gill and Macmillan.

Kissane, Bill, 2002. *Explaining Irish Democracy*. Dublin: University College Dublin Press.

Laffan, Michael, 1983. *The Partition of Ireland, 1911–25*. Dundalk: Dundalgan Press, for the Dublin Historical Association.

Laffan, Michael, 1999. *The Resurrection of Ireland: The Sinn Féin Party, 1916–1923*. Cambridge: Cambridge University Press.

Lee, J. J., 1989. *Ireland 1912–1985: Politics and Society*. Cambridge: Cambridge University Press.

Legg, Marie-Louise, 1998. *Newspapers and Nationalism: The Irish Provincial Press, 1850–1892*. Dublin: Four Courts Press.

Lyons, F. S. L., 1973. *Ireland Since the Famine*. London: Fontana.

McBride, Lawrence W., 1991. *The Greening of Dublin Castle: The Transformation of Bureaucratic and Judicial Personnel in Ireland, 1892–1922*. Washington, DC: Catholic University of America Press.

McCullagh, David, 1998. *A Makeshift Majority: The First Inter-party Government 1948–51*. Dublin: Institute of Public Administration.

McDermott, Eithne, 1998. *Clann na Poblachta*. Cork: Cork University Press.

McDowell, R. B., 1964. *The Irish Administration 1801–1914*. London: Routledge and Kegan Paul.

MacMillan, Gretchen, 1993. *State, Society and Authority in Ireland: The Foundation of the Modern State*. Dublin: Gill and Macmillan.

Manning, Maurice, 1987. *The Blueshirts*, new edn. Dublin: Gill and Macmillan.

Meghen, P. J., 1962. *A Short History of the Public Service in Ireland*. Dublin: Institute of Public Administration.

O'Brien, Justin, 2000. *The Arms Trial*. Dublin: Gill and Macmillan.

O'Day, Alan, 1998. *Irish Home Rule 1867–1921*. Manchester: Manchester University Press.

O'Halpin, Eunan, 1987. *The Decline of the Union: British Government in Ireland 1892–1920*. Dublin: Gill and Macmillan.

O'Halpin, Eunan, 1996. 'The army in independent Ireland', in Thomas Bartlett and Keith Jeffery (eds), *A Military History of Ireland*. Cambridge: Cambridge University Press, pp. 407–30.

Prager, Jeffrey, 1986. *Building Democracy in Ireland: Political Order and Cultural Integration in a Newly Independent Nation*. Cambridge: Cambridge University Press.

Purdon, Edward, 2000. *The Irish Civil War 1922–23*. Cork and Dublin: Mercier Press.

Rafter, Kevin, 1996. *The Clann: The Story of Clann na Poblachta*. Cork: Mercier Press.

Regan, John Martin, 1999. *The Irish Counter-Revolution 1921–1936: Treatyite Politics and Settlement in Independent Ireland*. Dublin: Gill and Macmillan.

Roche, Desmond, 1982. *Local Government in Ireland*. Dublin: Institute of Public Administration.

Sartori, Giovanni, 1976. *Parties and Party Systems: A Framework for Analysis*. Cambridge: Cambridge University Press.

Sinnott, Richard, 1995. *Irish Voters Decide: Voting Behaviour in Elections and Referendums since 1918*. Manchester: Manchester University Press.

Taylor, George (ed.), 2002. *Issues in Irish Public Policy*. Dublin: Irish Academic Press.

Townshend, Charles, 1999. *Ireland: The 20th Century*. London: Arnold.

Ward, Alan J., 1994. *The Irish Constitutional Tradition: Representative Government and Modern Ireland, 1782–1992*. Dublin: Irish Academic Press.

Website

www.ucd.ie/politics/irpols.html   Guide to Irish politics resources.

2 Society and political culture

John Coakley

In studying a country's political system, it can make sense to begin by analysing the constitution, where we will certainly find a detailed description of its political institutions and of the way in which they should operate. It is true that in most societies what the constitution says has an important effect on political life, and we consider the Irish constitution in Chapter 3; but the constitution does not operate in a vacuum. It is given substance by the set of political values and expectations that are dominant in the society within which it operates. The term 'political culture' has been coined to describe this set of attitudes; it refers to fundamental, deeply held views on the state itself, on the rules of the political game and on the kind of principles that should underlie political decision making.

This chapter begins with a discussion of the concept of political culture and an examination of its importance in political life. This will show that political cultural values do not exist in isolation; they are influenced by the social backgrounds and life experiences of those who hold them. We continue, therefore, by looking at the context within which Irish political cultural values have been acquired by examining the evolution of certain aspects of Irish society. We go on to examine the extent to which this pattern of evolution has generated a characteristic set of values. Finally, it is clear that no cultural pattern of this kind is homogeneous; we need therefore to consider the divisions within Irish political culture and the impact of the rapid pace of social evolution over recent decades.

Political culture and its importance

It is now taken for granted that political stability depends on compatibility between political culture and political institutions: the way in which a society is governed must not deviate too far from the system of government favoured by the politically conscious public. The political culture of a particular society need not, of course, be supportive of democratic institutions; attempts to impose liberal democratic constitutions – whether motivated by idealism or self-interest – in societies that do not share the kind of thinking that underlies them may well end in failure. This was what happened in many of the new states that appeared in central and eastern Europe after the First World War, in areas outside Europe (for instance, in the British Commonwealth) after the Second World War, in certain post-communist societies after 1989, and in such countries as Afghanistan and Iraq in the early years of the twenty-first century. What is important is that there be a match of some kind between political institutions and political culture; even authoritarian government presupposes a supportive political culture unless it is to rely entirely on rule by force, as the collapse of the communist regimes in central and eastern Europe in 1989 showed.

The widespread use of the term 'political culture' and the creation of a more systematic theory arguing its central importance in the political process date from the publication in 1963 of *The Civic Culture* by two American scholars, Gabriel Almond and Sidney Verba (Almond and Verba, 1989). A useful starting point for applying this in an Irish context is the suggestion by Almond *et al.* (2003: 51–8) that the political system has three principal levels and that these offer an appropriate framework for mapping the contours of its political culture. Furthermore, it appears that these three levels correspond approximately to three layers of values that a person acquires through the process of political socialisation – through the influence of family, school or peers, for instance.

- The *system* level refers to the state itself as a geopolitical structure and to people's attitudes towards it. This touches on a person's *core* values, absorbed during childhood and early adolescence; these relate to such matters as national identity, and tend to be stable and resistant to change in later life.
- The *process* level refers to the rules of the political game – the basic con-stitutional principles that determine how decisions are taken – and the public's view of these. Attitudes to these typically constitute a deep, *inner layer* of values, acquired during adolescence and early adulthood; these relate to fundamental principles of government, and may change, but not easily.
- The *policy* level refers to the actual outcomes of the decision-making pro-cess – the pattern of public policy that is followed by the state – and the extent to which it matches citizens' expectations. This corresponds to an *outer layer* of values, acquired for the most part in adult life; these relate to day-to-day political issues and tend to be consistent over time, but are more liable to change than the deeper ones discussed above.

While it might be possible to confine ourselves to describing Ireland's political culture in terms of this framework, it is important to remember that no political cultural pattern comes about simply by accident. The same kinds of structural forces help to shape it as influence political life more generally. We may group these into three broad areas (these are separate, but interact with and influence each other). First, the shape of a country's path of *socio-economic development* is of great importance: the extent to which society has industrialised or even passed through to a post-industrial phase, the nature of this process and its effects on social structure. The second dimension is the pattern of *cultural evolution*: the degree to which particular values (such as religious ones) have come to be dominant and the extent to which these are challenged by alternative values (such as loyalty to distinctive ethnic or linguistic groups). Third, a country's long-term *political experience* needs to be considered: external influences, patterns of past domination by distinctive groups and other consequences of the course of history may be of great significance.

This chapter rests on the assumption, then, that the pattern of political activity in any society is in large measure a product of the political culture of that society; and that political culture is, in turn, a product of a complex interplay of more fundamental societal factors. In other words, we would expect that such factors as level of socio-economic development, underlying cultural make-up (including features such as religious composition) and long-term political experience would each have an impact on people's political values at all levels, from the most profound and immutable to the most immediate and superficial. But causation need not be entirely in one direction. It is true that political culture gives substance to the institutions of state; but the direction of causation may also be reversed. Few states are merely passive victims of their political cultures; most attempt – some with exceptional vigour – also to shape their citizens' political values, and independent elites may also seek to do so, though with fewer resources. This may be done through speeches and other direct cues from political leaders, through central control or manipulation of the mass media or, most powerfully of all, through the education system. The teaching of such subjects as history and civics, in particular, may be a very effective mechanism for attempting to influence or even remould a political culture. Debates about the manner in which Irish history should be taught in schools constitute a good example (Coakley, 1994). Even more fundamentally, a state may in the long term seek to transform its own socio-economic infrastructure, to convert its citizens from one religion to another, or to bring about changes in patterns of linguistic usage – all with a view to promoting value change.

The Irish state, as we have seen in Chapter 1, came into existence in difficult circumstances at the same time as certain short-lived democracies in central and eastern Europe. Since it also shared many structural and historical characteristics with these states, it is important to ask why democratic institutions were apparently able to flourish here (see Kissane, 2002). We may find at least part of the answer in Ireland's political culture: in the set of deeply ingrained attitudes that caused Irish people to see democratic institutions and practices as normal and legitimate. This set of attitudes has had a double effect. On the one hand, the close conformity between political culture and political institutions reinforced the structures of the state. On the other hand, precisely because political cultural values normally change slowly, it is likely that these very values will act as an obstacle to future political evolution and that they will have an essentially conservative effect.

In the two sections that follow we look in turn at these two sets of characteristics: first at the set of long-term societal trends that have been relevant for Irish political culture, and then at the nature of this political culture itself. While the starting point of this discussion will be a set of generalisations that have been commonly accepted about Irish society and political culture, we qualify this by looking at the enormous changes that have taken place in recent decades. This approach oversimplifies the position by temporarily overlooking the heterogeneity of Irish political culture: the last section of the chapter seeks to compensate by turning to the issue of social and political cultural division.

Stability and change in Irish society

When the first systematic attempts to examine aspects of Irish political culture got underway in the early 1970s, it was still possible to describe Ireland as 'an agricultural country of small, scattered family farms'; the Irish people as being strongly attached to the Catholic Church and as adhering to a religion of 'an austere and puritanical variety that is somewhat cold and authoritarian'; and Irish society as being insulated from Europe by an all-pervasive British influence (Chubb, 1970: 51, 53, 46–7; see also Farrell, 1971: ix–xx; Schmitt, 1973). These characteristics, authors suggested, combined to produce a distinctive political culture which was characterised by such features as nationalism, authoritarianism, anti-intellectualism and personalism. Before going on to speculate in the next section about the extent to which such features survive in contemporary Ireland, we examine in this section the background characteristics in Irish society that are likely to have had a major impact on political values. The pattern we encounter will be one of relative stability, perhaps masking slow change, until the 1970s, but of accelerating change since then in each of the three domains that we have already discussed: economic transformation, cultural secularisation and geopolitical reorientation (on long-term Irish economic development, see Ó Gráda, 1995, 1997; Barry, 1999; on Irish society, Breen *et al.*, 1990; Clancy *et al.*, 1995; Goldthorpe and Whelan, 1992; Coulter and Coleman, 2003).

Socio-economic development

The outstanding characteristic of socio-economic development in Ireland, viewed over the long term, has been a fundamental shift in the nature of the economy and a radical change in social structure. In this Ireland has not been unique; researchers from different disciplines and ideological perspectives have pointed to the central importance of the revolutionary socio-economic transition through which all western societies have progressed, whether this is described as a transition from agrarian (or pre-industrial) to industrial society, from feudal (or pre-capitalist) to capitalist society, or from traditional to modern society. This change may best be appreciated by considering 'ideal types' (theoretical descriptions that do not necessarily exist in reality) of the two kinds of society. It should be noted that these types refer to more or less integrated packages of characteristics spanning a wide range of areas rather than being confined exclusively to economic change as implied in the narrow sense of the word 'industrial'. It has been argued that many western societies have indeed progressed beyond this, into a later 'post-industrial' phase, whose implications for political culture need also to be borne in mind; but our present focus is on the great historical transition from agrarian to industrial society, which had a lasting impact on socio-political attitudes.

Agrarian society has been typified as that in which the population, by definition, is overwhelmingly involved in the primary sector of the economy (with peasants relying on mixed subsistence agriculture, and the industrial sector being confined to small-scale cottage industries and crafts); with predominantly rural settlement patterns; mainly illiterate, and with an oral tradition dominated by village-based or regional dialects; with only a restricted transport network; and with poorly developed communications media. In industrial society these characteristics are reversed. The population is overwhelmingly involved in the industrial or services sectors (with large-scale, machine dependent industry and a small, surviving agricultural sector of specialised commercial farmers); with predominantly urban settlement patterns; mainly or even universally literate in a modern, standardised language; and with a high degree of mobility – of people and goods, and of ideas.

A yet more profound difference between the two types of society arises in the area of social relations. In agrarian society the individual is born into a particular rank in society, kinship group and village, and faces a fixed set of occupational options. Mobility prospects are restricted not just by society itself but also by the individual's own acceptance of his or her existing role as inevitable and natural. In industrial society, by contrast, regardless of the position into which an individual is born the prospects for spatial and occupational mobility are much greater not just because society is open to this, but because the individual's own perspective allows him or her freely to contemplate such roles. By contrast to agrarian society, where the existing order and the individual's role within it are accepted, in industrial society the typical individual has a capacity to envisage himself or herself occupying an unlimited range of roles.

Where does Ireland fit between the poles of agrarian and industrial society defined above – or might it even have developed so far that it is better described as post-industrial? The data on occupational structure and urbanisation in Appendix 1a are summarised in Figure 2.1, which also considers two other variables, language and literacy. If economic development was

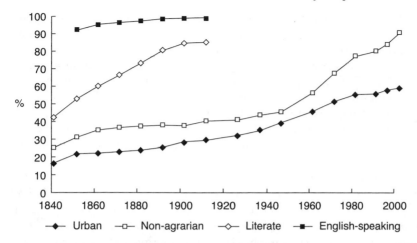

Figure 2.1 Urban population, non-agrarian population, literacy and language, 1841–
2002

Source: *Census of Ireland*, various years, 1841–2002.

relatively slow, with Irish society long remaining rural and agrarian, the
pace of other aspects of social change was relatively rapid. Although secondary education, in Ireland as elsewhere, was left to private interests or to the
church until recent decades, and third-level education had negligible impact
on the public until recently, the state intervened at an early stage in primary
education. After 1831 an ambitious network of 'national schools' was established throughout the country, and by the end of the nineteenth century the
great bulk of children of school-going age were attending these schools. The
impact of this system and of the efforts of other agencies on levels of literacy
was dramatic, as Figure 2.1 shows. Furthermore, between the 1880s and
1920s the stark cleavage between landlords and tenants (a common feature
of agrarian societies) was overcome as the process of state-sponsored land
purchase established and consolidated the principle of peasant proprietor-
ship and led to the disappearance of traditional landlords as a class.

The level of educational development in Ireland and the growth of
literacy, then, proceeded much more quickly than the more retarded pace
of economic development would have suggested. This anomaly draws
attention to one of the hazards of viewing socio-economic development in
isolation from external relationships and influences, especially those of
dependence. Although Ireland (or at least the south) was an economically
backward periphery, it formed until 1922 part of one of the world's most
advanced industrial states. The British government was prepared to promote a separate agenda for Ireland, overseeing the establishment there of
an advanced primary education system and of a developed transport infrastructure that included thousands of miles of roads and railways.

British educational policy in Ireland was not disinterested: it also contributed to the anglicisation of the country. The earliest reliable information on the linguistic structure of the population dates from 1851, and shows that already at that time almost all of the population (94 per cent of those in the present territory of the Republic) were able to speak English, and that a considerable majority (71 per cent) were able to speak English only. As the nineteenth century progressed the trend towards anglicisation continued, with the result that by the beginning of the twentieth century virtually the entire adult population was familiar with a single language of wider communication, English.

The right-hand side of Figure 2.1 points to a more recent and particularly striking phenomenon: it shows clearly that, after many decades of relative stability, the period since 1960 has been characterised by economic and social change that is almost revolutionary in scope. The proportion of the workforce engaged in agriculture has been plummeting and the urban population has expanded. The character of the non-agricultural workforce has been changing rapidly. Although the labourforce engaged in manufacturing industry increased only slightly between 1966 and 2002 (from 200,000 to 244,000), traditional food and clothing related industries accounted for 52 per cent of this in 1966, but only 22 per cent in 2002. Over the same period, chemical and metal related industries (incorporating new high technology manufacturing) increased from 20 per cent to 50 per cent. Furthermore, there has been a rapid growth in the services sector: over the three decades after 1966, the insurance, finance and business services sector increased five-fold, while professional services more than doubled (indeed, the rate of increase was even more dramatic within certain high-profile professions: the number of lawyers increased by 275 per cent and the number of accountants by 500 per cent between 1966 and 1996). All of this has been associated with yet another development that is also likely to have a considerable social effect: the growing wealth of Irish society. GDP per capita has been rising more rapidly than in the United Kingdom since 1960, and it has grown faster than the EU average since 1973. As a result, GDP per capita increased from about 60 per cent of the EU average in 1960 to about 85 per cent in 1997, having overtaken the UK level in 1996 (Haughton, 1998: 27–8). By 2002, Ireland had the second highest level of GDP per capita in the EU (Central Statistics Office, 2003: 16).

Dramatic though the statistics may be, they do not tell the full story: qualitative changes have also been taking place. The decline in the agricultural sector of the population, for example, does not mean simply that there are fewer farmers; the character of farming is being transformed from a way of life into just another enterprise, as small family farms are replaced by larger agribusinesses. Indeed, rural Ireland as it was traditionally conceived is disappearing as villages in the hinterland of larger urban settlements become dormitory towns. By the end of the 1990s, the national rail and bus

Table 2.1 Telephones, televisions and private cars, 1960–2000

Year	Telephones		Television licences		Private cars	
	Number	*Per 100 population*	*Number*	*Per 100 population*	*Number*	*Per 100 population*
1960	148,818	5.3	(92,675)	(3.3)	169,681	6.0
1970	291,478	9.8	415,918	14.0	440,185	14.8
1980	650,000	18.9	642,751	18.9	735,760	21.4
1990	967,000	27.4	806,055	22.8	796,408	22.6
2000	1,580,000	41.7	1,057,000	27.9	1,319,250	34.8

Source: Computed from *Statistical Abstract of Ireland, 1963–1997*, *Statistical Yearbook of Ireland, 2002* and other sources.

Note
The earliest data on television licences refer to 1962. Data on telephones relate to land lines only. To place these figures in context it should be noted that the number of houses per 100 population in 1991 was 28.5.

service interpreted the Dublin commuter area as being enclosed in a semi-circle whose circumference was defined by the towns of Dundalk, Carrickmacross, Mullingar, Tullamore, Portlaoise, Carlow and Gorey (towns ranging from 80 to 100 kilometres from Dublin). This erosion of urban–rural divisions is reflected in travel-to-work statistics: by 2002, 11 per cent of the working population was spending two hours or more per day travelling to and from work.

There are other respects in which the quality of Irish life has been changing. A communications revolution has occurred, with an explosion in access to a new, powerful medium – television – and greatly enhanced geographical mobility as a consequence of the increased availability of cars. The extent of these changes is indicated in Table 2.1, which covers the period 1960–2000. The most useful yardstick for interpreting these data is the number of households per hundred people. In 1991, there were 28.5 households for every 100 people (a ratio that has since risen a little); by 1990 the proportion of telephones had reached this figure, and the proportion of cars had reached it well before 2000. But this does not take full account of a new communications revolution. By the end of 2003, in addition to the land lines reported in Table 2.1, there were 3.2 million mobile phone subscribers, representing a market penetration rate of 83 per cent, only slightly below the EU average (Commission for Communications Regulation, 2003: 8). Between 1998 and 2003, the number of households connected to the internet increased from 5 per cent to 36 per cent (the EU average in 2002 was 39 per cent; Central Statistics Office, 2003: 29).

The extent of these changes is to be seen also in the educational revolution, which fuelled economic growth as well as being in part its consequence.

By 1996 the third-level student population numbered more than 100,000, having increased six-fold since 1966. By 2002, this had increased to 125,000, and 35 per cent of all of those aged 25–34 had received a third-level education (the overall EU level was 26 per cent; Central Statistics Office, 2003: 41, 43).

Another important concomitant of economic development has been change in the composition of the population. Given traditionally high levels of emigration, the sustained pattern of net immigration since 1996 is striking. In the eight years 1996–2003, a little over 400,000 people immigrated to Ireland – almost double the number who emigrated over the same period. By far the largest proportion of these were accounted for by a single country, the United Kingdom (38 per cent); 19 per cent came from other EU countries, 12 per cent from the United States and 31 per cent from other countries. The 2002 census shows that, in terms of birthplace, the non-EU countries accounting for the largest number of Irish residents were the USA (21,000), Nigeria (9,000), South Africa, Australia, Romania and China (6,000 each), Philippines and Canada (4,000 each), and Pakistan, India and Russia (3,000 each).

Religion and secularisation

Changes in the area of religious belief have also been dramatic. In terms of religious affiliation, a great majority of the population belongs to the Catholic Church (see Appendix 1a). The Protestant population, which in the nineteenth century constituted 25 per cent of the population of the island, amounted to a minority of only 10 per cent in the south after partition. Furthermore, many members of this community had been killed in the First World War; many had been associated with the old regime, and left after 1922; many were landlords who lost their estates or who were subjected to intimidation at around the same period, and who also left; while the remaining Protestant population had shrunk to 3 per cent by 1991, though it increased slightly in 2002 largely as a consequence of immigration.

From a comparative point of view, the position of the Catholic religion within Irish society has been rather remarkable. Unlike the position in central and eastern Europe (the most obvious part of the continent in which to look for comparable societies in a historical perspective), it was along religious denominational rather than along linguistic lines that political mobilisation took place in the nineteenth century. This arose in part from the perceived (but, in reality, imperfect) coincidence between the two main religions and two ethnic traditions – Catholic Irish natives, and Protestant British settlers. It was also related to the fact that the institutional Catholic Church in Ireland up to the nineteenth century was not a major landowner, was not linked with the old regime, and was neutral or sympathetic on the issues of democratisation and nationalism, rather than being suspicious or hostile, as in continental Europe.

In any case, Irish history offers many illustrations of the grip of the Catholic Church on the people. Even before the famine of 1845–9, when evidence suggests that only a minority of Catholics attended weekly mass, the Church had become intimately involved in popular political movements – first in the movement for Catholic emancipation, then in that for repeal of the Act of Union, both led by Daniel O'Connell. This involvement continued and intensified in post-famine Ireland. In what has been described as a 'devotional revolution', weekly mass attendance rates began to approach 100 per cent. Already before the new state was founded, Ireland was noted for the remarkable loyalty of Catholics to the Church and for the absence of a tradition of anti-clericalism (Whyte, 1980: 3–8). This relationship was cemented through the educational system, in which the Catholic Church has had an unchallenged role. Catholic identity – the self-perception of Catholics as an oppressed group, with both clergy and laity discriminated against by the state – became an important element of Irish national identity. Like all processes of collective mobilisation, of course, the political integration of the Catholic population had a negative aspect, its differentiation from others; in this case, the excluded group was the Protestant population.

The significance of interdenominational differences for an important aspect of development that has already been discussed – education – needs to be underscored. Historically, a preoccupation with education was characteristic of Protestant, not Catholic, societies; in the former, particular emphasis was placed on the need of every individual to be able to read the Bible and, hence, it was seen as imperative for all to be provided with rudimentary schooling. There is extensive evidence from Europe of large differences in Catholic and Protestant literacy levels, and the same trends are apparent in nineteenth-century Ireland. In 1861 in the present territory of the Republic, for instance, 47 per cent of Catholics were illiterate, as against only 12 per cent of Protestants. While these figures must be treated with some caution since Protestants were also, in general, of a higher social status than Catholics (and are for this reason more likely to have been exposed to education), they do draw attention to an important aspect of the interplay between cultural evolution and socio-economic development.

It is clear that until the 1970s the level of commitment to traditional Irish Catholicism was extremely high. This was reflected not just in the character of public debate but also in objective indicators such as church attendance, participation in church activities and clerical vocations. The pace of change since the 1980s has, however, been dramatic. Those attending church at least once weekly amounted to 91 per cent in 1973–4, and this figure remained steady throughout the 1970s, as Figure 2.2 shows; but it dropped a little in the 1980s, and much more dramatically in the late 1990s. By 2002, only 54 per cent declared themselves to be weekly churchgoers, and there was a striking breakdown in age profile: for those aged under 35, only 32 per cent attended at least once weekly; this rose to 52 per cent for the 35–54 age group, and to 80 per cent for those aged 55 or more (calculated from

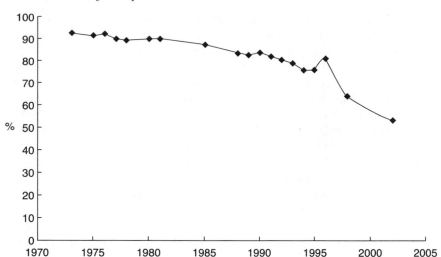

Figure 2.2 Weekly church attendance, Ireland, 1973–2002

Source: Calculated from Eurobarometer trend file, 1973–99, and European Social Survey, 2002.

Note: The data refer to those stating that they attend church at least once a week.

European Social Survey, 2002).[1] Between 1970 and 1995 the number of clergy had fallen from 33,000 to a little over 21,000, a drop of 35 per cent; but these figures hide a profound crisis in clerical recruitment. In 1996 there were only 111 vocations to religious life, a drop of 92 per cent over a 30-year period (Inglis, 1998: 212). Since a considerable number of those who respond to a religious vocation drop out before taking final religious vows, and since the general pattern is one of decline in religious vocations, the Catholic Church has already reached a point where it no longer has the personnel resources to staff its schools – or, in places, even its churches. Since the age profile of the Irish clergy is rapidly becoming older, the problem of staffing parishes is likely to become progressively more acute. Given the traditional centrality of the priest not just as a religious but also as a social leader in rural Ireland, the impact of this trend on the character of Irish life will be considerable.

It must be assumed that the decline in clerical recruitment and lapse in lay involvement reflect changes in underlying patterns of belief. It appears that many of the traditional devotional practices that were so characteristic of Irish Catholicism have been in decline, as numbers attending novenas, prayer vigils and outdoor processions have dropped; and of 3,000 holy wells recorded, no more than 200 were still in use by the 1990s (Inglis, 1998: 24–30). The number of visitors to St Patrick's Purgatory, an island in Lough Derg that has been famous as a destination for pilgrims since the Middle Ages, declined from 29,000 in 1987 to 11,000 in 2001 (Fuller, 2002: 278).

There is a good deal of evidence that in an increasingly secular Ireland 'a reformation of the Catholic Church, or a Protestantisation of Catholic belief and practice' has been taking place, in the sense that Catholics are increasingly guided by conscience rather than by church teaching (Inglis, 1998: 204). But quite apart from this trend, probably itself a consequence of broader social developments, the Catholic Church has suffered a crisis of authority, especially as a consequence of child sexual abuse scandals and the manner in which they have been handled – a major challenge for the future of Irish Catholicism (see Fuller, 2002: 237–68).

The decline in religious belief and practice recorded above may be in part a function of the socio-economic changes already discussed. Religious leaders themselves have not been immune from the pattern of value change in Irish society, and scandals associated with the clergy are likely to have further undermined the teaching authority of the church; but it must also be remembered that the falling trust in the church in Ireland is matched by a similar decline in trust in other major institutions (see Hardiman and Whelan, 1998: 82–5). The extent to which traditional church teachings in the domain of sexual morality and the family have been ignored is indicated in Figure 2.3. This shows the sharp increase in the proportion of births outside marriage that began in the 1980s; in the early years of the twenty-first century, more than 30 per cent of all births were to unmarried women, and

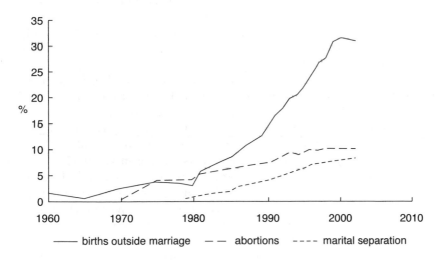

Figure 2.3 Births outside marriage, abortion and marital separation, 1960–2002

Source: *Statistical Abstract of Ireland,* various years; Office for National Statistics, Series AB, *Abortion Statistics for England and Wales,* no. 24, 1997 – no. 28, 2001; *Census of Ireland,* 1979–2002.

Note: Births outside marriage are expressed as a percentage of all births; abortions (based on British statistics for women having abortions in England and Wales and giving an Irish address) are expressed as a percentage of this figure plus total births in Ireland; marital separation refers to those who have been divorced, separated legally or otherwise or deserted, or whose marriages have been annulled, expressed as a percentage of the ever-married population.

this proportion increased in the younger age groups (in the last quarter of 2003, for example, 54 per cent of births to women aged under 30 took place outside marriage, as did 79 per cent of births to women aged under 25). Notwithstanding the increased availability of contraceptives, the number of abortions increased steadily until the beginning of the twenty-first century (here our data are based on women having abortions in England and Wales but giving Irish addresses). Marriage breakdown has also been on the increase, and the phenomenon of separated people entering new unions without the sanction of the church has been growing.

Political experience

Given the centuries-long British presence on the island, it is not surprising that the legacy of British rule has left a lasting imprint on the Irish political mentality. Whether or not Ireland was a willing recipient, Britain bequeathed to its neighbouring island its dominant language, much of its culture, many of its social practices and, most importantly for present purposes, its political vocabulary, concepts, institutions and patterns of behaviour. A large volume of Irish emigration to (and a smaller volume of reverse migration from) Britain has been characteristic of Irish population movement patterns. For long after independence a close economic relationship also remained, with the two countries sharing a common currency until 1979 and with a remarkably high degree of Irish trade dependence on the British market: for several decades after 1922 the greater part of Ireland's imports came from Great Britain, and approximately three-quarters of Irish exports were destined for Britain.

One of the most obvious aspects of the British legacy has been in the domain of language, as we have already noted. The British may have failed to assimilate the Irish to their religion; but where religious proselytism failed, anglicisation succeeded. The Irish language was in a very weak position by 1922, notwithstanding the energetic activities of revivalists. Little effort was made by the new state to halt its decline in Gaeltacht areas, though enormous resources were devoted to providing children in English-speaking Ireland with a rudimentary knowledge of the Irish language. While official statistics thus show a steady rise in the proportion claiming a knowledge of Irish (from 18 per cent in 1911 to 43 per cent in 2002), the language has continued to decay to the point of extinction as a living language. From a comparative point of view, its position has been unique and extraordinary. It has been given a powerful constitutional and legal position because of its status as the perceived ancestral language, yet most of the population fail to understand it and very few speak it on a daily basis. Although the language issue was used by the early nationalist movement, it was important as a symbol of Irish identity rather than as a medium of communication. The language revival movement was, strangely, made up overwhelmingly of people whose home language was English, and, by sharp contrast to the position in central and eastern Europe, the language boundary in Ireland did not separate two ethnic groups – speakers of the two languages felt equally Irish.

Geographical proximity and community of language thus continued to promote British influence in Ireland even after 1922. It was not only goods and people that travelled freely to Ireland from the neighbouring island; ideas could also do so. British newspapers have always circulated widely in Ireland. They accounted for at least 10 per cent of daily newspaper circulation in Ireland in 1968, and 21 per cent in 1992 (with the Irish edition of the *Star* accounting for a further 14 per cent); by the end of 2003, Irish editions of three British tabloids accounted for 45 per cent of circulation, and British-imported newspapers for a further 5 per cent, leaving three Irish dailies with a 50 per cent share. Of Sunday newspapers, British titles accounted for at least 40 per cent in 1968, though this figure had dropped to 31 per cent by 1992; by the end of 2003 it still stood at 32 per cent, including Irish editions of British papers (calculated from Chubb, 1970: 124–5; Wilson Hartnell, 1992: 17–18; Medialive, 2004). Irish people's first familiarity with radio and with the powerful medium of television came from Britain, and even with the development of Irish services competition from Britain has been intense, especially on the east coast. In 2003 it was estimated that the four Irish television channels had an overall market share of 55 per cent between them, but in those parts of the country where British channels could be received (accounting, in fact, for the great majority of homes) this dropped to 45 per cent, with BBC, UTV and other British channels accounting for 55 per cent (calculated from Medialive, 2004).

British influence has been imperfectly balanced by countervailing influences from elsewhere. The enormous Irish diaspora in the United States and in other English-speaking countries has had only occasional impact on attitudes at home. Links with the nearer countries of continental Europe, intense by contemporary standards until the eighteenth century, were rather weak in the nineteenth and early twentieth centuries; it is clear from data on the destinations of Irish emigrants that they were oriented almost entirely to the English-speaking world rather than to continental Europe. It is likely that American culture has been making inroads through the powerful medium of television (since the Irish channels carry a relatively high proportion of syndicated American material), but in this the Irish are likely to be only slightly ahead of the British and their other fellow-Europeans.

Paradoxically, the impact of the European Union, which in general has had the effect of breaking down borders between neighbouring countries, has had the opposite effect on Anglo-Irish relations. While the signing of the Anglo-Irish Free Trade Agreement in 1965 represented a further rapprochement between the two countries and might have been expected to lead to closer bilateral economic ties, Ireland's accession to the EC in 1973 acted as a counterbalance. There was a great increase in travel in general, and especially, in so far as we can measure it, in travel between Ireland and the continent. In 1960 a little more than a million passenger movements out of Ireland took place by ship and aeroplane, 7 per cent of them to destinations other than Great Britain; by 2001 this figure had increased to more than 11 million, and the proportion travelling directly to non-British destinations had increased to 34 per cent (calculated from *Statistical Abstract of Ireland*, 1961 and 2002). In addition, Ireland's trade relationships changed dramatically. In 1960, 46 per cent of Irish imports and 61 per cent of Irish exports were from or to Great Britain; by 2001 these proportions had dropped to 33 and 22 per cent, respectively (calculated from *Statistical Abstract of Ireland*, 1961 and 2002). Ironically, although in the long term the significance of the UK–Irish border is likely to diminish, over recent decades it has actually increased: different VAT rates, excise duties and the impact of the break in parity between the Irish and British currencies reinforced the border. Ireland's participation since 1999 in a European monetary union from which the United Kingdom has stayed aloof is likely to reinforce this trend, if only in the short term.

Ireland's changing political culture

The long-term economic and social processes discussed above have produced a society in which particular patterns of political cultural values are likely to flourish. We consider these at the three levels outlined at the beginning of this chapter:

- the issue of national identity, typically a core value with implications for the geopolitical status of the state (we will examine the extent to which *nationalism* is a key component in Irish political culture);
- the question of attitudes towards democracy and decision-making processes, which are typically deeply embedded in the political psychological makeup of the citizen (we will assess the extent to which a commitment to *democratic values* is characteristic of the Irish); and
- the domain of policy preferences, where people's values are less immutable (we will consider three areas, though rather more briefly than in the case of the more deeply embedded values discussed above: *conservatism*, a disposition to support socially and economically non-interventionist policies, *clericalism*, a tendency to defer to the political leadership of the church, and *isolationism*, a preference for a strategy of non-alignment in the area of foreign policy).

It is not our argument that discussion of Irish political culture can be reduced simply to analysis of these five features; indeed, this list is far from exhaustive. Rather, we will use these as a framework for discussing Irish political cultural values, illustrating the extent to which change appears to have taken place over time in each one. In each case, the discussion begins with an examination of the meaning of the term and its general implications, and continues with an assessment of such empirical evidence as is available – historical evidence of various kinds, electoral evidence and survey evidence.

Nationalism?

Although the term is elastic, *nationalism* implies at a minimum a sense of loyalty to one's nation – a type of community with which one primarily identifies. To the extent that this entails a willingness to sacrifice individual interests for the good of the community, this seems socially desirable, but it begs the question as to how the community is defined. If the community or nation with which people identify does not coincide with the state, then loyalty to it is likely to conflict with loyalty to the state (the collapse of the Soviet Union and of Yugoslavia were among the more drastic consequences of this form of conflict). Furthermore, when taken to excess, national loyalty can threaten other forms of human affiliation and can conflict with other ethical and political values (the ethnic 'purification' of Nazi Germany through the extermination of national minorities is an example).

It is clear that as Irish people mobilised politically in the nineteenth century the idea of an 'Irish nation' based on those who were of Catholic, Gaelic background became a central political ideal; its political programme entailed autonomy (or possibly even independence) for the island of Ireland. At this time, Irish nationalism was essentially *separatist*, and increasingly rejected the legitimacy of the United Kingdom government. The ultimate expression of this attitude followed Sinn Féin's victory in the 1918 general election, when a majority of Irish MPs refused to attend parliament and succeeded ultimately in establishing a separate state. Had the goals of Irish nationalism been fully achieved, it is possible that nationalist sentiment in this form would have faded away or been transformed. As we saw in Chapter 1, however, full formal independence was achieved only in 1949, and even then this did not extend over the whole island.

Irish nationalism after 1922 thus became in large measure *irredentist*: achieving territorial unification through annexation of Northern Ireland was a central aim. This was written into the constitution in 1937 in the form of a definition of the national territory as comprising 'the whole island of Ireland, its islands and the territorial seas', and the irredentist policy was vigorously pursued, apparently with significant popular support, in the 1940s and the 1950s. The growing violence in Northern Ireland in the 1970s appears to have convinced policy makers that this form of nationalism was actually subversive of the state; through their efforts, but also as a consequence of other social changes, the intensity of irredentism gradually diminished in the last quarter of the century. Furthermore, a progressive redefinition of the community appears to have taken place: identification with the population of the Republic of Ireland appears to be gradually replacing a form of identification that extended to people living north of the

border. It remains to be seen whether the tolerance of other groups (including those differentiated by race) that is associated with the national self-
image as a non-colonial state which is a net exporter of people can survive
the transition to membership of a post-imperial network of states in which
greatly increased immigration is likely to be the norm.

Electoral evidence broadly supports this interpretation. Even in the
turbulent 1920s, support for parties that rejected the legitimacy of the new
state never significantly exceeded 25 per cent, and the main anti-treaty
party's growing electoral success in the later 1920s and in the 1930s coincided with its increasingly moderate stance on the national question.
Since 1922, the mainstream parties have appeared to be increasingly content
with the status quo of partition. By the end of the 1990s, the decision by
Sinn Féin to abide by the terms of the Good Friday Agreement of 1998 (see
Chapter 15), to accept the right of Northern Ireland to determine its own
future and to grant full recognition to the institutions of government of
Northern Ireland, and the party's success in bringing the great bulk of its
electorate with it in this remarkable shift, marginalised fundamentalist
nationalism. The results of the May 1998 referendums in Northern Ireland
and the Republic (in which respectively 71 per cent and 94 per cent voted in
favour of the agreement) not only provided a popular mandate for the settlement but also symbolically revoked what fundamentalist republicans had
regarded as the irrevocable decision of the Irish people in 1918 in favour of
an independent, united Irish republic (see Coakley, 2002).

Survey evidence permits us to explore further the character of contemporary Irish nationalism. We may use this, and supplementary information
from other sources, to address a number of questions:

- *irredentism*: to what extent is the demand for territorial unity a continuing
  feature of Irish nationalism?
- *patriotism*: in what respects is Irish nationalism a force that is supportive of
  the state?
- *ethnocentrism*: to what extent are external groups regarded with hostility?

Perhaps inevitably, one legacy of partition has been increased differentiation between communities on either side of the border. Especially after
the outbreak of communal conflict in Northern Ireland, the attitudinal gap
between the south and Northern Ireland appears to have grown. There is
evidence, however, that following the declaration of the IRA ceasefire in
1994 the psychological distance that separated southerners from the north
has lessened, even if years of censorship of militant nationalist perspectives
'left huge gaps in understanding and many unrealistic expectations' (Ruane
and Todd, 1996: 255).

Survey evidence from 1988–9 confirms the north–south gap. Irish people,
it appears, felt considerably closer to English (or British) people than to the
Northern Irish of both communities, in terms of willingness to contemplate

marriage relationships, close friendship or neighbourliness. Indeed, large numbers felt that Northern Ireland and the Republic were two separate nations (49 per cent agreed, 42 per cent disagreed) and that 'Northerners on all sides tend to be extreme and unreasonable' (35 per cent agreed, though 46 per cent disagreed) (Mac Gréil, 1996: 225, 234). On the other hand, the extent of the rapprochement with the British is striking. In a survey conducted in September 2003, when people were asked how favourable or unfavourable their overall 'opinion or impression' of five large countries was, they placed the United Kingdom first (78 per cent 'mainly favourable' or 'very favourable'), followed by the United States (74 per cent), France (68 per cent), Germany (54 per cent) and Japan (39 per cent; British Council, 2003). Yet, irredentist, or at least pro-unity, sentiment has not necessarily disappeared. In a survey in summer 2002, 71 per cent agreed that 'the long term policy for Northern Ireland should be to reunify with the rest of Ireland', though only 13 per cent strongly agreed with this and, in any case, only 21 per cent felt that the issue was very important (calculated from Irish National Election Study, 2002).[2]

When we turn to examine the extent to which the character of Irish nationalism may be supportive of the state, it is true that we uncover patterns of patriotism that are in some respects stronger than those elsewhere in western Europe, and that in other respects are weaker. In surveys in 1981 and 1990 the Irish were significantly more likely than other Europeans to claim that they would be willing to fight for their country in the event of war, and a much higher proportion (76 per cent in 1990) declared themselves to be 'very proud' of their nationality; the average for other European countries was 37 per cent (Ashford and Timms, 1992: 90). Reported levels of national pride have been consistently high; a survey in autumn 2003, for instance, showed that 96 per cent of Irish respondents declared themselves proud to be Irish, well above the overall level in other EU states in respect of the same question (85 per cent). The same survey also confirmed the continuing power of national identification that earlier surveys had shown. When asked 'in the near future, do you see yourself as Irish only, Irish and European, European and Irish, or European only?', 49 per cent of Irish respondents answered 'Irish only', 43 per cent 'Irish and European', 4 per cent 'European and Irish' and just 1 per cent 'European only' (Eurobarometer no. 60, 2003).

In Ireland, as elsewhere, there is a darker side to nationalism: it can easily lead to intolerance and racism. Early survey evidence presented a mixed picture. Analysis of a large-scale survey in Dublin in 1972 suggested that there was a 'relatively high level of dormant or latent racialism' (Mac Gréil, 1977: 530). Although this had diminished by 1988, the level of ethno-centrism (prejudice against persons belonging to a nationality or culture other than one's own) had actually increased – rather ironically, but not surprisingly, since this coincided with efforts to bring the peoples of Europe together, which itself can aggravate inter-group tensions (Mac Gréil, 1996:

128–32). Of course, mistrust of other races tends to be related to the visibility of racial minorities: a 1990 survey showed the Irish to have a more tolerant attitude towards immigrants than the typical European one (Ashford and Timms, 1992: 14). This was confirmed in a 1993 survey of attitudes towards non-EC immigrants as well as people from other EC countries (Euro-barometer no. 39, 1993: A51–4). As late as 1997, surveys continued to convey the impression of Irish tolerance of ethnic minorities. Only 12 per cent said that they would not accept people seeking political asylum in the European Union (lower than the overall figure of 18 per cent for the EU as a whole), while only 19 per cent felt that there were too many foreigners living in Ireland (the corresponding figure in other EU countries averaged 45 per cent; Eurobarometer no. 48, 1997: 70–1).

These were the attitudes at a time when the proportion of foreign-born in Ireland was considerably lower than that in the typical European state. But to what extent are these attitudes likely to survive significant immigration? A growing literature addresses the issue of racism in Ireland (see Fanning, 2002; McVeigh and Lentin, 2002). Anecdotal and survey evidence indeed points to racist attitudes as an increasingly significant phenomenon (see O'Connell, 2003). When viewed in comparative perspective, though, indicators of racist attitudes in Ireland are not greatly different from levels elsewhere in Europe. A survey in spring 2000 found that 20 per cent of Irish respondents described the presence of people of another race as 'disturbing' (the overall EU level was 15 per cent; Eurobarometer no. 53, 2000: 88–9). Analysis of a survey conducted in late 2002 showed Irish respondents as being rather less negative towards refugees than their counterparts in most other west European states, and as not overestimating the numbers of immigrants in the country, a classic feature of racism (the median response gave the estimated proportion of foreign-born in Ireland as 10 per cent, exactly the proportion recorded in the census; calculated from European Social Survey, 2002).

Thus, it seems that Ireland's slow pace of economic and social development, juxtaposed with a much more developed Britain in a relationship of dependency, provide the raw material for the growth of Irish nationalism. This was reinforced by Catholic resentment at a heritage of oppression, and the church could see in self-government for Ireland a buttress against 'godless' ideas from across the Irish Sea. Britain did not help matters, arguably governing Ireland with insufficient wisdom to secure Irish loyalty to the united state established in 1800. While nationalist sentiment may have been substantially purged by independence after 1922, at least in the south, and by increasing self-confidence arising from the Republic's undisputed statehood and economic success, an unfamiliar new pattern of immigration may well encourage the growth of a new wave of ethnocentric or even racist attitudes, a development compatible with certain structural and other conditions in contemporary Irish society (Garner, 2004: 28–34).

Democratic values?

The existence of a political culture in which *democratic values* are dominant is clearly of central importance for the maintenance of democracy. By this we mean that those who are involved politically must be reasonably well informed about politics and be broadly supportive of democratic institutions. While observers of Irish political culture are agreed that a basic commitment to democratic values is a central feature, they disagree on the extent to which this is modified by other values of a more traditional character.

One book-length analysis of Irish political culture identified *authoritarianism* as one of its central characteristics (Schmitt, 1973: 43–54); a strong pressure towards political *conformism*, especially in rural areas, has been noted (Gallagher, 1982: 19–20); and *loyalty* (to leaders in church and state) and *anti-intellectualism* (in which a consensus on religious and political values was able for long to continue virtually unchallenged) have been seen as key elements, especially in the past (Chubb, 1992: 18–20). These terms belong to a common category to the extent that each of them implies commitment to opinions received from above, and a suspicion of those who are not prepared to accept these. (The term 'authoritarianism' is used here in a very specific and, perhaps, unusual sense; it is taken to refer not to a particular system of government but rather to a distinctive type of attitude that combines *deference* to the views of established leaders with *intolerance* of those who dissent from these views. The source of authority is not necessarily the will of the majority but some principle held to be objective and absolute, transcending individual preferences.)

A second set of political cultural features whose implications for democracy are rather negative appears at first sight to be incompatible with the set just discussed: *personalism* (Schmitt, 1973: 55–64) and *individualism* (Gallagher, 1982: 16–20). Personalism has been defined as 'a pattern of social relations in which people are valued for who they are and whom they know – not solely for what technical qualifications they possess' (Schmitt, 1973: 55). This recalls the complaint of Irish cynics that 'it's not what you know that matters, it's whom you know'. It also implies a tendency to evaluate and respond to persons in positions of power (such as the President, the Taoiseach or a local Dáil deputy) in terms of their personal character rather than in terms of the authority associated with their office. Its principal aspects include a closely integrated pattern of social and political relationships, and brokerage politics (see Chapter 9). It is entirely compatible with the broader concept of individualism, defined as 'a preference for individual action as opposed to co-operation' (Gallagher, 1982: 16), and has the same political consequences. This characteristic is similar to the 'amoral familism' detected by Edward Banfield (1967) in village life in southern Italy – a suspicion of and sense of competition with all those outside the immediate family, attributable to a low level of economic development and a legacy of foreign rule.

One of the strongest pieces of historical evidence that has been cited in support of the apparently strong commitment of the Irish to democracy has been the very survival of the liberal democratic institutions that were created in 1922. The prospects for democracy in the new states that appeared in Europe after the First World War were not bright: collapse was more common than survival (see Coakley, 1986). In Ireland, objective indicators (such as socio-economic development and political experience) were not promising. The very fact that the state and its constitutional system managed to survive so difficult a birth (see Prager, 1986) is clearly related to the pattern of existing political cultural values, even if this provides only a partial explanation (see Kissane, 2002). Irish voters adopted the country's democratic basic law, the constitution, in 1937, at a time when democracy was collapsing elsewhere in Europe. No significant voice has been raised against democratic institutions and practices, though certain fringe groups and personalities in the 1930s and the 1940s did advocate alternative forms of political organisation incompatible with democracy as we know it.

Electoral evidence relating to the character of Irish democratic values is also positive. Support for anti-democratic parties of the right and left has been negligible, and although individual deputies within the established parties may have wavered at times in their commitment to democracy, the parties themselves have remained firmly within the liberal democratic framework. Data relating to voting turnout confirm the similarity between the pattern in Ireland and that in other democracies. While a larger proportion of Irish people typically abstain from voting than is the case in continental Europe, Ireland compares favourably with other English-speaking countries, with an average turnout rate of 73 per cent in the 17 general elections over the period 1948–2002. The evidence for commitment to local democracy is less convincing. Apart from lower turnout levels (a characteristic shared with other Western democracies), observers have commented on the high degree of public acquiescence in decisions by governments to postpone local elections, or even to suspend local councils and replace them by appointed commissioners, and one observer has commented that 'the public is relatively unconcerned about local democracy' (Collins, 1987: 51).

Survey evidence in general bears out the view that the Irish are relatively supportive of liberal democratic government. The most useful evidence of this kind comes from polls that allow us to look at Ireland in comparative context. The first such survey, dating from 1970, replicated questions from the classic study of political culture published originally in 1963 (Almond and Verba, 1989). The researchers found that in certain areas Ireland was to be grouped with countries that had a political culture said to be conducive to democracy (Great Britain, the USA and, to a lesser extent, Germany), though in a comparative context, their level of 'subjective competence' (sense of having the capacity to influence the political process at local and national levels) was found to be low (Raven and Whelan, 1976: 22–6, 46).

More recent survey evidence confirms the similarity between Irish attitudes and those in other European states. We may assess this in terms of three areas:

- *knowledge about politics*: how well informed is the Irish public?
- *trust in political institutions*: how do the Irish regard the major state institutions?
- *political tolerance*: to what extent are the rights of minorities and individual rights generally accepted?

Irish people seem to be relatively well informed about politics. Thus, in a survey after the 2002 election, levels of recognition of politicians were high. Respondents were able to identify correctly the leader of Fianna Fáil (96 per cent), Fine Gael (90 per cent) and the newly elected leader of the Green Party (68 per cent); they were able to identify Ireland's EU commissioner (50 per cent) and one-third the Ceann Comhairle (34 per cent; calculated from Irish National Election Study, 2002). These figures may seem surprising, or even low, to those who are interested in politics, but they are relatively impressive by comparative standards. In terms of attitudes towards the EU at around the same time, although 24 per cent of Irish respondents (and 19 per cent in EU countries overall) felt that they knew little or nothing about it, they performed relatively well, by EU standards, in an actual knowledge quiz looking at such issues as EU history and membership (Eurobarometer no. 58, 2002: B27–B28).

In most important respects the Irish are significantly more favourably disposed towards major institutions than their European counterparts. Thus, a 1981 survey showed that the Irish were more likely than the 'average' European to express confidence in the police, the civil service, parliament and the press (Fogarty *et al.*, 1984: 179, 243). These findings were confirmed from the opposite perspective in a 1990 survey: the Irish were much less likely than the 'average' European to express lack of confidence in these same institutions, except the press; furthermore, Irish people's sense of subjective competence appeared now to be higher (Ashford and Timms, 1992: 16, 98). By 2001 the position had changed, as we may see in Table 2.2: trust in parliament was low, comparable with the position elsewhere in Europe, and trust in political parties was lower still: 57 per cent distrusted them. It is to be assumed that the political scandals that were uncovered in the 1990s have contributed to these high levels of mistrust and cynicism, which have also affected religious institutions. Interestingly, levels of trust in television and radio are high by European standards, but the print media are treated with some suspicion.

The cumulative impact of political developments on perceptions of the political system has been relatively positive. A series of surveys carried out

Table 2.2 Trust in selected institutions, Ireland and EU, 2001

Institution	Ireland		EU		Irish–EU differences (trust)
	Trust	Mistrust	Trust	Mistrust	
Political system					
The army	78	13	70	22	8
The police	70	22	67	28	3
The civil service	62	23	44	46	18
The legal system	61	29	51	42	10
Parliament	50	35	51	39	−1
The government	49	39	48	44	1
Political parties	28	57	18	73	10
Other organisations					
Charitable organisations	65	18	56	31	9
Religious institutions	51	35	44	45	7
Trade unions	48	34	39	49	9
Big companies	32	49	33	55	−1
Media					
Television	78	18	62	34	16
Radio	77	19	62	30	15
Press	53	40	46	48	7

Source: Eurobarometer no. 56, pp. B13–15.

Note
All figures are percentages.

regularly since 1973 has shown that a clear majority of those questioned has normally been satisfied with 'the way democracy works' (Eurobarometer trends 1974–93: 27–36, updated from later Eurobarometers). Over the period 1973–89 this proportion (those declaring themselves either 'very' or 'fairly' satisfied) has been relatively stable: it has averaged 53 per cent in Ireland, and 51 per cent in the EU overall. From 1992 to 1998 the level of satisfaction with democracy in Ireland averaged 66 per cent, fully 20 percentage points above that for the EU as a whole. Most surprisingly of all, this level peaked at 75 per cent in spring 1998, at a time when work relating to two tribunals of enquiry into possible political impropriety by senior politicians was getting underway – or, perhaps, because of this very fact. By autumn 2003, the Irish level of satisfaction was still 69 per cent, 15 points above the overall EU level (Eurobarometer no. 60, 2003: B55).

We have already raised the question of the level of political tolerance that is characteristic of the Irish. Early evidence suggested that this was relatively low. A survey in 1970 found that 61 per cent believed that they would be justified in imposing on others 'something which one believes to be good and right' and 78 per cent agreed that 'certain political groups must be curbed when they abuse freedom of speech' (Raven and Whelan, 1976: 47–8). A large survey in Dublin in 1972–3 led to the conclusion that there was a 'relatively high level of dormant or latent racialism, and a moderately high degree of intolerance against political and social outgroups', as well as 'a considerable degree of general intolerance and authoritarianism' (Mac Gréil, 1977: 530). If this were the case in Dublin, it might well be that such attitudes were even more common in rural Ireland, and later surveys indeed confirm this (Mac Gréil, 1996: 390–1). Further confirmation of these findings emerged in a 1990 poll, where Irish respondents very interested in politics came close to the bottom of a group of ten Western democracies in terms of their tolerance of the right to protest (Johnston, 1993: 16). Analysis of Irish survey respondents' views on such issues as respect for authority, protection of free speech and the existence of clear guidelines about what is good and evil suggest that 'the level of authoritarianism in Ireland, on these measures, is significantly above the average European level' (Hardiman and Whelan, 1994a: 126).

Since authoritarianism can rest on non-democratic processes of decision making, it is often accompanied by a willingness to rely on mechanisms other than the ballot box to give effect to political decisions. The cult of political violence has, indeed, played a significant role in Irish history, but the evidence suggests that the Irish have buried the rifle (Bric and Coakley, 2004). A 1970 survey showed that while a majority clearly opposed the use of force, a large minority (20 per cent) agreed that the use of force was at least sometimes the only way to advance an ideal (Raven and Whelan, 1976: 49), while a survey carried out in 1978 suggested that 21 per cent supported IRA activities (Davis and Sinnott, 1979: 97–9). On the other hand, despite the long tradition of revolutionary violence in Ireland, regular surveys since 1976 have shown that Irish people's attitudes to political change are not greatly different from those in other parts of the EC/EU: only tiny minorities are prepared to endorse attempts to change society by revolutionary means (Eurobarometer trends 1974–1993, May 1994: 43, 48–9). Survey data from 1990 show that Irish respondents are remarkably similar to those elsewhere in Europe in terms of their attitudes towards conventional forms of protest behaviour (such as signing a petition or attending a lawful demonstration) as opposed to unconventional ones (such as unofficial strikes and occupation of buildings or factories; see Hardiman and Whelan, 1994a: 112–17).

While the old debate about the quality of Irish democratic values is now largely obsolete, given political cultural similarities in this respect with other liberal democracies, we may see the evolution of this feature as the outcome of a battle between two underlying sets of pressures. On the one hand, a modest level of socio-economic development and the powerful attraction of British models encouraged the growth of democratic values (we note the ironic link between political opposition to British interference in Ireland and strong, if not uncritical, admiration for the British way of

political life). On the other hand, to the extent that socio-economic development was slow or uneven, and given the availability of alternative authoritarian models associated with the structures of the Catholic Church, we
can understand the late survival of more traditional, pre-democratic values.
Of course, in many respects Irish society is now post-industrial and it is
increasingly secular. To a growing extent, it is a 'typical' west European
society, and, while survey evidence may point to certain respects in which
the Irish deviate from other west Europeans in terms of their attitudes
towards democracy, these exceptions must be seen in the context of the
overwhelming reality that the broad thrust of Irish views in this area is
typically European.

Conservatism?

By *conservatism* we mean a leaning in the direction of support for traditional
values and in particular, in the context of liberal democracy, a suspicion of
state intervention. Conservatives generally support the existing social and
political order, favour low rates of taxation and prefer free enterprise to
state involvement in the economy.

The historical balance sheet is rather ambiguous on the question of Irish
conservatism. In the nineteenth and early twentieth centuries the major
political forces in Irish society were radical by European standards: they
stood for a dismantling of the existing system of land ownership and for the
pursuit of redistributionist policies. Radical egalitarian ideology was reflected
in the 1916 proclamation and in the 'democratic programme' of the first
Dáil, adopted in 1919. This was widely shared in the new state, especially
on the anti-Treaty side. But it is one thing to call for redistribution of wealth
when the privileged group can be portrayed as an alien minority whose
riches were gained by conquest; it is quite another to continue this call when
members of the former underclass have enriched themselves through their
own efforts. Egalitarian or socialist rhetoric has been notably muted in Irish
society since the new state consolidated its position. On the other hand,
conservative ideology has not been vehemently and coherently articulated
either; instead, policy makers experimented pragmatically with far-reaching
policies of state intervention, and public opinion appears in general to have
accepted this.

Electoral evidence indeed points towards conservative tendencies in Irish
society – or, at least, towards the relatively underdeveloped state of radicalism. Over the 17 elections from 1948 to 2002, the two largest parties –
both relatively conservative in orientation – have won on average 75 per
cent of the first preference vote, compared to 11 per cent for the Labour
Party (the rest of the left has been insignificant). It might be more accurate
to interpret this as evidence of the weakness of the left rather than of the
strength of the right. It is true that Fianna Fáil and Fine Gael identify themselves at European level as parties of the right (they are members, respec-

tively, of the conservative Union for Europe of the Nations group and the European People's Party, a group made up mainly of Christian Democratic parties), but both parties span a wide range of ideological positions, and neither can be seen as an archetypal conservative party.

Survey evidence has consistently shown that when Irish respondents are asked to identify where they are located on the left–right spectrum they place themselves significantly further to the right, on average, than other Europeans. Although it has been argued that the connotations of these terms may not be the same in Ireland as elsewhere, there is evidence of a close convergence between Ireland and the rest of Europe in terms of the correlation between left–right self-placement and other values classically associated with being on the 'left' or the 'right' (Hardiman and Whelan, 1994b: 162–3). On the other hand, surveys provide little evidence of commitment to ideologies of the extreme right. Indeed, survey data from 1979–83 placed the Irish in clear second position after the Greeks among EC peoples in their willingness to endorse classic economic policies of the left – many more of them were in favour of reducing income inequality (90 per cent), of more government management of the economy (72 per cent) and of more nationalisation of industry (64 per cent) than was the case in other west European states (Inglehart, 1990: 255). Data from 1990 position the Irish somewhere in the middle of a group of ten Western democracies in terms of their attitude towards heavier taxation of the wealthy (supported by 83 per cent) and provision of jobs by the government for all who want them (71 per cent), though Ireland was close to the top when it came to the question of whether the government has too much power (51 per cent agreed; Johnston, 1993: 13). There appears also to be considerable support for the kind of interventionist policies that have created so large a public sector in Ireland. While the political conservatism of the Irish is, then, undoubted, it coexists ambiguously with a rather pragmatic attitude towards economic development and an egalitarian attitude towards the distribution of resources.

In an obvious sense, this complex mixture of values may be related to the Irish path of socio-economic evolution, with the early disappearance of the traditional landed class, the installation of a strong farming class, late industrialisation and retarded development of class consciousness. It is also undoubtedly the case that the Catholic Church, with its traditional horror of communism and suspicion of socialism, has reinforced conservatism; in this context, the recent re-orientation of leading members of the Church in the direction of support for more egalitarian educational and social welfare systems has probably come too late to have much impact on deeply ingrained popular values. For its part, rapid economic growth appears to have led, predictably enough, not to an erosion in wealth inequalities but in a growing disposition to tolerate these, rooted in a new form of conservative individualism (O'Connell, 2001: 181–8).

Clericalism?

By *clericalism* we mean acceptance of the view that the teaching of the Catholic Church possesses such authority that it should be reflected in state legislation: it is argued that the political views of the clergy should be heeded, that the laws should reflect Catholic morals and social teaching, and sometimes that the church itself should be given a special place in the constitution. In continental Europe, clericalism was a political force opposed to the great liberal movement that dated from the time of the French Revolution, a movement that stood for the complete separation of church and state and protection of the individual against both.

Historical evidence of the significance of clericalism in Irish political life and its impact on social policy is so well documented that it needs little further comment (see Gallagher, 1982: 12–16 and Girvin, 1986, 1989, for short discussions and Whyte, 1980, for a more extended analysis). For many decades into the life of the new state public policy was firmly guided by Roman Catholic principles. The Labour Party dropped the expression 'Workers' Republic' from its constitution in 1940 and the government refused to support Noel Browne, Minister for Health, in his ambitious welfare programme in the so-called 'Mother and Child' controversy in 1951, in response to pressure from the Catholic bishops. More significant than the effect of episcopal intervention, however, is the fact its use was so rare. On other occasions public opinion was sufficiently supportive of the Catholic position to make clerical intervention unnecessary, and when the bishops did intervene in the two cases mentioned their position was compatible with dominant lay opinion.

As the twenty-first century began, however, the phenomenon of Irish clericalism appeared to be seriously under threat. Although the 1983 and 1986 referendums on abortion and divorce respectively resulted in conservative decisions, the very fact that these matters were subjected to a constitutional poll and the size of the minority vote were themselves indicators of change, and pointers to the ultimate narrow majority in favour of permitting divorce at the 1995 referendum. The liberalisation in 1993 of the laws relating to the sale of contraceptives and to homosexuality would have been inconceivable in 1973, or, perhaps, even in 1983. The authority of the Catholic bishops in speaking on matters of public morality was undermined by a pattern of social change linked with a climate of public opinion in which the press felt free to reveal that a prominent bishop had fathered a child in the course of a long-running affair, and suffered further as a consequence of a series of scandals relating to sexual abuse of children by clergy.

Electoral data do not readily lend themselves to indicating levels of clericalism in Irish society. In the past, the only parties which were avowedly anti-clerical, such as the Communist Party, were electorally insignificant. Almost all votes were cast for parties that were essentially clericalist; and to the extent that change has taken place, it has occurred within these parties, as first Labour, then Fine Gael and finally Fianna Fáil began to adopt positions that could be seen as being in conflict with official church views. Rather strikingly, fundamentalist Catholic parties altogether failed to make inroads into the space vacated by the secularising major parties in the 1990s.

We scarcely need survey evidence of the intensity of Irish clericalism in the past. Even in the late 1980s, although the authority of the Church to express its views in political areas began to be questioned, there remained significant differences between the perceptions of Irish people and of other Europeans on areas in which it was appropriate for the Church to speak out: the Irish were much more favourably disposed to the expression of church views (Ashford and Timms, 1992: 34–5). However, it is clear from public opinion polls that many people hold positions of which the Church has traditionally been critical, notably in the areas of divorce, abortion and availability of contraceptives, and impressionistic evidence would suggest that popular support for the view that Church leaders should be listened to with particular attention has been seriously eroded. An attitude scale on the issue of church–state relations based on 1990 data indeed shows little difference between Irish respondents and those in other Western democracies (Heath *et al.*, 1993: 58–9). Given the declining significance of religion in people's lives, as discussed above, it is likely that the decline of clericalism will accelerate. This may be due in large measure to the effects of economic growth and new wealth on individual psychological make-up, but it probably also reflects the greater exposure of Irish society to external influences. The conditions in which the Catholic Church could offer spiritual consolation to a poor but happy Irish nation, and provide moral guidance in its struggles in an often hostile world, have been changed out of all recognition.

Isolationism?

Like 'authoritarianism', we use *isolationism* here in a rather special sense: not to refer to a characteristic of the state but rather, for want of a better word, to refer to a predisposition to support a neutral position in the domain of foreign policy (see also Chapter 16). This feature, in Ireland as elsewhere, is derived from more profound values, such as nationalism.

Although the new state was anxious after 1922 to maximise international recognition by extending its external involvement in such bodies as the League of Nations and the United Nations, it always stopped short of any hint of participation in an external military alliance. While the justification for this (as expressed in rejection, for example, of NATO membership) was rooted in specific hostility to Britain because of its role in maintaining the partition of Ireland, in time the policy of military neutrality became valued in its own right, and it appears to have been transformed into a canon of Irish public opinion. Much of the evidence relating to Irish feelings on this subject is indirect. It is notable, though, that political parties have been reticent in tackling the issue of security co-operation, which is an inevitable concomitant of deepening European integration. However, it is true that the dominant parties have been moving to a more accommodating position on the issue of pan-European military alliances, while those parties which adopt an uncompromising policy on neutrality are weak in terms of electoral support, even if they are rather vocal on the issue.

Survey evidence has consistently shown that Irish respondents want control over security and military matters to be retained at national level. A clear majority of Irish respondents in a 1993 survey (71 per cent) wanted decision making in the sensitive areas of security and defence to remain at national level, but this position was supported by only 42 per cent of Europeans (Eurobarometer no. 39, 1993: A26–7). By 1998, the position had scarcely changed: 67 per cent of the Irish, but only 44 per cent of Europeans overall, wanted this form of decision making to remain at national level (Eurobarometer no. 49, 1998: B24–5). The early years of the new century showed little change in this position. It is true that overall attitudes to the EU were positive – more so, on balance, than in any other member state – at precisely the time that Irish voters rejected the Nice Treaty in 2001 (Eurobarometer no. 55, 2001). Strangely, at the same time, while 64 per cent of those with an opinion on the matter were reported as favouring Irish participation in a European rapid reaction military force, 82 per cent favoured maintenance of Ireland's policy of military neutrality (calculated from TNS-MRBI poll, May 2001).[3] But the result of the second Nice referendum in 2002 showed that voters appeared capable of reconciling these preferences with support for the treaty.

It is probable that this rather complex feature of Irish political culture arises from the country's distinctive 'colonial' and 'post-colonial' experience. But as this experience recedes into the more distant recesses of the collective memory, and as the full geopolitical implications of membership of an increasingly integrated European Union become clear, the depth of Irish commitment to traditional values of neutrality will be put to the test. At elite level, it appears as if there is a much greater willingness than in the past to contemplate participation in military alliances; it remains to be seen how long it takes for these ideas to achieve mass support, or at least acceptance.

A divided political culture?

The discussion up to now has focused on the 'typical' Irish person's political cultural values. Society, of course, is made up of individuals holding a great range of values; while we have drawn attention to areas where certain values are dominant or where the Irish adopt distinctive positions, we need to turn now to look at those who do not subscribe to these values and examine the extent of *fragmentation* in Irish society and in its political culture.

Social cleavages

Clearly, economic and social development did not proceed at a uniform pace in Ireland or in any other society; some groups always lagged behind others, and the process itself created some divisions while perhaps rendering others irrelevant. In the Irish case, this process, at least in its later stages, appears to have been associated with elements of a rural–urban and agrarian–industrial clash. It has also promoted divisions within each of these sectors, though many of these remain latent. On the agrarian side, although agricultural labourers, small subsistence farmers and large, commercially oriented farmers have conflicting interests, these are now rarely articulated. On the industrial side, an urban proletariat developed slowly, but levels of politicised class conflict remained low by European standards (though the level of industrial disputes was high). The spurt of economic growth that contributed to new levels of wealth in Irish society at the end of the twentieth century was not, however, accompanied by any diminution in the gap between rich and poor, and social inequalities remain endemic (see Hardiman, 1998).

In the religious domain, the most obvious historical division was that between Catholics and Protestants, and this survives, even though the Protestant minority is now of negligible size. Within the Catholic community, recent decades have seen the growth of secular values; although there is nothing corresponding to the secular subcultures of continental Catholic Europe, tensions between traditional Catholics and those with more liberal beliefs are likely to grow (see Girvin 1997a, b).

Contrasting perceptions of the past were also strongly held by different groups, with unionist, moderate nationalist and republican versions of history coexisting. Similarly, the degree of exposure to British, European and other influences tends to vary with region, class, occupation and level of education. We might expect these features, like the ones discussed in the last two paragraphs, to promote conflicting currents within Irish political culture; to what extent is there evidence for this?

Political cultural cleavages

The most fundamental political cultural cleavage faced by the new state related to the question of *nationalism*. In the early years, a strong 'republican' subculture struggled against the dominant values of the ruling group but, as we have seen, these two sets of values were largely accommodated to each other by 1948 at the latest. On the other hand, it could be argued that as mainstream Irish nationalist values became less strident a fundamentalist nationalist subculture, comprising those loyal to the old ideals, was increasingly clearly defined. The core beliefs of this subculture include rejection of the institutions of government of Northern Ireland, since partition was illegitimate, but also of the institutions of the south, for the same reason (fundamentalist nationalists continued to refer to the south as 'the Free State' until the early 1990s). This ideology rested on the assumption that the Irish people had made an irreversible decision in 1918 in favour of independent statehood for the entire island, and that armed resistance to anyone who opposes this decision is justified. Many held to this set of beliefs with passionate commitment (extending to a willingness to engage in an armed struggle or to die on hunger strike).

If the most appropriate yardstick to measure the strength of this subculture is electoral support for the party most obviously associated with it, Sinn Féin, we would be struck by the weakness of this tradition, at least in the south. Sinn Féin's recent Dáil presence dates only from 1997; but by this time the movement had itself been transformed, and no longer identified with the fundamentalist values described above. It is likely that its subsequent success at local elections and in the Dáil election of 2002 derived from an identification of the party with social radicalism rather than with fundamentalist nationalism. The party's acceptance of the Good Friday Agreement of 1998 is likely to have further marginalised those who still adhere to the traditional ideology. In any case, as the example of Northern Ireland shows, the cleavage between constitutional nationalism and Irish republicanism pales into insignificance beside the Catholic–Protestant cleavage over national identity. The history of Northern Ireland provides a good example of the force of this cleavage; but why has conflict of this kind been so strikingly absent in the south?

A number of contrasts between the northern and southern minorities help to explain this divergence between the two parts of Ireland. In demographic terms, the southern Protestant minority is much smaller and the long-term trend was of decline rather than increase as a proportion of the total population. In the socio-economic domain, this minority has traditionally been associated with a position of relative advantage, and has occupied more prestigious positions in a type of cultural division of labour. Politically, it was associated with a programme (maintenance of the union with Great Britain) that was quickly seen to be entirely unrealistic after 1922. Most significantly of all, however, it appears to have been culturally assimilated to the dominant group. Whereas at the beginning of the twentieth century southern Protestants were a national minority with their own ethnic symbols, myth of history and political programme, today they are essentially a denominational minority, distinguished from the majority mainly in terms of religious practice and belief (Coakley, 1998). In all of these respects, the position of the Catholic minority in Northern Ireland has been the reverse of this.

On the matter of *democratic values*, there appears to be a considerable degree of consensus, and challenges from groups adhering to sources of authority other than 'the people's will' have been few and weak. Nationalist authoritarianism – the belief that 'the nation' has a collective destiny which must be protected by an elite, if necessary against the wishes of a majority –

largely disappeared in the south after the 1930s. Religious authoritarianism – the belief that no electoral or political majority has a right to contravene the 'natural law', as defined, in an Irish context, by the Catholic Church – may, however, come to the fore as Catholic values are subjected to increasing challenge. Ironically, though, up to the early 1990s Catholic activists relied on public opinion and referendum results to defend their position, whereas their more 'progressive' rivals sought to bypass these and to use the courts and parliament to bring about change. The ease with which the will of the greater number may be translated into the dictatorship of the majority has not yet become the subject of public debate.

In terms of attitudes towards *public policy*, there are predictable divisions within Irish society. First, there is clearly a division between left and right, one side supporting interventionist economic policies, the other advocating privatisation and the free market. While the boundary between the two sides is not very precise, and does not correspond entirely with social class or with party political divisions, the two tendencies are nonetheless real. Second, there is an emerging division between secular and clerical forces, ranging Protestants and liberal Catholics against those disposed to accept church teaching more fully (Girvin, 1993, 1996). Third, there are elements of a division between cosmopolitan and isolationist views, the former arguing for a redefinition of Ireland's relationship with Europe and a reassessment of its policy of military neutrality, the latter defending the traditional position in these respects.

Conclusion

While political culture is an elusive concept and our instruments for measuring it are poor, the survey evidence reported in this chapter is sufficiently compatible with other evidence and with the perceptions of observers to allow us to make some generalisations about the nature of Irish political culture. First, there appears to be a consensus among the population in terms of core values relating to national identity: there is virtually universal agreement on one of the cardinal principles of Irish *nationalism* (the need for a separate Irish state), and the legitimacy of the Republic of Ireland is therefore now virtually unchallengeable. With a new, unfamiliar wave of immigration, however, it is possible that a distinctly racist ideological configuration will evolve in the years ahead. Second, commitment to *democratic values* appears to be solidly rooted within people's inner values, as in other Western societies. The challenge from *authoritarianism* is weak – nationalist authoritarianism has receded in recent decades, and religious authoritarianism has not so far been articulated in such a way that it constitutes a serious challenge to democratic principles. Third, in terms of people's values relating to principles of public policy, we can detect elements both of stability and of conflict. On socio-economic issues, *conservatism* appears to be dominant, even if the manner in which it is articulated has changed. On foreign policy issues, there may well be an emerging tension between positions that may be labelled *isolationism* and *cosmopolitanism*. Most obviously of all, however, on social and moral issues conflict between *clericalism* and *secularism* has emerged as a characteristic phenomenon of Irish life.

Political culture in Ireland, then, resembles that in other west European states rather closely, despite a significant lag in socio-economic development in this country. While the legacy of history and preoccupation with British dominance may have been a particular influence in the past, it is probably the pattern of underlying religious values in a slowly secularising society that will be responsible for the most distinctive elements in Irish political culture in the future.

Notes

1 The European Social Survey datafile is available to researchers from the Norwegian Social Science Data Services; see Irish Social Science Data Archive (http://www.ucd.ie/issda/) for further information.
2 Data from the Irish National Election Study will be deposited with the Irish Social Science Data Archive (http://www.ucd.ie/issda/).
3 The TNS-MRBI data are available from the Irish Social Science Data Archive (http://www.ucd.ie/issda/).

References and further reading

Almond, Gabriel A. and Sidney Verba, 1989. *The Civic Culture: Political Attitudes and Democracy in Five Nations*, new edn. London: Sage.

Almond, Gabriel A., G. Bingham Powell, Kaare Strøm and Russell J. Dalton, 2003. *Comparative Politics Today: A World View*, 7th edn. New York: Longman.

Ashford, Sheena and Noel Timms, 1992. *What Europe Thinks: A Study of West European Values*. Aldershot: Dartmouth.

Banfield, Edward, 1967. *The Moral Basis of a Backward Society*, new edn. London: Collier-Macmillan.

Barry, Frank (ed.), 1999. *Understanding Ireland's Economic Growth*. Basingstoke: Macmillan.

Breen, Richard, Damien F. Hannan, David B. Rottman and Christopher T. Whelan, 1990. *Understanding Contemporary Ireland: State, Class and Development in the Republic of Ireland*. Dublin: Gill and Macmillan.

Bric, Maurice and John Coakley (eds), 2004. *From Political Violence to Negotiated Settlement: The Winding Path to Peace in Twentieth-Century Ireland*. Dublin: University College Dublin Press.

British Council, 2003. *Through Irish Eyes: Irish Attitudes towards the UK*. Dublin: British Council.

Central Statistics Office, 2003. *Measuring Ireland's Progress, Volume 1 – 2003: Indicators Report*. Dublin: Stationery Office.

Chubb, Basil, 1970. *The Government and Politics of Ireland*. Stanford, CA: Stanford University Press.

Chubb, Basil, 1992. *The Government and Politics of Ireland*, 3rd edn. London: Longman.

Clancy, Patrick, Sheelagh Drudy, Kathleen Lynch and Liam O'Dowd (eds), 1995. *Irish Society: Sociological Perspectives.* Dublin: Institute of Public Administration.

Coakley, John, 1986. 'Political succession and regime change in new states in inter-war Europe: Ireland, Finland, Czechoslovakia and the Baltic republics', *European Journal of Political Research* 14:1/2: 187–206.

Coakley, John, 1994. 'The Northern conflict in Southern Irish school textbooks', in Adrian Guelke (ed.), *New Perspectives on the Northern Ireland Conflict.* Aldershot: Avebury, pp. 119–41.

Coakley, John, 1998. 'Religion, ethnic identity and the Protestant minority in the Republic', in William Crotty and David E. Schmitt (eds), *Ireland and the Politics of Change.* London: Longman, pp. 86–106.

Coakley, John, 2002. 'Conclusion: new strains of unionism and nationalism', in John Coakley (ed.), *Changing Shades of Orange and Green: Redefining the Union and the Nation in Contemporary Ireland.* Dublin: University College Dublin Press, pp. 132–54.

Collins, Neil, 1987. *Local Government Managers at Work: The City and County Management System of Local Government in the Republic of Ireland.* Dublin: Institute of Public Administration.

Commission for Communications Regulation, 2003. *Irish Communications Market Quarterly Key Data, December 2003.* Dublin: Commission for Communications Regulation.

Coulter, Colin and Steve Coleman (eds), 2003. *The End of Irish History? Critical Reflections on the Celtic Tiger.* Manchester: Manchester University Press.

Crotty, William and David E. Schmitt (eds), 1998. *Ireland and the Politics of Change.* London: Longman.

Davis, E. E. and Richard Sinnott, 1979. *Attitudes in the Republic of Ireland Relevant to the Northern Ireland Problem.* Dublin: Economic and Social Research Institute.

Fanning, Bryan, 2002. *Racism and Social Change in the Republic of Ireland.* Manchester: Manchester University Press.

Farrell, Brian, 1971. *The Founding of Dáil Éireann: Parliament and Nation-Building.* Dublin: Gill and Macmillan.

Fogarty, Michael, Liam Ryan and Joseph Lee, 1984. *Irish Values and Attitudes: The Irish Report of the European Value Systems Study.* Dublin: Dominican Publications.

Fuller, Louise, 2002. *Irish Catholicism since 1950: The Undoing of a Culture.* Dublin: Gill and Macmillan.

Gallagher, Michael, 1982. *The Irish Labour Party in Transition, 1957–82.* Dublin: Gill and Macmillan and Manchester: Manchester University Press.

Garner, Steve, 2004. *Racism in the Irish Experience.* London: Pluto Press.

Girvin, Brian, 1986. 'Nationalism, democracy, and Irish political culture', in Brian Girvin and Roland Sturm (eds), *Politics and Society in Contemporary Ireland.* Aldershot: Gower, pp. 3–28.

Girvin, Brian, 1989. 'Change and continuity in liberal democratic political culture', in John Gibbins (ed.), *Contemporary Political Culture: Politics in a Postmodern Age.* London: Sage, pp. 31–51.

Girvin, Brian, 1993. 'Social change and political culture in the Republic of Ireland', *Parliamentary Affairs* 46:3: 380–98.

Girvin, Brian, 1996. 'Church, state and the Irish constitution', *Parliamentary Affairs* 49:4: 599–615.

Girvin, Brian, 1997a. 'Ireland', in Roger Eatwell (ed.), *European Political Culture: Conflict or Convergence?* London: Routledge, pp. 127–38.

Girvin, Brian, 1997b. 'Political culture, political independence and economic success in Ireland', *Irish Political Studies* 12: 48–77.

Goldthorpe, John H. and Christopher T. Whelan (eds), 1992. *The Development of Industrial Society in Ireland: the Third Joint Meeting of the Royal Irish Academy and the British Academy*. Oxford: Oxford University Press.

Hardiman, Niamh, 1998. 'Inequality and the representation of interests', in William Crotty and David E. Schmitt (eds), *Ireland and the Politics of Change*. London: Longman, pp. 122–43.

Hardiman, Niamh and Christopher Whelan, 1994a. 'Politics and democratic values', in Christopher T. Whelan (ed.), *Values and Social Change in Ireland*. Dublin: Gill and Macmillan, pp. 100–35.

Hardiman, Niamh and Christopher Whelan, 1994b. 'Values and political partisanship', in Christopher T. Whelan (ed.), *Values and Social Change in Ireland*. Dublin: Gill and Macmillan, pp. 136–86.

Hardiman, Niamh and Christopher Whelan, 1998. 'Changing values', in William Crotty and David E. Schmitt (eds), *Ireland and the Politics of Change*. London: Longman, pp. 66–85.

Haughton, Jonathan, 1998. 'The dynamics of economic change', in William Crotty and David E. Schmitt (eds), *Ireland and the Politics of Change*. London: Longman, pp. 27–50.

Heath, Anthony, Bridget Taylor and Gabor Toka, 1993. 'Religion, morality and politics', in Roger Jowell *et al.* (eds), *International Social Attitudes: The 10th BSA Report*. Aldershot: Dartmouth, pp. 49–80.

Inglehart, Ronald, 1990. *Culture Shift in Advanced Industrial Society*. Princeton, NJ: Princeton University Press.

Inglis, Tom, 1998. *Moral Monopoly: the Catholic Church in Modern Irish Society*, 2nd edn. Dublin: University College Dublin Press.

Johnston, Michael, 1993. 'Disengaging from democracy', in Roger Jowell *et al.* (eds), *International Social Attitudes: The 10th BSA Report*. Aldershot: Dartmouth, pp. 1–22.

Jowell, Roger, Lindsay Brook and Lizanne Dowds with Daphne Arendt (eds), 1993. *International Social Attitudes: The 10th BSA Report*. Aldershot: Dartmouth.

Kissane, Bill, 2002. *Explaining Irish Democracy*. Dublin: University College Dublin Press.

Mac Gréil, Mícheál, 1977. *Prejudice and Tolerance in Ireland*. Dublin: Research Section, College of Industrial Relations.

Mac Gréil, Mícheál, 1996. *Prejudice in Ireland Revisited*. Maynooth: Survey and Research Unit, St Patrick's College.

McVeigh, Robbie and Ronit Lentin, 2002. 'Situated racisms: a theoretical introduction', in Ronit Lentin and Robbie McVeigh (eds), *Racism and Anti-Racism in Ireland*. Belfast: Beyond the Pale, pp. 1–48.

Medialive, 2004. Medialive: Ireland's Media Resource Centre. Available http:// www.medialive.ie/ [accessed 14 March 2004].

O'Connell, Michael, 2001. *Changed Utterly: Ireland and the New Irish Psyche*. Dublin: Liffey Press.

O'Connell, Michael, 2003. *Right Wing Ireland? The Rise of Populism in Ireland and Europe*. Dublin: Liffey Press.

Ó Gráda, Cormac, 1995. *Ireland: A New Economic History, 1780–1939*. Oxford: Clarendon Press.

Ó Gráda, Cormac, 1997. *A Rocky Road: The Irish Economy since the 1920s*. Manchester: Manchester University Press.

Prager, Jeffrey, 1986. *Building Democracy in Ireland: Political Order and Cultural Integration in a Newly Independent Nation*. Cambridge: Cambridge University Press.

Raven, John; C. T. Whelan and Paul A. Pfretzschner and Donald M. Borock, 1976. *Political Culture in Ireland: The Views of Two Generations*. Dublin: Institute of Public Administration.

Ruane, Joseph and Jennifer Todd, 1996. *The Dynamics of Conflict in Northern Ireland: Power, Conflict and Emancipation*. Cambridge: Cambridge University Press.

Schmitt, David E., 1973. *The Irony of Irish Democracy: The Impact of Political Culture on Administrative and Democratic Political Development in Ireland*. Lexington, MA: Lexington Books.

Whelan, Christopher T. (ed.), 1994. *Values and Social Change in Ireland*. Dublin: Gill and Macmillan.

Whyte, J. H., 1980. *Church and State in Modern Ireland 1923–1979*, 2nd edn. Dublin: Gill and Macmillan.

Wilson Hartnell, 1992. *The Irish Market: Facts and Figures*, 8th edn. Dublin: Wilson Hartnell Advertising.

Websites

www.cso.ie/principalstats/princstats.html   Useful information from the Central Statistics Office.

europa.eu.int/comm/public_opinion   Eurobarometer home page, with useful public opinion data.

3   The constitution and the judiciary

Michael Gallagher

Constitutions are important in liberal democracies. They lay down the ground rules about how political power is attained and how it can be exercised, about what governments can and cannot do. They set out rights of the citizens and often specify certain values, held to be central to the country's political culture, and deem it the duty of the state to aim to promote or defend these. Although most countries – Britain, Israel and New Zealand are among the best known exceptions – possess a document called 'The Constitution', in practice every country's constitution contains both a written and an unwritten component. That is, there are aspects of a country's political system that, perhaps through precedent and convention, have acquired the status of firm rules, even though they are not explicitly contained in the document called 'The Constitution'. For this reason, we cannot expect to get a full picture of the way in which a country's politics operates just by studying its written constitution. Constitutions might not explicitly acknowledge the existence of central features of modern politics such as large and disciplined political parties. Consequently, in this chapter we shall not examine those features of the constitution that regulate, for example, relations between government and parliament, or the rules governing the election of parliament – these are covered in other chapters – but will concentrate on the evolution of the constitution.

Constitutionalism – that is, the idea that the rulers are bound by rules that are not easy to change, and that certain fundamental rights of the citizens are protected absolutely, or almost absolutely – is an integral feature of contemporary liberal democracies, yet some have argued that there is an inherent tension between constitutionalism and democracy (Holmes, 1988: 196–8; Murphy, 1993: 3–6). Constitutionalism prevents the people, or their elected representatives, from carrying out certain policies that might have majority support, and can be criticised as 'rule by the dead', whose values the constitution embodies. Critics of constitutionalism such as Martin Shapiro (quoted in Holmes, 1988: 197) argue that when we examine a law we should ask not 'is it constitutional?' but 'do we want it to be constitutional?'; we should not be guided by 'certain dead gentlemen who could not possibly have envisaged our current circumstances' but instead should be guided by our collective decision about what sort of community we want to become. Defenders of the principle, in contrast, argue that there are certain rights so fundamental that they should be protected even against the wishes of a majority that wants them set aside. Although most liberal democracies feel that they have established a reasonable balance between constitutionalism and democracy, the tension undoubtedly exists, and has at times clearly manifested itself in Ireland.

The background: the Irish Free State constitution

Ireland's constitution (Bunreacht na hÉireann) dates from 1937 and, despite significant innovations, marked a development of previous constitutional experience rather than a decisive break with it. Its precursor, the 1922 Irish Free State constitution, was drawn up under the terms of the Anglo–Irish Treaty, so the British government insisted on modifications to the version produced by the Provisional Government, so as to ensure that it contained nothing that conflicted with the Treaty (for the Irish Free State constitution see Ward, 1994: 167–238). As a result, the final document was rather different from what the Irish government would have wanted (for an overview, see Farrell, 1988b). This British pressure manifested itself particularly in those articles that provided for a Governor-General, representing the Crown, and for the terms of an oath that all members of the Oireachtas (parliament) had to take, swearing to 'be faithful to HM King George V, his heirs and successors' (Article 17). The Free State was declared to be a member of the British Commonwealth (Article 1), and the constitution provided for an upper house, the Seanad, that was designed to give strong representation to the Protestant minority. Moreover, the introductory section of the Act establishing the constitution stated that if any provision of the constitution was, even after the British government's legal officers had scrutinised the document with a fine-tooth comb, in conflict with the Anglo–Irish Treaty, that provision was 'absolutely void and inoperative'.

Apart from these articles representing the result of arm-twisting by the British, the broad outlines of the governmental system also showed a strong British influence, as the constitution provided for government by a cabinet (the Executive Council), chaired by a prime minister (the President of the Executive Council). There were none of the rhetorical flourishes to be found in the 1937 constitution, and, unlike that document, the Irish Free State constitution was explicitly neutral as between religious denominations and, despite pressure from some quarters to make it so, could not have been described as a 'Catholic constitution'.

But although in some ways the constitution marked an attempt to codify some central aspects of the Westminster model of government, it did not represent a slavish acceptance of British practice. Mainly due to a desire to avoid an over-centralisation of power in the cabinet, the constitution contained some features designed to make the parliament more accountable to the people, and the government more accountable to the parliament, than was the case in the United Kingdom.

One of these was a proportional representation (PR) electoral system (the background to its adoption in Ireland is outlined in Chapter 4). There was also provision for referendums on both laws and constitutional amendments, for the legislative initiative (under which, if enough voters signed a petition calling for a particular change in the law, the Oireachtas would have either to make the change or to submit the issue to a referendum), and for judicial review of the constitution. In addition, the constitution allowed for the appointment of ministers who were not required to be members of the Dáil, an option that, had it been availed of, would have brought Ireland into line with the mainstream in western Europe. These 'extern ministers', as they were termed, would be appointed by the Dáil and answerable directly to it. However, apart from PR, most of these devices proved to be of little significance. No extern ministers were appointed after 1927, and even those who were appointed before then were all members of the Dáil. In 1928, when Fianna Fáil took the first steps towards forcing a popular vote on the oath of fidelity, the government hastily used its parliamentary majority to abolish both the legislative referendum and the initiative (Gallagher, 1996: 87).

The provision for judicial review did not prove much of a check on the government. For one thing, the Oireachtas itself could amend the constitution at will. The original version allowed it to do this (provided that any amendment came within the terms of the Treaty) for a period of eight years after 1922, after which amendment would require a referendum. But since this article itself could be amended, a simple extension of the period from eight to 16 years in 1929 ensured that the document was under the control of the Oireachtas throughout its unhappy life. Moreover, although constitutions are usually more powerful than ordinary legislation, so if the two conflict it is the constitution that prevails, the Irish Free State constitution was a weak document. Laws that contradicted the constitution, far from being thereby invalid, could simply incorporate a declaration that they amended the constitution to the extent necessary to render them constitutional (MacMillan, 1993: 196; Casey, 2000: 14; O'Neill, 2000: 311–12; Hogan and Whyte, 2003: 2161–2).

When Fianna Fáil came to power in 1932 it moved rapidly to remove those parts of the constitution that offended it most. In 1932 it abolished the oath, and in 1936 the Seanad and the office of Governor-General went the same way (Sexton, 1989: 165–6). It might be imagined that by now the resulting document was to Fianna Fáil's liking. Instead, it satisfied no one. Fianna Fáil had always viewed it with distaste, while even those who had clung so faithfully to it during the 1920s could not have felt much affection for it by 1937. Apart from the substance of the changes made by Fianna Fáil, the very fact that the document had been amended so many times (41 of the 83 articles had been changed) gave it a moth-eaten look. In any case, for Fianna Fáil the Irish Free State constitution was inherently illegitimate no matter how it read. Eamon de Valera in particular felt the need for the state to have an entirely new constitution, and to this end he initiated the process of drafting one in 1935 (Fanning, 1988; Keogh, 1988a; Hogan, 1997a). The resulting document was debated and finally passed by the Dáil in June 1937 (the vote on the final stage was 62 to 48). Although legally and constitutionally this new constitution could have been enacted by the Oireachtas as one long amendment to the existing constitution, that would have defeated the whole point of the exercise – it was vital symbolically to seem to make a new beginning, and to have the Irish people confer the new constitution on themselves. Accordingly, it was put to the people in a referendum on 1 July 1937, the same day as a general election. It was passed by 57 per cent to 43 per cent and came into effect on 29 December 1937 (see Appendix 2h on results of referendums).

The constitution has been the subject of two major reviews since it came into being. The first systematic assessment was made in 1966–7, when an all-party Oireachtas committee, which included former Taoiseach Seán Lemass, examined it article by article and issued a report recommending certain changes and assessing the merits of other possible amendments. The bipartisan approach adopted by this committee was brought to an abrupt end when Fianna Fáil went ahead the following year with its second attempt to change the electoral system, and little came of its work. In 1995–6 a root and branch assessment of the constitution was conducted by an expert committee, the Constitution Review Group (CRG), whose 350,000-word report can be read as an informed analysis of the constitution as well as an assessment of the arguments for change (CRG, 1996; for a critique of its work see Butler and O'Connell, 1998). The report of the CRG went to an all-party parliamentary committee on the constitution, which was set up in 1996 and re-established after the 1997 and 2002 elections, with the brief of undertaking a full review of the constitution and recommending specific steps.

The main features of the constitution

The promulgation of a new constitution was not purely symbolic, for despite the high degree of continuity, the 1937 constitution differed significantly in some respects from its predecessor. We shall examine some of its main features, without going in any depth into areas, especially those concerning the operation of government and parliament, that are covered in other chapters of this book.

Nation and state

Articles 1 to 3 relate to 'The Nation' and Articles 4 to 11 to 'The State'. These articles emphasise the importance attached to the constitution's role as a statement of the independence of the Irish state. Articles 1 and 5 both contain affirmations of sovereignty, and Article 6 says that all powers of government derive from the Irish people, emphasising that the institutions of the state should not be seen as having been in any way bestowed on the people by the British in 1922. Among this group of articles, Articles 2 and 3 came to cause most controversy. Article 2 defined 'the national territory' as 'the whole island of Ireland, its islands and the territorial seas'. Article 3 declared that, notwithstanding this, the laws enacted by the state shall, 'pending the re-integration of the national territory', apply only to the 26 counties, but by referring to the 'right' of the state's parliament and government to exercise jurisdiction over the whole of the national territory it affirmed a clear claim to Northern Ireland. Changes to these articles were demanded by northern unionists as part of the 1998 Northern Ireland Agreement, and, in a referendum in May of that year, the Irish people voted overwhelmingly to replace them by new articles. The changes came into effect when the Northern Ireland executive finally took office in December 1999. Article 2 now declares it the entitlement of everyone born on the island of Ireland to be part of the Irish nation, while Article 3 states that it is 'the firm will of the Irish nation, in harmony and friendship, to unite all the people who share the territory of the island of Ireland, in all the diversity of their traditions, recognising that a united Ireland shall be brought about only by peaceful means with the consent of a majority of the people, democratically expressed, in both jurisdictions in the island'.

The state was described as sovereign, independent and democratic. Its name remains unclear to many. Article 4 reads 'The name of the State is Éire, or in the English language, Ireland'. The 1948 Republic of Ireland Act refrained from giving a name to the state, so as not to violate this article; instead, its formulation is that 'the description of the State shall be the Republic of Ireland' (Casey, 2000: 29–32). In different contexts, the state is now known as 'Éire', 'Ireland', 'the Republic of Ireland', and even 'the Irish Republic', a confusion that the constitution does not entirely resolve.

Political institutions

Articles 12 to 33 deal with political institutions. As far as the operation of government was concerned, there was little major change from the Irish Free State constitution. There was to be an Oireachtas, consisting of a President and two houses. The office of the President was a major innovation, and is discussed further in Chapter 11. The lower house of parliament, Dáil Éireann, was to be directly elected by proportional representation, using the single transferable vote (see Chapter 4) as before. The re-emergence of the upper house, the Seanad, which de Valera had abolished only a year earlier, was surprising; given the nominally vocational basis of the Seanad (see Box 8.2 in Chapter 8), this may have been an adroit move to make a token concession to the transient clamour for the introduction of a vocationalist system of government (Lee, 1989: 272). The prime minister was now termed the Taoiseach (see Glossary), and his or her dominance within the government was strengthened in a number of ways – for example, the power to call a general election belonged now to the Taoiseach alone rather than to the government as a whole as before (see Chapter 11). It is clear, though, that for the most part the constitution merely reflected and summarised what had become existing practice rather than enforcing a change in that practice.

Constitutions are often more framework – setting the parameters within which the institutions must operate – than code, specifying the details of precisely what must occur at every step (Elazar, 1985). Thus the Irish constitution does not spell out, for example, exactly how the Taoiseach comes to be Taoiseach, or make any mention of the existence of coalition governments (Farrell, 1988d: 162). The absence of detailed rules to cover every possible situation means that there are some lacunae. For example, when a Taoiseach is defeated in a vote of confidence, yet the Dáil is unable to elect anyone else as Taoiseach, the Taoiseach is required to resign unless the President grants a dissolution (Article 28.10) yet continues in office until a successor is appointed (Article 28.11). The 1996 Constitution Review Group recommended that in such situations the outgoing government should conduct the state's business on a 'care and good management basis' only, for example refraining from making any non-essential appointments (CRG, 1996: 98–9), but the constitution does not make it clear just what powers a caretaker government and Taoiseach have.

The rights of citizens

The articles of the 1937 constitution that deal with citizens' rights (40–5) differed significantly from those of its predecessor. Like the earlier document, the new constitution guaranteed the usual liberal democratic rights – habeas corpus, free association, free speech, inviolability of dwellings, and so on – though (as is the case in most constitutions, and in the European Convention on Human Rights) almost invariably the ringing enunciation of a right is followed by a qualifying clause or paragraph asserting the power of the state to curtail it if, for example, 'public order', 'morality' or 'the exigencies of the common good' justifies that. The main difference was that the 1937 constitution also included rights articles that were strongly influenced by Catholic social thought (Whyte, 1980: 51–6; Keogh, 1988b). Two clauses of Article 44 gave Roman Catholicism a unique status. Article 44.1.2 read 'The State recognises the special position of the Holy Catholic Apostolic and Roman Church as the guardian of the Faith professed by the great majority of the citizens', while, in Article 44.1.3, the State merely 'recognised' a list of other and presumably less significant religions. Moreover, Article 41.3.2 prohibited the legalisation of divorce. These articles apart, admittedly, in many cases there is nothing visibly Catholic about the phraseology to the uninformed eye – only those familiar with Catholic social thought of the period would be able to identify the origins of the expressions used. Moreover, a number of additional rights not attributable to Catholic thought were enumerated.

The impact of Catholic thought on the constitution has led to its sometimes being branded a narrowly confessional document. However, this is to judge one era by the standards of another. The final formulation of Article 44 met with the approval of all the non-Catholic religions, while many in the Catholic Church were clearly disappointed, since they had hoped that theirs would be recognised as 'the one true church' and were reluctant even to accept that the word 'church' could validly be claimed by other religions (Keogh, 1988b: 111–17). The first large-scale protests against the religious articles came, 12 years later, not from non-Catholics but from the ultra-Catholic Maria Duce group, which wanted Article 44 amended to recognise the Catholic Church as the one true church (Whyte, 1980: 163–5). De Valera, far from imposing a sectarian constitution on a pluralistic society, was steering a middle course between non-Catholics on the one hand and triumphalist Catholics on the other, and he displeased the latter more than the former. Moreover, as Lee (1989: 203) observes, the explicit recognition given to the Jewish congregations was 'a gesture not without dignity in the Europe of 1937'.

Since 1937 the constitution has evolved in two ways. First, the constitution has been amended, initially by parliament and then by the people. Second, it has been developed by judicial interpretation.

Amendment of the constitution

The Irish constitution, like most constitutions, is more rigid – that is, less easily amended – than ordinary legislation. The constitution was amendable by parliament for a short period, but since then any amendment has required the consent of the people.

Amendment by parliament

The constitution contained, in Articles 51–63, transitory provisions to cover an interim period. These articles are no longer included in official texts of the constitution (they can be found in Hogan and Whyte, 2003: 2159–76) but continue to have the force of law. Article 51 permitted the Oireachtas to amend the constitution for a period of three years after the first President entered office, which meant up to 25 June 1941 – though the President had the right, if he chose, to refer any such amendment to the people for them to decide the matter by referendum. Any subsequent amendment would require the consent of the people. The loophole left in the Irish Free State constitution was addressed: Article 51 prevented the three-year transition period from being extended by the Oireachtas.

Two packages of amendments were made in this way (Casey, 2000: 24–5). The first, made in September 1939, altered only one article (28.3.3, the 'emergency' article), while the second, in May 1941, amended 16 different articles simultaneously. Some of the changes made in 1941 were minor 'housekeeping' changes, merely ironing out defects that had been detected in the articles affected. Other changes were more significant (though the President chose not to put any of them to a referendum), such as those relating to Articles 26 and 34, and especially to Article 28.3.3, which now looked quite different from the version approved by the people in 1937 (the annotated constitution in Foley and Lalor (1995) shows which sections were added by the Oireachtas). This article was designed to protect emergency legislation from scrutiny by the courts. In its original form, the article had stated that nothing in the constitution could be invoked to invalidate legislation designed to secure public safety and the preservation of the state in time of war or armed rebellion. The two amendments widened the scope of the article in circumstances where each house of the Oireachtas passes a resolution declaring that a national emergency exists affecting the vital interests of the state. After amendment, the article now says that 'time of war or armed rebellion' can include a time when an armed conflict is taking place that affects the vital interests of the state, even if the state is not directly involved, and a time after the war or armed rebellion has ceased but during which the Oireachtas takes the view that the emergency created by the conflict still exists. The Oireachtas declared a state of emergency after the outbreak of the Second World War in 1939, and this emergency remained in existence up to 1976, being lifted only by a resolution that simultaneously declared a fresh emergency arising 'out of the armed conflict now taking place in Northern Ireland', an emergency that was finally lifted in February 1995.

While it could plausibly be argued that the state's vital interests were indeed affected by the Second World War, in a way that persisted for some time after that war formally ended, it is easy to see that this article could potentially set at nothing all the rights guaranteed elsewhere in the constitution. At least at first sight, it appears that in order to pass any legislation it chooses, a government that has effective majority support in parliament, as most governments have, need only have the houses of the Oireachtas pass a resolution declaring that an emergency exists and then secure the passage of the legislation by declaring it to have the purpose of securing the public safety and preserving the state. In this way, it seems, legislation that, for example, proscribed opposition parties, outlawed elections or prescribed draconian penalties for even minor transgressions of the law would be immune from scrutiny by the courts.

However, a significant judgment of the Supreme Court in 1976, when it pronounced the Emergency Powers Bill constitutional, tempered the potential effect of Article 28.3.3. While not disputing the right of the Oireachtas to enact any legislation it saw fit in order to preserve public safety and the state once an emergency had been declared, the court said that it 'expressly reserves for future consideration' the question of whether it had the right to consider whether the Oireachtas was justified in declaring that a national emergency existed. No case has arisen subsequently to test the way in which the courts' thinking on this issue has developed, but the warning shot sounded in 1976 may have counterbalanced to some extent the action of the Oireachtas in 1939 and 1941 in widening the scope of Article 28.3.3. Both constitutional review committees recommended that a law declaring an emergency should have effect for three years only and should require annual renewal thereafter (Committee on the Constitution, 1967: 37–9; CRG, 1996: 94).

Amendment by the people

Ireland is one of the few countries where every constitutional amendment requires the consent of the people. Under Article 46, a proposal to amend the constitution must be passed by the houses of the Oireachtas and then be put to a referendum. Up to June 2004, 28 proposed amendments had been put to the people, of which 21 had been approved (see Box 3.1 and table in Appendix 2h; for an overview, see Gallagher, 1996; O'Mahony, 1998). Of the 27, eight related to moral or religious issues, seven to voting, and six to the European Community/Union. One was on Northern Ireland, one was on citizenship and the other five (in 1979, 1996, 1997 and 2001) were on relatively minor or technical matters that did not engender strong passions.

Of the eight referendums on moral or religious issues, the first proposal was passed comfortably in 1972, with the backing of all the parties and the opposition only of conservative Catholic groups. It removed from Article 44.1 the two subsections, already referred to, that recognised the 'special position' of the Catholic Church and the mere existence of a number of other churches. The two referendums of the 1980s were much more heated affairs, with deep divisions apparent within as well as between the

---

Box 3.1 Major changes made to the Irish constitution since it was adopted in 1937

Changes to the constitution have been made to allow:

- Ireland to take a full part in the process of European integration (1987, 1992, 1998 and 2002);
- recognition of the 'special position' of the Roman Catholic Church to be removed (1972);
- divorce to be legalised (1995);
- Ireland to fulfil its part of the Northern Ireland Agreement (1998).

parties. The first, in 1983, inserted what its proponents termed a 'pro-life' amendment, to the effect that the state 'acknowledges the right to life of the unborn' and undertakes 'by its laws to defend and vindicate that right' (Article 40.3.3). The second, in 1986, would have made it possible for the Oireachtas to legalise divorce in restricted circumstances, but was decisively rejected by the voters (Girvin, 1987).

The next three 'moral issue' referendums were held in November 1992 in response to the Supreme Court decision in the 'X' case (see Box 3.2 below). Amendments stating that Article 40.3.3 does not limit either freedom to travel outside the state or freedom to obtain information about services lawfully available in another state were passed with the support of both 'liberal' and 'centrist' voters and of all the political parties (for the complex background to these issues see Kennelly and Ward, 1993). A third proposal, which would have permitted abortions only in cases where a continued pregnancy would have meant a risk to 'the life, as distinct from the health, of the mother' (except where the risk to life arose from the possibility of suicide), was defeated, as both liberal and conservative voters opposed it, along with all the political parties except Fianna Fáil. In 1995 there was a second vote on divorce, and this time the decision was, albeit very narrowly, in favour of legalisation (Girvin, 1996; LeDuc, 2003: 131–7). Finally, in 2002 the government proposed an amendment along the same lines as the third of the November 1992 proposals, which would have restricted, without completely outlawing, the right to an abortion. It was narrowly defeated by a combination of relative liberals and a small purist section of conservative opinion, which rejected it on the ground that abortion should be completely prohibited rather than merely restricted (Kennedy, 2002). The pattern of voting was very similar at each of these referendums, with a great deal of consistency as to which constituencies were the most liberal and which were the most conservative. These moral issue referendums all brought to the fore the liberal–conservative cleavage in Irish society, as discussed in Chapter 2.

Of the seven proposals concerning voting, two, in 1959 and 1968, were unsuccessful attempts by Fianna Fáil to replace the PR-STV electoral system by the single-member plurality system (these referendums are described on pp. 108–9). On the second occasion, this proposal was coupled with one that was designed to permit rural voters to be over-represented at the expense of urban voters. The other four referendums caused little controversy between the parties. In 1972, there was all-party backing for lowering the voting age, and in 1979 an amendment to allow the university seats in Seanad Éireann to be reorganised got strong support among those sufficiently motivated to vote on the issue. In 1984 a proposal to permit the Oireachtas to extend the vote to non-citizens received general endorsement, and in 1999 voters agreed to an amendment that gave constitutional recognition to local government and stipulated that local elections must take place at intervals of no more than five years.

Joining, and the process of integration within, the European Community (EC) and European Union (EU) has been responsible for six referendums (these are discussed further in Chapter 16). Joining the EC required a referendum because the obligations of membership would otherwise have been in conflict with the constitution. Upon EC membership, the Community's institutions would have the power to make laws for the state and the EC's Court of Justice would be superior to Ireland's Supreme Court, thus creating an apparent conflict with at least two articles of the constitution (15.2.1 affirming the legislative monopoly of the Oireachtas, and 34.4.6 affirming the finality of all judgments of the Supreme Court). However, the decision was taken in 1972 not to amend those specific articles over which EC membership might cast a shadow but instead to introduce a catch-all amendment, by adding a new subsection (Article 29.4.3) allowing the state to join the EC and adding that 'No provision of this constitution invalidates laws enacted, acts done or measures adopted by the State necessitated by the obligations of membership of the Communities'.

The 1987 amendment allowed the state to ratify the Single European Act, and the 1992 amendment allowed it to ratify the Maastricht agreement (McCutcheon, 1992; Holmes, 1993). The 1998 referendum on the anti-climactic Amsterdam Treaty, which lacked a clear focus, was overshadowed by the simultaneous referendum on the Northern Ireland agreement, and the vote in favour reflected diffuse support for the EU rather than any enthusiasm for the contents of the Amsterdam Treaty specifically (Gilland, 1999). The Nice Treaty caused difficulty, when, for the first time, an EU treaty was rejected at a referendum in June 2001 (O'Mahony, 2001). This caused some uncertainty as to how to proceed; eventually, the treaty was put to a referendum a second time, and in October 2002 it was passed comfortably on a higher turnout (see Hayward, 2003 and Chapter 16).

The 1998 Belfast or Good Friday Agreement (for which, see pp. 416–26) was approved overwhelmingly by southern voters. One aspect of this was that it conferred an automatic right to Irish citizenship upon anyone born on the island; within a few years this had come to be branded by the government as an unintended 'loophole' and an inducement to 'citizenship tourism', and in June 2004 a proposal to remove this automatic right was approved by almost 80 per cent of voters (see Appendix 2h).

The referendum requirement in Article 46 has been a powerful check on governments wanting to make changes that do not have broad support across the political spectrum. On only one occasion (the referendum to approve the constitution in 1937) have the people approved a proposal not backed by the major opposition party – and even then the second opposition party, Labour, adopted a neutral position. Since 1937, whenever governments have put forward proposals not supported by the main opposition party – Fianna Fáil's attempts in 1959 and 1968 to change the electoral system and in 1992 and 2002 to restrict the circumstances under which abortion could be made legal, along with the Fine Gael–Labour coalition's proposed legalisation of divorce in 1986 – the people have rejected them.

The requirement that no changes can be made without a referendum may well enhance the status of the constitution, whose contents remain under the control of the people. The referendum requirement also means that such changes as are made, however controversial – for example, on divorce, Northern Ireland, or the EU – have a legitimacy that they would not have if the decision was made by politicians alone. However, it does have some drawbacks. One is that the expense involved in holding a referendum to make even the most insignificant and uncontentious amendment inhibits the process of change.

A second drawback concerns the modalities of the referendum process itself (see O'Neill, 2000; Whelan, 2000: 115–20). Before 1995, the government of the day felt free to use public funds to promote its side of the case exclusively. In the McKenna judgment of November 1995, the Supreme Court decided that this was unconstitutional, leaving the body politic with the dilemma of how to create a level playing field in future. For each referendum since 1995, the government of the day has established a 'Referendum Commission', composed of non-political figures (senior non-elected public officials such as the Ombudsman and a serving or retired judge) whose brief is to inform the public about the issues and arguments. From 1996 to 2001 inclusive it did this by making a public call for arguments (from individuals, interest groups or parties), and then putting these together in leaflets, newspaper advertisements and television and radio broadcasts. These invariably consisted of a number of arguments in favour of the proposal and an equal number of arguments against it. This approach was generally seen as unsatisfactory (Mansergh, 1999). Voters were often more confused or turned off than enlightened by the Commission's sometimes turgid presentation of the arguments. In particular, its highlighting of arguments against the 1998 Good Friday Agreement, indeed its ability somehow to find as many arguments against it as for it when all the political parties and 94 per cent of the voters favoured it, led to allegations that it was not so much creating a level playing pitch as tilting the pitch heavily in favour of a small minority.

The Commission's presentation of the arguments in the first Nice Treaty referendum of 2001, when its final broadcast was a kind of soup of alternating pro- and anti-Nice claims by actors playing partisans, was the last straw. Since then, its role has been changed (Kennedy, 2002: 117; All-Party Oireachtas Committee, 2001: 9–17, 24–33). It is no longer required to present (what it sees as) the main arguments for and against a proposal; its remit is simply to make the electorate aware that a referendum is taking place and to familiarise it with the issues at stake. Its performance in the second Nice referendum (2002) was described as having been a 'much more organised and accessible information campaign' than the 2001 equivalent (Hayward, 2003: 128).

Judicial development of the constitution

Given that a constitution lays down rules about what government and parliament can and cannot do, someone is required to keep an eye on them to make sure that they are obeying the rules, and this role is commonly performed by a judicial body. Judicial review can be defined as the power of a court to declare any law, any official action based on a law, or any other action by a public official, to be in conflict with the constitution and hence invalid (Abraham, 1996: 70). In most European countries, such as Austria, Germany, Italy and Spain, there is a special constitutional court, but in common law countries such as Ireland and the USA this function tends to be carried out by the regular courts.[1] The importance of judicial review in Ireland marks the country's gradual divergence from British practice, for whereas judicial review is significant in many countries, it has played little part in the governance of the United Kingdom.

The judges cannot alter the text of the constitution, but they decide what the text means. This power to interpret the constitution is considerable, since judges can, if they are so minded, 'discover' meanings that were never envisaged or intended by anyone initially; in the USA Charles Evans Hughes, who later became Chief Justice, bluntly declared in 1916 that 'the constitution is what the judges say it is' (Abraham, 1998: 356). Similarly, in an important Irish constitutional case in 1993, Mr Justice McCarthy observed that 'It is peculiarly within the jurisdiction of the courts to declare what the Constitution means' (Morgan, 1997: 32). In a number of European countries, the significance of judicial review is such that the judges could be counted among the policy makers (Stone Sweet, 2000; Gallagher *et al.*, 2001: 20–30; Guarnieri and Pederzoli, 2002). In Ireland, judicial review has proved to be the main method by which the constitution has been developed.

Constitutional cases can reach the courts by one of two routes. First, the constitution makes provision for a priori *abstract* review; that is, the constitutionality of a bill can be considered before it has become law and without reference to any specific case. Such review can be brought about only by a presidential referral of the bill to the Supreme Court. Second, there is provision for *concrete* review: it is open to anyone affected by a law to challenge its constitutionality before the High Court, with the possibility of appeal to the Supreme Court. The court decides whether the law is valid or must be struck down. In addition, any other act of the government (such as the signing of an agreement with another government) may be challenged in the courts as a violation of the constitution. In order to take a constitutional case, citizens must show that they have *locus standi* – that is, that they are in some way affected by the action or statute they are complaining about and are not merely busybodies.

Presidential referrals

The President of Ireland usually signs bills into law, but she or he has the power, under Article 26 of the constitution, instead to refer a bill to the Supreme Court for a decision on its constitutionality. In this event the Supreme Court hears arguments from lawyers assigned to put the case for and against the constitutionality of the bill, and delivers its judgment. If it decides that the bill is 'repugnant to the constitution', the President may not sign it into law.

This presidential power was employed on 14 occasions up to June 2004; on eight occasions the Supreme Court found the bill constitutional, and on the other six it found that the bill, or sections of it, were unconstitutional. The merit of this procedure is that the constitutionality of bills about which doubts have been raised can be definitively established before they become law; it prevents an unconstitutional law being in force until successfully challenged, a situation that could have consequences difficult ever to put right (CRG, 1996: 75).

However, there are two difficulties with the procedure. One is that Article 34.3.3 enshrines for all time a positive judgment in such cases: it states that the validity of a bill (or any part thereof) that is cleared by the Supreme Court after referral by the President may never again be questioned by any court. Even if the views of Supreme Court judges change over time, as of course they do, or if operation of the Act reveals aspects that no one had detected when the bill was argued about in abstract form, the Act is immune from all further challenge. The CRG thus recommended that Article 34.3.3 should be deleted and the all-party committee endorsed this (CRG, 1996: 76–80; All-Party Oireachtas Committee, 1999: 48, 112–13). The other difficulty is the opposite; it is that a bill may be struck down too readily, because the Supreme Court is not confined to the facts of any particular case. Whereas in the normal course of events the constitutionality of a law can be challenged only by an individual with a specific case to argue, in an Article 26 referral hypothetical suppositions can be conjured up and a bill could be found unconstitutional because of a possibility that might never arise in practice (Hogan, 1997b; cf O'Higgins, 1996: 281–2).

Judicial review

Once a bill is on the statute books, it is open to challenge by anyone whom it affects, and the courts are responsible, under Article 34.3.2, for delivering an authoritative decision on the constitutionality of legislation or the actions of public bodies. Judicial review has become more significant since the mid-1960s. Before then, the courts tended to interpret the constitution in a 'positivist' or literal manner, sticking closely to the letter of the document and taking the view that there was no more to it than the words it contained. The position then began to change, reflecting what has been seen as a virtually world-wide pattern (Tate and Vallinger, 1995). Due partly to the accession of a new generation of judges and partly to the general changes taking place in society and political culture at that time, the Irish judiciary began to adopt a more 'creative' approach (see Chubb, 1991: 60–78; Casey, 2000: 332–85). This was seemingly encouraged by the Taoiseach of the day, Seán Lemass, who in 1961 privately urged two newly appointed Supreme Court judges to be more activist in their approach to interpretation of the constitution (Sturgess and Chubb, 1988: 144). Judges began to speak of the general tenor or spirit of the constitution and of the rights that those living under such a constitution must by definition, in their view, enjoy.

An important article in this process turned out to be Article 40.3.1: 'The State guarantees in its laws to respect, and, as far as practicable, by its laws to defend and vindicate the personal rights of the citizen.' Although this may appear to be merely a pious declaration without much substance (as may, indeed, have been the intention), it has proved to be of great significance. Until the 1960s, it was assumed that the 'rights' referred to in Article 40.3.1 were only those specifically listed in Articles 40–4, but a landmark judgment in 1963 changed that. The plaintiff in the case of *Ryan v. Attorney General* argued that the fluoridation of water violated her right to bodily integrity, a right not mentioned anywhere in the constitution. In his judgment, Mr Justice Kenny accepted her contention that she – and by extension every other citizen – did indeed have such a right (unfortunately for her, he didn't accept that putting fluoride in the water violated it), and said: 'The personal rights which may be invoked to invalidate legislation are not confined to those specified in Article 40 but include all those rights which result from the Christian and democratic nature of the State.'

Subsequently, as the number of constitutional cases brought to the courts increased, judges 'discovered' many more 'undisclosed human rights' in the constitution (for a list of 18 such rights see CRG, 1996: 246; see also Hogan and Whyte, 2003: 1413–85). One of the most dramatic judgments came in 1973, when the Supreme Court (in the case of *McGee v. Attorney General*) accepted the plaintiff's claim that she had a right to marital privacy, and accordingly struck down the 1935 legislation banning the importation of contraceptives. Given de Valera's strongly Catholic views, and since it was his government's legislation that was being declared unconstitutional, it was apparent to all at this stage that the constitution was not, as indeed it never really had been, 'de Valera's constitution', the name sometimes applied to it. His creation now had a life of its own, and it was for the courts, not for any politician, to decide what its words meant. It is generally believed, incidentally, that de Valera did not anticipate judicial review being anything like as significant or extensive as it has proved, even though he was warned about the way things might turn out (Hogan and Whyte, 2003: xvii). The Irish courts have, indeed, proved much readier to identify unenunciated rights than their American counterparts (Beytagh, 1992).

The seemingly limitless number of unenumerated rights that might be lurking in the constitution has some self-evidently undesirable features. One is that the Oireachtas, despite striving as it does not to pass legislation that violates the constitutionally protected rights of the citizens, is placed in a position of uncertainty if it has no way of knowing exactly what these rights are. Another is that it seems to give considerable and perhaps undue power to the unelected judiciary, a point to which we return later in the chapter. Accordingly, the CRG recommended the replacement of the existing 40.3.1 by a comprehensive list, which would include those rights identified by the courts to date – together, perhaps, with those set out in the European Convention on Human Rights and the International Convention on Civil and Political Rights, and other rights as well (CRG, 1996: 257–65). The revised article would 'confine further recognition of fundamental rights by the courts to those necessarily implicit in the rights expressly listed' (p. 259). Whether this formula would bring about the certainty at which the CRG was aiming seems questionable, though, since it would still lie with the judiciary to decide which further rights are, in fact, 'implicit' in those listed.

Since 1973 the courts have made a number of decisions that have had major political implications, and we can give several examples (details of the main cases can be found in Doolan, 1994: 289–385; Beytagh, 1997: 43–111). First, they have defined and seemingly redefined the circumstances when the 'political offence' argument can be used by a defendant to avoid extradition, sometimes giving more weight to the apparent motivation of the perpetrator of a crime, at other times giving more weight to the nature of the crime. Second, in 1987, the Supreme Court, by its decision in the Crotty case, prevented the state from ratifying the Single European Act until the constitution was amended to permit this (see Thompson, 1991; Casey, 1992; McCutcheon, 1992). Third, in March 1992, in the 'X' case the Supreme Court declared that abortion was legal in certain circumstances (see Box 3.2). Fourth, in August 1992, the Supreme Court decided that the constitutional reference to collective cabinet responsibility (Article 28.4) entailed an absolute ban on all disclosure of discussions at cabinet meetings (Hogan, 1993). Fifth, in 1995, as mentioned earlier, in the McKenna judgment it decided that governments could not use public funds to promote only their own side of the case at referendums.

Furthermore, in addition to high-profile judgments such as these, there have been many less spectacular but nonetheless significant judgments in which the courts, relying on their power to interpret the constitution, have effectively changed the law. For example, in the *McKinley v. Minister for Defence* case of 1992, the plaintiff claimed that injuries (for which she held the defendants responsible) to her husband had deprived her of certain conjugal rights. Under common law, only a husband could claim compensation for the loss of these rights, and the state argued that this common law right was unconstitutional, discriminating as it did against married women, and hence had not survived the enactment of the constitution in 1937.

Box 3.2 The 'X' case of 1992

The 'X' case, which arose early in 1992, concerned a 14-year-old girl who had become pregnant, allegedly as a result of being raped. She intended to travel to Britain to obtain an abortion, but the Attorney-General, the legal adviser to the government, obtained a High Court injunction to prevent her travelling out of the country, on the ground that she intended to terminate the life of her unborn child, which he believed would be contrary to Article 40.3.3 of the constitution (the 'pro-life amendment' inserted by referendum in 1983). This decision caused an uproar in Ireland and earned the country wide unfavourable international publicity.

In March 1992 the Supreme Court overturned this injunction. It declared that Article 40.3.3 did in fact confer a right to an abortion on a woman whose life would be threatened by continuing with a pregnancy – including cases where this risk arose from the possibility of suicide by the mother.

This decision was welcomed by pro-abortion groups, and liberals in general, though there was concern that the Supreme Court had not explicitly affirmed that a woman had the right to travel out of the country no matter what her reasons for wanting to do so. It was bitterly criticised by anti-abortion groups, who complained that when the Irish people voted in 1983 to add the 'pro-life' amendment, they had intended this to have the effect of completely outlawing abortion. The judges, in their view, had undemocratically imposed their own idiosyncratic interpretation of the article in question. However, in the words of Charles Evans Hughes, quoted on p. 84, 'the constitution is what the judges say it is'.

Instead of taking this course, the Supreme Court 'developed' the rights in question so as to vest them in a wife as well (Casey, 2000: 474; Hogan and Whyte, 2003: 263, 1328–30). The cumulative effect of such judgments in invalidating old and unreformed statute and common law embodying anomalies or injustices should not be underestimated.

The power of judges

Provision for judicial review clearly carries potential dangers in a democratic state, because it puts significant power into the hands of unelected individuals who are not routinely accountable or answerable to anyone. It is true that under Article 35.4 of the constitution, judges can be dismissed by majority vote of the Dáil and Seanad for 'stated misbehaviour or incapacity', but the possibility of invoking this provision has only very rarely been considered. One such occasion came about in November 1994, when the Taoiseach belatedly realised the disastrous political consequences of a particular judicial appointment, but the government accepted that dismissing a judge was impossible unless there were 'solid reasons'.[2] A second arose in April 1999, when disquiet about apparent irregularities behind the reduction of a sentence on a convicted drunk driver led to an investigation, at the government's request, by the Chief Justice, whose report on the whole matter (which was dubbed 'the Sheedy affair') contained strong criticism of the behaviour of two judges. The government immediately made it clear that it wished the judges to resign, and there seemed no doubt that the Oireachtas would have debated and almost certainly passed a motion dismissing them, under the terms of Article 35.4, had they not reluctantly resigned within four days of the government making its views known. The idea of monitoring judges' behaviour has proved difficult to implement; the all-party committee recommended amending the constitution to create a 'Judicial Council' to review judicial conduct – as opposed to judicial decisions – but a government proposal to hold a referendum on this in June 2001 was withdrawn at a late stage when the opposition parties indicated that they were unhappy about some of the details (All-Party Oireachtas Committee, 1999: 21–4; *Irish Times*, 4 May 2001).

Mr Justice Kenny once said that 'judges have become legislators, and have the advantage that they do not have to face an opposition' (Hogan and Whyte, 2003: 1415n133) – he might have added that neither do they have to face the people, as politicians do. Judges in Ireland share a number of characteristics with their counterparts elsewhere: they are not elected, they enjoy substantial autonomy from control or scrutiny by elected representatives, and they are closed and secretive as to how they work. Their power to interpret the constitution makes them even more powerful than judges in many other countries. All of this raises the questions of who the judges are, how they came to be judges and what values they hold.

By law, Irish judges must be barristers of at least 12 years' standing or circuit court judges of at least four years' standing (solicitors of ten years' standing are appointable as circuit court judges and hence can make their way up the ladder to the Supreme Court – see Casey, 2000: 302–5; Morgan, 2001: 111–17; All-Party Oireachtas Committee, 1999: 5–8). They are appointed by the government, though in practice it seems that only the Taoiseach and the Minister for Justice (together with the other party leader(s) in the case of a coalition government) are involved in the selection, the rest of the government simply being informed of the name of the chosen person.[3] This being so, a record of support for one of the parties in government has, not surprisingly, always been an important factor. Until 1996 the procedure was an informal one, under which the names of appointees reached the government by a secret process involving the taking of soundings, with political connections playing an important role.

Since 1996 aspiring judges have been able to apply to the Judicial Appointments Advisory Board, which draws up an unranked seven-member shortlist and presents this to the government, which makes the final selection. However, the government is not bound to select someone from the board's list at all and, moreover, the board does not come into operation when the government decides to promote a judge from a lower court. Concerns have been expressed that the pool from which judges are drawn remains very narrow, and, moreover, legal academics seem not to be considered for appointment (Beytagh, 1997: 148–9). The only detailed study of judges' backgrounds was made over 30 years ago, and it found that most judges had a background of support for the party that appointed them (Bartholomew, 1971: 48). Most were from upper middle class backgrounds, over a quarter were sons of lawyers, and all were men – at least the gender balance has been redressed a little since then (see Table 10.6, p. 284).

Might governments not only look for appointees of the right political background but also take into account the views of those under consideration? There are suggestions that they do. Hogan speculates that the government's choice of a judge to fill a vacancy in 1940 on the Supreme Court just before a major constitutional case reached it may have been prompted by 'the belief that he would be, so to speak, a "safe pair of hands" on issues of this kind' based on his past record (Hogan, 2000: 259). An earlier study of judicial appointments concluded that in the mid to late 1960s the government, and especially the Department of Justice, was disturbed at the flurry of 'creative' decisions being made by the courts, and the Department decided to ensure that less activist judges were appointed in future (Tóibín, 1985: 17–20).

Most features of Irish judges' backgrounds are characteristic of judges almost everywhere. Across western Europe generally, judges tend to come from relatively privileged backgrounds, and appointment of judges is highly politicised. Irish practice is unusual in that the government alone appoints judges; the more common approach, used by most countries for their constitutional courts, is that cross-party agreement is needed for appointments, which means in effect that the process becomes a carve-up among the main political parties (Gallagher *et al.*, 2001: 30–2). The result of the judicial appointment process seems to be broadly similar everywhere: 'the men and women selected to judgeships almost always hold safe, sound, middle-of-the-road opinions', and are characterised by 'moderation and attachment to regime norms' (Jacob, 1996: 390–1).

The question of whether the political and socio-economic background of Irish judges may be related to the judgments that they deliver is strangely under-researched. No one has suggested that judges with a record as supporters of a particular party view elevation to the bench as an opportunity to conduct 'politics by other means' (Chubb, 1992: 295). But even if Fianna Fáil (or Fine Gael) supporters appointed to the bench do not see themselves as Fianna Fáil (or Fine Gael) judges, with a mission to use their positions to continue their political activities, it might still be true that the values that led judges to join one or other of the parties in the first place will inform the decisions they make. This sometimes seemed to characterise judgments in cases in the 1980s involving extradition of alleged members of republican paramilitary groups to Northern Ireland; judges with a background in Fine Gael tended to be less sympathetic to a 'political offence' line of defence than did those whose background was in Fianna Fáil. Examining the putative decisions of the five Supreme Court judges in an early constitutional case, Hogan relates these convincingly to their respective political backgrounds as well as to their jurisprudence (Hogan, 2000: 275–6). Or, more broadly, the prosperous middle-class background of most judges might lead them instinctively to be 'in favour of the individual rather than the community or the State' (Morgan, 2001: 108).

In the USA, critics have accused the judges of being as goal-oriented as political actors, using the constitution 'as a kind of letter of marque authorizing them to set sail at will among laws, striking down any they find displeasing' (quoted in Hodder-Williams, 1992: 16). In this perception, judges use the constitution simply to legitimise their own preferences when reaching a decision; as trained barristers, they are well able to make a plausible case for whatever argument they wish to make. Reviewing the decisions made by the judiciary in constitutional cases, Hogan points to the absence of any consistent approach on the part of the judges, with a strong suspicion that they utilise 'whatever method might seem to be most convenient or to offer adventitious support for conclusions they had already reached' (Hogan, 1988: 187; see also Chubb, 1991: 71–3; Morgan, 2001). When judges accept the existence of rights not specifically mentioned in the text of the constitution, such as the right to bodily integrity or the right to marital privacy, are they logically deducing the existence of these rights from the overall nature of the constitution, inferring them, discovering them, or calling into active life rights that, though hitherto unnoticed, have lain dormant within the constitution since 1937? Or are they, as critics might maintain, merely conjuring up or drawing out of the ether a 'right' in order to provide a convincing basis for a decision whose real progenitor is the judge's own attitude towards the case in question? Any attempt to explore this question would require a far greater depth of research into the politics of the judiciary in Ireland than has so far been undertaken.

If judges do not simply interpret the constitution to accord with their own preferences, on what basis should they interpret it? The 'originalist' perspective according to which the constitution should be interpreted in line with the intentions of the Irish people when they accepted the constitution in 1937 has obvious pitfalls: how can we know whether the people of 1937 would have felt that a law should or should not be constitutional, and, if we could know, why should the Irish people of the twenty-first century be bound by their views? Such an approach really would be akin to 'rule by the dead'. Yet, without such a constraint on the judges, the danger is that their judgments will be 'unmoored' in anything more substantial than the values and policy preferences of the judges of the day, or some vague notion of what constitutes the prevailing public attitude. It has been suggested that in practice, when it comes to the 'rights' articles (40–44), the courts have adopted a kind of middle way:

> there is a sense in which the actual text and the provenance of this text does not particularly matter. Instead, the accumulated sense of legal tradition and case-law, together with legal methodology and reasoning, make up a sort of *acquis constitutionnel* and it is this which really counts.
>
> (Hogan, 1997c: 373–4)

As we noted at the start of the chapter, there is an inherent tension between constitutionalism and democracy (at least, if the latter is equated simply with majority rule). The dilemma of judicial review is inherently unresolvable. It places a lot of power in the hands of a non-elected, unrepresentative, elite answerable to no one. But if judges were somehow made genuinely accountable to the government or parliament, they would cease to be an independent judiciary, one of the checks and balances of a liberal democracy. Judicial review has allowed judges to make important quasi-political decisions in areas such as extradition without reference to the people or their elected representatives. However, Irish judges have not come in for the type of criticism sometimes levelled against their counterparts elsewhere. Partly this is because, on the liberal–conservative spectrum discussed in Chapter 2, the judiciary has often seemed to be somewhat closer than the Oireachtas to the liberal end of the spectrum; given that public opinion has been becoming more liberal, the judiciary has been a few years ahead of, but not wildly out of line with, public opinion. For example, governments had shown no inclination to grasp the nettle of reforming the restrictive contraception laws until the courts forced their hand by the McGee judgment of 1973. One of the Supreme Court judges in this case later said that the court's judgment 'was seen by everybody, including the politicians, as having got the politicians off the hook' (Sturgess and Chubb, 1988: 125). The court's view that married couples should have access to contraceptives was radical in 1973 but mainstream within ten years.

Regardless of the policy content of judicial decisions, though, the merits of the 'creative' approach taken by the courts in the 1960s, and subsequently, have been increasingly questioned. The landmark decision of Mr Justice Kenny in the 1963 Ryan case, in which the judge spoke of the unenumerated personal rights that 'result from the Christian and democratic nature of the state' and quoted a recent Papal encyclical in support of his argument is open to innumerable criticisms (for a detailed analysis of this judgment see Hogan, 1994). Reviewing the unenumerated rights discovered by the courts over the years, Hogan concludes:

While the protection of such various unenumerated rights – such as the right to privacy, the right to earn a livelihood and the right of an unwed mother to custody and care of her child – may well be beneficial and salutary, it is often difficult to take this jurisprudence completely at face value, since there is nothing whatever in the actual text of the Constitution to show that these rights were intended to enjoy constitutional protection.

(Hogan, 1994: 114)

The search for one 'correct' standard to apply in determining which approach the judges should employ when interpreting the constitution is likely to be elusive (Kavanagh, 1997). In practice, attitudes to the judiciary often depend on 'whose ox is being gored', in the words of the American Governor Al Smith, and significantly, the strongest objections were voiced after the Supreme Court delivered its verdict in the 'X' case in March 1992 (see above), when anti-abortionists criticised both the specific judgments delivered (arguing that the judges had 'lost their way') and, it seemed, the principle of judicial review. Fianna Fáil Senator Des Hanafin, chairman of the 'Pro-Life Trust', declared that 'it is wholly unacceptable and indeed a deep affront to the people of Ireland that four judges who are preserved by the constitution from accountability can radically alter the constitution and place in peril the most vulnerable section of our society' (*Irish Times*, 6 March 1992). However, this seems to be a minority viewpoint. Calls for reform of the system of judicial appointment, for example by the introduction of US-style parliamentary assessments of proposed appointees, have up to now been voices in the wilderness, as the consensus among insiders appears to be that the present system, whatever its theoretical drawbacks, operates satisfactorily in practice. The tension between democracy and constitutionalism cannot in any case be eliminated by such devices; it can only be managed, with greater or less success, and thus far the record has not been a bad one.

The debate on constitutional change

Attitudes to the constitution have undergone a number of changes over the years. Until the mid-1960s there was remarkably little criticism of it, and, perhaps, limited awareness of how important a constitution was as the basic law in a functioning liberal democratic society. As societal attitudes began to change from the 1960s onwards, the constitution was increasingly seen as a symbol of the past and an obstacle to progress. For many, it was regarded as a product of de Valera's Ireland, a narrow Catholic and nationalist document that sought to impose the mores of the 1930s political elite upon a changing and modernising country. Numerous demands for 'a new constitution', free of the baggage of the past, were heard. Yet, at the same time, there was a growing awareness of the merits of the constitution and, due in particular to the work of the late Professor John Kelly, of the richness of the jurisprudence that was being constructed around it. When the fiftieth anniversary of the constitution was marked in the late 1980s by a spate of assessments, the tone was celebratory and appreciative rather than critical. Brian Farrell seemed to sum up the mood: '[Since 1937,] that Constitution, Bunreacht na hÉireann, has been amended, interpreted, re-shaped by judges, politicians, civil servants and the people. One man's document has become a political community's common charter – a living and effective guarantee of broadly based and expanding liberties' (Farrell, 1988c: viii). At the start of the twenty-first century, the standing of the constitution has never been higher.

This change in attitudes has resulted from the development of the constitution by the judiciary and from alterations to the wording of the constitution effected by referendum. The constitution no longer seems to pose an impediment to the 'liberal agenda', the 1995 removal of the ban on divorce having pretty much completed this. The rephrasing of Articles 2 and 3 for which the people voted overwhelmingly in 1998, i.e. the replacement of a claim over Northern Ireland by an aspiration to a peacefully united Ireland, similarly defused much of the criticism of the constitution as expressing old-style nationalism. This is not to say that there are no further political battles to be fought over the wording of the constitution (see Box 3.3). Article 41.2, incorporating the view that women's place is in the home, would find few defenders (see Dooley, 1998 and Connelly, 1999, for a fuller discussion), and the whole constitution contains innumerable examples of gender-specific language that the CRG (1996: xi) recommended be replaced by wording based on 'the principle of gender-inclusiveness'. The preamble to the constitution still conveys a very nationalist view of history in which unionists could not recognise themselves and, along with many other areas of the constitution, has a broadly Christian, often specifically Catholic, tone that does not match the political culture of the state as well as it did in 1937. Abortion is another issue fought out on constitutional terrain: since Article 40.3.3, inserted in 1983 by a referendum instigated by anti-abortion groups, was interpreted in the 1992 'X' case as allowing abortion in certain circumstances, the pro-life movement has called, with conspicuous lack of success, for the constitution to be amended again so that abortion can be completely outlawed.

The limited scope of the rights (both enumerated and unenumerated) guaranteed by the constitution has been criticised by those who believe that the constitution should actively promote equality of outcome and not merely equality of opportunity. Two members of the CRG argued that the constitution should have an article 'committing us to a democracy based on principles of social solidarity with the aim of eliminating poverty and promoting economic equality through a system of taxation based on principles of equality and progressiveness' (Lynch and Connelly, 1996: 590). Why, it is asked, should a right to adequate food, clothing, shelter, rest and medical

---

Box 3.3 Possible changes to the Irish constitution

Among the changes that have been suggested are:

- remove all examples of gender-specific language and ensure that the constitution contains only wording based on the principle of gender-inclusiveness;
- insert a comprehensive list of fundamental rights and seek to prevent the courts discovering further unenumerated fundamental rights;
- enshrine socio-economic rights (for example, to adequate housing and health care) to try to ensure equality of outcome rather than just equality of opportunity;
- qualify the right to private property so as to tilt the balance in favour of society as a whole;
- enshrine the principle of Irish neutrality in international affairs;
- continue to allow the parliament to declare a state of emergency but stipulate that any such state of emergency shall automatically lapse after a period of three years;
- give constitutional recognition to the office of Ombudsman (for which, see Chapter 9);
- give explicit recognition to the centrality of political parties to political life, and enunciate principles regulating parties' roles, rights and responsibilities.

---

care not be affirmed (Murphy, 1998: 167–81)? The former High Court judge Declan Costello observed that poverty and inequality were still widespread in Irish society, while the protection of the rights guaranteed in the constitution had undoubtedly been aided by their enshrinement in the constitution. Accordingly, he suggested, 'There is no reason to assume that the enjoyment of the economic and social rights of the underprivileged and deprived would not be similarly enhanced if they too were constitutionally protected' (Hogan, 2001: 183). This question was given topicality in February 2000 when, in the High Court, Judge Kelly directed the state to provide a number of units for children at risk, something that would clearly have entailed significant expenditure. On appeal, the Supreme Court overturned this judgment in what was seen as a reassertion of the separation of powers and a reaffirmation that decisions on how the resources of the state should be allocated are a matter for the executive and the legislature, not for judges (Coulter, 2001).

In this vein, the Minister for Justice Michael McDowell, an experienced barrister, expressed himself in 2003 against the constitutional provision of social and economic rights. Because of resource constraints, he argued, the exercise of rights to housing, health care and higher education had to be rationed by some mechanism, and decisions on how to do this 'are, in my view, the stuff of politics, and not at all appropriate to be decided by the courts . . . differences within societies concerning economic and social values and ends should, in the normal course of things, be resolved by the democratic political process' (*Irish Times*, 15 April 2003). A majority of the CRG, too, was opposed to the inclusion of specific personal economic rights. It took the view that matters such as freedom from poverty are essentially political questions, so it 'would be a distortion of democracy to transfer decisions on major issues of policy and practicality from the Government and the Oireachtas, elected to represent the people and do their will, to an unelected judiciary'. There was also the danger that the state would find itself compelled by the courts to pursue certain policies regardless of whether the necessary resources were available (CRG, 1996: 234–6; for a general discussion, see Hogan, 2001). The Irish constitution, it must be said, is very much in the European mainstream in guaranteeing the standard liberal rights while refraining from asserting that those under its jurisdiction possess justiciable economic rights. The same issue arises regarding, for example, suggestions that the constitution should be amended so as to enshrine the principle of neutrality in international affairs. A general objection to constitutionalising rights and policy positions in this way is that it takes the issue out of 'normal' politics, renders it immune from public debate and, moreover, resolves it favourably to one or other side – so, it has been suggested, 'a system that immunized from collective control the issues that produce the most conflict would hardly be democratic' (Sunstein, 1988: 339–40).

Those sections of the constitution that deal with the institutions of government are not generally seen as in pressing need of change. The CRG recommended the introduction of the 'constructive vote of no confidence', which would prevent the Dáil voting out a Taoiseach unless it was able to vote in a replacement, and it advocated giving constitutional recognition to both local government (this was effected in 1999) and the Ombudsman. It considered the arguments for change in the role and composition of the Seanad, and in the electoral system, but rather than make firm recommendations it called for further consideration of both questions. Many of these subjects are discussed in other chapters of this book. The CRG also considered possible changes of a less politically controversial and more narrowly constitutional nature. We have outlined many of these areas in this chapter already, such as the character of the 'emergency' article (28.3.3), the merits of the 'one judgment' rule (Articles 26.2.2 and 34.3.5), and the freezing for all time of the initial clearance of a bill following a presidential referral (34.3.3). The prospects for all-party consensus are much higher now than in the more divided 1960s and 1970s, given that the constitutional aspects of Northern Ireland and the liberal agenda have effectively been resolved, though it remains to be seen how high a political priority is accorded to what to some seems the arcane topic of constitutional reform.

Calls for a new constitution are now rarely heard. To scrap the existing constitution would risk losing the rights and liberties 'discovered' by judges in it, most of which have had the effect of enhancing the civic rights of citizens. Despite some past accusations that the constitution is excessively long and should be replaced by one that is confined to basics like the American constitution, in fact the Irish constitution is by no means verbose by world-wide standards; its length of about 14,000 words (in both English and Irish) compares with an estimated 15,900-word average length for 142 national constitutions examined by van Maarseveen and van der Tang (1978: 177). No political party advocates the drafting of a new constitution, and when the public was asked for its views in a May 1995 opinion poll, only 36 per cent wanted a new constitution compared with 55 per cent who wanted to retain the existing constitution and amend it as required (Market Research Bureau of Ireland, 1995: Table 1). The constitution as a whole possesses the kind of widespread acceptance and legitimacy that the Irish Free State constitution never attracted, and is likely to remain the fundamental law of the state for some time to come.

Notes

1 The constitutional court model was favoured by some of those drawing up the 1937 constitution but in the end was not chosen (Hogan and Whyte, 2003: xvii).
2 Comment of Brendan Howlin, a minister in the 1993–4 government, in Dáil Éireann: Select Committee on Legislation and Security, 1995, column 1069, 18 January 1995. The appointment in question, of Attorney General Harry Whelehan to be President of the High Court, caused the Labour Party to withdraw from the government, thus bringing about its collapse (see Garry, 1995).
3 Evidence of Ruairí Quinn, a minister in the 1993–4 government, Dáil Éireann: Select Committee on Legislation and Security, 1995, columns 937, 981, 17 January 1995.

References and further reading

Abraham, Henry J., 1996. *The Judiciary: The Supreme Court in the Governmental Process*, 10th edn. New York and London: New York University Press.

Abraham, Henry J., 1998. *The Judicial Process: An Introductory Analysis of the Courts of the United States, England and France*, 7th edn. New York and Oxford: Oxford University Press.

All-Party Oireachtas Committee on the Constitution, 1999. *Fourth Progress Report: The Courts and the Judiciary* (Pn 7831). Dublin: Stationery Office.

All-Party Oireachtas Committee on the Constitution, 2001. *Sixth Progress Report: The Referendum* (Pn 10632). Dublin: Stationery Office.

Bartholomew, Paul C., 1971. *The Irish Judiciary*. Dublin: Institute of Public Administration.

Beytagh, Francis X., 1992. 'Individual rights, judicial review, and written constitutions', in James O'Reilly (ed.), *Human Rights and Constitutional Law: Essays in Honour of Brian Walsh*. Blackrock, Co Dublin: Round Hall Press, pp. 147–62.

Beytagh, Francis X., 1997. *Constitutionalism in Contemporary Ireland: An American Perspective*. Dublin: Round Hall, Sweet and Maxwell.

Bunreacht na hÉireann (Constitution of Ireland). Dublin: Stationery Office.

Butler, Andrew and Rory O'Connell, 1998. 'A critical analysis of Ireland's Constitutional Review Group report', *Irish Jurist* 33: 237–65.

Casey, James, 1992. '*Crotty v. An Taoiseach*: a comparative perspective', in James O'Reilly (ed.), *Human Rights and Constitutional Law: Essays in Honour of Brian Walsh*. Blackrock, Co. Dublin: Round Hall Press, pp. 189–200.

Casey, James, 2000. *Constitutional Law in Ireland*, 3rd edn. Dublin: Round Hall, Sweet and Maxwell.

Chubb, Basil, 1991. *The Politics of the Irish Constitution*. Dublin: Institute of Public Administration.

Chubb, Basil, 1992. *The Government and Politics of Ireland*, 3rd edn. Harlow: Longman.

Committee on the Constitution, 1967. *Report* (Pr. 9817). Dublin: Stationery Office.

Connelly, Alpha, 1999. 'Women and the Constitution of Ireland', in Yvonne Galligan, Eilís Ward and Rick Wilford (eds), *Contesting Politics: Women in Ireland, North and South*. Boulder, CO: Westview and PSAI Press, pp. 18–37.

Constitution of the Irish Free State. Dublin: Stationery Office.

Coulter, Carol, 2001. 'Judges return decisions to politicians', *Irish Times*, 18 December.

CRG (Constitution Review Group), 1996. *Report* (Pn 2632). Dublin: Stationery Office.

Dáil Éireann: Select Committee on Legislation and Security, 1995. *Meeting of Sub-Committee, Inquiry into Events of 11 to 15 November, 1994*. Dublin: Stationery Office.

Doolan, Brian, 1994. *Constitutional Law and Constitutional Rights in Ireland*, 3rd edn. Dublin: Gill and Macmillan.

Dooley, Dolores, 1998. 'Gendered citizenship in the Irish constitution', in Tim Murphy and Patrick Twomey (eds), *Ireland's Evolving Constitution, 1937–97: Collected Essays*. Oxford: Hart, pp. 121–33.

Elazar, Daniel J., 1985. 'Constitution-making: the pre-eminently political act', in Keith G. Banting and Richard Simeon (eds), *The Politics of Constitutional Change in Industrial Nations: Redesigning the State*. London: Macmillan, pp. 232–48.

Fanning, Ronan, 1988. 'Mr de Valera drafts a constitution', in Brian Farrell (ed.), *De Valera's Constitution and Ours*. Dublin: Gill and Macmillan, pp. 33–45.

Farrell, Brian (ed.), 1988a. *De Valera's Constitution and Ours*. Dublin: Gill and Macmillan.

Farrell, Brian, 1988b. 'From first Dáil through Irish Free State', in Brian Farrell (ed.), *De Valera's Constitution and Ours*. Dublin: Gill and Macmillan, pp. 18–32.

Farrell, Brian, 1988c. 'Preface', in Brian Farrell (ed.), *De Valera's Constitution and Ours*. Dublin: Gill and Macmillan, pp. vii–ix.

Farrell, Brian, 1988d. 'The constitution and the institutions of government: constitutional theory and political practice', in Frank Litton (ed.), *The Constitution of Ireland 1937–1987*. Dublin: Institute of Public Administration, pp. 162–72.

Foley, J. Anthony and Stephen Lalor (eds), 1995. *Gill and Macmillan Annotated Constitution of Ireland*. Dublin: Gill and Macmillan.

Gallagher, Michael, 1996. 'Ireland: the referendum as a conservative device?', in Michael Gallagher and Pier Vincenzo Uleri (eds), *The Referendum Experience in Europe*. Basingstoke: Macmillan, pp. 86–105.

Gallagher, Michael, Michael Laver and Peter Mair, 2001. *Representative Government in Modern Europe*, 3rd edn. New York: McGraw-Hill.

Garry, John, 1995. 'The demise of the Fianna Fáil/Labour "Partnership" government and the rise of the "Rainbow" coalition', *Irish Political Studies* 10: 192–9.

Gilland, Karin, 1999. 'Referenda in the Republic of Ireland', *Electoral Studies* 18:3: 430–8.

Girvin, Brian, 1987. 'The divorce referendum in the Republic, June 1986', *Irish Political Studies* 2: 93–9.

Girvin, Brian, 1996. 'The Irish divorce referendum, November 1995', *Irish Political Studies* 11: 174–81.

Guarnieri, Carlo and Patrizia Pederzoli, 2002. *The Power of Judges: A Comparative Study of Courts and Democracy*. Oxford: Oxford University Press.

Hayward, Katy, 2003. ' "If at first you don't succeed . . .": the second referendum on the Treaty of Nice, 2002', *Irish Political Studies* 18:1: 120–32.

Hodder-Williams, Richard, 1992. 'Six notions of "political" and the United States Supreme Court', *British Journal of Political Science* 22:1: 1–20.

Hogan, Gerard, 1988. 'Constitutional interpretation', in Frank Litton (ed.), *The Constitution of Ireland 1937–1987*. Dublin: Institute of Public Administration, pp. 173–91.

Hogan, Gerard, 1993. 'The cabinet confidentiality case of 1992', *Irish Political Studies* 8: 131–7.

Hogan, Gerard, 1994. 'Unenumerated personal rights: *Ryan's* case re-evaluated', *Irish Jurist* 25–27: 95–116.

Hogan, Gerard, 1997a. 'The Constitution Review Committee of 1934', in Fionán Ó Muircheartaigh (ed.), *Ireland in the Coming Times: Essays to Celebrate T. K. Whitaker's 80 Years*. Dublin: Institute of Public Administration, pp. 342–69.

Hogan, Gerard, 1997b. 'Ceremonial role most important for President', *Irish Times*, 21 October.

Hogan, Gerard, 1997c. 'The constitution, property rights and proportionality', *Irish Jurist* 32: 373–97.

Hogan, Gerard, 2000. 'The Supreme Court and the reference of the Offences Against the State (Amendment) Bill 1940', *Irish Jurist* 35: 238–79.

Hogan, Gerard, 2001. 'Directive principles, socio-economic rights and the constitution', *Irish Jurist* 36: 174–98.

Hogan, Gerard and Gerry Whyte, 2003. *J. M. Kelly: The Irish Constitution*, 4th edn. Dublin: LexisNexis Butterworths.

Holmes, Michael, 1993. 'The Maastricht Treaty referendum of June 1992', *Irish Political Studies* 8: 105–10.

Holmes, Stephen, 1988. 'Pre-commitment and the paradox of democracy', in Jon Elster and Rune Slagstad (eds), *Constitutionalism and Democracy*. Cambridge: Cambridge University Press, pp. 195–240.

Jacob, Herbert, 1996. 'Conclusion', in Herbert Jacob, Erhard Blankenburg, Herbert M. Kritzer, Doris Marie Provine and Joseph Sanders, *Courts, Law and Politics in Comparative Perspective*. New Haven, CT and London: Yale University Press, pp. 389–400.

Kavanagh, Aileen, 1997. 'The quest for legitimacy in constitutional interpretation', *Irish Jurist* 32: 195–216.

Kennedy, Fiachra, 2002. 'Abortion referendum 2002', *Irish Political Studies* 17:1: 114–28.

Kennelly, Brendan and Eilís Ward, 1993. 'The abortion referendums', in Michael Gallagher and Michael Laver (eds), *How Ireland Voted 1992*. Dublin: Folens and Limerick: PSAI Press, pp. 115–34.

Keogh, Dermot, 1988a. 'The constitutional revolution: an analysis of the making of the constitution', in Frank Litton (ed.), *The Constitution of Ireland 1937–1987*. Dublin: Institute of Public Administration, pp. 4–84.

Keogh, Dermot, 1988b. 'Church, state and society', in Brian Farrell (ed.), *De Valera's Constitution and Ours*. Dublin: Gill and Macmillan, pp. 103–22.

LeDuc, Lawrence, 2003. *The Politics of Direct Democracy: Referendums in Global Perspective*. Peterborough, Ontario: Broadview Press.

Lee, J. J., 1989. *Ireland 1912–1985: Politics and Society*. Cambridge: Cambridge University Press.

Litton, Frank (ed.), 1988. *The Constitution of Ireland 1937–1987*. Dublin: Institute of Public Administration.

Lynch, Kathleen and Alpha Connelly, 1996. 'Equality before the law', in CRG (Constitution Review Group) *Report* (Pn 2632). Dublin: Stationery Office, pp. 586–91.

McCutcheon, Paul, 1992. 'The Irish constitution and the ratification of the Single European Act', *L'Irlande Politique et Sociale* 4: 19–41.

MacMillan, Gretchen M., 1993. *State, Society and Authority in Ireland: the Foundations of the Modern State*. Dublin: Gill and Macmillan.

Mansergh, Lucy, 1999. 'Two referendums and the Referendum Commission: the 1998 experience', *Irish Political Studies* 14: 123–31.

Market Research Bureau of Ireland, 1995. *Irish Times*/MRBI poll, 20–22 May. Dublin: Market Research Bureau of Ireland.

Morgan, David Gwynn, 1997. *The Separation of Powers in the Irish Constitution*. Dublin: Round Hall, Sweet and Maxwell.

Morgan, David Gwynn, 2001. *A Judgment too Far? Judicial Activism and the Constitution*. Cork: Cork University Press.

Murphy, Tim, 1998. 'Economic inequality and the constitution', in Tim Murphy and Patrick Twomey (eds), *Ireland's Evolving Constitution, 1937–97: Collected Essays*. Oxford: Hart, pp. 163–81.

Murphy, Tim and Patrick Twomey (eds), 1998. *Ireland's Evolving Constitution, 1937–97: Collected Essays*. Oxford: Hart.

Murphy, Walter, 1993. 'Constitutions, constitutionalism, and democracy', in Douglas Greenberg, Stanley N. Katz, Melanie Beth Oliviero and Steven C. Wheatley (eds), *Constitutionalism and Democracy: Transitions in the Contemporary World*. New York and Oxford: Oxford University Press, 1993, pp. 3–25.

O'Higgins, T. F., 1996. *A Double Life*. Dublin: Town House and Country House.

O'Mahony, Jane, 1998. 'The Irish referendum experience', *Representation* 35:5: 225–36.

O'Mahony, Jane, 2001. 'Not so Nice: The Treaty of Nice, the International Criminal Court, the abolition of the death penalty – the 2001 referendum experience', *Irish Political Studies* 16: 201–13.

O'Neill, Bairbre, 2000. 'The referendum process in Ireland', *Irish Jurist* 35: 305–44.

Sexton, Brendan, 1989. *Ireland and the Crown, 1922–1936: The Governor-Generalship of the Irish Free State*. Dublin: Irish Academic Press.

Stone Sweet, Alec, 2000. *Governing with Judges: Constitutional Politics in Europe*. Oxford: Oxford University Press.

Sturgess, Garry and Philip Chubb, 1988. *Judging the World: Law and Politics in the World's Leading Courts*. Sydney: Butterworths.

Sunstein, Cass R., 1988. 'Constitutions and democracies: an epilogue', in Jon Elster and Rune Slagstad (eds), *Constitutionalism and Democracy*. Cambridge: Cambridge University Press, pp. 327–56.

Tate, C. Neal and Torbjörn Vallinger (eds), 1995. *The Global Expansion of Judicial Power*. New York and London: New York University Press.

Thompson, Brian, 1991. 'Living with a Supreme Court in Ireland', *Parliamentary Affairs* 44:1: 33–49.

Tóibín, Colm, 1985. 'Inside the Supreme Court', *Magill* 8:7, February: 8–35.

van Maarseveen, Henc and Ger van der Tang, 1978. *Written Constitutions: a Computerized Comparative Study*. Dobbs Ferry, NY: Oceana Publications.

Ward, Alan J., 1994. *The Irish Constitutional Tradition: Responsible Government and Modern Ireland, 1782–1992*. Blackrock: Irish Academic Press.

Whelan, Noel, 2000. *Politics, Elections and the Law*. Dublin: Blackhall Publishing.

Whyte, J. H., 1980. *Church and State in Modern Ireland 1923–1979*. Dublin: Gill and Macmillan.

Websites

www.taoiseach.gov.ie/upload/static/256.pdf   Text of constitution.

www.courts.ie   Information on the judicial system.

www.justice.ie (link: organisation structure; link: courts policy)   Information on courts and judicial system.

Part II

Representative democracy at work

4 The rules of the electoral game

Richard Sinnott

Elections are the means by which voters directly choose their public representatives or other elected office-holders and indirectly choose between alternative political leaders, governments, and policies. Referendums are the means by which voters directly decide between competing alternatives of a constitutional or policy kind. Both processes have to be conducted according to a set of rules – the rules of the electoral game.

The electoral system is the most important feature of the rules of the electoral game. Electoral systems govern how votes are cast in an election and how seats are allocated on the basis of those votes. Electoral systems are a matter of institutional design: they have more or less identifiable effects on the functioning of the political system, and an electoral system can be selected or rejected with a view to achieving or avoiding certain consequences. The consequences of the Irish electoral system have been a recurring focus of debate and controversy.

This chapter begins by examining the way in which PR-STV (proportional representation by means of the single transferable vote) came to be adopted as the Irish electoral system in the first place and discusses the two referendums at which, contrary to the wishes of the incumbent government in each case, PR-STV was endorsed by the people. The chapter then explains how the system works, going through a full PR-STV count (Kildare North in 2002) to illustrate the process. The account of the electoral system concludes by analysing the effects of the electoral system on the proportionality between votes and seats, on government stability and party cohesion, and on the roles adopted by members of the Dáil. The final section of the chapter looks at recent developments in other aspects of the rules of the electoral game, focusing in particular on the issue of campaign financing.

The proportional representation option in Ireland

Proportional representation, in one or other of its many incarnations, is the most frequently used electoral system because the main alternative – dividing the country up into single-member constituencies and giving the seat in each constituency to the candidate with the most votes – can lead to egregiously unfair outcomes at national level. This latter system, generally known as the plurality or 'first past the post' system, is used for elections to the House of Commons in the United Kingdom (it is also used in Canada, India and the United States). The 2001 British general election illustrates its potential for bringing about an 'unfair' outcome: Labour won 41 per cent of the vote and a whopping 63 per cent of the seats, whereas the Liberal Democrats won 18 per cent of the vote and only 8 per cent of the seats. Such an outcome can occur because, within each constituency, the winning party takes 100 per cent of the representation (i.e. the one and only seat) while all the other parties or candidates receive zero representation. The imbalances at the constituency level tend to be cumulative, with the result that a party with considerably less than a majority of the votes can obtain a majority of the seats in parliament. The unfairness is compounded by the fact that the bonuses tend to go to the largest parties while the smaller parties suffer most.

Arguments in defence of this system stress the notion of elections as 'devices to choose viable governments and give them legitimacy' (Butler, 1981: 22) and maintain that the bonus given to the winning party is still the best way of doing that. However, since the middle of the nineteenth century and in tandem with the extension of the franchise, alternatives to this 'best system' have been sought. Proponents of PR have come up with a wide range of ideas and systems, the main distinction being between list systems on the one hand and PR-STV on the other. The former have been generally favoured in continental Europe and PR-STV was for a long time the preferred alternative of electoral reformers in Britain.

In a list system of proportional representation, each party presents a list of candidates in each multi-member constituency and the voter chooses between the various lists; the primary decision to be made by the voter is the choice of party. Seats are then allocated to parties on the basis of their share of the vote. In theory, a party obtaining, say, 35 per cent of the vote is entitled to 35 per cent of the seats, though how closely the outcome approaches this varies from system to system (for an overview see Gallagher *et al.*, 2001: 300–38). List systems vary in the methods they use to award seats to individual candidates within parties: in some, the matter is decided by the party organisation and is determined by the position of the candidates on a fixed list, while in others the voters can express preferences for specific candidates on their chosen party's list. Even in the latter systems, the fact remains that the vote cast is primarily a vote for the party and may end up assisting the election of a candidate to whom the voter is actually opposed (Bogdanor, 1983: 15).

In contrast, the primary focus of PR-STV is on the choice of individual representatives. Indeed, the originators of PR-STV in Britain were highly critical of political parties and of the role they played (Carstairs, 1980: 194). Reservations about the role of parties were also quite widespread in Ireland when PR-STV was adopted, and the party affiliation of candidates was not listed on ballot papers until 1965. PR-STV, therefore, involves a concept of the connection between the individual representative and his or her constituency that is much closer to the concept of representation implicit in the first past the post system than to the concept of party representation that underlies list systems.

PR-STV is not widely used, Malta being the only other country that employs it to elect the lower house of its national parliament (it is also used, with modifications, to elect the Australian Senate and in elections in Tasmania and Northern Ireland). How did this relatively uncommon system come to be adopted in Ireland? Developed simultaneously by Carl Andrae in Denmark and by Thomas Hare in England in the late 1850s, PR-STV was strongly advocated by electoral system reformers in Britain. In the early years of the twentieth century, the problem of minority representation in the event of Home Rule seemed to make PR particularly relevant in Ireland. A Proportional Representation Society of Ireland was formed, with Arthur Griffith, founder of Sinn Féin, among its first members. Inevitably, the views of electoral reformers in Ireland were substantially influenced by current thinking in Britain. An element of PR-STV was inserted in the abortive Home Rule Bill of 1912. In 1918 PR-STV was enacted for a single local council (Sligo Corporation) and an election was held there under the new provisions in January 1919. The next step was the decision by the British government to introduce PR-STV for the 1920 local elections in Ireland and then for the 1921 election to be held under the Government of Ireland Act.

Thus, by 1921, PR-STV had not only been endorsed by a significant section of the nationalist movement but had actually reached the statute book. It is not surprising, therefore, that when independence negotiations were under way and the issue of representation of minorities was being considered, the desirability of PR was common ground. The result was that PR was included in the 1922 Free State constitution. The constitution did not specify the precise form of PR to be used, but it was assumed that this would be PR-STV, and this was the system specified in the Electoral Act of 1923.

PR-STV has been implicitly or explicitly endorsed by the Irish electorate on three occasions. The first occasion was the approval of the new constitution in 1937. De Valera opted to include not just the principle of proportional representation in his draft constitution, as the 1922 constitution had done, but to spell out that this should be proportional representation by means of the single transferable vote (see Box 4.1). The matter did not give rise to extensive debate. Fine Gael had at one stage expressed some reservations regarding PR-STV (O'Leary, 1979: 25–6). However, in the debate on the draft constitution, John A. Costello of Fine Gael merely questioned why the details of the electoral system should go into the constitution rather than be left to the greater flexibility of ordinary legislation, to which de Valera replied that the matter was too important to be left to the vagaries of party warfare. The constitution was approved (see Chapter 3) and, in this fashion, PR-STV implicitly received its first endorsement by the Irish electorate.

Box 4.1 The constitution and the electoral system

The 1937 Constitution is quite specific about the Dáil electoral system. The main provisions are as follows:

Article 16.2
1 Dáil Éireann shall be composed of members who represent constituencies determined by law.
. . .
3 The ratio between the number of members to be elected at any time for each constituency and the population of each constituency, as ascertained at the last preceding census, shall, so far as it is practicable, be the same throughout the country.
. . .
5 The members shall be elected on the system of proportional representation by means of the single transferable vote.
6 No law shall be enacted whereby the number of members to be returned for any constituency shall be less than three.

Twenty years later, on the eve of his retirement as Taoiseach, de Valera proposed the abolition of PR-STV and its replacement by the plurality system. Although Fianna Fáil had been in power for 21 of the previous 27 years, it had won an overall majority of the seats on only four occasions, and, unless PR were abolished, might have been thought less likely to do so in the future without de Valera's leadership. Needless to say, the government did not put the case for change in such partisan terms. Rather, it argued, first, that PR has a disintegrating effect, creating a multiplicity of parties and increasing the probability of governmental instability. The second argument was that, whereas the plurality system enables the electorate to make a clear choice between two competing alternative governments, PR makes the formation of government a matter for post-election bargaining among parties, depriving the electorate of a direct say in the matter (for a useful summary of the Dáil debate on the issue, see FitzGerald, 1959).

Fine Gael stifled whatever doubts it may have had about PR-STV and led the opposition to change, with Labour also whole-heartedly against change. The opposition counter-arguments emphasised the issues of proportionality and fairness, particularly the question of the representation of minorities. Opposition speakers also attacked the proposal on the grounds that it would perpetuate Fianna Fáil rule indefinitely and undermine the parliamentary opposition. The proposal to abolish PR was narrowly defeated, with 48 per cent in favour and 52 per cent against (see Appendix 2h).

Obviously Fianna Fáil took some encouragement from the fact that it had lost by a narrow margin (33,667 votes). Otherwise it would be difficult to explain the party's decision to have another go just nine years later. An all-party Oireachtas committee established in 1966 to review the constitution failed to reach agreement on the question of the electoral system and simply set out the arguments for and against change (Committee on the Constitution, 1967). In the event the government opted for the same proposal as in 1959, i.e. to replace PR-STV with the plurality system. A second amendment proposed at the same time dealt with the issue of the ratio of members of the Dáil to population in each constituency, proposing that a deviation of up to one-sixth from the national average be allowed. The purpose of the change was to enable rural areas with declining populations to maintain their level of parliamentary representation. It did not go unnoticed, however, that the areas that would benefit from such a change tended to be areas in which Fianna Fáil had strong and stable support.

Essentially the same forces were ranged against the government on this occasion, the only difference being that the defenders of the status quo campaigned with more confidence and conviction (for a summary of the debate, see O'Leary, 1979: 66–70). The outcome was also more decisive: the result on the question of PR was 39 per cent in favour of abolition, 61 per cent in favour of retention, and the voting on the other proposed amendment was virtually identical (see the table of referendum results in Appendix 2h). The position of PR-STV in Ireland was undoubtedly greatly strengthened by this decisive popular endorsement. Certainly nothing more is likely to be heard about moving to the plurality system. However, plurality voting is not the only alternative and, beginning in the 1980s and gathering some momentum in the last ten years or so, there has been a renewal of the debate about the consequences of the system and about the desirability of altering it. Before turning to consider those consequences and that debate, it is necessary to take a detailed look at how the system actually works.

How PR-STV works

There are three distinct senses in which one can have an understanding of how PR-STV works: in terms of what is involved in the act of voting, in terms of the logic of the system and in terms of the mechanics of the count.

From the voter's point of view

From the voter's point of view, understanding the system is quite simple. The voter is presented with a list of candidates in alphabetical order and is required to indicate his or her order of preference among the candidates. Voters may indicate as many or as few preferences as they wish but each voter has only one vote (hence the term 'single transferable vote'). In essence, the voter issues a set of instructions to the returning officer as to what to do with that one vote, i.e. allocate it sequentially to the candidates in the order indicated. The simplicity of PR-STV from the voter's perspective is worth emphasising because a frequent (and misplaced) objection to the system in countries that do not use it is the claim that voters will not be able to understand it.

If one had in mind the second or third kind of understanding of the system mentioned above, this might well be so. The bulk of the voters probably have, at best, a hazy notion of the logic of the system and certainly do not understand its 'mechanics'. On this very issue, in the Dáil debate on PR prior to the 1959 referendum, the soon-to-be-Taoiseach Seán Lemass argued that: 'There are not half the Deputies in this House, much less half the electorate of the country, who can give an intelligent explanation of what happens [to] a No. 3 preference on a ballot paper. Is it not far better to give the people of the country a system of election they can understand?' (quoted in FitzGerald, 1959: 7). This misses the point, which is that PR-STV is easily understood in the sense in which the voter needs to understand it, and this does not include knowing the different things that may happen to a No. 3 preference. All that is needed in order to use the system to the full is an understanding of the notion of ranking a set of candidates according to one's preferences. This level of understanding is even enough to enable loyal party voters to participate in the vote management strategies adopted by some parties in some constituencies (see Gallagher, 2003: 108–10). For such strategies to work, the party managers need to know the subtleties of the system; the loyal party voter simply needs to know that the party wants him or her to express a particular preference order.

The logic of the system

The logic of PR-STV, or how it achieves what it achieves, is a somewhat more complex matter. In the case of the first past the post system, the logic of the system is clear: give the seat to the candidate with most votes, regardless of what proportion of the total vote that is. The majority or two-ballot system, as used in French presidential elections, introduces a refinement on this rule – in order to win a seat a candidate must reach the threshold of 50 per cent plus one, that is, an absolute majority. Again, the logic is clear. But what is the logic of PR-STV?

Understanding the logic of PR-STV is best approached by first considering how the system works when there is only a single seat to be filled, as in presidential elections and most by-elections in Ireland. Because multi-seat constituencies are an essential feature of PR – since a single seat cannot, obviously, be shared out proportionally – this is not actually PR-STV.[1] However, starting with this simpler situation allows us to examine the logic of the system by illustrating the nature of the quota and of the transfer process and then going on to see the effect of the introduction of multi-seat constituencies on both of these essential features.

Whatever the number of seats, PR-STV entails a quota – the number of votes that guarantees election. Once a candidate reaches this quota, he or she is declared elected. The quota is calculated as follows:

$$\text{Quota} = \frac{\text{Total number of valid votes}}{\text{Number of seats} + 1} + 1$$

Any fractional remainder is disregarded. When there is only one seat available this formula yields a quota that is identical to that used in French presidential elections, i.e. 50 per cent of the votes plus one. STV in a single-seat contest is in fact simply a sophisticated version of the majority system. The sophistication lies in how STV deals with the problem that arises when no candidate reaches the required absolute majority, which may well happen if there are more than two candidates. When this occurs in a French presidential election, all but the top two candidates are eliminated and the voters troop back two weeks later to choose between the remaining two – in effect, those who voted for eliminated candidates are asked to register a second preference. STV does not, as it were, waste the voters' time by asking them to come back later to register their second choice. Instead, it collects this information, along with information on third, fourth, fifth, etc. choices, all in one economical operation. Then, rather than disposing of all but the leading two candidates in one fell swoop, STV eliminates them one by one, reassigning the votes of each eliminated candidate according to the next preferences they contain. Thus, information on the preferences of the voters across the full range of candidates rather than, as in the case of the French presidential system, merely as between the two candidates who are in the lead after the first round of voting, is taken into account.

PR-STV is not, however, merely a refined version of the majority rule procedure, as it has the all-important additional feature of multi-seat constituencies. Multi-seat constituencies introduce two new elements into the logic of the system. The first is the systematic reduction of the quota as the size of the constituency (in terms of the number of seats) is increased. In the single-seat situation the quota is half the votes plus one. A quick look at the formula shows that this principle can be easily extended as follows: in a two-seat constituency, the quota is one-third plus one, in a three-seater it is one-quarter plus one, in a four-seater it is one-fifth plus one, and so on (see Table 4.1). Thus, as the number of seats is increased, the proportion of votes carrying an entitlement to a seat is progressively lowered – a nine-seat constituency would produce a quota of one-tenth plus one.

The second feature introduced by moving to multi-seat constituencies is the transfer of the surplus votes of elected candidates – these being the votes of an elected candidate over and above the quota, i.e. in excess of the number needed to guarantee a seat. If no such transfer were made, those who voted for such a candidate would not get the full share of representation

Table 4.1 Quota by district magnitude in PR-STV

District magnitude (TDs per constituency)	Quota (%)
1	50.0 + 1 vote
2	33.3 + 1 vote
3	25.0 + 1 vote
4	20.0 + 1 vote
5	16.7 + 1 vote

to which, as a group, they are entitled. For example, suppose that, in a three-seat constituency, just over 50 per cent of the voters vote for candidate A, and that A's supporters represent a particular point of view. Since the quota in a three-seater is 25 per cent plus one, and since therefore A's votes are far more than needed to elect A, then, if A's surplus were not redistributed, the second 25 per cent of the voters supporting A's point of view would achieve no representation. The problem is solved by transferring A's surplus votes to the other candidates according to the second preferences of the supporters of A. This is the point at which the mechanics of the counting procedure become somewhat complex but, fortunately, the complexities, which will be examined below, are not strictly relevant to grasping the logic of the system.

To summarise: the logic of PR-STV is that it ensures proportionality by (a) lowering the cost of a seat by using multi-seat constituencies, each additional seat bringing about a substantial reduction in the quota; (b) eliciting and using extra information on the voter's choice, i.e. his or her order of preference among the competing candidates; and (c) using this information not just in a process of elimination of the lowest candidates but also in dealing with the problem of what would otherwise be the under-representation of those who support candidates who exceed the quota.

The mechanics of PR-STV

Understanding the mechanics of the system is best achieved by working through an example. Again it is best to begin with the simple, albeit non-proportional, situation – a single-seat contest involving the transfer of the votes of an eliminated candidate. The presidential election of November 1990 provides a good illustration (see Table 4.2). The valid vote in that election amounted to 1,574,651, which, when divided by the number of seats plus one (i.e. by 2) yields 787,325.5. Disregarding the fraction and adding 1 to this number gives a quota of 787,326 votes. It is clear that Brian Lenihan was in the lead on the basis of first preference votes, but, since no candidate had reached the quota, the returning officer proceeded to eliminate the candidate with the lowest number of votes (Currie) and to distribute his

Table 4.2 The Irish presidential election, 1990

Candidate	First preferences	Transfer of Currie's votes	Second count result
Currie, Austin	267,902	−267,902	
Lenihan, Brian	694,484	+36,789	731,273
Robinson, Mary	612,265	+205,565	817,830
Non-transferable papers		+25,548	25,548

Notes
Valid votes: 1,574,651. Quota: 787,326.

votes in accordance with the second preferences indicated by Currie's supporters. On the second count[2] about three-quarters (205,565) of Currie's votes were found to carry a second preference for Robinson. This gave Robinson a total of 817,830 votes or 52 per cent of the total valid vote. This exceeded the quota (in this case the 50 per cent plus one rule) and Robinson was declared elected. Lenihan received only 14 per cent of Currie's second preferences, while nearly 10 per cent of those who supported Currie did not specify a second preference and their ballots appear in the 'non-transferable papers' row. Note that even if Robinson had not reached the quota, she could have been declared elected, provided that Currie's transfers were sufficient to put her ahead of Lenihan. This situation could have occurred if more of Currie's votes had been non-transferable.

Because PR-STV involves multi-seat rather than single-seat constituencies, counting the votes in general elections is a somewhat more complicated business. The process is best explained by working through a particular count. The Kildare North constituency in the 2002 election (see Table 4.3) provides an illustration of the basic points. In the 2002 election, Kildare North was a three-seat constituency with a valid poll of 32,980 votes. When the number of valid votes was divided by the number of seats plus one (i.e. by 4) and, disregarding the fraction, 1 was added to the result, the quota came out at 8,246 votes. One candidate (Charlie McCreevy, FF) exceeded the quota on the first count by a margin of 836 votes and was declared elected. Thus, the situation at the end of the first count was: one candidate elected (McCreevy); one candidate well-positioned to take the second seat (Emmet Stagg, Labour, who was 1,195 votes short of the quota); two candidates (Bernard Durkan, FG and Paul Kelly, FF) in contention for the third and final seat; and two candidates who had substantial blocks of votes (Kate Walsh, PD, on 3,919 and Anne Kelly-McCormack, Green, on 1,974) who would not in fact be in contention for the last seat and would, in due course, be eliminated. At this stage, Durkan (FG) was 618 votes ahead of Kelly (FF) in the race for the final seat. Thus, it was clear that the way the surplus votes and the votes of eliminated candidates transferred would determine

Table 4.3 Counting and transfer of votes in Kildare North, 2002 general election

Candidate	First count	Second count	Third count	Fourth count	Fifth count
		Transfer of McCreevy surplus	Transfer of Kelly-McCormack votes	Transfer of Walsh votes	Transfer of Stagg surplus
Durkan, Bernard J. (FG)	5,786	(+73) 5,859	(+318) 6,177	(+1,164) 7,341	(+684) *8,025*
Kelly, Paul (FF)	5,168	(+513) 5,681	(+242) 5,923	(+1,459) 7,382	(+508) 7,890
Kelly-McCormack, Anne (Green)	1,974	(+25) 1,999	(−1,999) −	−	−
McCreevy, Charlie (FF)	*9,082*	(−836) *8,246*	*8,246*	*8,246*	*8,246*
Stagg, Emmet (Lab)	7,051	(+117) 7,168	(+837) 8,005	(+1,467) *9,472*	(−1,226) *8,246*
Walsh, Kate (PD)	3,919	(+108) 4,027	(+446) 4,473	(−4,473) −	−
Non-transferable	−	(+0) 0	(+156) 156	(+383) 539	(+34) 573

Note
Votes of elected candidates in italics; distribution of transfers in brackets. Elected: Charlie McCreevy (FF), Emmet Stagg (Lab), Bernard Durkan (FG). Electorate: 60,094. Valid votes: 32,980. Number of seats: 3. Quota: 8,246.

which candidate and which party would win out at the end. The next step in the process was the redistribution of McCreevy's surplus.[3]

The destination of that surplus was determined by re-examining the entire set of 9,082 first preference votes for McCreevy. This was done by arranging McCreevy's votes in 'sub-parcels' beside the name of each of the continuing candidates according to the second preferences indicated on them. The total number of *transferable* votes (i.e. ignoring those that are non-transferable) was used as the base for calculating each continuing candidate's proportionate share of McCreevy's second preferences. These proportions were then applied to the 836 surplus votes that were actually available for transfer. Thus, if candidate X had obtained 50 per cent of the second preferences among McCreevy's transferable votes, he or she would have been entitled to 50 per cent of the 836 surplus votes. In the event, McCreevy's Fianna Fáil running mate, Paul Kelly, received just over 61 per cent of McCreevy's second preferences and so was entitled to precisely that proportion of the surplus, i.e. 513 votes. The remaining two-fifths of the surplus went mainly and fairly evenly to the Labour and PD candidates (117 and 108 votes respectively) with a smaller number (73) going to the FG candidate and a negligible 25 (3 per cent) going to the Green candidate. The reported non-transferable vote was zero.[4] At this stage the gap between Durkan (FG) and Kelly (FF) was down to 178 votes.

A significant and, one suspects, little understood aspect of the process of transferring surplus votes relates to which actual ballot papers are transferred and which remain with the elected candidate. The rule is: 'The particular papers to be transferred from each sub-parcel [i.e. each set of McCreevy second preferences lined up beside the name of each continuing candidate] shall be those last filed in the sub-parcel'. In other words, the surplus votes are physically transferred to each of the continuing candidates by taking the appropriate number of votes from the top of the relevant pile. The defence of this procedure is that the counting process requires that the papers be thoroughly mixed at the outset and that, therefore, the set of papers transferred in the way that has just been described is a random sample of the entire sub-parcel. However, it can be argued that the sample may not be strictly random and that it would be worth the extra effort to transfer all the papers in each sub-parcel at the appropriate fraction of their value, thereby avoiding any risk of bias or distortion – this is known as the 'Gregory method'. This is done in the counting of votes at Seanad elections and at Northern Ireland elections (for discussions of this point see Coakley and O'Neill, 1984; Gallagher and Unwin, 1986).[5]

As no one reached the quota on the second count, the next step was to eliminate the lowest candidate (Anne Kelly-McCormack of the Greens) and transfer her votes in accordance with the next available preferences. This is a simpler operation as all these votes are either transferable or non-transferable and there is no need to calculate proportions or to select which papers will be transferred. In the event, the largest block of Green Party votes (nearly 42 per cent) went to the Labour Party candidate (Stagg), putting him just 241 votes short of the quota. The next largest block (22 per cent) went to PD candidate Kate Walsh, and smaller amounts went to the two main contenders for the final seat – 16 per cent to Durkan and 12 per cent to Kelly; 146 votes (8 per cent) were non-transferable.

Again, no one had reached the quota and so the returning officer proceeded to eliminate the PD candidate and redistribute her votes. The PD transfers split three ways – approximately one-third to Kelly (FF), one-third to Stagg (Lab), and one-quarter to Durkan (FG); nearly 9 per cent (383 votes) were non-transferable. The substantial transfer Stagg received from the eliminated PD candidate (1,467 votes) put him well over the quota and he was declared elected. This left just one seat to fill and now, in the race for that final seat, Kelly (FF) had overtaken Durkan (FG) by 41 votes. The issue would be decided by the distribution of Stagg's surplus.

The approach to the distribution of a surplus that arises at this stage of the process is the same as that which applies to a surplus that arises on the first count, except that the votes that are examined for next preferences are not the entire block of votes credited to the elected candidate at that stage but the votes in the 'sub-parcel last received' by him, that is, the 1,467 votes Stagg (Lab) received from Walsh (PD). This procedure does involve substantial savings in time and effort. Its rationale is that the 'sub-parcel last received' is what put the elected candidate over the quota and in this way created the surplus. It could equally well be argued, however, that the procedure involves a potential distortion in that the distribution of next available preferences in the vote received by Stagg from Walsh may not have corresponded to the distribution of such preferences in the entire Stagg vote, and it would seem that the logic of the system requires that all those who voted for an elected candidate should have a proportionate say in the destination of the surplus in question. In the event, Stagg's surplus votes, which, because of the last-parcel-received rule, had originally been PD votes, went disproportionately to Durkan, the Fine Gael candidate, who got 176 votes more than Kelly (FF). The difference was enough to reverse the modest lead acquired by Kelly on the previous count and Durkan won the third and final seat by 135 votes. It is clear that, if PD voters had behaved differently, either by giving more transfers directly to the Fianna Fáil candidate when their own candidate was eliminated on the fourth count or by transferring to Fianna Fáil more than to Fine Gael after having transferred to Stagg (see the distribution of Stagg's PD-originating surplus on the fifth count), the result could easily have turned out to be a win for Fianna Fáil at the expense of Fine Gael. However, the behaviour of the PD voters was consistent with the PD strategy of warning the electorate against the dangers of giving their Fianna Fáil partners an outright majority (expressed most tellingly in the slogan 'One-Party Government? No thanks').[6]

The distribution of Stagg's surplus differed from McCreevy's in another way. This is because, unlike the McCreevy transfer, the Stagg transfer produced a reported non-transferable vote. This indicates that the number of transferable votes in the last parcel of 1,467 votes received by Stagg was less than his surplus of 1,226 votes. When this happens, all the votes that can be transferred are transferred (i.e. there is no need for the calculation of transfer ratios). Since the number of transferred votes is then less than the surplus, a number of 'non-transferable papers' that is sufficient to make up the difference between the number of transferred votes and the surplus is reported (in this case 34 non-transferables were reported). This implies that the actual number of non-transferable votes is the reported non-transferable vote (in this case 34) *plus* the difference between the total number of votes in the sub-parcel last received and the surplus (1,467 minus 1,226, in other words, all of the votes from the sub-parcel last received by Stagg that remained credited to him as part of his quota). In short, in the parcel of 1,467 votes transferred from Walsh to Stagg, there were 275 non-transferable votes and the real rate of non-transferability among these votes was thus 19 per cent rather than the 3 per cent one would arrive at if the reported proportion of non-transferable votes were to be taken at face value.

In summary, understanding how PR-STV works is quite simple in so far as the act of voting is concerned and the system has a rather elegant logic in the way it seeks to achieve a match between voters' preferences and the distribution of seats. On the other hand, the system can be quite complex when it comes to knowing how a surplus that has accrued on a count subsequent to the first count is transferred, though understanding this aspect of the matter is really only essential for returning officers, party strategists (and students of political science!). However, as well as understanding how the system works, we do need to understand its political consequences.

The political consequences of PR-STV

Identifying the consequences of an electoral system is not always straightforward, and sometimes there may be a tendency to assume too readily that a given feature of a country's politics must be brought about by the electoral system. In this section, we will explore the possible consequences of PR-STV in three areas: for the proportionality between votes and seats, for the stability of the party system and of governments, and for the role of the elected representative.

Consequences for proportionality

Disproportionality is measured by comparing parties' shares of the votes with their shares of the seats and noting the discrepancies. This is not quite as simple as it seems. First of all, the matter is complicated in the case of STV, given the system's focus on individual candidates rather than parties and given also the way in which transferred votes and not just first preference votes are a vital part of a party's overall level of support and can have a decisive effect on who wins. However, acknowledging those reservations, we have no option but to compare parties' first preference votes with their shares of the seats. Second, there are several competing measures of disproportionality (for a discussion see Lijphart, 1994: 58–62). Using Lijphart's preferred measure, the least squares index, we find that the average level of disproportionality, measured by this index, in Irish elections from 1923 to 2002 was 3.9 – ranging from a low of 1.7 in 1933 to a high of 6.6 in 2002. In a comparative analysis using this measure, Irish elections over the period 1948–89 emerge as much more proportional than those held under first past the post electoral systems, and as more proportional than some held under PR list systems; they were, however, less proportional than some elections held under some PR list systems, for example in Denmark, Finland, Germany, the Netherlands and Sweden (Lijphart, 1994: 160–2).

On average, Fianna Fáil's vote–seat deviation has been overwhelmingly positive, averaging +3.2 percentage points. Although its deviation has varied considerably in size (from −0.7 in 1944 to +7.6 in 2002), it has often been enough to put the party over the crucial threshold of 50 per cent of the seats, or at least to put it in a position to form a minority government. Fine Gael has generally also benefited from the system, though not to the same extent as Fianna Fáil, either in terms of the consistency of obtaining a bonus or of the average size of the bonus obtained (an average of 1.4 percentage points). Labour, on the other hand, has obtained a share of the seats that is smaller than its share of first preference votes in 18 of the 26 elections in the period 1923–2002, its average deficit being −0.8 percentage points). The minor parties and independents as a group have tended to be even more consistent losers in the vote–seat proportionality stakes.

It is important to emphasise that proportionality is crucially affected by the behaviour of the voters. Thus, in the period since 1948, Fianna Fáil's bonus was minimal in 1951, 1954, 1973 and in the three elections of 1981–82 – elections that were all marked by relatively high levels of transfers of preference votes between its main opponents (see Gallagher, 1978 and Sinnott, 1995: 208–16). On the other hand, this is not the only relevant factor – there was quite a high level of transfers between Fine Gael and Labour in 1977, yet Fianna Fáil ended up with its fourth highest bonus in seats over votes. Taking all of this into account and acknowledging that there can be considerable fluctuations in vote–seat deviations, one can nevertheless conclude that the system is reasonably satisfactory on the proportionality criterion – as Gallagher put it in an evaluation conducted for the Constitution Review Group: 'PR-STV in Ireland delivers a high degree of proportionality, virtually as high as that produced by electoral systems that have the achievement of proportionality as their sole aim' (Gallagher, 1996: 519).

Consequences for the party system and government stability

The classic case against proportional representation, argued mainly on the basis of case histories of Weimar Germany and of France and Italy in the 1950s, was that it leads to a proliferation of parties and thus to political instability or at least stalemate. These alleged effects of PR have been the subject of prolonged debate. In so far as the effect of PR on the number of parties is concerned, a consensus has emerged that can be summed up in Sartori's rewriting of one of Duverger's famous 'laws': 'PR formulas facilitate multi-partyism and are, conversely, hardly conducive to two-partyism' (Sartori, 1986: 64).

In fact distinguishing between two-party and multi-party systems and even the matter of determining the number of parties in a system are not always as straightforward as they might seem. In addressing these problems, Laakso and Taagepera (1979) have proposed an index, called the 'effective number of parties', that takes account of both the number and the relative size of the parties in a system. This index is particularly useful for comparing the number of parties in different countries, or in the same country at different points in time. The effective number of parties in Ireland declined from a peak in June 1927 and remained low throughout the 1930s. It rose sharply twice in the 1940s, but then fell back and settled down at a low level from 1965 to 1982. In 1987, it began a rise that continued over the next two elections, the rise being particularly pronounced in 1992 (see Sinnott, 1995: 91–4). It is clear from this that the number of parties is not simply a function of the electoral system. Ireland has had the same electoral system since the foundation of the state but the number of parties has fluctuated considerably.

Looking at the matter in comparative terms, the average effective number of parties in parliament in 19 western European democracies during the 1990s was 4.0; in Ireland the number in the same period was 3.2. This puts Ireland in joint thirteenth place (with France) on a scale of party fragmentation. The countries with the most fragmented systems were Belgium (8.5), Italy (6.9) and Switzerland (5.8). The least fragmented were Malta, which also uses PR-STV, with a score of 2.0, the United Kingdom (2.2) and Greece (2.3) (figures from Gallagher *et al.*, 2001: 322). Given this ranking and given the fluctuations in the effective number of parties in Ireland over time, the most one can conclude is that PR-STV in Ireland has, to use Sartori's terms, facilitated moderate multi-partyism when other factors were leading in that direction.

It should also be noted that a preoccupation with the number of parties and with the alleged problems of multi-partyism seems to be based on an assumption that multi-party systems lead to unstable government. As the Constitution Review Group (CRG) pointed out, this is not necessarily the case because, in the post-war European experience, any dangers that might arise from the presence of small parties have been countered by effective party discipline, an experience that is confirmed by the Irish case (CRG, 1996: 58). In this regard, the Irish experience would seem to run counter to a widely held theory that PR-STV leads to weaker party discipline and party organisation. Thus Taagepera and Shugart (1989: 28) argue that 'if strength of party organization is desired, STV is inappropriate, because either list PR (even with preference voting) or plurality (in the absence of U.S.-style primaries) gives far more leeway to party elites in deciding who the party's representatives may be'. This, however, is a relative observation. It does seem likely that, other things being equal, a list system of PR will lead to stronger party organisation. This does not mean that parties under PR-STV will be weak in some absolute sense. On the other hand, Katz (1980: 34) puts forward a more absolute version of the theory, hypothesising that 'Where intraparty choice is allowed, parliamentary parties will tend to be disunited' and noting that 'In the case of small districts this will be manifested in personalistic fractionalization'. Following Katz, Blais pushes the argument even further: 'There is strong evidence that the single transferable vote leads to a weaker party system . . . Electoral competition within the party hinders unity and cohesion . . . the single transferable vote, like preferential voting in general, is detrimental to the development of a responsible party system' (Blais, 1991: 248–9). Both authors point to the prevalence of intra-party personalistic competition in the area of constituency service as evidence for their theory. However, in order to save their hypotheses, both are also obliged to declare that the equally evident unity of Irish parliamentary parties (see Chapter 8) is 'illusory' (Katz, 1980: 107) and 'superficial' (Blais, 1991: 249). Neither author explains what illusory or superficial party unity is and neither provides evidence to demonstrate its existence or its consequences. It would seem more sensible to note that intense intra-party competition in the area of constituency service can coexist with a very substantial degree of party cohesion and party discipline, and that the latter are products of constitutional structure and inherited modes of politics and are not necessarily undermined by PR-STV.

In dealing with the question of stability it should be noted that the CRG's discussion focused exclusively on parties. By ignoring the way in which PR-STV facilitates the election of independent or non-party candidates, it may indeed have taken too sanguine a view of the Irish situation. The fact is that three Irish governments since the start of the 1980s have been explicitly dependent on the support of independent TDs. Two of these (those formed after the 1981 and February 1982 elections) collapsed within nine months. While this threat to the stability of government is occasional, since it depends on the parliamentary arithmetic after an election, no amount of party discipline can counter it. PR-STV contributes to the threat by increasing the probability of minority governments that may be tempted to rely on the support of a few independents rather than include another party in a coalition arrangement. It also facilitates the election of independents in the first place by focusing on individual candidates, by encouraging competition between deputies and candidates in the provision of local constituency service and, through the mechanism of the multi-seat constituency, by lowering the threshold of representation to a point at which it is within the reach of non-party candidates. In short, while it is true that PR-STV does not lead to unstable government by causing a multiplicity of parties or by diminishing party discipline, it does increase the probability of government reliance on independent deputies whose support may be delivered at a disproportionate price and even then may or may not be durable.

Consequences for the role of the TD

The issue of whether PR-STV imposes an excessive burden of constituency work on TDs hardly figured at all in the debates of 1959 and 1968. For example, a pamphlet by a civic-minded study group that aimed to provide an objective assessment of the arguments in 1959 devoted a page and a half to the issue of the quality of TDs, but only five lines of this dealt with the question of constituency service (Tuairim, 1959: 19–20). In contrast, the subsequent increase in the burden of constituency work led Farrell (1985: 14) to note in the mid-1980s that 'there is an evident consensus among deputies that the competition in constituency service has got out of hand'. The current Irish debate about PR-STV focuses mainly on the question of how far the electoral system is a cause of this preoccupation with constituency service and whether the system should be abandoned because of it. The fact that, over the years, the issues had been raised by current or former prominent politicians from both major parties (see, for example, Boland, 1991; FitzGerald, 1991, 2003; Martin, 1991; Hussey, 1993) suggests that there is a prima facie case to be examined. The debate received new impetus when, following the 1997 election, the cabinet position with direct responsibility for the conduct of elections (Minister for the Environment and Local Government) went to a TD (Noel Dempsey) with a strong personal commitment to getting rid of PR-STV.

Academic support for the proposition that the Irish electoral system leads to excessive emphasis on constituency work is not hard to find. Katz (1984: 143–4) argues that interpersonal competition tends to supersede interparty competition with the result that, ultimately, 'competition between parties tends to be on the basis of services rendered, rather than policy differences'. Carty emphasises the fact that PR-STV allows the voter to combine two criteria at once – party and personal service. He sees the electoral system as an independent contributory factor that adds to the already existing cultural impetus to brokerage:

> This dimension of electoral politics – local brokers competing for a party vote – has been institutionalised in Ireland by the electoral system. . . . With little to distinguish themselves from their opponents (particularly party colleagues), politicians are driven to emphasise their brokerage services to constituents, thus reinforcing cultural expectations.
>
> (Carty, 1981: 134)

The hypothesis underlying the above views is certainly plausible. The argument goes like this: the main competition for seats is between candidates of the same party. Since such candidates cannot differentiate themselves from one another on the basis of party policy, party record in government or party leadership, they compete on the basis of service to their constituents. This involves the kind of activity discussed more fully in Chapter 9: handling a large volume of casework, holding regular 'clinics' throughout the constituency, attending meetings of residents' associations and local pressure groups of all sorts, and being seen at local gatherings and functions from sporting events to funerals.

The report of the CRG was an important milestone in the debate about PR-STV. Overall, the report cautiously concluded that 'the present PR-STV system has had popular support and should not be changed without careful advance assessment of the possible effects'. It went on to note that, if there were to be change, a list system of proportional representation or a dual system that combines proportional and non-proportional components would 'satisfy more of the relevant criteria than a move to a non-PR system' (CRG, 1996: 60).

The report of the Constitution Review Group had not been intended to be definitive. That challenge was left to the follow-on All-Party Oireachtas Committee on the Constitution, which issued its report dealing with the role of parliament and, consequently, with the electoral system, in 2002. The All-Party Committee commissioned further research, conducted a survey among deputies and senators, received submissions from public representatives and from the general public and met at some length with Noel Dempsey (the Minister for the Environment and Local Government), with deputies Seán Fleming and Eamon Gilmore and with former Taoiseach, Dr Garret FitzGerald.

The main research report considered by the committee (Laver, 1998) dealt with the likely consequences of a switch to the Additional Member System (AMS), under which some TDs would be elected from single-member constituencies while others would be elected via party lists. It concluded that, whatever the other merits of AMS, and while that system would probably leave the broad party balance much as it would be under PR-STV, 'it seems likely that Fianna Fáil would win almost all the constituency seats, with the other parties winning all or most of their seats from the list-PR element of the system' (quoted in All-Party Oireachtas Committee, 2002: 17). Though the starkness of this prediction was queried in other evidence presented to the committee (All-Party Oireachtas Committee, 2002: 22), a degree of skewness in the distribution of constituency and list seats between the parties became an accepted assumption that almost certainly affected the committee's thinking. It may also have affected the thinking of many of the TDs who responded to the committee's survey, as the conclusions of the report were circulated with the request to respond to the survey. In all, 85 deputies or senators responded (a response rate of 38 per cent), and 69 percent (i.e. 59 individuals) wanted no change in the current system.

In concluding, the committee summarised the pros and cons of the PR-STV and the AMS systems, emphasising in particular that there are two sides to the argument about the effects of PR-STV on the constituency service role of TDs and that a defining, unavoidable and undesirable aspect of AMS is 'the resultant division of parliamentary representatives into two classes: constituency and list'. It then argued that:

> The fundamental and insurmountable argument against change is that the current Irish electoral system provides the greatest degree of voter choice of any available option. A switch to any other system would reduce the power of the individual voter. For all these reasons, we recommend against any change in this aspect of the Constitution.
>
> (All-Party Oireachtas Committee, 2002: 29)

Against the background of the evidence considered by the All-Party Committee, this conclusion would seem to have put the matter to rest, at least for now.

PR-STV: a balance sheet

PR-STV is a highly distinctive electoral system. It differs fundamentally from the other two major variants of electoral systems – from the plurality system by virtue of its proportionality, and from PR list systems by virtue of putting the emphasis on individual candidates rather than on political parties. Both these distinctive features are seen as weaknesses by its critics. The first line of criticism – that it produces results that are too proportional and that are conducive to unstable government – is easily dealt with. PR-STV produces moderate rather than extreme proportionality. In any event, high degrees of disproportionality are indefensible, and proportionally representative election outcomes do not necessarily lead to government instability and, by and large, have not done so in the Irish case.

The second main line of criticism – that it devalues parties – raises more fundamental issues. Katz (1984: 145) argues that 'the choice offered by [list system] PR . . . is a choice within party, while the choice offered under STV is a choice without regard to party. The effect has been to offer voters under STV a wider choice, but one which, in terms of the arguments used by its advocates, is less meaningful'. Instead of PR-STV, Katz argues for a small-district PR list system, in part on the ground that it provides 'the kind of parties needed for effective implementation of the public will'. It may be, however, that the party versus non-party dilemma is overstated by Katz in the phrase 'choice without regard to party'. It is true that the choice in PR-STV is not tied to party; rather, it is open and flexible, because it elicits more information from the voter and places less constraint on the kind of information that can be transmitted. But this means that voters can vote on a party basis if they wish, and the evidence from the analysis of transfer patterns suggests that, up to a point, they do (Gallagher, 1978; Sinnott, 1995: 208–16; see also Bowler and Farrell (1991) for a development of the argument that the system actually encourages an emphasis on party rather than individual candidacy).

The other side of the coin of the alleged devaluation of parties is the argument that PR-STV is responsible for the 'excessive' constituency orientation of TDs. That TDs do a great deal of constituency work is undeniable. That this is due in some definitive way to the electoral system is debatable. For one thing, it is clear that there are other causes of the constituency service role, among them being aspects of the political culture, the small size of Irish society, inadequate parliamentary resources and procedures, problems in the administrative system, and the weakness of local government (see the discussion in Chapter 9). In short, it is clear that the constituency service role is due to a number of different factors, and it is likely that the electoral system is a contributory factor but not the main determinant. It should also be noted that the constituency service role can have positive as well as negative aspects, namely that of keeping public representatives in touch with the real problems of ordinary people, enhancing their input into future legislative proposals and contributing to the accountability of the system. This is a reminder that, in evaluating the system, one must look not just at its alleged negative consequences but also at its positive aspects. The former are summarised in the Jenkins Report, which in the course of its evaluation of the options for a future British electoral system described STV in multi-member constituencies as:

> a system which has several substantial advantages. It maximises voter choice, giving the elector the power to express preferences not only between parties but between different candidates of the same party. It achieves a significantly greater degree of proportionality. It avoids the problem of having two classes of member, as is the case with the Additional Member System. It also avoids the likelihood of fostering a proliferation of small splinter parties, and does this without the need for setting any arbitrary threshold. It has long worked with on the whole beneficial results in the Republic of Ireland.
> (Independent Commission on the Voting System, 1998: 29)

One must also look at the alternatives that might be put in its place (Gallagher, 1987; for an overview of electoral systems see Farrell, 2001). For a variety of reasons, the plurality system, which has been twice rejected by the electorate, is a non-starter. At the other end of the spectrum, the list system is also unattractive for two main reasons – a closed list system would by definition do away completely with the candidate choice to which Irish voters are accustomed and attached; an open or preferential list system would not do away with the intra-party competition at the electoral level which is alleged to be the main disadvantage of PR-STV. This leaves a mixed system as the only plausible alternative. As noted in the constitutional reviews that have dealt with this issue, the prime candidate in this case is the Additional Member System (AMS). The danger in the Irish case is that such a system would exacerbate the two-tier character of the Dáil and the division between those with a mainly policy-making orientation and those with a mainly constituency-service orientation and that this division would, to a substantial degree, run along party lines. It is also not clear that an AMS system would eradicate inter-personal constituency-level competition. Experience in Germany and New Zealand suggests that many list members aspire to become constituency members and, with this in mind, informally attach themselves to a constituency. Thus one could well have a situation in which two or even three TDs would be assiduously cultivating a particular constituency; all the evidence indicates that in Ireland such competition would mainly take the form of constituency service.

Finally, although the issue does not figure much in public or political debate about PR-STV, a balance sheet of the pros and cons of PR-STV should mention the problem of what might be described as alleged theoretical flaws in the system. The flaws are theoretical because they are identified for the most part by imagining the preferences of a small set of hypothetical voters and showing that the outcomes can vary with minor changes in the assumed preferences in ways that violate certain abstract principles of how an electoral system ought to function (see, for example, Dummett, 1997: 89–108, 138–57; Nurmi, 1997). The most important violation is the phenomenon of 'non-monotonicity'. Monotonicity is the requirement that any increase in a candidate's vote should not diminish his or her chances of being elected. Because of the importance of the order of elimination in determining the outcome in PR-STV, the possible violation of this principle can be readily demonstrated with a hypothetical set of preferences. Furthermore, rare but real violations of the principle can be found in PR-STV election results (for example, Gallagher, 1999: 145–6). In assessing the significance of such issues from the voters' point of view, one must bear in mind that they depend either on assumptions or on retrospective knowledge about the order of elimination of the candidates and of the transfer behaviour of the voters. Such knowledge is not available to the voters and cannot enter into their calculations. This means that complex tactical voting under PR-STV can be imagined or retrospectively constructed; it cannot be realistically pursued by the voter. In summary, proponents of PR-STV should be wary of claiming that it is perfectly logical or that it disposes completely of the issue of tactical voting; at the same time, the problems identified in this regard remain in the realm of theory rather than practice and certainly do not justify Dummett's claim that the system is 'quasi-chaotic' (Dummett, 1997: 143).

Regulating electoral competition

While the electoral system is clearly the most important aspect of the rules of the electoral game, there are other rules or regulations that are essential for the conduct of free, fair and effective elections. The main regulations deal with the revision of constituencies, the arrangements for nomination of candidates, limitations on electoral spending and political donations, and the provision of public funding of parties and candidates. The regulation of electoral competition also encompasses the rules governing the conduct of referendums.

Constituency boundaries

The constitution stipulates that as, far as is practicable, the ratio between the number of Dáil deputies elected for each constituency and the population of each constituency shall be the same throughout the country (Article 16.2.3). Given population changes, meeting this constitutional requirement involves the regular redrawing of constituency boundaries and allocation of appropriate numbers of seats to each constituency.[7] Up to and including the 1977 election, this vitally important process was in the hands of the minister for local government (for a discussion see Coakley, 1980). This left incumbent governments open to the temptation to arrange the shape and size of the constituencies to the advantage of their own party or parties and certainly open to opposition accusations of doing so. Following the 1977 election, the government established an independent commission to advise on the redrawing of constituencies and the role of such commissions was established on a statutory basis by the 1997 Electoral Act. In setting out the terms of reference of the commission, the 1997 Electoral Act includes, *inter alia*, a requirement that the breaching of county boundaries should be avoided as far as possible and that due regard be given to geographic considerations. Other than that, the commission is obliged to draw the constituency boundaries as it sees fit without regard to the electoral consequences for particular parties or candidates.

Nominations

There is a general consensus that, in order to deter what are usually referred to as frivolous candidates, some regulation of access to the ballot paper is necessary. The traditional means of achieving this was the requirement that all candidates pay a deposit, which was returnable if the candidate received a certain level of electoral support. In the 1992 Act, the deposit was set at IR£300 (€381) and this was returnable if the candidate won at least one-quarter of a quota. However, this requirement was successfully contested in the High Court in 2001, Mr Justice Herbert finding that '. . . in the absence of some reasonable alternative route to the ballot paper, such as the nomination and signatures system . . . the fact that the deposit system, on the evidence, has the effect, even if unsought, of excluding from the ballot paper a considerable percentage of the adult citizens of this state who would be otherwise eligible to stand for membership of Dáil Éireann and the European Parliament renders that system unjust, unreasonable and arbitrary' (*Redmond v. Minister for the Environment*, IEHC 128, 31 July 2001). The government's response was to create a two-tier system regulating access to the ballot paper – a system of party authentication for candidates running on behalf of political parties and a requirement to obtain 30 signatures in the case of candidates not affiliated with a political party. The signature requirement was also challenged in the High Court by a number of independent candidates on the basis that it imposed an unfair burden on them but the challenge was unsuccessful.

Election campaign spending

Any attempt to regulate the financial aspects of electoral competition encounters a dilemma. On the one hand, it is desirable that political communication be as effective and free flowing as possible and, in the contemporary world, effective communication requires resources. On the other hand, it is equally clear that the outcome of an election should not be decided by possession of superior financial resources.

The 2002 election saw the imposition, for the first time, of spending limits in an Irish general election. The limits are related to the size of the constituency and, in 2002, were €25,395 in a three-seat constituency, €31,743 in a four-seat constituency and €38,092 in a five-seater.[8] The period within which the limits apply is defined as the period from the dissolution of the Dáil up to polling day, and the regulations emphasise that all property, goods or services that are used at the election during the election period fall under the spending limit no matter when the actual expense was incurred or the payments made. However, spending on items that are used before the campaign formally begins is exempt from the regulations, which gives an advantage to those who have money to spend.

The spending limit is applied to candidates, but a candidate can assign all or part of his or her spending to the party. The total amount available to the national agent to spend at the election is the sum of the amounts assigned by candidates to the party. In short, the limits per candidate noted above are comprehensive limits covering all expenditure undertaken by candidates and/or parties within the election period.

Donations

The financing of electoral campaigns is also regulated by controls on political donations. All political donations in excess of specified amounts are subject to disclosure and to a number of prohibitions. The disclosure requirement applies to candidates, to political parties and to what the legislation refers to as 'third parties'.[9] In the case of candidates, all donations in excess of €635 must be reported to the Standards in Public Office Commission. In the case of political parties, donations in excess of €5,079 must be reported. As implied by the definition in note 9 above, all donations to 'third parties' after the first €126.97 must be disclosed. There are limits on the size of donations that candidates can receive from any one source for an election, and candidates are also prohibited from receiving anonymous donations that exceed €126.97. In addition, parties may not receive donations from outside Ireland, unless these come from an Irish citizen or from a body that maintains an office in Ireland.

Public funding for candidates and parties

The final aspect of the financial regulation of elections has to do with the provision of public funding for candidates and for political parties. Funding for election candidates takes the form of reimbursement of some or all of the electoral expenses of candidates who, at any stage of the count, accumulate a number of votes equal to or greater than one quarter of the quota. In the 2002 election, such candidates received a reimbursement of €6,348.69 or thetotal amount of their actual election expenses, whichever was the lesser.

In contrast to this direct subvention of election campaigning out of public funds, the other two forms of public funding of political parties and elected representatives, which are described in Chapter 6, explicitly exclude the use of such funding for electoral purposes. Even so, it is clear that these substantial subventions to political parties are an indirect subsidy of the electoral process by the state in that the activities undertaken contribute to the long-run development of electoral strategy and free up resources for use in an election that would otherwise have to be used to fund the day-to-day activities of the parties.

Regulating referendums: campaign finance

A combination of legislative provisions and court rulings combine to regulate the financing of referendum campaigns. While all referendum expenditure by political parties and 'third parties' (see note 9) is subject to disclosure to the Standards in Public Office Commission, there are no spending limits in referendum campaigns. However, the limitations on the receipt of donations to political parties and 'third parties' noted above, including the prohibition of foreign donations, also apply in a referendum context. Moreover, political parties and political groups do not receive any public funding for referendum campaigning and political parties are expressly prohibited from using any portion of the state funds they receive on such campaigning.

The unavailability of public funding for referendum campaigning arises from the government's response to a 1995 Supreme Court judgment that prohibited the use of publicly funded resources to support referendum campaigning unless the resources are divided equally between the 'yes' and 'no' sides.[10] The government's response to the McKenna judgment was to establish a series of successive referendum commissions with varying terms of reference to assist in putting the issues in a referendum before the people. The Referendum Commission was given three main functions in the 1998 Referendum Act: (1) to prepare a statement containing a general explanation of the referendum proposal and statements of the arguments for and against the proposal, which statements must be 'fair to all interests concerned'; (2) to publish and distribute such statements by means that 'the Commission considers most likely to bring them to the attention of the electorate'; and (3) to foster and promote and, where appropriate, to facilitate debate or discussion in a manner that is fair to all interests concerned' (Referendum Act, 1998, section 3.1). Following the publication of the report on the referendum process by the All-Party Oireachtas Committee on the Constitution, the Referendum Act 2001 abolished the Commission's functions of preparing and publishing arguments for and against the proposal and of fostering and promoting debate and added the function of promoting public awareness of the referendum and encouraging the electorate to vote (Referendum Act, 2001, section 1). The Act did not, however, provide any public funding for the referendum, other than that provided for by the now neutral activities of the Referendum Commission (for a more detailed discussion of the issue of the funding of campaigning in referendums, see Sinnott, 2004).

Conclusion

Some 80 years ago, PR-STV appeared to be the natural choice as the fundamental element in the rules of the electoral game in the emerging Irish state. It offered the possibility of minority representation, it suited the anti-party mood of the time, and, most importantly, it was familiar. Having become part of the institutional apparatus of the Irish Free State, it was set out in some detail in Bunreacht na hÉireann in 1937. This constitutional embodiment meant that any change to the system would require a referendum. Change was rejected by the people on both of the occasions on which it was attempted – and by a very substantial majority on the second occasion. However, the merits of the system have recently been again extensively debated, in part on the initiative of a number of individual politicians seeking solutions to the problem of the burden of constituency service on elected politicians and partly through the work of the CRG and that of the All-Party Oireachtas Committee on the Constitution.

The criticisms of PR-STV are quite various. It is frequently criticised by observers unfamiliar with it on the basis that it is difficult for voters to understand. This is not a persuasive point. In the first place, what the voter actually needs to grasp is quite simple and, second, both its underlying logic and its (admittedly somewhat complex) mechanics can be made readily intelligible. It has also been argued that the system produces results that are too proportional and that, consequently, it undermines the stability of government. This argument is not sustainable. Likewise, there seems to be little support for the related argument that the system is destructive of party cohesion, though it must be conceded that it is conducive to the election of independent deputies and that this can have consequences for government stability.

This brings us to the most frequent and, superficially, the most plausible criticism of the system – that it imposes an excessive burden of constituency service upon those who are elected to the Dáil. There are two problems with this criticism. The first is that, in some of its versions at least, it appears to assume that all constituency service is a bad thing, that TDs should be legislators and nothing else, and that constituency service has no positive effect on the TD's legislative role. The second and the main problem with the criticism is that, rather than being due simply and solely to PR-STV, the excessive burden of constituency service experienced by TDs is due to a range of factors, as discussed in Chapter 9. Rather than treating alteration of the electoral system as a panacea, the more appropriate response would be to deal with the other contributory factors first. If this were done and if TDs still could not find an appropriate balance between their legislative and constituency service roles, there would then be a case for re-examining the range of alternative electoral systems to see if one of them could do better on this *and* on the other criteria of a good electoral system.

Regulation of electoral contests is not confined to the specifics of the electoral system, and electoral regulation in the broadest sense has become more extensive in recent years. The aspects covered range from drawing constituency boundaries to regulating campaign finance in both elections and referendums. Within the parameters set down in the constitution and in legislation, this regulation is currently achieved under the aegis of four separate commissions – the Constituency Commission, the Standards in Public Office Commission, the Referendum Commission and the Commission on Electronic Voting. Each of these commissions was established at different times in response to particular problems in the area of electoral competition. Given that all four bodies aim to ensure free, fair and effective electoral competition, the question arises as to whether or not it would be better to amalgamate the electoral regulation functions of all four in a single Electoral Commission that would take responsibility for all aspects of the regulation and administration of elections and referendums with a view to ensuring enhanced public confidence in the rules of the electoral game.

Notes

1   Technically, the single transferable vote in a single-seat contest is known as the alternative vote (AV). It is worth emphasising that this is not PR because, in debate about electoral reform in Ireland, the option of so-called 'PR in single-seat constituencies' is sometimes put forward. What is being referred to is in fact the alternative vote, which, for reasons that will become clear in a moment, cannot be a proportional system. The second reason for emphasising that the alternative vote and therefore the system used in Irish presidential elections is not a proportional system is to correct the mistaken impression conveyed by the constitution, which describes the system under which the President is elected as 'the system of proportional representation by means of the single transferable vote' (Article 12.2.3).

2   As Tables 4.2 and 4.3 show, the counting of the votes proceeds through a number of stages. Perhaps confusingly, each stage is commonly referred to as a 'count', and that term will be employed in this chapter, to conform with prevailing usage in Ireland.

3 Distribution of a surplus is postponed if the surplus is less than the difference between the votes of the two lowest candidates and is also less than the discrepancy between the share of the vote held by the next candidate to be eliminated and the threshold for reimbursement of electoral expenses (one-quarter of the quota). At the end of the first count in Kildare North, the first of these conditions obtained but not the second.

4 This is because the base used for calculating the transfer ratios was the total number of *transferable* votes in McCreevy's original vote (in other words, those with a second preference marked); it does not mean that absolutely no one plumped for McCreevy.

5 Implementation of this more precise approach would of course be greatly facilitated by the introduction of electronic voting. However, government plans to introduce electronic voting for the June 2004 local and European elections were withdrawn when an independent commission reported that it was unable to satisfy itself as to the accuracy and secrecy of the proposed system. If electronic voting is introduced sometime in the future, the issue of the Gregory method will no doubt be examined further. While on the subject of the minor anomalies in the system it is worth mentioning the alphabetical voting phenomenon. This arises because the candidates are listed on the ballot paper in alphabetical order of their surnames and some voters, presumably indifferent as to the individual candidates put forward by their preferred party, simply vote 1, 2, 3 for candidates of the party in the order in which they appear on the ballot paper. The result is an over-representation in the Dáil of individuals whose surnames begin with letters early in the alphabet (for example, in the 29th Dáil, which was elected in 2002, no fewer than 40 of the 166 TDs had surnames beginning with the letters A, B or C). The problem could easily be eliminated by arranging the names in a number of different randomised orders on different sets of ballot papers (see Robson and Walsh, 1974).

6 See Collins (2003: 26–8) for background on the PD election strategy. It is also worth noting that in the election as whole, PD to Fianna Fáil transfers were well down on 1997, but that Kildare North was the only seat where a PD failure to transfer to Fianna Fáil affected the destination of a seat (Gallagher, 2003: 107).

7 In fact, the constitution requires the Oireachtas 'to revise the constituencies at least once in every twelve years, with due regard to changes in the distribution of population' (Article 16.2.4).

8 These numbers are rounded to the nearest euro. The fractional amounts arise because the limits (which are laid down in the 2001 Electoral (Amendment) Act) were originally set in Irish pounds.

9 A third party is defined as any person, other than a political party or candidate at an election, who accepts, in a particular year, a donation for political purposes the value of which exceeds €126.97. The definition of political purposes in the 1997 Electoral Act as amended is very broad, covering not just activities in relation to an election but also a range of promotional activities in relation to a referendum or in relation to any campaign conducted with a view to 'promoting or procuring a particular outcome in relation to a policy or policies or functions of the government or any public authority'. Third parties are required to register with the Standards in Public Office Commission, to report donations received and proposed expenses in any year and to give an indication of their connection, if any, with any political party or candidate at an election.

10 The main cases have been *McKenna v. An Taoiseach* (No. 2) [1995] 2IR 10; *Hanafin v. An Taoiseach* [1996] 2 IRLM 171; *Coughlan v. Broadcasting Commission and RTE* [2000] 3 IR 1.

References and further reading ·

All-Party Oireachtas Committee on the Constitution, 2002. *Seventh Progress Report: Parliament*. Dublin: All-Party Oireachtas Committee on the Constitution.

Blais, André, 1991. 'The debate over electoral systems', *International Political Science Review* 12:3: 239–60.

Bogdanor, Vernon, 1983. 'Introduction', in Vernon Bogdanor and David Butler (eds), *Democracy and Elections: Electoral Systems and their Political Consequences.* Cambridge: Cambridge University Press, pp. 1–19.

Boland, John, 1991. 'Dáil can only be reformed if TDs are liberated from multi-seat constituencies', *Representation* 30:111: 42–3.

Bowler, Shaun and David M. Farrell, 1991. 'Voter behaviour under STV-PR: solving the puzzle of the Irish party system', *Political Behaviour* 13:4: 303–20.

Bowler, Shaun and Bernard Grofman (eds), 2000. *Elections in Australia, Ireland, and Malta under the Single Transferable Vote: Reflections on an Embedded Institution.* Ann Arbor: University of Michigan Press.

Butler, David, 1981. 'Electoral systems', in David Butler, Howard R. Penniman and Austin Ranney (eds), *Democracy at the Polls: a Comparative Study of Competitive National Elections.* Washington, DC: American Enterprise Institute for Public Policy Research, pp. 7–25.

Carstairs, Andrew McLaren, 1980. *A Short History of Electoral Systems in Western Europe.* London: George Allen and Unwin.

Carty, R. K., 1981. *Party and Parish Pump: Electoral Politics in Ireland.* Waterloo, Ontario: Wilfrid Laurier University Press.

Collins, Stephen, 2003. 'Campaign strategies', in Michael Gallagher *et al.* (eds), *How Ireland Voted 2002.* Basingstoke: Palgrave Macmillan, pp. 21–36.

Coakley, John, 1980. 'Constituency boundary revision and seat redistribution in the Irish parliamentary tradition', *Administration* 28:3: 291–328.

Coakley, John and Gerald O'Neill, 1984. 'Chance in preferential voting systems: an unacceptable element in Irish electoral law?', *Economic and Social Review* 16:1: 1–18.

Committee on the Constitution, 1967. *Report* (Pr. 9817). Dublin: Stationery Office.

CRG (Constitution Review Group), 1996. *Report of the Constitution Review Group.* Dublin: Stationery Office.

Dummett, Michael, 1997. *Principles of Electoral Reform.* Oxford: Oxford University Press.

Farrell, Brian, 1985. 'Ireland: from friends and neighbours to clients and partisans: some dimensions of parliamentary representation under PR-STV', in Vernon Bogdanor (ed.), *Representatives of the People? Parliaments and Constituents in Western Democracies.* Aldershot: Gower, pp. 237–64.

Farrell, David M., 2001. *Electoral Systems: a Comparative Introduction.* Basingstoke: Palgrave.

FitzGerald, Garret, 1959. 'PR – The great debate', *Studies* 48: 1–20.

FitzGerald, Garret, 1991. 'The Irish electoral system: defects and possible reforms', *Representation* 30:111: 49–53.

FitzGerald, Garret, 2003. *Reflections on the Irish State.* Dublin: Irish Academic Press.

Gallagher, Michael, 1978. 'Party solidarity, exclusivity and inter-party relationships in Ireland, 1922–1977: the evidence of transfers', *Economic and Social Review* 10:1: 1–22.

Gallagher, Michael, 1987. 'Does Ireland need a new electoral system?', *Irish Political Studies* 2: 27–48.

Gallagher, Michael, 1996. 'Electoral systems', in CRG, *Report of the Constitution Review Group*. Dublin: Stationery Office, pp. 499–520.

Gallagher, Michael, 1999. 'The results analysed', in Michael Marsh and Paul Mitchell (eds), *How Ireland Voted 1997*. Boulder, CO: Westview Press and PSAI Press, pp. 121–50.

Gallagher, Michael, 2000. 'The (relatively) victorious incumbent under PR-STV: legislative turnover in Ireland and Malta', in Shaun Bowler and Bernard Grofman (eds), *Elections in Australia, Ireland, and Malta under the Single Transferable Vote: Reflections on an Embedded Institution*. Ann Arbor: University of Michigan Press, pp. 81–113.

Gallagher, Michael, 2003. 'Stability and turmoil: analysis of the results', in Michael Gallagher *et al.*, *How Ireland Voted 2002*. Basingstoke: Palgrave Macmillan, pp. 88–118.

Gallagher, Michael and A. R. Unwin, 1986. 'Electoral distortion under STV random sampling procedures', *British Journal of Political Science* 16:2: 243–53.

Gallagher, Michael, Michael Laver and Peter Mair, 2001. *Representative Government in Modern Europe*, 3rd edn. New York: McGraw-Hill.

Gallagher, Michael, Michael Marsh and Paul Mitchell (eds), 2003. *How Ireland Voted 2002*. Basingstoke: Palgrave Macmillan.

Hussey, Gemma, 1993. *Ireland Today: Anatomy of a Changing State*. Dublin: Townhouse/Viking.

Independent Commission on the Voting System, 1998. *The Report of the Independent Commission on the Voting System*. London: Stationery Office.

Katz, Richard S., 1980. *A Theory of Parties and Electoral Systems*. Baltimore, MD and London: Johns Hopkins University Press.

Katz, Richard S., 1984. 'The single transferable vote and proportional representation', in Arend Lijphart and Bernard Grofman (eds), *Choosing an Electoral System: Issues and Alternatives*. New York: Praeger, pp. 135–45.

Katz, Richard S., 1997. *Democracy and Elections*. Oxford: Oxford University Press.

Laakso, Markku and Rein Taagepera, 1979. '"Effective" number of parties: a measure with application to West Europe', *Comparative Political Studies* 12:1: 3–27.

Laver, Michael, 1998. *A New Electoral System for Ireland?* Dublin: Policy Institute and All-Party Oireachtas Committee on the Constitution.

Laver, Michael, 2000. 'STV and the politics of coalition', in Shaun Bowler and Bernard Grofman (eds), *Elections in Australia, Ireland, and Malta under the Single Transferable Vote: Reflections on an Embedded Institution*. Ann Arbor: University of Michigan Press, pp. 131–52.

Lijphart, Arend, 1994. *Electoral Systems and Party Systems: A Study of Twenty-Seven Democracies, 1945–1990*. Oxford: Oxford University Press.

Marsh, Michael, 2000. 'Candidate centered but party wrapped: campaigning in Ireland under PR-STV', in Shaun Bowler and Bernard Grofman (eds), *Elections in Australia, Ireland, and Malta under the Single Transferable Vote: Reflections on an Embedded Institution*. Ann Arbor: University of Michigan Press, pp. 114–30.

Martin, Micheál, 1991. 'Fianna Fáil has a problem – it's time to deal with it', *Sunday Tribune*, 4 August: 12.

Nurmi, Hannu, 1997. 'It's not just the lack of monotonicity', *Representation* 34:1: 48–52.

O'Leary, Cornelius, 1979. *Irish Elections 1918–1977: Parties, Voters and Proportional Representation*. Dublin: Gill and Macmillan.

Robson, Christopher and Brendan Walsh, 1974. 'The importance of positional voting in the Irish general election of 1973', *Political Studies* 22:2: 191–203.

Sartori, Giovanni, 1986. 'The influence of electoral systems: faulty laws or faulty method?', in Bernard Grofman and Arend Lijphart (eds), *Electoral Laws and their Political Consequences*. New York: Agathon Press, pp. 43–68.

Sinnott, Richard, 1995. *Irish Voters Decide: Voting Behaviour in Elections and Referendums since 1918*. Manchester: Manchester University Press.

Sinnott, Richard. 2004. 'Funding for referendum campaigns: equal or equitable?', in Tom Garvin, Maurice Manning and Richard Sinnott (eds), *Dissecting Irish Politics: Essays in Honour of Brian Farrell*. Dublin: University College Dublin Press, pp. 160–77.

Taagepera, Rein and Matthew Søberg Shugart, 1989. *Seats and Votes: The Effects and Determinants of Electoral Systems*. New Haven, CT and London: Yale University Press.

Tuairim Research Group, 1959. *P.R. – For or Against?* Dublin: Tuairim.

Websites

www.environ.i.e (link: what we do: elections)   Information on elections, from the Department of the Environment.

www.electoral-reform.org.uk/votingsystems/systems.htm Detailed discussion of electoral systems.

5   The party system

Peter Mair and Liam Weeks

As we have seen in Chapters 3 and 4, the Irish constitution makes provision for state structures typical of those of a parliamentary democracy. It is true that the mechanics of the Irish electoral system are rather unusual, but its political effects are not arguably greatly different from those of the electoral systems of other European democracies. However, while the constitution and electoral law define the formal framework within which political parties compete, they tell us little about the content of politics or about the behaviour of politicians. It is through the study of party politics that some of the most fundamental processes in modern political life are to be encountered; the study of political parties indeed provides a key to our understanding of the manner in which modern states function in practice.

Before going on to look at parties as organisations in their own right in Chapter 6 and at their relations with the electorate in Chapter 7, we need to get an overview of the whole system of parties and party competition as it has evolved in independent Ireland. Since one of the best ways of approaching such an overview is to look at the Irish system from a comparative perspective, this chapter begins by looking at those features of the Irish party system that outside observers might regard as unusual and then goes on to examine how these features have evolved and how party competition has developed. The chapter concludes with an assessment of how the party system stands following the radical changes of recent years.

The Irish case in comparative context

Although the political science literature that compares the various European party systems is enormous – with a host of studies analysing the differing origins of party systems, their patterns of change and stability and the various ways in which they may be classified and compared – it often neglects the case of Ireland. There are two reasons for this. First, Ireland's status as a small peripheral state means that it often escapes the attention of studies which have inevitably focused mainly either on the larger European states (France, Germany, Italy and the United Kingdom) or on those clusters of smaller continental countries that share common traditions and cultures (the Benelux states or the Scandinavian countries). Second, comparative political research has also tended to overlook the Irish case because it seems that the Irish party system 'doesn't fit' into the more widely applicable models of party systems; it has long been believed that the patterns and structures of mass politics which are evident elsewhere in Europe have little relevance to the Irish case. For instance, unlike the European examples, the Irish party system is not structured on an unequivocal left–right social cleavage. The two main parties, Fianna Fáil and Fine Gael, tend to converge around the centre of the ideological spectrum, often crossing sides between centre-left and centre-right, or occupying both simultaneously. This can result in the policy differences between them being indistinct and vague, such that it can at times be difficult to clarify what distinguishes one from another, much like Tweedledum and Tweedledee.

The unusual Irish case

The Irish case seems especially peculiar when we look at one of the most common ways to compare and classify European party systems, which is to focus on the origins and genetic identity of the major parties which make up those systems, and then to group them into reasonably distinct sets of 'party families', such as socialists, conservatives, christian democrats and liberals (Mair and Mudde, 1998). There are several reasons why the Irish case seems exceptional in this regard. In the first place, when we look at support for parties of the political centre or the right, it can be seen that the average electoral support for such parties in Ireland far exceeds that in any neighbouring European countries. During the 1990s, for example, an average of almost 70 per cent of the vote in the two Dáil elections was won by parties of the centre-right (Fianna Fáil, Fine Gael and the Progressive Democrats), as against an average of just over 45 per cent in all the other west European countries taken together (Gallagher *et al.*, 2001: 230). Correspondingly, Ireland also records the lowest level of electoral support for left-wing parties. During the 1990s, the Irish left (the Labour Party, the Greens, the Workers' Party, Democratic Left and several fringe left-wing parties) polled an average of around 20 per cent of the vote, as against an average of over 40 per cent in the other west European countries. The closest approximation to Ireland in this regard was Switzerland, but even there the combined vote for left-wing parties during the 1990s was almost 30 per cent (Gallagher *et al.*, 2001: 204).

Second, Ireland also appears exceptional in terms of the sheer difficulty of fitting the major centre-right Irish parties into the principal European families. In general, for example, comparative treatments would seem to suggest that Fianna Fáil is best regarded as a 'secular conservative' party (see von Beyme, 1985). This means that it is a party of the centre-right which, at the same time, is not Christian Democratic in character, in that it did not originate as a party seeking to defend the position of the church against anti-religious forces. However, even this classification results in difficulties. For example, other than the new conservative groupings which have emerged in the political systems of Greece and Spain, as well as those emerging in post-communist Europe, the only other major traditional 'secular conservative' parties in Europe are the British and Scandinavian conservative parties, none of which is very similar to Fianna Fáil. These parties owe their origins to the defence of middle- and upper-class privileges in the nineteenth century, and to resistance to the rising tide of liberalism and socialism. None has the sort of radical, popular, anti-establishment heritage so treasured by Fianna Fáil (for a discussion of the party's origins and development, see below, as well as Dunphy, 1995, and Hannan and Gallagher, 1996); none has enjoyed such close links with the trade union movement; and none could, or can, come near Fianna Fáil in its traditional claims to represent the interests of the poor and underprivileged. Indeed, it is only in certain very specific circumstances – as, for instance, when comparing the Fianna Fáil brand of nationalism with the similar patriotic appeal of the Gaullists in France, with whom Fianna Fáil forged reasonably close links in the European Parliament – that one can identify connections between this largely idiosyncratic and very successful Irish party and some, at least, of its European neighbours.

Fine Gael has also proved relatively enigmatic in this regard. In comparative analyses it is often listed as a Christian Democratic Party, not least because it is now a full member of the transnational Christian Democratic federation, known as the European People's Party. But there the similarities largely end, and again it is in terms of its origins that the fit is least easily made. In general, most European Christian Democratic parties emerged in countries in which Catholics constituted a large part of the population, but those who were active or practising Catholics constituted no more than a large minority, thus leaving substantial room for the mobilisation of secular political forces (for example, in Belgium and Italy) and/or Protestant ones (for example, in the Netherlands) to challenge the Catholic influence on social and educational policy. This was clearly not the case in Ireland, where the vast majority of the population has traditionally been made up of active and practising Catholics (see Chapter 2). Following secession from the union with Britain, political Catholicism in Ireland emerged victorious, and Catholic values were very effectively enshrined in the political system. It is for this reason that, uniquely among the Catholic countries of western Europe, Christian Democracy has never emerged as a distinct political movement in Ireland. It was never needed by the church. Thus in terms of origins, to classify Fine Gael as Christian Democratic is to stretch the comparative argument. That said, Fine Gael in recent years has moved closer to the conventional Christian Democratic model, not just by affiliating with groups such as the European People's Party, but also in its failing attempts to forge a more distinct identity within what has become a very fluid party system.

Largely as a result of the pervasiveness of Catholic values, Ireland has also been exceptional in the absence of a traditional 'liberal' alternative: there has been no anticlerical party of the right in the classical southern European mould – that is, there has been no centre-right party seeking to defend the individual against state and church alike. This gap in the political spectrum was partially filled in the late 1980s with the success of the Progressive Democrats (see pp. 148–50). Traditional centre-left liberalism, on the other hand, which owes its origins to nineteenth-century secularist traditions, and which has always proved a persistent political force in Britain, still remains absent from the Irish political spectrum, despite occasional manifestations within Fine Gael in particular.

As far as the centre-right is concerned, therefore, we are confronted with a set of Irish parties that emerged from a unique experience in the period 1916–23, during which an intra-nationalist conflict and civil war centring on the country's constitutional status followed an armed independence struggle. Elsewhere in western Europe, by contrast, the parties of the centre-right grew mainly out of social conflicts, and out of the struggles of classes and other social groups for political – and later social – rights and privileges. Indeed, if one were to search elsewhere for echoes of the Irish experience, then the closest parallel might well be found in Finland, where the modern party system also grew out of a civil war fought over their relationship with a powerful neighbour (Russia) from whom the Finns had just won independence. As in the Irish case, this also resulted in a polarisation of society and in a new party system, although the Finnish divide did have stronger class connotations than that in Ireland (Gallagher, 1985: 6; Coakley, 1987).

One final oddity in the make-up of the Irish party system results from the strong presence of independent – i.e. non-party – TDs, whose number is often greater than the total elected to all other west European parliaments put together (Weeks, 2003: 221). Independents achieved their greatest success during the early years of the state, when the party system was in flux and when a stable pattern of competition had not yet been established. This was a similar experience to that in many emerging party systems, but where the Irish case differs is that the phenomenon has persisted: elsewhere in western Europe, independent representatives disappeared as list systems of proportional representation were introduced and as parties became the dominant actors in the political landscape. Indeed, in Ireland electoral support for independent candidates did tend to fall away in the 1960s and 1970s, but it has grown again since the 1980s, and a number of governments have proved dependent on the support of independent TDs in the Dáil. This recent resurgence appears to indicate a declining electoral attachment to the parties (also reflected in the lowering levels of party identification), and hence a weakening of the party system as such. It is also one further indication of how the Irish party system continues to differ from most other European cases.

Towards a European pattern?

For all of these reasons, the Irish system is often seen as a case apart, and, as such, at least in terms of much of the literature on comparative European politics, it is also often a case dismissed. These were also the reasons which motivated John Whyte (1974: 648) to note famously some time ago that 'it is then perhaps a comfort to comparative political analysis that Irish party politics should be *sui generis:* the context from which they spring is *sui generis* also' (see also Carty, 1981; for a generalised critique of the *sui generis* approach to Ireland, see O'Leary, 1990). Since the 1980s, however, there have been some signs to indicate that Ireland might well be losing its original off-shore distinctiveness, and that it might be drifting towards the more standard European models. Three of these in particular are worth noting.

First of all, and as noted above, a conventional liberal party has now emerged in the shape of the Progressive Democrats – a party which bears many resemblances to the more recent variety of reformist liberalism which has characterised such parties as Democrats '66 in the Netherlands and (notwithstanding its name) the short-lived Social Democratic Party in the United Kingdom. Liberal parties classically were opposed to state intervention in society, especially on aspects of economic policy such as trade restrictions. They also focused on the importance of individual legal and political rights. In this sense, the Progressive Democrats have been no different, and have now followed most of their European counterparts with policies that have been non-interventionist on both social and economic matters. Liberal parties in Europe also often exert a political influence far exceeding that suggested by their relatively weak electoral following, and are governing parties *par excellence* (Gallagher *et al.*, 2001: 219–20). This is true also of the Progressive Democrats, who have wielded a considerable influence in the ten years they have spent in government in their short lifetime, and who have registered this success on the basis of an average vote of less than 5 per cent since 1989.

Second, Ireland has also experienced the arrival of a 'Green' or ecology party, part of a new European political family that appeals to post-materialist values and that bases its support on the advocacy of a new style of politics. Like its counterparts in western Europe, the Irish Green Party first developed as a loose alliance of independent citizen movements in the 1980s (initially as the Ecology Party of Ireland in 1981, and then as Comhaontas Glas/Green Alliance in 1984), without any substantive policies beyond those relating to the protection of the environment. As elsewhere in Europe, they have since carved out a clear ideological left-wing position, reflected in policies which call for social redistribution and economic reform. The Irish Greens share their European counterparts' stance in favour of international disarmament and participatory democracy, two issues which have been at the forefront of their scepticism regarding a wider and deeper European Union. Since winning their first seat in 1989, their support has increased at every election, with their biggest success to date coming at the 2002 general election when they became the third largest party in Dublin in terms of seats.

Third, coalition politics, long the norm in Europe, but traditionally the exception in the English-speaking democracies, is now a recurrent feature of the Irish party system. The era of single-party majority governments appears to be at an end, with the last government of this type losing office in 1981. Since then, we have witnessed 20 years of coalition governments, whereas between 1922 and 1981 there were just ten years of coalitions. This transformation occurred for two reasons. First of all, the Dáil arithmetic of the 1980s and 1990s produced indecisive results, with neither Fianna Fáil nor a possible Fine Gael–Labour alliance achieving a majority of seats. Government formation proved increasingly difficult, and with a higher frequency of unstable administrations dependent on the support of independents, a shift in party strategies seemed inevitable. This strategic shift on the part of party elites proved to be a second factor, as Fianna Fáil, realising that it was unlikely to gain a majority in the near future, dropped its traditional hostility towards coalitions. Initially conceived of as a 'temporary little arrangement' in 1989, the party has gradually come to accept both the idea and the practice of coalition, such that it no longer appears simply an expedient to remain in power. This was confirmed in 2002, when, falling just three seats short of a majority, it re-formed its coalition with the Progressive Democrats (Mitchell, 2003), rather than forming a minority single-party government with the support of independents, as it had done in 1982 and 1987 with the same number of seats, and in 1951 and 1961, when it had won proportionally even fewer seats.

The origins of the party system

As we have seen in Chapter 1, the two major parties, Fianna Fáil and Fine Gael, originated from a split in the original Sinn Féin party, whose success in the 1918 Westminster election led to Irish independence in 1922. A crucial factor affecting the early alignment of the Irish party system was the fact that the nationalist issue remained unresolved. The division within Sinn Féin on this issue and the 1922–3 civil war created a strong polarisation between pro- and anti-Treaty sides for at least the first decade of the new state's life. The division was not solely political, as a marked social and economic cleavage also emerged to reinforce the political opposition, with anti-Treaty Sinn Féin (and later Fianna Fáil) tending to predominate in the economically and geographically peripheral west and south-west of the country. Their platform of economic autarky, together with an emphasis on the need for more generous social provisions, enhanced Sinn Féin's (and later Fianna Fáil's) appeal among the small farmers, the poor and the working class (Garvin, 1974; Rumpf and Hepburn, 1977: 87–107). At the same time, it initially alienated the party from the more privileged sectors of Irish society, who tended to prefer the more cautious and conservative pro-Treaty wing of Sinn Féin, later to become Cumann na nGaedheal.

The polarisation between the two sides was also reflected in the nature of the two parties. In general, parties formed within parliament tend to be less centralised, coherent and disciplined than those formed outside (Duverger 1964: xxxiv). The Irish case proves no exception here. Cumann na nGaedheal was a classic cadre party, which first formed as a parliamentary group around a group of local notables. Founded while in office and without winning any election, and lacking an effective opposition in the Dáil until 1927, the party adopted a complacent attitude to electoral politics. Ministers such as J. J. Walsh and Kevin O'Higgins shared a contempt for grass-roots organisations (Garvin, 1981: 147), while party leader Cosgrave rarely took part in canvassing. The result was that they never developed strong local organisations, instead relying on the personality of their notables to accrue votes.

Just as Fine Gael was shaped by its first few formative years, so too was Fianna Fáil (Logan, 1978; Dunphy, 1995). Formed in 1926 as an extra-parliamentary group, the party placed great emphasis on its organisation on the ground, with the local branches providing the foundations for its powerful grass-roots appeal. Its militant organisational skills also owed something to the adoption of the rural networks of the IRA, stemming from the war of independence. Indeed, IRA veterans constituted a large section of the thousands of unpaid volunteers who helped found a branch in every parish and canvassed intensely to build up the party. It is also necessary to underline that this contrast in organisational styles has survived remarkably well into the contemporary age, with Fianna Fáil retaining its character as an almost populist but at the same time ultimately professional political machine, and with Fine Gael still retaining its casual attitude to politics and political mobilisation (Mair, 1987: 94–137; Gallagher and Marsh, 2002: 41–55). The opposition between these two parties has persisted over the decades, even though, with the passing of time, and with the succession of new generations, both the original basis of their conflict and their mutual enmity have tended to wane (on the parties and the party system generally, see Manning, 1972; Carty, 1981; Gallagher, 1985; Mair, 1987; Sinnott, 1995).

Throughout the 1920s and 1930s, Labour played the role of the third party in the system, as indeed has been the case ever since. Labour's failure to develop into a major party along the lines of the prominent social democratic parties in the rest of western Europe has long constituted a focus of discussion among Irish political analysts, and there are two important factors which can be cited to account for the party's Cinderella status (see Gallagher, 1982; Mair, 1992). In the first place, and most obviously, the sheer salience of nationalist issues in the early years of the Irish state meant that there was simply little scope for a party which devoted itself almost exclusively to working-class socialist concerns. The working class itself was small, since Irish society at the time had a largely rural and agricultural character (see Chapter 2), and had no clear sense of class action, being typically willing to welcome socialist ideas only when these went hand-in-hand with the nationalist ideal (Rumpf and Hepburn, 1977: 67). This meant that many working-class voters were more likely to support Fianna Fáil, whose social programme was largely favoured by Labour. Indeed, unlike most left-wing parties in developed countries, Labour's support base was largely rural, being drawn mainly from the agricultural labourers in the farming heartlands, or the personal fiefdoms of Labour politicians; its appeal did not extend to urban areas until the 1960s, when it adopted a clear socialist programme (Garvin, 1981: 170).[1] Second, as Brian Farrell (1970) has argued, Labour's decision not to take part in the 1918 election played an important role in determining its subsequent poor fortunes. Given the very large proportion of newly enfranchised voters – two-thirds of the electorate were first-time voters in 1918 (Farrell, 1970: 487) – this can really be considered a 'critical' election in the sense of setting the political terms of reference for the new state. Had Labour participated, argued Farrell, then it would have had the opportunity of placing socialist issues on what was essentially a wholly new political agenda; in fact, Labour missed that opportunity, and thus in its own way it helped to pass the agenda over to almost exclusively nationalist concerns.

These arguments therefore place a particular emphasis on the patterns which developed at the very early stages of mass politics in independent Ireland. In the beginning was the Treaty, the argument goes, and since then nothing has changed. The pattern set in those years left the legacy which has been experienced ever since, and which is summarised in Figure 5.1: a strong if now slightly weakening Fianna Fáil, a rather less strong Fine Gael and a Labour Party that persistently takes third place.

But while the particular cleavage which divided the parties in these early years and the political context in which they were embedded may well have been unique, the more general phenomenon that very early patterns of politics become frozen into place is certainly not confined to Ireland. Indeed, as Lipset and Rokkan (1967) have shown in a now widely cited analysis, this is precisely the pattern which has tended to prevail throughout western Europe, with the cleavage structures (predominantly social or economic in character) which were dominant in the early twentieth century, when mass suffrage was first introduced, as well as the parties which mobilised on the basis of these cleavages, tending to remain frozen in place thereafter.

Even beyond the obvious evidence of 'the freezing of alternatives' in the Irish case, however, there have also been various attempts to fit Ireland into the substantive framework advanced by Lipset and Rokkan, building in particular on an emphasis on the importance of the so-called 'centre–periphery' cleavage (see Garvin, 1974). Sinnott (1984, 1987), for example, claims that the struggle for independence with Britain should be seen as a conflict between centre and periphery. This was the all-pervading political conflict on the island prior to independence, dividing the population into two

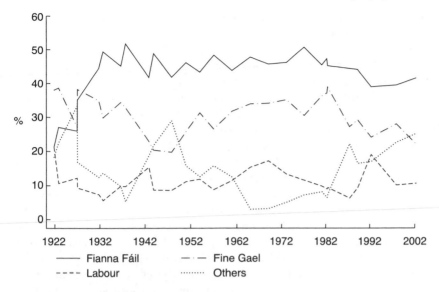

Figure 5.1 Electoral support for Irish parties, 1922–2002

Source: Calculated from Appendix 2b.

camps, Nationalists and Unionists, who together won nearly all the seats at parliamentary elections. The subsequent partition of the island gave each side its own domain, thus ensuring that rather than having one bitterly divided party system, there were to be two separate party systems, each with its own all-dominant cleavage. The new parties of the south, formed during the second phase of mobilisation post-1922, were thus structured on a cleavage over attitudes to the original nationalist issue, i.e. more nationalist versus less nationalist (Sinnott, 1987: 60).

In a country where a majority of the population was employed in agriculture, and where there existed a clear division between the rural west and the more urbanised east (see Rumpf and Hepburn, 1977), it is perhaps surprising that a rural–urban cleavage, and especially a powerful farmers' party, did not emerge. However, urban interests were never effectively mobilised beyond splinter parties or socialist-minded TDs, and were very much in a minority in a predominantly rural society. The main parties discouraged such social conflict, since they appealed to all sectors of society, and any such division had the potential to weaken their support (Gallagher, 1985: 152). It would appear that the rural way of life was elevated by much of the political elite as an ideal to which the country should aspire – an image encapsulated in a famous speech of de Valera's in 1943 which referred to 'a land whose countryside would be bright with cosy homesteads, whose fields and villages would be joyous with the sounds of industry, with the romping of sturdy children, the contests of athletic youths and the laughter of comely maidens, whose firesides would be forums for the wisdom of serene old age' (reprinted in Moynihan, 1980: 466–9).

To the extent that this view ruled, there was little fertile ground for the emergence of a rural–urban cleavage; hence, and in contrast to Scandinavia, although agrarian parties were occasionally established, they never became an enduring feature of the political landscape. The initial farmers' parties (such as the National Centre Party) of the 1920s and early 1930s catered for the interests of large farmers, whereas the farmers' party of the 1940s, Clann na Talmhan, represented the discontented small farmers of the west. Neither alternative survived for long. Moreover, ever since the final demise of Clann na Talmhan in the 1960s, no other farmers' party has emerged, not least because of the declining importance of agriculture in Irish society. Even at their most successful, however, these parties never gained much more than 10 per cent of the vote, and most farmers tended to vote for one or other of the two nationalist parties. In effect, any potential for a rural–urban conflict was lost when it was subsumed by the nationalist divide.

The formative years of Irish politics were therefore the crucial years, setting a pattern which has since proved almost impossible to shift. It is in this sense that people still continue to speak of the survival of 'civil war politics' and of the uniqueness of the Irish case. That said, we should be wary of assuming any sense of inevitability or fatalism in our understanding of the factors which determined the development of the Irish party system. In Ireland, to be sure, as elsewhere in Europe, the formative years played a very important role. But this is not the only relevant factor, and it is certainly not the only factor which can be cited to explain the continued survival of the old civil war parties and the long-term minority position of the Labour Party.

The dynamics of party competition

In seeking to understand the evolution of the Irish party system, we need to begin with one of its most characteristic features: its domination by a single party. This feature must in turn be seen in the context of the alliance options open to each of the parties, options that were a function of two other characteristics, one arithmetical, the other ideological: the mechanics and the nature of policy competition.

The electoral dominance of Fianna Fáil

The single most important element in determining the development of the Irish party system has been the persistently dominant position of Fianna Fáil (see also Dunphy, 1995). The notion of a dominant party is an important theoretical concept in political science, and draws attention to the importance of one particular actor in affecting both government formation and the nature of the party system. It is also a policy-blind concept, since it implies that parties are primarily interested in office, an assumption which many commentators would agree is a prevailing feature of Fianna Fáil. At the same time, however, the dominance of a party derives not just from its size, but also from its location within the system, and often from its ability to play one side of the system off against another. Following its accession to power in 1932, for example, Fianna Fáil began to consolidate its own preeminent position, not least because its governing status and increasingly moderate approach allowed the party to extend its support far beyond the small-farmer constituency in the peripheral west, and to begin to appeal to the more 'respectable' and privileged middle-class (and working-class) voters in the rest of the country (Garvin, 1974), thus stealing much of the ground from under the feet of Fine Gael, whose vote declined to a nadir of just under 20 per cent by the end of the 1940s.

Meanwhile, frustrated by the erosion of Fianna Fáil's original radical appeal, new parties had also begun to emerge in the 1940s. These included, as noted above, Clann na Talmhan, but also Clann na Poblachta, which mobilised on the basis of a strong republican and socially reformist programme. Labour also managed to reach a new peak in support by 1943, although in 1944 the party temporarily split into two. By the end of the 1940s, therefore, the party system was balanced between a relatively strong Fianna Fáil party, on the one side, and a fragmented and politically diverse collection of smaller parties, on the other. This was also a period in which there perhaps existed a greater potential for political realignment and change than had been the case for almost 20 years. In moving to the centre, Fianna Fáil had abandoned much of its original radicalism and had begun to disenchant many of its former supporters. Fine Gael, on the other hand, seemed to be heading towards the margins of Irish politics. Meanwhile, in the 1948 election, the two Labour parties, the two Clann parties and a variety of independents – all falling more or less outside the traditional mould of Irish politics – together won a total of almost 40 per cent of the vote.

Had the two new parties, and Labour, remained in opposition and pursued an independent line, they might well have mobilised an alternative politics, stimulating a major transformation and realignment of the party system itself. Had they remained in opposition, Fianna Fáil would have been forced to continue in office as a weak and stale minority government, while Fine Gael would probably have continued on a downward spiral, perhaps even to extinction. The old party system could have lost its meaning, and the alternative parties – perhaps linked to clearly defined social constituencies – might well have engineered its realignment. In the event, however, this was not to be. Instead, the various minor parties, together with some independent support, threw their lot in with Fine Gael in a loose and heterogeneous coalition, with the aim of putting Fianna Fáil out of office at last. Rather than building an alternative politics, therefore, they chose instead to build an alternative government.

Strategy, policy and party competition

The most important feature of this post-war configuration involved the constraints which it imposed on party competition and party strategy, constraints which resulted from the struggle for office between Fianna Fáil, on the one side, and all of the remaining parties on the other (see Mair, 1993). Given the size of its core electoral support and Dáil representation, Fianna Fáil was obviously the only party which was in a position to aim for a single-party majority government. As such, at least until 1989, it was also in a position to divide the party system into two camps – those who supported Fianna Fáil and those who did not – and to follow its own independent path, quite unconcerned with coalitions and alliances. If the party won a majority in the Dáil it would govern alone; if it failed to win enough seats to form a majority, then it would either form a minority single-party administration (as it did in 1951, 1961, March 1982 and 1987) or it would go into opposition (as it did in 1948, 1954, 1973, 1981 and December 1982). Indeed, in relative terms, Fianna Fáil has been one of the most successful parties in western Europe, winning on average 47.9 per cent of the seats and 44.7 per cent of the popular vote since 1948, of which the latter is approximately a quarter more than that polled by the largest party in the average western European system.

Fianna Fáil's opponents, on the other hand, were much less capable of developing a wholly independent strategy, largely because one of Fianna Fáil's core values was a rejection of coalitions. Indeed, as far as the struggle for government was concerned, their options were relatively simple, if also unappealing: both Fine Gael and Labour could plough their own independent furrows, which would mean that they would always remain in opposition; or they could form an alliance and share office together. In effect, the dominance of Fianna Fáil therefore forced these two smaller parties together, so that their choices were not simply coalition or opposition, but were rather, and more narrowly, coalition *with one another* or exclusion from government. It is in this sense that enormous constraints had been placed on the strategies that could be adopted in post-war party competition.

In the three decades which elapsed between the end of the second anti-Fianna Fáil coalition in 1957 and Fianna Fáil's own first coalition in 1989, the only major element of change in the structural configuration of the Irish party system was the composition of the non-Fianna Fáil alternative. The coalition experience in the 1950s, in which both governments were led by a Fine Gael Taoiseach, was sufficient to pull Fine Gael back from the brink and to restore its previously faltering political fortunes. Labour also benefited from the experience, while the two Clann parties, and many of the independents, found that their support had waned. By the 1960s, therefore, in the absence of an alternative politics, the old parties were back in style, and by 1969 their total vote share had risen to almost 97 per cent: 46 per cent for

Fianna Fáil, 34 per cent for Fine Gael and 17 per cent for Labour. By then, all other options had faded.

But while the old parties had consolidated their position once again, the logic of competition remained as it had been throughout the post-war period, with Fianna Fáil on the one side and a now reduced collection of opposition parties on the other. After 1957, Fine Gael and Labour did try to go their own separate ways, with each hoping, if perhaps only fancifully, that it might one day acquire sufficient support to challenge for government on its own. This pursuit of independent strategies meant that Fianna Fáil remained the only really feasible governing option during the 1960s. Thus, even though it never managed to poll a majority of the votes in any election in this period, it remained in office continuously between 1957 and 1973.

By the end of the 1960s and the beginning of the 1970s, there was a change in the patterns of policy competition. Both Labour and Fine Gael had moved to the left of the political spectrum and had begun to pursue what were essentially similar policy goals. The shift in Labour was most marked, even if largely rhetorical, and was symbolised most clearly in its slogan 'the seventies will be socialist'. But, perhaps surprisingly, Fine Gael had also moved to the left, abandoning many of the liberal, free-market policies which had characterised the party during the coalition period in the 1950s, and emphasising instead the need for social justice and redistribution, and for what it called 'The Just Society', the name given to the election programme which the party first launched in 1964.

Fianna Fáil, on the other hand, placed progressively less emphasis on such concerns, stressing instead the need for general economic development. It argued that any patterns of inequality and poverty could best be eradicated by increasing the size of the national cake. It stressed the need for social solidarity, framed in a more general corporatist ideology, which, by emphasising the importance of 'the national interest', deliberately set its face against any attempts to translate social conflict into politics. According to this ideology, all sections of society should work together to promote the interests of the nation as a whole – of which Fianna Fáil, in turn, was the most effective guardian (see Mair, 1987: 138–206).

Policy differences between the two sides were therefore sometimes quite marked, and this helped to give the eventual coalition programme that was hammered out by Fine Gael and Labour in 1973 the sort of coherence that was so noticeably absent from those in the late 1940s and 1950s. Beginning with this Fine Gael–Labour coalition, holding office from 1973 to 1977, governments alternated along the same pattern for 16 years, with Fianna Fáil returning in 1977, the coalition coming back once more in 1981 and then, following two short-lived alternating governments, the coalition returned to government once more in late 1982, before finally being displaced by a minority single-party Fianna Fáil government in 1987. By then, however, the common political agenda which had been forged by Fine Gael and Labour had become little more than a matter of historical memory.

The deep recession of the 1980s had encouraged Fine Gael's relatively well-to-do electorate to adopt a more self-interested view of politics and had undermined much of the party's commitment to redistribution. Fiscal rectitude now became the priority issue. At the same time, Labour had witnessed the gradual erosion of its electoral support during the coalition period, with its more conservative voters drifting towards Fine Gael or even Fianna Fáil, and with its more radical supporters turning towards the newly mobilised Workers' Party. This widening of the political spectrum in the 1980s, along with the emergence of an 'available electorate', placed a great strain on the shackles of the party system (Mair, 1987: 225). Having been constrained for so long, it was not surprising that a combination of these factors (and others) would result in a rejection of the limitations of the system at some stage in the 1980s, thereby changing the nature of Irish party competition.

The changing Irish party system

The notion of a party system implies a patterned set of interactions which becomes stabilised over time (Sartori, 1976: 43–4), and which is recognised as such by both voters and party leaders. Breaking such a pattern can therefore be fraught with difficulties, since it implies that new norms must be developed, and that expectations may be overturned. This is precisely what happened to the Irish party system in the mid-1980s. Old norms and shibboleths were discarded, even to the extent that Fianna Fáil, the party that had consistently preached against the evils of coalitions, has now led four coalition governments since 1989. The increased instability of party politics is reflected in five key events that have served to further fragment the system and to make it even more difficult to establish a structured set of relations that might guide its future shape. These were, first, the emergence of the Progressive Democrats; second, a departure from Fianna Fáil strategy and its entry into coalition with the Progressive Democrats; third, the formation of a Fianna Fáil coalition with long-standing rival Labour; fourth, the decline in the vote for the two main parties; and fifth, the rise in the vote for non-traditional alternatives. Let us look at each of these in turn.

The emergence of the Progressive Democrats

The Progressive Democrats, formed in 1985, resulted from a division within Fianna Fáil over the style of Charles Haughey's leadership, and its policy on Northern Ireland. The party made a major breakthrough in its first election in 1987, when it polled almost 12 per cent of the vote and won 14 Dáil seats. At the time, this proved the most volatile election since 1943, with aggregate electoral volatility jumping from just 3 per cent in 1982 (as measured on the standard Pedersen index)[2] to over 16 per cent, and it clearly shook the foundations of the party system. The Progressive Democrats helped to break the mould of Irish politics because they were not a civil war party, but rather a contemporary party seeking to mobilise on contemporary issues. For example, they had left Fianna Fáil over disagreement with the latter's irredentist nationalist line, and they preached a pluralist ethos (reflected in a proposed constitution for the state which dropped any reference to God in the preamble). Their emergence had a number of consequences. First of all, it broke apart the anti-Fianna Fáil bloc. Fine Gael moved to the right to combat the threat from the Progressive Democrats, while at the same time Labour was under pressure to move to the left to compete with the Workers' Party. A widening of the political spectrum ensued, as for the first time a clear left–right polarisation emerged in the party system, with Fine Gael and the Progressive Democrats on the right, competing against Labour and the Workers' Party on the left. The Progressive Democrats also had an effect on the electoral fortunes of the two main parties, preventing Fianna Fáil from gaining a majority in the short term, and perhaps also in the long term. They also spelled trouble for Fine Gael, whose middle-class heartland they threatened; indeed, Fine Gael has failed to make a breakthrough at any general election since this challenge to its centre-right ground, and has consistently remained below 30 per cent of the popular vote.

The Fianna Fáil coalition with the Progressive Democrats

Given Fianna Fáil's increasing difficulty in attaining an overall majority in the Dáil, it seemed rational by 1989 for the party to consider a coalition strategy. This was also a strategy that could enable it to take advantage of the new divisions that were opening up within the non-Fianna Fáil side of the party system. That said, the decision by Fianna Fáil to form a coalition with the Progressive Democrats in 1989 also carried certain risks for the party. As has been emphasised above, it was precisely Fianna Fáil's capacity to divide party alignments into an opposition between itself on the one hand, and all other parties on the other, which had structured and sustained the post-war party system, as well as Fianna Fáil's own position of dominance within that system. Once the political market was opened up in 1989, those parties which had been sustained most strongly by the old alignment, especially Fianna Fáil itself, were likely to become more vulnerable (see Mair, 1990).

The consequences of this new openness were to be seen in the elections of the 1990s. Since competition was no longer structured by the opposition of Fianna Fáil against the rest, it risked ceasing, in a sense, to be structured at all. Fianna Fáil clearly suffered from this change, electorally if not strategically, with its support falling to its lowest level since 1927. Fine Gael, whose role had long been reduced to that of leadership of the anti-Fianna Fáil alliance, also suffered, falling in 1992 to its lowest level of support since the nadir of 1948. At the same time, Labour, whose fortunes had been most seriously curtailed by the traditional alignment, finally found the space in which to begin shedding its image of electoral underperformance, and in 1992 polled its highest share of the vote since 1922.

In the event, the innovative Fianna Fáil–Progressive Democrat coalition did not survive, simply because Fianna Fáil was a party unused to working within coalition, and had no prior experience of sharing the cabinet table with another party. Soon after becoming Taoiseach in the new coalition government, for instance, Albert Reynolds went on record to assert that 'I will not allow anybody to think that Fianna Fáil needs to get its direction from another party' (Girvin, 1993: 9). Increasingly, the Progressive Democrat ministers felt themselves excluded from the government decision-making processes, and the eventual withdrawal of the smaller party from the cabinet and the collapse of the government in late 1992 came as no surprise (Girvin, 1993: 8–12).

The Fianna Fáil coalition with Labour

The coalition between Fianna Fáil and Labour in January 1993 was initially heralded as a moment of great importance, and as another break in the traditional Irish political mould. Since then, however, its expected consequences seem to have failed to materialise. Fianna Fáil's first coalition in 1989 had destroyed one pillar of the 'Fianna Fáil versus the rest' system, while this new coalition (Fianna Fáil joining with one of 'the rest') ended a second, thus signalling the death of the traditional party system (Mair, 1993: 172).

Labour had been very critical of Fianna Fáil during its coalition with the Progressive Democrats, an attack it continued during the election campaign of 1992. For these reasons alone, Labour might have been expected to cast its lot in with Fine Gael in the probable event that Fianna Fáil would fail to win a clear majority; this was also how Irish politics was believed to work. When Labour finally turned its back on Fine Gael, therefore, and entered a wholly novel coalition with Fianna Fáil, the reaction was predictable. The party was castigated in sections of the media and by senior figures in Fine Gael as having betrayed the expectations of its voters. Moreover, these accusations achieved a particular resonance since Labour had won a record electoral gain in 1992 while adopting a very critical stance towards Fianna Fáil.

In one sense, it can be argued that Labour's decision to enter this new coalition in 1993 was simply a repeat of the mistakes which it had made in the late 1940s and early 1970s. Then, following sporadic earlier electoral successes, the party had gone on to join new coalition governments, only to find that its identity had been undermined and its potential for further growth had been stymied. At another level, however, 1993 was clearly different. Labour was now a much larger party (with 33 seats), and the Dáil arithmetic had immeasurably strengthened its bargaining power. Indeed, given the unacceptability of other coalition options (for example, between Fianna Fáil and Fine Gael), no government was likely to be formed without it.

Unlike previously, Labour now had a number of options, and coalition with Fine Gael was not the only one. In the first place, it could of course take up the traditional option of a coalition with Fine Gael. This would not have capitalised on the party's electoral gains, however, and would once again have appeared to demonstrate to voters that there was little need to vote for Labour rather than Fine Gael. Second, it could form a coalition with Fianna Fáil in an attempt to reshape the party system. Rather than being confined to a 'Fianna Fáil versus the rest' system, where its only option was as a minor partner of Fine Gael, it could position itself like the Free Democrats in Germany, who had held the balance of power between the Christian Democrats and the Social Democrats from the late 1960s through to the mid-1990s, while averaging only some 6 per cent of the vote. With the decline of the Fianna Fáil vote, and the unlikely chance of its securing a clear majority in the future, Labour could alternate between Fianna Fáil and Fine Gael-led administrations, entering whichever coalition offered it the best deal regarding implementation of its policies. Third, Dick Spring, the party leader, could demand leadership of any government that his party would help to form. In the likely event that this demand would be rejected, he could have then gone into a new election campaign appealing for a transformation of the party system, and calling for voters to choose Labour as a party of government, and himself as Taoiseach, thus building on the party's 1992 gains.

Spring chose the second option, and initially it appeared to work. However, the souring of the relationships between the two parties, and a series of high-handed manoeuvres by Fianna Fáil which appeared to take no account of Labour sensitivities, led to the collapse of the agreement and to the return of Labour to participation in a new Fine Gael-led administration (Garry, 1995). Labour had thus fulfilled the ideal role of the pivotal coalition partner – when one administration collapsed, the party had merely switched sides. However, Labour failed to develop this role beyond 1997, and did not transform the mechanics of the party system in its favour. Spring dropped Labour's independent role at the 1997 election, ruled out coalition with Fianna Fáil, and stood as part of a coalition alternative with Fine Gael and Democratic Left. This discredited the policy he had chosen in 1992, and did not quell the disenchantment of many of his 1992 supporters. In 1997, the party's vote fell by almost half. Spring's successors as Labour leader – first Ruairí Quinn and later Pat Rabbitte – have since distanced themselves from his potentially ground-breaking policy. Although they do not rule out any future coalitions with Fianna Fáil (Collins, 2003: 30–3), the party's options again seem quite limited, and its potential for growth once more appears to be restricted by the constraints of the party system.

The decline of the two main parties

As with other European party systems, the traditionally dominant parties have fared poorly at recent elections. Fianna Fáil went through a tumultuous period in the 1970s and 1980s, one that lasted until Bertie Ahern became leader of the party in 1994 (see, for example, Collins, 2001). Its famed internal unity was torn apart by divisions over the leadership style of Charlie Haughey, and by an identity crisis over how to react to a changing Ireland, in terms of its policies on moral, social and Northern Ireland matters, many of which had not been altered since the party's foundation in 1926. Desperation to cling to power motivated it to shed a key strategic principle and to enter coalition. Rather than arrest its declining support, this merely accelerated it, however, leaving it with the uncertain status of being 'just another party'. Whereas its average vote from 1932 to 1989 was just over 46 per cent, it has since declined to less than 40 per cent. Fine Gael has gone through a far worse period since 1987, when its leader, Garret Fitz-Gerald, resigned. Under his leadership, the party tried to develop a clear social democratic profile, and presented itself as pursuing a so-called 'constitutional crusade' to 'pluralise' and liberalise Irish society. Since then, however, the party appears to have lost much of its *raison d'être*, and it has struggled to define itself in the party system in terms other than being simply the alternative to Fianna Fáil. Its vote has fallen from an average of 32 per cent between 1922 and 1987 to just 26 per cent since then, dropping to 23 per cent in 2002 (Gallagher, 2003: 94–7).

Fianna Fáil has recovered somewhat since the mid-1990s, and has learned how to play the coalition game. Its 1997–2002 coalition with the Progressive Democrats was the first government to win re-election since the return of Jack Lynch's government in 1969. But even though 2002 marked a small electoral gain for Fianna Fáil, it is still the third-lowest vote recorded by the party in 70 years. Indeed, the party has only been able to mask its overall electoral decline through its increasing ability to attract lower-preference transfers, itself a consequence of the opening up of the old 'Fianna Fáil versus the rest' system – hence its 7 per cent bonus share of seats over votes in 2002 (Gallagher, 2003: 111).

At the same time, the entry of Fianna Fáil into coalition politics has undercut the bargaining position of Fine Gael. Labour no longer needs Fine Gael to form a government, whereas the exclusion of a Fianna Fáil–Fine Gael coalition means that Fine Gael needs Labour. Minor parties may also follow the example of the Progressive Democrats, and look to Fianna Fáil for coalition, abandoning their once traditional preference for Fine Gael. Fine Gael's options for government thus appear very limited, and unless the other opposition parties develop an intense antipathy to Fianna Fáil that motivates them to create a Fine Gael-led coalition as in 1948 and 1951, the party is likely to suffer a prolonged spell in the electoral wilderness.

The rise of non-traditional alternatives

During the 1960s, at the high point of their joint popularity, Fianna Fáil and Fine Gael together won close to 80 per cent of the popular vote. In 2002, by contrast, the two parties together polled just 64 per cent. Given that the 2002 election was also marked by a record low turnout (Lyons and Sinnott, 2003), this translated to less than 40 per cent of the electorate. By the beginning of the new century, in other words, only four in every ten eligible voters were registering a preference for the parties that had forged the party system in the first place.

As voters have turned their backs on the old alternatives, minor groups have inevitably grown in strength. These have included in the first place the Workers' Party, a communist-style party most of whose Dáil group broke away to form Democratic Left in 1992, later merging with Labour in 1999. They have also included the Green Party and Sinn Féin, whose real breakthrough came in 2002, and a sizeable number of independents. What these groups have in common is that, apart from the Progressive Democrats, they are all 'opposition parties' and tend to promote an anti-establishment appeal. Indeed, a surprising factor has been the lack of a right-wing populist party among these groups, especially given the presence of increased popular disaffection with the traditional alternatives, a sentiment which fuelled the recent emergence of such parties in other European party systems. That said, it may be that in the Irish case it is Sinn Féin that will prove best able to tap into this constituency.

The anti-Fianna Fáil opposition has always been subject to change and reshaping, and, with Labour stagnating and Fine Gael in decline, this loose vote now tends to go to other groups and alternatives. In this sense, support for minor parties – if not for independent candidates – tends to reflect defections from Fine Gael, and to a lesser extent from Labour, rather than from Fianna Fáil, and is symptomatic of voter dissatisfaction with the traditional opposition parties. Indeed, the vote of over 25 per cent for minor groups in 2002 motivated talk of a new opposition, and was seen to take effect in the Dáil when the Greens, Sinn Féin, and various independents formed a technical group that outranked Labour in size, and thus in parliamentary status. Of course, the rise of such groups may well be just a temporary phenomenon like that of the 1940s and 1950s, and they may yet disappear into oblivion as most 'flash' parties tend to do. However, what is different now is that these groups can play an important role within the system, in that the opening up of the structure of party competition could offer them a key voice in a number of different coalition options – whether these involve aligning themselves in some way with Fianna Fáil, or against it (see Laver, 1999: 275).

Conclusion

In assessing the development of the Irish party system over the long term, we can identify three critical moments that have divided its history into rather distinct phases. The first of these occurred in the summer of 1927, when Fianna Fáil emerged from the wilderness and decided to take its seats in the Dáil. In so doing, the party ensured that the intense conflict which had once been fought out as a civil war would now become largely a focus for electoral competition. Politics, in this sense, genuinely became war by other means, with the major dimension of competition pitting Sinn Féin/Fianna Fáil against Cumann na nGaedheal/Fine Gael.

The second critical moment came in 1948, when the strategies chosen by the new minor parties, and by Labour, confirmed that in future the key dimension of competition would be that of Fianna Fáil versus the rest. Up until then, politics had revolved around the contest between Fianna Fáil and Fine Gael, but following 1948 that old version of 'civil war politics' no longer existed, and the pattern of competition that became consolidated echoed that of the simple two-party variety, with a single party (Fianna Fáil) on one side of the core divide and a varying collection of parties on the other (Mair, 1979). This new pattern was reflected in vote transfers; beginning with a switch in Labour transfers from Fianna Fáil to Fine Gael, a new trend emerged of anti-Fianna Fáil transfers, with voters for 'the rest' tending to reject Fianna Fáil in their lower preferences (Sinnott, 1995: 199–216). The 'Fianna Fáil versus the rest' pattern remained the key dimension of competition right through to the 1980s.

In 1989, however, this decades-old pattern finally began to open up. This year marked a third critical moment in the development of the party system, one that came about as a result of Fianna Fáil's decision to enter a coalition with the Progressive Democrats. This new watershed was important in two ways. Competition no longer revolved around 'Fianna Fáil versus the rest'. From this point on, Fianna Fáil was to become 'just another party', bigger and more successful than its opponents, to be sure, but certainly no different from them in any other important sense. Second, by playing the coalition game Fianna Fáil opened up the possibility that it could now remain almost permanently in office. As the biggest single party, and as the party which was perhaps closest to the centre of the political spectrum, it would probably always seem easier for Fianna Fáil to find a coalition partner than would be the case for most of the other parties.

The Dáil is now much more fragmented than before, and it will be increasingly difficult for any single party to win an overall majority. At the same time, and not least as a result of recent economic successes and the ceding of key decision-making power to the European Union, such policy differences as did exist between the parties have eroded significantly, and the once burgeoning polarisation of the late 1980s has now been left far behind. Within the Fianna Fáil–Progressive Democrat government that came to power in 1997, for example, a more or less clear consensus on budgetary and fiscal policy emerged, and in many respects this consensus also reached across to embrace many on the opposition benches. In addition, and sometimes in sharp contrast to the 1980s, a clear and openly stated all-party consensus on Northern Ireland has developed, while issues concerning church–state relations and traditional morality have also largely faded from the agenda. There is now less and less to choose between the competing protagonists, and less and less in principle that might prevent new forms of coalition or new governing arrangements. All parties are now coalitionable and, what is perhaps more important, all are also now more or less capable of coalescing with all others (with the possible exception of the populist Sinn Féin). In other words, not only have the parties become more coalitionable, they have also become more promiscuous.

This new politics of coalition-making is obviously something unprecedented in Irish politics, and has resulted in more protracted processes of government formation, with post-election bargaining becoming the principal determinant of which parties end up holding office. Of the nine governments formed since 1977, seven have involved protracted negotiations (see Chapter 8). Indeed, the Fine Gael–Labour administration of November 1982 and the Fianna Fáil–Progressive Democrat coalition of 2002 were the only governments that proved relatively easy to form (Mitchell, 2003). What this situation also means, of course, is that voters will inevitably retain fewer prior expectations about how governments should be formed, and this will also allow the parties greater freedom of manoeuvre.

It is certainly not easy to predict the future shape and direction of the new Irish party system. The degree of stability of party systems in general depends, among other factors, on two related elements, both of which are tied to voting patterns. The first derives from strong social cleavages, which pin voters down in particular alignments based on class, religion, region and other forms of collective identity. The second derives from a structured pattern of competition, which constrains voters by limiting the range of available alternatives. In Ireland, a country which was always supposedly characterised by politics 'without social bases' (see Chapter 7), only the second of these factors came into play, with overall stability being primarily ensured by the paramount need to choose between Fianna Fáil, on the one hand, and its opponents, on the other. However, the constraints of the system also began to work as a noose, and the more the parties attempted to break free, the more their behaviour became restricted. This came to a head in the 1980s when Ireland became one of a select few democracies to have five elections in one decade, with a series of indecisive election results threatening to send the party system into gridlock.

The opening up of the party system since 1989 has quelled the threat of stalemate, but has heralded in a period of instability, since there are now few patterns that can anchor the actions of parties and voters. Fianna Fáil on its own is now a much less credible alternative, but it is also much less easily distinguished from its traditional opponents, or they from it. If coalition with Labour is possible, then who is to argue against the future possibility of coalition with Fine Gael? The civil war factor has long since disappeared, as has the generation that experienced it, and even the arguments that warn against the dangers of a so-called 'grand coalition' are no longer plausible. After all, had a Fianna Fáil–Fine Gael coalition been formed after the 2002 election it would have had only ten more seats than the Fianna Fáil–Labour coalition of 1993–4. The terms of reference of Irish politics have finally changed, and for now, at least, the party system seems largely unstructured.

How future voters might respond to these changed terms of reference is of course difficult to foresee. If all parties are seen to be coalitionable, and if they also remain potentially politically unfaithful to their partners, then voters may have problems in choosing between them. One scenario that might therefore be envisaged is that voters will avoid the problem of choice altogether, with the new promiscuous world of Irish politics being accompanied by ever lower levels of electoral turnout. A second scenario might envisage many voters turning away from *party* politics as such, and relying more heavily on the competing personal appeals of the party leaders or even the local candidates, which could lead to even greater successes for independent, single-issue candidates. Yet a third scenario would suggest that voters begin to make their choices more or less at random, with little sense of consistency over time or between competing candidates, thus creating the possibility that electoral outcomes will be marked by ever-increasing levels of unpredictable volatility and instability. The 2002 election appeared to offer evidence for all three scenarios. Turnout has been declining since the 1980s, and in 2002 was lower than at any time since the establishment of the party system in the 1920s (Lyons and Sinnott, 2003); it was also one of the lowest levels of turnout recorded in post-war European history. The vote and seat share of independent candidates has also surged since the 1980s, and together they won nearly 10 per cent of the vote and 8 per cent of the seats in 2002. Finally, volatility has increased several times over since the 1980s; even though 2002 was not a record-breaking rate, it was still three times the level recorded in the early 1980s (see also Mair and Marsh, 2004).

To be sure, the traditional parties are still in place, although they are now more vulnerable than before. Part of the uncertainty about how voters might respond is the equally great uncertainty about how these parties will behave, and given that the old, established terms of reference have faded, the parties are necessarily going to develop a new language of politics. The one feature that has persisted, however, is Fianna Fáil dominance. Although smaller than before, the party has learned to take advantage of the new strategic opportunities afforded to it by the decline in the traditional structures of competition, and in this sense it remains part of the core logic of the system (Laver, 1999). Perhaps more so than its opponents, the party in recent years has realised that it can take neither success nor failure for granted.

Notes

1 For a revealing analysis of these particular Irish problems within the comparative context of class mobilisation, and in particular for a comparison of the Irish and Finnish cases, see Bartolini (2000: 441–54). Although Labour's early social profile contrasted strongly with that of Labour in the UK, it was similar in some respects to the social democratic parties in Scandinavia, where societies were also marked by a strong agrarian sector, and by quite a sizeable rural proletariat.
2 See Pedersen (1979). This index is the most commonly used indicator of aggregate electoral instability, and measures the total net gains of all winning parties, or, which is the same, the total net losses of all losing parties. For data on volatility levels in Irish elections see Sinnott (1995: 108–11) and Mair and Marsh (2004).

References and further reading

Bartolini, Stefano, 2000. *The Political Mobilization of the European Left, 1860–1980*. Cambridge: Cambridge University Press.

Beyme, Klaus von, 1985. *Political Parties in Western Democracies*. Aldershot: Gower.

Carty, R. K., 1981. *Party and Parish Pump: Electoral Politics in Ireland*. Waterloo, Ontario: Wilfrid Laurier University Press.

Coakley, John, 1987. 'Political succession during the transition to independence: evidence from Europe', in Peter Calvert (ed.), *The Process of Political Succession*. London: Macmillan, pp. 59–79.

Collins, Stephen, 2001. *The Power Game: Ireland Under Fianna Fáil*, 2nd edn. Dublin: The O'Brien Press.

Collins, Stephen, 2003. 'Campaign strategies', in Michael Gallagher, Michael Marsh and Paul Mitchell (eds), *How Ireland Voted 2002*. Basingstoke: Palgrave Macmillan, pp. 21–36.

Dunphy, Richard, 1995. *The Making of Fianna Fáil Power in Ireland 1923–1948*. Oxford: Clarendon Press.

Duverger, Maurice, 1964. *Political Parties: Their Organisation and Activity in the Modern State*, 3rd edn. London: Methuen.

Farrell, Brian, 1970. 'Labour and the Irish political party system: a suggested approach to analysis', *Economic and Social Review* 1:4: 477–502.

Gallagher, Michael, 1982. *The Irish Labour Party in Transition, 1957–82*. Manchester: Manchester University Press.

Gallagher, Michael, 1985. *Political Parties in the Republic of Ireland*. Manchester: Manchester University Press.

Gallagher, Michael, 2003. 'Stability and turmoil: analysis of the results', in Michael Gallagher, Michael Marsh and Paul Mitchell (eds), *How Ireland Voted 2002*. Basingstoke: Palgrave Macmillan, pp. 88–118.

Gallagher, Michael and Michael Laver (eds), 1993. *How Ireland Voted 1992*. Dublin: Folens and Limerick: PSAI Press.

Gallagher, Michael and Michael Marsh, 2002. *Days of Blue Loyalty: The Politics of Membership of the Fine Gael Party*. Dublin: PSAI Press.

Gallagher, Michael and Richard Sinnott (eds), 1990. *How Ireland Voted 1989*. Galway: Centre for the Study of Irish Elections and PSAI Press.

Gallagher, Michael, Michael Laver and Peter Mair, 2001. *Representative Government in Modern Europe*, 3rd edn. New York: McGraw-Hill.

Gallagher, Michael, Michael Marsh and Paul Mitchell (eds), 2003. *How Ireland Voted 2002*. Basingstoke: Palgrave Macmillan.

Garry, John, 1995. 'The demise of the Fianna Fáil/Labour "partnership" government and the rise of the "rainbow" coalition', *Irish Political Studies* 10: 192–9.

Garvin, Tom, 1974. 'Political cleavages, party politics, and urbanisation in Ireland: the case of the periphery-dominated centre', *European Journal of Political Research* 2:4: 307–27.

Garvin, Tom, 1981. *The Evolution of Irish Nationalist Politics*. Dublin: Gill and Macmillan.

Girvin, Brian, 1993. 'The road to the general election', in Michael Gallagher and Michael Laver (eds), *How Ireland Voted 1992*. Dublin: Folens and Limerick: PSAI Press, pp. 1–20.

Hannan, Philip and Jackie Gallagher (eds), 1996. *Taking the Long View: Seventy Years of Fianna Fáil*. Dublin: Blackwater Press.

Laver, Michael, 1999. 'The Irish party system approaching the millennium', in Michael Marsh and Paul Mitchell (eds), *How Ireland Voted 1997*. Oxford: Westview Press, pp. 264–77.

Lipset, S. M. and Stein Rokkan, 1967. 'Cleavage structures, party systems, and voter alignments: an introduction', in S. M. Lipset and Stein Rokkan (eds), *Party Systems and Voter Alignments*. New York: The Free Press, pp. 1–64.

Logan, Bruce, 1978. 'Parliamentary democracy in Ireland', unpublished PhD dissertation, University of Chicago.

Lyons, Pat and Richard Sinnott, 2003. 'Voter turnout in 2002 and beyond', in Michael Gallagher, Michael Marsh and Paul Mitchell (eds), *How Ireland Voted 2002*. Basingstoke: Palgrave Macmillan, pp. 143–58.

Mair, Peter, 1979. 'The autonomy of the political: the development of the Irish party system', *Comparative Politics* 11:4: 445–65.

Mair, Peter, 1987. *The Changing Irish Party System: Organisation, Ideology and Electoral Competition*. London: Frances Pinter.

Mair, Peter, 1990. 'The Irish party system into the 1990s', in Michael Gallagher and Richard Sinnott (eds), *How Ireland Voted 1989*. Galway: Centre for the Study of Irish Elections and PSAI Press, pp. 208–20.

Mair, Peter, 1992. 'Explaining the absence of class politics in Ireland', in J. H. Goldthorpe and C. T. Whelan (eds), *The Development of Industrial Society in Ireland*. Oxford: Oxford University Press, pp. 383–410.

Mair, Peter, 1993. 'Fianna Fáil, Labour and the Irish party system', in Michael Gallagher and Michael Laver (eds), *How Ireland Voted 1992*. Dublin: Folens and Limerick: PSAI Press, pp. 162–73.

Mair, Peter and Michael Marsh, 2004. 'Political parties in electoral markets in postwar Ireland', in Peter Mair, Wolfgang C. Müller and Fritz Plasser (eds), *Political Parties and Electoral Change*. London: Sage.

Mair, Peter and Cas Mudde, 1998. 'The party family and its study', *Annual Review of Political Science* 1: 211–29.

Manning, Maurice, 1972. *Irish Political Parties: An Introduction*. Dublin: Gill and Macmillan.

Marsh, Michael and Paul Mitchell (eds), 1999. *How Ireland Voted 1997*. Oxford: Westview Press.

Mitchell, Paul, 2003. 'Government formation in 2002', in Michael Gallagher, Michael Marsh and Paul Mitchell (eds), *How Ireland Voted 2002*. Basingstoke: Palgrave Macmillan, pp. 214–29.

Moynihan, Maurice, 1980. *Speeches and Statements by Éamon de Valera 1917–73*. Dublin: Gill and Macmillan.

O'Leary, Brendan, 1990. 'Setting the record straight: a comment on Cahill's country report on Ireland', *Governance* 3:1: 96–105.

Pedersen, Mogens N., 1979. 'The dynamics of European party systems: changing patterns of electoral volatility', *European Journal of Political Research* 7:1: 1–26.

Rumpf, Erhard and A. C. Hepburn, 1977. *Nationalism and Socialism in Twentieth-Century Ireland*. Liverpool: Liverpool University Press.

Sartori, Giovanni, 1976. *Parties and Party Systems: A Framework for Analysis*. Cambridge: Cambridge University Press.

Sinnott, Richard, 1984. 'Interpretations of the Irish party system', *European Journal of Political Research* 12:3: 289–307.

Sinnott, Richard, 1987. 'The voters, the issues and the party system', in Howard Penniman and Brian Farrell (eds), *Ireland at the Polls, 1981, 1982 and 1987*. Durham, NC: Duke University Press, pp. 57–103.

Sinnott, Richard, 1995. *Irish Voters Decide: Voting Behaviour in Elections and Referendums since 1918*. Manchester: Manchester University Press.

Weeks, Liam, 2003. 'The Irish parliamentary election, 2002', *Representation* 39:3: 215–26.

Whyte, John H., 1974. 'Ireland: politics without social bases', in Richard Rose (ed.), *Electoral Behavior: A Comparative Handbook*. New York: The Free Press, pp. 619–51.

Websites

www.politics.ie   Informative site on Irish politics. Very much current affairs-oriented.

www.electionsireland.org   Contains detailed results for all Irish general elections.

www.rte.ie/news/oireachtas   A guide to Irish politics by the state broadcaster, Radio Telefís Éireann (RTÉ).

See also the following party websites:

www.fiannafail.ie
www.finegael.ie
www.greenparty.ie
www.labour.ie
www.progressivedemocrats.ie
www.sinnfein.ie
www.socialistparty.net

6   Parties and society

Michael Marsh

Parties are at the centre of political life in Ireland. They provide the teams that contest elections, and the party label is usually critical in turning an aspiring politician into a serious candidate rather than an also-ran, as many voters use the label as a shortcut to help them make decisions about who to vote for (see Chapter 7). Candidates from a party can draw on a network of active supporters who will promote their cause and campaign on their behalf. After the election, party loyalties determine the choice of Taoiseach, and the Taoiseach in turn uses party as the first criterion when deciding appointments to the major offices of state and makes it a significant criterion in many other appointments. It is through party loyalty that governments are maintained in office, and the legislative programme of governments dominates the agenda of the Oireachtas. Parties thus provide the personnel and the policies that are central to political competition as well as providing a framework to assist the public to participate in elections, and, as party supporters, in day-to-day politics on a more regular basis.

Yet despite this central role in the democratic process, political parties in Ireland are typically treated as private organisations that are exempt from extensive public regulation. The conduct of elections in Ireland is regulated scrupulously by legislation and by the constitution, but the conduct of political parties – in choosing their candidates, selecting their leaders and drawing up their policies, for example – is not. The only direct regulation comes from the parties themselves and, indirectly, because parties need electoral support, from the voters, who can indicate approval or disapproval once every few years. The significant exception to this has been the public regulation of party financing since 1997.

Party teams are made up of a variety of players. There are the politicians who seek election and re-election, there are the officials who serve in the party organisation on a full-time basis, and then there are the ordinary members, some active, some not so active, who comprise the mass of the party. This chapter examines how they all fit together. We explore first how parties are organised: what the different units of the party are and what their relationship is to one another. In particular, we will consider whether the components are relatively autonomous, each pursuing its own course, or whether there is a considerable degree of influence by some parts over others. In other words, what is the quality of the participation that parties allow? In the second section of this chapter we will examine the finances of Irish parties, once a very murky subject indeed but now more open to public scrutiny. It will be seen that taxpayers' money is a vital source of political funding, which raises the question of why the public should fund parties and what the benefits of such a policy are for the quality of our democracy. Third, we look specifically at the members of the party: what it means to be a member, and how ordinary people come to be members. Members are a resource for parties, providing the foot soldiers in election campaigns and, perhaps no less importantly, giving voice to the party's message on a day-to-day basis. Parties need members but what do members get out of it? What sort of rank and file participation do parties allow? We will examine certain internal processes that are crucial to the role of parties in public life and ask how these are managed and, in particular, how important the ordinary party member is in each of them. These processes are the selection of candidates for election, the appointment of party leaders and the formation of party policy. Finally, we will conclude by discussing the overall vitality of Irish parties today.

Nineteenth-century parties typically placed little or no emphasis on membership and were sometimes scarcely more than clubs formed by members of parliament. In twentieth-century Europe some observers argued that the dominant form of party would be the 'mass' party. This typically has a large membership, which is expected to play a major part in determining a party's political outlook and strategy. Mass parties generally represent a particular social group and give this group political expression. However, in recent decades, this description of political parties has become increasingly inappropriate. Parties have become less identified with specific social groups. Their members have been described as being without influence and thin on the ground. Modern parties are seen to give top priority to electoral strategy; winning votes is more important than representing a particular social group; leaders and the group around them make all the main decisions and the role of the rank and file becomes peripheral and irregular. Political scientists refer to such parties as 'catch-all' or 'electoral-professional' parties (Katz, 1996). It will be seen that this description is broadly true of Irish parties, and in particular is true of the larger and more established parties represented in the Dáil – Fianna Fáil, Fine Gael and Labour. Where the experience of other parties is significantly different, this will be indicated.

Party structure

The organisational heart of an Irish party is its central office. This provides support for deputies and co-ordinates local branches that are scattered all over the country. Central office is staffed mostly by full-time officials these days. Fianna Fáil, Ireland's largest party, employs 33 full-time staff at head office, including nine in its parliamentary press office. These people are variously engaged in financial management and fund raising, in research and press relations, and in managing and co-ordinating the rank and file membership. These numbers are well up on what they would have been 20 or 30 years ago, and also higher than they were before state funding became more generous after 1997 (see pp. 165–6).[1] There has been a similar increase in other parties, though the overall numbers are smaller. However, while the trend is comparable to that elsewhere, the numbers remain small in comparison to equivalent parties in most other European countries (Farrell and Webb, 2000: Table 6.4).

The basic unit of most political parties is the local branch (called a *cumann* in Fianna Fáil and Sinn Féin). In the Greens (who call this a local group) and the Progressive Democrats it is a constituency-based body, but more typically it represents a smaller unit. Local branches are based on the parish in the case of Fianna Fáil and Fine Gael, but this level of organisation makes little sense for smaller parties. Branches vary in size, but each party sets a formal minimum membership. This is ten for Fianna Fáil and Fine Gael, and five for Sinn Féin and, in rural areas, for Labour. Sinn Féin, unusually, has imposed a maximum size, 12 in the past, now 24. A party normally has a number of branches in each Dáil constituency, and these send delegates to a constituency council (variously called) that handles the conduct of elections. For larger parties there is also an intermediate tier at the level of the local government constituency, which deals with local elections. Irish party organisations are thus constructed from the 'grassroots' upwards.

Local branches are seen as the real link between parties and communities, promoting (at least in theory) the policies and ideas of the party in local areas as well as providing a route through which local concerns can be fed upwards to party decision makers. In practice, as we shall discuss later, the linkage may be minimal. Despite their status as the building blocks of party organisations, party branches can be rather fragile. Some may be moribund outside of the election season and others may exist only on paper, being designed only to give local figures voting power at party selection bodies; many will be no larger than is required by party rules. Even so, Fianna Fáil, for example, estimates that it has about 2,500 *cumainn* and Fine Gael just over 1,000, but each may have more that are not registered in any particular year. This can be set against 6,000 polling districts nationwide in which parties would like to have a local presence.

At the summit of this organisational pyramid is what Labour and the Progressive Democrats call a national conference (called an *ard-fheis* in Fianna Fáil, Fine Gael and Sinn Féin and a convention by the Greens). In theory this is the supreme policy-making body of the party, comprising delegates from the branches, public representatives and party officials. It is typically a large and unwieldy body meeting infrequently, usually once a year, and such meetings tend to be major social and political occasions. Whatever their limitations as policy-making bodies, the national conferences function as rallies designed to reinforce the faith and commitment of the rank and file and to allow the party to demonstrate unity and enthusiasm to the outside world. Weekend conventions are now giving way in some parties, notably Fine Gael, to more low-key one-day events, tailored much more to the demands of the broadcast media than to participation by delegates. Financial and media considerations provide the main justification for such changes, but they also may be taken to indicate the declining importance of ordinary party members. Between one national conference and the next, management of the party rests in the hands of an executive committee. Though its name and precise composition vary from party to party, this normally comprises people elected by members, plus others representing party TDs (for more details on party organisation in Ireland, see Mair, 1987 and Farrell, 1994; see also websites at the end of this chapter's list of References and on p. 159). Figure 6.1 shows a typical party structure, in this

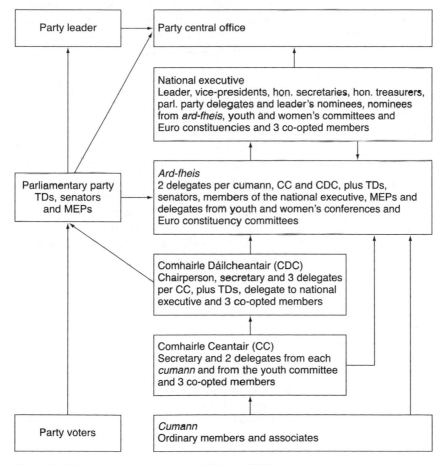

Figure 6.1 Organisational structure of Fianna Fáil

case that of Fianna Fáil. It shows the *cumainn* at the base, sending delegates to local and Dáil constituency organisations. Each of these units in turn sends representatives to the *ard-fheis*. Between meetings of the *ard-fheis*, the party is under the authority of the national executive, which supervises the party bureaucracy located in central office. The parliamentary party is represented strongly in the national executive. There are some differences of detail between this structure and those of the other Irish parties, but the essential features are the same.

Party finance

Whatever their organisational structure, political parties need money, and Irish parties are certainly no exception. It may once have been enough to have an army of dedicated volunteers willing to knock on doors, stuff envelopes and drive people to the polls on a wet and windy night, all for the love of the party – though this is doubtful. Certainly, this is not sufficient nowadays. Volunteers remain a vital part of the election campaign in the constituencies (Marsh, 2004), but a modern high-tech election campaign also depends upon a coterie of specialists and a lot of expensive equipment. Computers must be bought, staff must be employed, offices must be rented and phone, fax and postage bills must be paid. There are opinion polls to be commissioned, videos to be produced, posters to be printed, campaign buses and helicopters to be hired, manifestos to be published and so on, all of which require money. Quite apart from these campaign needs, parties need money for a range of purposes other than elections such as the general administration of the party, the co-ordination of the activities of its branches and party members, the training and education of members and officials and the formulation of policy.

Where does all this money come from, who spends it and what do they spend it on? Until recently, the short answer to all these question was that nobody knew, precisely. As both Michael Gallagher (1985: 130) and Peter Mair (1987: 106) have noted, this matter has traditionally been 'shrouded in secrecy'. This was because, while most parties received some state support, most also received quite extensive contributions from private sources about which they were most unwilling to give any information at all. Such money might come in to parties centrally but it also came to individual politicians and local branches and was never subject to external (or sometimes even internal) scrutiny.

The traditional perception was that Irish parties received little or no public funding, with their money coming from donations and collections made by party members together with some larger sums from affiliated bodies (in the case of Labour) and business interests. However, parliamentary party leaders have in fact long received public money in the form of 'leaders' allowances'. This system was reformed in 1996, to redress what had previously been systematic discrimination against smaller parties, and it has also been made more transparent. The reformed system retains the traditional principle that, since government parties can draw upon the resources of the civil service, the distribution of leaders' allowances is weighted in favour of the opposition. This is done by paying government parties only two-thirds of the sums due to them by virtue of the number of TDs they have (senators are not counted in this way). Smaller parties are also advantaged as the sums due per Oireachtas member decline as a party has more TDs and senators. In the past the money was spent entirely at the discretion of the party leader and was subject to no public controls. We now know, for instance, that the former leader of Fianna Fáil, Charles Haughey, used the money to help fund his extravagant lifestyle. This money must now be accounted for by parties (but not by individual independent candidates) in some detail and cannot be spent on election activities as such. Most of it goes on general administration and on secretarial support for TDs and senators (Standards in Public Office Commission, 2003a: Table G).

In addition to the leaders' allowances, Irish parties have traditionally received benefits in kind at election time, in the form of free airtime for 'party election broadcasts'. This airtime is made available to parties on the basis of a formula used by the state broadcasting station, RTÉ, that takes account both of a party's current Dáil representation and of the number of candidates nominated. This is a very significant asset, though difficult to quantify. It would certainly cost a lot if it had to be paid for. Since so many Irish homes now have access to a range of non-Irish television stations, however, it is difficult to know how many voters switch channels or turn the sound down when party election broadcasts fill the screen. Nonetheless, this facility does offer even small and poor parties a chance to make a case directly to the entire Irish electorate.

Notwithstanding such traditional public supports, the public funding of Irish political parties until very recently was at a much lower level than that to be found in many other European countries. However, the issue of party funding in Ireland came to a head in 1997 with reports of very large sums of money being paid by businessmen to senior politicians. Corruption was suspected. Most of these allegations remain the subject of various tribunals of inquiry (see Chapter 14), but the initial furore helped the passage of the Electoral Act, 1997, a piece of legislation that has had a fundamental impact on party politics in modern Ireland. This increased the levels of public subsidies available to parties but also imposed some transparency into the sources of all funding, some accountability into how money is spent and some limitations on expenditure on election campaigns.

The 1997 Act dealt, among other important matters, with public funding for political parties, the strict regulation of campaign spending, and the disclosure of political contributions. General funding under the 1997 Act goes to 'qualified parties' – registered political parties winning over 2 per cent of the vote in the previous election.[2] This funding has two components. The first is a contribution to parties' annual running costs; the second concerns the reimbursement of election expenses. The Act was amended by the Electoral (Amendment) Act, 2001, but while this changed details – most notably in increasing the level of funding – the fundamental principles remained intact.

Payments towards their annual running expenses are made to qualifying parties in proportion to their share of the total first preference votes won by all qualifying parties in the previous general election. All parties winning more than 2 per cent of the total vote received a basic sum of approximately €130,000, plus a proportionate share of a fund of almost €4 million. Once again, this money has to be accounted for and may not be used for narrowly defined electoral purposes; in 2001 the bulk of it went on general administration and the co-ordination of the activities of branches and members (Standards in Public Office Commission, 2003a: Table D). The 2001 Act also deals with partial reimbursement of election expenses up to a maximum of €6,348 for every candidate who contested the election with a minimal degree of success.[3]

All of this is summarised in Table 6.1. The total sums payable to Irish political parties from the public purse are thus now considerable. They amounted in 2002 (an election year) to over €4.5 million to Fianna Fáil, and almost €3.5million to Fine Gael; the Labour Party took almost €2 million, and the smaller parties and independents divided almost another €2 million between them. In sum, this amounted to almost €13 million of public money. By contrast, state subventions to parties in 1989 – prior to the passing of the 1997 Act – were only about €0.5 million at 1997 prices (Murphy and Farrell, 2002: Table 8.6). Even allowing for inflation, this amounts to a very dramatic increase.

Table 6.1 Approximate income for parties from the state, 2002 (in '000 €)

	Leaders' allowance	Exchequer funding	General election campaign reimbursement	Total
Fianna Fáil	2,100	1,900	670	4,670
Fine Gael	1,900	1,200	480	3,580
Labour Party	1,100	630	240	1,970
Progressive Democrats	330	300	90	720
Sinn Féin	180	350	160	690
Green Party	230	270	90	590
Socialist Party	50	–	12	62
Independents	500	–	160	660
Total	6,390	4,650	1,902	12,942

Source: Compiled from Standards in Public Office Commission (2003a, Tables E, G, H).

Balancing the largesse in recent legislation, there has been an effort to clean up political funding and remove some of the potential for allegations of political corruption. The Acts deal very strictly with the disclosure of political contributions, and set limits on campaign spending in general elections. The 2001 Act deals with a wide variety of benefits in kind as well as donations of cash; it prohibits any anonymous donation of more than €126.97 (IR£100) and compels candidates to declare all donations in excess of €634.87 (IR£500), as well as requiring parties to declare all donations in excess of €5,078.95 (IR£4,000). Moreover, candidates may not accept donations from any one individual in a single year exceeding €2,539.48 (IR£2,000), nor can candidates or parties accept donations from outside of the state unless these come from Irish citizens. These restrictions upon the size of party donations should be set against evidence given to tribunals of inquiry that in the past some politicians received sums of IR£30,000 and more, ostensibly towards election expenses, that remained hidden from public scrutiny.

Under the 1997 Act large donations to parties were still permitted. One well-known business donor, Denis O'Brien, gave IR£50,000 each to Fianna Fáil, Fine Gael and the Progressive Democrats in 2001 (IR£50,000 that he donated to Labour was returned in 2002). The 2001 Act prohibited any donation to a party in excess of €6,348.69 (IR£5,000) from the same source in a single year (a rule that hit Sinn Féin severely; it had declared almost $300,000 from one US donor). Thus the legislation relies not only upon making political donations transparent but also on prohibiting anything beyond relatively small donations.

The legislation also regulates spending by both candidates and parties at Dáil and European Parliament (but not local) elections. It goes to considerable lengths to prevent expenditure by people or groups friendly to political parties or candidates – so called 'third parties'– from escaping the regulatory net. The clear intention is to prevent the use of the type of 'political action committee', friendly to but formally unconnected with a candidate, which has become so prevalent in the United States as a way of getting around spending regulations.

There are clear limits on election spending by both candidates and national political parties. The limits on spending by parties flow indirectly from the limits on party candidates, which are fixed by the 2001 Act at €25,395 per candidate in three-seat constituencies, €31,743 per candidate in four-seat constituencies and €38,092 per candidate in five-seat constituencies (a significant increase on the 1997 limits: €17,700, €21,600 and €25,400). Total election expenses for a party and all of its candidates are limited to the total expenses allowed for all of the candidates of the party in question. These limits make little difference for small parties with limited resources, but for the larger parties they can be a real constraint on electioneering activities.[4]

Concerns over corruption linked to political parties helped to develop rules governing the financing of parties in a number of countries. The scandals ongoing in Ireland since the late 1990s (see Chapter 14) have certainly helped to create a radically new legal environment for party funding in Ireland. Much more public money is being provided, with a view to reducing the dependence of parties on anonymous private donors, and much more regulation is in place to limit campaign spending and to force the declaration of private donations. This is in line with trends elsewhere, and with recommendations of 'best practice' (Council of Europe, 2001; Venice Commission, 2001). The Irish pattern provides for a mixture of public and private funding, with donations from business and other supporters as well as contributions and fund raising by the members themselves. Funding is certainly not excessive, and Irish parties are still poorer than many of their European counterparts. Limits on donations are relatively strict, although election expenditure limits are not ungenerous to the more affluent parties. Altogether candidates spent just over €7 million in 2002, but only Fianna Fáil and the Progressive Democrats came even close to spending their full allowances, reaching 87 per cent of what was allowed, while the Greens and Sinn Féin, and in fact the average candidate, spent less than 50 per cent of the limit (Standards in Public Office Commission, 2003b). There are fears that public funding can insulate existing parties from competition, making it even harder for new parties to break into what becomes almost a cartel (Katz and Mair, 1995). Certainly funding is proportional to size and so more generous to larger parties, and would-be parties get no help at all other than some partial reimbursement of campaign expenses after an election should they pick up enough support to qualify. Not all questions about funding have been cleared up, as parties and politicians declare only the larger donations; it is certainly not possible to say with certainty how much money came into the hands of all politicians and would-be politicians in a given year, and spending controls are still weakened by the fact that they apply only to the formal campaign period (usually about three weeks). But overall the situation is much changed.

There is no doubt that the new regime has helped parties. Even the richest ones found it hard to raise the money needed to fund both their organisations and expensive election campaigns. Labour, Fine Gael and Fianna Fáil had chronic and severe debt problems. Parties spent money they did not have, particularly in the 1980s, when campaigns became far more competitive and capital intensive; by the end of 1992 the parties had fought six general elections in 11 years (Farrell, 1994). Organisations suffered; Labour's general secretary claims he was once reduced to paying wages out of his own personal funds (Kavanagh, 2001: 84). The restrictions on spending for electoral purposes brought more discipline into campaigning (Collins, 2003: 35). Support for legislators is now better, and the fact that most of the public money cannot be used for campaigning has also given party bureaucrats the resources to run their organisations more effectively; they no longer find the lion's share of the resources being siphoned off for another election. It is less certain that the new rules have done anything as yet for public confidence in politicians. Here, the problem was not funding scandals alone, but was probably a symptom of the much more intense and opportunistic competition of the last 30 years or so (Mair and Marsh, 2004). Nonetheless, confidence in politicians has plummeted over the last 20–30 years (Murphy and Farrell, 2002: 223–4) and if we are to judge from a Milward-Brown/*Sunday Tribune* poll, there is no sign yet of any recovery (*Sunday Tribune*, 24 October 2003).

Party membership

It is suggested popularly that this lack of confidence in politicians has an adverse effect at grassroots level, sapping the morale of activists and cutting membership levels. Party membership figures in Ireland were traditionally a combination of guesswork and wishful thinking. It is only recently that some parties have started to keep records of how many members (as opposed to branches) they have, and, indeed, Fianna Fáil still has limited records of members. Many party members, furthermore, are merely nominal and are certainly not active. Estimates of party membership, such as they are, are reported in Table 6.2. These figures are in some cases lower than those published several years ago but they do not necessarily indicate a decline. They may indicate only that records are better or estimates more realistic.

Table 6.2 shows the memberships of the different parties at the time of the 2002 general election, the votes won by different parties and the ratio between these figures. Fianna Fáil claims roughly one member for every 16 voters and Fine Gael one for every 20. It is striking that the ratio varies considerably across the other parties, with Greens having only one member for

Table 6.2 Party members and voters, 2002

	Members in 2002	Voters in 2002	Voters per member
Fianna Fáil	47,000	770,748	16
Fine Gael	21,000	417,619	20
Progressive Democrats	5,500	73,628	13
Labour	3,700	200,130	54
Sinn Féin	2,000	121,020	61
Greens	800	71,470	89
Total	80,000	1,654,615	21

Source: Membership figures supplied by the parties.

Note
The total excludes votes cast for 'other' parties and candidates. The membership figure for the Progressive Democrats represents party headquarters' best estimate.

every 89 voters and the Progressive Democrats claiming one for every 13. Well over 50 per cent of all those who belonged to an Irish political party belonged to Fianna Fáil. If this was indeed the case, then it clearly gave the party a real organisational advantage at election time.

Overall, of course, relatively few Irish people belong to political parties. The figures above suggest that only about 80,000 people were party members in 2002; that is, not even 3 per cent of the electorate, a level below that for most other democracies, although it is a level that many other countries are now approaching (Scarrow, 2000: Table 5.3). This is supported by survey evidence, most recently by that from the first wave of the European Social Survey (ESS), conducted in 2002. This found that fewer than 4 per cent of respondents reported having been members of a party within the previous 12 months. If we lump these with respondents who reported having made a financial contribution to a party or who said that they had actively participated or done voluntary work for a party in the same period, we find that no more than about 6 per cent directly supported party activities in 2002, an election year. This can be set against the comparable figure of 25 per cent for cultural or hobby groups, 13 per cent for humanitarian groups, 11 per cent for environmental groups and 10 per cent for consumer groups. Figures for membership in sporting, religious or professional/trade union organisations are very much higher. Party related activity is clearly something that involves only a very small minority of people in Ireland. Comparable figures for other countries covered by the ESS indicate that Ireland is not untypical, with countries such as Germany, Denmark, Italy, the Netherlands and Luxembourg all looking much the same, while Britain, Greece and Portugal record even lower levels of commitment to parties.[5]

Given these low figures it would not be surprising to find that party membership is in decline in Ireland, although it is unwise to assume it was ever very high and, as already explained, historical figures lack credibility. Fianna Fáil's estimate of less than 50,000, compared to almost 90,000 ten years ago, accounts for most of the decline, but it is hard to know how far that is simply a greater sense of realism or a sign of real change. Where the data are more reliable over a longer period, as in the case of Fine Gael in recent years, we can be pretty sure that there was a decline from a peak in the 1980s, but there is no reason to believe that there were fewer members in 2002 than there were, say, in the 1950s and 1960s (Gallagher and Marsh, 2002: 56–7). Labour, too, certainly had fewer members in 2002 than in its halcyon days when Mary Robinson was elected President and the party won almost 20 per cent of the vote (Murphy and Farrell, 2002: Table 8.4).

However, membership has actually increased in most parties over the last couple of years. In 2004, the Greens claimed 1,200 members compared to 800 in 2002; the Progressive Democrats claimed an increase in membership, not least in Laois–Offaly where new recruit and TD, Tom Parlon, has built a substantial base; Fine Gael reported 31,000 in 2004, up from around 20,000 in 2002; and Labour claimed almost 7,000 in 2004. Determined drives by the new leaders of the two last-mentioned parties, Enda Kenny and Pat Rabbitte, and candidate selection systems that give aspiring politicians a strong incentive to sign up as many new members as possible are the main reasons for the increase in Fine Gael and Labour, especially in view of the fact that local and European elections took place in 2004. This raises a question about the primary loyalties of such members: how far do they lie with the party and how far with the politician who mobilised them? However, there is nothing novel about that question in an Irish context. What the experience does demonstrate is that if parties want members, increases are possible. Sinn Féin's determination to increase its member base is particularly interesting. Formerly the party had been interested not in members as such but in activist members. Now the drive is on for members *per se*.

Even so, many might say, members are becoming less active. The smaller, more radical parties, such as the Workers' Party and Democratic Left in the 1980s and early 1990s, and Sinn Féin more recently, tend to place very heavy demands upon members and require a high level of year-round commitment. Most Irish parties, however, are essentially electoral organisations. Parties might wish that branches were busier, fulfilling the linkage role set down for them. Labour's website suggests that 'your local branch is there to bring the Labour Party to your community'; Fianna Fáil's site declares that the role of the *cumann* is to 'promote the interests of the Party in its area and secure public support for its policies'; and Sinn Féin's site explains that the *cumann* 'brings the policies of the party to the people of their local area'. From the perspective of the top, the role of the grass-roots organisation is to spread the party's message. The perspective from below might be a little different, with some members doubtless wanting to send messages upwards. However, the significance of party branches is broader than the policy domain. Branches will link local representatives to their community, passing on requests and concerns from constituents to councillors and TDs.

Branches may have problems in carrying out some of the more demanding roles expected of them. In particular, satisfying these expectations may require much more time than members really want to put in. In one extensive study, carried out on Fine Gael, it was found that the average member attended only one or two meetings a year (Gallagher and Marsh, 2002: Figure 5.1), and indeed the typical branch met no more often than this (Gallagher and Marsh, 2002: Table 5.10). While it was reported that discussion at meetings involved political and not merely organisational matters – and in particular local political issues – many members were critical of the role that branches played, or were allowed to play (Mockler, 1994; Gallagher and Marsh, 2002: 104–6). Parties have considered how they could attract more members and make them more active. One option is to make membership independent of branches, allowing direct registration with head office, as currently promoted by Fianna Fáil, who label such members 'registered supporters' (without voting rights, as they are not part of the branch structure). Another option, suggested by an internal commission of inquiry in Fine Gael, is the creation of 'functional' branches, grouping, for instance, 'teachers for Fine Gael' across a broader area than would be covered by a branch; but this has not been implemented. For the moment, almost all membership remains within the traditional branch structure.

Of course not all activity takes place at meetings. As in all organisations, informal activities may be as important as formal ones. Members acting outside the formal branch meeting may well pass on a constituent's demands to representatives; in fact, 60 per cent of Fine Gael members report doing that (Gallagher and Marsh, 2002: 89). They may also articulate the values of the party privately, and in other organisations (those who join parties also tend to join other organisations). This all provides a valuable service for the party. If branches were larger and more active the service could obviously be better but, even as it stands, it is clear to see why parties value members. What remains to be seen is what the members get out of the relationship. In particular, what impact can they have on the political process through their parties?

Party management

Parties like to see themselves as democratic organisations in two senses of the term – first, in contributing to democracy by providing candidates and policies so that the voters can determine how and by whom they are governed, and, second, in themselves being internally democratic, so that the candidates they nominate and the policies they put forward are influenced directly by their own members. They allow participation not simply at election time but on a continual basis. We will examine here what sort of role members play in Irish parties with particular emphasis on how election candidates and party leaders are selected, and how party policy is determined.

Selection of candidates and officials

Many observers have argued that candidate selection is the critical process as regards the distribution of power within parties (for a summary, see Hazan, 2002: 109–10). It may also be something that members care far more about than party policy, which has sometimes been seen as the chief concern of activists. In fact, members of Irish parties can play a significant role in deciding who becomes a politician, since the nomination of candidates for elections is for the most part a highly decentralised process, already allowing considerable participation by rank and file members (Gallagher, 1988). In recent years, however, there are signs that party leaderships are trying to exert more control over this.

The process of candidate selection varies somewhat between the parties. Typically, however, candidates are selected by members from the area in which the election is to take place. For Dáil elections, each branch in a Dáil constituency sends delegates to a constituency convention, which decides both how many candidates to select and who these people are to be. In the case of the Green party, candidate selection is handled directly by a convention open to any constituency member who wants to attend, rather than by a delegate convention. Fine Gael allows all members of eight weeks' standing, and belonging to a branch that has been registered for three months, to attend and vote at the candidate conventions. Labour has similar rules. This provides candidates with a good reason to get their potential supporters registered as party members well in advance of the selection. The Progressive Democrats' rules are flexible, and allow for both one-member-one-vote and delegate selection conferences as appropriate, with the former more common. All this means that direct membership participation in the candidate selection process can be quite extensive. In 2002, meetings ranged in size from just a handful to about a thousand people, depending on party and location (Galligan, 2003).

There are parties elsewhere where candidates must be party members. This is expected of candidates selected by Irish parties but it is evident that membership is sometimes of very short standing. Tom Parlon, for instance, was courted by Fine Gael before opting to join and run for the Progressive Democrats in the 2002 election, and there is considerable anecdotal evidence of parties nominating candidates whose potential vote-winning abilities outweighed any shortcomings they might have had in terms of experience as ordinary branch members. Parties nominate candidates; they do not necessarily nominate from their own ranks. The criteria for candidate selection in Ireland are essentially pragmatic. There are no formal grounds for eligibility. What is most valuable to an aspiring candidate is having a track record of winning votes. If a candidate has not stood for election before, the next best thing is to have a very solid local reputation. Neither the political views of the aspiring candidate nor his or her potential as a legislator seem to carry much weight. This was the conclusion drawn from a survey of Fine Gael members and also from surveys asking voters what they valued in a candidate (Gallagher and Marsh, 2002: 128–34; Marsh, 2003). When a party selects several candidates, there seems to be little concern to achieve any social balance – by age, gender or social class, for example. In rural areas, however, candidates will almost always come from different parts of the constituency and the procedures at the convention may well be designed to ensure this.

The nomination of candidates by local branches is subject to some control by central party organisations. The national executive or party leadership is typically able to veto a particular candidate, to nominate additional candidates, and to decide how many candidates should stand in any particular area – in fact, to take all key decisions on candidate selection. While it is quite common for the central party to determine how many candidates there should be in each constituency, the other powers have rarely been exercised. Local members have become accustomed to choosing candidates, and it is of course local activists who must do much of the gruelling legwork that helps to get any nominee elected. The local party, because of its knowledge of the constituency, may also have the necessary expertise to identify the candidates best equipped to win. But central organisations (including the party leader and general secretary, along with senior party figures and special advisers) are not always convinced that the local parties are the best judges. Since the late 1970s first Fianna Fáil and then Fine Gael and the other parties have sought more forcefully to impose some central control over local organisations.

Local parties may in practice often be effectively under the control of local deputies, whose personal supporters may occupy all key posts. This has sometimes meant that candidate selection has favoured the interests of particular local incumbents at the expense of the party in general. In Fine Gael in particular, many deputies were suspected in the past of engineering the selection of a weak running mate, or of no running mate at all, in order to protect their personal positions. In such cases, opportunities to win an extra seat were lost because the incumbent feared the risk to his or her own seat. The Fine Gael leadership intervened often in the 1980s to counteract this tendency, adding candidates to the list of those nominated (see O'Byrnes, 1986). Concern about the quality of deputies as legislators has also justified greater involvement by the party leadership, often informally and prior to the selection meeting. Fianna Fáil has changed its rules to weaken incumbents, and it has also ended the practice of nominations being made within the convention. Central organisations now seek to identify potential candidates well in advance, and work over a period to ensure that these are selected (Galligan, 2003).

These efforts do not always bear fruit. A determined but somewhat belated attempt by Fianna Fáil to replace a sitting but co-opted MEP by a TD with a proven record as a vote winner on its 2004 European Parliament election ticket was defeated at a well-attended selection convention, despite a postponement to allow a prolonged campaign on behalf of the TD by senior party figures (*Irish Times*, 1 March 2004). A similar fate befell the Labour leadership in 1994. Adding to the ticket candidates who were not selected initially may upset members and weaken their commitment to the ticket as a whole (Galligan, 2003).

In addition to candidates, members elect a number of other party officials. Branch members elect branch officials, as well as nominating delegates to constituency conventions and national conferences. A party's national executive committee also contains a number of people directly elected by the party conference. Although this committee is formally the decision-making body within the party between meetings of the party conference, in most parties it defers in practice to the party leader.

Selection of leaders

It is arguable that the choice of party leader is the most important decision facing any party. Elections are as much about *who* governs as about what is done *by* government, so that the party leader is a key figure in any party's campaign. In Fianna Fáil and Fine Gael, furthermore, the party leader is a potential Taoiseach, so that these parties, when they choose a leader, make a decision of major national significance.

While rank-and-file members tend to participate quite fully in the selection of local candidates, they often have no direct say in the choice of a national party leader. The selection of the parliamentary leader (who is effectively the party leader, even when there is some other formal post such as party president) in Fianna Fáil and Fine Gael is made solely by parliamentarians. Fianna Fáil restricts the vote to members of the Dáil on the basis that it is the Dáil that elects a Taoiseach; Fine Gael allows senators and members of the European Parliament a vote as well. An internal party report did suggest that all members should be involved in electing the Fine Gael party leader, but this was resisted by the party leadership. It was claimed that the exercise would be very costly, but undoubtedly there were also fears that the members would choose the 'wrong' person. In 2002 the suggestion was made again, this time by the annual conference. While the party deliberated on confirming this as accepted procedure, Enda Kenny was elected as leader under the old system. The party's branches subsequently rejected the more inclusive procedures.

The Labour Party adopted a much more open method of leadership selection in 1989, giving a vote to all party members (Marsh, 1993). However, it was a long time before the mechanism was used. The leader in 1989, Dick Spring, was never challenged under these rules; nor were they used for the election of Spring's successor Ruairí Quinn, because Spring resigned in 1997 before his second term was complete. However, when Quinn resigned in 2002 an election was held in which the membership as a whole could vote for both leader and deputy leader. This was preceded by a strict examination of who was eligible to vote – a clear illustration of the difficulty of defining members of party organisations. The election was fairly low key but campaigning was extensive and generally personal rather than through the mass media. About 90 per cent of eligible members voted and the experience may well make the method more attractive to other parties in future (Fitzgerald *et al.*, 2004). The Greens, as we might expect, have also adopted a very inclusive method of leader selection. For many years the party avoided having a single leader at all, but the exigencies of political competition eventually proved a stronger force and, at a selection convention that all members were eligible to attend, the party selected Trevor Sargent as its first ever leader.

Mary Harney was chosen by her parliamentary party to lead the Progressive Democrats in succession to Des O'Malley in 1993. Following new rules adopted by the party in February 2004, her successor will be chosen by an electoral college in which the parliamentary party (including any party members in the European Parliament) will have 40 per cent of the votes, the national executive and local councillors 30 per cent and rank and file members a further 30 per cent. Even where they have no formal role, rank-and-file members of any party may still have some indirect influence on who becomes leader. In the election of a new Fianna Fáil leader in 1992, for example, most deputies consulted their constituency members before the vote took place. Several local parties held meetings, following which clear messages were sent to local deputies. The voice of the ordinary party member was particularly evident in 1983, when the Fianna Fáil leader, Charles Haughey, in what became known as 'the night of the long phone calls', used his popularity amongst the party rank and file to put pressure on deputies on the eve of a challenge to his leadership.

When the decision on the party leadership is confined to parliamentarians, a single question seems to be uppermost in everyone's minds – who is most likely to boost party support in the next election? Most new leaders have been selected after a very muted campaign, and certainly not one that has put issues to the fore. As with candidate selection, it is the perception of a person's vote-winning ability that is probably decisive. It is possible that when the electorate is extended to all party members, who may have little to gain directly from election victories and may be more concerned with certain core values of the party, then the policy positions of potential leaders may become more important, although there was little sign of this in Labour's case.

In the smaller parties at least, then, there have been moves to make leadership selection more inclusive. Candidate selection is typically inclusive in any case, but in most parties this, too, has been opened up still further. This is not untypical of trends in other countries (Scarrow *et al.*, 2000). While in some parties, most obviously 'New' Labour in Britain, this greater inclusiveness was a means to dilute the role of activist members by mixing them in with more passive supporters, this is hardly the case in Irish parties, which have been driven more by the argument that members need to have a say in the party if they are to remain members. The opportunity for occasional participation is seen as providing an incentive which will attract and retain those that every party needs for its election campaigns.

Formation of party policy

While the ordinary member continues to have a real say in candidate selection and, in some parties, in leader selection, his or her voice may be no more than the faintest of whispers when it comes to deciding the policies on which candidates and their leaders fight elections. The formation of party policy in Ireland, as in most other democracies, presents some fascinating contrasts between theory and reality. In theory, as we have seen, the official policy of each of the main Irish parties is made at its annual or biennial conference involving a large number of party representatives, both local and national, as well as activists and ordinary members. In practice, this body is too large, too diffuse, and meets too rarely to make effective strategic decisions about party policy. A partial exception is the Labour national conference, which has in the past laid down the law on matters such as coalition – for example, binding the party leadership not to go into coalition without coming back to a special delegate conference for permission to do this. Sinn Féin's *ard-fheis* would perform the same role in the event of that party being invited to form a coalition.

For the most part, however, national conferences that fill large halls are far too cumbersome to generate effective party policy documents. This task normally falls to the party's national executive, or to an even smaller group. Small teams of people responsible to the party leader, for example, generally drew up party manifestos for the 1997 election. Although there was some consultation with members in some instances, no party engaged in any widespread formal participation in policy formulation (Garry and Mansergh, 1999). The 2002 election was no different.

When parties move into government, furthermore, policy making tends to become an even more centralised process. When only one party is in power, then the effective policy-making body of the party is the cabinet – it is as simple as that. A national executive might make some decision that conflicts with a cabinet decision, but it would have very little real control over the party leadership, and its decisions would have relatively little effect. In the popular mind, party policy would certainly be cabinet policy, not some policy propounded by the government party's national executive. A wise Irish voter who wants to discover Fianna Fáil's policy on third level education will be better advised to examine the speeches of the minister for education than the party's election manifesto.

Even when a party is in opposition, its parliamentary party designates a set of senior politicians to 'shadow' cabinet ministers in the Dáil and act as party spokespersons on the policy areas concerned. These people make the party's public statements on these policies, attack the government ministers concerned, and are the ones to whom the media turn for official party reaction. Members of this shadow cabinet develop policy expertise in the area for which they are responsible, and are in effect the main engines of policy development for their party, whatever the party rulebook might say.

Meetings of the parliamentary party, which take place weekly when the Dáil is in session, might on occasion force governments into a review of policy decisions (see pp. 225–6). These meetings certainly provide a forum at which views from the party at large may be articulated by members of the Oireachtas, but the role of this body is essentially reactive. It responds to policy; it does not make it.

Organisations and leaders: the balance sheet

Irish parties are often seen as falling outside the European mainstream, but in many respects they are not so different from their European counterparts. Many of the trends that we have identified in Ireland can be found elsewhere. Concerns about membership and financial difficulties characterise parties in many countries, as do moves to give members a direct say in selecting candidates and leaders. Election campaigns have also become more centralised elsewhere. All parties, whatever their origins, are coming to resemble one another in their central concern with fighting and winning legislative elections. This concern is very apparent in Irish parties, and goes some way to explain the increasing role of the party elite. The major role played by the parliamentary leadership in Ireland is also typical. Attempts to construct parties in which deputies are under the firm control of the party organisation have, for the most part, been unsuccessful. All this is not to say that modern Irish parties have no place for rank and file activity. Ordinary members do play a role, and this is not just confined to raising money; they can also exercise considerable influence on the choice of candidates who bear the party label at election time, a matter of considerable importance.

In an attempt to buck this trend, the Green Party in Ireland, like its counterparts elsewhere, has tried to construct a more democratic party organisation. There was initially no party leader, merely a 'co-ordinator' elected by its national executive. Although this changed with the election of a leader in 2001, other differences remain. Local groups elect 'facilitators'; delegates to higher bodies are expected normally to serve for a short, limited term to ensure rotation of office; and all members may attend any party meeting as observers. Decisions, according to the party's rules, should be reached by consensus wherever possible. Efforts are made to consult widely within the party before policy decisions are made. Yet before the party can really claim to be different, these procedures will have to be tested when it has a significant government presence. Sinn Féin too appears somewhat different at present, closer to old-style communist parties in the importance accorded to its membership. Activism has been valued more than membership, and membership is seen as important not least because it gives the party an opportunity to educate members in its values; it is perhaps less significant that, unlike the other parties, its leader, Gerry Adams, is not a member of the Dáil (though he is a Westminster MP and a member of the Northern Ireland Assembly). The forerunner of Democratic Left, Sinn Féin–The Workers' Party, had a somewhat similar character in its early years. It remains to be seen how far Sinn Féin will change as it grows, and whether it will enter into government with other parties, but if the experience of the European left in the twentieth century is anything to go by, it will in time come to resemble more closely the more established parties.

Conclusion

Elections in Ireland, as in all parliamentary democracies, are largely about parties. Parties nominate most of the candidates who stand in elections, and candidates with well-known party labels attract the overwhelming majority of votes. Parties dominate the campaign with their manifestos, their media events and their press conferences. Party leaders provide the personal focus of most media attention. And parties allow the relatively extensive participation of those who are interested in the selection of candidates. Yet parties get a bad press in Ireland, and the public is clearly sceptical about precisely whose interests are served by their activities.

Despite these reservations, there is no getting away from the fact that parties do organise and simplify much of the fundamental process of holding democratic elections. Without them, voters would have very little information about the choices on offer. They would have even less information about the link between the votes that they cast at an election and the political complexion of the government that was subsequently formed to run the affairs of the country. This is the basis of the argument that the vital role played by political parties in the essentially public processes of parliamentary democracy implies that parties need substantial resources, the bulk of which should be provided from the public purse. The public was never convinced of this argument, and most parties also argued against public funding, but recent scandals associated with secret contributions to politicians, potentially in exchange for political favours, have tilted that balance away from the latter view and towards public funding along with extensive regulation, and it is hard to see this being significantly reversed. Parties cost the taxpayer more than €12 million per annum, but in exchange there are now significant checks on the ability of wealthy people to influence them.

Increased public funding may have some negative effects on the internal life of Irish political parties. It may change the balance of power between the centre and the grassroots and downgrade the importance of the party membership. Irish parties do not have large memberships, but they do have enough members to give the larger parties a presence in most parts of the country. This provides a very important personal link between representatives in the Dáil and ordinary citizens. Party membership does, furthermore, allow more people to get involved in politics, and to participate more fully in the political process than those who merely vote at public elections. Moreover, parties still want members, and are making considerable efforts not simply to maintain but also to increase their membership levels. In some parties all members have also been given a significant and direct role in selecting candidates and leaders. Central control may be growing in some respects, perhaps assisted by the greater resources now available, but members are far from being superfluous, and it may be argued that greater funding could transform parties into organisations which can maintain much better links with their members. Parties certainly still need members, and they need to offer them something worthwhile if they are to attract and keep new ones.

The major parties have now been in existence for three-quarters of a century, and although they have undergone many changes in that period they show no signs of going away, whatever people may think of them. While public confidence in parties has declined, they remain as pivotal as ever in the political life of the country. Politics is still party politics, and those who want to be involved in politics must join parties. While independent candidates can sometimes be quite successful, and local party politicians can – as always, perhaps – build a support base that transcends their political labels, it is still parties who nominate most successful candidates, who structure electoral competition and who determine who governs and who opposes.

Notes

1 Figures for all parties up to 1999 are given in Murphy and Farrell (2002: Table 8.8). I have assumed these to include parliamentary press and research offices since these typically fall under the control of the general secretary and are essentially head office personnel.
2 To be registered a political party has to demonstrate that it has a formal structure and a number of supporters. This entitles it to nominate candidates at election time.
3 That is, who was either elected, or whose votes exceeded one quarter of a quota at some stage during the count.
4 No party spent up to its limit in 2002, but some parties, notably Fianna Fáil and Fine Gael, spent a larger share of what was permitted than others; see Standards in Public Office Commission (2003b).
5 Author's analysis. For more details on the ESS see http://www.europeansocial survey.org/

References and further reading

Collins, Stephen, 2003. 'Campaign strategies', in Michael Gallagher, Michael Marsh and Paul Mitchell (eds), *How Ireland Voted 2002*. London: Palgrave, pp. 21–36.
Council of Europe, 2001. *Financing of Political Parties*. Report of the Political Affairs Committee, May 4. Available http://assembly.coe.int/Documents/WorkingDocs/doc01/EDOC9077.htm [accessed 18 March 2004].
Dalton, Russell and Martin Wattenberg (eds), 2000. *Parties without Partisans*. Oxford: Oxford University Press.
Farrell, David M., 1994. 'Ireland: centralization, professionalization and competitive pressures', in R. S. Katz and Peter Mair (eds), *How Parties Organize*. London: Sage, pp. 216–41.

Farrell, David M. and Paul D. Webb, 2000. 'Political parties as campaign organisations', in Russell Dalton and Martin Wattenberg (eds), *Parties without Partisans*. Oxford: Oxford University Press, pp. 102–28.

Fitzgerald, Peter, Fiachra Kennedy and Pat Lyons, 2004. 'Results of a leadership election survey of party members: the 2002 Irish Labour Party leadership election', in Roger Scully, Paul Webb, David Broughton and Justin Fisher (eds), *British Elections and Parties Review*, Vol. 14, London: Frank Cass.

Gallagher, Michael, 1985. *Political Parties in the Republic of Ireland*. Manchester: Manchester University Press.

Gallagher, Michael, 1988. 'Ireland: the increasing role of the centre', in Michael Gallagher and Michael Marsh (eds), *Candidate Selection in Comparative Perspective: The Secret Garden of Politics*. London: Sage, pp. 119–44.

Gallagher, Michael and Michael Marsh, 2002. *Days of Blue Loyalty: The Politics of Membership of the Fine Gael Party*. Dublin: PSAI Press.

Galligan, Yvonne, 2003. 'Candidate selection', in Michael Gallagher, Michael Marsh and Paul Mitchell (eds), *How Ireland Voted 2002*. Basingstoke: Palgrave Macmillan, pp. 37–56.

Garry, John and Lucy Mansergh, 1999. 'Party manifestos', in Michael Marsh and Paul Mitchell (eds), *How Ireland Voted 1997*. Boulder, CO: Westview, pp. 82–106.

Hazan, Reuven, 2002. 'Candidate selection', in L. LeDuc, R. Niemi and P. Norris (eds), *Comparing Democracies 2: Elections and Voting in Comparative Perspective*. London: Sage, pp. 108–26.

Katz, R. S., 1996. 'Party organisations and finance', in L. LeDuc, R. Niemi and P. Norris (eds), *Comparing Democracies: Elections and Voting in Comparative Perspective*. London: Sage, pp. 107–33.

Katz, R. S. and Peter Mair, 1995. 'Changing models of party organisation and party democracy: the emergence of the cartel party', *Party Politics* 1: 5–28.

Kavanagh, Ray, 2001. *Spring, Summer and Fall: The Rise and Fall of the Irish Labour Party*. Dublin: Blackwater.

Mair, Peter, 1987. *The Changing Irish Party System: Organisation, Ideology and Electoral Competition*. London: Frances Pinter.

Mair, Peter and Michael Marsh, 2004. 'Political parties in electoral markets in postwar Ireland', in Peter Mair, Fritz Plasser and Wolfgang C. Müller (eds), *Political Parties and Electoral Change: Party Responses to Changing Electoral Markets*. London: Sage, pp. 234–63.

Marsh, Michael, 1993. 'Selecting party leaders in the Republic of Ireland', *European Journal of Political Research* 24:3: 295–316.

Marsh, Michael, 2003. 'Candidate centred and party wrapped: new evidence on electoral behaviour under STV', paper presented at the American Political Science Association Annual Meeting, Chicago, 28–31 August.

Marsh, Michael, 2004. 'None of your post-modern stuff around here: grassroots campaigning in the 2002 Irish general election', in Roger Scully, Paul Webb, David Broughton and Justin Fisher (eds), *British Elections and Parties Review*, Vol. 14. London: Frank Cass, pp. 247–69.

Marsh, Michael and Paul Mitchell (eds), 1999. *How Ireland Voted 1997*. Boulder, CO: Westview Press.

Mockler, Frank, 1994. 'Organisational change in Fianna Fáil and Fine Gael', *Irish Political Studies* 9: 165–72.

Murphy, Ronan and David Farrell, 2002. 'Party politics in Ireland: regularizing a volatile system', in Paul Webb, David M. Farrell and Ian Holliday (eds), *Political Parties in Advanced Industrial Democracies*. Oxford: Oxford University Press, pp. 217–47.

O'Byrnes, Stephen, 1986. *Hiding behind a Face: Fine Gael under FitzGerald*. Dublin: Gill and Macmillan.

Panebianco, A. 1988. *Political Parties: Organisation and Power*. Cambridge: Cambridge University Press.

Scarrow, Susan, 2000. 'Parties without members? Party organization in a changing electoral environment', in Russell Dalton and Martin Wattenberg (eds), *Parties without Partisans*. Oxford: Oxford University Press, pp. 79–101.

Scarrow, Susan, Paul Webb and David M. Farrell, 2000. 'From social integration to electoral contestation: the changing distribution of power within political parties', in Russell Dalton and Martin Wattenberg (eds), *Parties without Partisans*. Oxford: Oxford University Press, pp. 129–56.

Scully, Roger, Paul Webb, David Broughton and Justin Fisher (eds) 2004. *British Elections and Parties Review*, Vol. 14. London: Frank Cass.

Standards in Public Office Commission, 2003a. *Annual Report 2002*. Dublin: Standards in Public Office Commission; also available http://www.sipo.gov.ie/2826/ar02sipe.pdf [accessed 23 February 2004].

Standards in Public Office Commission, 2003b. *Review of Electoral Acts 1997 and 2001*. Dublin: Standards in Public Office Commission.

Venice Commission, 2001. *Guidelines on the Financing of Political Parties*. CDL-INF (2001) 8. Adopted at the 46th Plenary Session of the Venice Commission, 9–10 March. Available http://www.venice.coe.int/docs/2001/CDL-INF(2001) 008–e.html [accessed 19 March 2004].

Websites

www.sipo.gov.ie   Standards in Public Office Commission, which exists to monitor conformity to the legislation concerning parties.

www.coe.int (link: priority projects: democracy: activities: political parties)   Council of Europe political parties site.

www.idea.int   International Institute for Democracy and Electoral Assistance (IDEA).

See also the websites of the main parties on p. 159.

7 Voting behaviour

Michael Laver

People writing about Irish voting behaviour have often presented Irish politics as peculiar when set in a European context – a system of 'politics without social bases' (Whyte, 1974; Carty, 1981). Certainly, the differences between Fianna Fáil and Fine Gael, combined with the very modest long-term performance of the Labour Party, are not easy things for a specialist in Irish politics to explain even to the most sophisticated of European visitors (see Chapter 5). For the most part it is quite clear that Irish party politics has not been motivated, as it has in many other European counties, by a conflict between blue-collar and white-collar workers over the distribution of wealth. Neither has it been driven forward, as it has in many countries with a substantial Catholic population, by a conflict between pro-clerical Christian democracy and anti-clerical secular liberalism.

These general observations were combined by Richard Sinnott with the findings of earlier researchers into a comprehensive survey of the opinion poll evidence on the social patterning of Irish voting behaviour. He found that there was indeed some patterning, but that this is rather weak when seen in a wider European context (Sinnott, 1995: 181–8; see also the books in the *How Ireland Voted* series: Laver *et al.*, 1987; Gallagher and Sinnott, 1990; Gallagher and Laver, 1993; Marsh and Mitchell, 1999; Gallagher *et al.*, 2003). The main reason for this is the appeal of by far the most successful party in the state, Fianna Fáil, to voters from across a wide range of the social spectrum. Fine Gael and the Progressive Democrats are indeed somewhat more middle class in their support profiles than their main party rivals, but Fianna Fáil's populist appeal, combined with the resulting weakness of the Labour Party, are essentially what have led people to regard Irish party politics as a system without social bases. Sinnott did nonetheless find opinion poll evidence which indicated that things might be changing. Following a series of bitter referendum campaigns on divorce and abortion, he suggested that there may be signs of an emerging religious–secular cleavage in Irish voting behaviour (Sinnott, 1995: 193–5). Following the enormous transformation of Irish society that has resulted from a long trend of substantial migration from more rural to more urban areas, Sinnott's analyses of constituency variations in actual voting patterns also hinted at an emerging urban–rural divide that he felt merited further investigation (Sinnott, 1995: 114–44).

Useful though the opinion polls summarised by Sinnott and forming the basis of the received wisdom to date undoubtedly were, they were none-theless based on small and less-than-perfect samples of Irish voters, who were asked only a limited range of questions on behalf of the media organisa-tions that commissioned them. This situation changed radically in 2002, with the carrying out of the first Irish National Election Study (INES). This was a full-scale academic post-election survey, equivalent to those that have been conducted over a long period in most other Western democracies. During the course of the INES, a large sample of randomly selected voters were asked a comprehensive range of questions about their voting habits. Thanks to the INES, therefore, we now know far more than we did before about what makes Irish voters tick. This chapter thus goes beyond most traditional work on Irish voting behaviour and is largely based on the new insights offered to us by the INES. In what follows, we will explore three types of question:

- Why do Irish voters vote at all?
- Given the single transferable vote (STV) electoral system that requires Irish voters to rank individual candidates rather than political parties, do those people who do vote think more in terms of candidates than of political parties?
- To the extent that Irish voters do think in terms of parties, what condi-tions their choice of party?

Voting turnout

The question of why voters bother to turn out to vote at all has stimulated a lively debate within political science. This arises from the fact that it is extremely unlikely that the result of any major election will be decided by a single vote. Whether electors realise this or not, it is simple common sense that each individual vote, taken on its own, is almost certain not to make a difference to the eventual outcome of the election. Thus if voting is seen as an 'instrumental' act, undertaken to make some difference to the world, and if the act of voting is seen as costly in some sense, then going out and casting a vote does not seem a rational thing to do. Yet in the real world a lot of people do in fact vote. Does this mean that they wildly over-estimate the likely impact of their votes, or are they simply irrational? This question is often referred to as the 'paradox of turnout' or the 'calculus of voting' problem within the professional literature (for a good and accessible review of this see Hinich and Munger, 1997).

An alternative view of the act of voting is that this is not something that people instrumentally engage in so as to achieve some measurable effect, but is rather an act of self-expression that is valued in and for itself. On this account the benefit of voting comes simply from voting itself, from the value that citizens attach to using the ballot box to express their own personal views about politics (for a recent and lively review of this point of view, see Schuessler, 2002). If voting helps to fulfil voters' desires to express themselves politically, and there is of course no reason to regard people who think like this as either stupid or irrational, then the problem of why people turn out to vote becomes one of understanding which factors cause some people to get more, and others to get less, personal satisfaction from the act of voting.

For whatever reason, the percentage of the electorate turning out to vote in Ireland has been declining steadily over recent decades, a trend that Ireland shares with many other west European countries. Figure 7.1 shows levels of general election turnout in Ireland between the 1973 and 2002 Dáil elections and highlights an inexorable downward trend. This decline in turnout has certainly been viewed within the Irish political establishment as a serious problem and various remedies have been explored – including extending voting hours, holding elections on different days of the week, slightly relaxing provisions for postal voting, and, with a view to assisting functionally illiterate voters, even including pictures of the candidates on the ballot papers.

We get at least something of an idea about what is affecting levels of voter turnout by looking at the very obvious variations of turnout rates between different types of constituency. Lyons and Sinnott (2003) remark on the striking contrast between urban and rural constituencies in the 2002 election (continuing a long trend found in previous elections), with turnout lowest in Dublin South-Central at 51 per cent, and highest in Cork North-West at 72 per cent. Paradoxically, although actually getting to the polling station is often physically easier in urban than in rural areas, there is a striking tendency in Ireland for urban areas, and particularly Dublin, to have lower

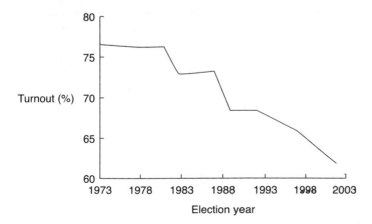

Figure 7.1 Turnout in Irish elections, 1973–2002

turnouts. Of course many of the 'urban' areas into which so many Irish voters have moved in recent years are in reality part of a huge and anonymous suburban sprawl around greater Dublin, which contrasts strikingly with the deeply rooted social structure of the traditional rural areas that, as we shall see, have proved much more resistant to political change.

Moving beyond patterns in constituency level election results to possible individual motivations for non-voting, the Irish National Election Study (INES) interviewed a sample of 2,663 people drawn from the electoral register – not just those who actually voted in the 2002 election. This means that we now have comprehensive information about both voters and non-voters in Ireland. The first thing to note in this regard is that the election study considerably overstates the level of turnout in the 2002 election. Of those who agreed to be interviewed, 81 per cent said they voted in the 2002 election,[1] as opposed to the 62 per cent of the electorate that we know actually did vote in reality. Overstating turnout is a general trend in election studies, suggesting either that there is a 'selection bias' in these studies that arises because people who do not vote in elections are also much less likely to co-operate with academic surveys, and/or that survey respondents interviewed a few weeks after the election have, shall we say, a somewhat rosy view of what they did in the past. Either way, we might reasonably infer that the pattern of systematically over-reported turnout in election studies suggest that non-voters do not seem particularly proud of their behaviour.

Nonetheless, we can find information in the INES on a substantial number of declared non-voters in the 2002 general election. Indeed, we can go further, since there were in fact three occasions in 2001 and 2002 on which Irish voters were asked to turn out and vote. In addition to the general election, there were referendums on the Nice Treaty in 2001 and on abortion in 2002 (the second Nice referendum, in October 2002, took place after the fieldwork for the survey had been completed). If we add up the number of times that voters claim to have turned out on these three days, this number can be anything from zero to three, giving a more complete picture of which types of people are really committed to voting and which are not.

Figure 7.2 shows the impact of gender, age and educational attainment on the propensity of people to vote in modern Ireland. While we must bear in mind the impact of selective recall on absolute levels of reported turnout, differences in turnout rates between different social groups are nonetheless very instructive.

First, from the top panel of Figure 7.2, we see that gender does not have a huge impact on turnout rates. Nonetheless, concentrating on hard-core non-voters, we do see that about 14 per cent of male electors claimed they did not vote at all despite the three opportunities offered them during 2001 and 2002, as opposed to about 8 per cent of women. Women were, in contrast, slightly more likely to have voted twice or all three times, but

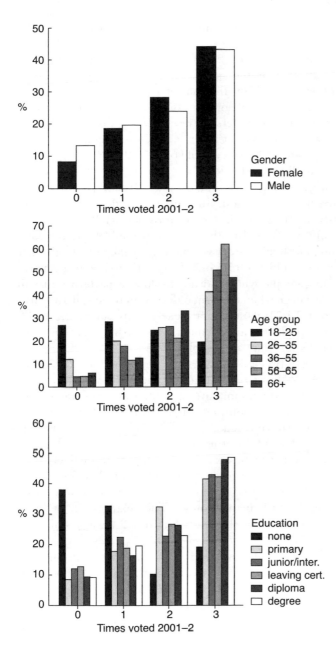

Figure 7.2 Demographic factors affecting voting turnout

differences in turnout rates between Irish men and women do not seem to be large.

Second, the middle panel of Figure 7.2 shows us that turnout during 2001 and 2002 was greatly affected by the age of the voter – a finding echoing that in most of the other research on the matter (see, for example, Lyons and Sinnott, 2003). The impact of age on turnout rates really is very striking, with about 28 per cent of voters in the 18–25 age group not voting at all in this period, as opposed to about 5 per cent of those aged between 36 and 65.[2] In contrast, only about 20 per cent of voters in the 18–25 age group claimed to have voted in all three elections, as opposed to well over 60 per cent of those aged between 56 and 65. Young people in Ireland, as elsewhere, do seem very much less likely to turn out and vote than older electors. With only one election study at our disposal, it is not possible to tell whether this is a 'lifecycle' or a 'cohort' effect. In other words, it could be that young people tend not to vote, but tend to start voting as they move through their lifecycles and get inexorably older. Or it could be that there is now a generation, or cohort, of young people who tend not to vote, a pattern that will continue to manifest itself even when they get older. Nonetheless, if low turnout is seen as a 'problem' in Ireland, as it clearly is by some, the INES makes it clear that it is a problem caused much more by high levels of non-voting among younger electors than among older ones.

Third, and again echoing previous work (Lyons and Sinnott, 2003), the bottom panel of Figure 7.2 shows us that educational attainment, and in particular a very low level of educational attainment, is also associated with non-voting. Electors who did not complete their primary education were very much more likely not to have voted in any of the three elections or referendums of 2001 and 2002. Beyond this, the patterns are not strong, although those with some post-second level education were distinctly more likely than others to claim to have voted in all three elections. Overall, therefore, hardcore non-voting tends to be associated with being male, having low levels of education and particularly with being young. The relationship between income levels and non-voting is not shown in Figure 7.2 because this is in fact very weak.

Moving beyond basic social and demographic characteristics, it might be that the likelihood of voting is affected by electors' attitudes to the political system, in particular by whether people feel that their votes make a difference. We recall that people who believe their vote should make a difference, but who feel that it does not, may not consider it worth the effort of voting. The INES asked two questions directly relevant to this. People were asked to agree or disagree with the statement 'so many people vote, my vote does not make a difference to who is in government'. A second question referred to making a difference 'to which candidate is elected'. Strikingly, 69 per cent of respondents (in relation to government) and 72 per cent (in relation to candidates) either disagreed or disagreed strongly with these statements. Most Irish voters do not do the same sums as political scientists; they do feel their votes make a difference to the eventual result. Answers to these two questions can be combined into a single index measuring the extent to which people feel their vote makes a difference and respondents can then be categorised into those who feel that their vote makes a big difference, almost no difference, or something in between.[3]

The top panel of Figure 7.3 shows rates of voting turnout among those who felt their votes had a low, medium or high impact, respectively, on the outcome of the election. As we might expect, rates of voting were much higher among those who felt that their vote did have an impact on the election result, and much lower among those who felt it did not. Rates of hard-core non-voting (zero votes in the three elections) were almost six times higher among those who felt their vote had a low impact, than among those who felt it had a high impact. We must of course be alert in this context to a problem of cause and effect. Demographic factors cannot possibly be affected by voting patterns – voting a lot cannot, alas, make you younger or more highly educated. However, voting patterns may either affect, or be affected by, attitudes to voting. Thus it might be that people who think their vote has an impact are more inclined to vote for this reason, or the direction of causality might work the other way. It might be that those who vote a lot justify this to themselves by believing that their vote has an impact. This would be an example of the well-known psychological effect of people reducing the 'cognitive dissonance' between apparently contra-dictory aspects of their social attitudes and behaviour. People might be uncomfortable with the idea that they vote a lot despite the fact that they also believe voting makes no difference, and adjust their beliefs about the impact of their vote accordingly.

A second reason for not voting might be that, whatever difference people believe their vote to make to the result of an Irish election, they believe that Irish election results make little difference to their everyday lives. The INES asked a battery of questions on this matter.[4] These questions can be combined into an index measuring what we might think of as respondents' views on the impact Irish politics has on their world.[5] The middle panel of Figure 7.3 shows that, once more, the effects were in the expected direction. Those who think that Irish politics does not make much of a difference to what happens were much less likely to vote than those who think it does make a difference. At the other end of the scale, high levels of voting were more likely among those who felt that Irish politics does make a difference.

Finally, it may be that some people feel that they just don't know about, or understand, politics, and are less likely to vote as a result. The INES asked two questions on this matter. People were asked to agree or disagree with the following statements: 'Sometimes politics and government seem so com-plicated that a person like me cannot really understand what is going on'; and: 'I think I am better informed about politics and government than most people'. Again we can combine responses to these two questions into a scale capturing each respondent's sense of 'understanding' of politics.[6] The bottom

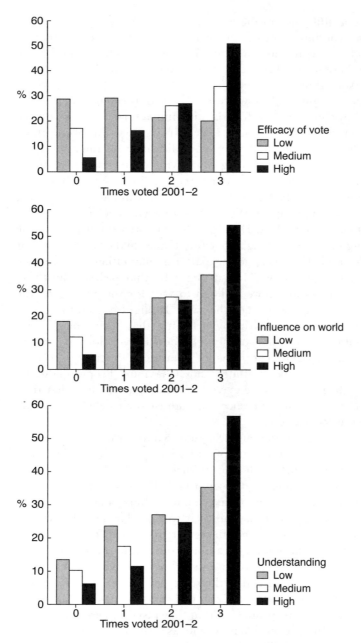

Figure 7.3 Attitudes to the political system affecting voting turnout

panel of Figure 7.3 shows the effects on turnout rates of these feelings about Irish politics. The effects are more modest than those we have just discussed. Nonetheless, they are very much in the expected directions. People who feel that they don't understand politics were more likely to be hard-core non-voters. People who feel they do understand politics are much more likely to be regular voters.

So far, we have looked at all of these effects of turnout one at a time, but obviously all effects are likely to be interrelated. Young or poorly educated people could feel that they can't understand politics well, for example, so it is important to get some idea of the impact of each factor on turnout levels, holding other factors constant. This can be achieved by using a particular technique of statistical analysis to predict whether or not respondents will be hard-core non-voters (never voting in 2001 and 2002), and whether or not they will be regular voters (voting three times) on the basis of the variables reported in Figures 7.2 and 7.3, holding all other variables, as well as household income, constant.[7] The results are not reported in detail here, but can be summarised easily.

Trying to explain hard-core non-voting, the significant effects come from gender, education, age, and how much impact the respondent thinks that his or her vote actually has. Men are almost twice as likely as women to be hard-core non-voters. People who did not complete primary education are over seven times more likely than others to be hard-core non-voters, as are people in the 18–25 age group. People in the 26–35 age group are between two and three times more likely to be hard-core non-voters. Finally, there is a strong and systematic link between feeling that the vote makes a difference to the result and the rate of voting. Turning to the syndrome of regular voting at elections, gender appears to have no effect on this, while the effects of age and education remain very strong. Poorly educated and younger people are very, very much less likely to be regular voters. The strongest predictors of regular voting are having a post-secondary education, being older and feeling that your vote makes a difference.

Candidates versus parties

It is common to describe Irish politics as being highly 'personalised', a product in part of a localised political culture, possibly reinforced by the STV electoral system (see Chapters 4 and 9). STV does indeed require voters to rank people, not political parties, when voting. The huge amount of constituency work done by most TDs, and even by aspiring candidates, combined with vigorously personalistic local campaigning and publicity, also mean that voters are strongly appealed to by individual candidates. On the other hand, of course, Irish governments are formed and run by political parties – on their own or in coalition with others. The business of the Dáil is run very much by the party whips. At the level of the national news media, the election campaign is fought out between political parties, and the key issue is often presented in terms of which party leader will become Taoiseach. The question that all of this poses, therefore, concerns whether Irish voters are primarily supporting a candidate or a party when they allocate their first preference vote.

The INES asked whether 'the party or the candidate' was 'more important in deciding how you cast your first preference vote in the general election', which might seem to settle the matter once and for all. Things are a little more complicated, however, since the larger Irish parties typically run more than one candidate in each constituency. Voters supporting such parties are thus forced to choose between different candidates of the same party when allocating a first preference – in this sense their choice of first preference is inevitably a choice between candidates rather than parties. Their answer to a simple 'party or candidate' question is thus ambiguous since those who said that they were choosing a candidate could 'really' be party voters allocating first preference votes between different candidates of the same first-choice party. A second INES question comes closer to what we want to know, asking: 'If this candidate had been running for any of the other parties would you still have given a first preference vote to him/her?' A respondent who answers 'yes' to this question is more unambiguously choosing a candidate rather than a party.

Table 7.1 reports and cross-tabulates answers to these two questions. Looking first along the bottom row we see that 62 per cent of respondents said they were choosing a candidate, while 38 per cent said they were choosing a party – this on the face of things makes Ireland appear a highly candidate-focused system. Looking next down the right-hand column, however, we get a slightly different picture. About 46 per cent said they would support the same candidate running for a different party – these certainly

Table 7.1 Party and candidate in deciding a preference vote, 2002

Would give first preference to same candidate if running for different party?	*Party or candidate most important in deciding first preference vote?*		
	Party	*Candidate*	*Total*
Yes	6	40	46
No	27	11	37
Depends on party	6	11	17
Total	38	62	100

Source: Author's calculations from INES.

Note
All figures are percentages. The valid number of cases was 2,072.

do seem to be people who put candidate over party. About 37 per cent said they would not, while 17 per cent said that this would depend on which other party was involved.

Looking inside Table 7.1 we first see a peculiar group of people: the 6 per cent of apparently bewildered respondents who said that party is more important than candidate when deciding how to cast their first preference vote, but who also say that they would definitely give their first preference vote to the same candidate if he or she ran for a different party.

Apart from this, we see that about 40 per cent of voters can be regarded as really committed supporters of candidates rather than parties. The candidate is more important for them than the party, and they would support the same candidate if he or she ran for any other party. Of the remaining 22 per cent of voters who said that candidates were more important than parties when allocating their first preference votes, about half said they would not support the same candidate running for any other party – these people seem much more like party than candidate supporters, choosing between different candidates of the party they want to support. About half said this would depend upon the party concerned – these voters clearly have parties in mind when allocating their first preference vote, even if the candidate is the most important factor.

The really hard-core party supporters make up about 27 per cent of respondents – these are the people who choose parties rather than candidates, and would not support the same candidate running for any other party. Another 6 per cent or so of respondents are party voters, but might support the same candidate running for another party – depending on what party that was.

In short, on the matter of whether voters choose candidates or parties, the INES allows us to carve up the electorate in 2002 as follows. About 40 per cent were dyed-in-the-wool supporters of some particular candidate, and would have followed that candidate across party lines. About 37 per cent of voters were party supporters, giving a first preference to a candidate only if he or she runs for that party. Another 17 per cent or so of voters take both party and candidate into account, being willing to consider supporting the same candidate running for a different party, but conditioning this on which party is involved. The remaining 6 per cent show contradictory views of the kind we often encounter in surveys. Crudely, about 40 per cent seem to be candidate voters, about 40 per cent party voters, with the remaining 20 per cent balancing the two motivations. Interestingly, age seems to have a systematic impact on voting motivation, with older people more likely to be committed party voters. About 30 per cent of 18–25 year-olds said they would *not* support the same candidate running for another party, as opposed to 50 per cent of those aged over 65.

Determinants of party support

As we saw in the introduction to this chapter, the Irish party system has been characterised as having no 'social bases' – a product largely of the cross-class appeal of the largest party, Fianna Fáil, and the long-term weakness of the Labour Party. The INES allows us to expand considerably on these conclusions, asking more people more detailed questions on their voting habits than ever before. This new information allows for the first time to begin at the beginning, with the political socialisation of voters when they were children in the family home, before going on to explore the impact of a range of different social characteristics on Irish voting behaviour.

Party choice and parental voting history

Perhaps the most primitive source of party choice is inherited from a voter's parents. Political scientists tend to see predispositions to vote for particular parties in terms of what they call 'party identification'. This is regarded as a kind of psychological 'closeness' to a given party, built up as the result of a process of political socialisation that begins in early childhood in the family home. Ever since the civil war, discussions of Irish politics have been replete with discussions of 'Fianna Fáil families' or even 'dynasties', 'Fine Gael families' and the like. Thus voters coming from 'Fianna Fáil families' are seen as being more likely to identify with and subsequently vote for Fianna Fáil, for example, and it is clearly an important matter to explore systematically the link between party choice and parental voting history.

Now that we finally have access to a full-scale election study in Ireland, anecdotal evidence about the impact of family political background on the voting choices of children in later life can be checked more systematically. INES respondents were asked 'when you were growing up', which party did your father and mother 'usually vote for'. From the answers to these questions it is easy to identify, at least for the two main Irish parties, respondents who recalled having two Fianna Fáil (or Fine Gael) parents, one or none. Respondents were also asked which political party, if any, they now felt 'close to'. In contrast to voters in many other countries, only about 25 per cent of respondents said that they felt 'close to' some party. The data confirm strongly that, for these people, feeling close to a party was strongly related to the choice of first preference party. Of those feeling close to Fianna Fáil, for example, 90 per cent voted for Fianna Fáil, while 83 per cent of those who felt close to Fine Gael voted for Fine Gael.

Table 7.2 explores, for Fianna Fáil voters, the relationship between family political background, 'closeness to' a party, and voting behaviour. The top panel confirms strongly that, when both parents supported Fianna Fáil, 86 per cent of respondents felt close to Fianna Fáil. In contrast, when neither parent supported Fianna Fáil, only 30 per cent of respondents felt close to Fianna Fáil. The top panel of Table 7.3 shows an even more striking pattern

Table 7.2 Attitudes towards Fianna Fáil and other parties, by number of parents supporting Fianna Fáil, 2002

	No. of Fianna Fáil parents		
	None	*1*	*2*
Party 'closest to'			
Fianna Fáil	30	54	86
Fine Gael	37	21	6
Other	33	25	8
Total	100	100	100
No. of cases	299	103	277
First preference party vote			
Fianna Fáil	32	47	64
Fine Gael	26	17	12
Other	42	36	25
Total	100	100	100
No. of cases	1,212	362	756

Source: Author's calculations from INES.

Note
All figures are percentages, except 'No. of cases'.

for Fine Gael. When both parents supported Fine Gael, 75 per cent of respondents felt close to Fine Gael; when neither parent supported Fine Gael, a mere 8 per cent felt close to Fine Gael. For both of the main parties, therefore, and spectacularly so for Fine Gael, feelings of closeness to the party show a strong tendency to be inherited from parents.

The bottom panels of Tables 7.2 and 7.3 show a strong relationship between the actual voting behaviour of voters and that of their parents. Respondents were twice as likely to support Fianna Fáil (64 per cent as opposed to 32 per cent), if both rather than neither of their parents supported Fianna Fáil. Even more strikingly, respondents were *four times* more likely to support Fine Gael (54 per cent as opposed to 13 per cent) if both rather than neither of their parents supported the party. Having a parent who supported the party seems to be much more of a prerequisite for a Fine Gael vote than having a Fianna Fáil parent is a prerequisite for supporting Fianna Fáil.

The data used to produce Tables 7.2 and 7.3 help us unravel the sequence of events leading from a person's family political background in Ireland to actual voting behaviour. We already know that a feeling of 'closeness to' a party is a very good predictor of voting choice, and from the top panels of Tables 7.2 and 7.3 that family political history is a very good predictor of feelings of closeness to a party. To take the analysis further: 80 per cent of those saying they felt close to Fianna Fáil voted for Fianna Fáil, even when

Table 7.3 Attitudes towards Fine Gael and other parties, by number of parents supporting Fine Gael, 2002

	No. of Fine Gael parents		
	None	*1*	*2*
Party 'closest to'			
Fianna Fáil	68	32	14
Fine Gael	8	55	75
Other	24	13	11
Total	100	100	100
No. of cases	520	60	96
First preference party vote			
Fianna Fáil	50	34	21
Fine Gael	13	32	54
Other	37	34	25
Total	100	100	100
No. of cases	1,821	211	299

Source: Author's calculations from INES.

Note
All figures are percentages, except 'No. of cases'.

neither parent had voted Fianna Fáil. When both parents had voted for Fianna Fáil, 88 per cent of those close to Fianna Fáil then voted for this party. The corresponding figures for Fine Gael show that 74 per cent of those close to Fine Gael voted for Fine Gael even when no parent had voted for Fine Gael, while 87 per cent did so when both parents had voted for Fine Gael.

There appear to be two things going on here. First, feeling 'close to' a party is such a strong predictor of voting for it, regardless of anything else, that many Irish respondents may simply be describing their voting behaviour when they talk of being 'close to' a party. Whatever its source, this sense of general party attachment, while felt only by about 25 per cent of INES respondents, is a potent predictor of voting behaviour. The political complexion of the parental home is, furthermore, a potent predictor of party attachment – and therefore of subsequent voting behaviour. Even among those who do feel close to some political party, the likelihood of voting for that party increases when both parents also supported the same party.

As always, we have to be alert to problems of cause and effect. The patterns in Tables 7.2 and 7.3 do not imply that having parents who supported some party is the *reason* why children tend to support the same party. Equally plausible is that there is rather little social mobility in the world, and that people who find themselves in the same social situations, as parents and children tend to do, tend to vote in the same way. Nonetheless, the Irish political folklore that voting runs in families is indeed borne out in a very systematic way by the results of the 2002 election study.

Party choice and social background

Irish voting behaviour is affected by much more than family background. Turning to the social demographics of party support in Ireland, for example, strong patterns do emerge. This is not surprising; notwithstanding the 'politics without social bases' tag that has been applied to divisions between Irish parties, small but significant differences between the parties have for long been recognised. This may be seen in the first instance in those characteristics, such as occupation, that are closely related to social class. One influential way of measuring 'class' is that proposed by Goldthorpe (1987). This categorises people as either non-manual (salaried, routine non-manual or petit bourgeois), manual (skilled or semi-skilled) or farmers. It was possible to generate these class groups from the INES and to relate class membership to voting behaviour. Provisional results indicate a slight manual (working-class) bias in Fianna Fáil support and a non-manual (middle-class) bias in the support base of Labour, the Progressive Democrats and the Greens. Perhaps surprisingly, Fine Gael did not appear to do disproportionately well among the non-manual groups (Garry, 2003). In terms of household income, the poorest supporters on average were those of Fianna Fáil, followed by those of Sinn Féin, Fine Gael and Labour, in that order. The party with the richest supporters on average was the Greens. Exactly the same pattern could be seen with educational attainment. The least well-educated supporters, on average, were those of Fianna Fáil, and the parties were rank ordered, in terms of the average educational attainment of their supporters, in exactly the same way as for income.

In addition, age distinguishes supporters of different groups of parties quite sharply. The INES suggests that the party with the oldest supporters in 2002 was Fine Gael; on average, Fine Gael supporters were born in mid-1954 and were thus 48 at the time of the election. Progressive Democrat supporters were on average a mere six months younger; Fianna Fáil supporters were about a year younger. This is in stark contrast with supporters of Sinn Féin (who on average were born in 1966) and the Greens (1967). The 'youthful' image of these two parties, as portrayed in media coverage of the election campaign, was thus justified. Green Party supporters were on average a full 13 years younger than supporters of Fine Gael. Labour fell right between these two poles, with Labour supporters born on average in 1960 and thus being about 42 at the time of the election.

There were some gender differences in party support, though these were not large. Standing out as the most 'male' party was Sinn Féin, 58 per cent of whose supporters were men, while the most 'female' party was the Greens, only 45 per cent of whose supporters were men. There was relatively little gender patterning of support for the other parties.

One background factor that is very strongly related to party choice concerns where voters lived. Election results are published at the level of Dáil constituencies, and one benefit of the 2002 election study is that the residence of voters was much more precisely classified. This can be defined according to whether the voter lived in open countryside, in a village or small town (of less than 10,000 people), in a larger town (of over 10,000 people), in one of the main Irish cities other than Dublin, in Dublin City (including Dun Laoghaire), or in the increasingly sprawling commuter belt of County Dublin – which in many ways represents the culmination of the process of 'urbanisation' that we have been seeing in Ireland in recent years. Table 7.4 breaks down party supporters in these terms and shows some striking patterns. Reading the columns of this table from left to right, we are in effect passing from 'traditional' to 'modern' Ireland, from people living in open countryside to those for the most part living in the new suburbs of the Dublin commuter belt. The level of Fianna Fáil support declines steadily as we move in this direction, while the level of Fine Gael support is three times higher among people living in open countryside than among those living in Greater Dublin. Combining support for the two traditional 'civil war' parties, Fianna Fáil and Fine Gael, this drops from 76 per cent of all people living in open countryside to a mere 44 per cent in County Dublin. Indeed in County Dublin, the combined total of the civil war parties was less than the combined 47 per cent won by the 'radical' parties challenging them – Labour, Greens, Sinn Féin and 'others' (the latter in the Dublin area almost exclusively comprising small parties of the radical left – Socialist Party, Workers' Party and Socialist Workers' Party). These more radical parties garnered negligible support among people living in open countryside. Table 7.4 thus paints a clear picture of what many might see as the growing rural–urban divide in Irish politics. The implications for the future arise because patterns of migration are having the effect that rural populations are declining inexorably, with urban, and especially suburban, populations growing at an explosive rate. On the evidence of Table 7.4, this pattern of social change does seem to be a potential engine of change in Irish party politics.

Party choice and social behaviour

Voting behaviour is also often associated with various forms of social behaviour that reflect how voters see their lives. Five key aspects of this were measured by the INES: church attendance, membership of the Gaelic Athletic Association (GAA), trade union membership, whether people worked in the public or private sector and whether they were self-employed. None of the conventional 'economic' behavioural traits – trade union membership, self-employment or public sector employment – was strongly

Table 7.4 First preference party, by residence of voter, 2002

	All voters	Residence of voter					
		Open country	Small towns and villages	Large towns	Other cities	Dublin City	Co. Dublin
Fianna Fáil	44	46	46	49	44	41	33
Fine Gael	20	30	20	13	20	11	11
Labour	11	6	11	16	9	15	13
Progressive Democrats	3	2	2	3	9	5	6
Greens	5	2	5	4	3	8	16
Sinn Féin	6	4	6	4	3	9	9
Independent	9	10	9	10	13	5	4
Other	2	1	0	2	0	6	9
Total	100	100	100	100	100	100	100
No. of cases	2,202	859	386	274	128	165	450

Source: Author's calculations from INES.

Note
All figures are percentages, except 'No. of cases'.

related to voting behaviour. However, the patterns in relation to church attendance and GAA membership were much more striking.

Table 7.5 shows levels of party support broken down by the frequency with which survey respondents claimed to go to church. The patterns are as strong as, and very similar to, those deriving from where people live. The level of Fianna Fáil support declines steadily as the voter's rate of church attendance goes down. The same pattern holds for Fine Gael. Thus the combined level of Fianna Fáil and Fine Gael support is about 75 per cent among those who go to church one a week or more, and goes down to 43 per cent among those who never go to church; the latter total is less than the combined level of support for Labour, Greens, Sinn Féin and others.

We can summarise and distil a lot of the information described above by constructing two stereotypical Irish voters. One is a 'traditional' Irish voter. He or she lives in open countryside, a village or a small town, goes to church several times or more a month and belongs to the GAA. The other is a 'modern' Irish voter, living in the Greater Dublin area, going to church once a year or less, and not belonging to the GAA. About 9 per cent of the respondents in the INES fit the 'traditional' stereotype; about 6 per cent fit the 'modern' stereotype. Table 7.6 compares the voting behaviour of these two types of voter and is highly instructive. Among 'traditional' Irish voters, 80 per cent support one of the two 'civil war' parties. After this they are most likely to support some local independent candidate. The combined level of support for the more radical parties is a mere 8 per cent among

Table 7.5 First preference party, by religious observance, 2002

	Religious observance					
	2+ times/ week	Once/ week	1–3 times/ month	Several times/year	Once/year or less	Never
Fianna Fáil	55	49	48	41	39	32
Fine Gael	21	26	23	12	15	11
Labour	7	7	9	9	17	15
Progressive Democrats	4	3	3	6	3	1
Greens	2	2	6	7	7	9
Sinn Féin	3	4	2	9	8	15
Independent	7	9	8	12	7	9
Other	1	0	2	4	5	9
Total	100	100	100	100	100	100
No. of cases	164	997	312	288	242	77

Source: Author's calculations from INES.

Note
All figures are percentages, except 'No. of cases'.

'traditional' voters, who are thus ten times more likely to support a civil war party than a more radical alternative. Among 'modern' Irish voters, the combined support total of the civil war parties slumps to 38 per cent, while the combined support total of more radical alternatives rises to 51 per cent. Thus the ratio of support for 'traditional' versus radical parties among traditional voters is 80:8; for 'modern' voters it is 38:51. This is a very strong pattern indeed.

Table 7.6 also suggests that, of the traditional Irish parties, Fianna Fáil is in very much better shape than Fine Gael. Support levels for Fianna Fáil decline, from traditional to modern voters, from 49 per cent to 31 per cent. Fianna Fáil remains the most popular party, by a wide margin, among 'modern' voters. Support for Fine Gael declines from 31 among traditional voters to less than a quarter of this, 7 per cent, among 'modern' voters. Fine Gael slumps from being the second most popular party among 'traditional' voters to the fifth most popular party among 'modern' voters, behind Labour, Sinn Féin and the Greens. Faced with the changing social face of modern Irish society – including, among many other things, migration from rural to urban areas and steadily declining church attendance – Fianna Fáil support appears to be far more resistant to social change than that of its traditional civil war enemy, Fine Gael.

Thus far, when we have considered various social factors that might affect voting behaviour, we have considered these one at a time. But many of factors are of course interrelated – rural people tend to be older and to go to church more, for example, while people with lower levels of education also tend to have a lower income. What we are really interested in are the

Table 7.6 First preference party, by voter stereotype, 2002

	Stereotype	
	'Traditional'	'Modern'
Fianna Fáil	49	31
Fine Gael	31	7
Labour	2	16
Progressive Democrats	1	4
Greens	1	10
Sinn Féin	4	12
Independent	12	7
Other	0	13
Total	100	100
No. of cases	209	128

Source: Author's calculations from INES.

Note
All figures are percentages, except 'No. of cases'.

independent effects of each of these factors, holding all others constant; this gives us a better idea of what might actually be affecting the vote, rather than just being associated with it. We can get some sense of this by looking at the simultaneous impact of all of the important effects we have so far considered, controlling statistically for the independent effect of each.[8] The results of doing this are summarised in Table 7.7, which indicates with '+' or '−' signs the direction and relative size of the significant independent effects of each factor. A '0' indicates factors that had no independent effect, controlling for the effect of all others.

Table 7.7 Social determinants of voter choice, holding other factors constant, 2002

	Fianna Fáil	Fine Gael	Labour, Green or Sinn Féin
Party parents	+++	+++	n.a.
Female gender	0	+	0
Older age	0	+	−−
Higher income	0	+	−
Less education	++	0	−−
Rural location	0	+++	−−−
More churchgoing	+	0	−−
GAA membership	0	0	−−

Source: Author's calculations from INES.

Note
n.a. = not available.

Very striking for both traditional parties is the fact that parental party support has a strong independent impact on the voting behaviour of children, even controlling for a wide range of social background factors. This suggests that parental party support does indeed affect children's voting, rather than that children vote like their parents because they tend to find themselves in the same social situation as their parents.

For Fianna Fáil, the 'dynasty' effect swamps most others, though it remains true that Fianna Fáil voters tend to be less well-educated than others, all other factors held constant, and that they tend to be more assiduous churchgoers. However, older age and rural location do not seem to have an independent effect on Fianna Fáil voting, once the impact of having Fianna Fáil parents and being a regular churchgoer are controlled for. GAA membership turns out not to have an independent effect on voting for either Fianna Fáil or Fine Gael; the patterns we observe in GAA membership seem to arise because both GAA membership and Fianna Fáil voting are related to the same social background characteristics.

The situation is rather different for Fine Gael. Once again, having Fine Gael parents is a factor with a very important independent impact on Fine Gael voting, but rural location is another very important independent factor (this reflects the fact that, as we have seen, Fine Gael has been much less successful in drumming up support in rapidly growing urban areas than has Fianna Fáil). Fine Gael voters are also significantly older and better off, holding other factors constant, and, controlling for other factors, they tend to be more likely to be women.

This support profile is not encouraging for a Fine Gael party trying to re-launch itself after a major general election setback, though it does give an insight into the party's apparently inexorable decline. Fine Gael support in 2002 was grounded in traditional Fine Gael families, in rural areas, and among older people. All of these factors are in long-term decline. It is clearly essential to its future survival for Fine Gael to reach out beyond its traditional base, as it did under the leadership of Garret FitzGerald in 1982 – the last time the party went into government on the basis of a general election result. Fianna Fáil can draw some comfort from the fact that its support is less strongly linked to the age structure of the population, or to traditional patterns of rural habitation. Its support is linked to religious observance, which is declining; but apart from this Fianna Fáil's fate seems less likely to be affected by the changing structure of Irish society.

All of this contrasts strongly with the independent effect of the various social background factors on support for Labour, the Greens or Sinn Féin (while it would have been nice to be able to treat each of these parties independently, the number of survey respondents supporting these parties means that they are taken together to give enough cases for confident statistical analysis). Apart from gender, which has no great impact, all of the background factors retain an independent impact on voting for the more radical parties. Their supporters tend strongly to be younger, to have spent longer in education, to be much more urban, to go to church much less, and not to be members of the GAA, and all of these factors have an independent impact on voting. Supporters of the more radical parties also seem to be somewhat less well-off than others. While we must be very careful about problems of cause and effect, these results do seem to imply a longer-term potential for change in Irish politics. Irish society is becoming more urban, people are going to church less, more people are spending longer in full-time education and the age structure of the Irish voting population is changing as a huge age bulge of younger people reaches voting age. All of this certainly offers a huge opportunity for the parties currently attracting younger and more urban voters, and a huge challenge for those not doing so.

Of course, in all of this we should not lose sight of one of the most important conclusions of the first part of this chapter, that young people are among the most recalcitrant non-voters. If non-voting by younger electors continues as a trend, this will retard the potential changes in the Irish party system that we have just discussed. Whatever parties young people might prefer, no change will happen if they do not turn out and vote for these. Indeed it seems likely, putting together the main conclusions of this chapter so far, that there would have been much more change in Irish party politics than we have already seen if young voters had been turning out at the same rate as their parents.

Choosing among candidates

As we have seen above, Irish electors have both candidates and parties on their minds when deciding how to cast their votes in a Dáil election. Considering first how voters might choose between the candidates on offer, the INES asked respondents to rate their first choice candidates on two key criteria: how good they would be at working for the local area; and how good they would be at contributing to national debate. What 'good' or 'very good' means in this context is possibly quite different for each respondent. Nonetheless, it is instructive to compare the same respondent's evaluation of the same candidate in terms of these two different criteria. Making this comparison of respondents' evaluations of both the national and the local contributions made by their first choice candidates, about 40 per cent rated these contributions equally, about 36 per cent rated the local contribution as better than the national, while about 24 per cent rated the national contribution as better than the local. There is thus a tendency, though not a massive one, for voters to rate their first choice candidates more in terms of their local than their national contributions. As long suspected by TDs who concentrate heavily on constituency service, Irish voters do seem more likely to value this than to value contributions to national political debate – though we cannot be confident that it is this that determines how they cast their votes.

Policy positions of voters

Thus far, despite the mythology of elections in modern democracies, which sees the voter as a policy-driven decision maker, the discussion in this chapter has ignored something very important – the role of policy issues in shaping electoral choice. We have got quite far in understanding party choice in Ireland without this, but the fact remains that real elections, on the surface at least, are fought by the political parties on the basis of their policies. Politicians don't say to voters, out loud anyway, vote for us 'because you are old', 'because you are young', 'because you are well-educated', or 'because you go to church a lot'. What they do say is vote for us 'because of all the policies we will enact if you give us the chance to do so'.

There are of course many, many policy issues in which people are interested, or in which they might conceivably be interested if stimulated. But common threads run though many of these. Thus if we consider economic policy we can think of public spending and, within this, of spending on many different types of public service. We can also think of taxation and, within this, of many different types of taxation. We can think of public ownership of the means of production, once more taking many different forms. The list goes on and on. But all of these matters are interrelated, both in theory and in the minds of many voters. If the government wants to spend more on some activity, other things being equal, it needs to cut spending elsewhere, to raise more in taxes, to borrow more or to tolerate higher levels of inflation. This is not a treatise on the public finances, but the bottom line is that there are common threads running through economic policy. In the same way, when people think about 'social' policy on matters such as abortion, divorce or homosexuality, particular sets of beliefs tend to mean that common threads run through this thinking. People associated with various religious denominations, for example, tend to disapprove of all three of these things at the same time, and to have a structure of moral values that reconciles these views. What all of this means is that, despite the huge variety of potential policy issues, we can think of a limited set of 'policy dimensions' that give structure to these. Such policy dimensions are a convenient way of summarising what in the real world is an inevitably more complex set of policy preferences within the electorate.

The INES explored voters' positions on a number of these policy dimensions, and we begin with one very simple one, considered by political scientists over the years to summarise a lot of how people feel about politics. Dating from the immediate aftermath of the French Revolution, when radical deputies gathered together on the left-hand side of the National Assembly, and conservative deputies gathered together on the right, it has been common to summarise policy positions in terms of a single 'left–right' dimension putting socio-economic radicalism on the left, and socio-economic conservatism on the right. INES respondents were asked to place themselves at one of eleven points on a left–right dimension, ranging from 0 on the far left, to 10 on the far right. The dead centre was thus represented by the position 5. The mean self-placements of INES respondents on this dimension, broken down by the party to which they gave their first preference vote, are shown in the first column of Table 7.8.

The bottom row of the first column of figures in Table 7.8 shows that the average Irish voter places him or herself at a position, 7.0, well to the right of centre on this dimension. There were, furthermore, smallish but nonetheless significant differences in these self-placements between supporters of different parties. The most right-wing supporters of all (7.4) were those of Fianna Fáil. Somewhat to the left of this and very much at the Irish centre-right average were three other sets of supporters, those of Fine Gael, of the Progressive Democrats and of independent candidates. Well to the left of this average, and the most left-wing set of party supporters, were those of the Greens. Slightly to the right of the Greens, we find supporters of 'other' (mostly left-wing) parties and Labour. Also to the left of the Irish average, we find Sinn Féin supporters. Ignoring others and independents, therefore, Irish party supporters were on average ranged from left to right in this classical left–right dimension in the order: Greens, Labour, Sinn Féin, Progressive Democrats, Fine Gael, Fianna Fáil (although the differences between the Progressive Democrats and Fine Gael, and between Labour and Sinn Féin, were too small to be statistically significant).

The remaining columns in Table 7.8 report the self-placements of party supporters on various issue dimensions defined in the same way as the left–right dimension we have already discussed. The first of these – contrasting 'God definitely does not exist' with 'God definitely does exist' is of course more a dimension describing general religiosity than any specific issue area, but as we shall see it ties together other issue dimensions. The bottom row shows that Irish voters in general are great believers in God, but this column of figures shows that there are distinct differences between groups of party supporters. The most God-fearing voters are Fine Gael and Fianna Fáil supporters, statistically indistinguishable from one another. The least (though still quite) God-fearing voters support the Greens and Sinn Féin. In between these can be found supporters of the Progressive Democrats and Labour. As might be expected in a predominantly Christian country, voter attitudes on abortion and homosexuality generally follow beliefs in God. Most opposed to abortion are supporters of Fine Gael, closely followed by Fianna Fáil and the Progressive Democrats. Leaning more distinctly in favour of abortion are supporters of Labour, Sinn Féin and the Greens, statistically indistinguishable from one another. Irish voters are slightly more liberal on homosexuality, but arrayed in more or less the same order. Fine Gael and Fianna Fáil supporters are the most conservative, and supporters of the Greens distinctively the most liberal. Sinn Féin and Labour supporters are also at the liberal end of the party range on homosexuality, with Progressive Democrat supporters also leaning in a more liberal direction on this issue.

Table 7.8 Mean respondent self-placement on various attitude scales, 2002

First preference party	Left–right self-placement	God does not/ does exist	Abortion: ban/make available	Homosexuality: never/always justified	Public/ private enterprise best	Insist on/ abandon united Ireland	Protect environment/ economic growth	EU: bad/good thing
Fianna Fáil	7.4 *0.09*	8.7 *0.07*	4.6 *0.12*	5.1 *0.10*	5.0 *0.09*	4.3 *0.10*	3.8 *0.08*	8.0 *0.07*
Fine Gael	7.0 *0.13*	8.8 *0.10*	4.2 *0.17*	4.9 *0.16*	5.5 *0.14*	4.6 *0.15*	3.7 *0.12*	7.8 *0.11*
Labour	6.1 *0.23*	7.9 *0.18*	5.4 *0.22*	5.8 *0.29*	4.4 *0.17*	4.4 *0.19*	3.5 *0.14*	7.7 *0.10*
Progressive Democrats	6.9 *0.27*	8.0 *0.30*	4.6 *0.36*	5.6 *0.39*	5.0 *0.31*	5.0 *0.31*	3.3 *0.21*	8.2 *0.23*
Green	5.7 *0.29*	7.0 *0.28*	5.7 *0.32*	6.5 *0.25*	4.6 *0.21*	4.6 *0.25*	2.7 *0.21*	7.3 *0.20*
Sinn Féin	6.3 *0.35*	7.0 *0.28*	5.5 *0.32*	5.8 *0.27*	4.9 *0.26*	2.9 *0.27*	3.3 *0.22*	7.3 *0.25*
Total	7.0 *0.06*	8.4 *0.05*	4.7 *0.08*	5.3 *0.07*	5.0 *0.06*	4.4 *0.06*	3.6 *0.05*	7.8 *0.05*

Source: Author's calculations from INES.

Note

All attitude scales run from 0 to 10; the low scoring option is the first mentioned in the column heading. Standard errors are reported in italics under estimated scale positions for each party. (Statistically, the standard errors measure the uncertainty associated with the estimated policy positions, with the 'actual' position expected to be within a range of two standard errors either side of the mean.)

Moving from God to Mammon, and the matter of whether public or private enterprises 'are the best way to provide the services people need', the bottom row of the table shows that the average Irish voters sits on the fence at the dead centre (5.0) of the policy spectrum. Rather to the right of this in favouring private enterprise are supporters of Fine Gael. Fianna Fáil and Progressive Democrat supporters are indistinguishable from each other and next in line, occupying the dead centre position. The most left-wing on economic policy are Labour supporters, followed by the Greens, with Sinn Féin supporters, despite their party's official claims to be a left-wing alternative, closer to the Progressive Democrats than to the Greens.

Policy on Northern Ireland is of course in many ways the founding issue for Sinn Féin, and Table 7.8 shows that Sinn Féin supporters do indeed have a very distinctively 'pro-united Ireland' policy stance. Quite a long way away from them on this dimension we find supporters of Fianna Fáil, closely followed by those of Labour and the Greens, with Progressive Democrat supporters the least likely to insist on promoting a united Ireland.

The environment provides the most distinctive public policy profile for the Greens, and Irish voters in general are inclined to say that they support measures to protect the environment, even at the expense of economic growth. Of the major party supporters, those of the Greens are indeed the most pro-environment, with Fianna Fáil supporters the least, though at the same time still at the pro-environment end of the spectrum. Apart from the Greens, however, there are not huge differences between the other parties.

Finally we move to the EU, and we see that Irish voters believe almost as firmly in the EU as they do in God. Differences between party supporters are, however, minor, with Progressive Democrat and Fianna Fáil supporters marginally most favourable to the EU, and Greens and Sinn Féin supporters, reflecting their parties' policy stances on the Nice referendum campaigns, marginally the least favourable.

So there are some modest policy differences between supporters of the various Irish parties, the largest being the pro-united Ireland position of Sinn Féin supporters and the pro-environment and gay rights positions of Green Party supporters. In general, Fine Gael supporters are the most conservative on specific issues, followed by those of Fianna Fáil. In general, supporters of Labour, Sinn Féin and the Greens are the most liberal, with Sinn Féin supporters tending towards the centre on the economy.

But does any of this make a difference to actual voting behaviour? The easy way to check this is to see whether adding information about voters' issue positions increases our ability to predict how they vote. This can be done by adding respondent positions on the seven specific issue positions in Table 7.8 to the set of socio-economic background characteristics whose independent impact was reported in Table 7.7 and considering the independent impact of all background characteristics and issue positions, taken together. There is no need for a new table to report the results of doing this, because the important finding is that knowing the issue positions of voters adds almost nothing to our ability to predict how they voted. For Fianna Fáil voters, of the seven specific issue dimensions discussed, only the EU policy dimension has an independent impact, with those liking the EU somewhat more likely to support Fianna Fáil. For Fine Gael voters, only the debate between public and private provision of services had an independent impact, with Fine Gael support somewhat more likely among voters favouring private provision. Issues had more independent impact for Labour/Green/Sinn Féin supporters, with support for these parties being more likely among those who liked the EU less, who favoured public provision of services, and who favoured a united Ireland, the latter no doubt reflecting Sinn Féin's distinctive contribution to this pool of voters.[9]

Overall, what we can conclude from this, regardless of the rhetoric of election campaigns, is that the various pools of party supporters are distinguished from each other much more by their socio-economic background characteristics, and especially their age, urban/rural location and parental partisanship, than by distinctive positions on prominent socio-economic issues. Supporters of different parties do tend to have somewhat different issue positions, but these have little independent effect on voting once the effect of socio-economic background characteristics is controlled for.

Conclusion

The findings about the behaviour of Irish voters reported in this chapter reveal intriguing paradoxes for Irish democracy. One of the main reasons we think of Ireland as a democracy, after all, is because Irish citizens are given the chance to choose their governments when they vote at Dáil elections. That choice is rationalised and simplified by political parties, who put competing policy programmes before the public during election campaigns, and offer rival potential governments. After the election results have been declared, furthermore, it is the leaders of political parties who bargain over the formation of a government. One of these party leaders will become Taoiseach and occupy *the* central role in the Irish political system

Notwithstanding all of this, we have seen that many Irish voters, when they cast their ballots at election time, are expressing preferences between rival candidates rather than between rival parties – about 40 per cent of voters, indeed, say that they would support the same candidate even if this person were to belong to a rival party. Despite all of the ballyhoo of an election campaign, furthermore, with the publication of rival party manifestos and the intense discussion of the issues of the day, it seems to be the case in Ireland, as elsewhere, that it is voters' social and demographic backgrounds, rather than their detailed policy preferences, that have the biggest impact on party choice. Indeed one of the best predictors of how people will vote today does appear to be how their parents voted in the past. Citizens in any democracy, of course, are free to choose how to vote using whatever criteria they see fit. It is striking, however, notwithstanding some of the grander principles of democratic theory, that many Irish citizens do not seem to be making up their minds at the time of a general election on the basis of a carefully balanced choice between the rival policy positions put before them.

While we will need to wait and see how things will develop over time, there are quite a few straws in the wind of the Irish National Election Study to suggest that Irish party politics might be on the brink of major change. Irish society has been transformed radically in recent decades – becoming younger, more urban, less religious – and as we have just seen there do seem to be major differences in voting behaviour between the 'old' and the 'new' Ireland. The two traditional major Irish parties – Fianna Fáil and Fine Gael – remain almost as popular as ever among the voters of the 'old' Ireland. But, among voters of the 'new' Ireland, they have lost a lot of ground to parties such as the Greens, Sinn Féin and Labour. Fianna Fáil's resilience even among this group of voters is also rather striking, however, and on the evidence from 2002 it is Fine Gael that has most cause to be seriously worried.

The only reason we have not already seen much more change in Irish party politics is that these citizens of the 'new Ireland' are also much less likely to turn out and vote at all. It is just possible that these voters will turn to Fianna Fáil or Fine Gael for comfort in their old age. But it is quite possible that, as these demographic and social changes work their way inexorably through the electorate, the face of Irish party politics will indeed change in a very striking way.

Notes

1 This and all subsequent findings reported from the INES are the result of the author's own calculations using the INES dataset.

2 This analysis is confined to those who would have been old enough to vote on all three occasions.

3 The two INES scales were added and the resulting scale inverted, so that high values reflected a high perceived impact of the vote. Scale values 1–3 were coded 'low', 4–10 'medium' and 11–13 'high'.

4 People were asked to agree or disagree with the following statements: 'In today's world, an Irish government can't really influence what happens in this country.' 'It doesn't really matter which political party is in power, in the end things go on much the same.' 'The ordinary person has no influence on politics.'

5 Responses to the three questions were added and the resulting scale inverted so that high scores reflected high perceived influence on the world. Scores 1–7 were coded as 'low' perceived influence on the world, 8–12 as 'medium' and 13–19 as 'high'.

6 The two INES scales were added after the first had been inverted so that high values reflected a high perceived understanding of politics. Scale values 1–5 were coded 'low', 6–8 'medium' and 9–13 'high'.

7 A binary logistic regression is a standard statistical technique that is used when what is being explained, the dependent variable, can take one of only two values – such as turning out to vote, or not, or voting for some particular party, or not. All

of the findings reported in the next paragraph are the independent effects of the variables discussed, holding constant the effects of all other variables.

8 This was achieved by using binary logistic regressions to predict 'FF voter', 'FG voter' and 'Labour, Green or SF voter', coded as binary variables, on the basis of the social background variables as coded in Tables 7.2–7.6, plus gender, year of birth, educational attainment and household income.

9 The binary logistic regressions on which Table 7.7 is based were augmented by the addition of seven of the eight new variables (excluding general left–right self-placement). Adding the seven issue dimensions reduced the role of church attendance to insignificance in predicting Fianna Fáil voting, but raised GAA membership to significance, while the effects of all other social background characteristics were the same. Apart from the other effects mentioned here, the effects of all social background characteristics were the same when the seven issue dimensions were added to the model predicting Fine Gael voting, and this was the case too in the model predicting Labour/Green/SF voting.

References and further reading

Carty, R. K., 1981. *Party and Parish Pump: Electoral Politics in Ireland*. Waterloo, Ontario: Wilfred Laurier University Press.

Gallagher, Michael and Michael Laver (eds), 1993. *How Ireland Voted 1992*. Dublin: Folens and Limerick: PSAI Press.

Gallagher, Michael and Richard Sinnott (eds), 1990. *How Ireland Voted 1989*. Galway: Centre for the Study of Irish Elections and PSAI Press.

Gallagher, Michael, Michael Marsh and Paul Mitchell (eds), 2003. *How Ireland Voted 2002*. Basingstoke: Palgrave Macmillan.

Garry, J., 2003. 'The impact of social characteristics and ideology on vote choice in the Republic of Ireland', paper presented at the American Political Science Association Annual Meeting, Chicago, 28–31 August.

Goldthorpe, J., 1987. *Social Mobility and Class Structure in Modern Britain*. Oxford: Clarendon Press.

Hinich, Melvin and Michael Munger, 1997. *Analytical Politics*. Cambridge: Cambridge University Press.

Laver, Michael, Peter Mair and Richard Sinnott (eds), 1987. *How Ireland Voted: The Irish General Election 1987*. Dublin: Poolbeg Press.

Lyons, Pat and Richard Sinnott, 2003. 'Voter turnout in 2003 and beyond', in Michael Gallagher, Michael Marsh and Paul Mitchell (eds), *How Ireland Voted 2002*. Basingstoke: Palgrave Macmillan, pp. 143–58.

Marsh, Michael and Paul Mitchell (eds), 1999. *How Ireland Voted 1997*. Boulder, CO: Westview Press.

Schuessler, Alexander A., 2002. *A Logic of Expressive Choice*. Princeton, NJ: Princeton University Press.

Sinnott, Richard, 1995. *Irish Voters Decide: Voting Behaviour in Elections and Referendums since 1918*. Manchester: Manchester University Press.

Whyte, John H., 1974. 'Ireland: politics without social bases', in Richard Rose (ed.), *Electoral Behavior: A Comparative Handbook*. New York: Free Press, pp. 619–51.

Website

www.tcd.ie/Political_science/elections/elections.html   Michael Marsh's Irish election data archive.

8 Parliament

Michael Gallagher

The Irish constitution, as we saw in Chapter 3, provides for a parliamentary system of government. Ireland's parliament, the Oireachtas, is bicameral: the lower and directly elected house, the Dáil, currently consists of 166 members (see Appendix 2c) elected from 42 constituencies, while the upper house, the indirectly elected Seanad, has 60 members. The power of the Seanad is very limited, and we shall concentrate on the Dáil in this chapter.

Classical liberal democratic theory ascribes a key role to parliament. The people elect a parliament, and this elects a government, makes laws and decides policies; the government then carries out these decisions of parliament and remains constantly accountable to it. This, in fact, is what enables democratic states to claim that they are democratic. Set against this theory, many people have found practice rather disappointing right across Europe, because it appears that once a government gets into office it can go its own way largely unchecked by parliament. And, even given these generally low expectations of how much control any parliament can really exercise over a government, together with the notorious difficulty of measuring the power of a parliament, it has frequently been argued that the Dáil is exceptionally weak. In the 1970s Ward described it as 'supine', in the 1980s Dinan adjudged it 'a woefully inadequate institution', and in the 1990s Chubb saw it as 'a puny parliament peopled by members who have a modest view of their functions and a poor capacity to carry them out' (Ward, 1974: 241; Dinan 1986: 71; Chubb, 1992: 189). In this chapter we shall look at what parliament is supposed to do and ask how well it does it.

Arend Lijphart (1999: 2) identifies two diametrically opposite models of democracy – the majoritarian (or Westminster) model and the consensus model – and when it comes to relations between parliament and government, and indeed in other ways too, Ireland displays features of both models, as we shall see during the course of the chapter. The Westminster model is characterised by, among other things, single-party and bare majority cabinets, cabinet dominance over parliament, a two-party system, a plurality electoral system, unitary and centralised government, unicameralism or unbalanced bicameralism, and the absence of a written constitution that seriously checks government freedom of action (Lijphart, 1999: 10–21). In contrast, among the characteristics of the consensus model are government by grand coalition, a genuine separation of powers between government and parliament, a multi-party system, a proportional representation electoral system, federal or decentralised government, strong bicameralism and a written constitution plus judicial review that imposes real constraints on government behaviour (Lijphart, 1999: 34–41). Given the major impact of the British style of government on the Irish system at independence, it is no surprise that Ireland has some features of the archetypal Westminster system, such as bare majority cabinets, no effective separation of power between government and parliament, unbalanced bicameralism and unitary and centralised government. Yet, at the same time, other aspects of the Irish political system are quite different: Ireland has a multi-party system (see Chapter 5), proportional representation (see Chapter 4) and a judicially interpreted written constitution (see Chapter 3). As a result, Irish practice does not conform fully to either a majoritarian or a consensus model.

The profile of TDs (members of the Dáil) is similar to that in many west European parliaments. In the 29th Dáil, which was elected in 2002, the average TD was aged 49, with three-quarters of TDs in their forties or fifties (details of TDs' backgrounds are based on Gallagher, 2003a: 113–15). Nearly half of all TDs have a professional occupation, with school-teachers the most common category; the great majority of TDs are in practice full-time politicians. Around half of Dáil members have a university degree. TDs have very strong local roots; nearly all live in their constituency, most were born and raised there, and around three-quarters were members of local government before being elected to the Dáil. Women are markedly under-represented (see Chapter 10).

Parties and parliament

Before we discuss the relationship between government and parliament in Ireland we should make the point that viewing the two as distinct bodies that vie with each other for supremacy would be quite unreal. Government and parliament are 'fused'. The government sits in parliament – in practice virtually all members of government are also TDs, as discussed in Chapter 12 – as opposed to being a body external to it. The government could be seen, as suggested by the nineteenth-century writer Walter Bagehot, as a committee of parliament, elected by it and acting in its name and with its authority. From this perspective, it is more realistic to see parliament as wielding power *through* the government that it has elected than to see it as seeking to *check* a government that has come into being independently of it.

Parliament, like every other aspect of modern political life, is dominated by political parties (Bowler *et al.*, 1999). When Dáil deputies vote on issues, they do so as members of a party, not as 166 atomised individuals. All around Europe, deputies follow the party line in votes in parliament and, if anything, parliamentary party cohesion is even higher in Ireland than the European average. It is extremely rare for deputies not to vote with the party; the norm is that every TD votes in accordance with the party line on every issue. There are powerful incentives to stay in line (Bowler *et al.*, 1999: 10–11; Heidar and Koole, 2000: 256). TDs voting against the party whip, or even abstaining, can expect to find themselves summarily expelled from the parliamentary party, with the prospect of remaining as independents until and unless the parliamentary party agrees to readmit them. In addition, TDs know that rebellion will probably harm their chances of promotion within the party.

However, TDs' obedience to the party line is not just a matter of fear of draconian punishments if they stray. The rules of a parliamentary party, after all, are made by its members, who choose voluntarily to bind themselves by such tight discipline. They do this because they believe it is in their and their party's interests. Deputies maintain discipline because they are reluctant to appear to be siding with the opposition, and because the party line is in any case likely to be broadly acceptable to them since they have their say on it at meetings of the parliamentary party. Their instincts are always to remain part of the party bloc, out of a sense of loyalty and common purpose. Moreover, the tough penalties imposed on defectors – provided these are rigidly enforced – make life easier in some ways. They make TDs less vulnerable to pressure from outside the party; TDs cannot be picked off, one by one, by pressure groups or local interests, because everyone knows that any threats such bodies can make against a TD for not doing their bidding pale into insignificance against the punishment the party will impose for displeasing it.

Viewed in this light, to consider parliament and government as two separate bodies competing with each other is to ignore the reality of party domination of parliament and government. Any effective increase in the role or power of 'parliament' *vis-à-vis* government means, in effect, an increase in the role or power of the opposition, not of parliament as a collective body. The role of government backbenchers, willingly accepted, is to sustain the government rather than to act as independent scrutineers of it; government backbenchers do not seek additional means of holding their own ministers to account. The ongoing battle of government versus opposition is paramount and tangible; the notion of a contest for power between government and parliament bears little relation to political reality.

Turning to a closer examination of what parliament does, the constitution assigns two main functions to the Houses of the Oireachtas. These are the appointment of the Taoiseach and the government (Articles 13 and 28) and law making, or more broadly policy making (Articles 15–27). The constitution also declares (Article 28.4.1) that 'The Government shall be responsible to Dáil Éireann'. This gives us three dimensions on which to assess the performance of the Dáil: the appointment of governments, policy making and scrutiny of government behaviour.

Appointment and dismissal of governments

The formal position, as laid out in Article 13.1 of the constitution, is that the Dáil nominates the Taoiseach and approves the composition of the government, whereupon the President appoints them. The Dáil can also dismiss a Taoiseach and a government, by passing a vote of no confidence (Article 28.10). In Westminster-model countries, the role of parliaments in appointing governments is negligible, because in practice governments are chosen at elections, and the vote of parliament after the election merely puts the seal on what the voters have decided. In consensus-model countries, in contrast, government formation can be a more complicated and time-consuming process; coalition government is the norm, and it may take weeks of negotiation to produce one (see Gallagher *et al.*, 2001, ch. 12). Indeed, in some such countries there might be frequent changes of government between elections.

Until the 1980s, government formation in Ireland was usually seen as a variant of Westminster practice, with coalitions and minority governments occurring only rarely. Certainly, there were elections that conformed very well to the model. For example, at the 1977 election Fianna Fáil won a majority of the votes and 84 of the 148 seats, and when the new Dáil met, the Fianna Fáil leader, Jack Lynch, was duly elected as Taoiseach on the block vote of the Fianna Fáil TDs. But a closer look at the record shows that single-party majority government was not as common as was sometimes assumed prior to the 1980s, while since 1981 it has disappeared (Mitchell, 2000). Over the whole period of the state, single-party majority governments have been in office for less than half the time. If we consider the period from 1948 to 2002, only four of the 17 governments were single-party majority ones, and these governments held office for only about 16 of those 54 years, during which period majority coalition government was more common (see Table 8.1). No election since 1977 has produced a single-party majority government. While majority government is the norm, minority governments have been in office for more than a third of the time (Mitchell, 2001).

There are three ways in which government composition might be settled: by an election at which a single party or a pre-agreed coalition wins a majority of seats; by political parties which, after an unclear election outcome, put together a majority coalition; or by the Dáil itself, which elects a government whose own strength alone does not suffice for a majority. In the first two cases, the Dáil's role could be seen as nominal, in that it is merely ratifying either a verdict of the people or a deal made among parties. The growing infrequency of single-party government means that elections are less likely to be the sole battleground that determines government composition: in the post-1948 period, only five elections have directly produced a government. On another seven occasions governments have not been chosen directly by the electorate but have resulted from post-election agree-

Table 8.1 Number and duration of governments, 1923–2002

	1923–2002			1948–2002		
	No. of governments	*Days in office*	*% of total days in office*	*No. of governments*	*Days in office*	*% of total days in office*
1-party majority	8	12,198	42.4	4	6,026	30.4
1-party minority	9	6,232	21.7	4	3,488	17.6
Coalition majority	6	7,041	24.5	6	7,041	35.5
Coalition minority	3	3,269	11.4	3	3,269	16.5
Majority governments	14	19,239	66.9	10	13,067	65.9
Minority governments	12	9,501	33.1	7	6,757	34.1
Total	26	28,740	100.0	17	19,824	100.0

Source: Details of governments from Appendix 3c.

Note
Governments are defined as lasting until either a change of partisan composition or an election. The three governments holding exactly 50 per cent of Dáil seats are classified as majority if the Ceann Comhairle (Speaker) was drawn from opposition ranks, as in 1965 and 1989, or minority when the Ceann Comhairle was a government TD (1937).

ments among parties (see Table 8.2). This leaves six occasions when the role of the Dáil has been decisive. In four of these cases, the Dáil elected minority Fianna Fáil governments; the other two occurred in 1981, when a minority Fine Gael–Labour coalition emerged, and in 1997, when a minority Fianna Fáil–Progressive Democrats coalition government was formed.

The role of the Dáil was central after some of the elections of the 1980s and 1990s. After the 1981 election, uncertainty as to who would form the next government persisted right up to the point when the vote was taken in

Table 8.2 Origins of governments, 1948–2002

Government composition settled by	*No. of cases*	*Date of cases*
Election: single party or pre-declared coalition wins majority of seats	5	1957, 1965, 1969, 1973, 1977
Parties: parties controlling a majority of seats put together post-election majority coalition	7	1948, 1954, Nov. 1982, 1989, 1992, 1994, 2002
Parliament: Dáil elects government that controls only a minority of seats	6	1951, 1961, 1981, Feb. 1982, 1987, 1997

the Dáil. Even though Fine Gael and Labour had agreed to try to form a coalition administration, these two parties had only 80 of the 166 seats and thus needed the backing of independent TDs to secure a Dáil majority. After the February 1982 election, it was Fianna Fáil that needed support from the Workers' Party and independent TDs to enable it to form a minority government (Farrell, 1987a: 17). In 1987, it seemed for a while after the election that no potential government would secure the Dáil's approval. When the Dáil met it was known that 82 of the 166 TDs would be voting for Charles Haughey as Taoiseach and 82 would be opposing him, with independent Tony Gregory uncommitted. The suspense continued until Gregory declared that he would abstain on the crucial vote, thus enabling Haughey to be elected Taoiseach on the casting vote of the Ceann Comhairle (Speaker) (Farrell, 1987b: 144). In 1989, for the first time ever, the Dáil was unable to elect a Taoiseach at its first post-election meeting. It took a further two weeks and two meetings of the Dáil before Fianna Fáil and the PDs agreed to form a government that controlled exactly half of the Dáil seats. Government formation after the 1992 election was an even more protracted process (Farrell, 1993). Finally, in 1997 neither of the competing coalitions commanded majority support, and both sought the support of independent and minor party TDs; the Fianna Fáil–Progressive Democrat combination was able to secure the backing of three of these TDs, enough to ensure its election by the Dáil (Mitchell, 1999a).

When we look at the Dáil's role in dismissing governments, a similar picture emerges: compliance neither with the purest version of the Westminster model nor with the consensus model. It is not the case that the Dáil regularly ousts governments; in fact, it has dismissed a government on only two occasions. The first was in November 1982, when the minority Fianna Fáil government was beaten by 82 votes to 80 on a confidence motion, precipitating the resignation of the government and a general election. Even this could be explained away as an aberration caused by the recent death of one Fianna Fáil TD and the absence through illness of another. The second was in November 1992, when the PDs left the government and joined the opposition benches, whereupon a motion of no confidence in the Fianna Fáil minority government was passed by 88 votes to 77 (Girvin, 1993: 12). At first sight, then, the record might look like that of an archetypal Westminster system, where the support of parliament can generally be taken for granted by the government.

However, there have been eight other occasions when the Dáil has, in effect, terminated the life of a government, which has chosen to resign rather than continue in a situation where defeat on a confidence motion seemed imminent. This happened in August 1927, 1938 and 1944, when the minority governments of the day were in a weak position and preferred to call a general election at a time of their own choosing rather than wait for the Dáil to pull the plug. Similarly, prior to calling the 1951 election the first inter-party government had been losing support from some of its own backbenchers in the wake of the traumatic 'Mother and Child' affair. Six years later the same fate befell the second inter-party government, and this factor was coupled with a weakening of its Dáil position due to by-election defeats. In January 1982 the minority coalition government was defeated in a vote on its budget, an item so basic to any government's programme that failure to get it through the Dáil is regarded as tantamount to losing a vote of confidence, and it resigned at once. In January 1987 Labour pulled out of the coalition government, leaving Fine Gael with only 68 seats and facing inevitable defeat had the Dáil met again. In 1994, Labour again pulled out of a coalition, this time with Fianna Fáil, and the rump Fianna Fáil government faced certain defeat in a confidence motion; on this occasion, in an unprecedented development, the government resigned but the Taoiseach did not seek a dissolution, and several weeks later a new government, with a different partisan complexion, was formed (Garry, 1995). In other words, one reason why governments have so rarely been dismissed by the Dáil is that when they have seen defeat staring them in the face, they have usually jumped off the cliff rather than waiting to be pushed.

The Westminster model, then, does not adequately capture the reality of the Dáil's role in appointing and dismissing governments. However, it remains true that Irish governments do not routinely fear dismissal by the Dáil; governments are not regularly made or broken on the floor of the house. In this, of course, the Dáil is in line with virtually every other parliament in western Europe. The idea of parliaments constantly making and unmaking governments is neither realistic nor attractive. The classic example of a parliament wielding this power occurred in the French Fourth Republic, where there were 28 governments in only 13 years. Few would recommend 'strengthening' the Dáil so that this pattern could be replicated. If parliament has a role, it must lie in one of the areas to which we now turn.

Making policy

The production of legislation

A minister wishing to introduce a bill puts a 'memorandum for government' to the cabinet, outlining the intended purpose of the bill, the views of all ministers concerned with the issue, and an outline draft of the bill. If the government approves the proposal, the cabinet secretary sends the Attorney General (the government's legal officer) a letter requesting that legislation be drafted in accordance with the memorandum for government. As in most common-law countries, the drafting of legislation is carried out by specialist barristers whose full-time duty this is rather than by civil servants. Specifically, legislation is drafted in the Office of the Parliamentary Draftsman, operating under the auspices of the Attorney General (Donelan, 1992: 3). The Attorney General has a role in scrutinising the draft legislation to ensure that it is compatible with the constitution – as we saw in Chapter 3, the Irish courts are active in hearing and, where appropriate, upholding challenges to the constitutionality of pieces of legislation. Once the bill has passed through this process, it goes to parliament for discussion.

Inevitably, the calm and methodical process that a formal description implies may not always occur in practice. Those responsible for drafting legislation complain that political actors do not always allow them sufficient time to do their job thoroughly. There are suggestions that if a minister comes under political pressure over some issue, he or she is prone to demand a bill hastily even if it has not been properly prepared. Bills are apt to be 'yanked out of' the parliamentary draftsman's office (in the words of one insider) before they are ready if the relevant minister sees some political advantage in this. Ministers, in turn, sometimes feel that the drafters can be overly fastidious in their approach and that if left unpressured they would take an unacceptably long time to complete their tasks to their own satisfaction. The frustration – due to this and many other factors – that can be felt by a minister attempting to have his or her ideas turned into legislation is expressed pungently by a former Labour minister in his memoirs (Desmond, 2000: 179–81).

Over the 58-year period from the start of the 12th Dáil in 1944 to the end of the 28th Dáil in 2002, 2,075 bills were passed – an average of 36 per year (details of all legislation can be found at www.irishstatutebook.ie). The number of bills passed per year is neither increasing nor decreasing over time; nor is there any difference in the rate of output as between majority governments and minority governments, or between coalitions and single-party governments. There is some sign that bill-production is linked to the electoral cycle, as, over this period, the average number of bills passed in the last full calendar year before an election was 41. One clear trend is that even though the number of acts passed by parliament is not increasing, the length of those acts is. The average number of sections in each act rose from 14 in 1956 to 23 in 1976, 27 in 1996 and 43 in 2001.

We should bear in mind that the volume of legislation may be increasing in ways not picked up by simply counting the number of acts of parliament, because of the phenomenon of 'delegated legislation', in the form of statutory instruments. This arises when parliament passes an act that expresses a broad goal and allows another authority – characteristically a specific minister – to make the detailed regulations (Morgan, 1990: 107–11). The rationale is that the central political issue at stake is discussed and decided by parliament, and the technical or administrative details are left to specialised authorities to work out. The potential disadvantage, of course, is that these authorities may be able, in effect, to draft and implement legislation that is immune from parliamentary scrutiny or any real publicity. The power given to a minister under these terms may be quite extensive, including, for example, the right to amend existing laws.

Statutory instruments are particularly common when it comes to transposing EU directives into Irish domestic law. In 1994 the Supreme Court upheld the validity of a statutory instrument that, in giving effect to a number of EU directives, amended some existing Irish legislation. It declared, in the words of the Constitution Review Group (CRG), that 'the sheer number of EU directives was such that membership of the Community necessitated the possibility of implementing directives in Irish law by means of statutory instruments rather than by Act of the Oireachtas, even where amendment of an Act of the Oireachtas was involved' (CRG, 1996: 115). The group expressed some concern about this, commenting that 'hundreds of statutory provisions, some important, have been expressly or impliedly repealed by statutory instruments often with a minimum of publicity' (CRG, 1996: 115).

Detailed examination shows that there has been a steady increase in the number of statutory instruments issued over the years. Their rate of issue in the 28th Dáil, at around 560 per year, was approximately twice that in the 16th, 17th and 18th Dála (1957–69). The number increased after Ireland joined the EU in 1973, and the most sustained increase has occurred since 1987. Delegated legislation is on the increase.

The Dáil's role in law making

The constitution, by assigning law-making powers exclusively to the Oireachtas (Article 15.2.1), reflects one of the central tenets of classical liberal democratic theory: the legislature (parliament) makes laws and the executive (government) carries them out. This might lead us to expect that the government is merely the striking arm of parliament, carrying out parliament's will whether it likes it or not. However, no one really expects to find this kind of relationship between government and parliament, and, as we have said, it is more common to find the view expressed that parliament, in Ireland even more than in many other countries, has come to be a mere 'glorified rubber stamp' (Dinan, 1986: 76) for whatever proposals government puts before it.

In the area of policy making, as in appointing governments, we can distinguish between the Westminster and consensus models. In the Westminster model, parliament is not seen as a real maker of laws. Rather, parliament provides a forum where the issues raised by a government proposal can be fully aired. The government is obliged to justify its measure and the opposition gets the chance to make the case against it (and, generally, to keep the government on its toes), but ultimately the government sees its plans approved by parliament pretty much as a matter of course. There is no feeling that the opposition's views need to be taken into account or that its agreement is required for the passage of legislation – after all, the opposition is the opposition precisely because it 'lost' the last election and the government won it. To bring the opposition into the policy-making process would reduce the significance of the choice made by the voters at elections and could thus be seen as anti-democratic. In the consensus model, in contrast, government is (or, at least, feels) obliged to take seriously the wishes of parliament, including the feelings of the opposition. While in the last resort it is the government that governs, governments prefer not to railroad their legislation through against strong resistance; they try to find a consensus within parliament for their proposals and are willing to take on board constructive suggestions from the opposition.

Ireland's law-making procedure is closely based, in the letter and in the spirit, on that of Westminster. Bills can be introduced in either house – in the past, almost all government bills were introduced in the Dáil, but in recent years there has been more use of the Seanad. The formal progress of a bill is the same through each house, but since in the event of a disagreement between Dáil and Seanad it is the former that prevails (see p. 233), we shall concentrate here on the Dáil. A five-stage process is provided for bills, though most bills can bypass the first stage (see Box 8.1).[1] The second stage is the general debate on the principle of the bill. The third (committee

---

Box 8.1 The stages of a bill initiated in Dáil Éireann

Stage   *Matters decided*

First stage   Formal introduction of bill, securing agreement that the bill proceed to second stage. Virtually all bills (government bills, and private members' bills introduced by a 'group' of at least seven deputies), can be presented to the house without needing this formal agreement, and enter the process at the second stage.

Second stage Debate on the broad principle of the bill. The details of the bill are not discussed at this stage, and the substance of the bill cannot be amended. The vote taken after the second stage debate (assuming there is one – a significant number of bills are passed by agreement of the house, without the need for a vote) determines whether the bill is allowed to proceed to almost certain acceptance or is rejected.

Third stage   Committee stage. The bill is examined in detail by a committee (in the past, almost invariably, the 'committee' consisted of the whole Dáil; since 2002, specialist 11-member committees have undertaken this task). The bill is discussed section by section. Amendments may be proposed, provided they do not conflict with the principle of the bill, since this was approved by the house at the second stage.

Fourth stage   Report stage. Usually a formal tidying up of amendments made at third stage. New amendments may be proposed provided that they are not substantively the same as amendments rejected at the third stage.

Fifth stage   The final and formal passing of the bill. Speeches at this stage tend to be shorter and more ritualistic versions of those on the second stage. The bill now goes to the Seanad for discussion.

Final stages   When it returns from the Seanad the Dáil discusses the changes, if any, proposed by the Seanad. If it accepts them, the bill is sent to the President, for signing into law or, in the President's discretion, for referral to the Supreme Court for a verdict on its constitutionality. If the Dáil does not accept the Seanad's suggested amendments, it sends the bill back to the Seanad for reconsideration. The Seanad may fall into line with the wishes of the Dáil or it may reaffirm its amendments, in which case it can delay but not veto the passage of the bill.

Note
Bills can also be initiated in the Seanad. In this case they then go to the Dáil after being passed, but, in the event of the Dáil's deciding to make amendments, they are treated as if they had been initiated in the Dáil (Article 20.2.2 of the constitution).

stage) involves a detailed examination of each section of the bill. The fourth and fifth stages consist of tidying up the decisions made at the committee stage and formally passing the bill. After this, bills go to the other house and then to the President, who signs them into law or, very rarely, refers them to the Supreme Court for a decision on their constitutionality (see pp. 85 and 308–9). In effect, only the second and third stages offer the house any real opportunity to affect the content of a bill.

Even though debating bills accounts for a high proportion of the Dáil's time, detailed studies of the legislative process have yet to be undertaken. There is no research, for example, on important questions such as the proportion of bills that are amended during their passage through the legislature (and, when bills are amended, why this occurs), or the proportion that are supported or at least agreed by opposition parties.

The second stage debates are, at least in theory, the big events in the life of the Dáil. However, in practice debates have a ritualistic quality about them. All too often they are highly predictable affairs. The relevant minister opens the event by outlining the rationale for the measure to be introduced, after which a succession of opposition deputies use the occasion to pour cold water on the bill under discussion or, at best, to welcome the legislation but criticise the government for the delay in bringing it forward. There is little incentive for the opposition to offer constructive alternative proposals since the likelihood of any government deputy crossing the floor to vote for them is practically zero.

TDs are not supposed to read speeches from a prepared text, but they may use 'notes', which are sometimes very extensive. Indeed, critics see Dáil debates as little more than an exchange of scripts being read tediously into the record. As one journalist puts it:

> It is not just proceedings that need a shake up but the standard of Dáil speeches, which are abysmal. . . . Today's Dáil speeches are flat. TDs and ministers rarely stand up to speak without a script in their hands. In most cases, a civil servant or party backroom worker has written the script, and the deputy or minister is often reading the speech for the first time when he or she gets on their feet. And it shows.
>
> (Sheridan, 2002)

Not surprisingly, then, second stage speeches, at least once the minister and the main opposition spokesperson have had their say, are not made to a packed and expectant Dáil chamber. It is not uncommon to find only a handful of TDs in the chamber for such speeches. Since the order of speakers is decided by the party whips – and not, as in the past, by the Ceann Comhairle choosing from among the TDs actually in the Dáil chamber – most TDs see no need to be present until a few minutes before they are due to speak. If the opposition is feeling recalcitrant, one of its TDs will demand a quorum (20 TDs), without which the Dáil technically cannot conduct its business. This means that government backbenchers have to stream out of their offices and into the Dáil chamber to make up the numbers for a while, but they soon drift back again and hope that the opposition tires of the tactic. Attendance used to be particularly low when Friday sittings took place.

While some profess indignation at the low level of attendance in the Dáil chamber, it is hard to criticise those TDs and ministers who conclude that they have more useful ways of spending their time. Dáil debates are often dialogues of the deaf, set pieces with a strong element of theatre in which TDs speak for the record or in order to get publicity at local level. Dáil deputies, when they speak in a debate, wonder whether anyone is listening. Newspaper coverage of parliamentary proceedings is far less than it was 20 or more years ago. Sheridan, quoted above, argues that this is because Dáil speeches are so boring: 'The result is that the media has turned off' (Sheridan, 2002). However, although TDs are criticised for never speaking without a script, they in turn complain that unless they supply a script to journalists, there is little or no chance of their words being reported in the press. Another journalist argues that the media are wrong to assume that all

Dáil speeches are hot air: 'often they are substantial, considered contributions, but they may as well be hot air for they are spoken into thin air, nobody noticing' (Browne, 2002). The press gallery is usually empty as 'political journalists seek their stories in the corridors rather than the chamber' (Burton, 2003). Thus, even those TDs who might be inclined to make the effort to produce a constructive and thoughtful contribution are offered little incentive to do so.

Proceedings have been televised since 1991, but the rigid rules laid down for the broadcasters by parliament have made the result rather dull viewing. As a result viewing figures have been low, and 'Oireachtas Report' ended up at one stage in 1998 being broadcast at 2.30 a.m., which Pat Rabbitte TD, then of Democratic Left, described as a time when 'only drunks and insomniacs' would be watching (as a result of such protests, its transmission was brought forward to midnight). TDs' feeling that the world takes little notice of them is shared by backbench parliamentarians almost everywhere. Attendance in the chamber tends to be low in nearly all parliaments these days, and a Danish joke has it that a deputy wanting to keep something secret should announce it from the rostrum of the Folketing, as then it is certain that nobody will hear it.

It is very rare for a government bill to be defeated at the second stage. If this were to occur, it would not be because some of the government's backbenchers become convinced by the brilliance of the arguments from the opposition; it is really likely to happen only in a situation of minority government, which, as we have seen, is quite common. In January 1982, as already mentioned, the minority coalition government's budget was defeated. The 1987–9 minority Fianna Fáil administration was defeated six times in the Dáil, though none of these defeats concerned legislation.

The assumption made so far is that all bills are government bills, because, with rare exceptions, only government bills can expect to pass into law. Indeed, the constitution states (Article 17.2) that no motion or resolution shall be passed, or law enacted, that involves spending public money unless the Dáil receives a written message, signed by the Taoiseach, recommending the measure on behalf of the government. This is a stipulation in many countries, the rationale being that were it not in force, parliament might vote for the spending of money but against government efforts to raise it. Moreover, when the 1987–9 Fianna Fáil government sustained Dáil defeats on motions apparently 'directing' it to take certain steps, it ignored the motions, dismissing them as being merely declaratory. Dáil standing orders contain provision for 'private members' bills', which are usually introduced by an opposition deputy.[2] From 1937 to 1988 only six such bills were passed, all in the 1950s (Morgan, 1990: 103, 231), though there were a few additional cases in the 1990s, along with some instances of governments accepting bills originating with the opposition. Such bills do not represent any temporary dominance of parliament over government, though, because they will be passed only if the government directs its own backbenchers to support them. Even unsuccessful private members' bills may have an impact, since the government sometimes secures the withdrawal or defeat of the bill by promising to take some action itself. Overall, government control of the parliamentary agenda is high in Ireland by comparative standards (Bowler, 2000: 166–7; Döring, 2001).

The opposition, then, is unlikely to secure the defeat of a government bill or the passage of a bill of its own. If the Dáil is to make any impression on legislation, this must come at the third, 'committee', stage of a bill's progress, where the opposition can hope to have some influence on the final shape of the bill. Prior to 1993, the 'committee' that considered bills in practice normally comprised the whole house. After several reforms, the position in 2004 was that all bills went to a specialist 11-member Dáil committee; there were 13 such committees on which the parties were represented in proportion to their Dáil strengths, with the government having a 6 to 5 majority on each. Although discussion on the broad principle of the bill is ruled out, this having been settled at the second stage, TDs can raise points about specific sections: they can point out anomalies, inconsistencies, loopholes, imprecise phraseology and so on. If the points raised are consistent with the basic intention of the bill, the minister might well accept them and modify the bill accordingly. If the minister does not want to accept opposition amendments, then they will fail. The atmosphere in a small committee may be less confrontational than in the full chamber – even when that chamber is in practice nearly empty – and ministers may be readier to take opposition proposals on board.

The fact that the plenary discussion of the principles of a bill precedes the committee stage is more significant than is often realised. In many countries, a bill is examined in detail by a small committee of parliament *before* it goes to the whole house; in the Westminster model, the sequence is usually the other way around and 'the committee is bound by the principle of the bill to which the House has agreed' (Laundy, 1989: 73). This is important in deciding the significance of parliamentary committees in policy making: 'If a committee can consider a bill before it is taken up on the floor, the chances of the committee influencing or determining the outcome tend to be greater than when the lines of battle have been predetermined in plenary meetings' (Shaw, 1979: 417). Small committees of deputies who have acquired some expertise in a particular area are more likely to reach a consensus if the issues at stake have not been heavily politicised by partisan debates on the floor of the house, and the chances of the government's proposals getting through unaltered are correspondingly lower. For this reason, governments in Westminster-model countries prefer to leave the committee stage until after the plenary discussion, so that any changes made by the committee are likely to be minor.

It is clear, then, that the Dáil cannot be seen as an active participant in the process of making laws, let alone broader policy. Governments are usually more concerned to bring the major interest groups round to their way of thinking (see Chapter 13) than to placate the Dáil, whose backing they tend to take for granted. The Dáil is often seen as legitimising legislation rather than really making it, though the role of legitimation should not be dismissed out of hand. Norton (1990b: 147) points out that parliaments play an important symbolic role, and that for many people the fact that all legislation has to be passed by a parliament consisting of the elected representatives of the people is more important in making them feel that they are ruled democratically than the question of how much real power that parliament wields.

It would be an exaggeration, though, to say that Ireland suffers from 'cabinet dictatorship' or an 'elected dictatorship' between elections. Quite apart from the extra-parliamentary checks on government, such as the constitution, the Dáil cannot be disregarded. The Dáil will do what the government wants provided, and only provided, the government has the backing of a majority of TDs. In situations of minority government, the government will be able to get its legislation through only if it takes care not to introduce any proposals that would induce the opposition to combine against it. For example, the minority Fianna Fáil–PD government of 1997–2002 suffered no defeats on any of its legislative proposals, but this is because it took care not to introduce proposals that would have been defeated, not because the Dáil was certain always to do its bidding.

Moreover, even when the government parties have a Dáil majority, it is easy to overlook the fact that the government has to pay a price to retain the backing of its TDs. Relations between governments and their own backbenchers are central to any understanding of the relationship between government and parliament (Andeweg and Nijzink, 1995). The real action may be taking place within the government parliamentary parties rather than in the Dáil chamber. Ministers have to show their backbenchers some respect in order to keep them trooping loyally through the government lobbies. When the party is in power, weekly meetings of its parliamentary party (attended by TDs, senators and MEPs) hear from ministers about their plans, and they expect this to be a genuine process of consultation. If a TD raises a doubt or a question, the minister would be unwise to brush this aside as dismissively as an opposition TD might be dealt with in the Dáil chamber – ministers, after all, want to be personally popular with their own TDs, for a variety of obvious reasons. A sensible minister will 'wear a velvet glove, albeit having a mailed fist within it', when dealing with government backbenchers (Rose, 1986: 14).

The power of the parliamentary party should not be overstated – evidently, the initiative in making policy lies with the government, not with backbenchers. But no government has a completely free hand from its own party; if a proposed policy or item of legislation arouses broad antagonism from government TDs at a parliamentary party meeting, it is unlikely to be pressed further, as occurred in 2001 when government proposals to abolish the dual mandate (the facility whereby TDs could retain their county council seats) ran into Fianna Fáil backbench resistance as well as opposition from the independent TDs backing the government. Between 1981 and 1987 there were at least 14 such examples of backbench rumbling, most of which brought about a change of government policy (Mitchell, 1999b: 279–80). Similarly, in the extremely rare event that government TDs are persuaded of a government measure's flaws by a critical speech from an opposition TD in the Dáil, this will be reflected not in TDs' voting against the measure in the chamber but in private pressure on the minister to amend or rescind the proposal. One of the few cases in Irish parliamentary history of a Dáil speech having such an impact occurred in 1985, when a lone crusade by the then independent TD Des O'Malley against a bill (designed to protect a cartel of airlines) that was backed by both the Fine Gael–Labour government and the Fianna Fáil opposition sowed seeds of doubt in the minds of many Fine Gael backbenchers, and as a result of the views they expressed in the privacy of parliamentary party meetings the minister significantly amended the bill. An awareness of what the parliamentary party will and will not stand for is bound to be a factor in determining what policies the government tries to introduce.

With this qualification, then, it is the government and not the rest of parliament that has the initiative in the shaping of laws and policies. Once again, the Irish pattern is not exceptional, even if the Oireachtas is less active in this area than are most parliaments. Of course, in presidential systems of government such as the USA, parliament can be quite strong, because the survival of a government is not at stake: if a presidentially backed bill is defeated in Congress, the administration does not fall. But things are very different in the parliamentary systems of government by which most European countries are governed. When a government is elected by, answerable to and dismissible by parliament, measures proposed by the government are very unlikely to be rejected by parliament. When bills go to a specialist committee before they reach the floor of the house, parliament can exercise significant influence over their final shape, but where the Westminster model prevails it would be unrealistic to expect a policy-making role for parliament. All that we might hope for is that the Dáil keeps a vigilant eye on what government is up to, the topic that we now examine.

Scrutinising the behaviour of government

The initiative in making policy, then, lies with government rather than with parliament. However, this does not freeze parliament out of the political process entirely. Even if it does pass virtually all the government's proposals, it still has a choice as to how to follow this up. Does it merely sit back and allow the government to act as it wishes? Or does it keep the government under careful scrutiny, checking on whether it has behaved as it said it would and on whether public money has been spent as the government promised, keeping the government on its toes and exposing its mistakes?

How effective is the Dáil in making the government answerable and accountable? The Dáil has three main methods of trying to compel the government to justify its behaviour: debates, parliamentary questions and committees.

Debates

As well as the debates on bills, which we have already discussed, the Dáil may debate other motions. Three that are relevant to the scrutiny function of the Dáil are, first, motions of confidence in the government; second, *ad hoc* motions on topical political issues; and third, formal motions on topics such as the adjournment of the house. From time to time an opposition party is prone to table a motion of no confidence in the government, to which the government almost invariably responds by tabling a motion of confidence in itself. The resultant debate, naturally, ranges over the entire gamut of the government's activity, with opposition TDs using the occasion to obtain publicity for their criticisms of the government rather than really expecting to oust it – as we have seen, only twice has a government actually lost such a motion. *Ad hoc* motions may be debated to allow the opposition to air a grievance or, alternatively, they may be occasions for the expression of broad cross-party consensus among TDs about some major development. The adjournment debate held at the end of some sessions (a debate ostensibly on a topic such as 'That Dáil Éireann do adjourn for the summer recess') is predictable in content, as various ministers defend the government's record while opposition TDs disparage it.

Parliamentary questions

The Dáil sits on Tuesdays, Wednesdays and Thursdays, and on each day an hour and a quarter is set aside for questions to a minister; ministers take it in turn to face these. The Taoiseach is questioned at the start of proceedings on Tuesdays and Wednesdays. Questions must be put down in advance, to give the minister and departmental civil servants time to discover the information sought. Most questions seek a written answer, which the TD receives within three working days, but others are put down for oral answer, which means that the TD must wait until the relevant minister's day for answering questions comes around; these questions must be put down four working days before they are due to be answered. Questions may seek very detailed information about an individual constituent or the constituency of the TD asking the question (this is characteristic of questions for written answer), or they may ask about a topic of national significance or a matter of government policy (characteristic of questions for oral answer). TDs can respond to the minister's reply to a question answered orally by asking a 'supplementary' question. A TD dissatisfied with the minister's reply can raise and elaborate upon his or her grievance during the 'adjournment debate' that occupies the last 50 minutes of each day's sitting, and the minister is obliged to reply more fully. Deputies may ask any number of questions for written answer, but no TD can put down more than two on any one day that seek an oral answer. The order in which the latter questions appear on the order paper (which determines which ones will be reached, since time constraints mean that on average only about 20 questions are answered orally each day) is settled by lottery. A number of opposition TDs therefore put down identical or near-identical questions in order to boost the chances of the question receiving a high position in the lottery.

The number of questions has risen greatly over the years, from around 1,200 a year in the mid-1930s to 4,000 a year in the mid-1960s and over 24,000 a year in the period 2001–3. Exactly the same pattern of a major increase in parliamentary questions over the years is found in several other west European countries (Gallagher *et al.*, 2001: 79). The variation in the number of questions put down by TDs concerning individual constituents suggests that many TDs find other less public ways of obtaining similar information. The fact that most questions are tabled by opposition TDs affirms the political motive of putting down a question – government deputies ask very few questions, even of a local nature.

Question time is highly politicised. Opposition TDs put down questions for oral answer not in an ingenuous search for information but, in most cases, as part of the ongoing war of attrition against the government, which they hope to be able to embarrass. Ministers treat question time in the same spirit, aiming to give away as little as possible. The culture is one of concealment, not of openness. The etiquette of parliamentary questions (PQs) requires not that answers be helpful or informative but only that they not be untruthful (though it has been alleged that answers given by certain Fianna Fáil ministers in the late 1980s and early 1990s relating to the beef industry failed to meet even this minimal requirement – see FitzGerald, 1994). Answers to a number of possible supplementary questions are worked out in advance, but the information contained in them is not disclosed unless the relevant supplementary is asked. In February 1998 an opposition TD, Liz McManus, received a written answer, which was mistakenly accompanied by a confidential memo – containing far more information than the bland answer – that had not been intended for her eyes. The chairman of the long-running Beef Tribunal (discussed further in Chapters 13 and 14) stated that if questions had been answered in the Dáil as fully as they had to be answered in the tribunal, the tribunal would not have been necessary. A senior civil servant appearing before the tribunal stated that in preparing answers to PQs, the policy was to answer the question but go no further; information, no matter how interesting it might be to the questioner, is not disclosed unless specifically sought (O'Toole, 1995: 257). A minister involved in the beef affair, Ray Burke, explained that if the opposition did not ask the right questions, they would not get the right answers (O'Toole, 1995: 256). Oppositions deplore this approach, and John Bruton, while opposition leader, suggested that the Ceann Comhairle be given additional power to insist that ministers answer questions fully and properly. However, entering government usually diminishes such reforming zeal and in February 1995, as Taoiseach, Bruton used exactly the same words as Burke when explaining on the radio that he had not disclosed a piece of information because the TDs questioning him had 'not asked the right question', to which the opposition responded that they could not possibly have asked the right question unless they had already known the answer.

Logistically, the odds at question time are stacked in the ministers' favour. After all, they have had at least four days to think of a reply and, besides, there is nothing to prevent them from giving an evasive reply. In addition, they need not answer supplementary questions at all, if necessary using the formula that 'that is a separate question', if by chance the supplementary asked is one that they did not anticipate and hence did not have their officials prepare an answer to. At question time, ministers have civil servants sitting across the aisle waiting to pass them the relevant information or documents, while the TD asking the question does not have access to this kind of back-up. Many opposition TDs are dissatisfied with the operation of question time, which, in the words of one insider, has 'gone to the dogs' (interview with author). The former Fine Gael minister Jim Mitchell wrote that 'question time, once the great tool of parliamentary accountability, has descended into an ineffective, unproductive, virtually unattended daily session' (Mitchell, 1999). In 2003 Fine Gael once again called for the Ceann Comhairle to be given 'additional powers' to compel ministers to answer the question they were asked, alleging that questions were all too often answered by way of a bland five-minute prepared script from a minister (*Irish Times*, 27 October 2003). If the answers are indeed getting longer, they are not necessarily becoming more informative.

Even so, there is a limit, in practical political terms, to the extent to which a minister can evade a question without giving the impression of having something to hide. The stature of a minister who seems unable to give convincing answers to questions will drop among both government deputies and journalists. Question time is the liveliest part of the Dáil schedule, so it gets relatively good media coverage. If a minister performs ineptly at question time, this may feature on television news, and journalists' assessments of the minister are less likely to be favourable. Consequently, parliamentary questions can be quite effective in probing some alleged ministerial misdemeanour. However, they are not designed to enable the monitoring of government policies on a continuous basis – if this is to be done, the most appropriate mechanism is a system of committees.

Oireachtas committees

Committees are a feature of almost all modern parliaments, but their significance varies greatly. Where government is not directly accountable to parliament, parliament may work mainly through committees: examples include the US Congress and the European Parliament. In parliamentary systems, committees tend to be more powerful in countries closer to the consensus model than where the Westminster model applies. In the traditional Westminster model, which Ireland took over in 1922, committees have no great significance.

When a fully fledged committee system is up and running, a typical parliament has a number of committees, each consisting of around 10 to 30 deputies, depending on the size of the parliament. Some committees monitor the performance of government in broad policy areas, such as agriculture or education. Others might be assigned to review policy on some specific question, such as taxation or pensions, and to examine or suggest legislation. If committees are to be strong and effective, they will have the power to insist that ministers and civil servants appear before them to explain their decisions, and they will also need the resources to hire outside experts and research staff in order to examine subjects systematically. If they are to work properly they need to operate to some extent on non- or cross-party lines, as otherwise they will merely replicate the division on the floor of parliament. Sometimes 'small group psychology' creates an identification with the committee that rivals, though rarely displaces, identification with party. Ministers and civil servants know that they might one day have to give detailed justifications of the decisions they make and so, it is hoped, they take more care to make the right ones.

Until the 1980s, Oireachtas committees were few in number. The most important was the Public Accounts Committee, always chaired by an opposition TD, which has the function of considering the accounts of government departments in the light of the annual reports of the Comptroller and Auditor General, who checks that public money has been spent in the way that the Oireachtas decided it should be (see Chapter 12). However, a study of the operation of this committee from 1961 to 1980 spoke of the unconscientious attitude of its members, superficial and unplanned questioning, and haphazard treatment of officials (O'Halpin, 1985, especially pp. 507–8). Other committees perform a 'housekeeping' function, regulating the internal affairs of Leinster House (the seat of the Oireachtas).

It is apparent to everyone that the only way in which the opposition – and government backbenchers – can be given a more meaningful role is through a well-designed committee system. Coming up with such a system has not proved easy. The Fine Gael–Labour coalition government of the 1980s introduced an ambitious scheme entailing a multitude of committees, but, despite some positive aspects, such as increasing the expertise of backbenchers who subsequently became ministers, it was clear that this particular configuration was not the answer. There were far too many committees, several committees had vague remits, and some major areas of government escaped scrutiny (assessments of the 1983–7 committees can be found in O'Halpin, 1986 and Arkins, 1988). Most of these committees were not re-established in the next two Dála (elected in 1987 and 1989), but after the 1992 election the committee system leapt into life again. This time, the range of committees was more logical than in the 1982–7 Dáil, and there was a significant innovation in that for the first time committees played a part in the legislative process, as the 'committee stage' of bills was conducted not by the entire Dáil but by the appropriate committee. However, in a repetition of the 1983 mistake, too much was tried too soon, with too many committee places to be filled, and TDs were over-stretched.

After the 1997 election, a new set of committees was established, and essentially the same set was re-established after the 2002 election (for a full list of these committees see Table 10.4, p. 278). The principle underlying this arrangement is that the structure of committees should closely match the structure of government departments, so there is more or less one committee per department (in practice, some committees handle two departments). Each of the 13 committees monitors the activities of its department, discusses its estimates, and deals with the third stage of legislation within the area of the department. The committees sit as joint committees (in other words, both TDs and senators take part) most of the time, but when they discuss the third stage of legislation that is passing through the Dáil, only TDs may participate. Of the 11 TDs on each committee, six are government TDs, but in addition the relevant minister is ex officio a member of the committee and has a vote. Even in the highly unlikely event of a government defeat on some matter, any committee decision can be overturned by the full Dáil. The other non-housekeeping committee is the Public Accounts Committee, whose role has been enhanced since a modernisation and extension of the remit of the Comptroller and Auditor General in 1993 (O'Halpin, 1998: 132; see also pp. 346–7).

TDs are assigned by the party whips to committees, though they are able to express preferences as to which committees they wish to serve on, and given that many TDs are indifferent, those who want to be on a particular committee have a good chance of being selected for it. The committee system is also a vehicle of patronage: on each of the non-housekeeping committees, there are four paid positions (chairperson, vice-chairperson, 'government whip' and 'opposition whip'). The position of committee chair usually goes to a government TD, and this position is undoubtedly used as a consolation post for TDs who have missed appointment as a cabinet minister or minister of state.

The post-1997 committee system is generally seen as having been more effective than its forerunners. The investigation by the Public Accounts Committee in 1999 of the non-payment of tax on certain non-resident accounts held in banks and building societies was regarded as a triumph for the entire committee system. On the other hand, committees had their wings clipped in November 2001, when the High Court ruled that the Oireachtas did not have the power to set up enquiries that are likely to lead to findings of fact or expressions of opinion adverse to the good name of individuals not belonging to the Dáil. Committees face abiding difficulties in raising a quorum, and it is common for meetings to be made quorate when they commence by the committee clerk rounding up a few TDs from an adjacent room and bringing them into the meeting (all TDs are entitled to attend any committee meeting).

Despite the generally positive evaluation of the post-1997 system, it would be unrealistic to expect dramatic consequences to flow from any reorganisation of the committees. There are a number of fundamental reasons why, despite the extensive reforms introduced in recent years, relations between government and parliament may be slightly adjusted by a well-designed committee system but will never be fundamentally changed.

First, most governments have not been keen to see a particularly probing committee system emerge. Government ministers, like everyone else, would prefer not to have to work under close scrutiny. Second, those who would most benefit from such a system have ambivalent views on the matter. Opposition frontbenchers would like to see the government on the rack, but they look forward to being in government themselves in the future and thus have some reluctance to see too many checks on ministers. Likewise, ambitious backbenchers dream of one day being a government minister, not of becoming a committee chair. Because of the relatively small size of the Dáil, a high proportion of TDs become ministers – for example, in the Dáil elected in 2002, 57 TDs (34 per cent of the total) were current or past cabinet or junior ministers, and the proportion is usually higher than this – so able TDs who are capable of dealing with national political issues know that they have a good chance of becoming ministers some day. TDs who are not in that category are unlikely to be interested in an effective committee system. A strong committee system would be of most appeal to TDs who, while interested in some aspect of the policy process, do not hope or expect to be ministers, and such TDs are rare.

Third, there are questions as to how far a strong committee system can be reconciled with a parliamentary system of government – especially when the Westminster model operates. A prudent government backbencher who wants promotion might well decide that going along with the party line is a safer option than becoming a trenchant inquisitor of his or her own party leaders in government. Fourth, while the resources available to TDs have improved greatly in recent decades, committees often have to share clerks and lack research support. In the absence of adequate resources, many TDs will continue to feel they cannot afford to spend too much time on committee work to the neglect of their constituency duties (for which see Chapter 9).

Seanad Éireann

Our discussion so far has concentrated mainly on the Dáil but, as we mentioned at the start of the chapter, the Oireachtas also has an upper house, Seanad Éireann. The lifespan of each Seanad matches that of the Dáil, except that Seanad elections take place a couple of months after the corresponding Dáil election. The Seanad has 60 members, who are elected in a particularly convoluted manner (see Box 8.2). The election of 43 members from quasi-vocational panels might give the impression that the Seanad consists largely of representatives of the main interest groups. However, the reality is otherwise because of the composition of the electorate (which is defined by law and not by the constitution). Not surprisingly, since the great bulk of the voters are practising party politicians, so too are the people they elect and, by and large, the senators elected from the panels are similar in background to TDs – indeed, they are often former or aspiring TDs, or both. The presence of the university senators remains contentious, with the principle of special graduate representation being criticised as elitist. The main argument in favour of the university seats is that these six senators, most of whom are not members of a political party, are often an innovative and independent force in an Oireachtas otherwise firmly controlled by the parties. The 11 senators appointed by the Taoiseach are usually chosen so as to ensure that the government has a secure majority in the Seanad, and to give a boost to politicians who have a chance of winning an extra seat for the party at the next Dáil elections.

The Seanad is by far the weaker of the two houses. A few of the powers of the Houses of the Oireachtas, it is true, are shared equally among both chambers; thus, the declaration of an emergency (see p. 79), the impeachment of a President or the removal of a judge (see pp. 88–9) need acquiescence from both Dáil and Seanad. In the area of legislation, the Dáil is unequivocally the superior chamber. Bills come before the Seanad, but at most it can merely delay them for 90 days. If it rejects a non-money bill, reaches no decision or suggests amendments that are unacceptable to the Dáil, the Dáil can simply overrule it (Article 23.1 of the constitution). In the case of a money bill, the Seanad is given only three weeks in which to make its 'recommendations', which again the Dáil may overrule (Article 21). If it rejects a bill (other than a bill to amend the constitution) and the Dáil overrules it, it may invoke the 'Article 27 procedure', under which a majority of senators and a third of the members of the Dáil may petition the President not to sign the bill but instead to submit it to a referendum. No such petition has ever been presented – indeed, the Seanad has not rejected a government bill since July 1964. Anecdotal evidence suggests that the minister sponsoring a bill is much more receptive to suggestions from senators if the bill is being introduced in the Seanad than in the case of a bill that goes to the Seanad after passing through the Dáil. The government nearly always has majority support within the Seanad, especially given the

---

Box 8.2 The composition of Seanad Éireann, 2004

Of the 60 senators, 43 are elected from five 'panels', six are elected by university graduates and the other 11 are appointed by the Taoiseach.

The five panels are Agriculture, Culture and Education, Industry and Commerce, Labour, and Public Administration, and those nominated for a panel are required to have 'knowledge and practical experience' of its subject (Article 18.7.1 of the constitution). The electors for the 43 panel seats are members of city and county councils, the Dáil and the outgoing Seanad – those qualified under more than one heading receive only one vote. At the 2002 Seanad election, the electorate for the panel seats comprised 970 people, of whom 811 were affiliated to one of the three main parties (Gallagher and Weeks, 2003).

The six university senators are returned from two panels. Graduates of the National University of Ireland return three senators, with the other three elected by graduates of Trinity College Dublin. The details of representation give more weight to Trinity graduates than to the more numerous NUI graduates, not to mention graduates of other third-level institutions who are excluded from the election.

The remaining 11 senators are appointed by the Taoiseach.

Several schemes have been proposed to broaden the Seanad electorate. In 2002 an Oireachtas committee advocated the direct election of 48 of the 60 senators. In 2004 a Seanad committee proposed the direct election of 26 members of an expanded 65-member Seanad; this scheme, unlike the 2002 one, recommended retaining the election of a number of senators by graduates and by members of county councils.

Taoiseach's right to nominate 11 of the senators. The Seanad meets less frequently than the Dáil (for an average of 70 days a year in 2001–3, compared with the Dáil's 86 days) and senators are paid only about 60 per cent of a TD's salary.[3]

Not surprisingly, the Seanad is often dismissed as a mere 'talking shop', and some have called for its abolition, pointing out that comparable chambers were abolished, without noticeably adverse consequences, in Denmark (in 1953), New Zealand (1950) and Sweden (1970). Defenders of the Seanad argue that despite its lack of power, it plays a useful role in the legislative process, as debates on bills are usually conducted in a more reflective, constructive, and non-party spirit than in the Dáil. In addition, the task of setting up an effective Oireachtas committee system would be even more difficult without the 60 senators. In March 2002 the All-Party Oireachtas Committee on the Constitution recommended that the method of election should be fundamentally changed, with 48 senators being directly elected from national lists (All-Party Oireachtas Committee, 2002; Laver, 2002). In April 2004, a Seanad committee came up with the fullest scheme for Seanad reform yet devised, proposing an extension of the functions of the body and a radical reform of its method of election (Seanad Éireann Committee, 2004). It called for the Seanad to be given a role in EU affairs – examining draft EU legislation and providing MEPs with a domestic forum – and in assessing public policy, reviewing the performance of government departments and state agencies. The committee suggested that the Seanad should be expanded to 65 members, of whom 26 would be directly elected in a national list system and six would be elected by graduates. Twenty senators would be elected by the current electorate (that is, county councillors and Oireachtas members) and 12 would be appointed by the Taoiseach. The final member would be the outgoing Cathaoirleach (speaker), who would be re-elected automatically. Whether the political will can be found to implement this scheme remains to be seen.

Weakness of parliament

From what we have said so far, it is evident that government is the dominant actor in its relations with the rest of parliament, but as its most powerful committee rather than as a body that competes with it – though in the increasingly frequent situation of minority government, the position is not quite so clear cut. There are many reasons for governmental dominance, some applicable to most parliaments – hence the frequent references to a 'decline of parliaments' since the nineteenth century – and some specific to the Oireachtas.

For one thing, the role of the state, and hence of government, has grown considerably over the past 100 years. Government business has become much more complex, and it is more difficult for all but those directly and continuously involved to monitor its work. The level of specialisation and expertise required is such that everyone else, including the backbench member of parliament, is effectively an amateur in the policy-making process.

Second, the development of the mass media has provided an alternative and often more effective means of making governments accountable. Ministers cannot so easily wriggle out of awkward situations when being grilled by an interviewer on the television as they can in parliament.

Third, parliaments tend to be conservative institutions, slow to adapt to changes in the outside world. The Dáil has tended to look only as far as another notoriously conservative parliament, the House of Commons, when considering reforms. The Oireachtas was very slow to demand that its members declare their interests in a register maintained for that purpose. Only with the passage of the Ethics in Public Office Act (1995) did this become necessary. TDs and Senators are now obliged to declare whether they have income or property above certain levels – and, if so, from what source – under a number of headings (though they are not obliged to declare the value of such income or property). Moreover, critics maintain that the Dáil does not meet as often it should and that it would be stronger if it sat for more hours per year. Usually, it sits for around 30 weeks per year (fewer in election years) and for three days per week – thus it sat for 94 days in 2001, 67 in 2002 and 97 in 2003. Opposition parties regularly demand longer sitting hours and allege that the government's refusal to accede to this is motivated by an aversion to being held accountable. One cross-party difficulty in extending sitting hours per week is a conflict between deputies based in or close to Dublin and those who cannot commute on a daily basis to Leinster House. The former would prefer the Dáil to sit for four days a week and keep 'normal' nine-to-five hours, while the latter want their sojourn away from their homes to be kept to a minimum and hence would prefer fewer but longer sitting days.

Fourth, new patterns of decision making virtually bypass parliament. In many European countries, including Ireland, the major interest groups, especially the employers' and farmers' organisations and the trade unions, play a central role in economic policy making (see Chapter 13). When the government agrees a package with these interests (such as the 2003 'Sustaining Progress'), parliament can do little except retrospectively discuss a *fait accompli*. Interest groups naturally concentrate their lobbying efforts on government ministers and senior civil servants, where the real power lies, leaving ordinary TDs with few interests to represent other than those of their constituents. In addition, a growing number of policies are made at EU level, again undermining the traditional notion of domestic parliaments as law-making bodies (see Chapter 16). Moreover, the courts, utilising their role as interpreters of the constitution, have become increasingly active in effectively changing the law in a number of respects (see Chapter 3).

Fifth, as we have already observed, TDs have other demands on their time, especially constituency work (see Chapter 9). Even the most nationally oriented deputies cannot spend all their political lives on parliamentary work, because they are expected to service the needs of their constituents and fear losing their seats if they neglect this work.

Finally, and most importantly, as we observed at the start of the chapter, deputies behave not as individuals but as members of a party. When it comes to the crunch, deputies in most parliaments follow the party line; when political life is dominated by political parties, as is the case throughout Europe, deputies' orientation to party is stronger than their orientation to an abstract notion of 'parliament'. This is not necessarily a bad thing – to govern effectively, governments need to be able to rely on their own back-benchers to support them through thick and thin. In Ireland, government backbenchers have proved very reliable indeed.

The 'fusion' of government and parliament, with virtually all ministers simultaneously being TDs, greatly affects the way in which TDs, especially government backbenchers, see their role. Fusion is a characteristic feature of Westminster-model countries, and as such is by no means typical of European practice generally. While in Ireland all ministers must be members of parliament, in certain European countries (notably France, the Nether-lands, Norway and Sweden) the offices of MP and government minister are incompatible. Whereas in Ireland only two of the approximately 150 ministers since 1922 have not previously been MPs, the average European figure is 25 per cent. In the Netherlands and Norway around half of all ministers have never been MPs (De Winter, 1991: 48–50). In such countries, there are to some extent different parliamentary and governmental career structures, and a greater psychological separation between parliament and government. In Ireland, certainly as far as government backbenchers are concerned, there is little or no such separation.

This list of causes of the weakness of parliament as a check on government puts into perspective occasional calls for 'reform' of the Oireachtas so as to make it stronger. For example, Ward (1996) deplores the Constitution Reform Group's ready acceptance of the dominant position of the govern-ment and suggests a number of reforms, such as having the Dáil sit for more days per year, increasing the size of the Dáil, and generally improving 'the performance of the Dáil in legislation, estimates or scrutiny of the executive' (p. 60). Yet, as O'Halpin (1998: 132) points out, 'the appropriate tools of enquiry and analysis are now to hand'; the Dáil does not challenge the government, not because it does not meet for a sufficient number of days or because its procedures are inadequate but because backbench government TDs want to back the government – indeed, ultimately to become members of it – and not to harass it. Giving government TDs more teeth will not alter the role of the Dáil if these TDs do not wish to bite the government.

Conclusion

The relationship between government and parliament is often seen in adver-sarial terms, and the question is asked: which controls which? We have argued in this chapter that the question makes little sense in the context of a political system where government sits in parliament and is backed, as a matter of principle rather than on an *ad hoc* basis, by a majority of deputies.

If government and parliament were seen as competing for power then, clearly, we should have to conclude that government has the upper hand. Virtually all government bills are passed, with opposition amendments taken on board only as the government sees fit, while hardly any legislation originating with the opposition is passed – certainly not against the wishes of the government. Extracting information from the government that it does not wish to disclose, through debates or parliamentary questions, is an uphill struggle. Other than in times of minority government or coalition break-up, the government need not fear being ejected from office by the Dáil.

Nonetheless, Irish government does not amount to cabinet dictatorship. The Dáil's provisions for scrutiny of government do allow the opposition to harass the government and bring into the light matters that it would prefer to keep concealed. The government also has to pay a price for the continued loyalty of its own backbenchers; it usually has to clear its plans with its TDs in advance, and takes care not to introduce measures that its TDs indicate they could not support. Even if its legislation is virtually certain to be passed, the opposition has plenty of opportunities to state its own criticisms.

If it were desired to make the Dáil a more significant actor, the most obvious step would be to build on the existing committee system and to use committees to discuss legislation before rather than after it goes to the full parliament. The reforms instituted since the 1997 election implement some of these ideas, yet it is clear that changes to the rules alone will never transform the position of parliament. Parliament would become more powerful if TDs of the government parties ceased to see their main role as supporting the government and became, instead, quasi-neutral observers of the political process, ready to back or oppose the government depending on their view of the issue at hand. Such a development, which is improbable in the extreme, would undoubtedly transform the role not only of parliament but of the entire process of government – and not necessarily for the better.

Notes

1 Because of the privileges enjoyed by 'groups' of seven or more TDs, after the 2002 election TDs of the Green Party and Sinn Féin (neither of which had as many as seven TDs), along with independent TDs, formed a 'technical group' to qualify for these benefits.
2 Private members' bills should be distinguished from private bills, which differ from public bills in that they apply only to certain bodies or localities (an example is The Altamont (Amendment of Deed of Trust) Act, 1993). Private bills, of which there are only a handful per decade, must be introduced in the Seanad and have a distinctive method of enactment (for details see Morgan, 1990: 103–4; Dooney and O'Toole, 1998: 60–1).
3 Payments to both TDs and senators are far from transparent because of the range of allowances, tax breaks, pension rights and so on (Gallagher, 2003b: 197–8).

References and further reading

All-Party Oireachtas Committee on the Constitution, 2002. *Seventh Progress Report: Parliament*. Dublin: Stationery Office.
Andeweg, Rudy B. and Lia Nijzink, 1995. 'Beyond the two-body image: relations between ministers and MPs', in Herbert Döring (ed.), *Parliaments and Majority Rule in Western Europe*. Frankfurt, Campus Verlag and New York: St Martin's Press, pp. 152–78.
Arkins, Audrey, 1988. 'The committees of the 24th Oireachtas', *Irish Political Studies* 3: 91–7.

Bowler, Shaun, 2000. 'Parties in legislatures: two competing explanations', in Russell J. Dalton and Martin P. Wattenberg (eds), *Parties without Partisans: Political Change in Advanced Industrial Democracies*. Oxford: Oxford University Press, pp. 157–79.

Bowler, Shaun, David M. Farrell and Richard S. Katz, 1999. 'Party cohesion, party discipline, and parliaments', in Shaun Bowler, David M. Farrell and Richard S. Katz (eds), *Party Discipline and Parliamentary Government*. Columbus: Ohio State University Press, pp. 3–22.

Browne, Vincent, 2002. 'When the Dáil is relegated to a sideshow', *Irish Times*, 20 November.

Burton, Joan, 2003. 'Five years on and looking for some sparkle in a dull Dáil', *Irish Times*, 16 August.

Chubb, Basil, 1992. *The Government and Politics of Ireland*, 3rd edn. Harlow: Longman.

Constitution Review Group, 1996. *Report*. Dublin: Stationery Office.

Desmond, Barry, 2000. *Finally and in Conclusion: A Political Memoir*. Dublin: New Island.

De Winter, Lieven, 1991. 'Parliamentary and party pathways to the government', in Jean Blondel and Jean-Louis Thiébault (eds), *The Profession of Government Minister in Western Europe*. Basingstoke: Macmillan, pp. 44–69.

Dinan, Des, 1986. 'Constitution and parliament', in Brian Girvin and Roland Sturm (eds), *Politics and Society in Contemporary Ireland*. Aldershot: Gower, pp. 71–86.

Donelan, Edward J., 1992. 'The role of the Parliamentary Draftsman in the preparation of legislation in Ireland', *Dublin University Law Journal* 14: 1–18.

Dooney, Seán and John O'Toole, 1998. *Irish Government Today*, 2nd edn. Dublin: Gill and Macmillan.

Döring, Herbert, 2001. 'Parliamentary agenda control and legislative outcomes in western Europe', *Legislative Studies Quarterly* 26:1: 145–65.

Farrell, Brian, 1987a. 'The context of three elections', in Howard Penniman and Brian Farrell (eds), *Ireland at the Polls 1981, 1982 and 1987*. Durham, NC: Duke University Press and American Enterprise Institute, pp. 1–30.

Farrell, Brian, 1987b. 'The road from 1987: government formation and institutional inertia', in Michael Laver, Peter Mair and Richard Sinnott (eds), *How Ireland Voted: the Irish General Election 1987*. Swords: Poolbeg and PSAI Press, pp. 141–52.

Farrell, Brian, 1993. 'The formation of the partnership government', in Michael Gallagher and Michael Laver (eds), *How Ireland Voted 1992*. Dublin: Folens and Limerick: PSAI Press, pp. 146–61.

FitzGerald, Garret, 1994. 'Paying too high a price for techniques of obfuscation', *Irish Times*, 13 August: 10.

Gallagher, Michael, 2003a. 'Stability and turmoil: analysis of the results', in Michael Gallagher, Michael Marsh and Paul Mitchell (eds), *How Ireland Voted 2002*. Basingstoke: Palgrave Macmillan, pp. 88–118.

Gallagher, Michael, 2003b. 'Ireland: party loyalists with a personal base', in Jens Borchert and Jürgen Zeiss (eds), *The Political Class in Advanced Democracies*. Oxford: Oxford University Press, pp. 187–202.

Gallagher, Michael, Michael Laver and Peter Mair, 2001. *Representative Government in Modern Europe*, 3rd edn. New York and London: McGraw-Hill.

Gallagher, Michael and Liam Weeks, 2003. 'The subterranean election of the Seanad', in Michael Gallagher, Michael Marsh and Paul Mitchell (eds), *How Ireland Voted 2002*. Basingstoke: Palgrave Macmillan, pp. 197–213.

Garry, John, 1995. 'The demise of the Fianna Fáil/Labour "Partnership" government and the rise of the "Rainbow" coalition', *Irish Political Studies* 10: 192–9.

Girvin, Brian, 1993. 'The road to the election', in Michael Gallagher and Michael Laver (eds), *How Ireland Voted 1992*. Dublin: Folens and Limerick: PSAI Press, pp. 1–20.

Heidar, Knut and Ruud Koole, 2000. 'Parliamentary party groups compared', in Knut Heidar and Ruud Koole (eds), *Parliamentary Party Groups in European Democracies: Political Parties behind Closed Doors*. London: Routledge, pp. 248–70.

Laundy, Philip, 1989. *Parliaments in the Modern World*. Aldershot: Dartmouth.

Laver, Michael, 2002. 'The role and future of the upper house in Ireland', *Journal of Legislative Studies* 8:3: 49–66.

Lijphart, Arend, 1999. *Patterns of Democracy: Government Forms and Performance in Thirty-Six Countries*. New Haven, CT and London: Yale University Press.

Mitchell, Jim, 1999. 'Scandals show reform of Dáil is badly needed', *Irish Times*, 17 December.

Mitchell, Paul, 1999a. 'Government formation: a tale of two coalitions', in Michael Marsh and Paul Mitchell (eds), *How Ireland Voted 1997*. Boulder, CO: Westview and Limerick: PSAI Press, pp. 243–63.

Mitchell, Paul, 1999b. 'Coalition discipline, enforcement mechanisms, and intra-party politics', in Shaun Bowler, David M. Farrell and Richard S. Katz (eds), *Party Discipline and Parliamentary Government*. Columbus: Ohio State University Press, pp. 269–87.

Mitchell, Paul, 2000. 'Ireland: from single-party to coalition rule', in Wolfgang C. Müller and Kaare Strøm (eds), *Coalition Governments in Western Europe*. Oxford: Oxford University Press, pp. 126–57.

Mitchell, Paul, 2001. 'Divided government in Ireland', in Robert Elgie (ed.), *Divided Government in Comparative Perspective*. Oxford: Oxford University Press, pp. 182–208.

Morgan, David Gwynn, 1990. *Constitutional Law of Ireland*, 2nd edn. Blackrock: Round Hall Press.

Norton, Philip (ed.), 1990a. *Parliaments in Western Europe*. London: Frank Cass.

Norton, Philip, 1990b. 'Conclusion: legislatures in perspective', in Philip Norton (ed.), *Parliaments in Western Europe*. London: Frank Cass, pp. 143–52.

O'Halpin, Eunan, 1985. 'The Dáil Committee of Public Accounts, 1961–1980', *Administration* 32:4: 483–511.

O'Halpin, Eunan, 1986. 'Oireachtas committees: experience and prospects', *Seirbhís Phoiblí* 7:2: 3–9.

O'Halpin, Eunan, 1998. 'A changing relationship? Parliament and government in Ireland', in Philip Norton (ed.), *Parliaments and Governments in Western Europe*. London: Frank Cass, pp. 123–41.

O'Toole, Fintan, 1995. *Meanwhile Back at the Ranch: The Politics of Irish Beef*. London: Vintage.

Rose, Richard, 1986. 'British MPs: more bark than bite', in Ezra N. Suleiman (ed.), *Parliaments and Parliamentarians in Democratic Politics*. New York: Holmes and Meier, pp. 8–40.

Seanad Éireann Committee on Procedure and Privileges, Sub-Committee on Seanad Reform, 2004. *Report on Seanad Reform*. Dublin: Stationery Office.

Shaw, Malcolm, 1979. 'Conclusion', in John D. Lees and Malcolm Shaw (eds), *Committees in Legislatures: a Comparative Analysis*. Oxford: Martin Robertson, pp. 361–434.

Sheridan, Kathy, 2002. 'Dáil needs to swap rhetoric for reform', *Irish Times*, 18 October.

Ward, Alan J., 1974. 'Parliamentary procedures and the machinery of government in Ireland', *Irish University Review* 4:2: 222–43.

Ward, Alan J., 1996. 'The Constitution Review Group and the "executive state" in Ireland', *Administration* 44:4: 42–63.

Websites

www.irlgov.ie/oireachtas/frame.htm   The main Oireachtas site. It is one of the most informative sites possessed by any national parliament. All Dáil and Seanad debates going back to the foundation of the state are on the web and electronically searchable, and all legislation passed over the same period is listed, along with standing orders of the Dáil and Seanad. The main page contains a link to the *Parliamentary Bulletin*, published quarterly since 2001 and downloadable in pdf format, which contains data on the number of sitting days, parliamentary questions asked, bills passed and meetings of committees, as well as changes to Dáil and Seanad standing orders and information about every aspect of the work of the Oireachtas.

www.irishstatutebook.ie   The complete text of all legislation passed since the founding of the state.

www.ipu.org   The International Parliamentary Union's valuable site.

9　The constituency role of Dáil deputies

Michael Gallagher and Lee Komito

In Chapter 8 we looked at the legislative and scrutinising roles of Dáil deputies. In this chapter we concentrate on a different aspect of the work of TDs, looking at the business on which they spend a lot of their time, namely constituency work. Some people wonder whether constituency work is really part of the duties of a TD at all; after all, the Irish constitution says nothing about it. Yet, judging by the large amount of time it occupies, it seems in practice to be more important in the working life of a TD than narrowly defined parliamentary duties such as speaking in the Dáil chamber or examining legislation. In most countries, it is taken for granted that parliamentarians will work assiduously to protect and further the interests of their constituents, and that constituency work forms part of an MP's parliamentary duties rather than conflicting with them, but in Ireland there is a body of opinion that sees a constituency role as aberrant and outdated, criticises it as 'clientelism', or believes that it is taken to excess. We shall ask whether there is anything distinctive about Irish practice in this area, looking at the reasons why TDs do so much constituency work, and then consider the consequences it has for the political system

The nature of constituency work

In all parliaments, members have both a formal, national, parliamentary role and a local, often more informal, constituency role. In the former they are expected to play a part in legislative business and in monitoring government behaviour, as was discussed in the previous chapter. In their local role they keep in touch with the people who elected them, looking after the interests both of their constituencies generally and of individual constituents. This role has several components (Searing, 1994: 121–60; Norton, 1994: 706–7). First, there is a 'welfare officer' role, in which the deputy sorts out, usually by interceding with the local or central civil service, a problem on behalf of an individual or group. Second, there is the 'local promoter' role, the deputy being expected to advance the interests of the constituency generally by helping to attract industry to the area, avert factory closures, secure public investment, and so on. Third, the deputy has the role of 'local dignitary', and will be invited to, and expected to attend, a variety of functions in the constituency. The first two of these require some elaboration, though it is worth making the point that whereas in Britain Searing concludes that most constituency-oriented MPs consciously choose either the welfare officer role or the local promoter role, in Ireland most TDs feel that they have little choice but to try to fulfil both.

The Dáil deputy as welfare officer

Those labelled 'welfare officers' by Searing are those 'whose primary focus falls on individual constituents and their difficulties' (Searing, 1994: 124). Examples of what this can involve are advising constituents about the benefits for which they are eligible; advising them how to get one of these benefits (a grant, allowance, pension or livestock headage payment); taking up with the civil service an apparently harsh decision or a case of delay; and helping, or seeming to help, someone to obtain a local authority house or even a job. Some of these activities allegedly involve pulling strings, for example in smoothing the path for dubious planning applications, so for some observers constituency work has negative associations because it is regarded as using undue influence to give particular people unfair advantages. Whatever it entails, it is very time-consuming. A former TD, Máire Geoghegan-Quinn, graphically describes the way in which the welfare officer role imposes on the life of a TD:

> Once you get elected you instantly become public property. You are on call 24 hours a day, 365 days a year. . . . As a TD you become responsible for whatever it is that any one of your 100,000 constituents wants you to be responsible for. They will raise these issues with you when you are out shopping, relaxing in the pub on Sunday night or at any other time they happen to run into you. Alternatively they might decide to, and indeed often do, call to your home to discuss their problems . . . the Dáil only really operates from Tuesday to Thursday. But working in the Dáil alone doesn't tend to get you re-elected. So on Friday, Saturday and Monday you will find TDs criss-crossing their constituencies holding clinics, attending meetings and dealing with local problems. If they are based in any of the larger constituencies they will put up more than a thousand miles a week in their cars. Their evenings are spent at a mixed bag of political and public functions.
>
> (Geoghegan-Quinn, 1998)[1]

TDs do a lot of constituency work – indeed, they spend most of their time doing it, holding several clinics each week in the constituency and exchanging letters or phone calls with constituents and with officials to follow up cases. The evidence relating to the volume of this work is consistent if rather outdated (most of it was conducted prior to 1990), and Kelly's figure of around 60 cases a week is probably the most reliable estimate for the 1980s (Kelly, 1987: 139). It was clear that the volume of constituency work had gone up greatly since earlier surveys in the 1960s (Roche, 1982). The main subject matter of representations was delay, usually concerned with the Department of Social Welfare or local authority housing.

Who contacts TDs, how and why? The 2002 Irish National Election Study found that, since the previous general election five years earlier, more than a fifth of respondents had contacted a TD (Table 9.1). Applying this proportion to the size of the electorate at the 2002 election gives us a figure of around 637,000 people who had contacted a TD over the previous five years so, if we were to assume that each of these people had contacted only one TD (in practice some contact more than one), the average TD would have been contacted by a little over 4,000 different people over the lifetime of the Dáil. If each of these people contacted a TD just once this would work out at around 16 cases per week, and since the number reported by the studies we have mentioned is well in excess of that, it must be assumed that those who do make contact make multiple contacts.

Making contact with a TD is a practice that crosses all social and geographical boundaries, though there are some interesting variations. Rural dwellers are somewhat more likely to do this than those living in towns or cities (see Table 9.1). Middle-aged people are the most likely to contact a TD and the youngest are least likely, as Table 9.1 shows. Moreover, those who are most active generally seem to be most likely to contact a TD; those who reported voting in 2002 were more likely to contact a TD (in other words, it is not true that those who are alienated and detached from the political system are above-average users of TDs' services). In addition, the more interested someone is in politics, the more prone they were to contact a TD (Table 9.1) – though, of course, it may be that contacting a TD heightens interest in politics rather than vice versa. However, many of the other characteristics that we might expect to be related to propensity to contact a TD are not. Social class, education, public/private sector employment and gender are unrelated to the likelihood of contacting a TD, for example. Housing tenure is not significantly related to it, though local authority tenants are a bit more likely than other people to have contacted a TD (26 per cent of them have done so). Most of those who contact a TD seem to be satisfied with the experience, as 88 per cent of them say they would do the same in future in similar circumstances.

Constituents may make contact with TDs by one of a number of routes. The traditional clinic still seems to be the most common, with a further third making contact by telephone (Table 9.2). Smaller numbers wrote or made contact through another person; these intermediaries may well belong to a TD's network of supporters, since a survey of Fine Gael in 1999 found that 61 per cent of members sometimes pass on to TDs requests from constituents (Gallagher and Marsh, 2002: 86). Most commonly, contact is made to take up a matter on one's own behalf, with about a quarter making contact on

Table 9.1 Contact between citizens and TDs, 1997–2002

	Have contacted a TD in last five years (%)		No. of cases
	Yes	*No*	
All	21	79	2,663
Lives in			
Open country	24	76	947
Village or town	20	80	779
City	19	81	859
Age			
18–34	15	85	858
35–54	27	73	834
55–64	26	74	278
65+	20	80	359
Interested in politics?			
Very	33	67	332
Somewhat	22	78	1,175
Not very	19	81	812
Not at all	9	91	316

Source: Irish National Election Study, questions B35, E5, B41.

Note
Total number of cases varies slightly because of missing cases. Cases weighted to ensure that socio-demographic balance reflects that of population as a whole. 'City' includes Dublin city, Dublin county, Cork city, Limerick city, Waterford city and Galway city.

behalf of their family or a friend and slightly fewer acting on behalf of an organisation (Table 9.2). Although education does not affect the overall inclination to make contact with a TD, it is strongly related to the mode and purpose of contact. Among those with no education beyond the junior or inter cert level, 57 per cent had made contact via a clinic, but this figure dropped to 25 per cent among those with a university degree, who were more likely to use the phone. Likewise whereas those whose education did not go beyond the junior or inter cert were mainly making contact on their own behalf (64 per cent), only 46 per cent of those with a degree were doing this; in contrast, 37 per cent of graduates were making contact on behalf of a group compared with only 11 per cent of those with at most the junior or inter cert. In other words, those with least education characteristically visit TDs' clinics to take up a personal problem; those with most education typically phone to lobby on behalf of a group.

Evidently, then, there is a lot of contact between TDs and constituents, and TDs devote a great deal of time to constituency work. Does all this activity serve any useful purpose – do people benefit from asking TDs for

Table 9.2 How and on whose behalf constituents make contact with TDs

	%	*No. of cases*
How was contact made?		
By letter	10	57
By telephone	31	173
Visit to a clinic	50	276
Through another person	9	49
On whose behalf was contact made?		
Self	56	312
Family or friend	26	143
Committee or organisation	19	104
Total	100	555/559

Source: Irish National Election Study, questions B35, B37, B38.

Note

Question B37 did not ask about contact by email. N varies slightly because of missing cases. Cases weighted to ensure that socio-demographic balance reflects that of population as a whole.

assistance? Early studies came to very different conclusions. Bax, whose research was in County Cork, maintained that TDs have considerable power; they could install an associate in a position of power locally and use him or her thereafter. He painted a picture of corruption, string-pulling and bribery (for example, Bax, 1976: 49, 64). In contrast, Sacks, who conducted research in County Donegal, concluded that politicians could achieve very little. They nonetheless manage to create and retain bodies of support by dispensing what he calls 'imaginary patronage' – that is, they convince people that they have achieved something for them even though in reality they haven't (Sacks, 1976: 7–8). Nearly all the constituency work TDs do is carried out, he implies, solely to create the impression that the TD is making an effort. Certainly, some of it might be of this nature: many requests concern cases where the constituent will get the benefit anyway without anyone's help (such as an old age pension) or won't get it as he or she is simply not eligible.

From the civil service side of the fence, Dooney and O'Toole tend to share Sacks's perception. They write sternly that 'officials are not impressed by representations' from politicians and that the 'elaborate and expensive' representations procedure 'very rarely has the effect of having administrative decisions reversed' (Dooney and O'Toole, 1998: 236–7). The implication is that TDs are largely going through the motions in order to impress their constituents with their industry rather than genuinely expecting to have any impact on decisions already reached by the civil service. However, it might seem implausible that TDs can build up, and preserve for many years, a reputation as hard-working and effective constituency politicians simply by dispensing imaginary patronage, unless their constituents are exceptionally gullible.

Moreover, *pace* Bax, there is not much evidence to back up claims of widespread 'string-pulling'. Of course, it is possible that there is more such activity than meets the public eye. When a former minister, Michael Lowry, fell from grace in 1997, with a tribunal finding that he had been benefiting from the black economy since shortly after he was first elected to the Dáil, reporters found considerable local support for him from people who saw him as helpful in various though not precisely specified ways. In the words of one: 'He will help secure finances for certain things. He will help you if you are buying land or setting up your own business. Whatever it is, you can go to Michael, he will be there and if he can he will sort it out.' However, one supporter maintained that Lowry did not get people things to which they were not entitled; he was simply 'an absolute master at cutting through red tape' (quotes from Ingle, 1997). The practice of TDs' making or passing on to the Minister for Justice representations on behalf of constituents charged with or convicted of crimes has attracted criticism, one commentator castigating 'a rampant clientelism in which the political messenger-boy takes no moral responsibility for the message which he is delivering' (Fintan O'Toole, quoted in Collins and O'Shea, 2003: 103). Data released under freedom of information legislation in 2002 showed that 89 of the 166 TDs had made such representations in the previous 22 months (*Irish Times*, 23 October 2002). In April 2002 the political career of Bobby Molloy, a TD and junior minister, was ended after a judge complained that attempts had been made on Molloy's behalf to contact him about a case he had heard (Murphy, 2003: 17).

Overall, though, politicians' scope for pulling strings is not great, and is certainly less than it once was. The principle of appointment on merit rather than through string-pulling was established early on, with the creation of the Civil Service Commission and the Local Appointments Commission. Over the years, the writs of these bodies have been progressively extended. Rate collectors were one of the last sizeable job categories excluded from their scope, and with their inclusion there are now very few types of civil service job where a politician's support can help an applicant. However, the army, the police and the boards of semi-state companies are exempted from the scope of these commissions.

In other words, it is very unlikely that much of the constituency work of TDs involves pulling strings on behalf of constituents, if only because ordinary TDs do not have many strings to pull. It is true that government ministers have the power to make decisions that will benefit or damage individuals, and there have been allegations that string-pulling and corruption have surfaced at this level (see Chapters 13 and 14). Moreover, at local level, scope for enrichment exists because rezoning of land may result in a substantial financial gain for the landowner, and charges of corruption in this area have led to tribunals of inquiry and to criminal prosecutions (see Chapter 14). Even so, all the evidence is that the bulk of the constituency work conducted by ordinary backbench TDs is more mundane and less ethically questionable than this. A consensus has emerged that TDs can be helpful to constituents, but not by getting them things to which they are not entitled. Instead, the value of contacting a TD lies in the fact that this can enable people to find out about the existence of – and/or how to obtain – benefits, grants or rights of which they would otherwise have been unaware.

This was the conclusion of research conducted in Dublin in the late 1970s and early 1980s. It found that the claim of politicians 'to power or influence rested on their ability to monopolise and then market their specialist knowledge of state resources and their access to bureaucrats who allocated such resources' (Komito, 1984: 174). Politicians could tell people what they were eligible for and how to secure it; this involved little work for the politician but saved constituents, many of whom are 'bureaucratically illiterate', a lot of work. In addition, a TD's intervention sometimes forced a case to be reviewed, a decision to be speeded up or a service to be provided (Komito, 1984: 182–3).

Kelly found much the same from her analysis of the caseload of Michael D. Higgins, a Galway West TD. Despite the picture presented by Dooney and O'Toole (1998: 235–7), according to which representations from politicians rarely have any effect, Kelly (1987: 145) found that in many instances the TD was able to secure a benefit for people after they had initially been turned down by the civil service, and he also got cases speeded up. He achieved this not by pulling strings but because of his expertise: his knowledge of how best to present the case and of what sort of supporting documentation was needed. Some people had been corresponding with the wrong department, while others had omitted steps such as quoting their social welfare number or obtaining a doctor's certificate to back up their case. The point that some people really do benefit from contacting a TD was put colourfully in 1997 by a renowned exponent of constituency work, P. J. Sheehan, a Fine Gael TD for Cork South-West from 1981 to 2002. During his successful re-election campaign, he posed the rhetorical question:

> In rural Ireland, many don't have the confidence, or the knowledge about where to go or how to fight for their rights . . . as long as we have the present system and bureaucracy exists, there will be a need for a helping hand and a friendly ear. If this service isn't needed, why are my clinics from the Head of Kinsale to the Dursey Sound overflowing with people every weekend?[2]
>
> (*Southern Star*, 31 May 1997, p. 3)

The notion that the bureaucracy operates unproblematically and that constituents really have no need to take any problems to a TD is also disputed by a Dublin deputy, Róisín Shortall of the Labour party:

I represent an area with a very high level of unemployment, poverty, housing problems, and people who spend their lives in queues, trying to sort out social welfare issues. I get up to 250 letters a week, and the follow-up on all these takes time. I wish it were not so. I wish people were sufficiently empowered to sort out their own problems. I wish they could go to their citizens' advice bureau and get the help they need. But this doesn't happen.

(*Irish Times*, 13 June 1995, p. 11)

So researchers have not found evidence of TDs interfering on a major scale with the equitable operation of the political or administrative system, but, equally, it is not true that TDs cannot achieve anything and that those who attend their clinics are suffering from a collective delusion. The picture to which most research points is that constituency work mainly involves rather routine activity, attending many clinics and local meetings, writing letters, helping people to sort out their social welfare problems and so on, rather than anything more corrupt or devious. The TD's welfare officer role, in fact, resembles that of a lawyer, who operates not by bribing the judge but by ensuring that the case is presented better than the ordinary citizen would be able to present it. In many ways, politicians' brokerage activities are similar to the activities of a range of professional mediators (such as priests, advice centre personnel and trade union officials); the difference derives from their special access to the state bureaucracy and their specific motives in carrying out brokerage functions.

The Dáil deputy as local promoter

The local promoter role is concerned primarily with making representations about 'the constituency's collective needs, which may be economic, environmental, or social' (Searing, 1994: 130). It may involve activity on behalf of a community, town, or residents' association, for example to persuade central or local government to improve water or sewerage services, street lighting, or roads. As when acting in the welfare officer role, this might involve the TD in contacting civil servants to try to get a decision reversed or speeded up. Another aspect of the local promoter role is that a TD is expected to fight to increase the constituency's share of whatever cakes exist: that is, to attract new industries to the area, to prevent existing industries closing, to get state backing for local projects, and generally to ensure that the constituency does well out of the disbursement of government resources.

Voters in many constituencies seem to feel that their area is hard done by, so at elections TDs and other candidates invariably stress their determination to rectify matters. A recurrent theme in the campaigns of non-incumbents is that the sitting TDs have failed to 'deliver' for the constituency (or a part of it), which has been neglected for many years, getting only 'crumbs from the Celtic Tiger', as one candidate put it in 2002. At the

Box 9.1 **Irish politicians and the delivery of largesse**

Between 1997 and 2002 the minority Fianna Fáil–Progressive Democrat administration reached agreements with four independent TDs under which the latter would support the government in exchange for spending on specified projects in their constituencies. One of these TDs, Mildred Fox, said her constituency of Wicklow had gained the following from this deal (*Irish Times*, 10 August 2000 – £1 was equal to €1.27):

- CAT scanner for Loughlinstown hospital – £500,000
- District Veterinary Officer for Wicklow town
- secondary school at Kilcoole – £4 million approximately
- Bray garda station – £3 million
- improvement on N81 road in west Wicklow – £1.15 million allocated for 2001
- one-stop shop for Wicklow County Council at Blessington
- CCTV system for Bray
- refurbishment of courthouse in Baltinglass
- library in Baltinglass
- additional funding for Wicklow jail museum.

The other TDs concerned (Harry Blaney, Tom Gildea and Jackie Healy-Rae) made similar claims about their own success in getting public spending commitments.

Critics from other constituencies argued that it was wrong that money that should have been spent in the national interest was going disproportionately to four constituencies simply because these TDs were in a pivotal position. At the same time, others suggested that there was no evidence that the TDs could claim legitimate credit for the projects and that the government was securing the support of the independent TDs without actually doing anything it would not have done anyway.

Ministers are expected to secure largesse for their home base or for the constituency as a whole. Names such as Pádraig Flynn in Castlebar, Ray MacSharry in Sligo, and Michael Lowry in Thurles are cited in this context, along with Dick Spring, who held senior positions in governments from 1982 to 1987 and from 1993 to 1997. When Spring stepped down as Labour Party leader in November 1997, a reporter found many testimonies to his ability to deliver 'pork' to his constituency and especially to his own base in Tralee, such as a leisure centre, a heritage project, a marina, hotels, a new sewage treatment plant, a regional college, a technology park, and so on, all of which were attributed to his efforts and influence. The reporter concluded: 'Modern-day Tralee is almost unrecognisable compared to a decade ago. The town is on the crest of a wave. The man who made it happen is Dick Spring' (Hogan, 1997).

In December 2003 the government announced a plan to decentralise government departments from Dublin to locations around the country. The junior minister Tom Parlon immediately issued leaflets in his constituency headed 'Parlon Delivers! 965 jobs!', listing the five towns affected and the number of jobs each was set to receive – though it was later alleged that he had played no part in the decision but had merely got wind of it before it was announced.

---

election of that year, John Connor, one of the three Fine Gael candidates for the two-county constituency of Longford–Roscommon, said:

> The north and west [of Roscommon] are the most neglected parts of the whole county, not having benefited at all from what it should have benefited from. We didn't have a voice in the last five years in north and west Roscommon to speak up when decisions were being made. Unless we have deputies [in this area of the county] we are going to be left out again. . . . There's a widespread knowledge that this part of the county has been left out and has not been delivered to. That goes right across the political lines – nobody can deny this part of the constituency has done badly and shouldn't have done in times of the most unprecedented prosperity we have ever seen.
>
> (*Longford News*, 3 May 2002, p. 7)

Essentially the same sentiments are expressed by many other candidates around the country at every election.

Given his or her very limited power, though, there is not a great deal that the ordinary TD can achieve – unless they happen to be an independent TD holding the balance of power. The four independents in this position in the 1997–2002 Dáil gave their support to the government in exchange for commitments of public expenditure in their constituencies (see Box 9.1). Other than this, TDs can do little except to lobby hard those, primarily ministers, who make the important decisions. If a TD becomes a minister, constituents' expectations will rise accordingly, as there is a belief that a minister who is sufficiently hard-working and adroit can 'deliver' in a big way for the constituency. Ministers may help foster this impression. In 1999, when a factory closed in his Longford base, Albert Reynolds said that this would not have happened had he still been Taoiseach: 'The truth is that I have no more political clout where it matters and the IDA [Industrial Development Agency] and Enterprise Ireland only respond to political pressure' (*Irish Times*, 7 October 1999). Both bodies, incidentally, immediately denied that any of their decisions were swayed by political factors.

Examples abound of ministers who are said to have secured largesse – 'pork', in American terminology – for their constituency, or at least for their own base within it (see Box 9.1). In this way, voters have an incentive, when choosing their TDs, to elect candidates of perceived ministerial ability. As we saw in Chapter 4, the Irish electoral system provides for intra-party competition for electoral support, and supporters of the largest parties usually have a choice of candidates. Despite suggestions that voters' desire for good constituency representation might lead them to choose active locally oriented representatives at the expense of people of national ability, and hence lower the calibre of parliamentarians (part of the argument of Carty, 1981: 137), in fact voters making their choices purely on the basis of local considerations have a strong incentive to support candidates of ministerial ability, because a minister can deliver the goods locally on a much grander scale than a permanent backbencher. Ironically, then, a desire for good local representation can lead to the election of nationally-oriented politicians.

Constituency work and clientelism

Some people use the term 'clientelist politics' to describe politics in Ireland; journalists and politicians alike are prone to speak of 'our clientelist system'. The picture painted by Bax and Sacks, as we have outlined, is one of politicians doing favours (real according to Bax, imaginary according to Sacks) for people and in return being rewarded by a vote at the next election. The suggestion is that politicians gradually build up a sizeable and fairly stable 'clientele' of people who are under some obligation to them; the politicians are able to 'call in the debts' at election time. Most voters, it is implied, are part of some politician's clientele.

However, the word 'clientele' would not be very apposite to describe those who give a first preference vote to a particular Dáil candidate. TDs simply do not possess 'clienteles'. Most people, as we saw earlier (Table 9.1), do not contact TDs at all. Moreover, even those who are helped by a TD cannot be taken for granted. For one thing, some of them 'do the rounds' of the clinics, hoping to improve their chances by getting several TDs to chase up their case. For another, even if a TD does something for a constituent, the secrecy of the ballot means that he or she has no way of knowing whether the favour is returned at the ballot box. Many of the key characteristics of clientelism, such as the solidarity binding 'clients' and 'patrons', are simply not present in Irish electoral politics (Farrell, 1985: 241; Collins and O'Shea, 2003: 88–90).

Thus, an earlier study concluded that 'politicians believed that they were inevitably dependent on the votes of anonymous constituents with whom

they could have no direct links' (Komito, 1984: 181). Far from resting comfortably atop pyramids of loyal supporters, they come across as 'professional
paranoids', permanently insecure, always busy at constituency work but
never sure that any of it will pay electoral dividends. They promote a high
community profile, advertise clinics, turn up at residents' association meetings and so on, not to build up a clientele – which is impossible – but simply
to earn a reputation as hard-working people. They hope that even people
who never actually need their services are impressed and will conclude that
the TD will be there if they ever need him or her. Much as TDs might wish
that they could build up solid clienteles by their constituency work, its
rewards are uncertain.

This being so, the word 'clientelism' is not appropriate to describe what
TDs do in their role as constituency representatives. It is more realistic to
see TDs as being engaged in 'brokerage', a distinct concept. A broker deals
in access to those who control resources rather than directly in the resources
themselves; there might be situations in which a person wants something
but is unable or unwilling to obtain it from the actor who has it, in which
case the services of a broker may be useful. Once the service has been provided, the brokerage relationship ends. The main difference between brokerage and clientelism is that clientelism implies a more intense, more
permanent relationship. It involves 'clients', people who are in some way
tied in to the person who does things for them, whereas 'brokerage' implies a
relationship that is not institutionalised. Thus to say that Irish politics is
characterised by clientelism would suggest that TDs have clienteles, sizeable
bodies of people who are linked directly to them and who are in some way in
their debt. 'To describe a political system as clientelistic is to imply persistent
and diffuse relations of exchange in a closed system where all participants
are either leaders or followers, and never simply uninvolved' (Komito, 1984:
176). To say that Irish politics is characterised by brokerage would imply
that there are many people who do not have any dealings with TDs, and
that even the people who do use TDs as brokers are not under any direct
obligation to them as a result. Although the loosely-used term 'clientelism'
has caught on in some circles as a way of describing constituency work, most
reliable research suggests that brokerage rather than clientelism, as defined
above, is the appropriate term to characterise TDs' constituency activities.

The term 'clientelism' may be used by some commentators partly because
of its pejorative and nefarious connotations; it has overtones of manipulation
and string-pulling, of a mode of behaviour that some feel Ireland should be
moving away from, in contrast to the more neutral 'brokerage'. Eisenstadt
and Roniger (1984: 18) observe that the tendency develops in many societies
to perceive less formalised relations of this kind as 'slightly subversive to the
institutionalised order, to fully institutionalised relationships or to membership of collectivities'. As we shall see later, constituency work in Ireland has
been criticised on precisely these grounds.

Constituency work in comparative perspective

Before going on to examine the reasons why TDs engage in so much constituency work, we will look briefly at patterns in other countries; this should dispel any illusion that the constituency role of Irish parliamentarians is somehow unusual. 'Grievance chasing' is part of the role of the parliamentarian virtually everywhere: 'members of every type of legislature say that they are subjected to an incessant flow of such [casework] demands, and they indicate that coping with them requires a substantial portion of their time and resources' (Mezey, 1979: 159). More broadly, relationships (which may or may not be of the patron–client form) based on personal linkages tend to exist in all types of society – modern or traditional, western or eastern, developed or pre-modern (Eisenstadt and Roniger, 1984).

For example, in France the role of the *député* is seen by voters as 'interceding with central government on behalf of individuals or councils, rather than as a legislator or watchdog over executive power or debater of the great issues of the day', and so deputies spend most of their time on constituency work (Frears, 1990: 46). Even members of the United Kingdom House of Commons, sometimes seen as relatively nationally oriented, are on the receiving end of a sizeable volume of constituency demands; just as in Ireland, the leisurely pace of the past has been replaced by a pattern of frenetic activity. In 1971 constituency work accounted for less than a fifth of the hours worked by MPs during parliamentary sessions, but by 1996 it had increased to two-fifths, and to three-fifths during recesses. By 1997, a clear majority of MPs of all parties saw their constituency role as more important than either their national parliamentary role or their party role (Rush, 2001: 210–11, 216).

Wood and Young, directly comparing recently elected British MPs with Irish TDs on the basis of a 1995 survey, found that the MPs did less constituency work than the TDs, but not very much less. MPs spent 1.8 days a week in their constituency compared with 2.5 days for TDs; MPs devoted 35 hours a week to constituency work compared with 49 hours for TDs; MPs spent 47 per cent of their time on constituency work compared with 58 per cent for TDs (Wood and Young, 1997: 221). Most TDs believed that their re-election prospects would be damaged if they cut back on their constituency work, but most MPs did not believe this. Why, then, do MPs in Britain do so much constituency work? The main factor, another study concludes, is the psychological satisfaction that comes from doing it, 'combined with a general sense that casework is an important public duty of representatives' (Norris, 1997: 47).

The only data that are directly comparable to those presented in Table 9.1 come from a cross-national study in which respondents were asked whether they had contacted an MP in the last 12 months (as opposed to the last five years, as in the Irish survey). This found that an average of 11 per cent had made such contact in the 19 countries studied; the figure ranged from 3 per cent in Spain up to 26 per cent in New Zealand (Curtice and Shively, 2000: 10). There is no way of knowing whether a figure of 11 per cent per year represents a higher or a lower level of contact than the Irish figure of 21 per cent over five years – the most that can be said is that the Irish pattern does not seem too far from the mainstream.

Given this pattern, it would be very surprising if Irish members of parliament did *not* have heavy constituency workloads. Defending and promoting the interests of one's constituents to the best of one's abilities is 'part of the job' for a member of parliament, and it is hard to imagine a job specification for TDs that does not include this role. Perhaps, as Collins and O'Shea (2003: 106) suggest, the contrary view derives partly from a 'deeply-held' bureaucratic idea that politicians, certainly ministers, should confine themselves to broad issues of policy and that any involvement in administration is thus inappropriate interference. The constituency role is recognised by law, even if not in the constitution, in that some of the payments and facilities made available to TDs are expressly for the purpose of carrying out their constituency work (O'Halpin, 2002: 113). Perhaps, indeed, what requires explaining is not why TDs do a lot of constituency work but, rather, why anyone should think it strange that they do. However, this question, interesting as it is, falls outside the scope of the present chapter.

Causes of constituency work

Even though members of parliament almost everywhere have a heavy constituency load, the perception of Irish politics as 'clientelist' and somehow anomalous seems to be so widespread that it is worth trying to explain the high volume of casework descending on TDs. Four factors in particular are frequently mentioned: political cultural attitudes to the state, the small scale of society, the electoral system, and the nature of the Irish administrative system. The potential impact of the ever-wider use of new technology is also discussed.

Political culture

Two aspects of Irish political culture are relevant to the constituency role of TDs. First, past attitudes to the state may still have a bearing on current attitudes. Second, the nature of elite political culture means that TDs regard serving their constituents as one of their most important roles.

First, historical factors may have led to some alienation from the state. In all peasant societies, the capital city and the machinery of central government tend to be looked on with some suspicion, and in Ireland this was reinforced by the non-indigenous nature of the ruling elite. Chubb (1992: 210) suggests that brokerage is:

deeply rooted in Irish experience. For generations, Irish people saw that to get the benefits that public authorities bestow, the help of a man with connections and influence was necessary. All that democracy has meant is that such a person has been laid on officially, as it were, and is now no longer a master but a servant.

The argument is that the political culture of the nineteenth century and before, when central government was for obvious reasons perceived as alien, remote and best approached via an intermediary, has carried on into the post-independence state. Former Taoiseach Garret FitzGerald comments that Dublin 'is still widely perceived in rural Ireland as if it were even today a centre of alien colonial rule' (FitzGerald, 1991: 364). Given that so many other aspects of pre-independence political culture have a bearing on contemporary politics (see Chapter 2), this is perfectly plausible, and indeed surveys testify to people's belief that a TD is the best person to approach if one wants to be sure of getting one's entitlements (Farrell, 1985: 243; Komito, 1992).

This cultural explanation would become dubious, however, if linked too closely with the notion of a 'dying peasant culture' or with a suggestion that people's tendency to approach their TDs springs from an atavistic misconception of the way in which officialdom works. After all, the volume of brokerage seems to be increasing rather than decreasing as urbanisation and the decline of agriculture proceed. Political culture and the legacy of the past are part of the explanation, but we need to look also for causes in present-day Ireland: 'rather than an outmoded style of behaviour, brokerage is an effective solution to a particular set of problems' (Komito, 1984: 191). This also means that there is no reason to expect brokerage work to go away as 'modernisation' continues.

Second, elite political culture leads TDs to regard local and constituency representation as 'normal', rather than as something that 'takes them away from their real job'. TDs interviewed by Mary-Clare O'Sullivan reported that their constituency, rather than the nation as a whole or a specific sectional group, was their main representational focus (O'Sullivan, 2002: 206–7). When TDs were asked what they had hoped to achieve when they entered politics, a plurality replied 'promote the interests of the local area' (O'Sullivan, 2002: 209). Some TDs drift away from this aim and come to prioritise national policies, while others, who find their initial national-level goals to be unachievable, acquire a stronger local focus over time (O'Sullivan, 2002: 211–12). TDs did not, though, see the local role as excluding a nationally oriented one, for more of them identified 'legislating and influencing policy' as being among the most important duties and responsibilities of a TD than identified 'representing the constituency' (O'Sullivan, 2002: 237). In other words, TDs accept that active constituency representation comes with the job, though they do not see this as being incompatible with a nationally focused role.

Small size of society

In all societies, informal networks of trust exist within and alongside formal structures. Such networks may be particularly significant in small societies where many people have some kind of direct or indirect access to decision makers that bypasses the formal structure. The Republic of Ireland is clearly, in relative terms, a small society, with only four million people, and this has an impact on people's perceptions of their deputies' role. At the 2002 election, for example, there was one deputy for every 18,085 electors and for every 11,192 valid votes. Very few other countries have as high a ratio of deputies to voters.

One might expect that the fewer people each member of parliament represents, the lower his or her constituency workload will be. Yet, at the same time, the fewer people each member represents, the more contact voters are likely to expect with him or her. In the USA, it has been found that the smaller the number of people represented by each Senator, the more those people are likely to define the Senator's role in pork-barrel terms and the more contact they are likely to have with their Senators (Hibbing and Alford, 1990). With such a small number of voters to represent, it is hardly surprising that deputies find themselves asked to play the role of 'mediator-advocate *vis-à-vis* the local and national administrative bureaucracies', as Farrell (1985: 242) puts it. At the 2002 election, 71 per cent of voters had spoken personally to the candidate to whom they gave their first preference.

A reinforcing factor in Ireland is the high degree of centralisation of decision making, nearly all of which takes place in Dublin. Local government is weak, with very few powers (see Chapter 14), and there are no intermediate (regional or provincial) tiers of government. It is noticeable that the casework loads of Belgian MPs dropped dramatically once federalism was introduced in the mid-1990s (De Winter, 2002: 100). The upshot of the absence of significant sub-national government in Ireland is that national parliamentary representatives get requests for assistance with what in many other countries would be purely local matters. This is reinforced by the fact that most TDs come to the Dáil via local government, and in the past have tended to remain on local councils after becoming TDs. Indeed, according to the 2002 election survey, TDs are contacted much more than councillors; only 11 per cent of voters had contacted a councillor in the previous five years (and a mere 2 per cent had contacted a senator), compared with 21 per cent for TDs. It remains to be seen how this changes following the outlawing of the dual mandate since June 2004 (see Chapter 14).

The electoral system

The electoral system is sometimes suggested as a cause of brokerage since, as we saw in Chapter 4, PR-STV puts candidates of the same party in competition with each other and thereby forces them to establish an edge over their so-called running mates. Running mates are a definite danger. Between 1922 and 1997, 34 per cent of all TDs who suffered defeat at an election, and 56 per cent of defeated Fianna Fáil TDs, lost their seat not to a rival party's candidate but to one of their running mates (Gallagher, 2000: 97). Moreover, as we saw in Chapter 8, backbench deputies cannot easily establish a reputation as outstanding parliamentarians and fight internal party battles on this terrain. So, once the demand for brokerage activity arises, TDs feel they have to respond to it. When surveyed by Wood and Young (1997: 221), 60 per cent of recently elected TDs said they felt they could lose their seat if they reduced their constituency work.

TDs are probably right to believe that their electoral fortunes are affected by their reputations as constituency workers. Surveys have consistently shown that voters, when asked to rank a number of factors as determinants of their votes, attach more importance to 'choosing a TD who will look after the local needs of the constituency' than to anything else (Garry *et al.*, 2003: 125). Even if some of those who say they want a TD who will look after the constituency are in fact expressing a choice *within* party rather than a choice regardless of party, it is clear that voters attach importance to this role. Party members, certainly in Fine Gael, regard the local brokerage role as more important than the national parliamentary one (Gallagher and Marsh, 2002: 131–2). Newly elected TDs, as part of their informal socialisation process in the Dáil, learn the conventional wisdom among politicians that ignoring constituency work is electoral suicide.

The electoral system gives a strong incentive to TDs to respond with alacrity to the demand that they do constituency work, but it doesn't really explain where this demand comes from in the first place. Even accepting that TDs eagerly advertise their availability and actively seek problems to solve, and maybe thereby generate more constituency work than would arise otherwise, this still leaves a lot that arises from other causes.

Emphasis on the electoral system as a significant cause of the constituency role of TDs implies that under a different electoral system the volume of constituency work might diminish significantly. This is very doubtful; members of parliament in countries with a range of completely different electoral systems undertake a lot of constituency work (Gallagher, 1996: 512–18). Even if Ireland moved to a closed-list PR system, where the voters simply have to accept the candidates selected by the party organisation without being able to choose among them, MPs might still do a lot of constituency work, as Belgian MPs did under such a system in the 1990s. They did this in order to discharge what was felt to be a duty, together with the gratification that comes from achieving something tangible for a constituent, as well as establishing one's position as a VIP in the constituency, in contrast with the anonymity of life as a backbencher. In addition, the candidate selectors, i.e. the local party members, when deciding how to order the candidates on the party list, favoured candidates who were active in dealing with casework

(De Winter, 1997). The evidence does not support a belief that a new electoral system would reduce or remove the burden of constituency work.

Administrative structures

The argument here is essentially that some citizens need brokers to obtain their entitlements. This is the conclusion of Roche and Komito and implicitly of others, such as Valerie Kelly, as well as TDs such as Róisín Shortall and P. J. Sheehan whom we cited earlier. As Roche (1982: 103) puts it: 'Irish complaint behaviour is a manifestation of a breakdown at the interface level between Ireland's public institutions and the Irish public.' In other words, some people turn to TDs to help them due to the frustration that results from their own direct dealings with the state apparatus.

This arises because of the nature of the machinery with which citizens come into contact. All bureaucracies tend to develop certain characteristics, such as inflexibility, rigid adherence to the rules and perhaps impatience with people who do not fully understand these rules. In Ireland, there is very little occupational mobility between the public service and the wider economy. There may be a bureaucratic tendency to send out standard replies that do not address a specific query, not to explain fully what someone is entitled to or why some application has been turned down – and inevitably there will be cases of delay. One TD in an interview stated that 'a lot of the work you get is a matter of red tape and . . . really we shouldn't be dealing with it – if officials at various levels were more consumer friendly . . . we wouldn't have half the workload we have' (O'Sullivan, 2002: 291).

All of this leaves many people wanting assistance from someone willing to help them, and contacting a TD often seems the most attractive option. The civil service has an appeal procedure, but those whose problems spring from 'bureaucratic illiteracy' are unlikely to be able to make much use of this. Moreover, in the past some appeal procedures have been viewed more as extensions of the bureaucracy that made the initial adverse decision than as independent structures (Hogan and Morgan, 1998: 275–82). A more promising step is to seek assistance from a Citizens Information Centre (CIC). There are 86 such centres around the country; they operate under the auspices of the state-funded Comhairle (formerly the National Social Service Board (NSSB)) but are run largely by volunteers. Their services are used much more by women than by men, and those under 35 make up more than half of their clients (Browne, 1999: 57–8); in both these respects their clients' profile differs from that of those who contact TDs, which we discussed earlier (pp. 244–5). CICs not only give information on social welfare entitlements but, where appropriate, also take up cases with the relevant office or department, though the great majority of cases involve only imparting information (Browne, 1999: 34). In 2002 they dealt with around 459,000 queries, nearly four times as many as in 1996 (Comhairle, 2003: 22). In addition, OASIS, a public service information system on the internet, received

960,000 queries in 2002, and a further 236,000 went to CIDB, a database provided by Comhairle containing information on rights and entitlements (Comhairle, 2003: 22, 27). This is clear evidence of public demand for assistance in dealing with the state bureaucracy. However, the restricted opening hours of CICs, and, perhaps, the limited ability of their volunteers to persuade public officials to reverse a decision, mean that these centres and services clearly do not meet the full demand.

One potentially valuable channel for obtaining rectification of grievances is the office of the Ombudsman, which was established in January 1984 (see Hogan and Morgan, 1998: 337–93, for the powers and operation of the office). This office has the role of investigating complaints from members of the public who feel that they have been treated unfairly by public bodies. The Ombudsman has the power to demand any information, document or file from a body complained against and can summon any official of that body to give information about a complaint. The number of cases coming in to the Ombudsman is not large. Over the five-year period 1998–2002 the office received on average about 2,400 valid cases a year, plus a further 1,400 that fell outside its jurisdiction.[3] Nearly half the valid complaints related to the civil service (47 per cent of them), with 32 per cent concerning local authorities, 18 per cent health boards and 3 per cent An Post. Of the valid cases, only 22 per cent were fully or partially resolved, with assistance being provided in a further 28 per cent; 35 per cent were not upheld and 15 per cent were discontinued. Details of some of the cases outlined in the annual reports of the office show how difficult it has sometimes been even for the Ombudsman, endowed as the office is with statutory powers to demand all the files relating to a case, to persuade the bureaucrats concerned that they should review a decision, highlighting the difficulties that ordinary citizens can encounter.

However, given the earlier estimates of TDs' caseloads, Dáil members collectively are contacted by nearly 700,000 people over a five-year period, and clearly most of these do not come to the Ombudsman, given that the office received only 19,527 cases (over a third of which fell outside its jurisdiction) over the five years 1998–2002. When the Ombudsman's 1996 annual report was debated in the Dáil, several TDs made the point that the office seemed to be handling hardly any more cases than the average TD. One commented that when the Ombudsman solves someone's problem, his work was praised as vindicating the rights of the ordinary citizen, yet when TDs do the same their activities are frowned upon and dismissed as 'an antiquated practice of parish pump politics' (Michael Noonan, *Dáil Debates* 480: 1483–4, 2 October 1997). One reason, no doubt, for the disparity in the numbers of cases received is that TDs seem more available and accessible than the Ombudsman, despite the latter's willingness to be of assistance. A survey carried out in October 1996 discovered that only 34 per cent of adults seemed to be aware of the office of Ombudsman (*Annual Report 1997*: 8). It is clear that the office has, to say the least, not established itself in the public mind as the first port of call when assistance in dealing with the bureaucracy is needed. Another reason why most people do not go to the Ombudsman is that many cases coming to TDs result from a lack of information as to how best to utilise the administrative system (or just disgruntlement with a decision) and do not involve possible maladministration; as John Whyte (1966: 16) put it, they are problems on 'a humbler scale' than would warrant the attention of the Ombudsman. In the words of the NSSB, 'the problem for most people in writing to the various Departments seems to be (i) not knowing exactly which section to address their letter to and (ii) the standard letter of reply may not deal satisfactorily with their enquiry' (NSSB, *Annual Report 1991*: 7).

So, almost by default, people wanting assistance turn to public representatives, who cannot afford to be abrupt or offhand – TDs' jobs, unlike those of civil servants, may depend on how helpful and approachable they are. Moreover, through experience TDs probably can be of genuine assistance: as one TD put it, 'there is hardly a Deputy in this House who is not at least as conversant with the supplementary welfare allowance scheme as are the community welfare officers' (Proinsias De Rossa, *Dáil Debates* 428: 834, 25 March 1993). TDs are very visible, available, highly responsive, and possessed of relevant expertise.

To suggest that the nature of the Irish administrative system is part of the explanation for the high volume of brokerage demands made to TDs might seem to imply that civil servants are not doing their jobs perfectly. In one sense this is true, in that if the Irish public service dealt with all cases effectively, promptly and to the complete satisfaction of the citizen, there would be no need for brokers. But no large organisation does or ever will work this way, so such a standard is unrealistic. It would be unfair to put all the blame on civil servants. Individual civil servants may not have enough training to be as helpful to the public as they would like to be and besides, as Collins and O'Shea (2003: 105) observe, traditionally 'the public servant is not rewarded for being helpful and approachable'.

Civil servants could stifle the brokerage system only by refusing to entertain any representations from politicians. They do not do this, partly because that system suits both politicians and civil servants, especially at the local level (Komito, 1984: 188–9). It protects the bureaucrats to some extent, since politicians form a barrier between them and the public. Without politicians acting as brokers, many more people would be tackling them directly; as it is, politicians form an unofficial complaints tribunal. In this capacity politicians also provide an unpaid monitoring service; they can differentiate those who have been dealt with harshly or have lost out on the benefit of the doubt from those whose complaint is groundless. If a TD or councillor then makes a firm complaint about a particular case, the official can be fairly sure that it has some basis, since politicians will not risk jeopardising their ongoing relationship with the official on behalf of an undeserving constituent. So, in effect, politicians do some preliminary screening of cases and then present the strongest among them in a manner tailored to the expectations of the civil service, which helps the officials. In return, civil servants may well give special priority to representations from TDs and respond more sympathetically than to letters of complaint or injury from ordinary members of the public; for over a decade there has been a special exclusive 'hotline' in the Department of Social Welfare to enable TDs to enquire about individual cases (statement by Minister for Social Welfare – *Dáil Debates* 421: 778–9, 23 June 1992). In addition, officials consider politicians to be more 'trustworthy'. Politicians have a stake in maintaining good relations with officials, so officials can rectify errors without any adverse comment. Members of the public, having no stake in the status quo, cannot be similarly trusted; officials are less likely to admit, and hence to rectify, errors.

Impact of new technology

The problems people experienced in dealing with the state bureaucracy were exacerbated in the 1960s and 1970s by the rapid growth in both the number of services being provided and the number of people looking for these services. Long delays in processing a social welfare claim, for instance, were the result of increases in the number of people applying for assistance and of an increasingly complex application procedure to decide eligibility. More recently, though, new technology has alleviated some of the difficulties. Structural improvements (such as computerisation) have reduced processing delays; the result may not suit the applicant, but at least the answer is known more quickly. Moreover, the need for assistance simply to find out where in the queue an application sits is somewhat less. This has reduced the scope for brokerage interventions by politicians – their ability to get fast answers is now a less valuable commodity.

New technology and the advent of the 'information society' might reduce the need for politicians' assistance still further by changing the relationship between government, TDs and voters. The amount of information made available has increased dramatically in recent years. The government has invested in web-based information systems that enable citizens to discover what their entitlements are and, in some cases, to apply for these electronically. This has reduced the monopoly that politicians previously enjoyed over information about entitlements and claiming procedures. Individuals can apply for services and benefits and monitor the progress of their application without recourse to politicians or even officials. Even those without access to the internet can use freephone or low-call numbers to access officials directly and these officials can provide immediate answers to individual queries. This is due partly to a changed attitude in the civil service, which is now more encouraging about citizen queries, but it also results from a change in the information system that enables civil servants to answer such queries for a relatively low 'transaction cost'. Part of the reason for going to politicians before was that the 'cost' of answering a query was relatively high. The person dealing with the query had to be located, the necessary file had to be dug out, details might have to be checked with other bureaucrats, and so on. Only a politician was important enough to warrant such an investment of time. With new office technologies, the cost of dealing with the query has been significantly reduced, so answering a citizen's query is now affordable.

There is also, perhaps partly as a result of corruption investigations and tribunals, more transparency in how scarce resources (such as public housing) are allocated to applicants and so less scope for political intervention in the administrative process. Anecdotal evidence suggests that this may have decreased the constituency work load of politicians to some extent, but that it has not made a huge impact on the previous level of activity. It also seems to have increased the level of general policy interventions that politicians are requested to make (as opposed to interventions for personal services). However, local queries ranging from parking and the painting of railings in public buildings still arrive for TDs.

New technologies are also having an impact on communication between politicians and constituents. An increasing number of politicians (31 out of 166 TDs and six out of 60 senators in early 2004) have their own web sites in order to enhance their visibility. Typically, these have information about the politician's activities, both local and national, as well as information about how to contact him or her. Many TDs, especially in urban areas, encourage constituents to contact them electronically. This has two advantages for politicians. First, it reduces their work load, as electronic queries can be received and processed by administrative assistants and the outcome of the query can simply be communicated electronically to the constituent. The second advantage is that it provides additional contacts for the TD's database. Politicians keep track of constituent queries on electronic databases, which are the basis for mailing lists that are used to electoral advantage. Constituents can receive personalised mail shots at elections as well as newsletters between elections. They can also be sent an electronic newsletter detailing the activities of the politician – this is much less expensive to print and circulate than the printed version and is a cost-effective means of maintaining visibility in the constituency. In middle-class constituencies, constituents' ability to contact TDs via email or telephone reduces the number of clinics that TDs need to hold. However, in poorer urban areas, as in rural areas, the level of clinic activity continues as in previous years.

New technology does not render the constituency role of TDs redundant. The increase in efficiency has not been matched in most areas by any marked increase in transparency: the rules for determining eligibility remain complex, and thus the need for the assistance of someone who understands the system remains. Those citizens whose resources for dealing with the bureaucracy are fewest are also the least likely to be able to make meaningful use of the information society. Furthermore, there has been no great increase in the amount of trust extended to civil servants and their activities, and thus the need for someone who can be trusted to act on one's behalf remains.

Consequences of TDs' constituency work

Some of the consequences of the constituency role of TDs are highly tangible, while others are less so. Brokerage work affects the operation of the political and administrative systems, and some suggest that it plays a part in shaping political culture. We shall look at its impact on the Dáil, the government and the civil service, and consider its effects on people's attitudes towards politics generally.

Impact on the Dáil and the government

This is the most obvious and tangible area in which brokerage has an impact. Dealing with casework reduces the time available for formal parliamentary duties such as examining legislation and discussing policy, which weakens the Dáil's ability to provide effective scrutiny of government and to contribute to policy formation, and for these reasons some deplore TDs' immersion in constituency duties. However, as we saw in Chapter 8, there are obviously many other reasons why the Dáil is weak, and it is open to question how much stronger it would be if TDs had less constituency work. Moreover, there is no reason why, with an adequate provision of support staff, politicians should not be able both to provide a service for constituents and to be active parliamentarians (Chubb, 1992: 210).

It is also sometimes suggested that even ministers are overburdened with constituency work and are unable to devote enough time to government business (FitzGerald, 2003: 93). However, in recent years ministers have used civil servants to do most of their constituency work for them. A series of parliamentary questions tabled by Eamon Gilmore in 2003 asked about the size of each minister's private office and constituency office. It turned up the information that the 15 cabinet ministers and 17 ministers of state collectively had 393 civil servants in their private offices and looking after their constituency work, at a cost of around €11.5 million a year (*Dáil Debates* 568: 1225–411, 17 June 2003). Around 134 of these were specifically described as looking after the ministers' constituency work at a cost of around €4 million, but the line between this and the 'private office' may not be clearcut; indeed, one minister acknowledged in 1993 that 'staff are not formally divided between constituency and other duties. The situation varies from day to day in each office and staff carry out appropriate duties as the need arises' (Joe Walsh, Minister for Agriculture, *Dáil Debates* 427: 1854, 11 March 1993). Given that each cabinet and junior minister has, therefore, an average of 12 civil servants, paid for by the taxpayers, to assist in his or her constituency and political work, it is hard to believe that brokerage can be a major burden on the shoulders of ministers.

Impact on the work of the civil service

The constituency work of TDs serves many useful functions for citizens, but this does not mean that all of its consequences are beneficial, or that there is no such thing as excess. We noted earlier that TDs may do some preliminary screening of cases before deciding which ones to take up with officials. However, even if a TD realises that a particular case is hopeless, he or she may not want to say this bluntly to the constituent. The safer option is to forward the case to the civil service, perhaps even putting down a parliamentary question, though of course without using up credit with contacts in the civil service by flagging it as a deserving case. When this happens on a large scale, there is an obvious cost to the civil service in terms of time and money, and indeed in 1962 a senator characterised the constituency work of TDs as 'going about persecuting civil servants', a phrase that was later used as the title of a very influential article (Chubb, 1963). Each question has to be followed up fully and all the details have to be investigated, even if the answer turns out to be something straightforward such as the person's simply not being eligible. Tales abound of civil servants or ministers, faced with even minor decisions, discovering that the matter is the subject of correspondence from several TDs and perhaps councillors too. Sometimes, undoubtedly, TDs do make representations even if they can see that a case is 'a dead duck' because 'it can be the only way to get people off your back'; only a response in writing will satisfy the constituent that nothing more could have been done (Éamon Ó Cuív TD in *Irish Times*, 13 April 2002). Examining these representations also costs civil servants time that could be spent dealing with other things so, ironically, some TDs, by clogging up the works with pointless representations, may exacerbate the delays they complain about (Dooney and O'Toole, 1998: 237). Whether it really follows that citizens would get a better service were it not for TDs taking up the cudgels on their behalf is, of course, another matter.

Individualisation of social conflict

Higgins (1982: 133) argues that clientelism 'disorganises the poor'; it encourages them to seek an individual solution to a problem such as poverty rather than to see the problem as fundamental to society and take part in collective action to try to redress it. It encourages vertical links, from the TD to the constituent, rather than horizontal ones between people in the same position, such as the poor or the unemployed. Clientelism encourages competition rather than co-operation between people in similar vulnerable positions. It reinforces and perpetuates individualism – social conflict is individualised. Thus, he concludes (p. 135), it is 'exploitative in source and intent'. Its origins lie in the dependency of the poor, 'the structural fact of poverty', and in the uneven distribution of resources such as wealth, knowledge and access, and it perpetuates this dependency by heading off any demand for more fundamental changes. Hazelkorn also argues that clientelism redirects incipient class conflict into channels that emphasise the role of individuals rather than of classes: 'the effect has been to retard the political development and consciousness of the economically dominated classes' (Hazelkorn, 1986: 339). She suggests that for left-wing TDs 'to operate in constituencies through clinics could be politically disastrous in the long-term', as this would reduce the chances of horizontal class links building up among the dominated classes (Hazelkorn, 1986: 340).

This is all very well, but what exactly is meant by 'clientelism' in these accounts? Hazelkorn seems to regard all the constituency work of a TD as clientelism: 'Irish clientelism involves individuals who seek out their TD . . . in order to acquire some benefit or service which they feel they would not receive by their own, or their group's efforts' (Hazelkorn, 1986: 327; cf. Higgins, 1982: 118–19). If politicians who help constituents sort out problems that the constituents could not resolve by themselves are behaving in a 'clientelistic' fashion, then clientelism exists in virtually every country in the world and cannot explain much about Ireland specifically. Higgins later became a TD, and was once asked on television whether he now engaged in the clientelistic practices that he had earlier deplored. His answer drew a distinction between, on the one hand, politicians attempting to give the impression that they were achieving results through manipulation and, on the other hand, politicians helping people to obtain their rights (RTE 1, 'Prime Time', 25 February 1997). The feeling remains that the term 'clientelism' is being used very loosely in these arguments.

TDs' readiness to offer helpful advice to constituents would come well down the list as an explanation for the absence of socialism in Ireland. It may well be that politicians' brokerage work reduces the level of alienation among those who seek their assistance, and thereby acts as a force for the stability of a social structure marked by clear inequalities rather than for radical transformation of it. However, it is far-fetched to imagine that if politicians refused to help their constituents with their problems, the result would be an unstoppable build-up of demand for collective action that would rectify all of society's ills. It is hard to see how a widow concerned about a delay in her pension payment, say, can tackle the immediate problem except in individual terms, and it is not necessarily irrational for individuals to seek to solve their own short-term problems rather than to try to transform society first. Although it is true that the 'welfare officer' role of members of parliament involves solving the problems of individuals – as it does in every country – the 'local promoter' role entails work for collectivities. The case against constituency work as a barrier to the left in Ireland remains unproven.

Impact on perceptions of the political system

There is some disagreement about how constituency work affects perceptions of the political system. Some, such as Bax (1976: 51–2), feel that it has an integrative effect; it brings citizens and the central state machinery closer together. TDs, by providing a 'helping hand and a friendly ear', as P. J. Sheehan (quoted above) put it, can serve the functions of humanising the state in the eyes of people who would otherwise see it as remote and countering the cynicism that attaches to 'politicians' generically. As has been noted in Britain, the effect is to build support for the political system by making people feel that there is at least someone who will listen to their problem and is 'on their side' (Norton and Wood, 1993: 50–5). Moreover, through constituency work, information is transmitted in both directions; politicians are kept fully in touch with their constituents, and will be quickly alerted to any general problems, for example about the way in which a department is implementing a policy. Thus, according to a senator, constituency work ensures that people's concerns are 'reflected in and inform contributions to Oireachtas debates', and injunctions to write constituents out of the agenda are 'a particularly naive form of elitism' (Mansergh, 2004). Of course, the system may not always respond appropriately to signs that something is amiss; as one writer observes, there is a tendency for departments to deal with each case as *sui generis* rather than as an indicator of some systemic weakness (O'Halpin, 2002: 119).

Others take a negative view, believing that brokerage perpetuates a mistaken belief that government and the civil service do not work in a fair and rational manner. Dick Roche, a public administration specialist as well as a TD, argues that the practice of approaching a politician with complaints about the civil service has 'a corrosive impact on political life. It undermined the confidence in the administrative system and its impartiality, and it also gave rise to the view that just about everything could be fixed' (*Dáil Debates* 482: 929, 6 November 1997; cf. Dooney and O'Toole, 1998: 237). Sacks (1976: 221–5) also believes that much constituency work propagates the notion that citizens improve their chances of getting something from the state by approaching it via a TD, and this perpetuates citizens' negative and suspicious views of the political system. In turn this reinforces personalism and localism, the tendency to trust only those with whom one has some personal or local connection, which Sacks sees as being important elements in Irish political culture. However, as we pointed out earlier, the bureaucratic view according to which people's use of TDs is irrational has been disputed by detailed research, according to which TDs can be of genuine help to constituents, not by 'fixing' matters improperly but by securing the legitimate redress of grievances or, at least, obtaining a satisfactory explanation of a decision.

Conclusion

Irish citizens expect their members of parliament to be active constituency representatives, taking up their personal or communal problems or grievances with the relevant government department. Although some have sought distinctively Irish explanations for this, a heavy constituency workload is the norm for parliamentarians around the world, and the main reason tends to be the same everywhere: quite simply, representing one's constituents is a central part of the job of a member of parliament in every country. The volume of constituency work takes time that TDs could, at least in theory, devote to their formal parliamentary responsibilities, and also has an impact on the functioning of the civil service. Among some observers of Irish politics, constituency work tends to be regarded as a negative phenomenon. It is often branded 'clientelism', a term with a multitude of unfavourable connotations (largely due to the private and individual, rather than public and collective, nature of politician–voter interactions), yet it is clear that Irish politics are not clientelistic in the conventional sense of the term. As in other countries, constituency work has both negative and positive consequences: it may weaken the ability of parliament to provide effective scrutiny of government and to make an input to policy making, yet it provides a vital link between citizen and state, reduces alienation, and provides feedback on the effects of government policies. The constituency role of TDs is a central aspect of the Irish political system, and its consequences continue to generate argument and discussion.

Notes

1 Máire Geoghegan-Quinn was a Fianna Fáil TD for Galway West from 1975 to 1997. In the 1990s the constituency was represented by five TDs, with a population at the 1997 election of 100,251. Most TDs hold 'clinics' in their constituency, setting aside a certain amount of time at designated places where constituents can come and discuss their problem with the TD.
2 The Head of Kinsale and the Dursey Sound are approximately 80 miles apart.
3 All figures calculated from the *Annual Reports* of the Ombudsman. Figures exclude complaints relating to Telecom Éireann; such cases made up 8 per cent of complaints in 1998 but were removed from the Ombudsman's jurisdiction in July 1999 upon the privatisation of Telecom.

References and further reading

Bax, Mart, 1976. *Harpstrings and Confessions: Machine-style Politics in the Irish Republic.* Assen: Van Gorcum.

Browne, Michael, 1999. *Citizens' Information: Theory, Current Practice and Future Challenge.* Dublin: National Social Service Board.

Carty, R. K., 1981. *Party and Parish Pump: Electoral Politics in Ireland.* Waterloo, Ontario: Wilfrid Laurier University Press.

Chubb, Basil, 1963. '"Going about persecuting civil servants": the role of the Irish parliamentary representative', *Political Studies* 11:3: 272–86.

Chubb, Basil, 1992. *The Government and Politics of Ireland*, 3rd edn. Harlow: Longman.

Collins, Neil and Mary O'Shea, 2003. 'Clientelism: facilitating rights and favours', in Maura Adshead and Michelle Millar (eds), *Public Administration and Public Policy in Ireland: Theory and Methods*. London: Routledge, pp. 88–107.

Comhairle, 2003. *Strategic Plan 2003–2006*. Dublin: Comhairle.

Curtice, John and Phil Shively, 2000. *Who Represents us Best? One Member or Many?* Oxford: CREST Working Paper 79, available at www.crest.ox.ac.uk.

De Winter, Lieven, 1997. 'Intra- and extra-parliamentary role attitudes and behaviour of Belgian MPs', in Wolfgang C. Müller and Thomas Saalfeld (eds), *Members of Parliament in Western Europe: Roles and Behaviour*. London: Frank Cass, pp. 128–54.

De Winter, Lieven, 2002. 'Belgian MPs: between omnipotent parties and disenchanted citizen-clients', in Philip Norton (ed.), *Parliaments and Citizens in Western Europe*. London: Frank Cass, pp. 89–110.

Dooney, Seán and John O'Toole, 1998. *Irish Government Today*, 2nd edn. Dublin: Gill and Macmillan.

Eisenstadt, S. N. and L. Roniger, 1984. *Patrons, Clients and Friends: Interpersonal Relations and the Structure of Trust in Society*. Cambridge: Cambridge University Press.

Farrell, Brian, 1985. 'Ireland: from friends and neighbours to clients and partisans: some dimensions of parliamentary representation under PR-STV', in Vernon Bogdanor (ed.), *Representatives of the People? Parliaments and Constituents in Western Democracies*. Aldershot: Gower, pp. 237–64.

FitzGerald, Garret, 1991. *All in a Life: An Autobiography*. Dublin: Gill and Macmillan.

FitzGerald, Garret, 2003. *Reflections on the Irish State*. Dublin: Irish Academic Press.

Frears, John, 1990. 'The French parliament: loyal workhorse, poor watchdog', in Philip Norton (ed.), *Parliaments in Western Europe*. London: Frank Cass, pp. 32–51.

Gallagher, Michael, 1996. 'Electoral systems', in Constitution Review Group, *Report*. Dublin: Stationery Office, pp. 499–520.

Gallagher, Michael 2000. 'The (relatively) victorious incumbent under PR-STV: legislative turnover in Ireland and Malta', in Shaun Bowler and Bernard Grofman (eds), *Elections in Australia, Ireland, and Malta under the Single Transferable Vote: Reflections on an Embedded Institution*. Ann Arbor: University of Michigan Press, pp. 81–113.

Gallagher, Michael and Michael Marsh, 2002. *Days of Blue Loyalty: The Politics of Membership of the Fine Gael Party*. Dublin: PSAI Press.

Gallagher, Michael, Michael Marsh and Paul Mitchell (eds), 2003. *How Ireland Voted 2002*. Basingstoke: Palgrave Macmillan.

Garry, John, Fiachra Kennedy, Michael Marsh and Richard Sinnott, 2003. 'What decided the election?', in Michael Gallagher, Michael Marsh and Paul Mitchell (eds), *How Ireland Voted 2002*. Basingstoke: Palgrave Macmillan, pp. 119–42.

Geoghegan-Quinn, Máire, 1998. 'Loss in salary and privacy price of becoming a TD', *Irish Times*, 28 March, p. 14.

Hazelkorn, Ellen, 1986. 'Class, clientelism and the political process in the Republic of Ireland', in Patrick Clancy, Sheelagh Drudy, Kathleen Lynch and Liam O'Dowd (eds), *Ireland: A Sociological Profile*. Dublin: Institute of Public Administration, pp. 326–43.

Hibbing, John R. and John R. Alford, 1990. 'Constituency population and representation in the US Senate', *Legislative Studies Quarterly* 15:4: 581–98.

Higgins, Michael D., 1982. 'The limits of clientelism: towards an assessment of Irish politics', in Christopher Clapham (ed.), *Private Patronage and Public Power*. London: Frances Pinter, pp.114–41.

Hogan, Dick, 1997. 'Spring's influence can be seen in north Kerry', *Irish Times*, 6 November.

Hogan, Gerard and David Gwynn Morgan, 1998. *Administrative Law in Ireland*, 3rd edn. Dublin: Round Hall Sweet and Maxwell.

Ingle, Róisín, 1997. 'Tipperary voters stand by their man despite damning report from tribunal', *Irish Times*, 30 August, p. 9.

Kelly, Valerie, 1987. 'Focus on clients: a reappraisal of the effectiveness of TDs' interventions', *Administration* 35:2: 130–51.

Komito, Lee, 1984. 'Irish clientelism: a reappraisal', *Economic and Social Review* 15:3: 173–94.

Komito, Lee, 1992. 'Brokerage or friendship? Politics and networks in Ireland', *Economic and Social Review* 23:2: 129–45.

Mansergh, Martin, 2004. 'New year resolve to eschew "me, me, me"', *Irish Times*, 3 January.

Mezey, Michael L., 1979. *Comparative Legislatures*. Durham, NC: Duke University Press.

Murphy, Gary, 2003. 'The background to the election', in Michael Gallagher, Michael Marsh and Paul Mitchell (eds), *How Ireland Voted 2002*. Basingstoke: Palgrave Macmillan, pp. 1–20.

Norris, Pippa, 1997. 'The puzzle of constituency service', *Journal of Legislative Studies* 3:2: 29–49.

Norton, Philip, 1994. 'The growth of the constituency role of the MP', *Parliamentary Affairs* 47:4: 705–20.

Norton, Philip and David M. Wood, 1993. *Back from Westminster: British Members of Parliament and their Constituents*. Lexington: University of Kentucky Press.

NSSB (National Social Service Board), *Annual Reports*. Dublin: National Social Service Board.

O'Halpin, Eunan, 2002. 'Still persecuting civil servants? Irish parliamentarians and citizens', in Philip Norton (ed.), *Parliaments and Citizens in Western Europe*. London: Frank Cass, pp. 111–27.

Ombudsman, *Annual Reports*. Dublin: Stationery Office.

O'Sullivan, Mary-Clare, 2002. 'Messengers of the people? An analysis of representation and role orientations in the Irish parliament', unpublished PhD thesis, Trinity College Dublin.

Roche, Richard, 1982. 'The high cost of complaining Irish style: a preliminary examination of the Irish pattern of complaint behaviour and of its associated costs', *IBAR – Journal of Irish Business and Administrative Research* 4:2: 98–108.

Rush, Michael, 2001. *The Role of the Member of Parliament since 1868: From Gentlemen to Players*. Oxford: Oxford University Press.

Sacks, Paul M., 1976. *The Donegal Mafia: an Irish Political Machine*. New Haven, CT and London: Yale University Press.

Searing, Donald, 1994. *Westminster's World*. Cambridge, MA: Harvard University Press.

Whyte, John, 1966. *Dáil Deputies: Their Work, its Difficulties, Possible Remedies*. Dublin: Tuairim pamphlet 15.

Wood, David M. and Garry Young, 1997. 'Comparing constituent activity by junior legislators in Great Britain and Ireland', *Legislative Studies Quarterly* 22:2: 217–32.

Websites

www.irlgov.ie/oireachtas/frame.htm (link: members)   Site of the Oireachtas, from which there are links to the sites of those TDs who have personal websites.
www.oasis.gov.ie   Site of OASIS, a public service information system.
www.comhairle.ie   Site of organisation overseeing Citizens Information Centres.
www.ombudsman.gov.ie   Site of Ombudsman.

10 Women in politics

Yvonne Galligan

In November 2003, President Mary McAleese was deemed by the public to be the most popular politician in Ireland.[1] Her approval rating of 84 per cent, replicating levels of popular support enjoyed by her predecessor, Mary Robinson, indicated a continued affirmation of women's presidential office-holding. On the basis of this level of popularity, one would reasonably expect to find women well integrated into political life in Ireland, with strong representation in various arenas of power, locally and nationally. There is no doubt that some women politicians have become household names: Mary O'Rourke and Mary Harney, for example, enjoy instant public recognition. Yet the high media profile enjoyed by some prominent women politicians only compounds the illusion that Irish politics is well advanced in its representation of women. In practice, this is not the case, and this chapter seeks to uncover some explanations as to why this is so. In order to assess the relationship between women and politics in Ireland we will first look at the pattern of women's representation in political and social decision making. We will then explore possible causes of the under-representation of women before examining the extent to which women's interests are presented and considered in the political decision-making framework. Finally, we assess the consequences for women and for society of providing one half of the population with a little over one-tenth of the political voice.

Women in political institutions

Irish women who campaigned for the vote in the late nineteenth century saw this as the key to increasing women's influence in national life. The Irish suffrage movement, strongly influenced by the women's franchise campaign in Britain, sought to bring a feminist voice to Irish politics. However, the strengthening independence movement led to this aim being joined, and arguably overshadowed, by the demand for national sovereignty promoted by prominent Sinn Féin women (Cullen-Owens, 1984; Cullen, 1997: 272). The supremacy of the nationalist discourse over that of feminism within the ranks of the suffragists is important in understanding the low representation of women subsequent to independence. While winning the vote was presented as a victory for feminists in Britain, the extension of the franchise to all women in Ireland in 1923 was interpreted as a step on the way to self-government. From this point on, women's representation in political life was linked to their association with the 'national question', and the few women who made it to political office in the post-1918 decades invariably had close family and personal connections with the revolutionary era. In the following sections, we trace the participation of women in Irish political life to the present, focusing on their representation in national and local politics and their involvement in political parties.

Head of state

In 1990 the Irish electorate chose Mary Robinson as the country's president, making Ireland only the second country in Europe (after Iceland) to have a woman head of state elected by popular vote. In 1997, President Robinson was succeeded by Mary McAleese. This in itself was quite a remarkable event, for nowhere else has an elected female head of state been followed into office by another woman. Indeed, Robinson's election victory and the success of her presidency seemed to influence political parties to nominate women as candidates for the 1997 presidential election: four of the five candidates were women, representing diverse strands of political opinion. However, the recognition of women as winning presidential candidates is a recent phenomenon in Irish politics. Of the six presidential elections held between 1938 and 1997, the first four were all-male affairs.

Government

With the exception of the appointment of Countess Markievicz as Minister for Labour in the government elected by the first Dáil in 1919 (a largely symbolic gesture in the circumstances of the time), no woman held a cabinet post until December 1979, when Máire Geoghegan-Quinn became Minister for the Gaeltacht. Of the 157 people who held full ministerial positions from 1922 to 2002 inclusive, only nine (6 per cent) were women. Although there is an identifiable increase in the number of women holding government office from 1979 onwards, the pattern varies from administration to administration (see Table 10.1). The 1994–7 'rainbow' coalition comprising Fine Gael, Labour and Democratic Left saw six (20 per cent) women being appointed to ministerial office (cabinet ministers and ministers of state), while women's ministerial presence was reduced in the Fianna Fáil and Progressive Democrat 2002 coalition to four (13 per cent). Thus, any gains made by women in government office-holding are not guaranteed to be consolidated. In total, 18 women held ministerial or junior ministerial rank in the 11 governments formed between 1979 and 2002, accounting for 11 per cent of all government office-holders in this 25-year period.

Table 10.1 Government office-holding by gender, 1979–2002

Government	Year	Men	Women	% women
Fianna Fáil	1979	29	1	3
Fine Gael/Labour	1981	26	2	7
Fianna Fáil	1982	24	1	4
Fine Gael/Labour	1982	28	2	7
Fianna Fáil	1987	28	2	7
Fianna Fáil/Progressive Democrats	1989	27	3	10
Fianna Fáil/Progressive Democrats	1992	28	2	7
Fianna Fáil/Labour	1993	25	5	17
Fine Gael/Labour/Democratic Left	1994	24	6	20
Fianna Fáil/Progressive Democrats	1997	26	5	19
Fianna Fáil/Progressive Democrats	2002	28	4	13

In 1997, Mary Harney became Tánaiste (deputy prime minister), the highest government office ever held by a woman (Box 10.1). However, the office of Taoiseach has so far remained an all-male stronghold, as have, at the time of writing, the influential ministries of Finance and Foreign Affairs and the position of Attorney General.

Parliament

Of the 68 women elected to the Dáil between 1922 and 2002, two-thirds (65 per cent) came to office after 1977. Before 1977, the average Dáil con-

---

Box 10.1 Firsts for women in politics

1918 Votes for women over 30; first woman elected (Countess Markievicz, Sinn Féin)

1919 First woman government minister (Countess Markievicz)

1923 Votes for all women

1969 First woman on a parliamentary legislative committee (Evelyn Owens, Labour)

1979 First woman government minister in modern times (Máire Geoghegan-Quinn, Fianna Fáil)

1982 First woman Cathaoirleach of the Seanad (Tras Honan, Fianna Fáil)

1982 First woman chairperson of a parliamentary committee (Nora Owen, Fine Gael)

1990 First woman president (Mary Robinson)

1993 First woman party leader (Mary Harney, Progressive Democrats)

1997 First woman Tánaiste (Mary Harney)

2002 First woman government chief whip (Mary Hanafin, Fianna Fáil)

Table 10.2 Women candidates and TDs at elections, 1977–2002

Election	Candidates			Deputies		
	Total	Women	%	Total	Women	%
1977	376	25	6.6	148	6	4.1
1981	404	41	10.1	166	11	6.6
1982 (Feb.)	366	35	9.6	166	8	4.8
1982 (Nov.)	365	31	8.5	166	14	8.4
1987	466	65	13.9	166	14	8.4
1989	371	52	14.0	166	13	7.8
1992	482	89	18.5	166	20	12.0
1997	484	96	19.8	166	20	12.0
2002	463	84	18.1	166	22	13.2

Source: Author's calculations.

Note
The actual number of women contesting the 1987 general election is distorted due to the fact that one independent candidate, Barbara Hyland, ran in 13 constituencies.

tained only four women; since then the average has increased to 14 (see Appendix 2d). The figures for women TDs and candidates in 1977, low as they were, represented record levels at the time and marked a turning point in women's parliamentary seat-holding. However, since then, progress has been relatively modest (Table 10.2).

The 2002 election returned 22 women to the Dáil (13 per cent), but that fell far short of the 40 per cent gender balance sought by the women's movement during the election campaign (Healy, 2002: 3). Indeed, Ireland's record on women's parliamentary representation consistently disimproved during the 1990s compared with that of other European countries. In 1993, Ireland held sixth position among the 12 EU member states. By 2004, it had dropped to seventeenth place among the 25 EU members (see Table 10.3), with some way to go to meet the average of 25 per cent seats held by women in the EU's national parliaments (www.ipu.org).

When seen in the context of parliamentary representation in the national and devolved legislatures on the islands of Ireland and Britain, the relative invisibility of women's Dáil presence is all the more striking. There are equal numbers of women and men in the Welsh Assembly and 42 per cent of Scottish parliamentarians are women. However, for reasons that we will discuss below, the reality remains that it is particularly difficult for Irish women to win a seat in the Dáil.

The pattern of women's representation in the Seanad, the upper house, is not very different. Over the 40-year period from 1937 (when the Seanad was established) to 1977, only 19 female senators in total made it to the second chamber. There was a perceptible increase in the number of women senators after 1977, when the Taoiseach, Jack Lynch, included three women

Box 10.2 Leading women politicians

Irish government has been largely male-dominated since the foundation of the state. Only since the start of the 1980s have women politicians gained access to any of the levers of power, but they still remain very much in a minority in the governmental system. Since 1922 only nine women have been members of an Irish government:

Máire Geoghegan-Quinn (born 1950), Fianna Fáil. In 1979 became the first female cabinet minister, and served in subsequent Fianna Fáil administrations in the 1980s and 1990s.
Eileen Desmond (born 1932), Labour. Appointed Minister for Health and Minister for Social Welfare in 1981.
Gemma Hussey (born 1938), Fine Gael. Appointed Minister for Education in 1982.
Mary O'Rourke (born 1937), Fianna Fáil. Appointed Minister for Education in 1987 and Minister for Private Enterprise in 1997. She became the first woman deputy leader of Fianna Fáil in 1994.
Niamh Bhreathnach (born 1945), Labour. Appointed Minister for Education in 1993.
Nora Owen (born 1945), Fine Gael. Appointed deputy leader of her party in 1993, became Minister for Justice in 1994.
Mary Harney (born 1953), Progressive Democrats. Became leader of her party in 1993 and appointed to the office of Tánaiste and Minister for Enterprise, Trade and Employment in 1997.
Síle de Valera (born 1954), Fianna Fáil. Appointed Minister for Arts, Heritage, Gaeltacht and the Islands in 1997.
Mary Coughlan (born 1965), Fianna Fáil. First elected to the Dáil at the age of 22, she was appointed Minister for Social and Family Affairs in 2002.

In addition, the country has had two female Presidents:

Mary Robinson (born 1944). Elected President 1990 with the backing of Labour, the Workers' Party and the Green Party.
Mary McAleese (born 1951). Elected President 1997, standing as the Fianna Fáil candidate with the support also of the Progressive Democrats.

Table 10.3 Women's parliamentary representation in
EU states following most recent election

Country	Election	% women MPs
Sweden	2002	45.3
Denmark	2001	37.9
Finland	2003	37.5
Netherlands	2003	36.7
Spain	2004	36.0
Belgium	2003	35.3
Austria	2002	33.9
Germany	2002	32.2
Latvia	2002	21.0
Poland	2001	20.2
Luxembourg	2004	20.0
Slovakia	2002	19.3
Portugal	2002	19.1
Estonia	2003	18.8
United Kingdom	2001	17.8
Czech Republic	2002	17.0
Ireland	2002	13.3
France	2002	12.2
Slovenia	2000	12.2
Italy	2001	11.3
Cyprus	2001	10.7
Lithuania	2000	10.6
Hungary	2002	9.8
Malta	2003	9.2
Greece	2004	8.7

Source: Inter-Parliamentary Union, www.ipu.org/parline

among his 11 appointees. The 2002 Seanad election resulted in eight women
being returned on the electoral panels with a further two appointed by the
Taoiseach, bringing the representation of women in the Seanad to 17 per
cent, slightly lower than in the previous Seanad. Once again, Ireland compares unfavourably with many other European countries on this measure.
The Netherlands, Spain, Germany and Austria had higher percentages of
women in the upper house in 2003, though France and Italy had lower
percentages than Ireland.

When women obtain seats in the Oireachtas, the question arises of what
positions of influence they hold there. The most obvious place to look for
indicators of women's influence in parliament is their participation in parliamentary committees. Oireachtas committees now have relatively important
legislative and investigative functions and being chairperson of a committee
is an influential and much-prized position (see Chapter 8, pp. 230–2, for a
more detailed discussion). In terms of committee membership, women's participation closely matches their legislative presence: women TDs make up
12 per cent of the membership of Dáil legislative committees (Table 10.4).

Table 10.4 Women's participation in legislative and standing committees in the 29th Dáil

Committee	Membership	Women (No.)	Women (%)
Select			
Agriculture and Food	11	1	9
Arts, Sport, Tourism, Community, Rural and Gaeltacht Affairs	11	2	18
Communications, Marine and Natural Resources	11	0	0
Education and Science	11	3	27
Enterprise and Small Business	11	1	9
Environment and Local Government	11	0	0
European Affairs	11	2	18
Finance and the Public Service	11	1	9
Foreign Affairs	11	1	9
Health and Children	11	3	27
Justice, Equality, Defence and Women's Rights	11	2	18
Social and Family Affairs	11	0	0
Transport	11	1	9
Standing			
Committee of Public Accounts	12	0	0
Procedure and Privileges	19	2	10
Working Group of Committee Chairpersons	17	1	6
Committee on Members' Interests	5	0	0
Joint House Services Committee	18	2	11
Joint Committee on Broadcasting and Parliamentary Information	8	2	25
Joint Committee on Consolidation Bills	6	0	0
Total	228	24	11

Source: www.irlgov.ie; Oireachtas committee secretariat (Nov. 2003).

However, there is only one woman (8 per cent) holding the position of chairperson (Arts, Sport, Tourism, Community, Rural and Gaeltacht Affairs) from among the 13 positions available. Women's committee membership is also variable, with no women on three of the Dáil select committees, while there are three women TDs on the committees of Education and Science and of Health and Children.

Along with the committees with a legislative brief, there are a number of other house committees regulating major aspects of Dáil business. Of these, the important Committee on Procedure and Privileges has only two (11 per cent) women, while there are no women on the Committee on Members' Interests or on the Joint Committee on Consolidation Bills. None of these house committees has a woman chair. In addition, the influential Committee of Public Accounts has no women members. It is quite evident, then, that as the committee system has become professionalised, women TDs have but a minor voice in legislative and house affairs. It could be argued that women parliamentarians indicate specific policy interests and priorities through their participation in committees dealing with health, education and other 'soft' issues. This view is however, a rather superficial conclusion to draw from the evidence in Table 10.4. Indeed, women's participation, or lack of participation, in Dáil committees is influenced by two other factors: one is that they are few in number and therefore are not available to 'populate' committees, and the second is that the committees on which women serve are likely to be least favoured for membership by their male colleagues. Given that in a recent survey 44 per cent of women TDs identified the environment and local government as their foremost policy interest, ranking education second and health third, there is some evidence to support the claim that women lose out in the party power struggle for membership of certain committees (Galligan *et al.*, 2000: 49).

Local government

The pattern of women's representation in local government has been similar to that in the national parliament. The wide gap in gender representation on local councils matters as local government service is seen as a route to national politics. With the outlawing of the 'dual mandate' (under which TDs and senators could simultaneously belong to a local council – see Chapter 14) from the June 2004 local elections, existing double office-holders, of whom there were 121, were encouraged to vacate their local seats in the lead-up to these elections. This provided a chance for political hopefuls to stake a claim to local representation. In the event, many TDs and Senators took the opportunity to retain links with local government by nominating family members, including wives and daughters, to their local council seats. However, the percentage of councillors who were female changed little, with the 1999 figure of 15 per cent rising only to 17 per cent in 2004. This can be compared with a figure of 22 per cent across the EU as a whole in the late 1990s (CEMR, 1999).

Local decision-making sites have expanded greatly since the beginning of the 1990s, with the creation of county enterprise boards and other agencies for the promotion of regional structural and economic development (see Chapter 14). These bodies afford opportunities for local community spokespersons and leaders to become involved in shaping the commercial, economic, service and infrastructural development in their areas. Funded by government and EU programmes, women's representation on the 34 county enterprise boards stands at 22 per cent. The most positive record of women's participation in local decision making is in the Area Partnership Companies where a policy of 40 per cent gender balance at board level has resulted in women's membership of these local boards reaching 31 per cent (Muintearas *et al.*, 2002: 28–9).[2] This achievement is the exception rather than the rule, for women continue to be under-represented across a wide range of local decision-making bodies (Muintearas *et al.*, 2002).

Political parties

While women continue to be significantly under-represented in electoral arenas, there are indications that political parties have become more conscious of the need to bring more women into internal decision-making fora. This is an important shift in party leadership thinking, given that parties dominate the selection process and that this process is overtly influenced by party headquarters (Galligan, 2003). Cross-national studies seem to indicate that party service at national executive level enhances women's (and men's) electoral ambitions, mainly through socialising prospective candidates into the norms and rules of political decision making, providing future candidates with a profile within the party and enabling party leaders to evaluate the electoral potential of senior party members. In addition, an increase in the percentage of women on the national executive at one point in time tends to be reflected in an increase in the percentage of women in parliament around ten years later (Caul 1999: 88–90). The level of women's participation in party politics has remained broadly static in terms of membership since the 1990s, with women comprising between one-third and a half of party members. In 2003, women constituted about 25 per cent of Fianna Fáil party members, Fine Gael had slightly higher female membership of 29 per cent, Labour had 35 per cent women members, while women were in the majority (51 per cent) in the Green Party (information supplied by political parties). Nonetheless, the numbers of women holding positions on the national executives of the main parties is generally not proportional to their membership (Table 10.5). In parties where one can find a sizeable propor-

Table 10.5 Women's representation on national executives of the main political parties, 1983–2004 (%)

	Fianna Fáil	Fine Gael	Labour	Progressive Democrats
1983	16.6	23.5	8.3	–
1985	11.1	12.5	13.8	–
1987	16.6	21.6	16.2	n.a.
1989	21.0	n.a	15.4	37.5
1991	7.9	27.0	17.0	27.5
1993	12.6	23.7	21.0	n.a.
1995	16.8	28.0	22.0	32.0
1998	30.0	21.4	26.3	46.6
2004	26.6	28.6	32.4	n.a.

Sources: For 1983–9 Farrell (1992: 444); 1991–2004 data supplied by the political parties; n.a. = not available.

tion of women in the executive, such as in the Green Party (41 per cent), Sinn Féin and latterly in Labour, this is usually due to the adoption of positive action strategies and a strong commitment to balancing gender representation by party leaderships.

The form the commitment to gender equality takes and the extent to which it is acted upon varies from party to party (Galligan and Wilford, 1999). In Fianna Fáil, for instance, past practice has been to rely on rhetorical encouragement to increase the supply of women candidates and party office-holders, though there are indications of a growing awareness that rhetoric needs to be accompanied by some form of affirmative action. During the 1990s, party strategists realised that it was necessary to encourage women's candidacies in order to win extra votes. Although formal positive actions were not implemented, senior party leaders encouraged women's political ambitions. A 1999 progress report on women's participation in the party contained support for the establishment of quotas and targets as a medium-term strategy. The party also instructed constituency executives to guarantee a gender balance on the slate of candidates and to hold early selection conventions to build local profiles (Long, 2003). However, exhortation alone did not yield results, as women's candidacies remained around 10 per cent at both the 1997 and 2002 general elections. The reason given for not implementing any formal affirmative action programme to support women's candidacies rested on adherence to the merit principle. The 'best' candidates were chosen, and measures favouring women were seen as undermining a female candidate's position in relation to her male colleagues. However, there has been some shift in traditional party thinking with regard to women's representation, suggesting that the wider public debates around gender equality issues during the 1990s have had some impact on the views of party members.

After a period of modernisation within Fine Gael accompanied by an acceptance of the value of positive action in bringing more women into politics, the party's record did not subsequently live up to its rhetoric. Fine Gael continued to favour male candidacies during the 1990s and later, with women accounting for only 18 per cent of the party's candidates in 2002. However, in line with the trend in Fianna Fáil, the party appointed an equality officer in mid-2003, indicating a renewed interest in opening electoral opportunities for women.

The Progressive Democrats, formed in 1985, eschew formal commitments to gender equality, in line with their party's liberal political thinking. The party has successfully integrated women members into office-holding positions and electoral politics without the use of gender quotas or other forms of affirmative action. Being a small and relatively new party, there are clearly more opportunities for women to become involved in decision making, and with a female party leader, it is more difficult for gender discrimination to take root within the organisation. The party's stance on positive action, which effectively ignores the gendered nature of power, is shared by other European parties such as the Swedish Centre Party and the Hungarian Democratic Forum.

On the left of the political spectrum, the Labour Party gradually built upon the modest 20 per cent gender quota it established for internal positions in 1991, and the informal 25 per cent target it aimed to reach in candidate selections. Since then, a one-third gender quota has been introduced to the 15 directly elected seats on the party's National Executive Committee. In 2003, women comprised one-third of Labour's executive body. In 2003, the party set a target of one-third for female candidacies at the 2004 local elections, though in the event only 20 per cent of Labour's candidates were women. Thus, while not yet embracing parity democracy, the Labour Party has adopted quotas as a way of bringing more women into political office.

The Green Party, a relative newcomer to the Dáil, has consistently advocated equality between women and men in political life, and has a policy of reaching a target of 40 per cent female candidacies, which it reached for the 2004 local elections. Within the party a gender quota of 40 per cent is applied to all officer positions, although this is not quite filled at constituency level where 31 per cent of constituency chairpersons are women. Sinn Féin also advocates equal participation for women and men in political decision making, and in 2003 implemented a gender equality policy for the 12 party-elected positions to its national executive body. While Sinn Féin has yet to have women constitute a significant proportion of party candidates in the Republic, it fielded 12 (32 per cent) women in the 2003 elections to the Northern Ireland Assembly.

Across all parties, however, women's office-holding at constituency level – varying between 20 and 30 per cent – does not reflect the gender composition of party membership. Interestingly, it is also generally lower than women's representation in a party's national executive. While a full explanation for this discrepancy must await further research, it would seem that at constituency level prevailing social attitudes towards women's public involvement – which we discuss more fully below – are replicated within party organisations. This is borne out by an examination of the positions occupied by women who do participate as party officers in the constituency organisation. Across the major parties, very few women hold the leadership, a pattern that has been quite consistent over the last decade and more. Instead, women are more likely to be found in the supportive roles of constituency secretary and treasurer. Although responsible posts in their own right, these positions are not seen as enhancing the leadership profile of an aspiring candidate. Indeed, the gendered pattern of constituency office-holding is a strong indicator of the nature and extent of attitudes towards gender equality within the wider party organisation.

Women in society

The dearth of women in positions of power in parties and political life is, of course, only part of the wider pattern of women's absence from decision-making centres generally. In this section we shall provide a brief summary of the levels of women's representation on state boards and in the civil service, judiciary, trade unions and other economic interest groups, and discuss the extent of women's participation in the paid workforce.

Over three decades ago, the Commission on the Status of Women noted that there was only one woman among the board members of the ten leading state-sponsored bodies. As of 2004, the effect of government policy to achieve a target of 40 per cent minimum representation of women and men on state boards has resulted in women comprising 28 per cent of all public appointments. In a survey of the board membership of 47 public bodies, 11 boards (23 per cent) met government guidelines, 18 boards (38 per cent) had less than 20 per cent women members, while the gender distribution of members on the remaining 18 boards ranged from 20 to 40 per cent (National Women's Council of Ireland, 2002: 16–17). On taking office as Minister of State at the Department of Justice, Equality and Law Reform in 2002, Willie O'Dea announced his intention to legislate for a 40 per cent gender balance if there was no improvement in women's presence on state boards. Although government has control over approximately 40 per cent of public appointments, and in general has an improving record on gender balancing its appointments, non-governmental nominating bodies do not feel under any obligation to defer to government policy in this matter, especially if they are restricted to putting forward one representative only. Despite repeated efforts to arrive at a solution, the problem of women's presence in public decision making falling far short of the government-prescribed minimum continues.

More progress has been made in tackling the poor record of women's representation in senior levels of the civil service. In the late 1990s there was only one woman (4 per cent) in charge of a government department, 10 per cent of the assistant secretaries and 12 per cent of principal officers were female, and the majority of women employed in the civil service filled the lower clerical and typing grades (Humphreys *et al.*, 1999). The persistent gender imbalance at the top of the civil service had been rationalised as a long-term effect of the 'marriage bar', removed in 1973, that excluded an entire generation of women employed in the civil service from continuing in their jobs once they married. An ineffective equal opportunities policy dating from 1986 was replaced in 2001 by a more robust policy requiring government departments to set targets and timetables for progress in bringing more women into senior positions. Some slight progress has been made in opening up senior positions to women – in 2004 while only one woman had made it to the top position of Secretary General, a further nine (12 per cent) held the post of Assistant Secretary (IPA, 2003: 16–17). By 2005 it is

Table 10.6 Women in the judiciary, 2003

Court	Total no. of judges	No. of women	% women
Supreme Court	8	2	25.0
High Court	28	3	10.7
Circuit Court	31	9	29.0
District Court	51	11	20.7
Total	120	25	20.8

Source: Bacik *et al.* (2003: 63–4).

expected that one-third of Assistant Principal posts, the grade from which senior civil servants are recruited, will be held by women (Department of Finance, 2001: 7).

The judicial arena remains more resistant to change than either public appointments or the bureaucracy. Although the total number of women working as justices doubled over the 1990s, with significant increases in the proportion of women serving at high court, circuit court and district court levels, women hold only 21 per cent of all judicial positions (see Table 10.6). This gender imbalance is more pronounced within the profession. Only 9 per cent of all senior counsel are women, and women solicitors are more likely to be employees than to be partners or owners of legal practices. Yet, the profession is becoming increasingly female, with women comprising 41 per cent of solicitors and 34 per cent of barristers (Bacik *et al.*, 2003).

The trend towards the feminisation of professions is not confined to the law. Young women account for 58 per cent of students in Irish universities and comprise 60 per cent of students graduating with law, business and social science degrees and 43 per cent of students graduating from science, mathematics and computing courses (www.hea.ie). However, these impressive educational qualifications do not translate into a gender equal sharing of economic power. Women make up only 2 per cent of CEOs of large private sector firms, 21 per cent of all small and medium-sized companies are owned or managed by women, and women account for 29 per cent of academics in the higher education sector (www.ndpgenderequality.ie/statdata). Trade union and employer organisations follow a similarly gendered pattern. Although women comprise 44 per cent of trade union members, only four (14 per cent) of the 29-member Irish Congress of Trade Unions executive council are women. The representation of women on the Irish Business and Employers Confederation executive board is slightly better, with two (22 per cent) women on its nine-person board.

It has been noted in other countries that the level of women's participation in employment affects the extent of their participation in other areas of public life. Although Irish women's labour force participation was restricted for many years, this began to change in the 1970s, and over the following two decades women either remained in work for longer periods or returned to work once family commitments eased. By 2000, women's labour force participation rate, at 47 per cent, was the same as the European average. This compares with a participation rate of 71 per cent for men. While the numbers of married women engaged in economic activity fluctuated a little over the 1990s, married women's labour force participation stood at 46 per cent in 2001, as compared with a married male rate of 77 per cent (www. ucd.ie/issda/qnhs). These figures show that while women have increasingly entered the workforce since the early 1990s, there are still strong pressures for married women, especially those with children, to remain in the home. Women constitute over three-quarters (76 per cent) of all part-time employees, which goes some way to explaining the persistence of a 20 per cent gender pay gap (www.ndpequality.ie/statdata). Thus many working women seek to balance employment with family responsibilities, and this dual role, with its attendant career, financial and social implications, has not diminished over the last decade.

Causes of the under-representation of women

The previous pages have examined the extent of the under-representation of women in politics and decision-making centres. We must now look at the reasons for this under-representation. In doing so we will discuss some of the factors that have acted as barriers to women's participation in public life, beginning with attitudes towards women's role in society and ending with a focus on obstacles inherent in the Irish political system that have developed from social expectations and practices.

Social attitudes

The main factor inhibiting women's participation in decision making is generally recognised as being the degree to which a society holds negative attitudes towards the involvement of women in politics. In a study of obstacles to women's political participation in Ireland, Randall and Smyth (1987: 200) noted that:

> Irish women have until the very recent past been subject to a particularly intense, if complex, process of socialisation, through the agency of family, school and the Church, into an acceptance of an extremely traditional division of labour between the sexes and its implications for women's political role.

Thus, as Randall and Smyth observe, the socialisation process, which transmits traditional assumptions about women's role in society (a feature, to varying degrees, of all societies in the liberal democratic world), has been reinforced in Ireland through the Roman Catholic Church, which prioritised a home and family-based role for women (see Chapter 2). Although Irish Catholics are less attached to religious observance than in the past, social attitudes remain heavily influenced by traditionalist assumptions regarding women's place in society. This becomes very evident in the responses to equal opportunity surveys and social values studies. In a 1997 study of equal opportunities for women and men across Europe, almost half (48 per cent) of men and women believed that women are forced to choose between having a career and having children, with more Irish women than men recognising it as a particular difficulty. Clearly, childcare facilities and flexible working options are seen as fundamental to providing women with the opportunities for continuing employment. Irish women favoured more childcare facilities and additional financial help with childcare in about equal amounts – broadly in line with the European women's average of 49 per cent and 46 per cent respectively – while Irish men indicated a preference for financial supports (45 per cent) over additional childcare facilities (40 per cent). Irish women were more in favour of homeworking as a solution to childcare than men (49 per cent as against 44 per cent). Irish men were among the most reluctant in the EU to interrupt their careers to bring up a child (20 per cent in favour) and the difference in Irish gender attitudes on this measure (30 per cent) was among the largest in the EU (European Commission, 1997: 42–7). These results indicate the persistence of a view among men that child-rearing is primarily a woman's responsibility, one that is not expected to impinge on the working lives of men. This revealing survey suggests that the patriarchal assumptions underpinning traditionalist perspectives of women's and men's social roles are still very intact in Ireland, and this conclusion is reinforced when one examines wider indicators of an orientation towards decision making.

Contradicting a popular perception, the Eurobarometer survey reveals that Irish people's interest in discussing politics is lower than the EU average. Whereas 77 per cent of men and 63 per cent of women across Europe discuss politics often or occasionally with friends, only 66 per cent of Irish men and 49 per cent of Irish women do so. Significantly, the gap in political interest between men and women in Ireland is among the largest in the EU, indicating that politics and political matters are viewed as a male preserve. This perception of disempowerment of women carries over into workplace decision making, where more women (45 per cent) than men (33 per cent) believed that the workplace was dominated by men who did not trust women to take appropriate decisions (European Commission, 1997: 49–57). Furthermore, more women (66 per cent) than men (56 per cent) felt that their family responsibilities prevented them from taking on decision-making positions.

Thus, it appears that in general people in Ireland continue to expect women to pursue a traditional family role while balancing the obligations flowing from this role with job and career demands. It is not surprising, therefore, to find the public sphere dominated by men. For women with political ambitions, the practicality of pursuing this time-consuming career in tandem with child-rearing is an issue of greater significance than it is for their male colleagues. Data from a comprehensive survey of women legislators pointed to family responsibilities as the most significant source of difficulty in pursuing a political career – demands that are exacerbated when a politician is from a constituency outside Dublin (Galligan *et al.*, 2000: 41–2). This point is indicative of the weight of traditional cultural attitudes in Ireland, even among women who have managed to get elected to the highest legislative office. It suggests that in Ireland, as elsewhere, 'culture continues to be a significant influence on the proportion of women parliamentarians, even with the introduction of prior structural and institutional controls' (Norris and Inglehart, 2001: 32).

Local base

If, as research has repeatedly shown, both education and occupation are relevant factors in the development of a political career for both women and men, then one must ask in what way they are significant. The standard of education of the average parliamentarian has increased over time, and the business of being a member of parliament has become a full-time occupation in its own right. Women TDs are mainly drawn from the professions or service sector employment while their male colleagues come from more varied employment backgrounds (Table 10.7). This employment pattern indicates that women are at least as well educated as their male counterparts and are therefore equally competent to undertake the task of legislating.

Educational achievement alone does not ensure electoral success for either women or men. Indeed, in an Irish context, one of the most important

Table 10.7 Occupation of TDs in 29th Dáil, by gender

Occupation	Total	Female TDs		Male TDs	
		N	%	*N*	%
Manual employee	3	0	0.0	3	2.1
Non-manual employee	35	7	31.8	28	19.4
Commercial	28	0	0.0	28	19.4
Farmer	21	0	0.0	21	14.6
Lower professions	37	9	41.0	28	19.4
Higher professions	41	5	22.7	36	25.0
Other	1	1	4.5	0	0.0
Total	166	22	100.0	144	100.0

Source: Gallagher (2003: 115, 252–7).

determinants of political success continues to be the strength of a candidate's local support. One of the most effective methods of establishing this is through local government service. However, as we have seen, there are relatively few women in local government due to the persistence of conservative party selection practices. One way of overcoming this disadvantage is through the development of local networks based on occupation. Professions such as teaching, medicine, law and business are generally seen as conferring status within a local community. They involve extensive interaction with the local electorate, and can be used as a foundation for personal bailiwick-building. In addition, these occupations bring economic independence and relative flexibility of time, two additional advantages for a person ambitious to hold political office. It was no accident that teaching was the occupation of the majority of women in the Dáil in the 1990s. While it still provides women political aspirants with a very significant local networking base, women TDs' working lives have diversified to include other occupations with the potential to generate a high local profile such as social work, law and business. These forms of employment combine three important factors facilitating political career-building: income security and financial independence, opportunities for local contact and time in which to pursue support-building activities.

Local voluntary activity presents another method of building a public profile, either on its own or combined with work-related activities. Previous research suggested that women's participation in organised voluntary and community groups and activities did not necessarily bring women into political life, and this finding remains substantially true (O'Donovan and Ward, 1999). However, more detailed research into the backgrounds of political women indicates that, for them, involvement in voluntary and community initiatives played an important part in their political socialisation. This 'grassroots' route to political office was identified as an important factor by almost half (45 per cent) of women parliamentarians (Galligan *et al.*, 2000: 40).

It appears that women with political ambitions try to follow the common routes of entry to political life and if these routes are closed to them, they seek alternative ways to gain credibility as a potential candidate. The influence of localism is one that many aspiring women politicians find difficult to counteract if they have not had the opportunity to break into a brokerage network through local authority service, occupational activity, or grassroots involvement. In other words, the opportunities for building recognition and credibility as a candidate are more limited for women than for men. Women political hopefuls are more likely to look to their party leaders for 'sponsorship' at the candidate selection stage in order to compensate for a lower level of access to local networks.

Finally, while family connections have been important in determining routes to political power in Ireland, this has traditionally been a more significant factor for women than for men. From 1927 to 1973 the majority of women elected to the Dáil were related through family or marriage to former TDs. This trend broadly continues, with 41 per cent of women elected in 2002 having a family connection with national politics (Gallagher, 2003: 114). More specifically, one can observe the trend over time where the 'widow's seat' has been replaced by a father–daughter succession, with no widows elected to the Dáil after the 1970s (Galligan *et al.*, 2000: 35).

Candidate selection

However, the above explanations, which focus on social and economic factors, do not fully account for the small number of women in politics. We must also look at the barriers embedded in the political system itself, and particularly at the selection processes of the political parties. In recent years, explanations for women's political under-representation have focused on internal party selection processes as the single most important obstacle to women's political participation (Norris and Lovenduski, 1993; Russell, 2000). In the 2002 election, women comprised 19 per cent of all candidates, with Fianna Fáil fielding 13 women candidates (12 per cent) and Fine Gael selecting 15 women (18 per cent). Research in the UK indicates a growing awareness of the important role discriminatory attitudes among party activists play in curtailing women's opportunities for selection (Shepherd-Robinson and Lovenduski, 2002). Although Irish party central organisations are now more directly involved in the candidate selection process, and indeed make rhetorical remarks about the need for more women candidates, parties have not yet rectified a gender imbalance in candidate tickets, indicating that discriminatory attitudes also persist among Irish selectors (Galligan, 2003: 49–50).

One of the reasons for this low selection rate of women candidates that is traditionally put forward by party activists is that voters prefer men. Evidence from survey research in this area opens up the complex dynamic between party members' perceptions of what the voter wants and what voters actually do seem to want. There is a developing strand of research investigating party members' attitudes towards women candidates that seems to highlight a view among party members that women prioritise family over politics. There are mixed reactions to this explanation among women and men party members, with women in Fine Gael more inclined than men to agree that women's family commitments keep them out of electoral politics (Gallagher and Marsh, 2002: 133). The significant time demands of a family are also perceived by women legislators as an important inhibitor to women's political careers, and this finding is supported by a worldwide survey of women legislators that found balancing the amount of time devoted to family and public activities to be the single most cited inhibitor (67 per cent) of office-seeking (Inter-Parliamentary Union, 2000).

The same strands of research also investigate demand-side explanations for women's under-representation, for instance that selectors fear that women will lose votes and therefore are not attractive candidates to put forward. This proposition is strongly rejected by Fine Gael party members (Gallagher and Marsh, 2002: 133). When asked the fundamental question of whether women and men have equal opportunity to participate or be selected as a candidate within their party, women in Fine Gael were less likely than men to agree that their party provided equal opportunities to women and men. Thus, the perception of obstacles to women's political participation recognises that the problem of supply is not the sole explanation for the few women coming forward for selection. Instead, there is a general awareness of the structural and attitudinal barriers to women's participation, with women, not surprisingly, being more acutely aware of this impediment.

Other research tackles the question of women candidates from another perspective – that of voter preference. There are no clear conclusions arising from this research, partly because of the low numbers of women going forward for election. An analysis of voter choice at the 1997 election indicated that voter attitudes had become more positive than before towards women as parliamentary representatives. When factors such as age, incumbency and previous political experience were controlled, no significant gender bias was found among voters. The factors that really mattered in winning election were party and incumbency. Thus, it would be expected that male TDs from the larger parties would have a greater chance of being re-elected than a female TD or female newcomer (Galligan *et al.*, 1999). A study of the 2002 election results confirmed this general finding. Overall, men won around 600 more votes than women candidates and male incumbents were much more successful in getting elected than female candidates. However, women had the edge on newcomer men (Gallagher, 2003: 90–1). These findings must remain tentative until significantly more women contest Dáil elections.

Consequences of the under-representation of women

The term 'under-representation', when used in the context of women's presence in parliamentary assemblies, is taken to have three different, yet related, meanings. One is the representation of interests – do women represent women's concerns, are they expected to do so by the voting public, and do they feel they have a specific duty to speak for women's interests? The second is the representativeness of the legislature – is a parliament truly democratic if it excludes women or only minimally incorporates them among its members? The third meaning is associated with equal opportunity and suggests that women's relative absence from parliament is caused by discrimination at one or more points in the electoral process, preventing them from having an equal right to act as representatives. As we have already discussed party positions on selecting women as candidates, this section will focus on the two previous points and assess their application to the political experience of Irish women.

Interest representation

Studies of women parliamentarians appear to indicate that women legislators seek in some way to speak and act for women in the community and also show that there is some expectation among women voters that women politicians will share their concerns (Childs, 2002: 143; Sawer, 2002: 8–9). Indeed, many of the discriminatory policies enacted against women in Ireland from 1937 onwards are seen as the product of a male-dominated political order. It is clear that during the 1970s, when women's parliamentary representation was almost negligible, government and parliament were only partially responsive to the growing voice of gender reform. The articulation and representation of women's rights fell to the emerging feminist movement, a reform-minded judiciary and the European Commission. According to Scannell (1988: 129–30), these agencies were more important catalysts in the initiation of change in the status of women than either politicians or parliament, suggesting that the political system was forced to respond to external pressures rather than initiating change. While European directives on employment and judicial decisions on individual rights acted as an important spur to specific legislative changes, the re-emergence of the women's movement in the early 1970s prompted a public discussion of discrimination against women in law and public policy.

Evidence suggests that women's lobby groups have had a more immediate influence on specific aspects of public policy than the efforts of women TDs (Galligan, 1998). In 1972, the Commission on the Status of Women, established by government two years earlier in response to lobbying from women's groups, recommended that action be taken to remove discrimination against women in the areas of the home, employment, social welfare, taxation, family law, jury service, public life and education. Twenty years later, the report of the Second Commission on the Status of Women – again a government response to women's groups' demands for gender equality – made a further 211 recommendations in broadly similar areas. Both reports provided important blueprints for gender equality and raised many important issues with respect to women's lives that had not previously, or had only marginally, been the subject of political attention. In addition to the policy changes advocated in these documents, the women's movement became effective lobbyists for legislative reform on specific issues such as family law (AIM – Action, Information, Motivation), domestic abuse (Women's Aid) and sexual violence against women (Rape Crisis Centres). The political voice of women became represented by the Council for the Status of Women, later known as the National Women's Council of Ireland (NWCI), to which over 200 women's groups were affiliated in 2002. In the

1990s, NWCI representatives were admitted to the highly corporatised economic and social decision-making social partnership as one of a number of
representatives from the community and voluntary sector, thus giving
women's interests an entry – although little more – into a highly influential,
primarily economic interest-based, elite. The resulting three-year economic
and social programmes that shaped the allocation of Ireland's financial
resources throughout the 1990s and beyond (see Chapter 13) contained only
minor provisions for gender equality, mainly in the area of equal pay.

If lobbying efforts were not sufficient to secure change, national and
European judicial systems served as agencies of progress. The McGee (1973),
de Búrca (1976) and Airey (1979) cases, which respectively established the
right of married couples to import contraceptives for their personal use, the
right of women to serve on juries, and the right of women to free legal aid,
are seen as important cases in leading to legislative reform of benefit to
women. The principle of equality for women in social welfare entitlements
was conceded by the government in 1990 following a judgment from the
European Court of Justice in a case brought by two women, Cotter and
McDermott, against the state. The contentious issue of abortion was also
placed on the political agenda through court findings – from the European
Court of Justice in 1991, the European Court of Human Rights in 1992 and
the Irish Supreme Court in 1992 (Connelly, 1999: 20–2). In particular, the
Supreme Court judgment in the 'X' case (see Box 3.2, p. 88) brought about
three referendums in November 1992 that sought to clarify public policy on
the abortion issue. The results were indeed clear, if not to the taste of many
politicians – there was a clear majority against an absolute ban on abortion
and in favour of affirming the right of a woman to travel to procure an
abortion. There was also a majority in favour of information being made
available on abortion services outside the state (Kennelly and Ward, 1993).
As Kennedy (2002: 115) observes, the outcome of the 1992 referendums
meant that the position on abortion remained that as ruled by the Supreme
Court – abortion was lawful where there was a real and substantial risk to
the life of the mother. Another referendum was sought by 'pro-life' groups
wishing to institute a complete ban on abortion in the state, and in 2002 a
further three-part effort by the government to restrict the implications of
the Supreme Court ruling was defeated (see Appendix 2h).

The representation of women's interests, then, has largely been conducted
by voices outside the legislative system through lobbying and legal activities,
forcing a generally reluctant government to respond. Nonetheless, there
have been feminist voices within the Dáil – mainly from the ranks of Fine
Gael and Labour – seeking to address women-specific issues. The first
minister for women's affairs, Nuala Fennell, oversaw important legislative
changes in women's family status in the mid-1980s (Galligan, 1998).
Women with connections to the feminist movement (Monica Barnes,
Gemma Hussey and Frances Fitzgerald of Fine Gael) and social democratic
politics (Eithne Fitzgerald, Niamh Bhreathnach and Joan Burton of Labour)

consistently advocated and promoted woman-friendly policies, while Liz O'Donnell of the Progressive Democrats also adopted a woman-centred view on public policy issues. Most of these individual women belonged to women's organisations before moving into politics, and consequently brought an awareness of gender and gender-related issues into their political perspectives. However, these singular voices over a 25-year period cannot be said to amount to a strong, coherent feminist voice within the Dáil. Indeed, in a survey of women parliamentarians that sought, *inter alia*, to identify their policy priorities, advocacy of women's issues was ranked seventh in a list of 14 policy areas. However, before rushing to judgement on women politicians, it is important to note that they ranked education, health, social affairs and equality in their top five priorities – policy areas with particular implications for women's lives (Galligan *et al.*, 2000: 49–50). Reluctant to be over-identified (or, in some cases, even associated with) feminist issues, and unwilling to be typecast as speaking for women, the few women TDs in parliament favour interest in more general 'soft' policy concerns as a substitute for articulation of a feminist view on wide-ranging policy issues. They should not be too strongly criticised for taking this stance, for, as a visible minority in parliament and in a political context where party discipline is strong, women TDs have little option but to moderate their views to fit in with the masculinist culture and norms pervading Dáil business.

Democratic deficit

Linked closely with the above discussion is the question of the representativeness of the Dáil. At no time has the proportion of women in the Dáil exceeded 14 per cent – leaving 86 per cent of Dáil seats in the possession of men. The 'democratic deficit' caused by the under-representation of women in legislatures and in decision making generally became a matter for attention among international bodies from the mid-1990s onwards. This international agenda for gender equality has received a positive response in some national contexts, resulting in the French 'parity' law linking funding for parties to the selection of equal numbers of female and male candidates, the adoption of equal opportunities as a fundamental working principle in the Scottish Parliament and Welsh Assembly, and the development of party-specific positive action measures in social democratic politics across Europe. However, the issue of gender parity has had little impact on the workings of the Oireachtas or, as we have already seen, on the priorities of political parties. Although criticised by the UN's Commission on the Status of Women for the low representation of women in elected office, and urged to adopt 'temporary special measures' such as quotas to address the gender deficit in the legislature, the Irish government has firmly resisted instituting any initiatives for institutional change. Instead, public funding has been made available to political parties to encourage, support and train women political hopefuls, but this strategy of exhortation and encouragement will not result in a rapid re-balancing of gender representation in the Dáil.

The attention given to the under-representation of women in the Dáil is important, not alone on justice-based arguments for gender equality but also on grounds of the legitimacy of national decision making. Restricting the participation of one half of the population in public affairs at the highest levels can be deemed to be fundamentally undemocratic. However, concerns about democracy are not prone to awaken the conscience of political power-holders, and so arguments based on justice and democracy must be accompanied by a utilitarian perspective. Bringing more women into electoral office increases the pool of talent available to undertake the business of governing, provides fresh perspectives on old policy problems and brings new policy issues to the political agenda. As a self-interested strategy, parties may seek to improve their image and widen their support base by fielding women in winnable seats. These are among some of the utilitarian arguments used to some effect in parties across Europe, but Fianna Fáil and Fine Gael appear unconvinced. In many ways, the scarcity of women in the Dáil represents the continuing unequal status of women in Irish society – the message conveyed is that politics is not for women, that women are not capable of doing the job of representing others, and that if they wish to become politicians they must abandon their own woman-formed beliefs and values.

A growing body of literature on women's parliamentary activity increasingly points to women making a distinctive contribution to the legislative process (Dodson, 1998; Childs, 2002; Grey, 2002). This contribution has an impact on the style and substance of politics: a significant female presence in the legislature promotes a more consensual and less conflictual style of decision making, it brings a new perspective to bear on 'traditional' policy concerns, and it highlights previously ignored issues. In the case of Ireland, the positive effects of such a contribution are not possible to identify, given the low numbers of women in the Dáil. In addition, party discipline dictates that members of the Oireachtas need to present a unified front in parliament and dissent from the party position is seldom tolerated (see p. 213 above). Yet, in Westminster, even though women account for only 18 per cent of MPs, there is a strong sense among them of wishing to change the confrontational political style while also speaking for women. More than three-quarters of female MPs elected since 1997 consider that their presence in parliament has brought women in their constituencies into closer contact with the legislative process:

> It has been useful to be able to use that position as a woman MP to high-light that [domestic violence] and I'm glad to say I've done so. I knew those issues were there and were relevant and I wanted them to make sure that their woman MP was there with them.
>
> (British woman MP, quoted in Childs, 2002: 150)

As Sawer (2002: 13–14) notes, when women's representation in parliament is low, women parliamentarians tend to feel more comfortable in the more 'intimate' arenas of parliamentary committees than in confrontational plenary sessions. In these settings, where discussion is promoted and there is a more consensual style of decision making, women parliamentarians can make their mark on the substance and style of the proceedings. In Scotland, the new parliament has been an ideal laboratory to test whether women in numbers have had a moderating effect on the traditional confrontational style of parliamentary politics. The findings show that such was the case, and indeed that the presence of substantial numbers of women gave men also the freedom to develop a more consensual political style (Russell *et al.*, 2002).

Thus, there is a range of evidence emerging to indicate that having more women in parliament, even in Westminster-style parliaments where cross-party voting is not condoned, can have an effect on the style and substance of political debate. However, this is not a straightforward matter, as evidence from New Zealand shows. Being a woman MP is not enough to engender change in the parliamentary business or in the way it is conducted. The dominance of social conservatism in parliament, party cleavages, a backlash against women MPs from the male majority and the adoption of aggressive debating tactics by women legislators meant that in New Zealand a 'critical mass' of 29 per cent women parliamentarians in 1996 was not sufficient to impact on the parliamentary culture or decisions (Grey, 2002: 28). This example serves as a reminder that progress in terms of women's numerical representation cannot be automatically linked with a more woman-friendly parliament and with parliamentary outcomes sensitive to the redress of gender inequalities.

The institutionalisation of women's interests

Gradually, as issues of women's rights and status in society came onto the political agenda in Ireland, political structures evolved that institutionalised the expression of these demands. Later, the focus shifted to mainstreaming women's policy concerns across all areas of government. First, the Women's Representative Committee was established by the Fine Gael–Labour coalition government in 1974 to oversee the implementation of the recommendations of the Commission on the Status of Women. It was replaced in 1978 by two organisations, the Employment Equality Agency (a statutory body) and the government-funded independent women's representative organisation, the Council for the Status of Women (later the National Women's Council of Ireland). The establishment of the junior ministry for Women's Affairs and Family Law Reform in 1982 and the Joint Oireachtas Committee on Women's Rights in 1983 fostered a woman-centred focus on policy and gave women's rights groups a path into the legislative process. Social and economic conservatism from the middle of the 1980s had a negative impact on the development of gender equality and in developing the institutionalisation of women's interests.

A renewed political commitment to the principle of equality was indicated in 1993 with the appointment of a cabinet minister with responsibility for equality and law reform. On this occasion, the concept of equality was given a generic meaning, and gender equality was a significant component, but not the only concern, of this ministry. In 1997 the office was amalgamated with the Department of Justice and once again given junior status, which it has retained. In 1997 also, a restructuring of parliamentary committees led to the women's affairs committee being subsumed into the committee on justice and equality and within it, the creation of a sub-committee on women's rights in 1998. These 'downgrading' institutional initiatives have been compensated for, however, by a government commitment to 'mainstreaming' a gender dimension into all policy concerns. Since 1993, for instance, policy proposals brought to cabinet for consideration must expressly consider the impact of the proposal on women. Given that such memoranda are confidential, it is not possible to assess the effectiveness of the gender impact made in these documents, but it is likely that in many instances the assessment is one of minimal gender implications.

Of greater significance is the internationalisation of the domestic gender equality agenda, influenced by government commitments to progress on United Nations and European Union equality policies, of which gender mainstreaming[3] is an important tool for monitoring and evaluating public policies (Galligan, 2000: 13–15). To support this endeavour, a Gender Equality Unit was established within the Department of Justice, Equality and Law Reform to oversee, co-ordinate and facilitate equal opportunities between women and men in the implementation of the National Development Plan (NDP 2000–6) (Government of Ireland, 2002: 39–40). The Gender Equality Unit supports the NDP Equal Opportunities and Social Inclusion Co-ordinating Committee whose task is to provide practical advice to the various NDP programmes on facilitating and implementing equal opportunities between women and men. Clearly, the government is making an effort to deliver on gender equality in the context of the NDP. The National Employment Action Plan (NEAP), too, has a gender mainstreaming requirement, as a result of European policy on equal opportunities between women and men in employment. However, these initiatives come to an end in 2006. In addition, they do not cover all aspects of public policy, as they are concerned with the mainly economic-related measures of the NDP and NEAP.

The adoption of gender mainstreaming as a mechanism for facilitating gender equality is an ambitious one, and as is inevitable with substantial analytical tools of this kind, putting the concept into practice falls short of the ideal. General criticisms voiced about the government strategy for mainstreaming include the lack of a comprehensive bank of gender disaggregated statistics to provide the fundamental information for gendered policy analysis. A related critical comment highlights the absence of an agreed set of indicators facilitating objective policy evaluation. A further critique coming from the women's movement is the low level of consultation with women by government in devising the NDP and NEAP gender equality strategy. Efforts to address these concerns have included the compilation of an extensive database of gender-disaggregated statistics, the commissioning of research into gender equality indicators, and wide consultation on the draft National Plan for Women. The larger public policy and administration lessons to be gleaned from these developments reveal the difficulty modern governments face in developing an integrated, responsive policy on gender equality while also providing for the specialist knowledge and information required to plan and evaluate policy effectiveness. Nonetheless, one can conclude that over the course of the 1990s, public policy on gender equality shifted from the equality of treatment model implied in the reform of discriminatory laws and practices to the equality of impact model focusing on the differential impact of policy outcomes on women and men. At its core, this is quite a radical shift in policy perspective offering the prospect of a more gender equal society in the longer term. Furthermore, as Carney (2002: 22) observes, gender mainstreaming has institutionalised 'femocrats' – feminists within the bureaucratic structure working for policy change – moving the gender equality agenda from a piecemeal approach to one with the clearly defined goal to 'address and rectify persistent and emerging disparities between men and women' (Carney, 2002: 23).

Conclusion

The relationship between women and politics in Ireland has become more complex over time. Women considering a career in public life continue to do so in a cultural environment that expects them also to fulfil traditional home-based duties. In partial response to these pressures, women are postponing having their first child until later in life and one-child families are becoming increasingly common. Ireland ranks low on the European scale in terms of women's representation in political life, yet there is no significant bias among the electorate against women candidates – incumbency is the main criterion of further success in electoral politics. Women remain underrepresented as election candidates and although parties are developing some initiatives to redress this imbalance there remains an important obstacle at the 'gatekeeping' candidate selection stage. Given this analysis, and despite the strong role models presented by Mary Robinson, Mary McAleese and others, the likelihood of a substantially increased presence of women in political life is slim without the adoption of strong affirmative action measures by parties. The continuing absence of women from parliament poses challenges to the context, style and substance of political representation as Ireland's democratic structures move into the twenty-first century.

Some progress has been made in policy terms. A range of issues raised by women since the 1970s, particularly those relating to women's rights within the family and in employment, were addressed in the 1980s and 1990s. A number of institutional reforms have taken place that have impacted on gender equality issues. Some of these have marginalised gender equality from the formal political channels, others have enhanced the implementation of gender equality in substantive policy concerns. The internationalisation of Ireland's gender equality agenda has brought about important shifts in policy focus, but has also brought with it renewed opportunities for empty political rhetoric and an accountability to non-national institutions far from the critical gaze of local activists. In sum, the relationship between women and politics in Ireland is undergoing a fundamental re-orientation, the outcome of which is not yet clear.

Notes

1 *Sunday Tribune*/Millward Brown IMS poll reported in *Sunday Tribune*, 2 November 2003, News section, p. 9.
2 Area Partnership Companies were established in the early 1990s to 'tackle exclusion and marginalisation resulting from long-term unemployment, poor educational attainment, poverty and demographic dependency' (IPA, 2000). The 31 per cent representation of women at board level has attracted continuing criticism from women working in local development as being an inadequate share of decision-making power given their contribution to local community development initiatives.
3 Gender mainstreaming has become a generic term for the inclusion of women's perspectives in policy making. However, the European Commission defines it more narrowly as follows: 'mobilising all general policies and measures specifically for the purpose of achieving gender equality by actively and openly taking account at the planning stage of their possible effects on the respective situations of men and women (the gender perspective)' (quoted in Mullally and Smith, 1999: 9).

References and further reading

Bacik, Ivana, Cathryn Costello and Eileen Drew, 2003. *Gender Injustice*. Dublin: TCD Law School.
Carney, Gemma, 2002. 'Feminism, the women's movement and the internationalisation of gender equality policy: the case of gender mainstreaming', *Irish Political Studies* 17:2: 17–34.
Caul, Miki, 1999. 'Women's representation in parliament: the role of political parties', *Party Politics* 5:1: 79–98.
CEMR (Council of European Municipalities and Regions), 1999. *Men and Women in European Municipalities*. Paris: CEMR.
Childs, Sarah, 2002. 'Hitting the target: are Labour women MPs "acting for" women?', in Karen Ross (ed.), *Women, Politics and Change*. Oxford: Oxford University Press, pp. 143–53.

Connelly, Alpha, 1999. 'Women and the constitution of Ireland', in Yvonne Galligan, Eilís Ward and Rick Wilford (eds), *Contesting Politics: Women in Ireland, North and South*. Boulder, CO: Westview Press and PSAI Press, pp. 18–37.

Connolly, Linda, 2002. *The Irish Women's Movement: From Revolution to Devolution*. Basingstoke: Palgrave.

Cullen, Mary, 1997. 'Towards a new Ireland: women, feminism and the peace process', in Maryann Gialanella Valiulis and Mary O'Dowd (eds), *Women and Irish History*, Dublin: Wolfhound Press, pp. 260–77.

Cullen-Owens, Rosemary, 1984. *Smashing Times: A History of the Irish Women's Suffrage Movement 1889–1922*. Dublin: Attic Press.

Department of Finance, 2001. *Gender Equality Policy for the Civil Service*. Dublin: Department of Finance.

Dodson, Debra, 1998. 'Representing women's interests in the US House of Representatives', in Sue Thomas and Clyde Wilcox (eds), *Women and Elective Office*. New York: Oxford University Press, pp. 130–49.

European Commission, 1997. *Equal Opportunities for Men and Women in Europe?* Special Report, available at http://europa.eu.int/comm/public_opinion/

Farrell, David M., 1992. 'Ireland', in Richard S. Katz and Peter Mair (eds), *Party Organizations: A Data Handbook on Party Organizations in Western Democracies, 1960–90*. London: Sage, pp. 389–457.

Gallagher, Michael, 2003. 'Stability and turmoil: analysis of the results', in Michael Gallagher, Michael Marsh and Paul Mitchell (eds), *How Ireland Voted 2002*. Basingstoke: Palgrave Macmillan, pp. 88–118.

Gallagher, Michael and Michael Marsh, 2002. *Days of Blue Loyalty: The Politics of Membership of the Fine Gael Party*. Dublin: PSAI Press.

Gallagher, Michael, Michael Marsh and Paul Mitchell (eds), 2003. *How Ireland Voted 2002*. Basingstoke: Palgrave Macmillan.

Galligan, Yvonne, 1998. *Women and Politics in Contemporary Ireland: From the Margins to the Mainstream*. London: Pinter.

Galligan, Yvonne, 2000. *The Development of Mechanisms to Monitor Progress in Achieving Gender Equality in Ireland*. Dublin: Department of Justice, Equality and Law Reform.

Galligan, Yvonne, 2003. 'Candidate selection: more democratic or more centrally controlled?', in Michael Gallagher, Michael Marsh and Paul Mitchell (eds), *How Ireland Voted 2002*. Basingstoke: Palgrave Macmillan, pp. 37–56.

Galligan, Yvonne and Rick Wilford, 1999. 'Gender and party politics in the Republic of Ireland', in Yvonne Galligan, Eilís Ward and Rick Wilford (eds), *Contesting Politics: Women in Ireland, North and South*. Boulder, CO: Westview Press and PSAI Press, pp. 149–68.

Galligan, Yvonne, Michael Laver and Gemma Carney, 1999. 'The effects of candidate gender on voting in Ireland, 1997', *Irish Political Studies* 14: 118–22.

Galligan, Yvonne, Eilís Ward and Rick Wilford (eds), 1999a. *Contesting Politics: Women in Ireland, North and South*. Boulder, CO: Westview Press and PSAI Press.

Galligan, Yvonne, Kathleen Knight and Una Nic Giolla Choille, 2000. 'Pathways to power: women in the Oireachtas 1919–2000', in Maedhbh McNamara and Paschal Mooney (eds), *Women in Parliament, Ireland: 1918–2000*. Dublin: Wolfhound Press, pp. 27–69.

Government of Ireland, 2002. *Ireland: Report to the United Nations on the National Plan for Women 2002 on the Implementation of the Beijing Platform for Action*. Dublin: Stationery Office.

Grey, Sandra, 2002. 'Does size matter? Critical mass and New Zealand's women MPs', in Karen Ross (ed.), *Women, Politics and Change*. Oxford: Oxford University Press, pp. 19–29.

Healy, Gráinne, 2002. 'In the general election – vote to make a difference for women!', *Womenzone* 10 (April). Dublin: National Women's Council of Ireland.

Humphreys, Peter, Eileen Drew and Candy Murphy, 1999. *Gender Equality in the Civil Service*. Dublin: Institute of Public Administration.

Inter-Parliamentary Union, 2000. *Politics: Women's Insights*. Geneva: Inter-Parliamentary Union.

IPA (Institute of Public Administration), 2003. *Yearbook and Diary*. Dublin: Institute of Public Administration.

Kennedy, Fiachra, 2002. 'Abortion referendum 2002', *Irish Political Studies* 17:1: 114–28.

Kennelly, Brendan and Eilís Ward, 1993. 'The abortion referendums', in Michael Gallagher and Michael Laver (eds), *How Ireland Voted 1992*. Dublin: Folens and Limerick: PSAI Press, pp. 115–34.

Knight, Kathleen, Yvonne Galligan and Una Nic Giolla Choille, 2004. 'Equalising opportunities for women in electoral politics in Ireland: the views of women members of parliament', *Women and Politics* 26:1.

Long, Kathleen, 2003. 'Parity democracy: an examination of gender in the Republic of Ireland'. Paper presented to PSAI Annual Conference, Portmarnock, Dublin, 16–18 October.

Muintearas, Ballymun Women's Resource Centre, Longford Women's Centre, 2002. *'Ait ag an mBord': Representation of Women in Decision Making Structures for Local Development in Ireland*. Sligo: Jaycee Printers.

Mullally, Siobhán and Louise Smith, 1999. *Gender Proofing and the European Structural Funds: Outline Guidelines*. Dublin: Department of Justice, Equality and Law Reform.

National Women's Council of Ireland, 2002. *Irish Politics Jobs for the Boys! Recommendations on Increasing the Number of Women in Decision Making*. Dublin: National Women's Council of Ireland.

Norris, Pippa and Joni Lovenduski, 1993. *Gender and Party Politics*. London: Sage.

Norris, Pippa and Ronald Inglehart, 2001. 'Cultural obstacles to equal representation', *Journal of Democracy* 12:3: 126–40.

O'Donovan, Órla and Eilís Ward, 1999. 'Networks of women's groups in the Republic of Ireland', in Yvonne Galligan, Eilís Ward and Rick Wilford (eds), *Contesting Politics: Women in Ireland, North and South*. Boulder, CO: Westview Press and PSAI Press, pp. 90–108.

Randall, Vicky and Ailbhe Smyth, 1987. 'Bishops and bailiwicks: obstacles to women's political participation in Ireland', *Economic and Social Review* 18:3: 189–214.

Russell, Meg, 2000. *Women's Representation in UK Politics: What Can be Done within the Law?* London: Constitution Unit.

Russell, Meg, Fiona Mackay and Leslie McAllister, 2002. 'Women's representation in the Scottish Parliament and the Welsh Assembly: party dynamics for achieving critical mass', *Journal of Legislative Studies* 8:2: 49–76.

Sawer, Marian, 2002. 'The representation of women in Australia: meaning and make-believe', in Karen Ross (ed.), *Women, Politics and Change*. Oxford: Oxford University Press, pp. 5–18.

Scannell, Yvonne, 1988. 'The constitution and the role of women', in Brian Farrell (ed.), *De Valera's Constitution and Ours*. Dublin: Gill and Macmillan, pp. 123–36.

Shepherd-Robinson, Laura and Joni Lovenduski, 2002. *Women and Candidate Selection in British Political Parties*. London: Fawcett.

Websites

www.ndpgenderequality.ie/statdata/statdata.html   This site is maintained by the Gender Equality Unit in the Department of Justice, Equality and Law Reform and provides extensive gender-disaggregated social statistics across a wide range of policy areas covered by the National Development Plan such as employment, education, transport, demography and others.

www.ucd.ie/issda (link: QNHS)   This site hosts a wide range of Irish social statistics and survey data disaggregated by sex, such as the Quarterly National Household Survey. Maintained by the Institute for the Study of Social Change in University College Dublin, the site also holds important European social survey data, which enables researchers to place social attitudes in Ireland in a European context.

www.hea.ie (link: statistics)   This site, hosted by the Higher Education Authority, provides extensive statistics on female and male participation rates in third-level education. It also makes available policy and research documents on aspects of higher education, including gender equality.

www.ictu.ie   The Irish Congress of Trade Unions website provides useful information on women's participation in trade union activity and links with individual unions.

www.ibec.ie   The site of the Irish Business and Employers Confederation which gives the employer perspective on labour-related issues, including workplace childcare provision.

www.ipu.org   This is a very useful site, maintained by Inter-Parliamentary Union, providing extensive information on women in parliaments worldwide and a host of additional information on women and politics.

www.qub.ac.uk/cawp   This site is hosted by the Centre for Advancement of Women in Politics in Queen's University Belfast. It provides data on women in politics in Ireland, Northern Ireland and Britain, including women candidates at elections. The site also makes available a range of documents on women and politics and has links to other women and politics sites.

Part III
Policy and administration

11 The President and the Taoiseach

Robert Elgie and Peter Fitzgerald

As we have seen in Chapter 3, the political life of the Republic of Ireland is overshadowed by two figures: the President of Ireland, who is the head of state and a mainly symbolic figure, and the Taoiseach, who is the head of government and is responsible for political leadership. This chapter explores the foundations of executive power in the Republic. It begins by assessing the role of the President. Why is the presidency such a weak institution and should the office be reformed or even abolished? It then considers the dominant position of the Taoiseach. What resources can the Taoiseach mobilise and what obstacles are placed in the way of individualised political leadership?

The President

In terms of protocol, the 1937 constitution indicates that the President takes 'precedence over all other persons in the State' (Article 12.1). Furthermore, the constitution also states that the President is not 'answerable to either House of the Oireachtas or to any Court for the exercise and performance of the powers and functions of his office' (Article 13.8.1). In practice, though, the Irish presidency has been perceived in a European context as 'the weakest presidency to be filled by direct election' (Gallagher, 1999: 104). There is no doubt that the presidency is a secondary political office and there are no expectations that the President should exercise political leadership or be actively involved in political issues of the day. Indeed, any attempt to do so would be treated as an unnatural interference in the normal workings of the political process. For example, when President McAleese commented on the Nice Treaty referendum during a state visit to Greece in July 2002, a number of politicians expressed the view that her intervention went beyond that allowed by her role; John Gormley of the Greens, for instance, advised her to 'butt out' of the political debate (*Irish Examiner*, 22 July 2002). A number of factors contribute to the relatively weak position of the presidency: the party-dominated method of election, the absence of constitutional powers and the tradition of limited presidentialism that has been the norm since 1937.

Presidential elections

The constitution provides for the election of the President by a direct vote of the people every seven years. In order to stand for office, candidates must be nominated by at least 20 members of the Oireachtas or four county or county borough councils (Article 12.4.2); in addition, former or retiring Presidents may nominate themselves (Article 12.4.4). The effect of the nomination process has been to place the selection of presidential candidates almost exclusively in the hands of Fianna Fáil, Fine Gael and Labour Party elites. In the past, these parties have tended to choose candidates who are either elderly or not quite at the forefront of active politics rather than senior politicians still in the prime of their active political career – though, in any event, the limited powers of the office have meant that the latter are rarely tempted to run for it. In this way, Presidents have come to office either without ambition or without the party political means to achieve what few goals they might have set themselves in the first place. Moreover, party elites can collude to prevent an election from taking place at all. The constitution states that where 'only one candidate is nominated for the office of President it shall not be necessary to proceed to a ballot for his election' (Article 12.4.5). In such a case, presidents are deprived not just of political authority but of popular legitimacy as well. Since the office was instituted, there have been five uncontested elections (1938, 1952, 1974, 1976 and 1983) and six have been contested (1945, 1959, 1966, 1973, 1990 and 1997; see Appendix 2g). Whatever the nature of the contest, though, successful candidates have been in no position to claim a mandate for leadership even if they had ever wished to do so. In this way, one of the conditions for presidential leadership has been absent from the system.

Arguably, though, the context in which presidential elections take place may be changing, albeit marginally. First, parties have tended recently to nominate rather younger and more dynamic candidates. Moreover, in the elections of 1990 and 1997 the Labour Party chose a candidate (Mary Robinson and Adi Roche respectively) whose links with the party organisation were relatively weak. The selection of Mary Robinson in 1990 was quite significant. She certainly had a history of Labour Party politics, having been a Labour senator and an unsuccessful Labour candidate at two Dáil elections. However, she resigned from the party in 1985 and during the 1990 election campaign stressed that she was an independent candidate. As a result, while in office she was relatively unconcerned with maintaining close relations with her sponsor party and there were persistent rumours about the difficulties between her and the then Labour Party leader, Dick Spring. Indeed, when the 1993–4 government, which included representatives from the Labour Party, refused to let President Robinson chair a committee looking at the future of the United Nations, the President 'implied strongly, in correspondence with Albert Reynolds, that she believed Dick [Spring] had leaked some of the details of the row. He in turn had been furious at this innuendo, and had written a sharp letter to the President' (Finlay, 1998: 284). All told, if the trend towards nominating younger, more independent-minded candidates continues, then at some stage in the future a party may find that it has helped to elect someone who wishes to maintain and perhaps even promote his or her own separate political agenda while in office.

Second, the 1997 election set an important precedent in that for the first time ever candidates were able to obtain sufficient support from county councillors to be validly nominated (Dana Rosemary Scallon and Derek Nally). This was a clear sign that the grip of party elites on the nomination process was loosening. It might be argued that this innovation opens the way for non-party, even populist, candidates to be nominated in the future. So, while not having the support of a party organisation may make it difficult for independent candidates to be elected president, all the same such candidates may change the nature of the political contest and this may have an impact on the presidency itself. For example, in 1997 Dana Rosemary Scallon came third, winning a respectable 14 per cent of the vote, and she did so without the backing of a major political party. Overall, if elected, such candidates would most likely cause problems for the traditional view of the President as figurehead. Currently, though, it is this vision of the presidency which, despite these changes, still prevails.

Presidential functions

Over and above the context of the election process, presidents have very few constitutional powers of which to avail. Indeed, so limited are these powers that a populist, reformist or even mildly independent-minded president would soon come up against the constraints of the office. The President has both non-discretionary and discretionary powers (Ward, 1994: 286–95). However, the former can scarcely be classed as 'powers' at all as the President has no room for independent action whatsoever. For example, Article 13.1.1 states that the 'President shall, on the nomination of Dáil Éireann, appoint the Taoiseach'; in other words, the President must accept the Dáil's nominee. The same principle applies to all other roles under this heading. In addition, the President may not even leave the state without the express agreement of the government (Article 12.9). The Taoiseach must keep the President informed on matters of domestic and international policy (Article 28.5.2), but there is no indication of how often the two must meet or how detailed the information must be. Indeed, Liam Cosgrave is reported to have seen President Ó Dálaigh only four times in two years in 1974–6. All told, presidents themselves have usually steered clear from taking any action that runs the risk of creating political controversy. More than that, on occasion governments have advised presidents to refrain from certain activities. Thus, in 1991 the government asked President Robinson not to deliver the Dimbleby Lecture in London, and in 1993 it asked her to decline to chair a Ford Foundation committee on the future of the United Nations, as mentioned above; on each occasion the President accepted this advice without forcing a confrontation (O'Leary and Burke, 1998: 153, 220–2). In all of these ways, then, the President's room for manoeuvre is not just limited; it is altogether absent.

In the case of discretionary powers, the President has a somewhat greater degree of freedom. That said, the scope of these powers is very small. There are six such powers, three of which are of minor significance (they relate to the President's role as an arbiter in the case of disputes between the Dáil and the Seanad). In fact, so far only one discretionary power has been invoked with any degree of significance (Article 26.1.1) and only one other remains potentially important (Article 13.2.2).

Article 26.1.1 allows the President, after consultation with the Council of State, to submit a bill to the Supreme Court to test its constitutional validity (see p. 85 above). The Council of State comprises the Taoiseach, Tánaiste, Chief Justice, President of the High Court, the chairs of both the Dáil and the Seanad and the Attorney General, as well as any former President, Taoiseach or Chief Justice who is willing to serve, plus up to seven presidential nominees. Its role in this, as in any other matter on which the President consults it, is purely advisory; the President need not follow its recommendations. There are certain limits to the President's power to submit bills to the Supreme Court. 'Money bills', meaning legislation that relates to the public finances as certified by the Ceann Comhairle, bills containing proposals to amend the constitution and bills that have been rushed through the Seanad in accordance with Article 24 cannot be referred. All the same, from 1937 to 2003 presidents used this power on 14 occasions (see Table 11.1). On one occasion, it was the cause of controversy (Gallagher, 1977). In September 1976, President Ó Dálaigh had referred the Emergency Powers Bill to the Supreme Court. This bill was designed to give additional power to the state authorities when dealing with suspected IRA members. On its referral, the bill was declared constitutional by the Supreme Court, but shortly afterwards the Defence Minister, Patrick Donegan, described President Ó Dálaigh as 'a thundering disgrace' for having referred the bill at all. The Taoiseach, Liam Cosgrave, refused to sack the minister for his comment and a Dáil motion of no confidence in Donegan was narrowly defeated. Following the vote, President Ó Dálaigh tendered his own resignation.

Article 13.2.2 states that the President 'may in his absolute discretion refuse to dissolve Dáil Éireann on the advice of a Taoiseach who has ceased to retain the support of a majority in Dáil Éireann'. In fact, this power has never been exercised. However, it remains controversial because at times of extreme political tension it draws the President into the party political process whether or not the article is actually invoked. Either to grant or to refuse a dissolution might lay the President open to charges of favouring one political party over another. Moreover, this article is doubly controversial because it politicises the presidency in circumstances which are not clearly

Table 11.1 Bills referred to the Supreme Court by the President

Bill		Outcome
1	Offences against the State (Amendment) Bill, 1940	Signed into law
2	School Attendance Bill, 1942	Found to be unconstitutional
3	Electoral Amendment Bill, 1961	Signed into law
4	Criminal Law (Jurisdiction) Bill, 1975	Signed into law
5	Emergency Powers Bill, 1976	Signed into law
6	Housing (Private Rented Dwellings) Bill, 1981	Found to be unconstitutional
7	Electoral (Amendment) Bill, 1983	Found to be unconstitutional
8	Adoption (No. 2) Bill, 1987	Signed into law
9	Matrimonial Home Bill, 1993	Found to be unconstitutional
10	Regulation of Information Services Outside the State for Termination of Pregnancies Bill, 1995	Signed into law
11	Employment Equality Bill, 1996	Found to be unconstitutional
12	Equal Status Bill, 1997	Found to be unconstitutional
13	Illegal Immigrants (Trafficking) Bill, 1999	Signed into law
14	Planning and Development Bill, 1999	Signed into law

Sources: Dooney and O'Toole (1998: 117–18); BAILII (2003).

spelt out in the constitution. Who is to say when the Taoiseach has actually lost the support of the Dáil? Is it simply when the government has lost a vote of confidence, or when it has been defeated over a single item of legislation, or when a party announces that it is leaving the governing coalition, or even when an independent TD withdraws his or her support? On several occasions the significance of this article has been apparent. In 1944 President Hyde agreed to dissolve the Dáil after a government defeat on a minor piece of legislation because he considered that there was no alternative administration in waiting. In January 1982 President Hillery again agreed to dissolve the Dáil after a government defeat on a part of the annual budget, even though this time the leader of the opposition, Charles Haughey, was apparently willing to try to form a government without recourse to an election. Finally, President Robinson made it known that she would have refused a dissolution had Albert Reynolds requested one following the fall of the Fianna Fáil–Labour coalition in 1994 (Gallagher, 1999).

These examples illustrate the ambiguities that surround Article 13.2.2. As a result, in 1996 the Constitution Review Group stated in its final report that 'the introduction of a constructive vote of no confidence would be preferable to the involvement of the President in the government-formation process' (CRG, 1996: 98). In other words, it recommended that the constitution be changed so as to oblige the Dáil to nominate an alternative Taoiseach at the same time as it voted on a motion of confidence. This would prevent the President from participating in any such political controversies and put an end to any lingering problems associated with this article.

Presidential office holders

Against this general background, the tradition of a limited presidency was established from the first incumbent, Douglas Hyde, onwards. The fact that he was the sole nominee, that he was associated with the cultural rather than the party political world, that he was aged 78 at the time of his election and that de Valera, as Taoiseach, was still at the peak of his political authority all went to ensure that power continued to reside with the head of government. This tradition was then reinforced by Hyde's successor, Seán T. O'Kelly. In contrast to Hyde, he was elected (at least in 1945) and he had previously enjoyed a long party political and ministerial career. However, he made no attempt to break the mould that had just been set. Indeed, Hussey comments that O'Kelly held office 'safely and unremarkably' until 1959 (Hussey, 1995: 11). Thereafter, most presidents appear to have been happy with a role as figurehead. For example, President Hillery has written that he wanted to do the job with 'the minimum of self-projection' and, in an oblique reference to the events of January 1982, when he dissolved the Dáil despite attempts by Charles Haughey to suggest that formation of an alternative government might be possible, he stated that 'the most important use of [presidential] powers was sometimes not to employ them at all' (*Irish Times*, 12 November 1997). All told, the desire to exercise presidential leadership has generally been absent from the system.

In fact, it appears that only two or three presidents have had the will to test the limits of the office. The first, Erskine Childers, enjoyed considerable political authority and public affection. However, his attempts to reform the office were met with outright resistance from the Taoiseach of the day, Liam Cosgrave. For example, Garret FitzGerald reveals that the head of government vetoed the President's desire to fulfil a campaign pledge to set up a 'think-tank' to examine the long-term needs of the country (FitzGerald, 1991: 254). In the event, Childers's presidency was brought to an abrupt end by his sudden death. The second, Mary Robinson, was the most popular and, arguably, most successful president to date. She demonstrated that it was possible for a president to shape the political agenda at least at the margins. Most notably, on a visit to West Belfast in 1993 she shook the hand of Sinn Féin president, Gerry Adams, at a time when the first IRA cease-fire had yet to be called and when the party was still treated as a pariah. Equally, she made a series of high-profile visits to Rwanda and alerted the public not just in Ireland but also elsewhere to the atrocities that were being perpetrated there. Needless to say, there was a great deal of opposition to some of her actions. For example, in 1995 her comments in a US television interview were interpreted as a call for a 'yes' vote in the divorce referendum and, hence, were criticised by those who were campaigning on the opposite side and by elements of the media. At the same time, though, she was truly able to incarnate the concerns of many sections of Irish life in her championing of women, the disadvantaged, travellers and the diaspora.

For her part, Mary McAleese has also been involved in a number of controversies. Her intervention in the referendum to ratify the Nice Treaty provoked a limited party political backlash (see p. 305 above). In the main, though, President McAleese's interventions have been outside the strict confines of the political arena. For example, in December 1997 she flouted the Catholic Church's teaching that it is not permissible for Roman Catholics to take communion in Protestant churches. Equally, in May 2003 at the 'Re-imagining Ireland' conference in Virginia, USA, she stated that 'the Irish love of conviviality has its dark side in the stupid wasteful abuse of alcohol' (McAleese, 2003). These events provoked a great deal of public and social comment. However, they were not really the source of political debate. Thus, President McAleese has abided by the basic norm that the President is allowed to comment on matters that relate to social issues, but not in a way that impacts upon the party political agenda. In fact, like other presidents before her, one of President McAleese's main roles during her term of office has been to support the government's diplomatic and trade efforts abroad. The President has undertaken a number of high-profile foreign visits where she has supported the government's efforts to extend Ireland's cultural and economic relations abroad (see Table 11.2). Her visit to China in October 2003 was a good case in point. Here, she was accompanied by 174 business people representing 82 Irish companies on the largest ever Irish trade mission abroad and addressed a number of meetings on the issue of trade links with Ireland (*Irish Times*, 4 October 2003).

Table 11.2 President McAleese's state visits abroad 1997–2003

Year	Countries visited
1997	Lebanon
1998	England (four times), France, USA (twice), Australia, New Zealand, Canada, Belgium
1999	Italy, Honduras, Mexico, England (three times), USA (twice), South Africa, Czech Republic, Scotland
2000	Hungary, USA, England (twice), Germany, Monaco, France, Bosnia-Herzegovina, Kosovo, Egypt, Oman
2001	USA, Finland, Estonia, Slovenia, Uganda, Kenya, England
2002	USA (three times), England (twice), Greece, Egypt, Thailand, Malaysia, Portugal, Wales
2003	Australia, USA, Poland, Slovenia, Scotland, England, China, Italy, Luxembourg, France, Belgium.

Sources: Áras an Uachtaráin, 2003.

Note
The 1997 data begin on 11 November. President McAleese has also visited Northern Ireland on 41 occasions during the above period.

Overall, the President is a symbolic head of state with a ceremonial role, such as receiving the credentials of foreign ambassadors; she has an acknowledged right to comment on social matters in a non-political way; and she is sometimes called upon to support Ireland's national interests abroad. However, the President is not a major political leader.

The case for abolition or reform

The weakness of the presidency is such that its very existence has periodically been called into question. In 1967, the Committee on the Constitution identified two arguments in favour of abolishing the office, stating that the Taoiseach could quite happily exercise the few powers that the president does enjoy and that abolition would bring about budgetary savings (Committee on the Constitution, 1967: 8). However, the Committee also identified three counter-arguments, stating that it would not be realistic for the Taoiseach to act as guardian of the constitution, that it would be a severe burden for one person to carry out the duties of both head of state and head of government, and that the amount of budgetary savings would be minimal. More than that, it is generally felt that there is a real need for a non-political figure to personify in a disinterested manner the aspirations of the people as a whole. In this vein, the Constitution Review Group (1996: 28) concluded that 'there is no public demand or good reason for abolition of the office'.

What about reforming the presidency? According to one writer, the basic problem is that as things stand the presidency is neither truly political nor truly non-political (Gallagher, 1977: 382). As the above examples demonstrate, there are occasions when presidents cannot avoid being drawn into the political process. At the same time, on the occasions when they might wish to make their mark presidents do not have the powers with which to do so. It might be argued, therefore, that the presidency should be reformed either to increase the set of presidential powers so as give the incumbent the potential to be a significant political player or to reduce them even further so as to place the institution completely above the political fray. In fact, if there is to be reform then it is likely that it will take the second of these two courses. All countries require a symbolic figure to personify the state. This is the role that the President is currently in a position to perform successfully. Moreover, the Taoiseach is already charged with exercising political leadership. There is therefore a case for a further reduction of the President's powers with a view to eliminating the lingering suspicion that the presidency is anything other than a purely symbolic office. Indeed, this logic led the Constitution Review Group to recommend that executive authority should be reserved for the government and that the President should be placed 'above politics' altogether.

The Taoiseach

If the Irish presidency is perceived to be one of the weakest of all directly elected heads of state, then the Taoiseach is usually considered to be one of the strongest of all heads of government. For example, Anthony King places the Taoiseach alongside the British, German, Greek, Portuguese and Spanish prime ministers in the category of heads of government who have the highest degree of influence within their own systems of government (King, 1994: 152). Brendan O'Leary goes one further. He states that: 'Within his own political system the Irish prime minister is potentially more powerful than any other European prime minister, with exception of his British counterpart' (O'Leary, 1991: 159). However, the key word here is 'potentially'. In practice, the power of the Taoiseach varies from one office holder to another. Even if the Taoiseach is usually pre-eminent amongst his colleagues, the 'precise degree of this pre-eminence, however, may well vary from Taoiseach to Taoiseach' (Chubb, 1974: 13). The reality, then, is a system in which there are a number of constitutional, administrative and political resources at the disposal of the office. However, it is also a system in which the Taoiseach faces a number of constraints. Most notably, the power of the Taoiseach is shaped by party political factors, and these go a long way towards accounting for the strength of an individual Taoiseach.

Constitutional, administrative and political resources

The constitution officially designates the Taoiseach as head of government (Articles 13.1.1 and 28.5.1). In this capacity, the Taoiseach meets and negotiates with heads of state and heads of government throughout the world, attends meetings of the European Council on behalf of the state, pays particular attention to the situation in Northern Ireland and is the government's main spokesperson at home. In all, the Taoiseach is the person upon whom the responsibility for leadership is most visibly incumbent.

The constitution also provides the Taoiseach with a considerable power of appointment. For example, Article 13.1.2 gives the Taoiseach the right to appoint the other members of the government, subject, of course, to Dáil approval. Although the appointment of junior ministers, or ministers of state, is vested by law in the government, in practice the Taoiseach plays no less significant a role here. In addition, Article 30.2 provides the Taoiseach with the right to appoint the Attorney General, who has a seat at the cabinet table. It should be noted, though, that there are formal limits to the Taoiseach's power of appointment: the number of cabinet ministers is limited to between seven and 15 (Article 28.1), the Tánaiste and Minister for Finance must be members of the Dáil (Article 28.7.1), the choice of ministers is restricted to members of the Oireachtas and no more than two ministers at any one time can be members of the Seanad (Article 28.7.2). There are also informal limits which are outlined below.

Despite these limits, there is no doubt that heads of government have used the power of ministerial appointment to shape the membership of the cabinet to their own advantage. This was particularly noticeable in 1992 when Albert Reynolds failed to appoint a number of senior Haughey supporters to his first cabinet. Moreover, Article 28.9.4 states that the 'Taoiseach may at any time, for reasons which to him seem sufficient, request a member of the Government to resign' and that if the minister refuses to comply, the Taoiseach may simply dismiss him or her. Accordingly, Jack Lynch dismissed Charles Haughey and Neil Blaney during the 'arms crisis' in 1970, while Haughey himself dismissed Brian Lenihan in 1990, and he dismissed Albert Reynolds and Pádraig Flynn for refusing to back his leadership in 1991. All other things being equal, then, the Taoiseach has the opportunity to determine the composition of the cabinet not just at the beginning of an administration but at any time throughout its life.

In selecting the government, the Taoiseach also determines the portfolios of individual ministers. By giving a particular policy area a ministry to itself, the Taoiseach bestows a level of importance on that area. For example, when the 1993–4 government included a Department of Equality and Law Reform, which engaged in a process of reform of family law culminating in the divorce referendum of 1995, the Taoiseach, Albert Reynolds, stated that the 'issues involved are regarded as so fundamental to the character of our society that they require to be the responsibility of a member of the Government' (*Irish Times*, 13 January 1993). Similarly, in bundling policy areas together in a ministry, the Taoiseach can effectively demote certain policy areas as government priorities. For example, in 2002 the area of equality and law reform was added to the responsibilities of the Department of Justice. According to the Taoiseach, Bertie Ahern, this decision was taken to 'reflect or . . . emphasise new priorities in government' (*Irish Times*, 27 June 1997). In effect, this downgraded the importance of issues relating to this area.

In addition, the Taoiseach may also reserve certain policy portfolios for himself or herself. For example, from 1932 to 1948 Eamon de Valera combined the post of Minister for External Affairs with the position of head of government. In the period when Anglo-Irish affairs dominated Ireland's external relations and the central issues concerned the jurisdiction and sovereignty of the state, de Valera's own interest in these areas propelled him to the view 'that this was a post which should, if possible, be held by the Head of Government, so that there might be no doubt as to the authority with which the minister spoke' (Longford and O'Neill, 1970: 275). More recently, from 1987 to 1992 Charles Haughey was both Taoiseach and Minister for the Gaeltacht. Haughey's decision to combine these posts seems to have reflected a personal interest in the cultural aspects of the latter portfolio and also perhaps doubts as to whether it warranted the full-time attention of a cabinet minister. Whatever the reason, by virtue of holding this post the Taoiseach took personal charge of presenting a number of pieces of legislation in the Dáil and the Seanad, including the An Blascaodh Mor (Great Blasket Island) National Historic Park Bill (1989).

Over and above the power to select the government, the Taoiseach nominates 11 members of Seanad Éireann (see Chapter 8, p. 233). This is usually sufficient to guarantee that the government of the day has a majority in the upper house. So, in 2002 Fianna Fáil won only 24 of the 49 elected seats to the Seanad but the incoming Taoiseach, Bertie Ahern, was then able to use his power of appointment to ensure that the Fianna Fáil–Progressive Democrat coalition enjoyed a comfortable majority in the 60-seat chamber. In addition, the Taoiseach nominates members of his or her own party to fill Oireachtas committee posts. In 2002, Bertie Ahern nominated members of Fianna Fáil to fill 14 committee chairmanships (the chairmanship of the important Public Accounts Committee goes to a member of the largest opposition party). There are also committee vice-chairs, convenors and chairs of subcommittees to be nominated (all of which earn the holders a higher salary). Finally, Article 13.2.1 provides the Taoiseach with the power to dissolve the Dáil and call a general election. The probability that this power will be used depends on the likelihood that the government will win the ensuing election, but it was successfully used by de Valera in the 1930s to maintain and reinforce his position in office. However, an attempt by John Bruton to emulate this feat in 1997 backfired when, despite high satisfaction ratings, the government failed to win an election that was called five and a half months before the natural end of the Dáil term. In short, when the circumstances are right the head of government, who comes to office thanks to the favour of the lower house, has the right to determine the parliamentary lifetime of the members of that house.

In addition to the power of appointment, the Taoiseach also has the capacity to shape the day-to-day process of policy making. The Taoiseach has important prerogatives with regard to the operation of the cabinet, even though coalition government is now the norm and has somewhat restricted the head of government's powers in this respect (see p. 320). In general, as Farrell states: 'The Taoiseach determines the order in which items on the cabinet agenda are taken, the time given to consideration of each item, who is to speak, and when a decision should be reached – or postponed . . . in practice, ministers do not challenge the Taoiseach's control of the agenda' (Farrell, 1996: 176). In this context, Farrell quotes an anonymous cabinet minister as saying: 'Really you can't get an item discussed for five seconds at a cabinet meeting if the Taoiseach isn't with you' (Farrell, 1994: 80).

Furthermore when the issue under discussion is one that is close to the Taoiseach, it is difficult to halt its progress. For example, Finlay (1998) describes how a tax amnesty was pushed through cabinet in 1993 by the Taoiseach of the day, Albert Reynolds, despite serious misgivings on the part of many around the cabinet table including the Tánaiste, and the Minister for Finance. A further example of the power of the Taoiseach in cabinet is the way Bertie Ahern pushed ahead with a referendum on abortion in 2002 (the twenty-fifth amendment to the constitution – Protection of Human Life in Pregnancy Bill) despite a lack of enthusiasm from his coalition partners (Murphy, 2003: 16). While there are limits to how far a Taoiseach can push an unpopular item, particularly in coalition governments, confronting the Taoiseach at cabinet involves expending considerable political capital, and this encourages the avoidance of such confrontation. Outside the cabinet, the number of permanent cabinet committees is small. In one sense, though, this factor further strengthens the position of the Taoiseach. It obliges the head of government to be personally concerned with all departmental policy matters and requires the Taoiseach to be more than just a policy co-ordinator. As such, although the head of government must bear in mind the sensitivities of coalition partners, the Taoiseach is in a position to direct rather than simply manage the flow of governmental business and is thus able to follow the full course of policy making from inception through to approval at the cabinet table.

The Taoiseach is in a similar position with regard to the legislative aspect of the policy-making process (see Chapter 8). For example, Article 25 of the Dáil's standing orders allows the Taoiseach to determine the order in which government business will be taken each day. In this sense, the Taoiseach controls not just the cabinet's business but the Dáil's agenda as well. In addition, the Taoiseach regularly defends the government's record during question time and on other occasions. The Taoiseach answers pre-submitted formal questions every week when the Dáil is in session. Elgie and Stapleton (2003) have found an overall increase in the parliamentary activity of Taoisigh since the foundation of the state. In particular, there was a sharp increase from the beginning of the 1960s in activities such as the presentation of the daily order of business, question answering and statement making. However, this overall rise masks a decline in certain forms of activity, such as set-piece speech-making and minor interventions in debates. Moreover, the aggregate level of parliamentary activity of the Taoiseach remains low when compared with heads of government in other countries, such as the UK and Canada. Indeed, in the years to come the average level of the Taoiseach's parliamentary activity may begin to decline again because since late 2002 Bertie Ahern has answered parliamentary questions on two rather than three days a week. Overall, the Dáil is often perceived as one of the least influential legislatures in western Europe (see Chapter 8), and it is the Taoiseach who is the main beneficiary of this situation.

The Taoiseach's position is further strengthened by the administrative support which the office commands. The most important institution in this respect is the Department of the Taoiseach. The department comprises approximately 300 people in a number of different sections or divisions. Their role is to co-ordinate government policy and contribute to its formulation. There are separate sections in various areas such as Economic and Social Policy, European and International Affairs and Northern Ireland. The department also includes the Taoiseach's private office, the Office of the Chief Whip, the Government Secretariat and the Government Information Service. Collectively, these institutions carry out many of the essential tasks of government on the Taoiseach's behalf. For example, one of the most pivotal organisations is the government secretariat, the main task of which is to prepare cabinet meetings and to execute its decisions. In this capacity, the secretary general to the government attends cabinet meetings in a non-voting capacity to take the minutes.

More generally, though, the secretariat co-ordinates the work of the government as a whole. It liaises with government ministers to ensure that decisions are being made and deadlines are being met. In this way, it is central to the working of the cabinet system. As O'Leary notes, its existence 'is no proof of overweening monocratic power' (O'Leary, 1991: 155). At the same time, though, to the extent that the secretary general to the government is one of the Taoiseach's closest interlocutors, then it allows the head of government to maintain a privileged overview of the cabinet system. As Morgan argues, it 'equips the Taoiseach to exercise better-informed powers of surveillance over his Government's activity' (Morgan, 1990: 55). Also significant in this respect is the Government Information Service, which is headed by the Government Press Secretary. The press secretary is a political appointee chosen for his or her loyalty and knowledge of the media. There is no doubt that the press secretary is privy to the most sensitive of all government discussions (see, for example, Duignan, 1996). There is also no doubt that the presence of an experienced and skilled individual at this post can be of enormous public and political benefit to the Taoiseach personally.

The final resource upon which a Taoiseach may draw is electoral and party political. As will be shown below, party politics is also the main reason why the power of the Taoiseach varies. However, when the party situation allows, the head of government can draw upon three electoral and party-based resources. First, the Taoiseach derives authority from the electoral process. General election campaigns are highly personalised. In the words of Basil Chubb, they 'often take the form of gladiatorial contests between two designated party leaders' (Chubb, 1992: 185). In 2002, Bertie Ahern clearly won the popularity battle between the two main party leaders. For example, one analysis indicates that Bertie Ahern was viewed as the 'best Taoiseach' by 52 per cent of those asked, compared to 13 per cent for Michael Noonan (Garry *et al.*, 2003: 129). As a result, the Taoiseach could claim that the party's increase in seats was at least partly due to his personal popularity and he could insist on a degree of loyalty from both cabinet and parliamentary party colleagues.

Second, the Taoiseach can benefit from the fact that the formation of the government is approved by a vote in the Dáil. As Coakley notes, this system forces 'parliament to define at the outset its attitude to any new prime minister and compels would-be dissidents within his party to choose between open rebellion and conformity' (Coakley, 1984: 413–14). Thus, after the

2002 election the incoming government led by Bertie Ahern successfully marshalled its own troops to muster a working majority with the PDs.

Third, the Taoiseach is not just head of government but also party leader (John A. Costello, Taoiseach in 1948–51 and 1954–7, is the sole exception to this rule). This is a significant power because Fianna Fáil and Fine Gael are highly centralised political parties. The leader has the power to appoint staff members at party headquarters, influence candidate selection and party rules and, hence, create the conditions for party support (see Chapter 6).

Structural and conjunctural constraints

All of the above points might suggest that there is a system of prime ministerial government in the Republic of Ireland. And yet, such a conclusion would be premature. Although it is certainly the case that the Taoiseach is the principal political figure within the executive, it is also the case that there are distinct limits to the Taoiseach's powers. Some of these limits are structural, others are conjunctural. That is to say, some are built into the system and are inescapable, whereas others depend on the particular context within which the Taoiseach has to operate. With regard to the latter, the most important variable is the nature of the party political situation with which the government is faced.

As a result of structural factors, the Taoiseach's position within government is always less than absolute. Most notably, running the business of government is an extremely complicated and time-consuming affair. The Taoiseach cannot be expected to master every detail of policy and there is pressure to prioritise some policy areas, such as foreign and European policy, Northern Ireland policy and social and budgetary policy, at the expense of others (see FitzGerald, 1991: 425).

Moreover, the Taoiseach's power of ministerial appointment is, in effect, quite restricted. In addition to the constraints of coalition government (see p. 320), the pool of potential ministers is always relatively small. For example, in 2002 there were only 81 Fianna Fáil TDs in total, while in December 1994 there were only 46 Fine Gael deputies from whom the Taoiseach was able to choose. Furthermore, the Taoiseach must pay attention to both the loyalty and seniority of party colleagues when making appointments. There are certainly times when it is best to appoint potential dissidents so as to bind them to the principle of collective governmental responsibility. There are also times when the Taoiseach may wish to appoint a complete Dáil newcomer to ministerial office, such as Niamh Bhreathnach in 1993, and evidence indicates that TDs are being promoted more quickly to ministerial office than in the past (Farrell, 1987: 146). However, in general terms the Taoiseach will wish to reward loyalty and there may be certain long-standing deputies whose presence at the ministerial table is almost a given. In these ways, the Taoiseach's freedom of choice is further restricted.

Equally, there may be pressure to appoint ministers from particular geographical areas in the hope of reaping future electoral reward. So, there will be strong pressure to appoint a number of deputies from Dublin and from the other major cities to ministerial office. In recent times, gender has also become an important factor. It is now almost obligatory to include a number of female ministers in the cabinet. In 2002, two of the 15 cabinet positions went to women. Where there is a reshuffle of the cabinet or a party has remained in government after an election, the Taoiseach may also be lobbied to retain certain ministers in their current portfolios. For example, lobbying by fellow ministers and by figures in the agribusiness industry was seen as playing a role in the retention of the Ministers for Defence and Agriculture following the 2002 election (Mitchell, 2003: 223). Finally, the Taoiseach must at least bear in mind the policy expertise of potential appointees. This is not to say that the Minister of Education has to be a former teacher or that the Minister of Health must be a former doctor. It is simply to suggest that the Taoiseach may wish to take into account the role played by junior ministers or opposition party spokespersons when appointing people to full cabinet posts. Overall, there is certainly a sense in which the Taoiseach's power of ministerial appointment is always more restricted than a simple reading of the constitution may suggest.

In addition to structural limitations the Taoiseach's power is subject to conjunctural constraints. In terms of the Taoiseach's power within government, the most important conjunctural variable is party political. As O'Leary asserts, 'the Taoiseach's ability to fulfil his policy-initiating role within the government is primarily determined by party-government variables' (O'Leary, 1991: 159–60). The Taoiseach is a professional party politician who comes to power by way of a party-dominated process and who remains in power only for as long as party support can be maintained. Thus, party politics pervades the political process. At times, the Taoiseach can be liberated if the conjunction of party forces is favourable. At other times, though, the Taoiseach can be imprisoned by party politics if the conjunction of these forces is disadvantageous. Accordingly, his or her power and freedom to manoeuvre is shaped by whether there is a coalition or a single-party government, whether there is a majority or a minority government and whether the main governing party is united or divided.

All other things being equal, the position of the Taoiseach is stronger during periods of single-party government than coalition government. All told, from 1922 to 2003 single-party governments held power for 52 years and coalitions for 29. For the most part, then, heads of government have not had to operate within the confines of coalition constraints. This is one reason why commentators such as Anthony King (as we saw above, p. 313) have classed the Taoiseach as such an influential domestic actor in a comparative context. However, there has been a coalition government of one sort or another since 1989 due to the fact that Fianna Fáil has been unable to win an overall majority on its own and that it no longer refuses to envisage a coalition agreement (see Chapter 5). As coalition government becomes the norm, the overall position of the Taoiseach has become weaker and judgements such as the one cited earlier by Anthony King may need to be revised accordingly.

The impact of coalition government can be seen in four ways. First, the Taoiseach's power of appointment is restricted; it is shared with the leaders of the other parties participating in the coalition. The head of government must accept ministerial nominations that are made by the coalition partner, and may even be forced to make imaginative compromises. For example, the agreement which sealed the formation of the so-called 'rainbow coalition' in 1994 included the understanding that an additional junior minister would be allowed to attend cabinet meetings as Democratic Left's second representative, even though the constitutional limit of 15 cabinet ministers had already been reached.

Second, in office, representatives of the coalition partner may be in a position to shape the policy of the departments that they head. So, for example, in the government that took office in 2002, Michael McDowell was a high-profile Progressive Democrat Minister for Justice, Equality and Law Reform.

Third, coalition government may also mean that the Tánaiste becomes a significant political actor. There is a convention that the Taoiseach appoints the leader of the main coalition partner to this post. From this vantage point, the Tánaiste is in a position to participate in the most important decisions of the government (see Box 11.1). For example, Mary Harney's opposition to the proposed construction of a national stadium at Abbotstown, outside Dublin, in 2002–3 had a key role in sidelining the project. It is certainly the case that her Labour Party predecessor, Dick Spring, was influential in shaping foreign and, arguably, Northern Ireland policy from 1993 to 1997. Indeed, during this time he headed a specially created Office of the Tánaiste which was agreed as part of the January 1993 coalition agreement with Fianna Fáil and which was designed to provide the incumbent with administrative support along the lines of the Department of the Taoiseach. The Labour leader thus received all government papers and not simply those relating to his own ministerial portfolio of foreign affairs. Overall, such was the position of Dick Spring during this time that Brian Farrell wonders whether there was a subtle shift from the role of Tánaiste as deputising Taoiseach to the Tánaiste as deputy Taoiseach (Farrell, 1996: 179). This experiment, though, did not continue after 1997, when the Office of the Tánaiste was abolished.

Fourth, if the Taoiseach rides roughshod over the concerns of the coalition partner, then the government runs the risk of collapse. There is nothing inherently unstable about coalition governments, but circumstances can conspire to render them extremely fragile, as the coalition break-ups of 1992 and 1994 showed.

Box 11.1 **The Tánaiste**

Tánaiste is an old Irish language word which means 'heir apparent' or 'second in rank'. Indeed, some of the original proposals for what would become the 1937 constitution used the English language term 'deputy-prime minister' to describe the position (Smith, 1995). In the constitution, the Tánaiste's main role is to deputise for the Taoiseach. Article 28.6.2 states that the Tánaiste acts 'for all purposes in the place of the Taoiseach if the Taoiseach should die, or become permanently incapacitated' and Article 28.6.3 states that the Tánaiste 'acts for' the Taoiseach in his or her temporary absence. In practice, though, the Tánaiste is rarely called upon to carry out this role. In fact, the only occasion when the Taoiseach has had to be replaced for any length of time was when Eamon de Valera travelled to the Netherlands for treatment for his failing eyesight and was absent for four and a half months (Collins, 2000: 150). Instead, as a minister like any other, the Tánaiste's main role is to carry out his or her duties as head of a government department. For example, in the government appointed in 2002 the Tánaiste, Mary Harney, held the position of Minister for Enterprise, Trade and Employment. Article 31 of the constitution grants the Tánaiste ex officio membership of the Council of State. The Tánaiste is appointed by the Taoiseach (Article 28.6.1). (For a list of incumbents, see Appendix 3b). The only condition imposed on who can be appointed is set down in Article 28.7.1 which requires that the Tánaiste be a member of the Dáil (in other words a Taoiseach's nominee to the Seanad cannot be Tánaiste).

In recent times, there has been some speculation that the position has become more important and that the Tánaiste now acts more like a deputy rather than a deputising prime minister. For the most part, this is because coalition governments have become the norm. In these situations, the post has tended to be filled by the leader of the second largest party in government, although it might be noted that during the 1989–92 Fianna Fáil–Progressive Democrat coalition the position was held by the deputy leader of Fianna Fáil rather than the leader of the Progressive Democrats. In addition, the post was particularly important in 1993–7 under Dick Spring. During this period, there was a separate Office of the Tánaiste, the role of which was set out by the Taoiseach in answer to a Dáil question in 1993: 'The role and functions of the Office will encompass briefing and advising the Tánaiste generally on all government policy matters; representing the government on the new National Economic and Social Forum and thereby

continued on next page

ensuring direct liaison through the Tánaiste between the forum and the government; joint responsibility, together with the Minister of State and Chief Whip attached to my Department, for the implementation of the provisions under the heading "Broadening our Democracy" which are contained in our Programme for a Partnership Government, 1993–7; representing the Tánaiste on a committee of programme managers to monitor the implementation of the programme for government; representing the Tánaiste on the Central Review Committee under the Programme for Economic and Social Progress [and] any successor to that committee under any further such programme and representing the Tánaiste on the Interdepartmental Committee on the Co-ordination of EC Affairs' (*Dáil Debates* 426: 356, 17 February 1993). However, the Office of the Tánaiste was abolished when the rainbow government lost office in 1997. Overall, what power the Tánaiste has tends to be derived from his or her position as a minister and coalition party leader rather than from anything inherent in the position itself.

Over and above the number of parties in government, the power of the Taoiseach is also affected by the government's position in the Dáil: whether or not it enjoys majority support. Again, in general terms, the position of the Taoiseach is stronger during periods of majority government than minority government (where government parties fail to command 50 per cent of the seats in the Dáil). From 1922 to 2003, minority governments (either coalition or single-party) were in office for about a third of the time, as we saw earlier (see Chapter 8, p. 215). Most heads of government, then, have benefited from the support of a parliamentary majority. This provides a further reason why most commentators have categorised the Taoiseach as such an influential political actor. Nevertheless, some minority governments have remained in office for a considerable period of time. This was particularly the case with the de Valera government from 1951 to 1954 and the Lemass government from 1961 to 1965. These were both single-party Fianna Fáil administrations which capitalised on the lack of cohesion amongst the opposition parties in order to remain in office. Moreover, it is also the case that governments which are only just short of a majority have encouraged non-aligned TDs to give them their ongoing support. This happened in 1982 in the case of the so-called 'Gregory deal' (Joyce and Murtagh, 1983). It also happened in 1997 when the minority Fianna Fáil–Progressive Democrat government looked for the support of independents, such as Harry Blaney and Mildred Fox. This indicates that a minority government need not necessarily be a fragile government.

At the same time, though, the absence of a parliamentary majority does constrain the power of the Taoiseach. This is because the government constantly runs the risk of being defeated. Its head must then negotiate more, bargain more and compromise more. For example, in 2001 the minority Fianna Fáil–Progressive Democrat coalition found itself having to shelve proposals to bar members of the Dáil from also holding local authority seats because of the objections of four independents on whose votes it relied. The proposal was reintroduced only after the general election of 2002 when the Fianna Fáil–Progressive Democrat coalition was returned with an overall majority and no longer relied on independents. Moreover, if negotiations break down, bargaining positions are inflexible and compromise cannot be reached, then the government runs the further risk of being forced out of office altogether. Thus, the short-lived 1981–2 Fine Gael–Labour minority coalition was brought down when an independent deputy decided on the spur of the moment to vote against the budget. Overall, despite the fact that minority governments can exist for a considerable period of time, the Taoiseach's position is still somewhat less comfortable when the government fails to enjoy majority support in the Dáil than when it does.

Finally, the power of the Taoiseach depends on the extent to which the main governing party is unified. Generally speaking, the position of the Taoiseach is stronger under a unified party than a divided party. In this respect, the experience of the historic leaders of both Fianna Fáil (de Valera and Lemass) and Cumann na nGaedheal/Fine Gael (William T. Cosgrave), who were the subject of a certain 'cult of leadership' and were capable of inspiring not just followership but also a certain degree of devotion in some cases, contrasts starkly with the experience of John A. Costello, who was not even the leader of Fine Gael when he held office and who had to share power with the party leader, Richard Mulcahy. That said, at least until the mid-1960s most heads of government enjoyed the almost unqualified support of their own parties. This is yet another reason why commentators have traditionally described the Taoiseach as a powerful leader. In recent times, though, the degree of party discipline has generally weakened. Jack Lynch and Charles Haughey were the particular focus of backbench plotting during their terms as Taoiseach. Furthermore, on occasion internal party problems have found expression not so much in rebellions against the parliamentary party whip but more in behind-the-scenes scheming and public 'heaves' against the leadership. In Fianna Fáil, the level of intra-party disaffection was particularly significant from the election of Jack Lynch in 1966 to the accession of Bertie Ahern in late 1994 (see the account in Marsh, 1993). Overall, the result is that the link between the Taoiseach and the party is more conditional now than in the past. As with the trend towards coalition government, this suggests that the overall position of recent heads of government is now weaker than was previously the case and requires King's view of the power of the office to be further qualified.

Chairman or chief?

The Taoiseach, then, occupies an office which can call upon many political resources but which also faces both structural and conjunctural constraints. In practice, the power of the Taoiseach is potentially great but it is also subject to considerable variation. In this context, how do we make sense of the role of the Taoiseach? One useful approach has been outlined by Brian Farrell (1971, 1996). He distinguishes between 'chairman' and 'chief' images of the office. He defines a 'chairman' as someone who is 'prepared to allow others to share resources, responsibilities and publicity, reluctant to move beyond established procedures and slower to act'. By contrast, he defines a 'chief' as someone who is distinguished 'by a tendency to accumulate political resources, concentrate decision making or control of decision making in their own hands, and – above all – make use of their strategic position to mobilise the machinery of government for action' (Farrell, 1996: 179–80). Although in practice a Taoiseach may exhibit a mixed set of characteristics, these 'ideal-type' images capture two of the main ways in which incumbents can exercise power.

Farrell argues that whether a particular Taoiseach should be classed as a chairman or a chief depends not just on the personality of the leader concerned, but also on the particular circumstances that the leader faces, the character of the political system and the style of authority within society. On this basis, he argues that the 'growing size, intensity and complexity of the modern governmental machine, have concentrated power in the office of chief executives generally, including the Taoiseach (Farrell, 1971: x). Thus, there is a tendency for Taoisigh to act as 'chiefs'. At the same time, the power environment they face means that they may end up having to settle for the role of 'chairman' (Farrell, 1971: 84). In short, whether or not the Taoiseach emerges as a 'chairman' or a 'chief' depends on a number of factors. In the first place, the Taoiseach is an individual political actor and so each incumbent 'will bring their own policy concerns and preferences to the office; they will enlist new supports, acquire new debts, recruit new men, confront new political situations' (Farrell, 1971: 8). Even so, as Farrell also correctly indicates, it is 'his position, not his personality, which puts him into the centre of the political stage' (Farrell, 1971: 3). In other words, the office enjoys considerable powers and even reluctant heads of government have leadership responsibilities thrust upon them. And yet, even if the office enjoys considerable political resources and public attention, the incumbent also has to operate within the 'value systems of the community' (Farrell, 1971: 83) and 'to switch roles according to circumstance' (Farrell, 1988: 45). This serves to limit the role of the office holder.

In this context, perhaps the most notable finding of Farrell's original study was that there was a strong tendency towards 'chairmen'. He argues that William T. Cosgrave 'set the pattern by eschewing an innovatory policy and establishing a role . . . corresponding to that accorded to the Prime

Minister in nineteenth-century Britain' (Farrell, 1971: 84). Perhaps surprisingly, Farrell also places Eamon de Valera in the chairman category, suggesting that he acted as a chairman partly because he headed a cabinet that was quite divided, for example, between Seán Lemass and Seán MacEntee in their respective ministries, and partly because of his own insistence on unanimous cabinet agreement for government policies. Thus, it is partly because of political circumstances and partly because of de Valera's own personality that he is classed as a chairman. In fact, what is somewhat surprising is that of the five taoisigh who held office in the period up to the beginning of the 1970s, Farrell classed only Seán Lemass as a chief.

In the more recent period, a similar pattern emerges. So, for example, Farrell argues that Charles Haughey's instinct was to act as a 'chief', but this ambition was 'curtailed by factionalism within his party, failure to secure a parliamentary majority, and economic circumstance' (Farrell, 1996: 186). For his part, Garret FitzGerald clearly took an active role in the decision-making process. Indeed, his role in the negotiation of the 1985 Anglo-Irish Agreement has been well documented (FitzGerald, 1991: 494–575). All the same, as the leader of a coalition government he was obliged to operate within a collective decision-making context. The same is true of John Bruton, who was able to manage a wide-ranging coalition government particularly well. In so doing, however, he was obliged to act more as a chairman-style figure than a chief. Finally, Bertie Ahern could be considered as the epitome of the Taoiseach as chairman. Though admittedly constrained by coalition politics, his reluctance to force through his own 'pet' projects, such as the plan to build a national stadium at Abbotstown outside Dublin, is a clear sign that he valued office before image. Overall, he has acted as a manager rather than a leader. However, even he has at times acted like a chief, such as when he got government backing for the referendum on abortion in 2002. This situation is similar to the case of Jack Lynch in the 1970s. Though a compromise candidate when he became leader of Fianna Fáil, during the 'arms crisis' of 1970 he is described as having 'established a rock-like authority over the members of Fianna Fáil' (Arnold, 2001: 165). So, while the chairman or chief distinction provides a useful way of categorising different leadership styles, taoisigh are likely to have to exhibit both styles at some stage during their term of office as they react to the problems caused by differing circumstances.

Conclusion

The President and the Taoiseach stand at the apex of the executive system. The President is there in a symbolic capacity as the representative of the nation. As such, though, the President has little or no opportunity to control decision making. Yet, there is still a need for at least one high-profile public representative to be 'above politics' and to incarnate in a disinterested way the legitimacy of the state. In this way, the President performs an important function. In contrast to the symbolic position of the President, the Taoiseach is a 'working' part of the constitution. The Taoiseach has the potential to control decision making and there is an expectation that the incumbent will do so in order to address the pressing issues of the day. However, there sometimes exists a gap between the potential to shape public opinion and the actual capacity to do so. In this context, a Taoiseach must sometimes be content simply to articulate popular concerns, to administer party relations and to facilitate the business of government. Depending on the context, then, the Taoiseach may act as either leader or manager.

References and further reading

Áras an Uachtaráin, 2003. Engagements. Available http://www.irlgov.ie/aras/engagements/index.htm [accessed 31 October 2003].

Arnold, Bruce, 2001. *Jack Lynch: Hero in Crisis*. Dublin: Merlin Publishing.

BAILII (British and Irish Legal Information Institute), 2003. Supreme Court of Ireland decisions. Available http://www.bailii.org/ie/cases/IESC/2000/ [accessed 30 October 2003].

Chubb, Basil, 1974. *Cabinet Government in Ireland*. Dublin: Institute of Public Administration.

Chubb, Basil, 1992. *The Government and Politics of Ireland*, 3rd edn. Harlow: Longman.

Coakley, John, 1984. 'Selecting a prime minister: the Irish experience', *Parliamentary Affairs*, 37:4: 403–17.

Collins, Stephen, 2000. *The Power Game: Fianna Fáil since Lemass*. Dublin: O'Brien Press.

Committee on the Constitution, 1967. *Report of the Committee on the Constitution*. Dublin: Stationery Office.

CRG (Constitution Review Group), 1996. *Report of the Constitution Review Group*. Dublin: Stationery Office.

Dooney, Seán, and John O'Toole, 1998. *Irish Government Today*, 2nd edn. Dublin: Gill and Macmillan.

Duignan, Seán, 1996. *One Spin on the Merry-Go-Round*. Dublin: Blackwater Press.

Elgie, Robert and John Stapleton, 2003. 'The parliamentary activity of the head of government in Ireland (1923–2000) in comparative perspective', *Journal of Legislative Studies* 9:1: 37–56.

Farrell, Brian, 1971. *Chairman or Chief? The Role of Taoiseach in Irish Government*. Dublin: Gill and Macmillan.

Farrell, Brian, 1987. 'The road from February 1987: government formation and institutional inertia', in Michael Laver, Peter Mair and Richard Sinnott (eds), *How Ireland Voted: The Irish General Election 1987*. Galway: PSAI Press, pp. 141–52.

Farrell, Brian, 1988. 'Ireland: the Irish cabinet system: more British than the British themselves', in Jean Blondel and Ferdinand Müller-Rommel (eds), *Cabinets in Western Europe*. London: Macmillan, pp. 33–46.

Farrell, Brian, 1994. 'The political role of cabinet ministers in Ireland', in Michael Laver and Kenneth A. Shepsle (eds), *Cabinet Ministers and Parliamentary Government*. Cambridge: Cambridge University Press, pp. 73–87.

Farrell, Brian, 1996. 'The government', in John Coakley and Michael Gallagher (eds), *Politics in the Republic of Ireland*, 2nd edn. Limerick: PSAI Press, pp. 167–89.

Finlay, Fergus, 1998. *Snakes and Ladders*. Dublin: New Island Books.

FitzGerald, Garret, 1991. *All in a Life*. Dublin: Gill and Macmillan.

Gallagher, Michael, 1977. 'The presidency of the Republic of Ireland: implications of the "Donegan affair"', *Parliamentary Affairs* 30:4: 373–84.

Gallagher, Michael, 1999. 'Republic of Ireland', in Robert Elgie (ed.), *Semi-presidentialism in Europe*. Oxford: Oxford University Press, pp. 104–23.

Garry, John, Fiachra Kennedy, Michael Marsh and Richard Sinnott, 2003. 'What decided the election?', in Michael Gallagher, Michael Marsh and Paul Mitchell (eds), *How Ireland Voted 2002*. Basingstoke: Palgrave Macmillan, pp. 119–42.

Hussey, Gemma, 1995. *Ireland Today: Anatomy of a Changing State*. London: Penguin.

Joyce, Joe, and Peter Murtagh, 1983. *The Boss: Charles J. Haughey in Government*. Dublin: Poolbeg Press.

King, Anthony, 1994. '"Chief executives" in Western Europe', in Ian Budge and David McKay, *Developing Democracy: Comparative Research in Honour of J. F. P. Blondel*. London: Sage, pp. 150–63.

Longford, The Earl of, and Thomas P. O'Neill, 1970. *Eamon de Valera*. London: Hutchinson.

Marsh, Michael, 1993. 'Selecting party leaders in the Republic of Ireland', *European Journal of Political Research* 24:3: 295–316.

McAleese, Mary, 2003. Speech by the President of Ireland, Mary McAleese, at the 'Re-imagining Ireland' conference, Charlottesville, Virginia, 7 May. Available http://www.irlgov.ie/aras/speeches/070503.html [accessed 30 October 2003].

Mitchell, Paul, 2003. 'Government formation in 2002: "You can have any kind of government as long as it's Fianna Fáil"', in Michael Gallagher, Michael Marsh and Paul Mitchell (eds), *How Ireland Voted 2002*. Basingstoke: Palgrave Macmillan, pp. 214–27.

Morgan, David Gwynn, 1990. *Constitutional Law of Ireland*, 2nd edn. Blackrock: Round Hall Press.

Murphy, Gary, 2003. 'The background to the election', in Michael Gallagher, Michael Marsh and Paul Mitchell (eds), *How Ireland Voted 2002*. Basingstoke: Palgrave Macmillan, pp. 1–20.

O'Leary, Brendan, 1991. 'An Taoiseach: the Irish prime minister', *West European Politics* 14:2: 133–62.

O'Leary, Olivia and Helen Burke, 1998. *Mary Robinson: The Authorised Biography*. London: Hodder and Stoughton.

Smith, Murray, 1995. 'The title An Taoiseach in the 1937 Constitution', *Irish Political Studies* 10: 179–84.

Ward, Alan J., 1994. *The Irish Constitutional Tradition: Responsible Government and Modern Ireland, 1782–1992*. Blackrock: Irish Academic Press.

Websites

www.gov.ie/aras/   Website of the office of the President of Ireland.

www.taoiseach.gov.ie   Website of the Taoiseach's department, with links to other departments.

12 The government and the governmental system

Eileen Connolly

In several chapters of this book, most notably Chapter 8, we have seen that the government is a very powerful actor. It tends to dominate parliament, and, as we shall see in Chapter 13, it has a central role in the policy-making process. In this chapter, rather than emphasise the government's dealings with other actors, we look inside the government itself. This chapter thus provides an outline of how Irish government actually works, and of the forces, values and assumptions that influence its operation. That involves both an outline of the main structural and operational features of the system, and consideration of its decision-making processes. It requires examination of the roles both of the titular masters of the government machine – members of the cabinet and ministers of state – and of their officials in the national bureaucracy, the civil servants sometimes described in the media as the 'permanent government' because, while ministers and parties enter or leave power every few years, civil servants remain at their posts at the heart of the government machine. It also necessitates consideration of recent developments in the way that Irish cabinet government operates.

Cabinet government

After independence Ireland adopted a system of government that broadly followed the British 'Westminster model' of party government, in a set of arrangements that ensure that the government will not in practice be seriously constrained by the legislature (see Chapter 8). While the Irish and British systems have diverged considerably over the years, this basic relationship remains unaltered. The relationship is not entirely one-sided. The government is not directly elected by the people: rather, it is chosen by the Dáil, through the election of a Taoiseach and the approval of his choice of ministers who are collectively responsible to the Dáil for every aspect of the government's activities. The government cannot survive if it loses the support of the Dáil.

Article 28 of the constitution lays down the basic powers, functions and responsibility of the government (while the term 'cabinet' is frequently used colloquially instead of 'government', this term has no legal basis). While the constitutional provisions do not adequately describe the process of government formation and operation, they remain the bedrock upon which the day-to-day conduct of national affairs is based, and as such they require enumeration.

The constitution fixes the size of the government at not less than seven and not more than 15 members, all of whom must belong to one of the Houses of the Oireachtas. Up to two ministers may come from the Seanad, but the Taoiseach, the Tánaiste (deputy prime minister) and the Minister for Finance must all be TDs. In practice, almost all ministers have been TDs: only three senators have been appointed since 1922 (in 1932, 1957 and 1981). All members of the government have 'the right to attend and to be heard' in both Houses of the Oireachtas: a minister from the Dáil can participate in Seanad debates and, similarly, a minister from the Seanad can attend the Dáil.

The constitution places the Taoiseach in a very powerful position as the head of the government, as we saw in Chapter 11. In a single-party government at least, all ministers are nominated by him for formal appointment by the President following approval by the Dáil. The Taoiseach decides on the distribution of responsibilities amongst ministers, and can sack them. If the Taoiseach resigns, all ministers are deemed to have resigned also. The Taoiseach alone can approach the President to request a dissolution of the Dáil, and the President is bound to accept such a request other than in the specific circumstances discussed in Chapter 11.

Making the government

The constitution provides a basic framework under which governments are formed: the Dáil votes a government into existence by first choosing a Taoiseach and then endorsing his choice of ministers. As a result, the nominee of the political party in the majority or the nominee of a group of political parties acting in coalition will inevitably be elected. This outcome seems to support a 'pure' model of party–government relations where parties influence government and governments are dependent on parties (Blondel and Cotta, 1996: 250). In practice the process is more complex than either the Irish constitution's provisions or the 'pure' model of party–government relations suggest. This is because the Irish constitution ignores the role of political parties and, as Blondel and Cotta (1996: 259) argue, the 'pure model' overestimates 'the weight of parties and underestimates the role of governments as well as the ability of these governments to resist the influence of parties and in turn exercise influence on parties'. Government exerts influence on parties because the leaders of the political parties are also usually the leaders of the government and therefore the party elites can use the powers of government in areas such as the appointment of ministers, policy making, and the exercise of patronage to control and influence their parties.

In the absence of one party receiving an overall majority, government formation is the result of post-election bargaining between the various political parties and sometimes, as in February 1982 and in 1997, of negotiations with independent TDs who may hold the balance of power. In 2002 the post-election negotiation on the formation of the government took place between Fianna Fáil and the Progressive Democrats (PDs). Although there had not been a formal election pact, Fianna Fáil had indicated its preference for the continuation of the coalition with the PDs even though it could have governed with the help of independents. The weakness of the other two main parties, Fine Gael and Labour, made Fianna Fáil the only desirable coalition option for the PDs (Mitchell, 2003: 220). In Ireland the history of coalition negotiations 'can be conveniently divided into three periods: before 1973, 1973–89, and after 1989' (Mitchell, 2000: 129). Between 1932 and 1973 Fianna Fail dominated electoral politics as a single-party government and was replaced on only two occasions by diverse coalitions made up of a number of parties. From 1973 the issues underlying coalition negotiations remained unchanged – Fianna Fáil versus the rest – 'but the "rest" had now been streamlined into just two parties', Fine Gael and Labour (Mitchell, 2000: 130). Although no party has won an overall majority of seats in the eight elections since 1977, it was only in 1989 that the rules of the government formation game changed dramatically. This happened because, in that year, Charles Haughey of Fianna Fáil ditched his party's so-called 'core value' of never entering a coalition by concluding an unlikely alliance with his most bitter political enemies in the PDs (Mitchell, 2000: 131; see also pp. 149–50 above). Haughey's embrace of coalition as a means of retaining power was a contributory factor in his eventual ousting as party leader, but neither of his immediate successors was any more successful in getting the party into government without the support of other groups. Since 1989, Ireland has seen continuous coalition government (see Chapter 5).

Fianna Fáil's pragmatic conversion to coalition politics, just at a time when the state's acute public finance problems were fading and when the first evidence of economic improvement was emerging after a decade of disaster, helped to remove the aura of perpetual crisis management that had previously surrounded coalitions. The unprecedented growth of the 'Celtic Tiger' economy, together with the dramatic achievements of the Northern Ireland peace process in the 1990s, were overseen by a succession of coalition governments. These successes disposed of the old argument that coalitions were simply a poor substitute for single-party government and could not provide strong and resolute direction of national affairs. In the 2002 election the perception of coalition governments as successful was underlined by the PDs' campaign that emphasised the point with the slogan 'Coalitions work better' (Mitchell, 2003: 218).

Prior to 1994 it was assumed that there would not be a change of the party composition of the government without an intervening general election. However, following the collapse of the Fianna Fáil–Labour coalition in

November 1994, a month later the Dáil installed a three-party 'rainbow' coalition under John Bruton of Fine Gael, which included Reynolds's previous coalition partners Labour. Also in mould-breaking fashion, after the 2002 election the outgoing government was returned for the first time in 33 years and both incumbent parties increased their share of Dáil seats (Kennedy, 2002: 95). Coalition government appears to have become an integral part of Irish politics.

The selection of ministers

The process of deciding who is to be included in the government, and who gets what department, is always sensitive and is the most visible aspect of the relationship between political parties and government (Blondel and Cotta, 1996: 249). This relationship is emphasised in Ireland where, unlike in other European democracies, ministers must be members of parliament. In a single-party government, the party leader will have made many of the decisions prior to the election result. In the case of coalition governments, the allocation of ministerial portfolios becomes part of the coalition negotiation process. The outcome of this aspect of negotiations is linked to the policy ambitions of the parties involved, as comparative research confirms that within coalition governments in European countries the party affiliation of a minister has a definite bearing on the policy programme pursued in a given department, although allowances must always be made for the fact that some ministers are more effective than others in bringing their policy ideas to fruition (Laver and Shepsle, 1994: 308). The coalition bargaining process can often see the reorganisation of government departments and the redistribution of functions between them in order to balance out the portfolios assigned to ministers of different parties. For example, as a result of the formation of the Fianna Fáil–PD coalition in 1997 the Department of Equality and Law Reform established by the 1993–4 Fianna Fáil–Labour coalition was merged with the Department of Justice (from which some of its divisions had been transferred on its foundation) to produce a Department of Justice, Equality and Law Reform. In addition, a Department of Public Enterprise was formed from parts of the Department of Enterprise, Trade and Employment and of the Department of Transport, Energy and Communications; and a Department of the Marine and Natural Resources emerged through the transfer of responsibility for forestry and other matters from the Department of Agriculture and Food (see Appendix 4). There is a degree of cynicism within the civil service about such innovations, which are carried out entirely without reference to their impact on civil service effectiveness and often disappear with the government that introduced them.

There is a clear ranking in the perceived importance of ministerial portfolios, with Finance generally accepted as the most important (after the Taoiseach, of course) because of its responsibility for economic management and for public expenditure. Foreign Affairs is also considered a senior department, given its key role in European Union business (Laver, 1994: 157). Establishing a ranking order of departments is made more difficult by the way in which departments are frequently chopped and changed when a new government is formed. In addition to the natural desire of all parties in a coalition to have important seats at the cabinet table, individual parties will be influenced by their particular policy priorities in the coalition bargaining process. For example, the position of Minister for the Environment, while not a glamorous portfolio, is considered a strategic one because of the opportunities it offers to allocate public investment in physical infrastructure such as roads and housing (Finlay, 1998: 8). Fairly or not, it is taken for granted that the constituency and region from which the incumbent minister hales will benefit disproportionately from public policy decisions during his or her term of office.

A Taoiseach's selection of ministerial colleagues will be influenced by a number of factors. There are always more aspiring ministers than there are cabinet seats available, and so some disappointment is inevitable. After the 2002 election Bertie Ahern demoted four politicians who had been ministers in the previous government, in order both to accommodate the PDs with an additional cabinet seat to reflect their increased Dáil representation and to introduce new blood into the cabinet. It was widely reported that he had originally planned also to drop two of the oldest members of his previous cabinet, Michael Smith and Joe Walsh, but changed his mind as a result of strong lobbying on their behalf from 'prominent businessmen and politicians' (Mitchell, 2003: 223). Other factors affecting the selection of the cabinet will be the need to have competent colleagues in key departments and to make sure that all sections of the party are represented as far as possible so as to prevent the growth of factions. There may also be electoral considerations, such as whether to reward colleagues whose efforts have produced a premium of seats for the party in their constituencies, or to avoid the charge that some region is underrepresented and by implication disadvantaged – this is often where the less important departmental portfolios are useful. Finally, since 1982 every government has included at least one woman minister, and it is highly unlikely that any Taoiseach would entirely ignore gender representation in constructing a government.

Once the personnel and the allocation of portfolios have been finalised – in the case of a single-party government by the Taoiseach, in the case of a coalition by the Taoiseach and the other party leader(s) – the Dáil will be asked to confirm the Taoiseach's nominees en bloc. This is usually a formality, since a government could not be formed if it could not command a Dáil majority for such a vote. The same usually applies when a minister leaves office and is replaced, but we should note the important case of the withdrawal of Dr McDaid's nomination as Minister for Defence in 1991 under pressure from Fianna Fáil's coalition partners the Progressive Democrats, who objected to his nomination.

Following the appointment of the government, the Taoiseach will in due course nominate up to 17 'ministers of state' (junior ministers) outside the cabinet. With the exception of the chief whip, these are not entitled to attend government meetings unless invited specifically to talk about some matter affecting departmental responsibilities (although during the rainbow coalition of 1994–7 the Democratic Left junior minister Pat Rabbitte was allowed to attend all meetings, and the same facility was extended to the PD junior minister Bobby Molloy in the following government). Even more than in filling government posts, a Taoiseach will be mindful of regional and constituency considerations in appointing junior ministers, and may also wish to bring in new blood who in time will graduate to the cabinet. In coalitions junior ministers are also deployed in key departments so as to provide a balance of representation between the participating government parties. While problems often arise between ministers and junior ministers within departments, such tensions appear to stem more from personal competition for good publicity and credit for policy successes than from genuine party or policy differences. It is said that ministers of state are commonly starved of high profile work by their senior colleagues, although some have established considerable reputations for themselves in areas such as European Affairs, where the workload is so heavy – and, arguably, the constituency payback so low – that a cabinet minister is glad to have a junior colleague to share the burden.

The central institutions of the government

The cabinet

Like most of its European counterparts, the Irish constitution is fairly vague on the actual organisation of cabinet government, concentrating instead on the conditions under which governments may be formed or may fall (Blondel, 1988: 5–6). In practice the cabinet determines the overall policy programme and aims of the government, it takes all major policy decisions, and it approves the government's budget and all other legislation to be submitted to the Dáil. It is the decision-making body of a structure of government composed of the Department of the Taoiseach, which includes the office of the chief whip and the various ministerial departments, with their attendant ministers of state.

The constitution describes the government as 'collectively responsible' to the Dáil for all its decisions and actions. This principle lies at the heart of cabinet government. In theory, it means that all members of the cabinet are bound by, and must stand over, all cabinet decisions. This is also true of coalition governments, 'coalition discipline is typically very strong in Ireland with parties behaving as if they were unitary actors' (Mitchell, 2000: 140). Farrell (1994), in his examination of government practice, found that ministers did not regard the cabinet as a 'mere rubber stamp' for departmental decisions. Rather, it was perceived as a considerable restraint on individual ministers. Gemma Hussey (1990: 12), a former minister for education, said that the Department of Finance 'rarely agreed to any spending proposal and fought the battles out at full cabinet'. The negotiations for the 'partnership' agreements (see Chapter 13, pp. 359–62) also give an indication of the active role played by the cabinet, which certainly goes well beyond a rubber stamp for decisions taken elsewhere. One participant in the 1997 talks recalled that issues identified as 'bottom line' for the voluntary and community sector were agreed only after consideration at two cabinet meetings and were included in the final text only hours before it went to print (Crowley, 1998: 78). Perhaps the clearest indication that cabinet meetings, in spite of their crowded agenda, do produce debate and conflict and are not merely an official stamp for an already agreed position is the care with which party leaders in both single-party and coalition governments seek to manage the cabinet agenda. Depending on the issues and the personal style of the Taoiseach involved, meetings can be brisk or 'staggeringly interminable' (Finlay, 1998: 15).

Once a decision has been taken by cabinet it becomes a government position to which all members of the cabinet must give public support. The doctrine of cabinet confidentiality (Article 28.4 of the constitution) also requires that all cabinet discussions remain confidential and that all policy proposals and initiatives by individual ministers are discussed and approved by cabinet before being made public. Cabinet confidentiality permits free discussion of policy issues among ministers unconstrained by the impact that the espousal of particular views may have on the electorate. It also allows for the free discussion of sensitive material. If the cabinet is to maintain a united front and unanimously support all policy decisions taken by the government, it cannot make disagreements at cabinet public knowledge. Cabinet minutes, because of the requirement of cabinet confidentiality, are very brief, being little more than a record of decisions taken. Individual ministers are circulated only with the decisions relevant to their departments, not with the full minutes.

The absolute nature of cabinet confidentiality was called into question during the Beef Tribunal in 1992, when the tribunal wished to ask ministers about cabinet discussions (Hogan, 1993: 131). The issue was taken to the Supreme Court, which ruled that collective cabinet responsibility and hence cabinet confidentiality were absolute constitutional principles and the tribunal could not hear reports of cabinet debates. A referendum in October 1997 on cabinet confidentiality explicitly enshrined the principle in the constitution, while relaxing the strict Supreme Court judgment very slightly.

The confidentiality of government decision making more generally was liberalised to a significant degree in the Freedom of Information Act, 1997, which we discuss further later in the chapter. This Act creates for the first time a general right of access to government documents, qualified by a number of exemptions including diplomatic and security material. Hitherto such papers were covered by the Official Secrets Act and were generally not made available. Indeed, even historical documents were made widely available only under the National Archives Act, 1986, which released most government papers once they were more than 30 years old. The Freedom of Information Act, by allowing access to contemporary papers, clearly has a more immediate impact on the policy process. Cabinet papers are exempt but background and factual briefing papers must be available as soon as a government decision is announced. Other government papers must be released after ten years unless exempt under some other provision such as national security. The international experience, while varied, suggests that such legislation tends to improve standards of administration, as civil servants respond to the fact that documents could be made public quite quickly (Doyle, 1996: 77).

Box 12.1 How do we know how the government works?

Finding out how the government works entails drawing upon a number of sources. There are *basic documents* such as the constitution and laws, which describe the formal outlines of the system; in addition, there are off-the-record comments by officials and politicians giving their personal perceptions of how the system actually works. In between is a range of *official sources*: official publications; the reports of tribunals; the records of government meetings and of departments. As well as these, there are *informal sources*, including academic studies; the published recollections of former ministers and officials; newspaper reporting.

Furthermore, the *Freedom of Information Act*, which came into operation in April 1997, significantly adds to our knowledge of the workings of government. Finally, a great deal of information about government organisation and procedures is now available via the *internet* (see http://www.irlgov.ie/irlgov/Contents.htm).

It is important to realise that no single kind of source sufficiently describes the way Irish government works, and that sources often conflict on matters of fact and interpretation. Take the example of the drive to eradicate human tuberculosis that began in the late 1940s. The Minister generally credited with responsibility for this, Noel Browne, gave his account in his celebrated autobiography *Against the Tide*. His department's chief medical officer recalled affairs very differently, while a respected academic study also offered an altogether more complex story (Browne, 1986: 110–24; Barrington, 1987: 15–61; Deeny, 1989: 165–73).

The cabinet customarily meets weekly in Government Buildings on Upper Merrion Street in Dublin (on Tuesdays when the Dáil is sitting, on Wednesdays at other times of the year). In principle, all ministers are required to attend; in practice, depending on the agenda and on ministers' other commitments, some ministers may be missing. There is no quorum for the meetings. Additional meetings may also be convened if required at short notice. The government Chief Whip and the Attorney General also attend, while the Secretary General to the Government (a civil servant) takes the minutes and advises the meeting on aspects of procedure and precedent. Papers relating to the agenda are circulated beforehand to ensure that all ministers' departments will have had the opportunity to comment on any matters for decision that might affect them. Ministers of state and even some officials may be invited to attend to assist in the discussion of particular items. The Secretary General to the Government manages the government secretariat with a staff of civil servants – its role is a coordination one. Prior to 1979, the secretary of the Taoiseach's office also served as secretary to the government. Since then, the Secretary General to the Government has had the primary role of making sure that the business of government is properly coordinated.

In one respect Irish cabinet government does depart markedly from the European norm. This is in the area of cabinet committees to help reduce the workload of the grossly overburdened cabinet agenda. Blondel (1988: 10) describes the use of cabinet committees as widespread – but not universal – and as having widely varying functions and status in the different European states. In general the function of cabinet committees 'is to propose (or in some cases even "take") decisions for the cabinet meeting. Often the result is that they tend to take decisions and filter to the cabinet meeting only those matters on which agreement has been achieved' (Blondel, 1988: 10). Ireland lacks an institutionalised system of cabinet committees comparable to European practice, though it does make some use of more informal or *ad hoc* sub-committees, especially during coalition governments.

Such committees have been constituted from time to time, but have often been transient in nature rather than developing into permanent features of the cabinet landscape. Even those that have lasted in one form or another for decades under different administrations – for example on Northern Ireland and on security – have never developed their own secretariats and pools of official expertise independent of the succession of ministers who serve on them. They thus remain genuine sub-sets of each government, rather than forces for continuity in analysis and policy from one administration to the next. In coalition governments cabinet committees have been used to smooth the wheels of interparty government. In 1994, during the disagreements between the Fianna Fáil and Labour coalition partners over the appointment of Attorney General Harry Whelehan to the High Court, it was agreed that a cabinet sub-committee be set up 'to defuse the conflict' (Garry, 1995: 194). However, the general lack of a committee structure means that the majority of questions facing the government, major and minor, come to the cabinet table for discussion and decision.

During coalition governments a system of informal meetings between the party leaders has sometimes operated to circumvent unnecessary argument at cabinet. These meetings finalise the cabinet agenda and generally ensure that issues that are not capable of immediate resolution between the parties do not appear on the agenda until a compromise has been reached (Farrell, 1993: 158). However, there have been times when the junior party in a coalition has been 'left largely in the dark about key aspects of government business' by the Taoiseach, usually at times of strain between the parties (O'Halpin, 1997: 79; Finlay, 1998: 70–1). Zimmerman (1997: 538), drawing on interviews with former ministers and civil servants, also reports that rules governing cabinet meetings and procedures relating to the circulation of material have been on occasion over the years quite deliberately broken.

The cabinet exerts a considerable degree of control over the Dáil through its ability to control parliamentary business. The Dáil may debate and enact legislation, but the cabinet decides what it will debate and the time allocated to different topics. In Ireland the cabinet's control over parliamentary business is almost total (Laver and Shepsle, 1994: 294–5). This contrasts with practice in many other European states, for example in Austria and Norway where the parliamentary agenda is partly determined by a body within the legislature (Laver and Shepsle, 1994: 294). Cabinet supervision of the work of ministers is equally tight; all policy proposals by individual ministers require the approval of cabinet, and procedures are in place to ensure that all relevant ministers and departments have been properly consulted about any policy initiatives before these come to cabinet for a final decision. This is spelt out in the official guidelines for ministers, which are given to all cabinet members upon appointment: 'where proposals for legislation relate to matters on which government policy has not already been laid down, or where they include a new development or a material departure from existing policy, they should first be submitted to the Government by way of a memorandum for a decision in principle' (Department of the Taoiseach, 1998a: 26). The Taoiseach's power as chairman of the cabinet is reflected in the rule that no item can be put on the government agenda without his approval.

The Department of the Taoiseach

In 1988 Jean Blondel observed that the role of the prime minister in most European states had grown substantially in importance since the early 1970s, and as a result prime ministers had also become more dominant figures in cabinet (Blondel, 1988: 9). In Ireland as elsewhere, that trend has continued for a combination of reasons, amongst them the growing emphasis on meetings of heads of government in European Union affairs and the increasing complexity of public business. The power of the Taoiseach, as we saw in Chapter 11, stems from the control he has over the composition of the government and over the conduct of cabinet business, and usually also on his influence as the leader of a political party – as well as from his position as actual and symbolic head of government. Officially the role of Taoiseach is described as one of providing leadership; he is responsible for 'ensuring that government policy as a whole is geared to meet the economic, social and infrastructural needs of Ireland in the twenty-first century' and must 'have a corresponding involvement in all major policy areas, for example Northern Ireland, economic and social issues, and European and wider international policy' (Department of the Taoiseach, 2003: 7). From this three primary functions of the Taoiseach can be distinguished: a general leadership role, especially important in key policy areas such as Northern Ireland, European Union affairs and international negotiations; an agenda setting role; and the overall management of the business of government. These roles are given organisational expression in the structure and organisation of the Department of the Taoiseach.

The department is organised essentially by function. The Taoiseach's private office coordinates the day-to-day official activities of the Taoiseach, and also liaises with the Government Information Services, which act as a public relations arm of the department. The office of the Chief Whip is responsible for organising and coordinating government business in the Oireachtas. As well as keeping government deputies and senators in line, the chief whip acts as a channel of communication between government and opposition parties. The office also monitors the preparation of draft legislation within the bureaucracy.

Under the Secretary General to the Government are three divisions – the government secretariat, protocol, and European and international affairs – providing for interdepartmental coordination and the smooth and efficient functioning of government (Department of the Taoiseach, 1998: 5). The government secretariat services all government meetings, drawing up the agenda, circulating documentation to ministers and communicating decisions to government departments. The protocol division provides state protocol services, and also advises the government on its constitutional relationship with the president. The European and International Affairs division supports the Taoiseach as a member of the European Council of the EU and in any other international responsibilities that he may have. The work of this division reflects the high degree of penetration of EU policy and administration into the process and outcomes of the Irish government's policy programme. The division works closely with the Department of Foreign Affairs in particular in identifying and responding to issues at EU level that affect Ireland's core interests. In such areas tensions can sometimes arise between the Department of the Taoiseach and other departments, which may resent what they perceive as interference in their policy areas.

Under the direction of the Secretary General to the Department of the Taoiseach there are, in addition to two divisions dealing essentially with routine housekeeping matters, three divisions dealing with policy areas in which the Taoiseach plays a key leadership role – Northern Ireland, Economic and Social Policy, and the Irish Financial Services Centre. The Northern Ireland division supports the essential input of the Taoiseach as leader of the state. All recent Taoisigh have appointed special advisers on Northern Ireland to work in the Department of the Taoiseach, the most prominent of whom has been Martin Mansergh, who worked for all Fianna Fáil Taoisigh since Charles Haughey until his election to the Seanad in 2002. Officials of the department have played a key role in the development of state policy on Northern Ireland. The Economic and Social Policy division deals with the management and renegotiation of the social partnership agreements that have become a cornerstone of domestic policy since the Programme for National Recovery was negotiated in 1987 (see Box 13.1, p. 360). Since the negotiation of that first partnership agreement, the policy scope of such understandings has broadened beyond their initial focus on the macro-economic policy parameters and pay bargaining to include a wide range of social issues. The centrality of the Department of the Taoiseach to the management of relations with and between the social partners reflects both its coordinating role and the imperative that the Taoiseach must take a leadership position on this fundamental and central aspect of the overall policy programme of the state. In the Partnership 2000 negotiations the core of the government's negotiating team came from the Department of the Taoiseach, 'supplemented by ministers and senior civil servants from various departments, depending on the issue that was being discussed' (O'Donnell and Thomas, 1998: 132).

The three policy divisions under the Secretary General of the department, and the European and international affairs division under the Secretary General to the Government, give the Taoiseach and the officials of his department a central role in policy development in almost all the key areas of the government's policy programme.

The role of the Tánaiste

The constitutional role of the Tánaiste is a limited one, that of deputising for the Taoiseach in circumstances where the Taoiseach may be temporarily incapacitated or outside the state (see Box 11.1). Traditionally this was the role assigned to the Tánaiste even in coalition governments, although as a minister he or she had plenty of departmental work to do. The Tánaiste's role was, however, radically recast during the 1993–4 Fianna Fáil–Labour coalition. This was because the Labour leader Dick Spring, who was also Minister for Foreign Affairs, insisted on the creation of an Office of the Tánaiste that in some respects resembled, and was designed to shadow, the Department of the Taoiseach in its leadership and policy oversight role. This development was perceived partly as a response to the way in which the previous Fianna Fáil–PD coalition had ended amidst recriminations about alleged failures to follow cabinet procedures, and partly to provide the Tánaiste with a proper overview. As one Labour official put it, the Tánaiste 'must have the same breadth of understanding as the Taoiseach – but the Taoiseach has a hundred or more civil servants to help him do his job' (Finlay, 1998: 156). The Fianna Fáil–PD coalition that formed the government in 1997 abandoned this and other innovations. In spite of this Mary Harney, as Tánaiste in both the 1997 and the 2002 coalition governments, has been perceived as a significant and influential figure; a better relationship between the party elites has apparently substituted for more formal measures.

Government departments

The role of the minister

Ministers are the political heads of government departments. They are charged with setting the policy parameters of their departments and with making all policy (rather than administrative) decisions. The minister takes policy decisions, but civil servants play a key role in the detailed development and implementation of that policy.

Ministers' workloads are extremely heavy: as well as departmental duties, they are members of the cabinet, leading figures in their political parties, and prominent constituency politicians. The time constraints on an individual minister may result in there being little political input into ongoing policy development even in key areas, with such matters being dealt with mainly by civil servants. Yet, with the exception of the successful 'programme managers' experiment between 1993 and 1997, in which officials from inside and outside the public service were given the job of ensuring the implementation of the programmes for government agreed between the parties forming both the Reynolds–Spring government of 1993–4 and the rainbow coalition of 1994–7, there has been no attempt to develop the ministerial *cabinets* that are a feature of policy making and of political control of administration in many other European states. The originator of the programme managers concept had in fact planned a full-blown *cabinet* system, but, in the words of a Labour official, 'to our surprise, there was immediate opposition' from the Department of the Taoiseach and the proposal was dropped (Finlay, 1998: 156).

Even for the most energetic and creative of ministers, policy innovation is limited by the need to get prior approval from the cabinet. The general policy direction and practical control of government business is exerted by the Taoiseach through the cabinet, while the Department of Finance keeps a nervous eye on any policy proposals that would involve additional expenditure (as almost every policy development does). Farrell points out that 'the concentration on the cabinet itself as the clearing house for information and the centre of all government decision making severely restricts the independence of individual ministers'. On the basis of interviews with former ministers he concluded that 'with the rarest exceptions' ministers 'will always seek cabinet approval in policy matters', a necessary discipline if collective responsibility is to be maintained (Farrell, 1994: 77). The four categories of decision making in which they felt unable to act on their own initiative were: issues involving cost, innovation, coordination [i.e. with other departments] or those regarded as politically sensitive. Cabinet ministers are bound into a formal system of consultation on policy initiatives and in the preparation of legislation that gives both the Department of the Taoiseach and the Department of Finance an oversight role, allows for consultation with other departments, and gives cabinet the final voice on the output and shape of policy. To be effective, a minister must therefore, in addition to being a convincing advocate for his or her department, be an influential member of the wider cabinet team. Within these constraints, however, cabinet ministers are ultimately judged by their colleagues, by the media and by the public to a large degree on their perceived performance in charge of a department, responsible not only for policy development and new legislation but also for the efficient and fair execution of existing law and policies.

The decisive role of ministers at crucial moments, as well as their ultimate responsibility for decisions reached, is indicated in a study by an Irish official of the crucial negotiations of the 1997 Treaty of Amsterdam. This highlights the degree to which even the most intricate EU agreements, for which committees of officials from the member states, the Council of Ministers and the European Commission make the most painstaking and intricate preparations, are ultimately concluded virtually unaided by ministers of the member states in marathon meetings (MacDonagh, 1998: 190–5).

The civil service

Until the advent of the Public Service Management Act, 1997, senior officials of government departments in legal terms had no independent role in policy making or in the management of government departments, and no accountability or responsibility for the actions of the civil servants within their department (Millar and McKevitt, 2000). Under the Ministers and Secretaries Act, 1924, each minister is a 'corporation sole', the effect of which is that (with a few stated exceptions) civil servants can act only in the name of the minister (O'Halpin, 1991: 295–6; Garvin, 1991: 51). The 1985 White Paper *Serving the Country Better*, the first sustained attempt since the 1924 Act to change the way that the civil service worked, did not alter the basic 'corporation sole' principle. Instead, it placed new emphasis on changing the administrative process, invoking concepts such as quality of service, accessibility, improved management of resources within departments, and the imaginative use of information technology, as well as encouraging staff mobility between departments at every level (Department of the Public Service, 1985; Boland *et al.*, 1986). These concepts were elaborated on in the

1994 Strategic Management Initiative, which in turn led on to the Public Service Management Act, 1997. This Act recast the role of the most senior official in each department – now styled the Secretary General – giving clearer powers to manage than had been the case under the Ministers and Secretaries Act, 1924, the linchpin of the administrative system since independence. The then Taoiseach in introducing the measure argued that its success would depend on ministers 'releasing their grip' to some extent, an attitude that runs counter to the 'clientelist nature of much of Irish politics' which 'puts significant pressures on politicians to involve themselves in detailed matters' (quoted in Boyle *et al.*, 1997: 6).

The impact of the legislation has to be assessed in conjunction with other developments that have taken place in the relationship between ministers and their civil servants. Politicians even prior to this legislation had begun to introduce a 'buffer zone' into the administrative system in the form of ministerial advisers (Millar and McKevitt, 2000: 50). Ministerial advisers were a response to a number of factors: the hectic work schedules of ministers, the complexity of modern policy making and the need for a new form of oversight in coalition governments. The ministerial advisers, who are usually recruited from outside the civil service, provide an alternative source of advice for the minister; they can monitor the progress of legislation and policy through the administrative system and in many respects act as an 'extension of the minister' (Mitchell, 2003a: 438). These advisers are not an entirely new phenomenon – Richie Ryan acted as an adviser for James Everett, Minister for Justice in the 1954–7 government – but they became a widespread feature of government only in the 1990s. This practice was institutionalised in the Public Service Management Act, 1997, which legally provides for the appointment of a special adviser to each minister or minister of state (Millar and McKevitt, 2000: 50–1). The coalition governments of the 1990s introduced a special form of ministerial adviser, the programme manager, when in 1993 the Fianna Fáil–Labour coalition appointed a group of programme managers to assist with the implementation of the Programme for a Partnership Government (Millar and McKevitt, 2000: 51). A key aspect of the programme manager's responsibility 'was to submit policy implementation to detailed tracking, to overcome bureaucratic and political obstacles to policy delivery, and generally to make sure that the party's policies were actually implemented' (Mitchell, 2003a: 438). While this experiment was repeated by the 'rainbow' coalition of 1994–7 it was subsequently scaled down by the Fianna Fáil–Progressive Democrat coalitions that followed 'partly because the PDs in particular had criticised the creation of the new political appointees as wasteful' (Mitchell, 2003a: 438). Ministerial advisers and programme managers are intended to correct the disadvantages faced by ministers compared to their senior civil servants in terms of the detailed knowledge of a particular policy area and the advantage civil servants have in not having the same level of competing demands on their time as do senior politicians.

The degree of influence over policy outcomes that is exerted by the civil service has been and continues to be a matter of debate. Research by Zimmerman reveals conflicting opinions from the former ministers and civil servants whom he interviewed. Overwhelmingly, interviewees believed that ministers did not play a 'direct role in the internal management of their departments' – this function was left entirely to the civil servants (Zimmerman, 1997: 540). Former ministers did not view the department secretaries as their principal advisers (even in the absence of an outside ministerial adviser or programme manager), although it would be general practice to consult departmental secretaries on major policy issues, where their experience would make their advice invaluable (1997: 538). Retired department secretaries, while they corroborated this view, also played down the frequency with which 'major policy issues' arose. They laid stress on the incremental, continuous nature of policy making, with major changes in policy occurring only rarely (1997: 538). It was this incremental approach that the Labour Party set out to change while in government between 1993 and 1997, so that there would be far greater party political input into national affairs (Finlay, 1998: 149).

It is probably in the incremental dimension of policy making that civil servants exert their greatest influence, not only through their preparation of information and the evaluation of policy alternatives, but also through their ongoing contact with a wide range of interest groups concerned with policy development in a particular department. Although interest groups may occasionally get to meet the minister or minister of state (see Chapter 13 for a fuller discussion), their usual point of contact is with civil servants in the department, working on policy areas that are of concern to them. Such dealings between interest groups and the civil service are growing and becoming more systematic (O'Halpin and Connolly, 1999). Contacts of this sort are a two-way exchange of information, and the civil servants directly involved pass material that they consider significant up the line within their departments. Ultimately a senior official will determine how much material should reach the minister.

The position of the senior officials in a department allows them, should they choose, both to block policy with which they disagree and to promote policy of which they are in favour. The extent to which these tactics are employed by the civil service is a matter of some dispute. Farrell (1994: 83) found diverse views. Although only a handful of ministers thought that the obstruction of particular policy initiatives was 'usual', a larger number thought it occurred sometimes. There was more support from former ministers for the idea that civil servants were inclined to promote their own policy preferences, with varying assessments as to how successful this strategy was. These assessments ranged from the view that ministers in general had only a small impact on eventual legislation, to the opinion that ministers could easily spot and therefore take into account the overselling of particular lines of policy by civil servants (Farrell, 1994: 84). However, as discussed earlier, the introduction of political advisers and programme managers was intended to tip the balance in favour of the minister by providing advice and policy oversight from outside the administrative system of the civil service.

The question of how much influence the higher civil service does and should exert on policy is not unique to Ireland. Laver and Shepsle state that the 'power of the civil service is acknowledged almost everywhere' in European states, particularly with regard to 'routine decisions, dealing more with the implementation of policy'. However in France, the Netherlands, Norway and Sweden, the senior civil servants have comparatively more power, as their 'professional knowledge' in certain policy areas is acknowledged (Laver and Shepsle, 1994: 303). In Ireland, by contrast, the relationship between ministers and senior civil servants was until 1997 defined by the Ministers and Secretaries Act, 1924, under which ministers were legally responsible for everything done by their officials, from the formulation of policy to the administration of departments and the most basic and routine clerical duties. Ministerial responsibility acted like a shield, behind which the actual policy role of senior civil servants was hidden from public view. This position has now been somewhat altered by the Public Service Management Act, 1997, which for the first time identified the role and responsibilities of senior civil servants and distinguished these responsibilities from those of the minister. The Act gave a public, legal accountability to the secretary general of each government department and acknowledged the key strategic and managerial role that holders of this office play.

A number of controversies in the 1990s – among them the allegation that senior civil servants were aware that Anti-D blood supplies were infected with Hepatitis C in 1996 – added weight to the need for an overhaul of the civil service system, whose image had deteriorated in the eyes of the Irish public (Millar and McKevitt, 2000: 55). The Public Service Management Act, 1997, is, therefore, part of a two-pronged change in the culture of government departments, aimed at making their operation both more efficient and more transparent. A process of public sector reform, strengthened by commitments in Partnership 2000, plus the drive towards open government embodied in the Freedom of Information Act, 1997, are significantly altering the ethos of government. Departments are now required (also under the Public Service Management Act) to produce detailed strategy statements that are freely available public documents. This is a further development of the Strategic Management Initiative (SMI) introduced by the government in 1994 'as an attempt to enhance strategic capabilities in the civil service' (Boyle *et al.*, 1997: 3). The strategy statements detail the goals and objectives of the individual departments and set out how the department will achieve them. The Secretaries General at the Department of the Taoiseach expressed the view that not only would the strategy statement provide 'a blueprint' for the work of the department but it would also provide 'the basis for formal delegation of responsibility and accountability'

(Department of the Taoiseach, 1998: 7). Also arising from the 1997 Act, and the recommendations of Partnership 2000, is the introduction of 'partnership committees' in the departments to allow management, unions and staff to come together to facilitate the process of change and reform in the civil service 'by empowering staff at all levels to engage in a continuous process of improvement' (Link Newsletter, 1999). There does appear to be a strong commitment to civil service reform, which aims to increase the effectiveness of the service but also more openly acknowledges the actual role played by the upper echelons of the civil service in policy making.

This wider process of public service change is placing a new emphasis on the effective management of resources, on the incorporation of strategic planning as a dynamic element of management, on customer consciousness, and on openness and transparency in policy formulation and decision making (Murray and Teahon, 1998: 55–8). As part of the drive for ethical government senior civil servants must observe the provisions of the Ethics in Public Office Act, 1995, concerning the submission of an annual statement of personal interests, including gifts or benefits of one kind or another, that might influence them in the performance of their duties.

Monitoring Irish government

Over the past 25 years, the degree to which the government and the administrative system can be subjected to public scrutiny and held accountable for its actions has been greatly enhanced, with the pace of change accelerating in the 1990s. Four pieces of legislation are primarily responsible for this change: the Ombudsman Act, 1980, the National Archives Act, 1986, the Comptroller and Auditor General Act, 1993 and the Freedom of Information Act, 1997 (which has already been briefly discussed). Together, these have greatly increased external oversight of administrative practices and decision making, and cumulatively they represent a sea change in public knowledge of the activities of central government.

Individual citizens have been able to have their grievances against central government departments (and from 1986, also against local authorities and the health boards) investigated by impartial officials from the Office of the Ombudsman since 1984, when the Ombudsman Act, 1980 came into operation (see also Chapter 9, p. 260, for discussion of the role of this office). This has put the actions and administrative practices of officials under unprecedented review. Since the Ombudsman began his work, investigations have uncovered not only individual cases of unfairness, maladministration, or mistakes by civil and public servants, but systemic problems with the decision-making processes within the public service. For example, the Ombudsman has discovered serious anomalies in pensions regulations, which resulted in great unfairness to some individuals. The office continues to face some problems in increasing awareness amongst both the general public and the political system of its capacity to help people – as in other countries, the Ombudsman has found that it is the least well off in society and those most dependent on the state's social services who are the least likely to seek his or her help. Nevertheless, there can be no doubt that the office has had a considerable impact on the approach of national, local and health board officials to their dealings with the public.

The National Archives Act, 1986, came into operation in January 1991. It has transformed the way that students of Irish policy making and political history do their work. Under the Act, departments are obliged to make all records more than 30 years old available to the public for research (subject to a few exceptions where records dealing with sensitive matters such as state security can be withheld). This Act has provided a wealth of material for people studying every aspect of politics and administration, and has transformed the study of Irish politics and public affairs since independence. It has enabled the writing of systematic and detailed studies of all aspects of Irish government from foreign policy to the development of local government (Daly, 1997; Skelly, 1997; Kennedy and Skelly, 2000; Fanning *et al.*, 2002). It has also seen the uncovering of unpleasant truths about aspects of policy making and administration in the past, most notoriously in relation to the treatment of Jewish immigration and of the state's complicity in the unethical and sometimes illegal transport of Irish children for adoption in the USA without the consent (or even the knowledge) of their natural parents (Milotte, 1997: 94–122; Keogh, 1998: 207–8, 210). Although such studies are necessarily historical, they inform and can have a considerable impact on public debate about contemporary challenges and problems in such areas.

The Comptroller and Auditor General Act, 1993, is another crucial piece of legislation. The Comptroller and Auditor General (C&AG) is responsible for ensuring that all public money is properly handled and accounted for by the state. Although the C&AG is protected by Article 33 of the constitution, historically holders of the office were severely hampered in their work by three factors. The first was a lack of resources, linked to civil service dislike of their activities. The second was a lack of Oireachtas interest, which is probably explained by the winner takes all, majoritarian culture of the Dáil. The third was archaic legislation – the C&AG's powers came principally from the Exchequer and Audit Departments Act, 1866, a British measure introduced by the Chancellor of the Exchequer William Ewart Gladstone in the rather different circumstances of mid-Victorian Britain. Attempts by successive C&AGs to interpret their powers of audit and review in a more modern fashion ran into civil service obstruction for years (O'Halpin, 1985: 506–7). In the late 1980s and early 1990s, however, under the guidance of an unusually assiduous chairman, the Fine Gael TD Jim Mitchell, the Dáil Committee of Public Accounts belatedly took an interest in these problems. A consensus emerged on the desirability of radical change. As well as closing crucial loopholes, the resulting 1993 Act empowered the C&AG to carry out Value for Money (VFM) audits, including comparative studies across the public sector. These have already occasioned much embarrassment for the institutions whose financial practices come under scrutiny, for example the impact of the 'waiting list initiative' for public hospitals which failed to reduce waiting lists in emergency departments despite additional funding (Comptroller and Auditor General, 2003). They also have an important exemplary function, providing an incentive for other public sector institutions to handle state funds with due care so as to avoid criticism in the future.

The Freedom of Information Act, 1997, Ireland's first piece of legislation of this type, is a powerful measure that confers three new legal rights on individuals: the right to consult official records held by government departments and other state agencies, subject to some security, commercial confidentiality, privacy and other provisos; the right to have personal information held on them corrected or updated if incomplete, inaccurate or misleading; and the right to be given reasons for decisions, taken by public bodies, that affect them. In 2002, the Act was widened to incorporate 18 more public bodies, ranging from the National Statistics Board to the Irish Film Board. The public have enthusiastically used the provisions of the Act. In 2001, 15,428 requests were made to an ever-expanding list of public bodies under the Act, a figure up by 12 per cent from 2000, and 34 per cent from 1999 (*Irish Times*, 1 March 2003). The legislation also allows for a court of appeal, in the form of the Information Commissioner, and further appeals to High Court on a point of law are possible.

After five years of operation the Act was again altered by the Freedom of Information Amendment Act, which came into effect in April 2003. The main aim of this amendment was to alter the original provision of the Act that allowed for the release of government papers once they were more than five years old. The Taoiseach, Bertie Ahern, claimed that the five-year rule was impracticable and dangerous since it could lead to the release of Belfast Agreement negotiating papers (*Irish Times*, 1 March 2003). This is a questionable argument, as any papers relating to the Belfast Agreement would be exempt under the security and international relations clauses. It does however reflect the finding of a review of the 1997 legislation by five leading civil servants, that stated that the five-year rule could '. . . stop free expression at Cabinet' (*Irish Times*, 28 February 2003).

The amendments include a number of changes that restrict the original legislation. In addition to the abolition of the five-year rule, curbs on the publication of correspondence between ministers have been introduced. The definitions of what constitute cabinet papers and a government meeting have been dramatically widened, and the right to appeal to the Information Commissioner in relation to a refusal to see policy papers is being completely set aside where the policy process is certified as ongoing. Furthermore, reports from cabinet subcommittees and civil servants groups will be inaccessible if departments rule that the reports were for the direct support of government deliberations. In this regard the Freedom of Information Amendment Act has maintained the strength of cabinet confidentiality, which could have been weakened by the release of relatively recent papers. In addition to these formal restrictions new fee structures introduced under the amendment have also restricted the ease by which the public can use the legislation, with a standard fee of €15 for an initial request, rising to as high as €150 for a review by the Information Commissioner.

Even with the watering down of the Freedom of Information Act the legislation still represents a reversal of the presumption of secrecy that has underpinned Irish government since independence (Doyle, 1996: 78–81). It is, for example, in practice a far more powerful investigative instrument than a parliamentary question, until now the main overt means by which information could be dragged out of a government unwilling to release it voluntarily (see Chapter 8, pp. 227–9). Furthermore, the Act is underpinned by a number of provisions designed to ensure that public bodies do not dodge their responsibilities by obfuscation, and officials are required actively to help requesters to frame their questions in a way that ensures they find the material they are seeking.

Conclusion

This chapter has looked at the Irish government system in a process of change. How fundamental or significant that change will be remains to be seen, but it is undeniable that the 1990s saw real change that has affected the way government operates in the twenty-first century. The Freedom of Information Act has ensured greater openness in government, while the Ethics in Public Office Act was a belated acknowledgement that corruption is a problem in the Irish as in all other European political and administrative systems. The Public Service Management Act has altered the relationship between top civil servants and ministers in a way that may make the internal workings of the departments more transparent and that, by defining the responsibilities of senior civil servants more clearly, may encourage ministers to concentrate more on policy questions. Other measures have strengthened oversight of government. These changes have been driven by a number of diverse forces – the experience of coalition government, the need to deal with political scandals, public pressure for more openness in government, the development of social partnership as an energising force in public policy development, and the impact of new approaches to public management in the public service. The Irish government system is in some respects recreating itself following the trauma of scandals and the unsettling shifts in voter behaviour. However, in spite of the many welcome changes that are taking place the fundamentals of the system have remained intact. The Taoiseach and the cabinet will remain in an overwhelmingly dominant position, and their deliberations will continue to be secret; the degree of control, of innovation and of integrity exhibited by ministers of all parties will continue to vary widely; and senior civil servants will continue to play a crucial and largely unseen role in policy development.

References and further reading

Barrington, Ruth, 1987. *Health, Medicine and Politics in Ireland, 1900–1970*. Dublin: Institute of Public Administration.

Blondel, Jean, 1988. 'Introduction', in Jean Blondel and Ferdinand Müller-Rommel (eds), *Cabinets in Western Europe*. Basingstoke: Macmillan, pp. 1–15.

Blondel, Jean and Maurizio Cotta, 1996. 'Conclusion', in Jean Blondel and Maurizio Cotta (eds), *Party and Government: An Inquiry into the Relationship between Governments and Supporting Parties in Liberal Democracies*. Basingstoke: Macmillan, pp. 249–62.

Boland, John, John Dowling and Eunan O'Halpin, 1986. 'Serving the country better: a debate', *Administration* 34:3: 287–301.

Boyle, Richard, Tony McNamara, Michael Mulreaney and Anne O'Keeffe, 1997. 'Review of developments in the public sector in 1996', *Administration* 44:4: 3–41.

Browne, Noel, 1986. *Against the Tide*. Dublin: Gill and Macmillan.

Comptroller and Auditor General, 2003. *Report on Value for Money Examination: Department of Health and Children – The Waiting List Initiative*. Dublin: Stationery Office. Also available http://audgen.gov.ie/documents/vfmreports/vfm-waiting list.pdf.

Crowley, Niall, 1998. 'Partnership 2000: empowerment or co-option?', in Peadar Kirby and David Jacobson (eds), *In the Shadow of the Tiger: New Approaches to Combating Social Exclusion*. Dublin: Dublin City University Press, pp. 69–81.

Daly, Mary E., 1997. *The Buffer State: The Historical Roots of the Department of the Environment*. Dublin: Institute of Public Administration.

Deeny, James, 1989. *To Cure and to Care: Memoirs of a Chief Medical Officer*. Dublin: Glendale Press.

Department of the Public Service, 1985. *Serving the Country Better*. Dublin: Stationery Office.

Department of the Taoiseach, 1998. *Strategy Statement, 1998–2001*. Dublin: Stationery Office. Also available http://www.irlgov.ie/taoiseach/publication/smi/smi.htm.

Department of the Taoiseach, 1998a. *Cabinet Handbook*. Dublin: Stationery Office. Also available http://www.taoiseach.gov.ie/index.asp?docID=225.

Department of the Taoiseach, 2003. *Strategy Statement, 2003–2005*. Dublin: Stationery Office. Also available http://www.taoiseach.gov.ie/index.asp?docID=1530.

Doyle, John, 1996. 'Freedom of information: lessons from the international experience', *Administration* 44:4: 64–82.

Fanning, Ronan, Michael Kennedy, Dermot Keogh and Eunan O'Halpin (eds), 2002. *Documents on Irish Foreign Policy: Vol. 3, 1926–32*. Dublin: Royal Irish Academy.

Farrell, Brian, 1993. 'The formation of the partnership government', in Michael Gallagher and Michael Laver (eds), *How Ireland Voted 1992*. Dublin: Folens and PSAI Press, pp. 146–61.

Farrell, Brian, 1994. 'The political role of cabinet ministers in Ireland', in Michael Laver and Ken Shepsle (eds), *Cabinet Ministers and Parliamentary Government*. Cambridge: Cambridge University Press, pp. 73–87.

Finlay, Fergus, 1998. *Snakes and Ladders*. Dublin: New Island Books.

Garry, John, 1995. 'The demise of the Fianna Fáil/Labour "Partnership" government and the rise of the "Rainbow" coalition', *Irish Political Studies* 10: 192–9.

Garvin, Tom. 1991. 'Democracy in Ireland: collective somnambulance and public policy', *Administration* 39:1: 42–54.

Hogan, Gerard, 1993. 'The Cabinet Confidentiality case of 1992', *Irish Political Studies* 8: 131–7.

Hussey, Gemma, 1990. *At the Cutting Edge: Cabinet Diaries, 1982–1987*. Dublin: Gill and Macmillan.

Kennedy, Fiachra, 2002. 'The 2002 general election in Ireland', *Irish Political Studies* 17:2: 95–106.

Kennedy, Michael and Joseph Morrison Skelly (eds), 2000. *Irish Foreign Policy 1919–1966: From Independence to Internationalism*. Dublin: Four Courts Press.

Keogh, Dermot, 1998. *Jews in Twentieth-Century Ireland: Refugees, Anti-semitism and the Holocaust*. Cork: Cork University Press.

Laver, Michael, 1994. 'Party policy and cabinet portfolios in Ireland 1992: results from an expert survey', *Irish Political Studies* 9: 157–64.

Laver, Michael and Ken Shepsle, 1994. 'Cabinet government in theoretical perspective', in Michael Laver and Ken Shepsle (eds), *Cabinet Ministers and Parliamentary Government*. Cambridge: Cambridge University Press, pp. 285–309.

Link Newsletter, 1999. Available http://www.irlgov.ie/taoiseach/publication/link/frmain.htm, 26 January 1999.

MacDonagh, Bobby, 1998. *Original Sin in a Brave New World: An Account of the Negotiation of the Treaty of Amsterdam*. Dublin: Institute of European Affairs.

Millar, Michelle and David McKevitt, 2000. 'The Irish civil service system', in Hans A. G. M. Bekke and Frits M. van der Meer (eds), *Civil Service Systems in Western Europe*. Cheltenham: Edward Elgar, pp. 36–57.

Milotte, Mike, 1997. *Vanished Babies: The Secret History of Ireland's Baby Export Business*. Dublin: New Island Books.

Mitchell, Paul, 2000. 'Ireland: from single party to coalition rule', in Wolfgang C. Müller and Kaare Strøm (eds), *Coalition Governments in Western Europe*. Oxford: Oxford University Press, pp. 126–57.

Mitchell, Paul, 2003. 'Government formation in 2002: "You can have any kind of government as long as it's Fianna Fáil"', in Michael Gallagher, Michael Marsh and Paul Mitchell (eds), *How Ireland Voted 2002*. Basingstoke: Palgrave Macmillan, pp. 214–27.

Mitchell, Paul, 2003a. 'Ireland: "O what a tangled web . . ." – delegation, accountability, and executive power', in Kaare Strøm, Wolfgang C. Müller and Torbjörn Bergman (eds), *Delegation and Accountability in Parliamentary Democracies*. Oxford: Oxford University Press, pp. 418–41.

Murray, Frank and Paddy Teahon, 1998. 'The Irish political and policy-making system and the current programme of change', *Administration* 45:4: 39–58.

O'Donnell, Rory and Damien Thomas, 1998. 'Partnership and policy-making', in Seán Healy and Brigid Reynolds (eds), *Social Policy in Ireland: Principles, Practice and Problems*. Dublin: Oak Tree Press, pp. 117–46.

O'Halpin, Eunan, 1985. 'The Dáil Committee of Public Accounts, 1961–1980', *Administration* 32:4: 483–511.

O'Halpin, Eunan, 1991. 'The civil service and the political system', *Administration* 38:3: 283–302.

O'Halpin, Eunan, 1997. 'Partnership programme managers in the Reynolds–Spring coalition, 1993–4: an assessment', *Irish Political Studies* 12: 78–91.

O'Halpin, Eunan and Eileen Connolly, 1999. 'Parliaments and pressure groups: the Irish experience of change', in Philip Norton (ed.), *Parliaments and Pressure Groups in Western Europe*. London: Frank Cass, pp. 124–44.

Skelly, Joseph Morrison, 1997. *Irish Diplomacy at the United Nations, 1945–1965: National Interests and the International Order*. Dublin: Irish Academic Press.
Zimmerman, Joseph F., 1997. 'The changing roles of the Irish department secretary', *Public Administration Review* 57:6: 534–42.

Websites

www.taoiseach.gov.ie   This is the official site of the Department of the Taoiseach. It contains a wealth of material on the role of the Taoiseach, the ministers and the government programmes. It explains the organisational structure of the Department of the Taoiseach and contains links to news, press releases and information on government policy.

www.maryharney.ie   The constituency website of the Tánaiste and leader of the Progressive Democrats, Mary Harney.

www.taoiseach.gov.ie (link: taoiseach and government: the government: list of ministers and ministers of state)   A part of the Department of the Taoiseach site containing a full list of all Government Ministers and Ministers of State with links to both government departments and Minister's web pages.

www.taoiseach.gov.ie/upload/publications/233.pdf   This page contains an electronic copy of the Cabinet Handbook, a set of detailed guidelines which have been developed to assist Ministers in their departmental role and in their relationship with cabinet. It covers topics such as bringing policy recommendations to cabinet for consideration. Generally it is a guide for ministers on how the cabinet functions.

www.bettergov.ie (link: publications: Link Magazine)   Home page of the *Link* magazine, a magazine which is circulated to all civil servants to keep them informed about internal issues in the organisation and management of the civil service, with industrial relations issues and perhaps most importantly with developments in the internal modernisation process. Back issues as far as 1998 are also available online.

ue.eu.int/en/summ.htm   This is the home page of the Council of the European Union. It illustrates the role of the Irish government in the EU and contains links to news, press releases, upcoming meetings, publications, etc.

13 Interest groups in the policy-making process

Gary Murphy

This chapter examines the role of interest groups and seeks to explain the central role that they play in the policy-making process. The importance of interest groups has varied over time since they became an accepted part of the political process in the early 1960s. At times they have been outside the political mainstream as a mere voice in the wilderness. Yet since the advent of social partnership in 1987 they have been serious players in the Irish political market. We will explore their influence and examine the role that interest groups play in the policy-making process, assessing whether their impact is positive or negative.

Defining interest groups is a perennial problem, especially given the proliferation of organisations that have attempted to influence the policy process in recent years. As one commentator has asked, should we conclude that 'any organisation which seeks to any degree to influence public policy is to be regarded as an interest group?' (Wilson, 1991: 7). Such a broad definition would embrace political parties. A satisfactory definition will stipulate two criteria: that the organisation has some autonomy from government and that it tries to influence policy (Wilson, 1991: 8). Thus, as a formal definition, the perspective of Kimber and Richardson, that a pressure group or interest group 'may be regarded as any group which articulates demands that the political system or subsystem should make an authoritative allocation' (Kimber and Richardson, 1974: 1), remains the most useful. Adding the rider that such groups do not themselves seek to occupy the position of authority has the effect of excluding political parties.

In Ireland some groups have in recent years attempted to stretch this definition by putting forward members of their groups for election at both national and local level, with varying degrees of success. The rise of independents as a major factor in Irish electoral politics has ensured that candidates representing various organisations such as hospital action groups and other similar issues have had an increased profile. A further feature of policy making in Ireland in recent years has been the increasingly vigorous lobbying on behalf of business or private interests, in an attempt to influence specific government policy, as distinct from the sectional demands of the wider business community. This has been a feature of evidence heard at the

Flood Mahon and Moriarty tribunals of inquiry into rezoning in County Dublin and payments to politicians respectively (see Chapter 14). Thus any discussion of interest groups now has to take into account private business interests as well as the cause-centred and sectional groups with which interest group study has been traditionally concerned. Furthermore, some commentators have begun to think of interest groups not as free-standing entities but as members of policy networks. With the proliferation of interest groups in recent years, policy making has taken on an increased complexity and the policy network approach is based upon the idea that decision making is rarely limited to key actors in a single organisation but rather involves a whole range of actors across many bodies trying to seek agreement. Thus what interest group scholars now have to contend with is a rapidly expanding area of politics which consists of four separate strands: sectional groups, cause-centred groups, private interests and policy networks.

Interest group politics in essence means trying to influence the formation, passage through the legislature, and implementation of public policy by means of contact with ministers, civil servants, political parties, individual politicians, the media and the public. It can also mean attempting to change existing legislation by lobbying within the relevant area of public policy (Punnett, 1994: 142). The methods of interest group activity are shaped by the crucial question of access through which influence is exerted. The main channels of access available to interest groups are through the government bureaucracy, the assembly, the courts, political parties, the mass media and various supranational bodies (Heywood, 2002: 280). Ultimately the existence of interest groups places constraints on governments in that the 'process of governing societies always involves some accommodation of the wishes of pressure and interest groups' (Richardson, 1993: 11).

Interest groups and the political process

The centrality of interest groups to the political process is clear as much of the process of governance can be seen as the management of the 'interface between governments and groups' (Richardson, 1993: 10). This can be vividly seen in western Europe. While modern European states have a tradition of strong political parties or administrative elites, which in theory should insulate them from particularist private demands (Aspinwall and Greenwood, 1998: 1), in practice the way governments interact with interest groups in the policy process is remarkably similar. A central element of western European democracy has been the so-called 'co-optation' of interest groups into the policy process, in which the interrelationship between governments and interest groups, depending on the specific policy area, can often be of greater significance for policy outcomes than general elections (Richardson, 1993: 12). Thus, notwithstanding the strength of political and administrative elites, interest groups have a substantial role to play in western European polities. As Heisler and Kvavik emphasised, a common

denominator of the European polity is 'a decision making structure characterised by continuous, regularised access for economically, politically, ethni-
cally, and/or subculturally based groups to the highest levels of the political
system, i.e. the decision making subsystem' (Heisler and Kvavik, 1974: 48).

Models of interest group activity

Where does Ireland fit into such a model? Within the decision-making
subsystem, two distinct models of interest group behaviour are particularly
useful: corporatism and pluralism.

The *corporatist* model suggests that interest groups are closely associated
with the formal political process and play a critical role in both the formulation and the implementation of major political decisions. Thus large and
powerful interest groups monopolise the representation of the interests of a
particular functional section of the population. This usually encapsulates
organised labour, the farmers and employers. Moreover these interest
groups are organised in a hierarchical manner, typically with a powerful
peak organisation. In the Irish case this would probably include the Irish
Congress of Trade Unions (ICTU), the Irish Business and Employers Confederation (IBEC) and the Irish Farmers' Association (IFA), co-ordinating
strategy at the apex of a pyramid of organisations. These organisations
proceed to negotiate with each other and with government to produce an
agreed outcome that minimises social and economic disruption.

One of the main problems associated with corporatism, however, is that
different scholars have used it in different ways, so there are multiple definitions. For some the term simply describes what is little more than centralised
pay bargaining in which government and the so-called social partners
(organised labour and business) sit round a table and thrash out a national
incomes policy. For others corporatism is rooted much more deeply in the
policy-making system and consists of a set of institutional arrangements that
entrenches major social groups in the overall management of the national
economy (Gallagher *et al.*, 2001: 400). One commentator reckoned that
24 different working definitions of corporatism were used by various authors
between 1981 and 1997 (Siaroff, 1999). For Siaroff, working from his
review of these definitions, corporatism involved 'within an advanced industrial society and democratic polity, the co-ordinated, co-operative and
systematic management of the national economy by the state, centralised
unions, and employers (these latter two co-operating directly in industry),
presumably to the relative benefit of all three actors' (Siaroff, 1999: 177).
Such a definition of course excludes the peak farming organisations, but can
we definitively say that corporatism excludes the farming community?
What sets corporatism fundamentally apart as a model of interest group
activity is the stress it places on policy implementation. To this end we
can include peak farming organisations if they are comprehensive in their

representation of the particular sector of society they represent, and are able both to protect their members' interests and to control their members. As Lehmbruch (quoted in Gallagher *et al.*, 2001: 401) points out:

> corporatism is more than a particular pattern of articulation of interests. Rather, it is an institutionalised pattern of policy-formulation in which large interest organisations co-operate with each other and with public authorities not only in the articulation of interests but . . . in the 'authoritative allocation of values' and in the implementation of such policies.

Thus if farming organisations are involved both in the articulation of interests and in the implementation of policies in conjunction with government, organised labour and business, we can include them as players in the corporatist model of interest group behaviour. This does not, however, exclude them from other models and we will later examine agricultural interests as part of our discussion on policy networks.

While a crucial element of corporatism lies in implementing such policies as are agreed by the government and other groups, it is important to note that the various groups involved are ready to oppose each other if they perceive that their interests are threatened. In consequence there is a certain element of validity in the metaphor of various groups sitting around a table thrashing out a deal on economic policies. Thus even within a corporatist model, the ability of interest groups to present their case forcefully is an important consideration. What is more important is that agreements made within a true corporatist system entail a comprehensive role for the social partners in the implementation of policy and they are applicable in wide policy domains, not simply the economy (Cawson, 1986: 37). Economic policy formulation that involves government, industry, trade unions and perhaps farmers is better described as tripartite. Some scholars have also used the term meso-corporatism to describe those countries where corporatist practices take place for some groups or issues with pluralism prevailing for other groups and issue areas (Cawson, 1985; Regan and Wilson, 1986: 394).

The *pluralist* model maintains that individual interest groups apply pressure on political elites in a competitive manner and attributes power in policy making to individual groups operating in particular areas at particular times. This competition is usually disorganised and its main essence is to exclude other interest groups from the policy process. Schmitter defines pluralism as:

> a system of interest representation in which the constituent units are organized into an unspecified number of multiple, voluntary, competitive, non-hierarchically ordered and self-determined (as to type or scope of interest) categories which are not specifically licensed, recognized, subsidized, created or otherwise controlled in leadership selection

or interest articulation by the state, and which do not exercise a monopoly of representational activity within their respective categories.

(Schmitter, 1974: 96)

Unlike corporatism, pluralism offers no formal institutional role to
interest groups in the decision making or implementation of policy. Interest
groups are assumed to be self-generating and voluntary. This allows government a critical role in mediating between groups that are competing with
each other to represent the interests of the same classes of people in similar
areas of economic and social activity. Indeed, group activity may be fragmented and group membership may only be a small proportion of the
possible total. Moreover, groups in the same field of interest may be poorly
co-ordinated by peak organisations, resulting in the emergence of a pluralist
rather than a corporatist model of behaviour. In the pluralist model, better
organised interest groups with more resources and more strategic social,
economic and political positions than others can be relatively powerful
influences on government (Budge *et al.*, 1997: 159).

In essence pluralist theories offer the most positive image of group politics,
emphasising the capacity of groups to both defend the individual from the
government and promote democratic responsiveness. The core expression of
pluralism is that political power is fragmented and widely dispersed with
decisions made through a complex process of bargaining and interaction
that ensures that the views and interests of a large number of groups are
taken into account (Heywood, 2002: 273). However, in practice pluralism
has tended to occupy an uneasy 'no man's land between being a "norma-
tive" theory of how politics ought to be conducted and a "positive" theory
of how groups actually do operate' (Gallagher *et al.*, 2001: 407). To that end
pluralism can be characterised as being more conflictual than consensual.

Interest groups in Ireland

Given the difficulty of measuring degrees of corporatism and pluralism,
there has been no consensus on the application of these models to the policy
process either generally or in relation to the Irish case. Beyond doubt, however, interest groups play a major role in policy formulation and implementation. For the purposes of this chapter they can be divided into two broad
categories. On the one hand are those with a *sectional base*, such as trade
unions, farmers' associations, business organisations and self-regulating
professional bodies such as the Irish Medical Organisation and the Institute
of Chartered Accountants of Ireland. The second category comprises *cause-
centred groups*, such as the Irish Wheelchair Association and Youth Defence,
which lobby to promote a particular cause – in these cases, the achievement
of full social, economic and educational integration of people with disabilities
and the anti-abortion agenda respectively.

In terms of numbers, those interest groups that we classify as sectional are increasing in number. For instance in 2002 there were 23 agricultural organisations, 23 teaching organisations, 9 civil service associations, 4 different Garda (police) representative bodies, 3 defence force representative bodies, 15 local government organisations, 57 trade unions affiliated to the Irish Congress of Trade Unions, 4 unions not affiliated to ICTU and over 270 other trade and professional bodies that were organised to represent the interests of their members. Within these there were a number of distinct business organisations, with IBEC having over 70 separate sector associations affiliated to it (Institute of Public Administration, 2003: 330–62).

Likewise there is an increasing number of cause-centred groups. Again in 2002, there were 80 different arts organisations, 72 health organisations, 25 Irish language organisations, 29 women's interest groups, 49 youth organisations and over 300 other organisations espousing various social, political and cultural causes (Institute of Public Administration, 2003: 174–80, 363–97). Moreover we can also categorise other organisations as occasional interest groups, in that, while their main function is not political, they often end up involved in political negotiations with governments. Chief amongst these groups would be the Roman Catholic Church and the Gaelic Athletic Association (GAA). The Roman Catholic Church, for instance, was an active advocate in the various abortion and divorce referendums in Ireland over the 20-year period 1983–2002 and is still a voice which makes itself heard on issues such as stem-cell research, on which it attempts to give leadership to its flock. Likewise, the GAA lobbied the Fianna Fáil–Progressive Democrat government very effectively for the financing of its flagship stadium Croke Park and was rewarded in December 1997 with the awarding of IR£20 million (over €25 million) of public funds for the rebuilding of the stadium, the largest amount ever granted to a sporting organisation in the country. Since that time the GAA has continuously engaged in lobbying the government, with various degrees of success, in relation to the funding of Croke Park. Staying with sport, both the Irish Rugby Football Union and the Football Association of Ireland have also been active lobbyists of governments and secured public funding for the redevelopment of Lansdowne Road as the national stadium in early 2004.

While the numbers for cause-centred groups might look high, membership of voluntary organisations in Ireland is low by west European standards (Therborn, 1995: 307), and in a west European context Ireland's proliferation of cause centred groups is not unusual. In a world values survey conducted at the beginning of the 1990s, the percentage of the population in Ireland belonging to a voluntary organisation was 49 per cent. This placed Ireland below Austria, Belgium, Britain, Denmark, Finland, Iceland, the Netherlands, Sweden and Germany, but ahead of France, Italy, Portugal and Spain. The most recent data for Irish membership of voluntary organisations show that 47 per cent of people are active on a weekly basis in

Table 13.1 Frequency of involvement in
civil society, 2001–2

	%
Several times a week	21.3
About once a week	25.7
About twice a month	11.4
A few times a year	13.9
Rarely or never	27.7
Total	100.0

Source: Irish Social and Political Attitudes
Survey, Irish Social Science Data Archive, Insti-
tute for the Study of Social Change, UCD,
Winter 2001/2.

Note
The table shows responses to the question 'How
often do you spend time with other people in
clubs or associations, religious organisations or
voluntary groups of one kind or another? (tick
one box only).'

meeting with other members of their organisation, and 58 per cent meet
fellow members at least twice a month (see Table 13.1).[1]

In terms of sectional groups, it is illuminating to compare Ireland's business and trade union interests to those in Germany. In Germany there are
only 16 major trade unions, all belonging to the German Federation of
Trade Unions. Their combined membership is around 12 million, constituting a good third of the total German employed labour force and about
80 per cent of all unionised employees. This peak organisation can be compared to ICTU in the Irish context. Moreover while there are hundreds of
employers' organisations, these again are part of a larger umbrella body,
the Confederation of German Employers' Associations, which deals with
social policy, including collective bargaining. There are two other peak
organisations in Germany: the Association of German Chambers of Industry
and Commerce, and the Federation of German Industries (Gallagher *et al.*,
2001: 405–6), but the key point is that all three organisations co-ordinate
their activities and often function as a single entity, similar to IBEC in
Ireland.

Sectional groups

Tripartite agreements

In this section we will look at the role of the sectional groups and examine
their influence in relation to social partnership and their impact on its
development. Ireland has had a tradition of tripartite consultation in the

public policy sphere since the early 1960s. It was during this era that the economic interests (farmers, trade unions and business associations) were invited to participate in the work of a number of national bodies who were concerned with formulating a new approach to economic management (Horgan, 1997: 228–49; Murphy, 2003a: 105–18). This approach – co-ordinated by the Taoiseach, Seán Lemass – had as its ultimate aim entry to the European Economic Community, which the government of the day assumed would happen sometime in 1963–4. It was with this goal in mind (and the perceived need to show a united front to western Europe) that the economic interest groups were co-opted into this tripartite arrangement towards economic management (Murphy 2003b: 115–22).

In the 1970s, however, the focus of state policy shifted; corporatist policies in the economic sphere were dropped and the process was no longer directly aided by government financial support (Hardiman, 1988). Notwithstanding this, the continuing high level of state intervention in the economy ensured an ongoing and important role for the Confederation of Irish Industry (McCann, 1993: 51). To a lesser degree, this was also the case with the trade unions and the farmers' organisations. While the sectional groups were not central to economic decision making, they were far from isolated voices in the wilderness. The tripartite approach to governance took centre stage again in 1987 with the coming to power of a minority Fianna Fáil government. This approach has since evolved into a system that aims to keep all the major interests reasonably happy by giving them a role within the broad economic approach of the state, which in turn will perpetuate a national economic and social coalition of sorts. This social partner-ship cements these economic interests, now known as 'social partners', to a coherent and consistent policy framework. This consensual approach mirrors that of northern European social democracies such as Sweden, Norway and Denmark; indeed since the mid-1990s Ireland has experienced the kind of economic success that was previously associated with such countries. In this respect the Irish approach has been markedly different to the dismissive tone sometimes taken by British governments in regard to organised labour in particular.

Social partnership in Ireland since 1987

It was during a period of deep depression in the mid-1980s that the social partners, acting in the tripartite National Economic and Social Council (NESC), agreed a strategy to overcome Ireland's economic difficulties. The NESC's *Strategy For Development* (1986) formed the basis upon which, in 1987, the new Fianna Fáil government and the social partners negotiated the Programme for National Recovery (PNR), which was followed by five other agreements (see Box 13.1). What made these agreements different from those of the 1960s and 1970s was that they were not simply centralised wage mechanisms but agreements on a wide range of economic and social policies

---

Box 13.1 Social partnership agreements in Ireland since the 1980s

A number of broadly tripartite agreements have been made between governments and the main economic interest groups since the mid-1980s, under the auspices of NESC (the National Economic and Social Council, an advisory body through which employers, trade unions, farmers and senior civil servants analyse policy issues). The first of these represented a strategy to escape from the circle of economic stagnation, rising taxes, increasing debt and massive unemployment that surrounded the Irish economy in the mid-1980s. Its success paved the way for further agreements in the 1990s and these agreements were widely seen as a major explanation for the rapid economic growth that Ireland enjoyed in the 1990s (the so-called 'Celtic tiger' economy). The main agreements have been:

- Programme for National Recovery (PNR) 1987–90;
- Programme for Economic and Social Progress (PESP) 1990–93;
- Programme for Competitiveness and Work (PCW) 1994–96;
- Partnership 2000 for Inclusion, Employment and Competitiveness 1997–2000;
- Programme for Prosperity and Fairness (PPF) 2000–3;
- Sustaining Progress 2003–5.

The negotiation of each of these social partnership agreement was preceded by a NESC strategy report, which set out the shared perspective of the social partners on the achievements and limits of the previous programme and the parameters within which a new programme would be negotiated.

---

such as tax reform and the evolution of welfare payments (O'Donnell and Thomas, 1998: 118). For instance, for the first time in the history of centralised bargaining in the state, Partnership 2000 provided an integrated package of pay rises and tax cuts that enabled trade union leaders to calculate the real value of the deal, the better to sell it to their members.

With the development of the Partnership 2000 agreement a watershed was reached as for the first time agencies from the voluntary sector, including charities and self-help groups, were included in consultation and ultimately negotiations. This new initiative resulted from complaints that the government and the economic partners were missing an opportunity to tackle social exclusion in an integrated fashion by ignoring the voices of other interest groups. The most graphic illustration of this widening of the social partnership parameters was the inclusion of the Irish National Organisation of the Unemployed (INOU) in the negotiations – the first time that the unemployed had been seen by the government as an actor with something to offer to social partnership negotiation. In all there were eight organisations involved in what was known as the second tier of interest groups in the negotiations leading up to Partnership 2000: the INOU, the Conference of Religious in Ireland, the National Women's Council, the National Youth Council of Ireland, the ICTU unemployed centres, the Society of St Vincent de Paul, Protestant Aid and the Community Platform, which included the travelling community and people with disabilities. The inclusion of such groups shows that while the main sectional groups (farmers, employers and trade unions) remain the critical players in the realm of social partnership, the development of a social pillar in terms of economic and social development has come to be accepted as intrinsic to the conclusion of any national development. What Partnership 2000 looked forward to was nothing less than the enactment of a new social contract. Yet the voluntary organisations felt they were ranked below business and labour in the hierarchy of interests, showing very clearly that in social partnership it was the employers and the unions who remained the pivotal actors.

A new pay agreement – Programme for Prosperity and Fairness (PPF), 2000–2003 – was negotiated in early 2000. The agreement still included the social pillar groups, but these had to be persuaded by government to remain in the process as in their eyes the new social contract promised in Partnership 2000 had not materialised. The pay terms, at about 15 per cent over 33 months, were substantially higher than in any previous agreement, while tax cuts gave a further boost of about 10 per cent to disposable income. Yet the agreement was in effect renegotiated when in response to a sharp rise in inflation during 2000, and increasing strains on the terms of the pay agreement in some sectors, the unions secured a further upward revision of the pay terms of the PPF in December 2000 (Hardiman, 2002: 11).

A sixth agreement – Sustaining Progress, 2003–2005 – was agreed in February 2003 after tortuous negotiations, especially between the employers' organisations and the trade unions. An uneven sectoral distribution of growth had placed considerable strain on the 'one size fits all' pay norm (Hardiman, 2002: 18). Within this framework it became increasingly difficult to reach a consensus as the union leaders were looking for an increased share of national wealth at a time when employers sought to reintroduce cost competitive constraints. Moreover the Community Platform, now consisting of 26 participative organisations, and the other voluntary organisations were becoming more disenchanted by what they perceived as the government's failure to treat them as equal partners in the process. Nevertheless they stayed in it and were party to the final deal. For the Taoiseach, Bertie Ahern, the agreement provided 'a coherent and focused strategy for managing the interlocking elements of the economy and the behaviour of economic and social policies' (Department of the Taoiseach, 2003: 2). The social partnership agreements had evolved considerably from 1987, when the first agreement was developed strictly as a means of responding to a grave fiscal crisis. They developed into a strategy for facilitating steady growth and the inward investment that fuelled such growth, over a much longer time period than was originally expected, and this strategy was central to the successes of the Irish economy from the mid-1990s.

There is some debate about the exact nature of social partnership in Ireland. Allen (2000) claims it is a myth and has functioned mainly as a means of sustaining inequalities in the outcome of growth by incorporating union leaders into the process and reinforcing their control over the ordinary membership. For O'Donnell and O'Reardon (2002: 252), it is best described as the 'formulation of a new concept of post-corporatist concertation' as the range of interests represented in social partnership goes beyond that arising from functional interdependence between business and labour. This challenges the representational monopoly of the confederations on each side that one would find in a classically corporatist arrangement. They argue too that new relationships have emerged between government policy-making institutions and interest groups at different levels with the result that traditional conceptions of neo-corporatism, premised on the effectiveness and power of central government, are outdated.

For Roche and Cradden (2003: 80–7), both these approaches have faults, and they argue that social partnership can best be understood in terms of the theory of competitive corporatism. The resurgence of neo-corporatist social pacts in a number of European countries, including Ireland, in the 1990s differed substantially from superficially similar agreements in the 1960s and 1970s. The later agreements concentrated on pay deals that were consistent with the enhancement of national competitiveness, on sustainable levels of public expenditure, the reform of taxation and welfare systems, and the upskilling of the labour force. Previous aspirational policies such as managing income distribution gave way to the promotion of business objectives – particularly in terms of competitive advantage. To that end the social partnership pacts of the 1990s can be seen as examples of competitive corporatism, which has also been termed 'supply side' or 'lean' corporatism. Significantly, nine of the then 15 members of the European Union – Belgium, Finland, Germany, Greece, Ireland, Italy, the Netherlands, Portugal and Spain – put in place social partnership pacts of this competitive neo-corporatist kind in the 1980s and 1990s (Roche and Cradden, 2003: 73). Thus Ireland's social partnership experiment since 1987 can be seen as one of a number of similar agreements across the EU.

Other sectional group activity

Of course, interest groups involved in social partnership are also frequently in competition for favourable decisions from government. For example, the trade unions and employers' organisations have been at odds for many years over workers' protection in the building industry. Members of individual trade unions have also not hesitated to take protest action when they feel their interests are threatened, notwithstanding the fact that their membership is instrumental to social partnership. A good example of this kind of activity can be seen in the response of various individual trade unions to the Minister of Transport's attempts from 2002 onwards to break up Aer Rianta's operation, management and development of Dublin, Shannon and Cork Airports and make them private operators in competition with each other instead. Minister Séamus Brennan's attempts to deregulate the bus market in Dublin also met with opposition by the unions of Dublin Bus who took industrial action in opposition to these moves.

Moreover it should be borne in mind that not all sectional groups are involved in social partnership. Some remain outside it, such as the Vintners' Federation of Ireland (VFI), which lobbies on behalf of the publicans of the country. Established in 1973 from a number of smaller associations for the protection and betterment of the livelihood of the individual publican, the VFI has traditionally had the reputation of being an extremely successful lobby group. It played a very important role in opposing the plans of the Minister for the Environment to reduce the drink-driving limit during the 1993–4 Fianna Fáil–Labour coalition and states that one of its aims is to keep watch on all proceedings of the Oireachtas with a view to taking steps to promote and protect the interests of its members (see www.vfi.ie). The VFI claimed success in influencing government over the implementation of new licensing legislation in 2003. It successfully lobbied the government to strengthen the right of the publican to refuse service to any customer in this legislation after the Equal Status Act, 2000 outlawed discrimination in the provision of goods and services to the public. The VFI claimed that this legislation was making it impossible for its members to run effective and trouble-free public houses. It campaigned amongst local councillors and Oireachtas members to ensure that the licensing legislation reflected that publicans were in a unique situation, due to the intoxicating nature of alcohol, when it came to refusing service. The Intoxicating Liquor Act, 2003 transferred jurisdiction in discrimination cases from the Equality Authority to the District Courts. This provision was included following lobbying from publicans who claimed that members of the Travelling community were abusing equality laws because of the ease of taking cases before the Equality Authority. Yet the VFI's reputation as one of the most influential sectional lobby groups was seriously undermined when it failed to persuade the Minister for Health to exempt public houses from a smoking ban in the workplace in late 2003.

Cause-centred groups

Cause-centred groups have been significant players in the policy process since the early 1980s. Whether they are *ad hoc* groups formed to press for a single measure, as has become prevalent in the area of moral politics, or organisations with a permanent mission such as Greenpeace or the Simon Community, their activities and influence have become much more visible. Groups that formed in the hope of getting a single piece of legislation enacted have become quite vocal in recent years, particularly in the area of moral politics, for without doubt the politics of morality has been conducted in the domain of the interest group. Since 1983 there have been three referendums on abortion and two on divorce and in essence the campaigns have been conducted primarily through the medium of the interest group. The classic example is the divorce referendum of 1995. The campaign was primarily fought by concerned interest groups as the government deliberately pursued a low key approach with one minister claiming that the 'hysteria' associated with the 1986 divorce campaign would thereby be avoided (Girvin, 1996: 179). The fact that all the political parties stood back let the various interest groups come to the fore in the debate.

In the abortion and divorce referendums of the 1980s, the forces of moral conservatism had shown themselves to be far better skilled in modern pressure group techniques than those who sought to modernise Irish society. By the time of the 1995 divorce referendum, however, those groups in favour of the amendment such as the Divorce Action Group and the Right to Remarry Group had proven themselves to be efficient operators in the game of pressure politics.

Prior to this campaign it was those groups who wished to impose a distinctly Catholic view of morality on the state who were the acknowledged kingpins in the field of pressure group politics. Indeed the Society for the Protection of the Unborn Child sprang up completely unannounced in 1981 and within two years had, along with other like-minded groups under the umbrella of the Pro-Life Amendment Campaign, successfully persuaded the government of the day to call a referendum with the purpose of introducing an amendment which would in effect guarantee the rights of the unborn child and constitutionally outlaw abortion (Girvin, 1986). The Fine Gael–Labour government of the day appeared to be ill equipped to deal with such a highly organised pressure group and the result was a decade of social division, whose effects still linger as evidenced by the refusal of abortion to disappear as a political issue.

Two further abortion referendums took place in 1992 and 2002. This was because the 1983 referendum had exactly the opposite effect to that anticipated by those who had advocated the amendment (and probably all those who voted for it) when, in delivering its judgment in the 'X' case in 1992, the Supreme Court found that the threat of suicide provided grounds for having an abortion in Ireland within the meaning of the amendment (see Box 3.2, p. 88, for the 'X' case). Both of these referendums tell us much about the effects of cause-centred lobbying. In December 1991 the then Taoiseach Charles Haughey and his Minister for Foreign Affairs Gerard Collins had persuaded their European colleagues to insert into the Maastricht Treaty a special protocol to protect the 1983 amendment, having been convinced by anti-abortion activists that without such a protocol the constitution would not be able to protect the original amendment (Murphy, 2003c: 34). Once the Supreme Court issued its controversial ruling in the 'X' case in March 1992, the pro-life lobby groups sprang into action demanding that the new Taoiseach Albert Reynolds – appointed the previous month – call another abortion referendum before the Maastricht Treaty referendum. Reynolds refused and eventually held the Maastricht referendum in June, a full five months before the abortion referendums (see Chapter 3), believing that it was the duty of the government to lead in such areas; this shows that pressure group politics can work only if the government allows it to do so by its own ready acquiescence.

In March 2002 the Fianna Fáil–Progressive Democrat government decided to hold yet another referendum on abortion just two months before it would go to the country in a general election. The proposal itself followed an extensive consultation process with a whole variety of lobby groups including the medical profession, the Catholic Church, and both pro-life and pro-choice groups. The main pro-life groups, the Pro-Life Campaign and the Pro-Life Movement, gave the amendment their enthusiastic support but there is no evidence – as there was for the 1983 referendum, in particular – of pressure being brought successfully to bear on the government of the day. Indeed the pro-life ranks split with both Youth Defence and its ally the Mother and Child campaign opposing the amendment on the grounds that it would not protect the unborn from the moment of conception. Moreover, in a clear sign of voter disenchantment with the politics of morality being fought out via referendum, the 2002 turnout at 43 per cent was significantly lower than in 1992 and 1983 (Murphy, 2003c: 32; see also Appendix 2h).

While interest groups have come to the fore in fighting various referendum campaigns, it should be stressed that women's interest groups have been at the centre of political life since the early 1970s (see also pp. 291–2 above). Organisations such as AIM (Action, Information, Motivation) and Cherish (a single-mothers' organisation) became important lobbying agencies for changes in family law and the status of women. Moreover the National Women's Council of Ireland, which represented established women's organisations, sought to influence government policy in a wide range of areas affecting women (Galligan, 1998: 54). Both AIM and the Rape Crisis Centre were successful in having their demands accepted by policy makers, as each group was closely involved in shaping the detail of legislation relevant to them. The Rape Crisis Centre ran a sustained lobbying campaign between 1981 and 1990 in their attempts to reform the Criminal Law (Rape) Act, 1981. As Galligan notes, 'they presented a case for policy changes to government advisory bodies and to parliamentary committees; raised public awareness of the need to reform the legislation through use of the media; and finally negotiated with the Minister for Justice and government administrators on the reform proposals' (Galligan, 1998: 119). The ultimate result was the passage of the Criminal Law (Rape) (Amendment)

Act, 1990. AIM, for its part, was involved in a number of policy initiatives, most notably in its lobbying over a number of years for the introduction of divorce. As a cause-centred group it also had an input into such legislation as the Family Law (Maintenance of Spouses and Children) Act, 1976, the Family Home Protection Act, 1976 and the Judicial Separation Act, 1987 (Galligan, 1998: 104–5). It is not all a story of success, however, as regards women's interest groups, since they have had little success in the area of employment equality, for instance (Galligan, 1998: 170).

It is important to stress that cause-centred interest group activity in the policy process stretches well beyond the politics of morality. For example, in recent years the question of a rights-based approach to disability has been the central concern of a number of lobby groups. There are a number of organisations working to promote advocacy and a rights-based perspective seeking justice and equality in an inclusive society. In general, these organisations seek to share knowledge about the rights of people with disability and to empower people to engage in advocacy on their own behalf. The disability movement in Ireland has as one of its main aims the move from a charity-based model to a rights-based model. The Disability Federation of Ireland (DFI) is the national umbrella organisation of voluntary disability organisations in Ireland. Its member organisations lobby for and provide services to people with hidden, intellectual, physical and sensory disabilities. DFI currently has over 72 full members that form its national council, and an association with up to 296 voluntary disability-related organisations throughout its regional networks in Ireland. Underpinning the activities of each member organisation is the right of people with disabilities to full and equal citizenship. While the DFI is theoretically a co-ordinating body for the numerous disability organisations, each of these sees itself as promoting different aspects of the same objective. Consequently each looks out for its own interest in terms of lobbying and all seek the receipt of funds, in various guises, from different government departments. DFI also supports the broader voluntary and disability sector through its representation of the disability strand within the Community and Voluntary pillar of the social partnership process, as a social partner at the National Economic and Social Forum, and in other fora at regional, national and European level (www.disability-federation.ie).

Influencing public policy

The question of access is crucial for all interest groups, which pursue their aims and exercise their influence on policy through public or private channels, directly or indirectly. Thus the major sectional economic interests have representatives on the boards of state companies, on various advisory and review bodies, and at the European level. They have adequate resources to carry out their own research and to analyse relevant decisions that might be taken at various levels. They have excellent access to the bureaucracy at both the national and international level and they lobby continuously. As an illustration, we will look at the main sectional interest groups: the IFA, ICTU and IBEC.

The major sectional groups in action

The IFA represents about 85,000 members and is organised into 940 branches countrywide (information from www.ifa.ie). It has over 3,000 elected voluntary officers who work with individual branches to ensure that local views are received by the leadership. In addition the IFA has the back-up and support of 60 staff working at regional and national level. For its members the greatest benefit of the IFA is its strong representative voice on issues of concern to Irish farmers both in Ireland and in Europe. The IFA spends nearly half of its income from farmers every year on its European lobbying efforts and claims that its influence in Europe is far greater than its numerical strength would indicate. This influence is achieved by maintaining a permanent office in Brussels which is manned by the IFA's director of European Affairs who, the IFA maintains, plays a vital role in promoting and defending Irish farmers' interests in Europe and acts as an effective communications link with EU decision makers. The IFA's Brussels office provides advice and research of a technical and political nature, which is vital to IFA representatives when lobbying abroad. It monitors Council of Ministers meetings and EU summits, and gives regular policy briefings to the EU institutions. The IFA has the back-up of 25 expert staff in its head office in Dublin who are well versed in European policy, and it attempts to ensure that all IFA policies are drafted in a manner that commands the support of EU farm organisations across member states as well as being acceptable to the European Commission and the European Parliament.

   The key point about lobbying is that the structures put in place by organisations such as the IFA are of little benefit unless they can be used effectively to influence the decision makers in the government, the EU and agribusiness. Thus, central to any efficient pressure group, including the IFA, is to have good communication links with sympathetic parties. The IFA has both formal and informal links with Fianna Fáil and Fine Gael, at professional and voluntary levels. Indeed, in rural areas almost a third of Fine Gael members also belong to a farming organisation, and most of these are involved in the IFA. The result is that in some areas 'party meetings might look a little like a sub-committee of the local farmers' association meeting' (Gallagher and Marsh, 2002: 66). Such links ensure that when governments change, the organisation's influence on the parties in government is not diminished.

   At local level the IFA uses its voluntary officers and links with individual political parties, whether backbenchers or county councillors, to lobby on various issues, using these political representatives to try to secure its objectives. If this is not enough to deliver its aims, other strategies such as national demonstrations will be considered to keep the pressure on decision makers. Ever since a ground-breaking farmers' march in Dublin in 1966, the IFA has been the foremost interest group engaged in demonstrating outside government offices. Farmers still account for 6 per cent of the total workforce and when mobilised can be a potent force. This was seen to good effect in an IFA march in January 2003 when 1,500 tractors descended on Dublin in a protest over declining farm incomes. The IFA has used other novel tactics such as bringing flocks of sheep into the Department of Agriculture to protest at the low price of lamb in September 1999.

The other main economic interest groups, the trade unions and the business organisations, have similar access to the decision-making process and employ lobbying techniques akin to those of the farming organisations. While the trade union movement was substantially weakened during the early 1980s (Weinz, 1986: 100), its re-emergence as a central player in the social partnership context since 1987 has made it an intrinsic part of the fabric of public policy in Ireland. As a social partner, ICTU has represented unions in the negotiation of national agreements on social and economic issues, as well as on pay and conditions of workers. ICTU is the central authority for the trade union movement in Ireland, with 98 per cent of trade union membership in the country affiliated to it. It has 64 affiliated unions, 48 of them in the Republic where about two-thirds of the membership is based, and its membership is growing. Affiliated membership of ICTU was somewhat below the growth in employment in the Republic up to 2001 but has equalled or exceeded it in 2002 and 2003. According to Congress there are 543,882 members in the Republic of Ireland (www.ictu.ie).

ICTU's main function is to co-ordinate the work of trade unions operating in Ireland and to represent the interests of workers in respect of economic, employment, taxation and social protection issues, especially with government. It is represented on government advisory bodies and it proposes and names representatives of labour for nomination to a number of bodies, such as the Labour Relations Commission and the Labour Court. It furthermore provides information, advice and training to unions and their members, assists with the resolution of disputes between unions and employers, regulates relations between unions, and rules on inter-union disputes. Congress plays a major role, along with the other social partners, in influencing the government's economic and social policies through direct contacts and via the national social partnership process, as we have seen.

The business community is represented through IBEC, which believes that the industry's bargaining position is strengthened through representation of the widest range of members across the fullest range of issues in a single organisation (McCann, 1993: 52). IBEC represents and provides economic, commercial, employee relations and social affairs services to about 7,000 companies and organisations – up from 4,000 since the late 1990s – from all sectors of economic and commercial activity, and is in general the umbrella body for Ireland's leading sectoral groups and associations (www.ibec.ie). To that extent it is the national voice of Irish business and employers. It attempts to shape policies and influence decision making in a way that develops and protects its members' interests and it does this by representing these interests to government, state agencies, trade unions, other national interest groups and the general public. IBEC is also active on the European level, and works through its Brussels office, the Irish Business Bureau, on behalf of business and employers to ensure that European policy is compatible with IBEC's own objectives for the development of the Irish economy. These objectives are to create and sustain a competitive business environment that encourages enterprise and growth.

The access to the structure of decision making that both ICTU and IBEC have gives them powerful leverage in their attempts to protect their members' interests. For instance, the very semblance of a threat from any of the social partners to withdraw from one of the agreements usually precipitates intense discussions to ensure that the demands of the sector are met without jeopardising the remit of the agreements. This, as we have seen (p. 361 above), was the case with the revision of the pay terms of the PPF in December 2000. There is evidence, however, that IBEC is becoming somewhat disenchanted with social partnership. It initially refused to enter into discussions on the renegotiation of the Programme for Prosperity and Fairness arguing that there was no facility for this in the original agreement. IBEC eventually agreed to the additional 5 per cent in pay and gained in return a strengthened 'industrial peace' clause (Roche and Cradden, 2003: 83). After making much noise about not entering into another partnership agreement, IBEC eventually signed up to Sustaining Progress in 2003, but only after gaining agreement that the compliance terms of the pay agreement would be stronger than in PPF and would involve binding arbitration by the Labour Court in certain circumstances.

Policy networks

The policy network theory of interest group behaviour is based on the idea that in the complex policy environment of liberal democracies, 'decision making is rarely limited to key actors in a single organisation; rather it involves bargains and agreements made between actors across many bodies' (Cole and John, 1995: 90). In the Irish case, agricultural policy has been viewed as a network in that the close relationship between the IFA and the Department of Agriculture allows privileged access to one sector of the community and, more importantly, can limit or restrict access to outsiders (Collins, 1993; Adshead, 1996). Moreover while personnel within the network may change positions they rarely move outside its rarefied confines. Over a number of years, for instance, senior policy members of the IFA have been former civil servants dealing with agriculture at both a national and European level, while other IFA members have been co-opted into the Department of Agriculture as special advisers (Collins, 1993: 115). Granting access to organised groups in this way is seen as making the system more effective in supplying public needs, with the result that Irish agricultural policy maintains a stable network capable of limiting access to outsiders (Evans and Coen, 2003: 14). Within this policy network theory, it can be argued that the IFA has had a number of successes. For instance, it was able to insist on a number of compromises in terms of licensing when the Environmental Protection Agency sought to bring agriculture within its regulatory grasp (Taylor, 2001: 75). Likewise, it was able to dilute the impact of the Rural Environment Protection Scheme as an effective instrument for environmental protection by persuading the Minister for Agriculture to halve the rate of inspection (Taylor and Murphy, 2002: 95). Nevertheless, the policy network theory is incomplete as an explanation of interest group relations in Ireland. The IFA has had an input into government policy on agriculture since 1964 (Murphy, 2003b: 110–11). Yet in the 40 years since then, it has as often as not been in conflict with elected governments and has engaged in a number of bitter disputes with the Department of Agriculture. While it might have an inside track, successful influence can never be taken for granted. As one commentator has argued in relation to the organic agriculture industry in the United Kingdom and Ireland, the centrality of governments in policy change remains clear (Greer, 2002: 471).

The pursuit of influence

Interest groups pursue their goals through a number of different channels. These include public and private pressure on government, individual politicians and other interest groups and use of the mass media. Yet despite all the other avenues open to groups it is still the Oireachtas and its members who remain the prime focus, principally because parliament is the centre for information, access and publicity for such groups. TDs have access to insider information, can generate publicity (particularly given the televising of Dáil proceedings), and are in a position to put pressure on governments and individual ministers by tabling parliamentary questions. In fact all the political parties as well as TDs and county councillors report receiving an ever increasing amount of material from interest groups and lobbyists (O'Halpin and Connolly, 1998: 132).

The ability of interest groups to extract concessions from government was evident in the difficulties experienced by the 1973–7 Fine Gael–Labour coalition over its introduction of a wealth tax. This tax was part of Labour's price for participation in government and was one aspect of a wider initiative in tax reform, intended to increase the tax burden on the better off (Sandford and Morrissey, 1985: 61). It was accepted with great reluctance by Fine Gael, as, besides being open to legitimate technical criticism, it was inherently unattractive to most Fine Gael members of the government. With the government fundamentally divided on the issue, the main interest groups involved – the farmers and the business organisations – launched a wave of attacks on the proposal in an attempt to gain concessions for their members (Sandford and Morrissey, 1985: 71–81). The result was that the government came under increasing pressure from a number of directions. The agricultural lobby was represented by about 25 different organisations, which all made detailed submissions to the government and encouraged their members to lobby their local TDs. All these organisations argued that Irish agriculture was under-capitalised and farmers did not have the income to pay the wealth tax (Sandford and Morrissey, 1985: 76). While the agricultural lobby was the most vocal pressure group, the government also came under intense pressure from business interests, with the hotel lobby being particularly outspoken. In reply to this wave of pressure, the government made concessions to the agricultural lobby, the commercial lobby and the tourist lobby with the result that the proposed tax ultimately became 'an ineffectual tax with limited support' and yielded less than a quarter of what had been originally anticipated (Morrissey, 1990: 33–4). The wealth tax suffered its final ignominy when Fianna Fáil abolished it in 1979 after returning to office.

The story of the implementation of residential property tax (RPT) over the course of its existence between 1983 and 1997 was similar. RPT was a self-assessment tax and spent the first ten years of its existence as a rather minor, low-yielding tax. Brought in at the behest of the Labour Party, it did not lead to any real ideological conflict with Fine Gael (Rafter, 2000: 68). In the 1994 budget the Fianna Fáil–Labour coalition government decided to tinker slightly with the tax and raise the levels at which it was payable. The result was a clamour of protest from both the political opposition and more crucially a host of lobby groups including the Construction Industry Federation, the Irish Auctioneers and Valuers Institute, and the tax officials' branch of the Impact trade union. Some lobby groups, such as the Combat Poverty Agency, did advocate tax reform and the extension of property tax but they found themselves left out of the debate, which quickly became very one-sided and dominated by the opponents of RPT. The result was that the 'campaign waged against the 1994 changes to RPT illustrates how a number of lobby groups with media backing can place sustained pressure on policy makers' (Rafter, 2000: 81). In December 1996 RPT was finally abandoned – a victim of interest group pressure as the wealth tax had been two decades earlier.

Cause-centred groups, in their attempts to influence policy, have used a variety of methods to raise public consciousness. Some have run candidates at elections in the hope of having a disproportionate influence on government should their candidate get elected and hold an influential position within parliament. For example, the Roscommon hospital candidate Tom Foxe was elected in Longford–Roscommon in 1989, and he used his pivotal position in the Dáil to secure guarantees concerning the status of Roscommon hospital in exchange for his support in a crucial vote in 1990. Similarly, in 1997 Tom Gildea, running as a television deflector candidate on behalf of a group concerned that their ability to watch British television channels at low cost was under threat, was elected in Donegal South-West (Murphy, 1998: 132). In November 1998 he reached an 'understanding' with the government under which a number of issues in the constituency would receive sympathetic treatment and he announced that he would henceforth support the government. Such cause-centred candidates tend to be at their most influential when they have minority governments looking for their vote. The 2002 general election saw a number of independent hospital candidates elected but with the Fianna Fáil–Progressive Democrat government having a comfortable overall majority, these independent deputies were pretty powerless to influence government health policy.

While cause-centred groups have only recently discovered the advantages of having representatives elected to the Dáil, some of the main sectional interest groups have had links to various political parties going back many years. The Labour Party, indeed, was conceived by the Irish Trades Union Congress in 1912 to act as the political voice of organised labour and came into being in 1922 as a party committed to defending workers' rights. Over the years the trade union movement has played an important financial role within the Labour Party through affiliation fees. The links were strengthened in the early 1960s when the number of unions affiliated to the party increased. In 2003 12 trade unions were officially affiliated to the Labour Party; these included SIPTU (Services, Industrial, Professional and Technical Union) and the Amalgamated Transport and General Workers' Union, which between them account for about 44 per cent of union membership in the Republic. Moreover the trade union movement has long been a breeding ground for politicians on the left, with many Labour TDs, including its current leader Pat Rabbitte, having been trade union officials. However, despite its close ties with the trade union movement, the Labour Party has remained historically weak. Indeed, Fianna Fáil has also had traditionally close links with the organised trade union movement, which has often preferred dealing with Fianna Fáil governments than with coalition governments including a Labour component.

For its part, the Irish Farmers' Association has had links with both Fianna Fáil and Fine Gael. Former Fine Gael leader Alan Dukes was at one stage an economist with the IFA, while Alan Gillis (who was elected as a Fine Gael MEP in 1994) and Paddy Lane (elected as a Fianna Fáil MEP in 1989) were both former leaders of the IFA. In January 2002 another former IFA leader, Tom Parlon, declared that he would stand for the Progressive Democrats in that year's general election, having turned down an invitation from Fine Gael. Parlon went on to take a seat and was appointed a minister of state.

It is also clear that both Fianna Fáil and Fine Gael have received substantial donations from business interests. In its second interim report of September 2002 the Flood tribunal ruled that the former Minister for Foreign Affairs, Justice and Communications, Ray Burke, had received corrupt payments from a succession of builders. It also ruled that Burke, during his time as Minister for Communications in the late 1980s, had made decisions that were not in the public interest after receiving payments from a private radio station's main backer, Oliver Barry (Tribunal of Inquiry, 2002: 65). The link between business contributions to political parties – and by extension to the political process – and favourable treatment for such business interests was proven to Justice Flood's satisfaction. It is important to note, though, that through the duration of the Flood and Moriarty tribunals not one politician has admitted that such a link exists (see Chapter 14).

Private interests and the question of access

A further development in interest group politics has been the growth of professional lobbyists – or public affairs consultants, as they like to be known. The list of lobbyists in Ireland now includes former government press secretaries, former officials of all the major parties, some ex-TDs and a host of former journalists. While these lobbyists originally catered primarily for foreign interests wishing to operate in Ireland, they are now involved in much more mainstream lobbying. Politicians argued that in the past private companies made donations to political parties not for particular purposes but for the access to government that such donations provided. It would appear that companies and others are paying lobbyists for the same purpose, though now on a more formal footing. In general lobbyists claim that what they are doing is providing advice and access to the decision-making process for business people who are ignorant of the public policy process and need a specialist to introduce them to the complex workings of government. Most lobbyists now working in Ireland have long experience of how the political and administrative system works and claim that the people they represent, in practically all cases large business interests, have no idea of how government works.

Lobbyists talk of trying to convince their clients that there is rarely if ever any point in talking to the relevant government minister and that it is more important to talk to the senior civil servant who is handling the specific file. This is where their role is questionable in a parliamentary democracy. While all lobbyists claim that the lobbying system is above board, there are no guidelines governing the interaction between lobbyists and civil servants, who are after all servants of the state and are supposed to offer advice impartially without recourse to any interest group pressure.

In any case, advice from the civil service can be ignored by the minister – as was shown at the beef tribunal in the early 1990s. This tribunal found that Albert Reynolds, as Minister for Industry and Commerce, was legally entitled to make all the decisions he had done in relation to export credit insurance and had done so in good faith. Reynolds, however, through the whole period under investigation by the tribunal had systematically overruled the advice of his senior civil servants in relation to export credit insurance (O'Toole, 1995: 79–85). The tribunal could find no link between such decisions and the relationship between highly powerful beef industry figures and either politicians or political parties in general. What the tribunal did find was that one such beef figure, Larry Goodman, profited from advance business information which he had acquired because he was on the 'inside political track'. Goodman, the tribunal found, 'had reasonably ready access to members of the government . . . for the purpose of discussing his plans for the development of his companies and his exports. It is clear that he had similar access to previous governments' (Collins and O'Raghallaigh, 1995: 706).

The closeness of relations between senior members of various governments and the business community would seem to cast doubt on the view of the majority of lobbyists that dealing with the civil servant, not the minister, is what counts. One Irish lobbyist is convinced that the ear of the minister is the key. He maintains that politicians are swamped with paperwork and that the case has to be made to them in a personal way: 'Our job is to get our client into a position to make their case but at the end of the day the decisions are made by the politicians themselves' (Collins, 1998). While lobbyists deny that it matters who is in power, many major companies are now covering their options by having different lobbyists cover approaches to different political parties; this is now quite easy as there are so many former officials and government press secretaries involved in the lobbying business. Indeed some consultants can even be sitting TDs. In evidence at the Moriarty tribunal in 2003 into the awarding of the state's second mobile phone licences, the entrepreneur Denis O'Brien told the tribunal that he first met Michael Lowry in early 1995, a few months after Lowry was appointed Minister for Transport, Energy and Communications. The tribunal heard that the meeting was organised by the late Jim Mitchell, then a Fine Gael TD, who was acting as a consultant to O'Brien (*Irish Times*, 14 November 2003). The conflicts of interest that have arisen out of the various tribunals led to the Public Relations Institute of Ireland's drafting a code of conduct in 2003 which stated explicitly that TDs should not engage in public affairs consultancy, nor should those employed in the public service or engaged as full-time advisers to government.

It would seem that TDs have taken this on board. The Ethics in Public Office Act, 1995 provided for the first time a register of interests of members of Dáil Éireann. The publication of this register for the period covering February 2002 to January 2003 sheds no light whatsoever on interest group activity in the policy arena. When the first register of interests appeared only one interest group, the Irish Music Rights Organisation, was mentioned as employing three TDs as 'Consultant/Advisers'. However, the register issued in June 2003 shows that not one interest group employed any member of the Oireachtas to lobby on its behalf.

Interest groups and parliament

One very good example of how interest groups lobby parliament, and the Minister for Finance in particular, is in relation to the framing of the annual government budget. The budget is prepared through an elaborate process that starts with the estimates campaign, where each government department submits its proposals for expenditure for the forthcoming year. Parallel to these departmental bids for resources is the process of pre-budget submissions from the social partners and from various interest groups that wish to put their own case to the Department of Finance and the minister. The social partners, as we have seen, have been involved since 1987 in the negotiation of economic governance (Hardiman, 2002) and issue a substantial wish list as part of their budget submission. But a whole host of other groups also prepare detailed pre-budget submissions. There were, for instance, 186 submissions for the 2001 budget (Montague, 2001: 5). These are sent in writing to the Department of Finance, and then some groups are invited to meet the minister and his officials. The minister will have a comprehensive brief prepared by his officials as to the merits or otherwise of the case being made but the exercise is pretty much a one-way street as the organisation makes its case, is listened to and is then sent on its way to be replaced by the next organisation in the queue. Ruairí Quinn, Minister for Finance between December 1994 and June 1997, has commented on the cosmetics of this exercise:

> Pre-budget submissions by the leadership of the organisations were as much an exercise in communicating with their own members as they were an excuse in convincing the Minister for Finance. . . . Pre-budget submissions take up a lot of time of the organisations and the civil servants. The exercise is designed to keep the members of organisations content in the belief that their executive and secretariat are representing their interests effectively. In other cases it is for the optics of the wider public. It is not transparent, nor is it accountable to democratic institutions.
>
> (*Irish Times*, 25 November 2002)

Quinn abolished this system in 1995 and replaced it with one where all pre-budget submissions were not just sent to the Department of Finance but were also referred to the Finance Committee of the Oireachtas, whose members could meet in public session with the organisations. This was to enable public representatives to question the lobby groups as to why special concessions should be made to them. Some lobby groups opposed this measure, and Quinn's successor, Charlie McCreevy, reverted to the traditional system. The demands of groups can vary widely, with some groups seeking up to 100 concessions and others making just one specific demand. There is evidence to suggest that those who lobby for a specific demand are much more likely to succeed in influencing the minister and the department than those who have an excessively long wish list, with Ruairí Quinn maintaining that a bullet is preferable to a shotgun approach. As examples he points out that successful approaches to the department during his tenure as minister included the Small Firms Association's proposals to cut corporation tax and the Society of the Irish Motor Industry's car scrappage scheme proposal. The shotgun approach was typified by the IFA 'with their 57 varieties of issues, with no political benefits for the government' (Montague, 2001: 33).

The committee system of the Oireachtas has also increasingly become a forum for interest groups to articulate their concerns to the legislature. While Oireachtas committees have had a patchy record over the past two decades (see Chapter 8), they have at least provided an avenue for interest groups to attempt to influence public policy. The Joint Committee on Small Businesses, for example, which sat from 1983 to 1987 and produced 68 reports in all, most of which were mere wish lists for small business, was largely dependent on research support and topics for inquiry on a unit of the Confederation of Irish Industry (O'Halpin and Connolly, 1998: 133). The committee system is useful as a conduit between the Oireachtas and various interest groups. The practice of Oireachtas committees in receiving representations from interest groups provides what could be seen as a valuable forum for such groups to air their grievances, but this should be tempered with a word of warning. As O'Halpin and Connolly point out:

> Given the shortage of research and administrative support for Oireachtas committees of all kinds, it is probable that they will remain exceedingly soft targets for any coherent pressure group, however selective its data or outlandish its case, wishing to set the agenda and to influence thinking and ultimately policy.
>
> (O'Halpin and Connolly, 1998: 133)

While this is substantively true, it should be said that when interest groups operate officially through such committees, and through government channels in general, this would seem to be a far more open and accountable way of influencing government than the lobbying of individual ministers and senior civil servants, which, as we have seen, is becoming increasingly prevalent in Ireland today.

Interest group activity assessed

A strong case can be made for or against the involvement of interest groups in the policy process. Realistically, interest groups are certain to be involved, but we can identify the advantages and disadvantages this entails (see Box 13.2).

***Box 13.2* The benefits and disadvantages of interest group activities**

Andrew Heywood (2002: 277) summarises the balance sheet as follows.

On the positive side, interest groups may:

- provide some kind of check on government power; they help to ensure that the state is balanced by a vigorous and healthy civil society;
- strengthen representation by articulating interests and advancing views that may be overlooked by political parties;
- provide an alternative to conventional party politics and offer opportunities for grassroots activism;
- maintain political stability by constituting an additional channel of communication between government and the people;
- promote debate and discussion by creating a better informed and more educated electorate.

On the negative side, interest groups may:

- exercise non-legitimate power, in that their leaders, unlike politicians, are not publicly accountable and their influence bypasses the representative process;
- be divisive, given that they advance minority interests against those of society as a whole;
- entrench political inequality by strengthening the voice of the wealthy and privileged in particular;
- create an array of vested interests that are able to block government initiatives and make policy unworkable;
- make the policy process closed and secretive by exerting influence through negotiation and deals that are not subject to public scrutiny.

In an Irish context, one can find numerous examples to exemplify both the benefits and the dangers. In the 1980s, many interest groups were criticised for looking for ever more resources from the overstretched state. A former secretary of the Department of Finance complained that such behaviour by sectional groups over a number of years had had disastrous consequences for the national finances (Doyle, 1987: 72). Similar criticisms were echoed by those in the private sector over the trade unions' demands during the so-called benchmarking process of linking public sector pay in the early 2000s. Regarding cause-centred groups, the level of influence some groups can have on governments, while other groups and even parliament are excluded from major policy-making decisions, can be seen as detrimental. As one commentator pointed out regarding the 1991 Maastricht protocol decision (O'Reilly, 1992: 139):

> The key issue here of course was that such a private debate should ever have been conducted by the government with the non-elected lobbyists. What right did they have to make demands and seek consultations when the elected representatives of the people, the opposition parties, did not even know what was going on?

There can be little doubt, however, that interest groups have also played a beneficial role in Irish politics and society. The Irish National Organisation of the Unemployed, for instance, has filled an important gap in representing the unemployed, a group that for many years did not have a formal voice in relation to policy making. Likewise, as we have seen, there are now many groups representing people with disabilities who for so long were marginalised in Irish society. As for the main sectional interests, while they have often been criticised by outsiders and indeed by each other, there is no doubt that they play an important role as a conduit to government for their members, who otherwise would not have any ready access to the decision-making process. Moreover, cause-centred groups, through their efforts in consciousness raising, create a better informed electorate. In this way interest group behaviour may benefit society generally, not just the membership of the organisations themselves.

Conclusion

Is there a specific model of interest group activity that is applicable to Ireland today? As far back as 1986, Regan and Wilson came to the conclusion that interest group activity in Ireland was neither corporatist nor pluralist and argued that a new theory had to accommodate the continuation of both corporatist and pluralist features, while allowing for practices and structures that groups and governments might evolve as part of the policy-making debate (Regan and Wilson, 1986: 410). Recent research into Irish organised interests in the sphere of privatisation has argued that different patterns of such organised interests may co-exist in different areas of economic policy because of the varying institutional dynamics in a polity over time (Chari and McMahon, 2003: 30–1). In the decade after 1987, the year when the Programme for National Recovery was launched, interest group activity in Ireland attained centre stage with the tripartite agreements of the 1990s cementing social partnership. With the implementation of Partnership 2000, with its unique social pillar, and the continuation of this structure in both the Programme for Prosperity and Fairness and Sustaining Progress, the number of interest groups associating with government has grown quite substantially.

Given the various definitions of interest group involvement in the policy process, it would seem that all countries in western Europe are nationally specific, with none of them fitting any model of interest group activity precisely. Some countries, such as Austria, tend more towards corporatist ideas of policy making, and others, such as Britain, towards more pluralistic versions. In 1999 Ireland was ranked twelfth out of 18 European democracies in terms of how close it was to the idealised model of the corporate state (Siaroff, 1999: 198). This particular study argued that within Europe there were three major corporatist countries: Austria, Norway and Sweden. These were followed by countries that were ranked as moderately corporatist – including the Netherlands, Germany, Denmark and Switzerland at the more corporatist end and Luxembourg, Iceland and Belgium at the less corporatist end. Then there were countries that were described as hardly corporatist at all, which included Ireland, France and Britain; these were followed in turn by Portugal, Italy, Spain and Greece, which ranked lowest of all. Yet from the evidence we have presented it seems that Ireland is far more corporatist than Siaroff allows for and can in no way be categorised as similar to Britain. It appears from Siaroff's evidence that those countries with a dominant left or social democratic control of government in the post-war era are more likely to be corporatist in orientation. The outlier to this is the Netherlands where Christian democracy held sway in this time period and as such the Netherlands resembles some of the more moderately corporatist countries such as Germany, Switzerland and Belgium (Gallagher *et al.*, 2001: 401–2).

While Ireland records the lowest levels of support for left-wing parties in western Europe (see Chapter 5), the reality is that Fianna Fáil has since its inception attracted votes from across the political spectrum and has been particularly successful in gaining working class support (see Chapter 7). In the 2002 election, for instance, 44 per cent of those voters classified as working class voted for Fianna Fáil while only 12 per cent voted Labour (Garry *et al.*, 2003: 131). In the light of this evidence it is much more appropriate to classify Ireland as at least part of the moderate group of corporatist countries, while the weakness of the left in Ireland tells us little in terms of whether Ireland is corporatist or not. From the mid-1980s major sectional interest groups gained access to government and an input into public policy that brought the political process to a position where social partnership was seen as the sole route to economic success and social inclusiveness. While Ireland has seen a comprehensive role for the social partners since 1987, Partnership 2000 came under a variety of strains as individual interests pressed their claims on the government in a way that was practically pluralistic. Moreover the PPF had to be renegotiated half way through, such were the pay demands of the unions. In that context Sustaining Progress was in severe danger of never seeing the light of day.

Ireland finds itself now very much in the mainstream of western European politics in relation to interest group influence, which has witnessed a blurring of the distinction between corporatist and pluralist models of group behaviour. It is pretty much redundant to ask whether a particular system is corporatist or pluralist, as behaviour is now more concentrated on policy making within particular sectors (Gallagher *et al.*, 2001: 420). Corporatists see this as sectoral corporatism while pluralists distinguish between sectors characterised by particular policy networks. Such networks can include some groups and exclude others or be more traditionally competitive in terms of pluralist competition between groups. It is within these parameters that interest group activity finds itself in Ireland today. This activity continues to grow and is likely to expand even further in the future.

It is thus likely that the Oireachtas and its members will remain the central focus of attention for those who want to influence public policy. From the evidence presented in this chapter we can safely say that interest group activity has been increasing in contemporary Ireland. The Oireachtas itself is aware of the phenomenon. In 1999 its Public Accounts Committee sub-committee on certain revenue matters while investigating the evasion of DIRT tax found that there was a particularly close and inappropriate relationship between banking interests and government: '[t]he evidence suggests that the State and its Agencies were perhaps too mindful of the concerns of the banks, and too attentive to their pleas and lobbying' (Committee of Public Accounts, 1999: 5). This gives certain credence to the view that those groups with money can be a corrosive influence on the body politic. It is clearly a political truism that those with more money can wield more influence and to that extent interest group activity in Ireland remains both deeply uneven and problematic.

Note

1 I am grateful to Fiachra Kennedy of the Institute for the Study of Social Change at UCD for providing me with these data.

References and further reading

Adshead, Maura, 1996. 'Beyond clientelism: agricultural networks in Ireland and the EU', *West European Politics* 19:3: 583–608.
Allen, Kieran, 2000. *The Celtic Tiger: The Myth of Social Partnership in Ireland*. Manchester: Manchester University Press.
Aspinwall, Mark and Justin Greenwood, 1998. 'Conceptualising collective interest in the European Union: an introduction', in Justin Greenwood and Mark Aspinwall (eds), *Collective Action in the European Union: Interests and the New Politics of Associability*. London: Routledge, pp. 1–30.
Budge, Ian, Kenneth Newton *et al.*, 1997. *The Politics of the New Europe: Atlantic to Urals*. London: Longman.
Cawson, Alan (ed.), 1985. *Organised Interests and the State: Studies in Meso-Corporatism*. London: Sage.
Cawson, Alan, 1986. *Corporatism and Political Theory*. Oxford: Basil Blackwell.

Chari, Raj and Hilary McMahon, 2003. 'Reconsidering the patterns of organised interests in Irish policy making', *Irish Political Studies* 18:1: 37–50.

Cole, Alistair and Peter John, 1995. 'Local policy networks in France and Britain: policy co-ordination in fragmented political sub-systems', *West European Politics* 18:4: 89–109.

Collins, Neil, 1993. 'Still recognisably pluralist? State–farmer relations in Ireland', in Ronald J. Hill and Michael Marsh (eds), *Modern Irish Democracy: Essays in Honour of Basil Chubb*. Dublin: Irish Academic Press, pp. 104–22.

Collins, Neil and Colm O'Raghallaigh, 1995. 'Political sleaze in the Republic of Ireland', *Parliamentary Affairs* 48:4: 697–710.

Collins, Stephen, 1998. 'Do you want your old lobby washed down, sunshine?', *Sunday Tribune*, 12 July.

Committee of Public Accounts, Sub-committee on Certain Revenue Matters, 1999. *Parliamentary Inquiry into DIRT: First Report*, Dublin: Stationery Office.

Department of the Taoiseach, 2003. *Sustaining Progress: Social Partnership Agreement 2003–2005*. Dublin: Stationery Office.

Doyle, Maurice, 1987. 'Comment', in Sean Cromien and Aidan Pender (eds), *Managing Public Money*. Dublin: Institute of Public Administration, pp. 71–6.

Ethics in Public Office Act, 2003. *Register of Interests of Members of Dáil Éireann, 1 February, 2002 to 31 January, 2003*. Dublin: Houses of the Oireachtas.

Evans, Mark and Liam Coen, 2003. 'Elitism and agri-environmental policy in Ireland', in Maura Adshead and Michelle Millar (eds), *Public Administration and Public Policy in Ireland: Theory and Methods*. London: Routledge, pp. 1–19.

Gallagher, Michael and Michael Marsh, 2002. *Days of Blue Loyalty: The Politics of Membership of the Fine Gael Party*. Dublin: PSAI Press.

Gallagher, Michael, Michael Laver and Peter Mair, 2001. *Representative Government in Modern Europe: Institutions, Parties and Governments*, 3rd edn. New York: McGraw-Hill.

Galligan, Yvonne, 1998. *Women and Politics in Contemporary Ireland: From the Margins to the Mainstream*. London: Pinter.

Garry, John, Fiachra Kennedy, Michael Marsh and Richard Sinnott, 2003. 'What decided the election?', in Michael Gallagher, Michael Marsh and Paul Mitchell (eds), *How Ireland Voted 2002*. Basingstoke: Palgrave Macmillan, pp. 119–42.

Girvin, Brian, 1986. 'Social change and moral politics: the Irish constitutional referendum 1983', *Political Studies* 34:1: 61–81.

Girvin, Brian, 1996. 'The Irish divorce referendum, November 1995', *Irish Political Studies* 11: 74–81.

Greer, Alan, 2002. 'Policy networks and policy change in organic agriculture: a comparative analysis of the UK and Ireland', *Public Administration* 80:3: 453–73.

Hardiman, Niamh, 1988. *Pay, Politics and Economic Performance in Ireland 1970–1987*. Oxford: Clarendon Press.

Hardiman, Niamh, 2002. 'From conflict to co-ordination: economic governance and political innovation in Ireland', *West European Politics* 25:4: 1–24.

Heisler, Martin O. and Robert B. Kvavik, 1974. 'Patterns of European politics: the European polity', in Martin O. Heisler (ed.), *Politics in Europe: Structures and Processes in Some Post Industrial Democracies*. New York: David McKay and Co.

Heywood, Andrew, 2002. *Politics*, 2nd edn. Basingstoke: Palgrave.

Horgan, John, 1997. *Seán Lemass: The Enigmatic Patriot*. Dublin: Gill and Macmillan.

Institute of Public Administration, 2003. *Administration Yearbook and Diary, 2003.* Dublin: Institute of Public Administration.

Kimber, Richard and Jeremy J. Richardson (eds), 1974. *Pressure Groups in Britain.* London: Dent.

McCann, Dermot, 1993. 'Business power and collective action: the state and the Confederation of Irish Industry 1970–1990', *Irish Political Studies* 8: 37–53.

Montague, Pat, 2001. 'Persuasive influence: an assessment of how Irish groups campaign around the budget'. Unpublished MA thesis, School of Communications, Dublin City University.

Morrissey, Oliver, 1990. 'Scanning the alternatives before taxing with consensus: lessons for policy making from the Irish wealth tax', *Administration* 38:1: 21–40.

Murphy, Gary, 1998. 'The 1997 general election in the Republic of Ireland', *Irish Political Studies* 13: 127–34.

Murphy, Gary, 2003a. *Economic Realignment and the Politics of EEC Entry, Ireland 1948–1972.* Washington, DC: Maunsel.

Murphy, Gary, 2003b. 'Towards a corporate state? Seán Lemass and the realignment of interest groups in the policy process 1948–1964', *Administration*, 51:1–2: 105–18.

Murphy, Gary, 2003c. 'Pluralism and the politics of morality', in Maura Adshead and Michelle Millar (eds), *Public Administration and Public Policy in Ireland: Theory and Methods.* London: Routledge, pp. 20–36.

NESC, 1986. *A Strategy for Development, 1986–1990.* Dublin: National Economic and Social Council, Report No. 83.

Neville, Pat, 1990. 'The 1989 general election in the Republic of Ireland', *Irish Political Studies* 5: 69–76.

O'Donnell, Rory and Damian Thomas, 1998. 'Partnership and policy making', in Seán Healy and Brigid Reynolds (eds), *Social Policy in Ireland: Principles, Practice and Problems.* Dublin: Oak Tree Press, pp. 117–46.

O'Donnell, Rory and Colm O'Reardon, 2000. 'Social partnership in Ireland's economic transformation', in Giuseppe Fajertag and Philippe Pochet (eds), *Social Pacts in Europe: New Dynamics.* Brussels: European Trade Union Institute, pp. 237–57.

O'Halpin, Eunan and Eileen Connolly, 1998. 'Parliaments and pressure groups: the Irish experience of change', in Philip Norton (ed.), *Parliaments and Pressure Groups in Western Europe.* London: Frank Cass, pp. 124–44.

O'Reilly, Emily, 1992. *Masterminds of the Right.* Dublin: Attic Press.

O'Toole, Fintan, 1995. *Meanwhile Back at the Ranch: The Politics of Irish Beef.* London: Vintage.

Punnett, R.M., 1994. *British Government and Politics*, 6th edn. Aldershot: Dartmouth.

Quinn, Ruairí, 2002. 'Pre-budget submission system needs an overhaul', *Irish Times*, 25 November.

Rafter, Kevin, 2000. 'Making it up as they went along: Residential Property Tax and the process of policy change', *Irish Political Studies* 15: 63–82.

Regan, Marguerite C. and Frank L. Wilson, 1986. 'Interest-group politics in France and Ireland: comparative perspectives on neo-corporatism', *West European Politics* 9:3: 393–413.

Richardson, Jeremy J. (ed.), 1993. *Pressure Groups.* Oxford: Oxford University Press.

Roche, William K. and Terry Cradden, 2003. 'Neo-corporatism and social partnership', in Maura Adshead and Michelle Millar (eds), *Public Administration and Public Policy in Ireland: Theory and Methods*. London: Routledge, pp. 69–87.

Sandford, Cedric and Oliver Morrissey, 1985. *The Irish Wealth Tax: a Case Study in Economics and Politics*. Dublin: Economic and Social Institute, ESRI paper 123.

Schmitter, Philippe C., 1974. 'Still the century of corporatism?', *Review of Politics* 36: 85–131.

Siaroff, Alan, 1999. 'Corporatism in 24 industrial democracies: meaning and measurement', *European Journal of Political Research* 36:6: 175–205.

Taylor, George, 2001. *Conserving the Emerald Tiger: the Politics of Environmental Regulation*. Galway: Arlen Press House.

Taylor, George and Cathi Murphy, 2002. 'Environmental policy in Ireland', in George Taylor (ed.), *Issues in Irish Public Policy*. Dublin: Irish Academic Press, pp. 88–98.

Therborn, Goran, 1995. *European Modernity and Beyond: The Trajectory of European Societies 1945–2000*. London: Sage.

Tribunal of Inquiry, 2002. *The Second Interim Report of the Tribunal of Inquiry into certain planning matters and payments*. Dublin: Stationery Office [this tribunal was chaired by Mr Justice Flood].

Weinz, Wolfgang, 1986. 'Economic development and interest groups', in Brian Girvin and Roland Sturm (eds), *Politics and Society in Contemporary Ireland*. Aldershot: Gower, pp. 87–101.

Wilson, Graham K., 1991. *Interest Groups*. Oxford: Basil Blackwell.

Websites

www.nesf.ie   National Economic and Social Forum.

www.ictu.ie   Irish Congress of Trade Unions.

www.ibec.ie   Irish Business and Employers Confederation.

www.ifa.ie   Irish Farmers' Association.

14 Multi-level governance

Neil Collins and Aodh Quinlivan

For many people, the idea of politics may suggest the endless theatre of politicians, journalists, judges and activists that compete with the 'soaps' and with sport for our attention on the television and in the newspapers. Another way to experience politics, however, is to suffer the delays caused by new road projects or under-invested railways, to enjoy subsidised theatre or public parks or to seek permission to build or extend a house. In other words, politics is about almost every aspect of life where public agencies provide benefits, impose duties or redistribute resources from some citizens to others through taxes and other charges. In this political process, the government, parliament and bureaucracy in Dublin described in the previous chapters of this book are an important factor. But government at the state level is only part of the story. The everyday pattern of public provision is the responsibility of many other agencies, few of which feature in the model of politics as a daily drama. Some of the complexity of everyday politics, and the traditional political science question of 'who gets what, when and how', is captured in the phrase 'multi-level governance'. This expression is used in the present chapter to capture some of the growing intricacy that marks the way politics in the form of public services is delivered, particularly by public bodies outside the central government.

The chapter begins with a discussion of the concept of multi-level governance and its implications for political life. The next section examines the development of local government in the Republic and discusses the impact of its increasing complexity. Similarly, the changing contribution of the state-sponsored sector is discussed in the light of new approaches to public sector service delivery. Finally, the chapter focuses on the ever more vexed issue of public accountability in the context of multi-level governance.

The concept of multi-level governance

The term 'governance' has established itself in many fields of activity. For example, reference is frequently made to 'global governance' or 'corporate governance'. The easiest way to define the concept in this broad sense is the capacity of a social system to steer or control events. It is much broader than the term 'government', though the traditional institutions of central and local government are included. As Hughes (2003: 76) explains, 'government is the institution itself, where governance is a broader concept describing forms of governing which are not necessarily in the hands of the formal government'. As with such vogue terms generally, the literature on governance is rather diverse and complex, and much of it is based on detailed case studies of individual policy areas that can result in insights related to that field, but leave the rest of the world out of sight. Fortunately, Hooghe and Marks (2003) have provided us with a useful and simple twofold typology of governance that will help structure the discussion here and facilitate easier comparison of the Republic of Ireland with other jurisdictions. Though they do not label their categories, we refer to them here as 'structured' and 'flexible'. These terms indicate the main differences and, in a broad sense, suggest the trend, i.e. for governmental structures to become less rigid:

Type I: structured

- sub-central government is multipurpose;
- memberships of sub-central bodies do not overlap;
- there is a defined number of levels of authority;
- the whole system follows one uniform design.

This type is easily recognisable in Ireland and is exemplified by the county and city councils that have been largely unchanged in their spatial form since 1898. The county in particular has become the focus of sporting, cultural and social loyalty.

Type II: flexible

- individual agencies are task-specific;
- these agencies have overlapping memberships;
- their remit does not coincide with other boundaries;
- there are several types of agency with different structures.

Type II may seem unnecessarily complex but it increasingly describes a pattern found in western liberal democracies. In Ireland, for example, the urban planning function is shared by a variety of agencies focusing on transport, housing, educational provision and all the other interrelated features of life in towns and cities. Some of these bodies are traditional local authorities or sections of government departments but others are pressure groups, single-purpose agencies or public and private enterprises. The exact pattern of such bodies varies greatly as the demands of policy change.

The idea that governance is multi-level is suggested by the observation that every citizen's life is affected by global, regional, national and local organisations. In Ireland, these might include supra-national bodies such as

the World Trade Organisation and the EU as well as government departments. Similarly, multi-level governance extends to local authorities, health
boards and those voluntary groups to which the delivery of many important
personal services are devolved. It also emphasises both formal and informal
interactions between actors at various levels of government. Keating and
Hooghe (2001: 242) refer to the process of multi-level governance as having
emerged due to the parallel processes of Europeanisation and region-
alisation, thus creating new political arenas and frameworks for economic
activity. Chapter 16 looks in some detail at EU organisation; the focus here,
therefore, is on sub-national agencies. It is worth noting, however, that at
EU level the debate on multi-level governance is couched in comparable
terms. Are similar procedures and laws (the so-called *acquis communautaire*) to
apply everywhere or should the European project allow multiple regimes in
different policy areas ('variable geometry')?

The efficiency and accessibility of local councils, health boards and the
local offices of government departments dealing with employment or social
welfare have always been important to the quality of everyday life. The
term multi-level governance, however, alerts us to a new complexity in how
services are delivered. All over the world governments are questioning the
idea that they need to meet social needs directly through traditional public
agencies. They are adopting the idea of 'steering not rowing'. This phrase
was coined by the American authors Osborne and Gaebler (1992) who urged
governments to get things done by working through other social actors
including markets, hierarchies and networks. Government may still be the
most important provider of services but by no means the exclusive provider.
Ironically, this is a pattern with which Ireland is familiar because education,
health and social services were to a significant degree delivered by religious
communities and others on behalf of the state for many years. Similarly,
professional bodies, farm unions and chambers of commerce have all co-
operated in implementing state policies in their own spheres in exchange for
an important influence on policy direction in particular areas.

While the EU has become more influential in Ireland, some powers have
also been transferred from Dublin to sub-national levels. This has not
always been obvious because of a growing mismatch between the units to
which citizens feel loyalty, such as counties, and the way in which services
are organised. The economics of waste management, health and hospital
services and of transport and road development, for example, dictate
different ways of providing services that were once more obviously 'local'.
This has caused a certain amount of confusion and unease. Issues such as
these have become the basis of new pressure group campaigns, some of
which have led to the election of single-issue independent TDs. At the same
time, local politicians have had their influence on such issues reduced. As
multi-level governance theorists might express the problem, there is a tension between efficient service delivery and political legitimacy.

Multi-level governance is a feature of the two jurisdictions in Ireland, both separately and, since the Good Friday Agreement, together. New cross-border agencies, all-Ireland forums and links between Britain and Ireland have, to use Carmichael's (2002) characterisation, made governance arrangements 'messy', or less straightforward than they used to be. In the Republic, however, there is an additional complexity in the transfer to all levels of institution of the idea of 'social partnership', which has been credited with sustaining economic and social progress at the centre. Social partnership, as currently practised, began in 1987 when the 'social partners' agreed the *Programme for National Recovery* (see Chapter 13). Although social partnership now covers social and other issues, this first agreement was largely about wage restraint. By the time the *Partnership 2000* agreement was negotiated in 1997, partnership at all levels was being urged. This found concrete form in different local government arrangements that, as will be outlined below, challenged the existing structures of local government.

Local government

Local government in the Republic of Ireland is organised on the basis of a three-tiered system. Eight regional authorities play a monitoring role with regard to the use of European Union structural funds and also co-ordinate some of the activities of sub-county authorities. At county and city level there are 34 local authorities.[1] These comprise five city councils and 29 county councils which have an equal standing and which cover the entire land area and population of the state. The cities and counties are regarded as the primary units of local government in Ireland and the mainline providers of services. At sub-county level, a network of 80 town authorities carry out a representational role for urban areas with a varying range of local government functions.

Structures of local government

Each of the areas specified above (cities, counties, boroughs and towns) has its own local authority as elected by the local population. Elections for the local authorities are held every five years, by virtue of Article 28A of the constitution, enacted in 1999. Membership is open to persons aged 18 years or over, although there are some excluded categories, including members of the European Parliament and members of the national parliament (Dáil Éireann and Seanad Éireann) – in other words, a 'dual mandate' is now prohibited.[2] Elections are undertaken by means of proportional representation with the single transferable vote, as in the case of Dáil elections.

The results of local elections since 1967 (see Appendix 2e) highlight a certain political stability in Irish local government. The 1999 local elections saw a consolidation of the position of the two main parties, Fianna Fáil and

Fine Gael, and reproduced the traditional occupational backgrounds of councillors, with a heavy representation of such groups as teachers and farmers. Local elections are often treated by voters as an opportunity to give the government of the day a mid-term shock. That pattern was broken in 1999, when Fianna Fáil had a good result (Kenny, 1999: 21), but was re-affirmed in 2004, when Fianna Fáil support dropped to its lowest ever level (see Appendix 2f). While the main political parties vigorously contest elections at local level, Gallagher (1989: 28) and Coakley (2001: 86) note that non-party and independent candidates tend to do relatively well. In all, 90 independents were elected to city and county councils in 2004.

The current system of proportional representation for local elections has been in place since 1919, and local elections have been held at fairly regular intervals since the foundation of the state (see Chapter 1, p. 31). All residents aged 18 or more are eligible to vote, but there was an obvious downward trend in turnout figures for local elections over the 1967–99 period (though turnout increased in 2004). Kenny (2003: 107) notes that 'in the space of one generation public participation at local government elections declined by one-fifth'. An urban–rural divide in turnout levels has for long been clear, with voters in the larger cities turning out at the polls in significantly lower numbers than their rural counterparts (Kenny, 2003: 108). In Dublin, some areas do not even register a 30 per cent turnout.

Each council elects its own chief official. A lord mayor is elected on an annual basis in Cork and Dublin, and a mayor in the other city councils and in borough councils. The offices of lord mayor in Cork and Dublin enjoy a high prestige but, in reality, the positions are largely ceremonial. A 'chairman' or *cathaoirleach* is elected to the county councils and town councils, although the Local Government Act, 2001 allowed counties and towns to adopt the title 'mayor' for this post, and some have done this. The same act also provided for modest 'representational payments' to be paid to elected members. The sum for city and county councillors is based on one-quarter of the annual salary of a member of the Seanad.

Functions of local government

In comparison with other EU states, Ireland has a weak system of local government due to strict central control, a lack of financial independence and a narrow functional range (Daemen and Schaap, 2000). The functions of the local authorities are classified into eight programme groups in the Public Bodies (Amendment) Order, 1975, as follows:

- housing and building;
- road transportation and safety;
- water supply and sewerage;
- development incentives and control;

- environmental protection;
- recreation and amenity;
- agriculture, education, health and welfare;
- miscellaneous.

Roche (1982) states that this range of functions has emerged through a combination of history, accident and attachment to tradition. By international standards, the functions and powers of local authorities in Ireland are narrow. In fact, the sparse allocation of functions and powers to local authorities is one of the distinguishing features of the Irish administrative system. Daemen and Schaap (2000: 61) highlight this in their comparative study of 15 local democracies in Europe. They express surprise that Irish local authorities 'carry no responsibility for such areas as education, health, civic defence, and social welfare'.

One of the other defining characteristics of Irish local government is city and county management. In 1922 the new Irish Free State government created the Ministry of Local Government and the first legislative measure of the new parliament was the Local Government (Temporary Provisions) Act, 1923, which provided for the dissolution of local authorities that were not performing their functions and their replacement by commissioners. Commentators such as Roche and Barrington have cited this particular piece of legislation as influential in the creation of a centralised mentality. It should be observed, however, that Ireland at that time had been through a period of enormous turbulence, with the war of independence followed by a bitter civil war. A tight rein with strict centralised control was deemed appropriate for a small and troubled state with a new government seeking authority and respect. Ewen (1992: 5–6) comments:

> It was important for the new government to obtain order and discipline. It had taken over Ireland on behalf of the people and it had to show it was capable of running the country. The ministers were more committed to restoring order, achieving efficiency and putting an end to suggestions of local corruption and abuse than they were to local democracy. . . . These actions must be seen against the background of the time and understood as those coming from men of idealistic, often austere views who had been through a revolutionary experience and were progressing towards achieving independence after many attempts over the centuries.

Essentially, the needs of the time ensured a substantial intrusion by the central administration into local government, and centralism became an accepted facet of government in Ireland. In many ways, the new regime simply reinforced the centralism of the British authorities from which it took over the business of governing.

The management system

Since 1923 the system of local government in Ireland has developed at a leisurely pace, and the basic structures have remained virtually unaltered, save for the abolition of rural district councils in 1925 (these bodies had been created in 1898; see Chapter 1, p. 9). The distinctive management system has been the most significant advance, with Lyons (1973) claiming of the new Free State administration that much of its maturity and competence was owed to the 'managerial revolution' in local government. The management system emerged following the regular use of the power of dissolution. Roche notes (1982: 53) that 'the power of dissolution was used freely at first, and with breathtaking disregard of the antiquity and prestige of the victims. Whether dissolution was a deserved or appropriate fate is debatable, but the surprising thing was the quiet acquiescence of the citizens in these violent assaults on their civic privileges, such as they were'.

Within the first three years of the 1923 Act, 23 bodies were dissolved and replaced by commissioners. The Kerry and Leitrim county councils have the dubious distinction of being the first two authorities to be dissolved in May 1923, while the corporations in Dublin (May 1924) and Cork (October 1924) were other famous victims. The dissolution mechanism was originally designed as a temporary punitive measure to punish troublesome local authorities. However, the appointed commissioners who replaced the elected officials soon began to have a positive influence on local administration. Their reliability and administrative competence (the early commissioners were senior civil servants from the Department of Local Government) earned them praise and respect from both central government and the local electorate. The concept developed, and a strong supporting lobby group emerged in Cork city, with commercial and industrial interests to the fore. Despite strong opposition from councillors, the Cork City Management Act, 1929 was passed, and provided for a permanent official sharing power with (rather than replacing) the elected representatives. Dublin and Dun Laoghaire (1930), Limerick (1934) and Waterford (1939) adopted the Cork model and the system was finally extended to the entire country with the County Management Act, 1940. To the present day, it is this power-sharing relationship between management and elected members that is at the heart of understanding local government in Ireland.

The law regulating the management system recognises reserved functions (the responsibility of the elected members) and executive functions (the responsibility of the manager). Reserved functions tend to be in the policy domain, with executive functions concerned with day-to-day administration. These functions are carried out by means of a written manager's order and include decisions in relation to staff, fixing rent, acceptance of tenders and decisions on planning applications. In reality, as the system has evolved, the distinction between executive and reserved functions has become blurred. For example, it is primarily the manager, through his senior officials, who initiates new policies and is seen as 'the powerhouse of local government' (Chubb, 1970: 286). Local authorities throughout the country operate by means of a partnership arrangement between elected representatives and management. The quality of this relationship holds the key to the efficiency and effectiveness of the local authority. It is therefore appropriate to ask whether the management system in Irish local government can be deemed a success when there is a 'universally acknowledged discrepancy between what we read in the City and County Management Acts and what actually happens' (Roche, 1982: 113).

Reform and modernisation

By the 1940s, according to Barrington (1991: 157), 'intense centralisation and general subordination to central government' were the dominant themes, and the next two decades were largely uneventful ones in the local government arena. The 1960s brought prosperity and optimism on the back of the 1958 Programme for Economic Expansion (the first national strategy in Ireland and the first attempt at economic planning). The positive mood was reflected by the Local Government (Planning and Development) Act, 1963 which envisaged local authorities expanding their roles into 'development corporations'. The optimism soon dissipated and the potential of local government at this time was never realised, partly because 'arteries had grown too hard and bureaucratic sclerosis had become too far advanced' (Barrington, 1991: 158). The following decade saw local authorities relieved of their health functions and also of financial independence, in a process described as follows: 'in a disgraceful political auction between the two main national political parties, rates on domestic dwellings were abolished in 1977, on the premise of meeting the cost from the Exchequer, itself in heavy and rapidly increasing deficit' (Barrington, 1991: 160).

Rates on agricultural land were subsequently removed in 1982 following a High Court case (as upheld on appeal by the Supreme Court in 1984) which ruled that the use of the valuation system as a basis for levying rates was unconstitutional. The loss of rates revenue as an independent source of finance has severely restricted local authorities to the present time. The 1990s saw various reform efforts, with minimal impact on the overall structure or operation of the local government system. The Local Government Act, 1991 relaxed the *ultra vires* doctrine (which stated that a local authority had to be able to adduce legal authority for its actions) and enhanced the socio-economic role of the authorities. This legislation also paved the way for the establishment of eight regional authorities with responsibility for the co-ordination of local authority activity.

Another significant issue is the increasingly influential relationship between the European Union and sub-national government in Ireland. Links between the local and EU levels are increasing and are likely to continue to do so in a more direct way than was previously the case when everything was channelled through central government. Callanan (2003a: 428) explains that: 'A situation is evolving of complex structures of multi-layered governance with European, national and local actors all playing a part. Increasingly, networks are evolving to solidify relationships between these different layers.'

A criticism of the way in which the public sector provided services was that citizens must turn to too many departments or agencies to solve their problems. Thus, for example, a family in poor housing may have medical, employment, educational and other problems. To seek help from public agencies may involve several different parts of 'the government'. Similarly, for public servants, complex policy challenges can cut across departmental boundaries and fall between the cracks of a system built around vertically structured functional departments. To counter this type of problem, public management theorists introduced notions such as 'joined up' or holistic government, a system that allows co-ordinated responses to problems that are the responsibility of different agencies. In essence the holistic governance agenda can either increase centralisation or else encourage decentralisation and local pluralism. Chandler (2000) and Rhodes (2000) argue that it is inevitably centralising and 'there are good reasons to believe that centralisation is a poor strategy with which to pursue holism' (6 *et al.*, 2002: 188).

As Ireland moves from the Type I to the Type II model (see p. 385 above), it is becoming increasingly clear that central and local government have yet to fully understand the implications of moves towards a system of multi-level governance. There is little doubt that over the past decade the environment in which local authorities operate has radically altered. New relationships have had to be formed (or old ones reformed) with regional authorities, health boards and other central and regional agencies. Generally, management in the public sector is becoming more difficult. Peters (2001: 378–9) notes, 'Scarcity, changing social and cultural values, and increasing organisational and interorganisational complexity have all made it more difficult to accomplish assigned tasks through the public sector. Paradoxically, however, it becomes even more important for those in government to manage their operations effectively'. This is an accurate commentary for local government in Ireland as it strives to make the most out of each euro of public money.

State-sponsored bodies

Much of the service that the Irish state has traditionally provided to its citizens has been the responsibility of agencies that are neither government departments nor local authorities. State-sponsored bodies (SSBs), sometimes referred to as semi-state bodies, form a large part of the public sector, beginning with the Electricity Supply Board, the Dairy Disposal Company and the Agricultural Credit Corporation in 1927 and increasing in the intervening decades to about 130 at the end of 1998. Each SSB is established by statute. The constituent act prescribes its status, functions and powers. While state-sponsored bodies are largely independent of ministerial control in their day-to-day operations, the exercise of some functions, particularly financial ones such as capital development programmes, is subject to ministerial approval. They are also obliged to submit their annual reports and accounts to the minister for presentation to the Dáil. As the multi-level governance concept implies, the exact operational structure of SSBs is varied, and is influenced by the public management ideas that were fashionable at the time of their establishment and the recent impact of 'new public management'. There are two broad categories – commercial (trading) bodies, often referred to as public enterprises, and non-commercial bodies that have promotional, regulatory or semi-judicial functions. In 2003, state-sponsored bodies employed 66,300 people (57,500 in the commercial sector and 8,800 in the non-commercial sector).

Commercial state-sponsored bodies

As in other countries, the Irish commercial state-sponsored bodies now operate like private companies in the marketplace. Where possible they are expected to make profits, pay dividends and finance new investment. The basic belief is that business skills used in the private sector may be utilised to equal effect in the service of the state, thus combining public accountability and commercial success. This sector is being transformed particularly because of EU competition policy, embodying free trading, directives on liberalisation and the elimination and/or regulation of monopolies.

Some state-sponsored bodies were established when the government originally decided that a particular industry or service should be developed by a public authority. Examples include the Electricity Supply Board (ESB) and Córas Iompair Éireann (CIE, the public transport authority). In other cases, the activity was already in the public sector and operated by a department of state when it was decided that, in the interest of better management, it should be entrusted to a state-sponsored body that would have the professional expertise and business focus to develop it as a successful commercial enterprise. Examples are An Post, Telecom Éireann and Coillte (Forestry Authority). Very exceptionally, the government has taken over a private sector business that was failing.

As prescribed by the acts setting them up, the boards of directors of state-sponsored bodies (mostly non-executive) are formally appointed by the minister with responsibility for the industry or service concerned. The basis of selection varies. In some cases the statute prescribes no criteria, leaving choice entirely at the minister's discretion. In other cases, the minister may be obliged to select persons having special knowledge or experience, or persons representative of designated interests, or, occasionally, persons nominated by a statutory selection committee. The major commercial bodies have worker directors elected by their peers, as well as non-executive directors who are not involved in the day-to-day running of the company.

The heads of large semi-state or state-sponsored bodies, such as the chief executive of An Post or Aer Lingus, have a clear and direct role in public policy. They have open communications with ministers and senior civil servants in their 'parent' departments. Those that are commercial enterprises may also invest large sums of money in important infrastructural projects, and the government takes a close interest in their plans. Under pressure from the EU, Ireland is committed to examining the prospects for privatisation of state enterprises in whole or in part. As well as selling off state companies, various other ways of involving the private sector with state-sponsored bodies have emerged in recent years. For example, the funding of infrastructure developments increasingly involves the private sector. The first private investment in infrastructure in Ireland was the building of a toll bridge across the river Liffey in Dublin in 1984. While private operators have had an involvement in many projects since then, the current policy envisages the private sector being responsible for roads, water supply, waste management and sewerage projects in their entirety. Of course, not all public infrastructure projects would attract private interest and government will still be the major provider but, as the Type II (flexible multi-level) governance model suggests, governments are open to a variety of funding arrangements.

Non-commercial state-sponsored bodies

Across a range of government departments, independent bodies, removed from the influence of party politicians, have been established to ensure public confidence in their decisions. Some of their areas of responsibility are those that in many other jurisdictions would be carried out by local or regional government. In Ireland there is a reluctance to devolve powers to local government due to a lack of trust in central–local relationships. Callanan (2003b: 489) explains: 'Mistakes made by local authorities are sometimes used as the basis for intervention, and occasionally for appropriation of a responsibility, by the centre. The reverse does not seem to apply – mistakes made by central government are not held to justify devolution to local government.' So such bodies as the National Roads Authority (established in 1994) and the Dublin Transportation Office (1995) have removed major transport decisions from local authorities and from party politics. Transport is not alone. Major decisions on health policy rest with central government; but detailed management of all health and personal social services is left to a national body called the Health Services Executive, formed in 2004 under a board appointed by the minister. This body works under a management regime governing financial accountability and expenditure procedures that reflect the influence of new public management and seek to disengage the Department of Health and Children from detailed involvement in operational matters. This organisational structure was set up in response to a crisis of resources and confidence in the health service. It removes local politicians from involvement in controversial decisions on locating hospitals, managing waiting lists and approving consultant posts.

Examples of older state-sponsored bodies engaged in regulatory or semi-judicial functions are the Environmental Protection Agency and An Bord Pleanála (the planning board). These agencies have been used to take controversial decisions out of the party political framework. For example, while local authorities are the planning authorities for their area, an appeal against their decisions may be made to An Bord Pleanála. From 1963 until the establishment of this agency in 1976, the Minister for Local Government (now the Minister for the Environment and Local Government) had the power to deal with appeals, and there were ongoing complaints about the party political nature of decisions. Although An Bord Pleanála initially consisted of ministerial nominees, in 1983 the board was reconstituted to comprise a chairman appointed through a selection board and other directors representing bodies such as An Taisce – The National Trust for Ireland, Institute of Architects, the Irish Congress of Trade Unions and the Irish Business and Employers Confederation.

In comparison to other European countries, the concentration of power in central government across most policy areas is pervasive. The centralisation of the Irish system of government is reinforced by a Dublin focused and controlled national communications media. In an attempt to counter this Dublin orientation, the government announced a radical programme of decentralisation in December 2003. It is ironic, therefore, that this latest reform of the civil service involves no transfer of power from central government but simply the relocation of government departments to provincial towns. Whole government departments and 12,000 civil servants are scheduled to move to locations all around the state. The only obvious criteria for the new locations are political, since the redistribution does not seem to have been based on the National Spatial Strategy published in November 2002. If the programme is fully implemented, the result will be that power will still be held by the same central government departments, but these will now be less conveniently located in terms of parliamentary supervision, co-ordinated public management and access to organised national interest groups.

Public accountability

One question that demands greater understanding is whether there is a conflict between multi-level governance and public accountability – a conflict that may find dramatic expression in the form of political corruption. The study of corruption in Ireland has stressed the impact of domestic political events, though the intrusion of the Cayman Islands, Florida and Prague are colourful off-stage events that inform the local drama. It is possible, however, that Irish events are just a manifestation of broader trends in Western society as a whole. Certainly, according to Bull and Newell's (2003) assessment of political corruption, there has been 'an apparent growth in the phenomenon over the past decade' across many political systems in Europe and elsewhere.

Corruption has become a significant issue in Ireland in recent years or, more accurately, its existence has been highlighted recently by enquiries into the activities of former ministers and officials. It is not possible to tell whether political corruption – defined as the abuse of public office for private gain – is new in Ireland. Some observers suggest that corruption in the Republic increased dramatically since the 1960s when a new generation of politicians not directly involved in the founding of the state came to power. Others reject this 'sea-change' explanation and point to a few isolated cases in previous decades to imply that there were probably others undetected. It is hard to be definitive because corruption is essentially a covert activity. Collins and O'Shea (2001) suggest it occurs when:

- politicians have a direct role in deciding specific, individual policy decisions of high value to wealthy business interests such as planning at local government level;
- civil servants routinely exercise discretion over commercially important decisions in the context of lax systems of accountability and ambiguous policy objectives; and
- ministerial decisions are commercially charged and the policy criteria are insufficiently explicit.

These conditions have been most frequently met in the Irish context in relation to planning and economic development.

In the early 1980s, a series of scandals enveloped the Fianna Fáil government led by Charles Haughey. Most of these involved abuses of power such as unwarranted telephone tapping and interference with police administration, and they seemed confined to a small group within the Fianna Fáil party. More recent scandals investigated by the Beef, McCracken, Moriarty and Flood (now called the Mahon) tribunals and by the Dáil itself revolve around the issue of politicians, money and dealings with business, as may be seen in Box 14.1. An investigation into the beef industry in 1994 gave rise to considerable misgivings about inappropriate relationships between business interests and senior politicians. Several relatively minor incidents of impropriety led to ministerial apologies and resignations in 1995 and 1996. The next major *cause célèbre* unfolded following revelations in the *Irish Independent* in November 1996 about disclosures made during a court battle between members of the family that owns the major retail chain Dunnes Stores. As a result, a Fine Gael cabinet member, Michael Lowry, was accused of failing to disclose payments from Ben Dunne, one of the family, and it emerged that a prominent Fianna Fáil politician (later revealed to be Charles Haughey) had also received more than one million pounds from Ben Dunne.

Throughout 1997, a further series of revelations by the press kept the question of payments to individual politicians and to political parties at the forefront of public attention. An official enquiry, the McCracken Tribunal, established that there was no evidence that Michael Lowry had abused his position to help Ben Dunne, though he had left himself vulnerable to pressure from Dunnes Stores. The tribunal exposed a web of offshore accounts and convoluted transactions designed to avoid tax. Most spectacularly, the enquiry began to shed light on the sources of Mr Haughey's wealth. Very large sums of money were channelled to the former Taoiseach from a set of off-shore bank accounts in the Cayman Islands. So complex and secret were these accounts that a further tribunal under High Court Judge Michael Moriarty was set up to investigate all payments to politicians.

Local government decision making on land use planning has also been an area of suspicion for some years. Particularly in the Dublin environs, the rezoning of land to make it available for housing or industrial use very greatly increases its value. In September 1997, the Minister for Foreign Affairs, Ray Burke, was pressured into resignation after he confirmed reports in the *Sunday Business Post* that he had received £30,000 (€38,000) in cash from building interests in 1989. Mr Burke had already been a minister at the time but he insisted that no political favours had been asked for or granted. Nevertheless, the incident resulted in yet another enquiry, the Flood Tribunal, into the conduct of politicians and officials. Corruption and related topics continued to provide a theme for political stories in the media throughout 1998. In early 1999, Pádraig Flynn, a former minister and then EU Commissioner, became embroiled. It was alleged that in the late 1980s he had received £50,000 (€63,487) from a property developer; he claimed that this was a donation for the political party (Fianna Fáil) of which he was treasurer at the time. This allegation was considered at the Mahon Tribunal, as were several connected revelations about payments, offshore bank accounts and significant ministerial decisions.

Box 14.1 summarises the main incidents of political corruption, their primary focus and the initial results of their discovery. Much of what has been revealed is a result of the two major tribunals of enquiry set up by the Oireachtas and generally referred to by the names of their chairs, Justices Flood, Mahon and Moriarty. This summary omits a range of incidents that attracted wide publicity – relatively minor instances of tax irregularities or small undeclared donations to campaign funds, and enquiries into clerical abuse, police misconduct and health sector scandals, though each has raised the level of public concern about the misuse of power by people in authority.

Though many Irish people feel a true sense of scandal at the revelations about corruption, the most influential model for analysing its occurrence reflects no such emotion. Economists suggest that corruption is a response to 'rent seeking behaviour' – in other words, if the opportunity presents itself

Box 14.1 **Major political corruption revelations since 1994**

Instance	Issue	Outcome	Comment
Beef Tribunal (1994)	Govt mishandles export procedures	Criminal charges, destabilised government	Followed UK media story
Michael Lowry (1996)	Public duties, private interests	Resignation; and Moriarty Tribunal ongoing	Followed media investigation
Charles Haughey (1996)	Unethical receipt of money	Moriarty Tribunal ongoing	Followed media investigation
Ray Burke (1997)	Unethical receipt of money on planning and radio licensing issues	Resignation; Flood Tribunal; 2003 charged on serious tax offence; ongoing	Followed media investigation
George Redmond (1999)	Unethical receipt of money by senior official	Tax investigation by Criminal Assets Bureau; jailed 2003	Followed revelations at Flood Tribunal
Frank Dunlop	Unethical payment of money to councillors by PR consultant	Naming of councillors paid; resignations; ongoing	Revelations to the Flood Tribunal

Source: Adapted from Collins and O'Shea (2001).

Note
The Flood Tribunal is now known as the Mahon Tribunal following a change of chair.

then corruption will be found regardless of moral, cultural or historical circumstances. While this approach may be overstated, it does point to certain features of the strategies used internationally to combat corruption:

- reduction in the number of levels of decision taking, thus offering fewer opportunities;
- reduction in the incentives to engage in corruption, thus lowering the rewards;
- increasing the cost of being corrupt, or raising the penalties;

- increasing the chances of being caught, by providing an enhanced policing system in the area of corruption.

In the Irish case, this has translated into more laws and codes, harsher penalties, and new forms of checks and investigations. These measures include the Ethics in Public Office Act, 1995, the Electoral Act, 1997, the Standards in Public Office Act, 2001, the Electoral (Amendment) Act, 2001 and several other pieces of legislation designed to tighten existing provisions and to create new ones. It is easy to see, though, that from a 'rent-seeking' perspective, multi-level governance increases the possibility of corruption by providing more 'transactions' and by eroding traditional mechanisms of accountability.

Public accountability in Ireland operates, at central government level, through the doctrines of individual and collective responsibility of ministers and other members to parliament. By extension, Oireachtas members are answerable to the electorate. As Geddes and Ribeiro Netto (1999: 23) note: 'Ultimately . . . accountability depends on something more basic [than the idiosyncrasies of a particular political system]: the public's desire and ability to end the political careers of corrupt officeholders.' The Irish electorate has been relatively lenient in this respect. For example, Michael Lowry topped the poll in North Tipperary in 1997 and again in 2002, even after revelations about payments to him from Dunne and about tax evasion. Notwithstanding the voters' ambiguity, the role of periodic elections is too broad to be an effective instrument of public accountability. As McAllister (2000: 25) puts it, 'the principle of "throwing the rascals out" . . . assumes that electors are sufficiently well informed . . . [and] will be able to overcome their partisan loyalties, by perhaps voting against their favoured party in order to remove an unsatisfactory elected representative'.

In the simple model of parliamentary accountability, the focal point for an assessment of corruption is properly the Dáil and its committees. It is a common thread in many of the most significant instances of corruption in Ireland that parliamentary methods have been found wanting. If the legislature was working effectively, both through its elected members and their political staff, the system would be so transparent and accountable that political corruption should be minimal. The rise of more disciplined parties, the increased pace of the legislative process, and the wider remit of government have, however, militated against incisive parliamentary scrutiny. These factors are particularly acute in political systems such as Ireland's in which members of the legislature fill the cabinet and other government offices. The political fortunes of parliamentarians are closely linked to the popularity of the senior members of their party in the executive. This has led to the accusation that Dáil investigations are 'soft' on ministers.

Despite measures such as the Committees of the Houses of the Oireachtas (Compellability, Privileges and Immunities of Witnesses) Act, 1997, critics suspect that the odds against the detection of corruption are lengthening.

In recognition of similar misgivings, many parliamentary systems augment the role of the legislature with other watchdog agencies such as ombudsmen, special prosecutors and other quasi-judicial bodies. In Ireland, it is a feature of several of the incidents cited above that Dáil deputies were unable to elicit crucial information that was subsequently central to tribunal and other inquiries.

In relation to the causes of corruption one important theme deserves special attention because of the frequency with which it occurs both in Ireland and elsewhere. This is the alleged link between corruption and the financing of political parties and elections. As Heywood (1997: 14) notes: 'Many of the major scandals in democracies in recent years have been linked in some way to campaign and party finance. The democratic political process costs money – in ever increasing amounts.'

In Ireland, instances of corruption have been associated with the financing of political parties and, more frequently, the campaigns of individual politicians. The sums involved range from the trivial to the substantial. In the example cited above, former minister Pádraig Flynn claimed that the £50,000 (€63,487) cheque given to him by the property developer in 1989 was to cover his election expenses and was quite an accepted practice at the time. Under the current electoral act, which was introduced in 1997 and amended several times since, political parties can accept donations from one source of up to €6,348 in a given year, while donations to individual politicians are limited to €2,539 per donor (see Chapter 6). These limits are subject to amendment, but the figures are very much lower than some of the sums of money which changed hands in the guise of election contributions to the major figures in the various corruption tribunals. To deal with the confusion between personal and political spending, each candidate must now open a separate bank account for donations, and declarations must be made to the Standards in Public Office Commission. To counterbalance the fall-off in funds available to political parties as a result of the capping of donations, there has been an increase in the annual public funding made available to political parties, as we have seen in Chapter 6. Experience abroad suggests, however, that party financing will continue to be an area of potential corruption whatever the formal rules.

Conclusion

Multi-level governance presents many challenges for the way government in Ireland is organised, and in particular for 'the negotiated, non-hierarchical exchanges between institutions at the transnational, national, regional and local levels' (Peters and Pierre, 2001: 131–2). Millar and McKevitt (2000: 57) are correct in asserting that 'we need . . . to be aware that the objective of public service is support of the citizen and not simply the fashioning of "modern" administrative structures'. Progressive administrative reforms can lead to a higher degree of trust in government and in public administration generally. The fundamental challenge, however, in the world of multi-level governance is co-ordination. Whelan *et al*. (2004) argue that the structure of the Irish administrative system is not suited to the management of issues that cross the remits of single government departments or offices. Responsibility and accountability, politically and administratively, are rooted in an institutional focus (at civil service departmental level, or at local authority level), but major cross-cutting issues will require a more flexible and adaptive public management response in the future. Whelan *et al*. (2004) especially argue against the creation of too many single-issue agencies as a response. As multi-level governance appears to be moving inexorably from structured to flexible, citizens may find the resulting process of service delivery confusing and unsettling. Politics may not be endless theatre but, in the absence of expensive processes of coercion, it does depend on widespread popular consent. This in turn demands a clear focus of accountability. Multi-level governance, by making this link between known politicians and service provision less clear, carries the danger of lessening the quality of Irish democracy.

Notes

1 Traditionally, 26 counties are listed, but Tipperary has always had two county authorities, North Tipperary and South Tipperary. Following reforms in the early 1990s, the area of Dublin County that surrounds the boundary of Dublin city was divided into three local authorities, Fingal, South Dublin and Dun Laoghaire/Rathdown, giving a total of 29. In addition, there are five city councils, in Dublin, Cork, Limerick, Galway and Waterford.
2 The Local Government Act, 2003 disqualifies members of the Dáil or Seanad from membership of a local authority from the 2004 local elections onwards.

References and further reading

6, Perri, Diane Leat, Kimberly Seltzer and Gerry Stoker, 2002. *Towards Holistic Governance: The New Reform Agenda*. Basingstoke: Palgrave Macmillan.

Barrington, Tom, 1991. 'Local government in Ireland', in Richard Batley and Gerry Stoker (eds), *Local Government in Europe*. London: Macmillan, pp. 156–69.

Bull, Martin J. and James L. Newell (eds), 2003. *Corruption in Contemporary Politics*. London: Palgrave Macmillan.

Callanan, Mark, 2003a. 'Local government and the European Union', in Mark Callanan and J. F. Keogan (eds), *Local Government in Ireland: Inside Out*. Dublin: Institute of Public Administration, pp. 404–28.

Callanan, Mark, 2003b. 'Where stands local government?', in Mark Callanan and J. F. Keogan (eds), *Local Government in Ireland: Inside Out*. Dublin: Institute of Public Administration, pp. 475–501.

Callanan, Mark and J. F. Keogan (eds), 2003. *Local Government in Ireland: Inside Out*. Dublin: Institute of Public Administration.

Carmichael, Paul, 2002. 'Northern Ireland public administration in transition: an analysis of the civil service', *American Review of Public Administration* 32:2: 166–87.

Chandler, James A., 2000. 'Joined-up government: "I wouldn't start here if I were you" '. Paper presented at the Annual Conference of the Political Studies Association, London, London School of Economics.

Chubb, Basil, 1970. *The Government and Politics of Ireland*. London: Longman.

Coakley, John, 2001. 'Local elections and national politics', in Mary E. Daly (ed.), *County and Town: One Hundred Years of Local Government in Ireland*. Dublin: Institute of Public Administration, pp. 77–87.

Collins, Neil and Mary O'Shea, 2001. *Understanding Political Corruption in the Republic of Ireland*. Cork: Cork University Press.

Daemen, Harry and Linze Schaap, 2000. 'Ireland: associated democracy', in H. F. M. Daemen and L. Schaap (eds), *Citizen and City: Developments in Fifteen Local Democracies in Europe*. Rotterdam: Centre for Local Democracy, pp. 57–74.

Ewen, Richard J., 1992. Report on Local Government in Ireland and on the Process of Establishing Unitary Authorities in Wales (unpublished). New Zealand Society of Local Government Managers Study Award.

Gallagher, Michael, 1989. 'Local elections and electoral behaviour in the Republic of Ireland', *Irish Political Studies* 4: 21–42.

Geddes, Barbara and Artur Ribeiro Netto, 1999. 'Institutional sources of corruption in Brazil', in Richard Downes and Keith S. Rosenn (eds), *Corruption and Political Reform in Brazil: The Impact of Collor's Impeachment*. Boulder, CO: Lynne Rienner, pp. 21–48.

Heywood, Paul, 1997. *Political Corruption*. Oxford: Basil Blackwell.

Hooghe, Liesbet and Gary Marks, 2003. 'Unraveling the central state, but how? Types of multi-level governance', *American Political Science Review* 97:2: 233–43.

Hughes, Owen, 2003. *Public Management and Administration*, 3rd edn. Basingstoke: Palgrave Macmillan.

Keating, Michael and Liesbet Hooghe, 2001. 'Regions and the EU policy process', in J. Richardson (ed.), *European Union: Power and Policy-making*. London: Routledge.

Kenny, Liam, 1999. *From Ballot Box to Council Chamber*. Dublin: Institute of Public Administration.

Kenny, Liam, 2003. 'Local government and politics', in Mark Callanan and J. F. Keogan (eds), *Local Government in Ireland: Inside Out*. Dublin: Institute of Public Administration, pp. 103–22.

Lyons, F. S. L., 1973. *Ireland Since the Famine*. Glasgow: Fontana.

McAllister, Ian, 2000. 'Keeping them honest: public and elite perceptions of ethical conduct among Australian legislators', *Political Studies* 48:1: 22–37.

Millar, Michelle and David McKevitt, 2000. 'The Irish civil service', in Hans Bekke and Frits van der Meer (eds), *Civil Service Systems in Western Europe*. Cheltenham: Edward Elgar, pp. 36–57.

Osborne, David and Ted Gaebler, 1992. *Reinventing Government: How the Entrepreneurial Spirit is Transforming the Public Sector*. Reading, MA: Addison-Wesley.

Peters, B. Guy, 2001. *The Politics of Bureaucracy*. London: Routledge.

Peters, B. Guy and Jon Pierre, 2001. *Politicians, Bureaucrats and Administrative Reform*. London: Routledge.

Rhodes, R. A. W., 2000. 'Governance and public administration', in Jon Pierre (ed.), *Debating Governance: Authority, Steering and Democracy*. Oxford: Oxford University Press, pp. 54–90.

Roche, Desmond, 1982. *Local Government in Ireland*. Dublin: Institute of Public Administration.

Whelan, Patrick, Tom Arnold, Agnes Aylward, Mary Doyle, Bernadette Lacey, Claire Loftus, Nuala McLoughlin, Eamonn Molloy, Jennifer Payne and Melanie Pine, 2004. *Cross-departmental Challenges – A Whole-of-Government Approach for the Twenty-first Century*. Dublin: Institute of Public Administration.

Websites

www.environ.ie (link: what we do: local government)   Information on local government and links to local authorities.

www.gov.ie (link: all state organisations)   Links to commercial and non-commercial state sponsored bodies.

www.flood-tribunal.ie   Site of the Mahon (formerly Flood) tribunal of enquiry into payments to politicians linked to planning, with links to reports.

www.moriarty-tribunal.ie   Site of the Moriarty tribunal of enquiry into payments to politicians.

Part IV

Ireland in a wider world

15 Northern Ireland and the British dimension

John Coakley

Although the Ireland of the twenty-first century is in many respects a typical European state, there is one characteristic that marks it out as significantly different from others. This feature is symbolised in the very name of the state: 'Ireland' is a contested concept. The territorial extent of its frontiers, and the issue of whether these should include Northern Ireland, was for long the subject of bitter political dispute; and the identity of the state itself, and the extent to which it was formally and substantively independent of Great Britain, continued to be matters of contention well after 1922. These questions not only provided a distinctive dynamic to the Irish political process, as we have seen in Chapter 1; they also shaped the structure of the party system that emerged in the new state after 1922, as Chapter 5 has shown.

As recently as 1985, when the Anglo-Irish Agreement was drawn up, each of the two parties to the agreement produced their own variants on the text, and both versions were signed by the two sides. The official British text described that arrangement as an 'agreement between the Government of the United Kingdom of Great Britain and Northern Ireland and the Government of the Republic of Ireland'; the official Irish text described it as an 'agreement between the Government of the United Kingdom and the Government of Ireland'. The shorter Irish version was no mere matter of verbal economy. As a matter of principle, the Irish government was not prepared to acknowledge the *de jure* incorporation of Northern Ireland in the United Kingdom, something which is explicit in the full title of that state; and the British government did not wish to acknowledge the implicit claim to Northern Ireland in the official name of the Irish state (see Chapter 3; in the past, British official usage had referred exclusively to 'Éire' or to the 'Irish Republic', but from the 1970s onwards 'Republic of Ireland' – but never 'Ireland', *simpliciter* – gained currency among British officials as a way of referring to the 26 counties).

Behind this apparently trivial battle over names lie centuries of conflict between communities and islands (see Davies, 1999, for an interpretative overview). Chapter 1 has already described the historical relationship between Ireland and Great Britain, and examined the extent to which that has coloured the Irish political process. The present chapter begins with a similar topic, the relationship between north and south on the island of Ireland after partition. While this relationship had a dynamic of its own, though, its evolution can best be understood in terms of the broader context within which it operated: the changing relationship between Dublin and London after 1922, the topic we then address. Finally, it is important to note that both of these relationships were fundamentally redefined in the late 1990s; the last section of this chapter therefore looks at the nature of the Good Friday Agreement of 1998 and at the issues raised by efforts to implement it.

The north–south relationship

The roots of the partition of Ireland are deeply embedded in Irish history (for general historical background, see Brady *et al.*, 1989; Stewart, 1989; Bardon, 1992). At one level they lie in the seventeenth century 'plantations' that changed the face of Ulster, up to that point the most Gaelic of the provinces, giving it an Anglo-Scottish, Protestant character. By the nineteenth century, the northeastern part of the island was further distinguished from the rest of the island by socio-economic differences. In addition to the long-standing privileged position of Protestants (and especially Episcopalians, or members of the Church of Ireland), Ireland's industrial revolution had been substantially concentrated in the Lagan Valley, with the rapidly growing city of Belfast as its focal point, and the economic growth of the region left the rest of the island well behind. To these cultural and socio-economic differences were added political ones. As electoral mobilisation took off in the late nineteenth century, unionist Ulster became increasingly sharply differentiated from the rest of nationalist Ireland, as we have seen in Chapter 1. But there were further political differences between north and south. Organised unionism was itself divided: its main organisation, the Irish Unionist Alliance, extended after 1885 only over the three southern provinces where unionist support was thinly spread. Northern unionism was organised separately, taking permanent shape with the formation of the Ulster Unionist Council (still today the controlling body of the Ulster Unionist Party) in 1905. There were differences within nationalism, too, but these became obvious only in 1918, when nationalist candidates in several northern constituencies managed to withstand the Sinn Féin tide that engulfed the south – admittedly, aided by a pact brokered by the Catholic primate, Cardinal Logue.

When partition was finally introduced in 1920, then, the British could present it as a recognition of political realities (see Laffan, 1983). It is true that the new southern state comprised counties that were overwhelmingly nationalist; the county with the largest Protestant minority was Dublin (29 per cent). (Since religious affiliation at this time almost entirely determined political allegiance, we can use this as an indicator of political preference, relying on the 1911 census, which indeed formed the basis of later political calculations.) Furthermore, the new state of Northern Ireland contained two counties with large Protestants majorities, Antrim (79 per cent) and Down (68 per cent), and two with smaller but still significant majorities, Armagh (55 per cent) and Londonderry (54 per cent). But in the two remaining counties Protestants were a minority: Tyrone (45 per cent) and Fermanagh (44 per cent). Overall, according to the 1911 census, Protestants accounted for 65.6 per cent of the population of the six counties that would form Northern Ireland, and Catholics for 34.4 per cent.

Partition clouded north–south relations over the following decades for three main reasons (for general histories, see Harkness, 1983; Hennessey, 1997; Loughlin, 1998; Wichert, 1999). First, nationalists claimed, it was wrong in principle: electoral majorities in Ireland had voted for autonomy, and the unionist minority should have accepted this as a democratic decision of the Irish people. Second, it had in any case been unfairly implemented: rather than seeking to draw a border that would aim to follow the admittedly imprecise boundary between Protestant and Catholic Ireland, an effort had been made to maximise the territory of Northern Ireland even though this meant incorporating some overwhelmingly Catholic areas adjacent to the Catholic south. Third, nationalists argued, partition was maintained from the 1920s onwards by policies of discrimination, gerrymander and oppression directed against the Catholic minority.

From the northern Protestant perspective, of course, the picture appeared different. First, there was no particular reason why, if nationalist Ireland wished to opt out of the United Kingdom, Protestant Ulster could not opt out of nationalist Ireland; there was nothing sacred about using the island as the only decision-making unit (Gallagher, 1990). Second, although the new state extended over some predominantly Catholic areas, these had been included to maximise the number of Protestants that would be able to retain the valued link with Britain. Third, some unionists simply denied that any discriminatory or other unfair practices were directed against Catholics, while others, if they admitted these, justified them on the ground that Northern Ireland was entitled to protect itself against subversion by a disloyal minority; and both groups alleged that in any case the south discriminated against its own small Protestant minority (on the old system of government in Northern Ireland, see Birrell and Murie, 1980).

Against this background, the prospects for a productive political relationship between north and south were poor. But it is worth noting that they were not non-existent, at least initially. Although it has been called the 'partition act', the Government of Ireland Act, 1920 also sought to make provision for all-Irish institutions. Irish unity would continue to be symbolised by the continuance of certain long-established offices, and provision was made for a 40-member inter-parliamentary Council of Ireland, with 20 members each from the northern and southern parliaments. The responsibility of the Council was confined to a small range of matters initially, but provision was made for it to become an embryonic Irish parliament.

The Council of Ireland perished in two stages. First, it was overtaken by the Anglo-Irish Treaty of 1921, which greatly extended the political autonomy of the south (instead of being a self-governing part of the United Kingdom, and thus a mirror image of Northern Ireland, it was given separate status as a British dominion, outside the United Kingdom, as we have seen in Chapter 1). This had the effect of bringing to an end those few offices that would have symbolised the unity of the island, such as those of Lord Lieutenant and Lord Chancellor, and it led to the disappearance of the Irish Privy Council, of which northern and southern government ministers would have been members. Second, an agreement in 1925 between the Irish, British and Northern Irish governments to 'freeze' the north–south border as it then stood was accompanied by a further agreement to shelve the idea of a Council of Ireland; its few powers were transferred to the Belfast and Dublin administrations.

This ended whatever formal opportunities had existed for political contact between north and south. Northern unionists had not been particularly keen on the Council of Ireland, but the Northern Ireland parliament had selected its representation on it. The government of the Irish Free State, however, had found the Council a distasteful reminder of partition, had shown no enthusiasm to get it up and running, and gladly scrapped it in 1925 when the occasion arose. In the decades that followed, political contact between the two parts of the island was kept to a minimum, reaching a low point in the late 1940s, when the south not only left the Commonwealth but also began a vigorous and fruitless campaign to persuade the British to end partition (Kennedy, 1988). Co-operation between the two jurisdictions was kept to a minimum, covering only areas where it would have been difficult to avoid it (Kennedy, 2000).

The advent of political 'normalisation' between north and south had to await the arrival of a new political generation. This was represented symbolically by a visit by Taoiseach Seán Lemass to meet his counterpart, Prime Minister Terence O'Neill, in Stormont, Belfast in January 1965. But this development, and the thaw in relationships associated with it, was overtaken by events in Northern Ireland. There, the frustration of Catholics spilled over in 1968, a year of revolution throughout much of the world, behind a civil rights movement which aimed to win full equality before the law for all (see Purdie, 1990). The subversive potential of the civil rights movement lay in the fact that it did not represent a full frontal attack on the state, as pro-unity nationalist movements had traditionally done; instead of pursuing the rights of Irish nationals, it advocated the granting of rights of British citizens to all. This was a difficult demand for a unionist government to resist, and in 1968–9, under pressure from London, it agreed to a comprehensive reform package.

If the Northern Ireland problem had been simply about civil rights, it could have been resolved at a relatively early stage (for general background, see Darby, 1983; Whyte, 1990; Aughey and Morrow, 1996; Mitchell and

Wilford, 1999; Dixon, 2001; Tonge, 2002). But much more than this was at stake: having exposed the vulnerability of the state, nationalists pressed home with more far-reaching demands. Since the 1970s, these have taken two very distinctive forms. First, a new mainstream nationalist party, the Social Democratic and Labour Party (SDLP), appeared in 1970, and since then has pushed a dual agenda: for power sharing between the two main communities within Northern Ireland, and for institutional recognition of the Irish identity of northern nationalists by the creation of an 'Irish dimension', such as some kind of council of Ireland. Second, a new, militant force appeared at the same time: in December 1969 the Provisional IRA was created, and the armed campaign that it waged until 1994 was accompanied by a political movement, Sinn Féin, in pursuit of a more radical objective: the withdrawal of the British from Northern Ireland and the establishment of an all-Ireland republic (Bell, 2000).

This mobilisation on the nationalist side was matched by similar developments within unionism. As early as 1965, on the occasion of the Taoiseach's visit to Northern Ireland, a little-known clergyman, Rev. Ian Paisley, moderator of an even less well-known denomination, the Free Presbyterian Church of Ulster, made a vocal protest at Stormont, with placards reading 'No Mass, no Lemass' and 'IRA murderer welcomed at Stormont' (Moloney and Pollak, 1986: 119). A religious and political outsider, Paisley nevertheless articulated the fears of many unionists in the face of political change and apparent 'surrender' to civil rights demands, and in 1969 formed the Protestant Unionist Party (reorganised as the Democratic Unionist Party in 1971). This challenged mainstream unionism, which itself was deeply divided, and grew steadily in electoral appeal through the 1970s. In March 1972 the Ulster Unionist Party received its biggest jolt, one from which it was never to recover, when the British government suspended Northern Ireland's devolved institutions which had existed since 1921, and imposed direct rule from London under a Secretary of State for Northern Ireland, a member of the British cabinet.

Since the beginning of the 1970s, then, electoral politics in Northern Ireland has been dominated by two very distinctive forms of competition. First, nationalists have competed with unionists. After decades during which the combined representation of nationalists never exceeded a quarter of the seats in the Northern Ireland House of Commons, nationalist strength has been growing steadily. Nationalists won on average 26 per cent of the total vote (combining elections of all types) in the 1970s and 31 per cent in the 1980s (Mitchell, 1999: 101). In the 1990s this increased to 38 per cent, and in the early 2000s to 41 per cent, leaving unionists with little more than 50 per cent once allowance is made for votes for parties of the centre. This obviously reflects not just increased vote mobilising capacity on the part of nationalists but also a steady growth in the Catholic share of the population, from 35 per cent in 1961 to approximately 46 per cent in 2001. Second, there have been intense electoral struggles within the two communities.

On the nationalist side, the SDLP inherited the mantle of the old Nationalist Party, seeing itself as the voice of the community and managing to beat off the Sinn Féin challenge that appeared in the early 1980s. On the unionist side, the Ulster Unionist Party, whose long-standing hegemony had been frittered away in the 1970s, nevertheless managed to remain ahead of the Democratic Unionist Party for three decades. All of this was to change in November 2003, however, when the more militant parties on the two sides, Sinn Féin and the Democratic Unionists, managed to establish a decisive lead within their respective blocs.

This, then, was the political reality confronted by southern governments from the 1970s onwards (see Girvin, 1999). The south's traditional relationship with the old Nationalist Party continued on in the form of a similar but warmer relationship with the SDLP. Hints of an initial empathy with more militant republicans, reflected in early sympathy for the Provisional IRA, did not survive the armed campaign of the Provisional IRA, though, and Sinn Féin was not just regarded with hostility by Irish governments until the 1990s but was actively prevented from having open access to the southern state communications media (Sinn Féin members were not allowed to speak on radio or television from 1972 to 1994). To complete the picture, the Republic's relationship with all strands of unionism remained frosty until well into the 1990s, characterised more by mutual recrimination than by constructive dialogue.

The Irish–British relationship

As we have seen in Chapter 1, the relationship with Great Britain was a central, formative influence in Irish politics, leaving its imprint on constitutional norms, party development and political behaviour. In the early years of the state, this relationship was a major issue of political dispute, as Irish governments – especially after 1932 – sought to extend the state's independence, subject to existing constraints. The most important restrictions on Irish sovereignty were the continuing role of the King as head of state and Ireland's membership of the Commonwealth, both provided for in the Anglo-Irish Treaty of 1921. While the salience of these two fronts in the Irish nationalist campaign diminished over time, each remained a formal reality until 1949, when the Republic of Ireland Act came into effect, breaking such links as remained with the monarchy and the Commonwealth.

The unique character of Ireland's status in this respect was clear from the outset. The unity of the early Commonwealth was symbolised by the Crown, which was represented in each Commonwealth state by a Governor-General, by tradition a British nobleman. But the Irish Free State broke with this tradition from the beginning: the first Governor-General, Tim Healy, appointed on the nomination of the Irish government, was neither British nor a nobleman. Furthermore, he was discouraged by the Irish government from engaging in any kind of active role. His successor was forced to resign in humiliating circumstances in 1932 by the new Fianna Fáil government, which then went on to secure the appointment of a new Governor-General who was not only personally objectionable to the British but also fulfilled only the minimum constitutional functions of his office. Thus the termination of this office in 1936, though of some symbolic significance, had few practical implications for the British–Irish relationship, which had already lost the kind of link that bound other Commonwealth governments to London.

The restricted role of the Governor-General was of considerable practical significance. In other Commonwealth states, the office of the Governor-General at this time had many of the functions of a modern embassy; and the Commonwealth states, in turn, were represented in London by high commissioners, diplomats with quasi-ambassadorial status. Ironically, then, for almost two decades after 1922, Dublin had eyes, ears and a voice in London through its High Commission there; but London had no comparable channel of communication in Dublin. The pressures of international conflict made rectification of this position imperative following the outbreak of war in 1939, when the first British 'representative' in Dublin – his title deliberately vague – was appointed. It was not, however, until after 1949 that the holder of this post was designated an 'ambassador'.

Although the constitutional issue disappeared as a source of dispute after Ireland had finally severed its ties with Crown and Commonwealth in 1949, the territorial issue remained one of contention, and this was aggravated by irritation in Britain at Ireland's war-time policy of neutrality. The British responded to the Republic of Ireland Act with its own Ireland Act of 1949, which, while continuing to extend citizenship rights to Irish immigrants, declared that 'in no event will Northern Ireland or any part thereof . . . cease to be part of the United Kingdom without the consent of the Parliament of Northern Ireland'. The question of partition continued periodically to inflame relations between the two governments, especially after a new all-party anti-partition campaign, directed by the 'Mansion House Committee', was launched in Dublin in 1949. But the relationship also had its positive moments. Earlier, for example, the Anglo-Irish agreements of 1938 had ended the 'land annuities' dispute and resolved other outstanding differences, including British withdrawal from certain ports that had been retained under the terms of the 1921 Treaty (see Chapter 1). In 1965 the two governments signed the Anglo-Irish Free Trade Agreement, the most explicit acknowledgement of the need for practical co-operation up to that point.

The outbreak of the Northern Ireland troubles after 1968 once again cast a shadow on the Irish–British relationship – this time, at least initially, a substantial one (see Arthur, 2000). In addition to the political rhetoric and, indeed, constitutional provisions that presented the Republic as having at least an interest in affairs in Northern Ireland, public opinion was inflamed by the harsh treatment meted out to Catholics in such instances as the Derry civil rights march of October 1968, the Belfast riots of August 1969 and the killing of 13 unarmed civilians by British troops in Derry on 'Bloody Sunday' in January 1972. These had resulted in levels of sympathy that extended well outside the conventions of normal politics, as the 'arms crisis' of 1970 (when prominent ministers were accused of colluding with the smuggling of arms for use by northern nationalists) and the burning of the British embassy in 1972 showed (O'Brien, 2000). But efforts by the Irish government to influence the course of events in Northern Ireland were brushed aside by the British government on the grounds that this was an internal United Kingdom affair, and thus no business of the Irish government (for general background, see Arthur and Jeffery, 1996; Bew *et al.*, 1996; for reference material, see Elliott and Flackes, 1999; CAIN, 2004b; for chronologies, see Bew and Gillespie, 1999; CAIN, 2004a; on the British perspective see Boyce, 1996; Cunningham, 2001).

By 1972, though, it was clear that the circumstances had changed. The British government was moving closer to the SDLP position, implying acceptance not just of power sharing within Northern Ireland but also of involvement of the Republic in an institutionalised 'Irish dimension'. The outcome was the creation in 1973 of a new Northern Ireland Assembly which was required to produce an executive or government that would be 'broadly acceptable' throughout the community – code for power sharing between nationalists and unionists. Agreement on a three-party coalition comprising Ulster Unionists (themselves deeply divided on the issue), the SDLP and the small, centrist Alliance Party was duly forthcoming, and in December 1973 an agreement at Sunningdale, England, between the Northern Ireland executive-designate and the British and Irish governments made provision for a Council of Ireland with significant executive powers. This would comprise a 60-member interparliamentary Consultative Assembly, an intergovernmental Council of Ministers, and a permanent secretariat (for the text, see Elliott, 2002: 189–93).

The Council of Ireland agreed in 1973 was never to come into being. The Northern Ireland Executive did take up office in January 1974, but immediately ran into difficulties. Opponents of the Sunningdale agreement took control of the Ulster Unionist Party later in the same month; an election to Westminster in February 1974 registered a decisive majority for anti-Sunningdale unionists; and in May a political strike organised by the loyalist Ulster Workers' Council finally brought about the resignation of the executive (it was at this time, too, that the worst single set of incidents in all the troubles took place, when bombs in Dublin and Monaghan planted by loyalists killed 33 people). Subsequent efforts to revive this experiment failed, and the focus of British attention switched to security policy, expressed in a vigorous but unsuccessful attempt to defeat the IRA. As the 1970s advanced, the southern perspective, too, seemed to change, as politicians and the public lost their appetite for involvement in a conflict that was bloody, bitter and apparently intractable.

By the early 1980s, the time for a new initiative seemed right. In addition to the positive working relationship between the two governments that was also in part a product of 'normalisation' following the entry of both countries to the European Community in 1973, and to the need to find an alternative to a cycle of political violence that seemed unending, there was a concrete political reason for this. The two governments were worried by the rise of Sinn Féin, previously a marginal force in electoral terms, following the deaths of ten republican prisoners on hunger strike in 1981 and the mobilisation of republicans that this had provoked. The British undertook their own initiative in 1982, with the creation of an assembly on which executive powers might be conferred if there was substantial consensus in the assembly to this effect, in a so-called 'rolling devolution' scheme. This proved unsuccessful, since only two parties (the Democratic Unionists and the Alliance Party) participated consistently in the Assembly's affairs. Dublin, consigned to the sidelines, could do little other than reflect; but this it did with some energy in an inter-party New Ireland Forum that met in 1983–4. This sought to arrive at a nationalist consensus on the way forward, and its report, under pressure from Fianna Fáil leader Charles Haughey, identified a unitary Irish state as its preferred option. It also considered two other models: a federal or confederal state, and joint rule over Northern Ireland by the two sovereign governments (for a summary of the forum's conclusions, see Coakley, 2002a: 170–4).

Although the options considered by the New Ireland Forum were each dismissed by British prime minister Margaret Thatcher, she nevertheless engaged in intense negotiations with the Irish side, and these led to a far-reaching agreement signed at Hillsborough, Co. Down, in November 1985. The Anglo-Irish agreement of 1985 did not come close to satisfying the stated preference of nationalist Ireland, stopping well short of even the notion of joint rule, but its provisions were nevertheless remarkable (for the text, see Elliott, 2002: 194–9). There was to be an Anglo-Irish Intergovernmental Conference which would meet regularly and frequently to discuss matters of common interest, but which would have particular responsibility for a wide segment of matters impinging on relations between the two communities within Northern Ireland. Although sovereignty would continue to reside with the British, the Irish government would be entitled to express its views and make proposals on all matters falling within the ambit of the conference, and in the event of disagreement between the two sides 'determined efforts' would be made to resolve them. The work of the conference would be serviced by a standing secretariat drawn from the Irish and UK civil services.

The mere existence of these structures was significant, but the definition of the areas in which they were involved was even more striking. In general, these covered political, security and legal matters, including the administration of justice, and cross-border co-operation was also to be promoted. The language of the agreement made it clear that the two governments were moving increasingly towards recognition of the binational character of

Northern Ireland. The agreement was defined as comprising a framework 'for the accommodation of the rights and identities of the two traditions which exist in Northern Ireland', and for promoting 'reconciliation, respect for human rights, co-operation against terrorism and the development of economic, social and cultural co-operation'. It was agreed that the conference would consider 'measures to foster the cultural heritage of both traditions, changes in electoral arrangements, the use of flags and emblems, the avoidance of economic and social discrimination and the advantages and disadvantages of a Bill of Rights in some form in Northern Ireland'. The extent to which these measures were designed to improve the circumstances of nationalists in particular was underlined by the granting of an explicit right to the Irish government to make representations on behalf of that community. The agreement also went further than ever before in defining the circumstances under which Irish unity could come about, while also accepting current constitutional realities. It developed more explicitly one of the provisions of the Sunningdale agreement, stating that:

> The two Governments
> (a) affirm that any change in the status of Northern Ireland would only come about with the consent of a majority of the people of Northern Ireland;
> (b) recognise that the present wish of a majority of the people of Northern Ireland is for no change in the status of Northern Ireland;
> (c) declare that, if in the future a majority of the people of Northern Ireland clearly wish for and formally consent to the establishment of a united Ireland, they will introduce and support in the respective Parliaments legislation to give effect to that wish.

The agreement also endorsed the creation of a parliamentary body that would link the two jurisdictions. Unlike the agreement's other provisions, which took effect immediately, the British–Irish Interparliamentary Body (to give it its formal name) came into existence only in 1990. It was made up originally of 50 members drawn equally from the British and Irish parliaments, but its membership was enlarged to 66 in 2001, with the inclusion of representatives of the United Kingdom's three devolved regions and of the Channel Islands and the Isle of Man. The body has been useful as a bridge-building exercise and in constructing informal networks among its members; by the end of 2003, 27 plenary meetings had taken place.

The Good Friday Agreement

The Anglo-Irish agreement of 1985 did not provide a solution to the problems of Northern Ireland, and was probably not intended to do so in any kind of permanent way (for analyses of the problem, see McGarry and

O'Leary, 1996, 2004; Ruane and Todd, 1996). In attempting to enhance the status of the nationalist community, it strove to undermine support for the IRA; but that body continued its armed campaign. The agreement was perceived by unionists as damaging, unfair and one-sided, and they did their utmost to overturn it. But it had been designed to withstand the kinds of action that had brought down the power-sharing executive in 1974. The two governments in Dublin and London were far distant from Northern Ireland, and the new Anglo-Irish secretariat, though based outside Belfast, was physically out of bounds to protesters. The result was that the agreement was able to survive street protests, strenuous objections in parliament and even the force of unionist opinion (all 15 unionist MPs in the British House of Commons resigned their seats to force a set of by-elections on the issue in January 1986, but the net outcome was that one unionist seat was lost, to Séamus Mallon of the SDLP).

The agreement did, however, have a considerable impact on the positions of the various parties. For Sinn Féin it represented something of a setback: to the extent that it represented a victory for constitutional nationalism, it gave the SDLP an advantage. SDLP leader John Hume sought to build on this, engaging in talks with Sinn Féin leader Gerry Adams from 1988 onwards. These resulted ultimately in a document defining a shared nationalist position, and parts of this were incorporated in the 'Downing Street declaration' of 1993, a joint statement by the British prime minister and the Taoiseach to the effect that talks would be held on an open-ended agenda regarding the future of Northern Ireland, and that all parties not engaged in violence could participate in them. This led ultimately to the IRA ceasefire of August 1994, which was quickly followed by a loyalist ceasefire (for background, see Gilligan and Tonge, 1997; Mallie and McKittrick, 1997; Cox, Guelke and Stephen, 2000; Hennessey, 2000; Moloney, 2002). But the 1985 agreement also held out a carrot to unionists: it had provided that the Anglo-Irish Intergovernmental Conference would not have jurisdiction over any matters that were the responsibility of devolved institutions within Northern Ireland. If, therefore, agreement could be reached on the establishment of such institutions (even though the governments insisted that they would have to be based on the principle of power sharing), the Anglo-Irish agreement would be undermined. Alternatively, many unionists hoped that it would be possible to arrive at a new agreement that would supersede that of 1985; they thus had a vested interest in coming to the negotiating table (see Aughey, 1989; Cochrane, 1997).

Accompanying these shifting positions and perspectives was an intense process of discussion between the various parties (de Bréadún, 2001; Coakley, 2002b). The Irish government organised a Forum for Peace and Reconciliation in Dublin in 1994 that brought Sinn Féin in from the cold, to a forum where it could participate in meetings with the SDLP, the Alliance Party and the southern parties (the work of the forum ended in 1996, when the

IRA ceasefire collapsed in protest at Sinn Féin's exclusion from negotiations, though the ceasefire resumed in 1997). The British government organised elections to a Northern Ireland Forum (1996–8), whose main function was to provide teams for inter-party talks (most of these took place outside the forum, which the nationalist parties in any case did not attend). With the assistance of a great deal of informal diplomacy and external mediation (notably by a team headed by former US senator George Mitchell), talks between the Northern Ireland parties and the two governments in 1997–8 finally resulted in agreement on Good Friday, 10 April 1998, and this was approved by referendum on 22 May 1998, with the support of 71 per cent of those voting in Northern Ireland and 94 per cent in the Republic.

The Good Friday Agreement (also known as the Belfast Agreement) was remarkable for the range of parties that went along with its provisions and for the wide span of areas that it covered. The Democratic Unionist Party had withdrawn from the talks process in 1997 when Sinn Féin was admitted, but all of the other significant parties, including Sinn Féin and two small parties close to the main loyalist paramilitary organisations, had joined the British and Irish governments in approving the final draft. In terms of its scope, too, the agreement was remarkable. It covered not only the issues of power sharing within Northern Ireland and the 'Irish dimension' (now renamed 'strand one' and 'strand two' respectively); it also introduced a 'strand three' – the broader British–Irish relationship. But the agreement went even further than this, addressing long-term constitutional matters, short-term issues arising from decades of conflict and a number of specific areas of particular concern to one community or the other (see Box 15.1; for the text of the agreement, see Elliott, 2002: 223–34; for analyses, see Ruane and Todd, 1999; Cox *et al.*, 2000; Wilford, 2001).

Box 15.1 **The Good Friday Agreement, 1998**

1 Strand one: devolved government for Northern Ireland

- a 108-member legislative assembly with consociational provisions
- a First Minister and a Deputy First Minister elected on a cross-community basis
- an executive comprising up to ten ministers chosen by the D'Hondt formula
- a committee system with chairs and deputy chairs chosen by the D'Hondt formula

2 *Strand two: links between Northern Ireland and the Republic of Ireland*

- a north–south Ministerial Council bringing together ministers from the two administrations
- a north–south secretariat comprising civil servants from Belfast and Dublin (now based in Armagh)
- six north–south implementation bodies
- six areas of co-operation between the two administrations

3 *Strand three: links between Ireland and Great Britain*

- a British–Irish Council linking eight administrations
- a British–Irish Intergovernmental Conference linking the two sovereign governments
- a British–Irish joint secretariat comprising British and Irish civil servants (now based in Belfast)

4 *Other provisions*

Constitutional issues: the agreement acknowledged that a majority of the population of Northern Ireland wished to remain in the United Kingdom; the Irish government agreed to hold a referendum to drop its constitutional claim on Northern Ireland; and the British government agreed to facilitate Irish unity should a majority so wish.

Equality: the governments acknowledged the divided nature of Northern Irish society and committed themselves to respecting the equality of the two cultures, including a right to opt for either British or Irish citizenship, or both, whatever the overall territorial arrangements.

Policing and human rights: an independent commission on policing would recommend on a police force acceptable to the two communities; the criminal justice system would be reviewed; and a commission on human rights would be established.

Addressing the legacy of conflict: there would be an accelerated programme of early release of prisoners; structures to assist victims of the violence would be established; the parties to the agreement pledged themselves to work in good faith to remove all paramilitary weapons; and the British government agreed to a reduction in the security force presence.

Strand one: domestic politics in Northern Ireland

The core of the new arrangements was a set of devolved institutions in Belfast that were given responsibility for most matters of domestic policy making. The key, in turn, to the functioning of these is the balance of political forces represented in a newly created Northern Ireland Assembly. This has 108 members, elected by the single transferable vote system of proportional representation from 18 six-member constituencies (which correspond to those used as single-member constituencies in elections to the UK House of Commons). In line with provisions commonly to be found in consociational democracies, where elaborate power- and resource-sharing measures are designed to overcome deep societal divisions (see Lijphart, 1977), all members of the assembly (MLAs) are required either to designate themselves 'unionist' or 'nationalist', or to opt out and self-designate as 'other'. In a number of the most politically sensitive areas, the assembly is obliged to make its decisions 'on a cross-community basis', defined as enjoying support either by a majority of the assembly plus majorities within the unionist and nationalist blocs, or by a 60 per cent majority of the assembly plus support from at least 40 per cent of the members of these two blocs.

The main example of the first of these qualified majority systems in operation is the election of the First Minister and the Deputy First Minister. These are elected by means of a single vote, and must have majority support within each of the two blocs (thus ensuring, in effect, that one post will go to each of the two communities). Other posts are allocated rather differently, and in a way that significantly weakens the powers of the two first ministers. In selecting the ten-member executive, the D'Hondt electoral system (a proportional representation formula commonly used for parliamentary elections in continental European list systems) is used. The largest party is given the first seat, and subsequent seats are allocated following the conventional D'Hondt formula, each party selecting its preferred ministry as its turn arrives. There is also a strong committee system, the committees corresponding to government departments and reflecting party strength in the assembly; their chairs and deputy chairs, too, are selected in accordance with the D'Hondt formula.

The results of the two elections to the assembly that have taken place so far are reported in Table 15.1. Following the 1998 election, David Trimble (Ulster Unionist) and Séamus Mallon (SDLP) were elected First and Deputy First Minister respectively, and the party strengths in the assembly entitled the Ulster Unionists and SDLP to three ministries each, and the Democratic Unionists and Sinn Féin to two each. Because of prolonged haggling over other issues (with the failure of the IRA to 'decommission' weapons as a major stumbling block), the executive did not take office until December 1999. Even after that, though, it functioned in a stop-start way. Devolution was suspended and replaced by direct rule from London from 11 February to 29 May 2000, and was again suspended indefinitely on 14 October

Table 15.1 Results of elections to the Northern Ireland Assembly, 1998 and 2003

Party	1998		2003	
	Votes	*Seats*	*Votes*	*Seats*
Ulster Unionist Party	21.3	28	22.7	27
Social Democratic and Labour Party	22.0	24	17.0	18
Democratic Unionist Party	18.1	20	25.7	30
Sinn Féin	17.6	18	23.5	24
Alliance Party	6.5	6	3.7	6
United Kingdom Unionist Party	4.5	5	0.8	1
Progressive Unionist Party	2.6	2	1.2	1
Women's Coalition	1.6	2	0.8	0
Others	6.1	3	4.6	1
Total	100.0	108	100.0	108

Note
Following the 2003 election, three members of the Ulster Unionist Party moved to the Democratic Unionist Party, giving the former 24 members to the latter's 33.

2002 (there were also two short 'technical' suspensions on 10 August and 21 September 2001 arising from David Trimble's tactical resignation as First Minister and difficulties in securing his re-election). Furthermore, although the Democratic Unionists took up their two ministerial seats, in which, indeed, they functioned very effectively, they refused to attend meetings of the executive and continued to proclaim their opposition to the agreement.

The results of the second election to the assembly produced further stalemate. Ulster Unionists had refused to remain in office with Sinn Féin because of fears that IRA activities were continuing, but in any case the election saw the anti-Agreement Democratic Unionists take the lead on the unionist side. The continuing failure of the devolved institutions to function poses a serious threat to the Good Friday Agreement overall, because of the interlocking nature of all of the institutions: they were designed to function only as part of a comprehensive settlement, but not separately from this.

Strand two: the north–south dimension

Although unionists were prepared to swallow a form of power sharing within Northern Ireland that went much further than that implemented in 1973–4, they had particular difficulties with any attempt to revive the Council of Ireland concept agreed at that time. The result was the creation of a set of bodies with a more practical focus, and a less ambitious political super-structure (indeed, there had been a significant level of cross-border co-operation before this, much of it EU-funded; see Tannam, 1999). The most important of the new institutions is the North–South Ministerial Council, which, it was planned, would meet in three formats. In its plenary form, it includes the Taoiseach and the Northern Ireland First Minister and Deputy First Minister as its core, but the practice in the four meetings that have taken place to date has been for most Dublin and Belfast ministers to attend. In addition, by the time the institutions were suspended on 14 October 2002 a total of 60 sectoral meetings had taken place (though these were boycotted by the Democratic Unionist ministers). These consisted of the relevant southern minister, his or her northern counterpart, and a northern minister from the 'other' side (for example, if the northern minister was a member of the SDLP, an Ulster Unionist minister also attended). The council has also met once in a third, 'institutional', format to consider business that did not fall under any other heading.

The North–South Ministerial Council meets at different locations throughout Ireland, but it has a standing secretariat in Armagh. At the beginning of 2004, this was made up of 27 people seconded from the civil service in Dublin and Belfast, with approximately equal numbers from the two jurisdictions. Cross-border activities fall into two categories: the work of implementation bodies, and areas in which the two administrations function separately but cooperate formally.

Under the provisions of the agreement, six north–south 'implementation bodies' were set up. These are listed in Table 15.2, which also gives an indication of the staffing and the budget of each. Some of the bodies (such as Waterways Ireland, responsible for maintenance and development of all of the island's inland waterways, mainly for leisure purposes) have a relatively large staff and a highly visible impact; others (such as the Special EU Programmes Body) have a small staff and budget, but are responsible for administering much larger tranches of funds from the EU. Some (such as the Food Safety Promotion Board and InterTrade Ireland) are entirely new bodies; others (such as the Foyle, Carlingford and Irish Lights Commission) are based largely on existing bodies. Indeed, in the latter case, one of the

Table 15.2 North–south implementation bodies, 2003

Implementation body	Headquarters	Staff	Budget (€m)
Waterways Ireland	Enniskillen	333	35.9
Food Safety Promotion Board	Cork	29	8.6
InterTrade Ireland	Newry	42	14.3
Special EU Programmes Body	Belfast	44	3.2
Language Body	Dublin and Belfast	49	20.3
Foyle, Carlingford and Irish Lights Commission	Derry	41	5.1

Note
There is also a *de facto* seventh implementation body, Tourism Ireland, with 142 staff and a budget of €139.8m.

existing bodies, the Commissioners of Irish Lights, has been so securely protected by legislation since its foundation in 1786 that it has not been possible to bring it under the aegis of the new body (the fact that it forms part of a coastal protection system shared with Great Britain has made matters more complex). In the case of the language body, there are two agencies. One, Foras na Gaeilge, was made up of existing Dublin-based bodies that now have a 32-county function; the second, the Ulster-Scots Agency, is an entirely new body whose mandate is to promote the Ulster Scots' language and culture.

In addition to the areas where implementation bodies were established, it was agreed that in six other designated areas co-operation would take place through the medium of existing departments. The areas are agriculture, education, environment, health, tourism and transport. Actual levels of co-operation in these areas have been very uneven. In the area of tourism, for example, co-operation proceeded rapidly, though much of it had begun even before the Good Friday Agreement; the result was the creation of a new all-Ireland tourist promotion company, Tourism Ireland Ltd – in effect a seventh implementation body. In the transport sector, by contrast, where the case for co-ordinated planning is virtually unanswerable, there has been very little co-operation – largely because the relevant department in Northern Ireland was under the control of a Democratic Unionist minister.

Strand three: the British–Irish dimension

In many respects, the strand three provisions of the Good Friday Agreement were seen as a trade-off for the strand two provisions: nationalists were particularly keen on links with the Republic, and unionists were to the fore in demanding a strengthening of links with Great Britain. Here the central institution is a new British–Irish Council. This is intergovernmental in structure, and links the administrations of eight territories of very uneven status for purposes of policy co-ordination on matters of common interest: two sovereign states (the Republic of Ireland and the United Kingdom); three devolved administrations within the United Kingdom (Scotland, Wales and Northern Ireland); and three adjacent autonomous Crown territories (the Isle of Man and the Channel Islands of Jersey and Guernsey). By the end of 2003, five plenary meetings of the council had taken place, and modest progress had been made in a number of sectors (such as the environment, drugs and transport) where a common approach appeared sensible. Attention should also be drawn to the British–Irish Interparliamentary Body, discussed above, which was reconstituted in 2001 to match the territorial span of the British–Irish Council, though it lay entirely outside the terms of the Good Friday Agreement.

Rather less visible than the British–Irish Council, but considerably more significant, is the British–Irish Intergovernmental Conference, which brings together the two sovereign governments in respect of areas not devolved to the new institutions in Belfast. At first sight, it looks similar to its predecessor, the Anglo-Irish Intergovernmental Conference established in 1985, but in principle it also contains representatives of the northern parties, and thus of unionism, since there is provision for participation in its affairs by 'relevant' members of the new Northern Ireland executive. This may have helped to make it less objectionable to unionists than its predecessor, to which it plays a very similar role while Northern Ireland's institutions are suspended. It is serviced by a British–Irish joint secretariat, comprising British and Irish civil servants, that is now based in Belfast.

Resolving issues of contention

Reaching an accommodation on the shape of major political institutions was an outstanding achievement; but the Good Friday Agreement went further, also addressing a range of other issues that were exceptionally contentious. These included long-term constitutional issues; the question of equality between the two traditions in the economic, social, cultural and political domains; outstanding challenges in the area of security, policing and human rights; and the dilemma of making a transition from conditions of armed conflict, with its legacy of fundamental problems, to a more peaceful dispensation.

In the constitutional domain, nationalist Ireland made major concessions. The full significance of Article 2 of the Irish constitution in international law had never been established; it stated that 'The national territory consists of the whole island of Ireland, its islands and the territorial seas', a formulation which, together with the following article, was taken to embody a territorial claim to Northern Ireland. This was now replaced by a new wording which stated merely that 'It is the entitlement and birthright of every person born in the island of Ireland, which includes its islands and seas, to be part of the Irish nation', while the new version of Article 3 made it clear that Irish unity could come about 'only by peaceful means with the consent of a majority of the people, democratically expressed, in both jurisdictions in the island'. However, the agreement also sought to reassure nationalists by acknowledging that should a majority within Northern Ireland ever move to support Irish unity the British government would seek to implement this, and it would also hold a referendum to ascertain public opinion on this issue as necessary.

The agreement also acknowledged the divided nature of Northern Irish society, and the two governments committed themselves to respecting the equality of the two cultures, not just while Northern Ireland was part of the United Kingdom but also in the event of its incorporation into a united Ireland. As a practical illustration of formal equality, the two governments agreed that Northern Ireland residents could opt for either British or Irish citizenship, or both, again regardless of the overall territorial arrangements. The British government also pledged to push forward with measures designed to promote the economic and social development of the province in an even-handed way, and to address the marginalisation of subordinate cultures, most notably the Irish language.

The agreement further provided for a review of the criminal justice system, and for its replacement by one likely to be more generally acceptable to the two communities. Given Northern Ireland's history of civil rights controversies, it was agreed that a commission would be established to promote human rights in the province and to draw up a code to supplement the European Convention on Human Rights by taking account of the special circumstances of Northern Ireland. But policing was the most difficult issue of all. The Royal Ulster Constabulary, overwhelmingly Protestant in composition and carrying the baggage of decades of association with unionist governments, was unacceptable to nationalists, who had for long demanded its reform or abolition. The agreement went some way toward this, promising that an independent commission on policing would be established to recommend on the nature of a police force acceptable to the two communities. Chaired by former Hong Kong governor and later EU commissioner Chris Patten, the commission duly reported in September 1999, recommending fundamental reform and renaming of the police force. A restructured Police Service of Northern Ireland came into existence in 2001 in circumstances of some controversy. Its commitment to radically increasing the proportion of Catholic officers by means of a new 50:50 ratio of Catholic to other recruits and to adopting politically neutral imagery angered unionists, but were insufficient to win Sinn Féin support.

But it was in dealing with the legacy of the conflict that the agreement faced the greatest obstacles of all. Since the major paramilitary organisations had been on cease-fire since 1994 (broken temporarily in 1996 in the case of the IRA), the British government agreed to an accelerated programme of early release of prisoners, a measure designed not just to deal with an outstanding issue but also to win support for the agreement among the prisoners' families and communities – a respect in which it appears to have enjoyed some success. On the other hand, the release of prisoners would be deeply hurtful to their many victims, already suffering from the effects of their actions; it was agreed that structures would be established in an effort to assist victims of the violence. A Victims Commission had been set up already in 1997, and its work was continued by other agencies. But demilitarisation posed the biggest challenge of all. The parties to the agreement pledged themselves to work in good faith with an independent commission on decommissioning, with a view to removing all paramilitary weapons. Although the military and security significance of this issue was slight, it came to acquire crucial political importance for symbolic reasons, and failure on the part of the IRA to decommission appropriately became a central argument of the Ulster Unionist Party in withdrawing from the executive, and of the Democratic Unionists in refusing to participate fully in it. On the other hand, republicans could point to the fact that although the

British government had committed itself in the Good Friday Agreement to a reduction in the security force presence, signs of military involvement still continued to be highly visible in such areas as South Armagh.

Conclusion

If the Good Friday Agreement is seen as a marker of the progress of the north–south and British–Irish relationships in recent decades, we might expect the balance sheet to appear negative. The devolved institutions have collapsed, at least for the present, and given the interlocking nature of the different components of the agreement we might expect other areas, too, to have come unstuck. But this has not happened. In reality, once the agreement had been arrived at and measures to implement it had been set in motion, these acquired a life of their own. First, both sides have pocketed gains in areas where concessions have been virtually irreversible: prisoners have been released, the Irish constitution has been amended, and the Royal Ulster Constabulary has been transformed. Second, there are areas where practical needs and broader concerns have prompted the governments to prevent institutions from collapsing simply because of the absence of an executive in Belfast. Thus, the British–Irish Council has continued to meet, and, although no meetings of the North–South Ministerial Council have taken place since the devolved institutions were suspended in October 2002, the implementation bodies have continued to function, with the two governments supervising their activities on a 'care and maintenance' basis. The governments have, however, been particularly careful to stress the continuing centrality of the Good Friday Agreement as a blueprint for the future of relationships within Northern Ireland, between north and south and between Ireland and Great Britain.

While the character of constitutional and institutional arrangements may well be a barometer of the relationships between the various parties in these islands that have for so long been at loggerheads with each other, it is important in conclusion to note the significance of other political dynamics. The perspectives of the British and Irish governments have converged not just because of deepening policy consensus on the future of Northern Ireland, but also because their broader international interests, and especially shared concerns within the EU, promote this. The 1990s brought about a fundamental change in relationships between Ulster Unionists and nationalist Ireland, as the party leadership began to engage with the Republic; and the first decade of the twenty-first century may witness a similar engagement with the Democratic Unionists. Whether such entente between elites will suffice in resolving underlying problems is, however, another matter; mutual suspicion and political distrust between communities have proven extraordinarily resilient in the Northern Ireland of the twenty-first century, and although traditional southern antipathy towards Britain has abated there are indications that psychological distance from Northern Ireland remains considerable.

References and further reading

Arthur, Paul, 2000. *Special Relationships: Britain, Ireland and the Northern Ireland Problem.* Belfast: Blackstaff Press.

Arthur, Paul and Keith Jeffery, 1996. *Northern Ireland since 1968.* Oxford: Basil Blackwell.

Aughey, Arthur, 1989. *Under Siege: Ulster Unionism and the Anglo-Irish Agreement.* London: Hurst.

Aughey, Arthur and Duncan Morrow (eds), 1996. *Northern Ireland Politics.* London: Longman.

Bardon, Jonathan, 1992. *A History of Ulster.* Belfast: Blackstaff.

Bell, J. Bowyer, 2000. *The IRA, 1968–2000: Analysis of a Secret Army.* London: Frank Cass.

Bew, Paul and Gordon Gillespie, 1999. *Northern Ireland: A Chronology of the Troubles 1968–1999*, new edn. Dublin: Gill and Macmillan.

Bew, Paul, Peter Gibbon and Henry Patterson, 1996. *Northern Ireland, 1921–1996: Political Forces and Social Classes*, rev. edn. London: Serif.

Birrell, Derek and Alan Murie, 1980. *Policy and Government in Northern Ireland: Lessons of Devolution.* Dublin: Gill and Macmillan.

Boyce, D. G., 1996. *The Irish Question and British Politics 1868–1986*, 2nd edn. Basingstoke: Macmillan.

Brady, Ciaran, Mary O'Dowd and Brian Walker (eds), 1989. *Ulster: An Illustrated History.* London: Batsford.

CAIN, 2004a. A chronology of the conflict – 1968 to the present. Available http:// cain.ulst.ac.uk/othelem/chron.htm [accessed 12 March 2004].

CAIN, 2004b. Background on the Northern Ireland conflict. Available http:// cain.ulst.ac.uk/othelem/index.html [accessed 12 March 2004].

Coakley, John (ed.), 2002a. *Changing Shades of Orange and Green: Redefining the Union and the Nation in Contemporary Ireland.* Dublin: University College Dublin Press.

Coakley, John, 2002b. 'Conclusion: new strains of unionism and nationalism', in John Coakley (ed.), *Changing Shades of Orange and Greens: Redefining the Union and the Nation in Contemporary Ireland.* Dublin: University College Dublin Press, pp. 132–54.

Cochrane, Feargal, 1997. *Unionist Politics and the Politics of Unionism since the Anglo-Irish Agreement.* Cork: Cork University Press.

Cox, Michael, Adrian Guelke and Fiona Stephen (eds), 2000. *A Farewell to Arms? From 'Long War' to Long Peace in Northern Ireland.* Manchester: Manchester University Press.

Cunningham, Michael, 2001. *British Government Policy in Northern Ireland 1969–2000.* Manchester: Manchester University Press.

Darby, John (ed.), 1983. *Northern Ireland: The Background to the Conflict.* Belfast: Appletree Press.

Davies, Norman, 1999. *The Isles: A History.* London: Macmillan.

de Bréadún, Deaglán, 2001. *The Far Side of Revenge: Making Peace in Northern Ireland.* Cork: Collins Press.

Dixon, Paul, 2001. *Northern Ireland: The Politics of War and Peace*. Basingstoke: Palgrave.

Elliott, Marianne (ed.), 2002. *The Long Road to Peace in Northern Ireland*. Liverpool: Liverpool University Press.

Elliott, Sydney and W. D. Flackes, 1999. *Northern Ireland: A Political Directory, 1968–1999*, 5th edn. Belfast: Blackstaff.

Gallagher, Michael, 1990. 'Do Ulster unionists have a right to self-determination?', *Irish Political Studies* 5: 11–30.

Gilligan, Chris and Jon Tonge (eds), 1997. *Peace or War? Understanding the Peace Process in Northern Ireland*. Aldershot: Ashgate.

Girvin, Brian, 1999. 'Northern Ireland and the Republic', in Paul Mitchell and Rick Wilford (eds), *Politics in Northern Ireland*. Boulder, CO: Westview Press, pp. 220–41.

Harkness, D. W., 1983. *Northern Ireland since 1920*. Dublin: Helicon.

Hennessey, Thomas, 1997. *A History of Northern Ireland, 1920–1996*. Dublin: Gill and Macmillan.

Hennessey, Thomas, 2000. *The Northern Ireland Peace Process: Ending the Troubles?* Dublin: Gill and Macmillan.

Kennedy, Dennis, 1988. *The Widening Gulf: Northern Attitudes to the Independent Irish State, 1919–1949*. Belfast: Blackstaff.

Kennedy, Michael J., 2000. *Division and Consensus: The Politics of Cross-Border Relations in Ireland, 1925–1969*. Dublin: Institute of Public Adminstration.

Laffan, Michael, 1983. *The Partition of Ireland 1911–25*. Dundalk: Dundalgan Press.

Lijphart, Arend, 1977. *Democracy in Plural Societies: A Comparative Exploration*. New Haven, CT: Yale University Press.

Loughlin, James, 1998. *The Ulster Question since 1945*. Basingstoke: Macmillan.

Mallie, Eamonn and David McKittrick, 1997. *The Fight for Peace: The Secret Story behind the Irish Peace Process*, rev. edn. London: Mandarin.

McGarry, John and Brendan O'Leary, 1996. *Explaining Northern Ireland: Broken Images*. Oxford: Basil Blackwell.

McGarry, John and Brendan O'Leary, 2004. *The Northern Ireland Conflict: Consociational Engagements*. Oxford: Oxford University Press.

Mitchell, Paul, 1999. 'The party system and party competition', in Paul Mitchell and Rick Wilford (eds), *Politics in Northern Ireland*. Boulder, CO: Westview Press, pp. 91–119.

Mitchell, Paul and Rick Wilford (eds), 1999. *Politics in Northern Ireland*. Boulder, CO: Westview Press.

Moloney, Ed, 2002. *A Secret History of the IRA*. London: Allen Lane.

Moloney, Ed and Andy Pollak, 1986. *Paisley*. Dublin: Poolbeg.

O'Brien, Justin, 2000. *The Arms Trial*. Dublin: Gill and Macmillan.

Purdie, Bob, 1990. *Politics in the Streets: The Origins of the Civil Rights Movement in Northern Ireland*. Belfast: Blackstaff.

Ruane, Joseph and Jennifer Todd, 1996. *The Dynamics of Conflict in Northern Ireland: Power, Conflict and Emancipation*. Cambridge: Cambridge University Press.

Ruane, Joseph and Jennifer Todd (eds), 1999. *After the Good Friday Agreement: Analysing Political Change in Northern Ireland*. Dublin: University College Dublin Press.

Stewart, A. T. Q., 1989. *The Narrow Ground: The Roots of Conflict in Ulster*, rev. edn. London: Faber.

Tannam, Etain, 1999. *Cross-border Cooperation in the Republic of Ireland and Northern Ireland*. Basingstoke: Macmillan.

Tonge, Jon, 2002. *Northern Ireland: Conflict and Change*. London: Prentice Hall.
Whyte, John, 1990. *Interpreting Northern Ireland*. Oxford: Clarendon Press.
Wichert, Sabine, 1999. *Northern Ireland since 1945*, 2nd edn. London: Longman.
Wilford, Rick (ed.), 2001. *Aspects of the Belfast Agreement*. Oxford: Oxford University Press.

Websites

www.northsouthministerialcouncil.org   North–South Ministerial Council.
www.nio.gov.uk   Northern Ireland Office (British administration in Northern Ireland).
www.northernireland.gov.uk   Northern Ireland Executive, with links to other public bodies.
www.ni-assembly.gov.uk   Northern Ireland Assembly, including debates.
www.britishirishcouncil.org   British–Irish Council.

16 Europe and the international dimension

Brigid Laffan and Ben Tonra[1]

Ireland, according to Article 5 of the constitution, is a 'sovereign, independent, democratic state'. This assertion of the state's legal right to conduct its own affairs without outside interference is, however, an inadequate description of its relationship with the rest of the world. Forces of Europeanisation and globalisation have greatly increased Ireland's interaction with the international system and have embedded the state within it. It makes considerable sense to adapt the terminology often used by economists and to think of Ireland as a 'small open polity'.

Such an approach reminds us that the national political system is not self-contained but is subject to complex interactions with its external environment. On the one hand, Irish policy makers seek to project their values, preferences and interests onto the European and global stages. On the other, European and international institutions significantly impact upon events and policy in Ireland. In the first part of this chapter we identify the main characteristics of that environment, and show how geopolitical changes have affected Ireland's political development during the first 80 years of the state's existence. During the span of Irish independence, the Irish state found itself in a world dominated by great powers (1922–48), in a world of growing interdependence (1948–89) and, since 1989, following the collapse of communism, in an unsettled, unsettling and increasingly unipolar world, as American dominance steadily asserted itself. The two formative events of the contemporary international system were the breaching of the Berlin Wall on 9 November 1989 and the attacks on the twin towers in New York on 11 September 2001.

A key element in Ireland's international setting merits detailed analysis. The European Union (EU) – or European Community, as it was known when Ireland joined in 1973 – is a complex political system with a unique structure. Its influence on its members is pervasive and sometimes controversial. Macro-questions about the future development of the EU or issues concerning particular EU policies and programmes may become politicised at domestic level. The effects of the EU can be felt in politics, public policy and more widely in the state's constitutional and legal system. EU membership is not just a 'foreign policy' issue; in many respects it is an extension of national (or 'domestic') politics. Engagement with the Union creates a new type of politics that is neither international nor domestic but shares elements of both. For this reason, following an historical overview of Ireland's traditional external relations in the next section, we consider the nature of Ireland's relationship with the EU and we review the interplay of forces and interests between Dublin and Brussels, before turning in the last section to consider the significance of the EU dimension for Irish foreign policy.

In this context we ask whether Ireland really has a 'foreign policy', in the sense implied in the constitutional claim to independence quoted above. To what extent, and employing what means, do Irish governments pursue their values and interests in international politics in general? We shall see that much of this activity now takes place in conjunction with other EU states and through the complex web of multilateral networks that have been developed since the Second World War. This raises questions about the nature of specific policies, such as neutrality, and even about the continued existence of the 'sovereign, independent state'.

The external environment

Any state's external environment consists of all other international actors, together with the nature of the system formed by their relationships. Writers in the field of international relations have disagreed when it comes to identifying the most important characteristics of the international system (Baylis and Smith, 2001). We do not have to go very far into their contending theories to appreciate the complexity of the external environment, but their basic distinctions provide a starting point for an analysis of Ireland's position in world politics.

Followers of what is often called the 'realist' school stress the state as the focus of international politics, and look to 'power' as a major explanatory factor. Given the anarchic nature of the international system – there is no authority above states – the ever-present tendency to resort to force is seen as the most pressing problem of international life. In this view the foreign policy of a small state such as Ireland is above all a struggle for survival in a Hobbesian world of predatory great powers. Ireland's 'smallness' in these terms is rooted in its lack of 'power' – defined most clearly in military, political and diplomatic terms.

On the other hand, 'interdependence' or 'liberal' theorists have argued that states can co-operate in an anarchic world and can create mutually beneficial relationships directed towards collective problem solving. Such problems are largely defined in terms of maintaining peace and securing prosperity. Moreover, states are not the only actors on this international stage. International organisations, non-governmental organisations and non-state ('transnational') bodies such as multinational corporations may wield even more influence than some states. Ireland's vulnerability – as both a small open economy and a small open polity – is thus rooted in both economics and politics.

Both of the foregoing theoretical schools assume that states and state-actors (including diplomats and politicians) all act in a rational manner, pursuing their interests in something like a global poker game, with each state marshalling whatever resources it has at its disposal and then entering into complex negotiations from which it seeks successful outcomes. In some scholarship, this 'rational' approach has been challenged, and instead writers have chosen to focus upon the beliefs, values and identities of state actors and the communities of people(s) that comprise states. These approaches then study how such non-material factors impact on and some-times determine the foreign policy of a state and the consequent choices made by state actors. In such an approach, Ireland may be defined in a number of different ways, determined by the strength of contending and competing political discourses. These include seeing Ireland primarily as a post-imperial and post-colonial country with interests similar to those of states in the developing world; as a modern, cosmopolitan, European state co-operating with its partners in the European Union; or as a dynamic, free market-based society within the English-speaking world.

Whichever approach is adopted, it is clear that over time the international profile and even the role of the Irish state has evolved and changed. Such changes are, at least in part, a result of larger and sometimes revolutionary shifts in the external environment. Whether the Irish state contributes to or contests such change, it has no option – by virtue of its power, capacity and/ or sense of self-identity – but to adapt to these new realities. What is perhaps most interesting in looking at the evolution of the Irish state's international position is its considerable success up to now in negotiating the shoals and reefs of international politics.

Ireland in a world of great powers, 1922–48

From the establishment of the Irish Free State as a member of the British Commonwealth until the late 1940s, the international system was domi-nated overwhelmingly by the actions of the great powers, almost un-mediated by multilateral or international institutions. Although the League of Nations provided the new state with the opportunity to establish and develop its international credentials (Kennedy, 1996), the attempt to orga-nise an international rule of law through the League failed, and inter-national stability was eventually established only through force of arms. At first sight it seems paradoxical that Ireland's political independence was steadily consolidated during this period, but given that the overriding goal was one of independence from British domination this result is not so surpris-ing. British decline was a constant theme throughout the period as the age of empire began slowly to give way to the age of superpowers. Irish government representatives worked assiduously at both bilateral and multilateral levels first to establish and then gradually to strengthen the attributes of sovereign statehood. Over time, Ireland's ambiguous constitutional position (as a British dominion) was successfully exploited to secure the maximum leverage over Ireland's external affairs and ultimately to lay the groundwork for the 1948 decision to declare the state a republic.

These efforts began with multilateral negotiations within the British Commonwealth and the League of Nations, establishing the legal bona fides of the Irish state in international law and ultimately providing the basis for de Valera's unilateral revision of the 1921 Anglo-Irish Treaty in the form of the 1937 constitution (see Chapter 3). At this time the British government's policy of appeasement of Germany was mirrored on a much smaller scale by the appeasement of Ireland. Following a difficult period of bilateral conflict, including an 'economic war' with Britain, a resolution was achieved. This included – rather surprisingly given the wider European context – the handing over to Irish control in 1938 of naval ports originally retained by the British government in the 1921 treaty to provide for the effective defence of the British Isles. The return of the ports was an absolute prerequisite for the successful pursuit of Irish neutrality in the Second World War (Keatinge, 1986; Fisk, 1983).

The comparative success of Irish neutrality over the course of the Second World War, and the way in which the concept of neutrality came to be defined as the very leitmotif of Irish independence and sovereignty, should not obscure the basic limitations of Ireland's international position coming into the postwar era. Notwithstanding formal political independence, the economy remained almost wholly dependent on the fortunes (or more usually the misfortunes) of one of Europe's least successful economies, that of Britain. Moreover, partition was, if anything, more firmly consolidated, in spite of sporadic attempts to make it an international issue.

As the Cold War developed in the immediate postwar period, the weakness of the Irish position became all too clear. Early soundings on Irish membership of the North Atlantic Treaty Organisation (NATO) were rebuffed by Dublin when it became clear that the USA would not allow such negotiations to become embroiled in the partition issue (McCabe, 1991). Irish leaders hoped that playing the (Irish-) American card would mobilise Washington against London, but this card turned out to be of very limited value when the exigencies of a great power alliance such as that between the USA and Great Britain were at stake. Even though wartime neutrality had not been played strictly according to the rules (Fisk, 1983; Salmon, 1989) it had been played skilfully. In the end, however, its viability owed more to geopolitical realities than to government policy, and it left Irish negotiators without the kind of political capital they needed to pursue Irish interests internationally.

Ireland in the age of superpowers, 1948–89

A different kind of international system came into being after the Second World War. This 'bipolar' system, although marked by a major international conflict (the Cold War between the USA and the Soviet Union), came to acquire a much greater degree of stability than its predecessor. Against a background of unprecedented economic growth, 'international regimes' (a term that covers both formal organisations and looser arrangements) increasingly became the norm. Traditional distinctions between 'foreign policy' and 'domestic policy' lost some of their meaning, especially among the countries forming the core of west European integration.

Ireland, like some other small peripheral states in western Europe, was slow to adapt to this process. In the late 1940s traditional concerns with Anglo-Irish relations and partition seemed at least as important as the new issues, such as the Cold War, and geopolitical irrelevance facilitated an even less clearly defined policy of military neutrality. Economic dependence on the United Kingdom inhibited a close involvement in the European integration process, as British governments remained aloof from 'Europe'. However, a fundamental reappraisal of economic policy in the late 1950s brought about a more active interest in European integration. This led to an application to join the European Economic Community (EEC) in 1961, when the United Kingdom turned in this direction, only to be blocked by the veto on EEC enlargement in 1963 imposed by French President Charles de Gaulle against British membership.

Nevertheless, the state's internationalisation did make some tentative progress. A founding member of the Organisation for European Economic Cooperation (later to become the Organisation for Economic Cooperation and Development, OECD) and the Council of Europe in the late 1940s, Ireland was at last admitted to the United Nations (UN) in 1955. The delay had more to do with Cold War politics than with Irish policy, which had aimed at membership since 1946. Participation in the UN provided the basis of a peacekeeping role that soon emerged as a keystone of Irish foreign policy, and it also prompted the formation of policies towards the emerging 'third world' countries. In a UN dominated by wealthy industrialised countries and ex-colonial powers, Irish diplomats also played a significant role in several early UN debates such as those on China, on decolonisation and on nuclear non-proliferation (Skelly, 1997), thereby establishing something of a benchmark in what came to be seen as a 'golden age' in Irish foreign policy.

'Europe' – that is, the European Community, as the EEC and its associated treaty alliances were known – was, however, the focal point of government policy from the early 1960s onwards, for overwhelmingly economic reasons. When enlargement again became feasible in 1969, membership was negotiated and was approved in a referendum in 1972, by a majority of

83 per cent to 17 per cent in a turnout of over 70 per cent (see Appendix 2h). Thus from 1973 the state's involvement in international affairs became much more intensive, and its direct effects reached far into Irish public life (Keatinge, 1991). Economic growth rates accelerated significantly, while direct transfers from the European budget, initially through the common agricultural policy and then later and more broadly through the structural funds (regional, social and 'cohesion'), further contributed to Irish growth.

While Ireland suffered badly as a result of international recessions in the early and late 1970s – a trend exacerbated by poor domestic policy choices – it was evident by the late 1980s that European transfers, international investment, increased trade and better national economic planning were laying strong foundations for growth. Nonetheless, the dramatic increase in Irish growth rates in the second half of the 1990s (the so-called 'Celtic Tiger' phenomenon) caught most observers by surprise as the Irish economy outperformed all others in the European Union for more than a decade. In sum, this brought Irish per capita GDP from 66 percent of the EC average in 1972 to 115 percent of the average of the expanded EU in 2000. EU membership is not of itself a panacea for all economic ills – and indeed arguments rage about the comparatively sluggish pace of the European economy compared to that of the USA – but it does provide a systematic way of influencing a collective European response to global forces that are beyond the control of even the largest European economies.

The revival of momentum towards west European integration in the late 1980s confirmed the significance of Ireland's membership of the EC, which was transformed into the European Union (EU) following the Maastricht Treaty of 1992. Indeed, Ireland was seen by many of the smaller states in central and eastern Europe as a model success story, the narrative of which they wished to apply to their own early negotiations and ultimate membership of the European Union.

The collapse of the Soviet Union as one of the world's two 'superpowers' between 1989 and 1991 not only opened the path towards reform and enlargement of the European Union but it also – and more significantly – defined the end of the bipolar power system. The new global political system is characterised by major uncertainties: the strains of fundamental democratic and free market transition in the former communist world, and especially in the Russian Federation; the capacity and will of the USA to play the role of 'global policeman'; the proliferation of military technology of all sorts, especially weapons of mass destruction; and, arguably, a new situation in which 'threats' to the security of states may now arise not just from the actions of other states but from those of terrorist groups and even from individuals.

The extent and speed of change in Ireland's external environment is unparalleled. However, this unique transition has also been met by a uniquely formidable complex of multilateral organisations – the UN and its agencies, the Bretton Woods system (International Monetary Fund, World Bank and World Trade Organisation), collective security institutions (Organisation for Security and Cooperation in Europe, NATO), regional political or economic groupings (such as the North American Free Trade Area, Association of South East Asian Nations, African Union and Organisation of American States) and trade or economic institutions (such as Organisation of Petroleum Exporting Countries, Asia Pacific Economic Cooperation and OECD). None of these existed in any substantial form at the end of the Second World War and each has had to respond in its own way to the fundamental changes witnessed in the world since 1989. This institutional matrix has failed in some circumstances and only partially succeeded in others, but these institutions have softened the hard edges of a very painful transition.

The European Union is a central element in all of this, and thus Ireland is much more directly involved in the making of the global and regional systems than was the case in the late 1940s. The European Union produces about one-quarter of the goods and services consumed internationally and generates about one-quarter of global wealth. It does so not only from its own resources but through its trading and economic relationships with the rest of the world. The Union is thus a powerful economic and trading actor, with the capacity to define the shape and policy of international institutions. From an Irish perspective, it may be argued that the Union also offers something of a safe haven against the wilder and unpredictable winds of globalisation. While no state or group of states can stand alone against such tempests or sail indefinitely against international economic winds, the Union – by virtue of the size of its internal market and its economic and trading capacity – can offer its member states breathing space and serve to temper the sharpness and chill of such currents.

Ireland in a changing world

There is as yet no consensus as to how we should characterise the contemporary international system. In the immediate aftermath of the fall of the Berlin Wall on 11 November 1989 and the subsequent collapse of the Soviet Union, hubris and optimism defined the period as 'the end of history' and the final victory of liberal democracy over its twentieth-century adversaries, fascism and communism (Fukuyama, 1992). This was illustrated in 1990–1 when, in response to the Iraqi invasion and occupation of Kuwait, a large multinational coalition was forged to defend international law under American leadership through the auspices of the United Nations. Ireland did not join that coalition – citing its military neutrality – but it facilitated troop movements through Shannon airport. Hubris was evident in talk of new world orders sustained by universal global values, law and institutions. This optimistic vision was met by the offer of darker visions of an emerging conflict between civilisations being played out between and within states (Huntington, 1996). The 1991–5 wars in Yugoslavia and the 1994 genocide in Rwanda offered perfect case studies for such analyses. The failure of the international community to respond effectively to these challenges was seen by some as proof of the liberal illusion. When the borders between different cultural or civilisational groups failed to ignite elsewhere, attention began to shift again, and this time looked to earlier models of *realpolitik* and even to medieval metaphors – where once more the world would play the game of great states and princes. The central analytical question now was on the locus of international power. Would the international system settle into a battle of dominance between many or few 'poles' of power or was the USA, as the sole superpower, going to define a new *pax Americana* through its unipolar moment in history? The questions posed in the post-Cold War world were challenge enough without those that came to be asked in the aftermath of the terrorist attacks against the USA in New York and Washington, DC on 11 September 2001, when four commercial airliners were hijacked: two were deliberately crashed into New York's World Trade Center, and a third was flown into the Pentagon in Washington, DC (the fourth did not reach its intended target).

The cumulative impact that these attacks had on the external environment was to create a demand from the USA to its friends as well as to its allies to support a new global effort – a so-called 'war against terrorism'. In the case of Ireland, the response has been to work through the European Union to introduce new legislative provisions, to co-operate in devising new EU-wide security policies and to establish new bilateral EU–US structures to combat terrorism.

While most states in the international system and almost all multilateral institutions have pledged some measure of support to that endeavour, there remain important differences over strategy, tactics and an often fundamental divergence of understanding over the nature of the roots of this conflict. What it does overall, however, is to introduce a further element of instability to an already destabilised international system. While larger and more powerful states may have the capacity to contend with such issues – to steer their own course, as it were – smaller countries such as Ireland are left far more exposed.

For Ireland, the successful pursuit of security and prosperity has been made through its commitment to regional and multilateral institutions. Faced with rising levels of instability, the orthodox prescription for Irish foreign policy will be to cling even closer and harder to the moorings of international law and its institutional networks. For Ireland, the European Union is perhaps the centre of that matrix and it simultaneously offers Irish policymakers their greatest capacity to participate in the shaping of world events rather than simply be swept before them. We will now turn to Ireland's role within that entity.

The European institutions and Ireland

Over the years, the EU has developed a constitutional framework and a set of institutions to govern co-operation among the member states. The Union's constitutional and legal framework consists of a series of treaties and an extensive corpus of laws that have been agreed within the framework of the Union's institutions. This section analyses the key characteristics of the European Union and the interaction between European institutions and Ireland.

The European Union

The European Union is unlikely ever to assume the properties of traditional statehood, but it has undeniably altered our understanding of statehood in Europe. It differs from traditional forms of interstate co-operation in five main respects. First, the founders of the European Economic Communities in the 1950s set out to lay the foundations of a federal or supranational Europe. After the war, there was a strong movement favouring European unity. Although the European Union failed to live up to the expectations of the founding fathers, the idea of a common destiny among the states is part of the rhetoric of EU policies and provides an ideological underpinning to European integration. Moreover, when a country decides to opt for EU membership, it is accepting a political commitment to participate in an evolving political entity (Laffan *et al.*, 1999).

Second, the Union has a constitution that is based upon a set of earlier treaties (see Box 16.1). These treaties establish the range of public policies

---

Box 16.1 Treaties of the European Union

The main treaties are:

- Paris Treaty (establishing the European Coal and Steel Community), 1950
- Rome Treaties (European Economic Community and Euratom), 1957
- Merger Treaty, 1965
- Budget Treaties, 1970 and 1975
- Single European Act, 1987
- Treaty on European Union (Maastricht Treaty), 1992
- Treaty of Amsterdam, 1997
- Treaty of Nice, 2000
- Constitutional Treaty endorsed by the Convention on the Future of Europe, 2003. Negotiations to transform this into a European Constitution concluded in June 2004

that the Union may engage in and make provision for a set of institutions to manage collective governance among the member states. The treaties were condensed into a draft constitution in a convention that began work in March 2002 and completed it in July 2003. Law plays a central role in the workings of the Union, and EC law in effect represents an 'external constitution' for the Irish political system.

Third, the Union is endowed with a set of institutions to make and implement policy (see Box 16.2). The Union involves both traditional intergovernmental co-operation (that is, co-operation between sovereign states) and, at the same time, significant elements of supranational authority, in the form of institutions that are formally independent of the member states (Nugent, 2003). Intergovernmental relations are formalised in the Council system, while supranational authority is represented by the legal system, the Commission, the Court, the European Parliament (EP), the Court of Auditors and the European Central Bank. The Union's policy processes are a delicate balance between the powers of all of these institutions.

The fourth respect in which the EU differs from traditional forms of interstate co-operation is that it has an extremely ambitious policy reach. The treaties set out in considerable detail just what the Union should be doing, and the substance of much of what it does is economic. The EEC Treaty established the goal of integration as the creation of a customs union and a common market, in which there would be a free flow of goods, capital, workers and services. A large part of the Union's later policy developments have derived from the need to fulfil this goal. The central thrust of the Single European Act of 1987 was the '1992 programme', whose aim was the creation by the end of 1992 of an internal market in which economic

---

Box 16.2 Institutions of the European Union

The EU has five main institutions. These are:

- Commission
- Council of Ministers
- European Parliament
- European Court of Justice
- Court of Auditors, which was elevated to the status of a full institution in the Treaty on European Union

In addition, there are a number of Union bodies, such as the European Central Bank (ECB), the Economic and Social Committee, the Committee of the Regions and the Ombudsman. The ECB was given the status of a full institution in the Convention's draft constitution but this has not been agreed by all of the member states.

exchange between states would resemble economic exchange within a state. This involved nothing less than the abolition of border controls, the harmonisation of technical standards, the creation of a framework in which banks and insurance companies from one member state might set up in any other member state, liberalisation of the rules governing air transport, and the achievement of a degree of convergence in rates of indirect taxation. The Treaty of Maastricht established the framework for a single currency, the euro, which came into effect on 1 January 1999. The Treaty of Amsterdam (1997) established an ambitious programme for co-operation in justice, immigration and asylum. The Treaty of Nice (2000) finalised the institutional reforms necessary to provide for the enlargement of the Union.

Fifth, the Union has a presence in world politics. Some 156 states are accredited to it, with embassies in Brussels. Its international role has led to development co-operation with third countries, a number of association agreements with European and non-European states, the common commercial policy that makes the Union an important actor in the World Trade Organisation (WTO), and the system of foreign policy co-operation that is described below.

Since the mid-1980s, the EU has experienced a particularly dynamic period of development characterised by two big economic projects (the single market and the single currency), a series of additional treaties, and the accession of new states. As a consequence of an intensive period of treaty change, its governance structures became more complicated, with a myriad of rules and differing institutional roles. In addition, the growing visibility and salience of the EU in domestic affairs led to the politicisation of integration and growing unease about democracy and accountability in the Union. In all of the member states there has been contention about particular aspects of EU policies and about the future of the Union itself. The prospect of a continental enlargement to embrace the former socialist states gave renewed urgency to reform of the Union's institutions and ways of doing business.

The Commission

The Commission, originally conceived of as the EU's embryonic government, has 25 members drawn from the member states. Since 1973, there have been seven Irish commissioners (see Box 16.3). Although in principle the incoming president of the Commission should have a say over national nominees, in practice the government of the day decides who should get the Irish nomination. This may change under the provisions of a new European constitution. In future, it is envisaged that a member state will send the names of three nominees to the president-designate of the Commission, who will choose from these.

Apart from the College of Commissioners, as the EU's central bureaucracy the Commission interacts with the Irish political system in a variety of

Box 16.3 Ireland's EU Commissioners, 1973–2004

Commissioners are appointed by the respective national governments, and to date all the Irish commissioners have been established political figures. Most have been cabinet ministers, though both Peter Sutherland and David Byrne were Attorney General prior to their appointments. A commissioner is assigned a 'portfolio' in the Commission, much like a cabinet minister at national level, and there is considerable competition for the plum positions. Peter Sutherland was given Competition, which was seen as an important portfolio, when he joined the first Delors Commission in 1985. Agriculture, for which his successor Ray MacSharry was given responsibility in the second Delors Commission in 1989, is much sought after because the CAP commands a sizeable proportion of the Community budget. Pádraig Flynn's brief included Social Affairs, which is regarded as a middle-ranking portfolio. David Byrne won the politically sensitive portfolio – in the aftermath of BSE and various other food scares – of Health and Consumer Affairs. In July 2004 the government announced that Ireland's representative in the Barroso Commission, to take office in November of that year, would be Charlie McCreevy, who was then the Minister for Finance.

Commissioner	Appointing government	Period	Portfolio
Patrick Hillery	FF	1973–6	Social Affairs
Richard Burke	FG–Lab	1977–80	Transport, Consumer Affairs, Taxation, Relations with EP
Michael O'Kennedy	FF	1981–2	President's delegate, Administration
Richard Burke	FF	1982–4	Greek renegotiation
Peter Sutherland	FG–Lab	1985–8	Competition
Ray MacSharry	FF	1989–92	Common Agricultural Policy
Pádraig Flynn	FF	1993–9	Social Affairs
David Byrne	FF–PD	1999–2004	Health and Consumer Protection

ways. Irish civil servants and the representatives of interest organisations participate in Commission advisory bodies and working parties when legislation is being prepared for submission to the Council of Ministers. They are also involved in what are called the 'comitology' committees, which oversee the implementation of EU policies. The Commission plays a very important role in managing the flow of Brussels money to the member

Table 16.1 Referrals to the European Court
of Justice, 2001

Member state	No. of cases
Denmark	4
Finland	6
Sweden	6
Portugal	14
Netherlands	15
Austria	15
Luxembourg	17
UK	22
Belgium	23
Spain	26
Ireland	27
Germany	28
Greece	34
France	53
Italy	57

Source: European Commission, Com (2002), 324
final, 13.

states. Its officials sit on national monitoring bodies to ensure that EU
money is being well spent. In its capacity as guardian of the treaties, the
Commission is responsible for ensuring that the member states implement,
observe and enforce European laws, and that private companies adhere to
competition policy and to legislation on mergers. The Commission can issue
proceedings against a member state for failure to implement EC law.
Ireland, which had a reasonably good record on implementation in the
mid-1980s, then fell behind in the incorporation of legislation on the internal
market directives: a Commission report of December 1991 showed that only
Italy and Luxembourg had a higher rate of non-implementation (European
Commission, 1991: 57). The reasons for this included the absence of legal
expertise within Irish government departments, reliance on the overburdened parliamentary draftsman, staff shortages in some departments, and
the sheer weight of the Union's legislative programme. In 2001, there were
27 outstanding cases against Ireland, a large number given the country's
size and population (see Table 16.1). Ireland appears to have particular
difficulties in implementing directives in the fields of transport, the environment, and food legislation.

The Council of Ministers and European Council

The Council of Ministers is at the centre of the legislative process and is the
juncture where the Union meets with the national political systems.
Although the Council is legally just one body, in practice the appropriate

national ministers (such as foreign affairs, agriculture, environment or transport) meet to negotiate on Commission proposals that fall within the ambit of their responsibilities at national level. In addition, the Taoiseach has direct contact with his counterparts in other member states in the European Council. The European Council was made a formal part of the EU system in the 1987 Single European Act (SEA) although meetings between heads of state and government had been a routine part of the system from 1975 onwards. The Council of Ministers has a vast and complicated substructure made up of some 250 working parties and committees. During a typical working week in Brussels, Irish ministers, civil servants and officials from state-sponsored bodies will be attending working-party meetings in the Commission or in the Council. The frequency of flights from Dublin to Brussels at 40 per week on winter schedules (compared with 31 to Amsterdam, for example) underlines the impact of this additional layer on Irish government and politics.

The presidency, which was originally envisaged simply as a convenient mechanism to provide chairpersons for Council meetings, has become an important source of political direction within the Union. Member states hold the presidency on a rotating basis for a period of six months. Since joining the EU, Ireland has held it on six occasions: in 1975, 1979, 1984, 1990, 1996 and 2004, the last traditional presidency for which Ireland had responsibility. The pressure of enlargement and the problems of continuity caused by a succession of six-monthly chairs led to demands for changes in the chairing of the Council. The demise of the traditional presidency, although inevitable, deprives small states such as Ireland of an opportunity to enhance their status and involvement in international politics. Successive Irish governments have taken the presidency very seriously, seeing it as an opportunity to run the affairs of the Union in a businesslike fashion so as to build up a stock of goodwill in other member states. Ireland's 2004 presidency was particularly successful, culminating in the Taoiseach and his negotiating team securing agreement to a draft EU constitution at the June European Council meeting. Apart from the presidency, where Ireland has a very good record, it is difficult to judge how well Irish ministers and officials perform in the Council chamber and in working parties. Ireland's voting record suggests that there is a tendency to side with the emerging consensus. Between 1996 and 2000, Ireland abstained on only one vote and opposed seven – only Luxembourg, Austria and Finland cast fewer votes against an emerging consensus (see Table 16.2).

The European Parliament

The European Parliament (EP) is the Union's representative institution. It was conceived as a consultative body rather than a legislature by the founding fathers, and so it could only give its views on legislative proposals, though it could dismiss the entire Commission by a two-thirds majority of

Table 16.2 Number of votes where each EU country has not been on the winning side in European Council, 1996–2000

Member state	Abstained	Voted against
Belgium	5	11
Denmark	2	20
Germany	14	37
Greece	2	9
Spain	10	8
France	6	12
Ireland	1	7
Italy	9	28
Luxembourg	5	3
Netherlands	4	22
Austria	2	8
Portugal	9	6
Finland	0	5
Sweden	0	14
United Kingdom	6	16
Total	75	206

Source: Hayes-Renshaw (2002: 64).

its members. In 1975, the Parliament gained some budgetary powers. After 1979, when for the first time it was directly elected, its search for new powers was underpinned by its democratic credentials. During the successive treaty negotiations, the Parliament pressed for increased powers for itself, both in the legislative process and in relation to the Union's international role, and it was partially successful on each occasion, so the Council now has to take more heed of its views. In the 1992 Treaty on European Union (TEU) the EP gained the right of co-decision with the Council of Ministers. In effect this meant joint decision making between the EP and the Council and the possibility for the Parliament to reject a proposal if agreement could not be reached between the two institutions. When co-decision applies, the Parliament has become as powerful as the Council of Ministers.

The Parliament has 732 members, of whom 13 represent the Republic and a further three Northern Ireland.[2] While 13 seats might not appear that many, Ireland is generously represented in per capita terms; in 2004 each of the Irish MEPs represents some 225,000 voters whereas their German counterparts represent some 806,000. MEPs do not sit in national delegations but as part of political groupings that are largely based on Europe's traditional party families.

Irish MEPs are members of six of the Parliament's groups (see Table 16.3). When Ireland became a member of the Community in 1973, its political parties had to decide which EP group to join. This was relatively straight-

forward for Labour, which joined the Socialist group. For Fianna Fáil and
Fine Gael the decision was more difficult – for one thing, they could not join
the same group because of electoral competition at national level. Fine Gael
joined the largest of the conservative groups, the European People's Party
(the Christian Democrats). Participation in the Christian Democratic movement has widened the horizons of Fine Gael and has brought its senior members and some of its activists into contact with their counterparts in other
countries; around 18 per cent of Fine Gael members have attended an EPP
meeting (Gallagher and Marsh, 2002: 233). Fianna Fáil was left without a
political grouping for its first six months in the Parliament. The advantages
of belonging to a group – such as secretarial and research backup, speaking
time and membership of committees – forced it to link up with the French
Gaullists. This was an uneasy partnership, and it was limited to the Parliament; there were no party-to-party links of the sort found in the Christian
Democratic group or the Socialists. The departure of the Gaullists to the
European People's Party left Fianna Fáil in a group called the Union for
Europe of the Nations (UEN), a conservative grouping consisting of the
Pasqua–Villiers list from France and the Italian Alleanza Nazionale, a
conservative or 'post-fascist' party. This grouping is the second smallest in
the Parliament, weakening Ireland's voice, since a significant number of
Ireland's MEPs are in a group with limited influence and one that, furthermore, adopts a very critical stance on integration. The Progressive Democrats joined the Liberal grouping in 1989 while the Green Party, of course,
belongs to the Green group.

The five-yearly direct elections to the European Parliament constitute an
additional contest in the Irish electoral cycle (for the results of past elections,
see Appendix 2e). The constituency boundaries were redrawn for the 2004
elections and the Republic is now divided into four constituencies: Dublin
(four seats), East (three seats), South (three seats) and Northwest (three
seats). Election is by PR-STV, as in the case of Dáil elections (see Chapter 4),
though this could well change in the future since a common electoral system

Table 16.3 Irish party membership of EP groups, July 2004

EP group	Total	Ireland
European People's Party and European Democrats	268	5 (FG)
Party of European Socialists	200	1 (Labour)
European Liberal Democratic and Reformist Group	88	1 (Ind.)
Greens/European Free Alliance	42	0
European United Left/Nordic Green Left	41	1 (SF)
Independence and Democracy	33	1 (Ind.)
Union for Europe of the Nations	27	4 (FF)
Not attached/others	33	0 (Ind.)
Total EP	732	13

for all member states remains on the agenda and this would probably be some kind of list system of PR (see p. 106). Irish MEPs inhabit a rather different world from that of their counterparts in the Dáil. They must travel a lot and spend two or three weeks of every month outside Ireland at plenary sessions of the Parliament, attending committee meetings and dealing with the work of their political grouping. This makes it difficult for them to maintain contact with their very large constituencies and to maintain a profile in their political parties. In January 2002, Pat Cox, a member of the Liberal group in the Parliament, was elected president of the EP for a period of two and a half years – the highest elected office that an Irish person has won in the European Union.

The Court of Justice

Since its inception, the European Court of Justice (ECJ) has played a key role in providing the legal cement for integration. It has interpreted the treaties in a dynamic fashion rather than in a static manner, and its legal activism has strengthened the federal character of the EU. The Irish judicial system now feeds into the Union's legal order. Irish courts may seek rulings from the Court of Justice on the correct interpretation of EU law, and the Irish government and private citizens may find themselves before the court in Luxembourg. Ireland has been taken to court in such diverse areas as agriculture, fisheries, the internal market, taxation and the environment. EU law endows Irish citizens and groups with rights that they can pursue in the Irish courts and also at the Court of Justice in Luxembourg. The Irish courts are obliged to ask the ECJ for a preliminary ruling on matters of EU law, if these are raised by cases in the Irish system. Rulings from the ECJ have meant, for example, that the Irish state has had to pay compensation to women for discrimination in social security legislation and late implementation of EU directives (see p. 292). Issues of constitutional law and the compatibility of EC treaties with the Irish constitution were raised by the Supreme Court judgment in 1987 on the Crotty case, when it deemed title three of the Single European Act to be incompatible with the constitution, meaning that a referendum had to be held on the SEA.

The Court of Auditors

The Court of Auditors was given full institutional status in the Treaty of Maastricht. Its main task is to monitor the management of EU finances by EU institutions and the member states. This means that its officers have the right to investigate EU expenditure by Irish public and private agencies. It works closely with the Irish Comptroller and Auditor General (see pp. 346–7 above). The court was particularly critical of Ireland's management of the beef regime, a matter that came to public attention during the 1991–4 Beef Tribunal (see Chapter 14).

The EU and the Irish political system

Increasingly scholars of integration are analysing the impact of the EU on the national level – 'how Europe hits home' (Börzel and Risse, 2000). In this section four aspects of how 'Europe hits home' are explored. First, public opinion in Ireland and the outcomes of a series of referendums on European treaties are analysed. Second, the impact of Europe on public policy is assessed. Third, the manner in which the Irish executive and parliament have responded to the challenge of dealing with Brussels is examined and, fourth, the impact of EU membership on Irish foreign policy is considered.

Public opinion and referendums

Knowledge about Irish public opinion towards engagement with the European Union can be gleaned from twice-yearly public opinion surveys, known as Eurobarometer surveys, that are conducted by the European Commission, and the referendums that have been held in response to treaty change in the Union. The emphatic Yes vote in the 1972 accession referendum demonstrated that Irish public opinion was largely in favour of EU membership. In 1972, Fianna Fáil and Fine Gael both supported entry, along with the employers' and farmers' organisations, while Labour, the two Sinn Féin parties and the trade unions opposed it, in a campaign dominated by economic issues. Although integration itself faltered in the 1970s and early 1980s, the reform of the EC in the Single European Act (SEA) was approved by a second referendum in 1987. However, the result – 70 per cent to 30 per cent in a poll of only 44 per cent – reflected a measure of disillusionment, or at least of indifference (Gallagher, 1988). It may also indicate a degree of public bewilderment concerning a very complex political system. Again Fianna Fáil and Fine Gael supported the treaty whereas Labour did not take an official stance.

The SEA was followed by the Treaty on European Union (the Maastricht Treaty) which again required a change in the Irish constitution and hence a referendum in 1992 (Holmes, 1993). This was complicated by the issue of abortion: the government had inserted a protocol in the Maastricht Treaty, in order to protect Ireland's constitutional ban on abortion (Article 40.3.3), but the Supreme Court's subsequent interpretation of that article in the 'X' case (see Box 3.2, p. 88) led to confusion about the meaning and remit of the protocol. Both feminist and anti-abortion lobbies opposed the treaty, alongside traditional nationalists and supporters of neutrality. On the other side was found almost the whole political establishment and the major economic interests. The distribution of votes cast was similar to that in the SEA referendum (see Appendix 2h). In the circumstances this was a strong endorsement of Ireland's participation in the mainstream of European integration.

Although in 1992 there had been much uncertainty about the achievement of economic and monetary union, one of the main points of substance in the Maastricht Treaty, it was clear by 1998 that Ireland would be a founding member of the planned union. In May of that year the electorate was asked to give its verdict on a further revision of the EU's legal base, the Amsterdam Treaty of 1997. The outcome suggested some hesitation among the Irish electorate about the continuing process of treaty change in the Union, for just 62 per cent voted Yes, down from the 69 per cent support for the Maastricht Treaty in 1992. Yet by 1998, all political parties in the Dáil with the exception of the Green Party supported the treaty.

This was followed by the rejection of the Nice Treaty in June 2001 when a majority of the Irish electorate (54 per cent) voted No in the referendum (O'Mahony, 2001). This was a profound shock to the government, to its partners in the Union, and to the candidate states in central Europe. The government allocated only three weeks to the campaign and adopted a desultory approach to convincing the electorate of the merits of ratification. A lacklustre campaign failed to engage the electorate. The majority of voters stayed at home; only 34 per cent voted. Research conducted after the referendum found that turnout had a major bearing on the outcome; 53 per cent of those who had voted for the Amsterdam Treaty abstained on Nice whereas the abstention level among opponents of Amsterdam was only 36 per cent (Sinnott, 2001). The government was faced with a very difficult domestic and external agenda. It sought to persuade its partners and the candidate states that Ireland was still committed to enlargement while, at the same time, it sought to persuade its electorate that it had listened, knowing that it was under pressure to re-run the referendum.

The government pursued a strategy of creating the domestic conditions for holding a second Nice referendum by:

- the establishment of a cross-party National Forum on Europe (autumn 2001);
- enhanced parliamentary scrutiny of Ireland's European policy (July 2002);
- the Seville Declarations on Irish neutrality and a common defence (June 2002) (see Box 16.4, p. 458).

Following re-election in May 2002, the government was committed to re-run the referendum in October 2002 (Hayward, 2003). The result was a significant Yes vote of 63 per cent to 37 per cent with a turnout of 49 per cent (see Appendix 2h). There was a far higher level of mobilisation on the Yes side for the second Nice referendum. The two governing parties, and particularly Fianna Fáil, devoted considerable resources to the campaign and there was extensive mobilisation of civil society groups including the establishment of a new campaign organisation, the Irish Alliance for Europe. The experience of referendums on Europe suggests that a majority of the electorate accepts Ireland's membership of the EU and has been prepared to endorse treaty change within the Union. However, turnout in the referendums, added to a decline in the Yes vote, underlines the fact that a proportion of the Irish electorate have concerns about the deepening of integration and Ireland's place in the evolving Union.

In Eurobarometer surveys over many years until recently, well over 80 per cent of respondents stated their belief that membership had been good to Ireland. In recent years, however, that endorsement has appeared less settled. In spring 2003 (Eurobarometer no. 59), the Irish graph of support for European integration, as measured by the standard 'membership' indicator (thinking that country's membership of the European Union is a 'good thing'), registered a third successive fall, going from 83 per cent in autumn 2001 to 67 per cent in spring 2003 (Eurobarometer 59, 2003). Eurobarometer 60 in autumn 2003 recorded an upward swing with 73 per cent of respondents saying that EU membership was a good thing for Ireland. That figure was second only to Luxembourg at 77 per cent. On the question of whether the country had benefited from EU membership, 82 per cent of Irish respondents believed this to be the case, the highest figure in the EU (see Table 16.4). Support for Ireland's membership of the Union was not accompanied by high levels of knowledge about EU affairs, though. Ireland was one of four countries where respondents had a pronounced sense of lack of knowledge of the European Union, with 42 per cent of respondents feeling that they had a poor knowledge of the EU and its policies. The only two member states standing lower were the United Kingdom and Portugal (Eurobarometer 60, 2003).

Public policy

The development of the EU is not just an issue of 'high politics' during a referendum campaign; it has a continuing impact on a host of domestic public policy issues. This impact is felt through the Union's spending policies, its agricultural and regional funds, through the demands of the single currency and through European regulation. The dynamic of economic and political integration is felt in the nooks and crannies of public policy and its implementation.

Irish agricultural policy is almost entirely made in Brussels. Irish farmers, attracted by the prospect of improved farm incomes, strongly endorsed Ireland's membership of the EU in 1972. Since then, the Irish Farmers' Association and the Irish Creamery Milk Suppliers' Association have acted as powerful lobbies in support of the common agricultural policy (CAP). The high cost of the policy has led to sustained pressure for reform. The Department of Agriculture and the farming organisations have been key members, together with the French, of the CAP supporters' club. That said, a combination of budgetary pressures, successive enlargements, and pressure within the General Agreement on Tariffs and Trade (GATT) and World Trade

Table 16.4 Perceived benefits of EU membership among public in member states, autumn 2003 (%)

	Austria	Belgium	Denmark	Finland	Germany	Greece	France	Ireland
Benefited	40	57	67	40	37	75	48	82
Not benefited	45	31	21	47	37	17	33	9
Don't know	15	12	12	13	27	8	19	9
Total	100.0	100.0	100.0	100.0	100.0	100.0	100.0	100.0

	Italy	Luxembourg	Netherlands	Portugal	Spain	Sweden	UK	EU 15
Benefited	49	69	54	65	66	31	30	46
Not benefited	35	21	34	22	19	50	45	34
Don't know	16	10	12	13	15	19	24	19
Total	100.0	100.0	100.0	100.0	100.0	100.0	100.0	100.0

Source: Eurobarometer no. 60, 2003.

Note
The figures represent responses to a question as to whether respondents believe that their country has benefited from EU membership.

Organisation have forced change in the financing and instruments of agricultural support in Europe. The eastern enlargement in May 2004 has led to a decoupling of EU payments to farmers from agricultural production but has not led to a reduction in the size of the agricultural budget in the Union. Financial flows from the CAP have meant that the subvention of farm incomes in Ireland has been paid for by the European budget and indirectly by European consumers who pay higher prices for their food than they might otherwise do.

Other financial transfers from the EU budget became part and parcel of distributive politics, especially since the 1980s. The structural funds represented a very significant transfer from the EU budget to Ireland. EU largesse was channelled to Ireland in the form of three Community Support Frameworks (CSF), which ran from 1988 to 1993, 1994 to 1999 and 2000 to 2006. The Economic and Social Research Institute described the 1994–99 CSF as a notable success story because it enhanced medium-term financial planning, and represented a quantum leap in the provision of public infrastructure (Honohan, 1997). Central government invested heavily in the implementation of the various EU programmes, and Ireland is generally regarded as a state that uses structural funds well. Whereas the first CSF was developed and controlled by the Department of Finance, different regions, localities and community groups fought for influence over the second and third CSF. The flow of funding in the 2000–6 period represents a transition phase in Ireland's receipts of structural funds. For this period, the country was divided into two regions: the Borders, Midlands and West (known as the BMW region) and the Eastern region. The BMW region retained its status as one designated for a high level of EU subvention, whereas the Eastern region received considerably less. Although Ireland's GDP converged and then surpassed per capita incomes in other member states (it reached a per capita GDP 25 per cent above the EU average in 2002), Ireland remained a net beneficiary of the EU budget. In 2002, Ireland received a net transfer of 1.6 billion euro from the EU budget, a figure that amounted to 1.5 per cent of gross national income in that year. After 2006, Ireland's receipts from the structural funds will dramatically change, as EU transfers will be directed to the new member states. In the financial period 2007–13 Ireland will become a net contributor to the EU budget.

The single currency project is another area that has had a significant impact on Irish public policy. Following the ratification of the Maastricht Treaty, successive Irish governments signalled their desire to join the single currency in the first wave. This had a direct bearing on the framing of the annual budget from 1992 onwards, as the goal of policy was to meet the criteria for membership of European monetary union. This implied tight control over the public finances and a fiscal policy designed to promote low inflation. The position of the Central Bank and the Department of Finance was enhanced *vis-à-vis* the spending ministries, as Finance could hide behind the criteria in preparing the annual budgetary estimates. With the conversion to the euro, EU economic governance became even more important as there is now considerable pressure to coordinate macro-economic policies, including taxation, at an EU level. The long-term consequence of this for Irish politics is difficult to predict, other than to say that there will be increasing constraints on Irish government and a further narrowing of policy options.

The implementation of EU environmental law illustrates the manner in which Europe becomes part of the dynamic of politics at domestic level. The EU passed two environmental conservation directives – the Birds directive in 1979 and the Habitats directive in 1992 – that have proved very contentious and difficult to implement. These two directives altered the policy frame at national level by requiring the imposition of restrictions on private land use, thus impinging particularly on farmers. These directives are strongly supported by the environmental organisations, notably Birdwatch Ireland and the Irish Peatland Conservation Council. Farmers reacted angrily to the constraints imposed by these directives with the result that their implementation was delayed. The Commission, in an attempt to speed up implementation, brought Ireland to court on two occasions and threatened Ireland's receipts from the structural funds. The government found itself mediating between angry farmers who were turning up in their hundreds to Irish Farmers' Association meetings, the Commission seeking implementation of agreed European law, and environmentalists using Brussels to strengthen their hand in domestic politics. Within the administration there was a battle between the scientific logic of special areas of conservation, the generalist civil servants dealing with Brussels, and the politicians, who were unwilling to impose an unpopular EC directive on their constituents. Following agreement on adequate consultation and compensation, the directive is being implemented although considerable contention remains.

The management of EU business at home

The EU's complex policy process is but the tip of an iceberg that extends deep into the national political and administrative systems. Each member state must service the policy process in Brussels, the constant round of meetings held under the auspices of the Commission and the Council. Outside the formal legislative process, there are frequent informal meetings at various levels. During each set of negotiations and at all stages, Irish civil servants prepare briefing material and instructions for those going to Brussels to represent the Irish interest. The preparation of positions requires consultation and coordination both within and between departments. Moreover, Irish interest groups will seek to influence those formulating the Irish position. The farming organisations are active on all issues dealing with agricultural policy, and the employers and trade unions debate labour law issues within a European framework. Other groups such as the Irish National Organisation of the Unemployed, women's groups and environmentalists seek to lobby in the Union's multilevel system (see also Chapter 13). Politics may begin at home, but it no longer ends there (Laffan, 1996). Responsibility for the management of European affairs in Ireland is divided between the coordinators, at the heart of the system; the inner circle; and an outer band of departments with limited EU responsibility. The coordinators are the Taoiseach's department, Foreign Affairs and Finance. Together these departments form the core of the system (Laffan, 2001; Laffan and O'Mahony, 2003).

The Department of Foreign Affairs, responsible for keeping a watching brief over the flow of legislation through the policy process and over the main lines of policy development, is the centre of daily and weekly coordination. It has built up an extensive expertise on the Union, giving it a key role in the management of EU business in Ireland, and its responsibility for EU matters means that its importance within the administrative system has increased. With the growing importance of the European Council, the Department of the Taoiseach is heavily involved in European matters. The Department of Finance also forms part of the core because of its responsibility for the public finances. The inner core consists of those departments that have important European responsibilities, notably Enterprise and Employment, Agriculture, Justice and Law Reform, and Environment – all of which are heavily involved in EU business. The remaining departments form the outer circle, with limited European responsibilities.

All member states of the Union have established coordinating mechanisms to manage EC business, in order to ensure that the Brussels process is adequately serviced and that national priorities are highlighted. The traditional Irish style for managing EU coordination was relatively light, characterised by adaptable committees and policy groups. It was far less institutionalised and formalised than the systems in most other member states, and the committees that existed met with less frequency. The defeat of the first Nice referendum led to a re-appraisal of EU management in the core executive and an enhancement of horizontal processes for managing European affairs.

Since 1973 Irish policymakers have adopted a very pragmatic approach to the development of the EU and to the promotion of Irish interests. For many years there was little sustained thinking about the overall development of the Union and the needs of small states within it. The decision in the late 1980s by the Taoiseach, Charles Haughey, to ask the National Economic and Social Council to undertake an extensive review of Ireland's membership of the Community, and the subsequent publication of its report (NESC, 1989), marked an important move away from the *ad hoc* approach of the past. A further attempt to develop a more considered approach was the establishment in 1991 of an Institute of European Affairs, a non-governmental organisation that promotes interdisciplinary Irish research on EU matters. The lead-up to the first Nice referendum and the lacklustre nature of the campaign underlined a degree of drift in Ireland's European policy. The EU was no longer getting the priority it warranted from ministers. As a consequence, the system of coordination was enhanced and the priority given to European matters heightened.

Following membership of the Union, the Oireachtas lost the 'sole and exclusive power of making laws' bestowed on it by Article 15.2.1 of the constitution. Like other parliaments in the member states, it sought to qualify its loss of law-making powers by establishing mechanisms to oversee the government's behaviour in the Union. Besides being to some extent accountable through the traditional mechanisms of parliamentary questions and debates (see Chapter 8), the government is also committed to placing a report on developments in the EU before the Houses of the Oireachtas twice yearly. These reports generally arrive too late for parliament to give serious consideration to the issues they raise.

In addition, in 1973 the Oireachtas established a Joint Committee on the Secondary Legislation of the European Communities, a watchdog committee on EC matters. Since Ireland does not have a strong tradition of parliamentary committees, as we saw in Chapter 8, this committee was something of a novelty at the outset. It had 25 members (18 deputies and seven senators), with the political parties represented in proportion to their strength in the Oireachtas. Its terms of reference allowed it to examine and report to the Oireachtas on Commission policy proposals, legislative proposals, EC laws, regulations made in Ireland under the European Communities Act 1972, and all other legal instruments that flow from EC membership.

The joint committee suffered from a number of constraints that impeded the work of all parliamentary committees. Its terms of reference were very restricted, so it concentrated most of its energies on secondary legislation and did not maintain a systematic overview of the flow of EU policies through the legislative process. Nor could it examine major changes in the European landscape, notably the collapse of communism and German unification, that were certain to shape the EU of the 1990s. In the work that it actually did, a weakness of both financial and human resources hampered it. Neither the members nor the secretariat of the committee had the legal or technical expertise to examine many of the complex issues involved in EU law and policies; the time pressures on Irish politicians do not allow them to develop the kind of expertise required for a thorough examination of EU policies.

In response to these difficulties the Fianna Fáil–Labour government established a new Joint Oireachtas Committee on Foreign Affairs in the spring of 1993. This subsumed the work of the previous Committee on Secondary Legislation, and also covered a much broader agenda, encompassing the state's foreign relations as a whole. This development brought Irish parliamentary practice into line with other parliaments in Europe.

A separate Joint Committee on European Affairs was established in March 1995, because the work of the Foreign Affairs Committee left it with inadequate time for the scrutiny of European law, and both committees were re-established after the 1997 election. Neither committee had adequate research and administrative back-up to develop independent thinking on foreign and European issues. The committees were heavily dependent on briefing papers from the Department of Foreign Affairs and on external consultants. Moreover, attendance at the committees was patchy, given the constituency duties of Irish parliamentarians (for which see Chapter 9). There is some overlap – and hence tension – between the two committees on areas such as the common foreign and security policy. That said, the committees contributed to greater openness on foreign policy matters, and a small coterie of deputies and senators became engaged in these issues. The involvement of the European Affairs Committee in the Conference of Parliamentary Committees on European Affairs (COSAC) exposed Irish parliamentarians to practices in other member states.

The weakness of parliamentary scrutiny emerged as an important issue in the first Nice referendum. A former Attorney General, John Rogers, signalled that he would oppose the treaty on this basis. In the aftermath of its defeat on Nice, the government looked to enhanced parliamentary scrutiny as a means of legitimising a second referendum. The new system was put in place in July 2002. The former joint committee has been replaced by a select committee (i.e. it consists solely of TDs, with no senators) for European Affairs. All EU-related documents are deposited with the EU Co-ordination Unit of the Department of Foreign Affairs and passed on by this unit to the select committee. A sub-committee of this committee sifts through the documents and decides whether parliamentary scrutiny is warranted. A request for an explanatory memorandum from the relevant department can be made, and this must be received within one month. The select committee may then decide to ask one of the sectoral committees to scrutinise the proposal and to report on it. Although Ireland has not put a formal scrutiny reserve in place, ministers are obliged to take the views of the committees seriously when negotiating in the Council of Ministers. The preparation of explanatory memoranda known as 'notes', the increase in the amount of information given to the committee, and the more frequent attendance of ministers at the select committee and sectoral committees has strengthened parliamentary engagement with European issues.

An important factor in this was the more active engagement of deputies, particularly from Fianna Fáil, in the second Nice referendum. The Taoiseach made each deputy responsible for his or her electoral area and demanded a full campaigning effort from them. In addition, the National Forum on Europe, which consists of deputies from all parties in proportion to their presence in the Dáil, helped educate Irish parliamentarians on major European issues. They have been forced to take European issues more seriously, although this does not alter the executive-dominated nature of the Irish parliamentary system.

The EU and Irish foreign policy

If membership of the EU impinges to such an extent on what is conventionally thought of as the internal policy process, it might be asked whether we can expect a member state, especially a small one such as Ireland, to conduct its own foreign policy (Tonra and Ward, 2002). Not surprisingly, this activity does indeed largely take place in a collective setting, the Common Foreign and Security Policy (CFSP). Although it involves intensive consultations with all other member states, this 'second pillar' of the Union is a less closely integrated form of policy making than exists in the supranational first pillar described above. In spite of the introduction of qualified majority voting in the foreign and security policy arenas in the Maastricht and Amsterdam Treaties, the practical reality is that a consensus among all the member governments is required for any move beyond consultation to the expression of a common view ('declaratory policy') or the taking of common action, such as imposing economic sanctions (Keatinge, 1997).

National foreign policies have thus resisted the logic of integration to a considerable extent. Decisions on Irish foreign policy still rest, at least formally, with the government in Dublin, and the whole apparatus of national diplomacy – the Department of Foreign Affairs and its embassies abroad – grew in both size and political importance following Ireland's accession to the Community (Keatinge, 1978). When it has taken its turn for six months in the rotating EU presidency, the Irish government has actually been responsible for the management of CFSP, giving both the foreign minister and the Taoiseach a highly valued public role of international statesman. Routine access to their counterparts in the major European states, on top of the vastly enhanced information available to the Department of Foreign Affairs, is arguably as much a national resource as it is a form of exposure to external influences. Moreover, in so far as EU positions on major international issues are consistent with Ireland's interests and values, if they are advanced on behalf of nearly 400 million people they are likely to bear more weight than statements on behalf of a society of just under four million (Keatinge, 1991).

At this level of generalisation it may seem that, so far, an acceptable balance has been found between the way in which Irish governments see their national foreign policies and the obligations of the CFSP. This may not remain the case, though. Up to 1993 Irish governments arrived at many foreign policy decisions with minimum input from political parties, and enjoyed relatively large domestic freedom of manoeuvre so long as the Oireachtas was the only west European parliament without a standing foreign affairs committee. But two factors have changed in this policy environment.

First, the treaties of Maastricht and Amsterdam, by introducing and developing the European Security and Defence Policy (ESDP), may be seen increasingly to clash with a long-standing element of Irish foreign policy: the stance of military neutrality. The 1999 Helsinki European Council Summit established a series of 'headline goals', which included the creation of a 60,000-strong European rapid reaction military force, capable of international deployment within 30 days and maintained in the field for one year (Keatinge and Tonra, 2002). The force was mandated with the fulfilment of a series of potential missions defined in the Amsterdam Treaty as the so-called 'Petersberg tasks' – humanitarian and rescue tasks, peace-keeping tasks and tasks of combat forces in crisis management, including peace-making. Following a series of further summit agreements and the creation of an institutional framework (including a political and security committee, an EU military committee and EU military staff), the rapid reaction force was declared operational in 2003. While the Irish government has pledged approximately 850 troops to it, it has done so on the condition of its 'triple lock' (see Box 16.4).

A second change occurred closer to home: what might be called the 'democratisation' of the foreign policy process (Keatinge, 1998). In addition to the introduction of parliamentary committees, an elaborate consultative process was launched in 1995 prior to the publication of the first ever comprehensive White Paper on foreign policy in 1996 (Department of Foreign Affairs, 1996). These developments have been matched by the emergence of a proliferation of non-governmental organisations, suggesting at least the potential for the advocacy of 'bottom-up' foreign policies that may be at odds with those of Irish governments or an EU consensus (Tonra, 2001a).

Nevertheless, Ireland's participation in the CFSP over more than 30 years on the whole supports the proposition that opportunities to pursue foreign policy objectives were enhanced by EC and later EU membership (Tonra, 2001b). Some examples may illustrate the point. So far as east–west relations were concerned, the EC member states jointly were an important positive influence in the Conference on Security and Cooperation in Europe (the 'Helsinki process'), which maintained a modicum of diplomatic engagement with the USSR during the tension of the 'new Cold War' of the early 1980s. In the Middle East, the Irish government's position on the Arab–Israeli conflict was mirrored in Europe's gradual receptiveness to the Palestinian case. For most of this period Ireland remained, as it had been before joining the EU, a consistent and credible contributor to United Nations peace-keeping operations, and governments developed a more substantial and systematic approach to relations with the third world (Holmes *et al.*, 1993).

This is not to suggest that Ireland's policy (or that of the EU as a whole) was an unequivocal success story. Trying to influence the unruly game of international politics is best approached in the Olympic spirit – 'it is not to have won that matters, but to have taken part'.

***Box 16.4* The Seville Declarations and Irish neutrality**

In response to the public rejection of the Nice Treaty in June 2001, the government sought to clarify Ireland's position on its military neutrality and towards an emerging European Security and Defence Policy. Two Declarations were agreed and published at the European Council Summit at Seville on 21 June 2002. The first was a Declaration by Ireland's EU partners that '. . . the Treaty on European Union does not impose any binding mutual defence commitments. Nor does the development of the Union's capacity to conduct humanitarian and crisis management tasks involve the establishment of a European army.' It also insists that 'like all Member States of the Union, Ireland would retain the right, following the entry into force of the Treaty of Nice, to take its own sovereign decision, in accordance with its Constitution and its laws, on whether to commit military personnel to participate in any operation carried out under the European Security and Defence Policy. Ireland, in its national Statement, has clearly set out its position in this regard.'

A National Declaration was then attached to the EU Council Declaration. It provides that 'Ireland confirms that its participation in the European Union's common foreign and security policy does not prejudice its traditional policy of military neutrality.' The National Declaration goes on to say that the participation of contingents of the Irish Defence Forces in overseas operations, including those carried out under the European security and defence policy, requires (a) the authorisation of the operation by the Security Council or the General Assembly of the United Nations, (b) the agreement of the Irish government, and (c) the approval of Dáil Éireann, in accordance with Irish law. This last is characterised as the 'triple lock' on Irish military force deployment overseas.

As part of the referendum providing for Irish ratification of the Nice Treaty, the constitution was also amended to exclude Irish membership of any common European Defence. The amended Article 29.4 now provides that: *The State shall not adopt a decision taken by the European Council to establish a common defence pursuant to Article 1.2 of the Treaty referred to in sub-section 7 of this section where that common defence would include the State.*

Conclusion: a small open polity

Ireland's external environment has been an important influence on the state's political development. In the turbulent international system up to the end of the Second World War the British connection provided the main focus, in which the new state's political independence was demonstrated by the policy of neutrality during the war. After that war Ireland was gradually drawn into a broader, more stable and increasingly interdependent international system. Membership of the European Union since 1973 provided this small open polity with a framework within which it could mediate the forces of growing interdependence and, more recently, globalisation. The EU was not just about managing the outside world, however, as membership had a major impact on political life in Ireland. Politics and public policy are moulded by engagement with the EU. Within the Union, Ireland is faced with a continuing process of treaty change and further enlargements beyond 25 members. As the geographical reach of the Union expands, Ireland will find itself a member of a much larger entity. As representatives of a small state, Irish policymakers will have to be smart as they navigate the new Union that is emerging. After over 30 years of membership, they have built up considerable expertise on European issues but cannot afford to be complacent. As we saw during the Nice referendums, many Irish voters have concerns about the evolving political structures of the Union.

The collapse of communism in 1989 and the terrorist attacks on the twin towers in September 2001 altered the dynamic of world politics, in many ways making the world a more unpredictable and difficult place for all states – especially small open polities. The boundary between internal and external security has blurred and security threats are more likely to come from unstable or failed states, the proliferation of weapons of mass destruction and non-state terrorist actors. In this new world disorder, Europe finds itself in a relatively benign environment given the successful transition in most of the eastern half of the continent. That said, there remain difficult questions about Europe's role in the world and its relations with the USA. These questions and challenges have an impact on the substance and conduct of Irish foreign policy. Particularly difficult questions remain about the future of neutrality and Irish security policy in a changing global system.

Notes

1 The authors would like to acknowledge the contribution made by Patrick Keatinge to this chapter. He was co-author with Laffan of the corresponding chapter in previous editions of the volume.
2 Prior to the 2004 enlargement, Ireland had 15 seats in a 626-member parliament. The reduction to 13 seats reflects the institutional consequences of enlargement and the growing scale of the Union.

References and further reading

Baylis, John and Steve Smith (eds), 2001. *The Globalization of World Politics: An Intro-duction to International Relations*. Oxford: Oxford University Press.

Börzel, Tanja and Thomas Risse, 2000. 'When Europe hits home: Europeanization and domestic change', *European Integration Online Papers* 4: 15. Available http://eiop.or.at/eiop/texte/2000-015a.htm [accessed 25 March 2004].

Department of Foreign Affairs, 1996. *Challenges and Opportunities Abroad: White Paper on Foreign Policy*, Pn. 2133. Dublin: Stationery Office.

European Commission, 1991. *Report on the Implementation of Measures for Completing the Internal Market*, 2491 final, 19 December.

Fisk, Robert, 1983. *In Time of War: Ireland, Ulster and the Price of Neutrality 1939-1945*. London: André Deutsch.

Fukuyama, Francis, 1992. *The End of History and the Last Man*. New York: Free Press.

Gallagher, Michael, 1988. 'The Single European Act referendum', *Irish Political Studies* 3: 77-82.

Gallagher, Michael and Michael Marsh, 2002. *Days of Blue Loyalty: The Politics of Membership of the Fine Gael Party*. Dublin: PSAI Press.

Hayes-Renshaw, Fiona, 2002. 'The Council of Ministers', in John Peterson and Michael Shackleton (eds), *The Institutions of the European Union*. Oxford: Oxford University Press, pp. 47-70.

Hayward, Katy, 2003. '"If at first you don't succeed . . .": the second referendum on the Treaty of Nice, 2002', *Irish Political Studies* 18:1: 120-32.

Holmes, Michael, 1993. 'The Maastricht Treaty referendum of June 1992', *Irish Political Studies* 8: 105-10.

Holmes, Michael, Nicholas Rees and Bernadette Whelan, 1993. *The Poor Relation: Irish Foreign Policy and the Third World*. Dublin: Trócaire.

Honohan, Patrick (ed.), 1997. *EU Structural Funds In Ireland: A Mid-Term Evaluation of the CSF 1994-99*. Dublin: Economic and Social Research Institute.

Huntington, Samuel P., 1996. *The Clash of Civilizations and the Remaking of World Order*. New York: Simon and Schuster.

Keatinge, Patrick, 1978. *A Place Among the Nations*. Dublin: Institute of Public Administration.

Keatinge, Patrick, 1986. 'Unequal sovereigns: the diplomatic dimension of Anglo-Irish relations', in P. J. Drudy (ed.), *Ireland and Britain since 1922*. Cambridge: Cambridge University Press, pp. 139-60.

Keatinge, Patrick (ed.), 1991. *Ireland and EC Membership Evaluated*. London: Pinter.

Keatinge, Patrick, 1997. 'Strengthening the foreign policy process', in Ben Tonra (ed.), *Amsterdam: What the Treaty Means*. Dublin: Institute of European Affairs, pp. 97-105.

Keatinge, Patrick, 1998. 'Ireland and European security: continuity and change', *Irish Studies in International Affairs* 9: 31-7.

Keatinge, Patrick and Ben Tonra, 2002. *The European Rapid Reaction Force*. Dublin: Institute of European Affairs.

Kennedy, Michael J., 1996. *Ireland and the League of Nations, 1919-1946: International Relations, Diplomacy and Politics*. Dublin: Irish Academic Press.

Laffan, Brigid, 1996. 'Ireland', in Dietrich Rometsch and Wolfgang Wessels (eds), *The EU and Member States: Towards Institutional Fusion?* Manchester and New York: Manchester University Press, pp. 291-312.

Laffan, Brigid, 2001. *Organising for a Changing Europe: Irish Central Government and the European Union*. Dublin: Policy Institute, Trinity College Dublin.

Laffan, Brigid and Jane O'Mahony, 2003. *Managing Europe from Home: The Europeanisation of the Irish Core Executive*. Dublin: OEUE Phase 1 Occasional Paper, 1.1–04.03.

Laffan Brigid, Rory O'Donnell and Michael Smith, 1999. *Europe's Experimental Union: Re-thinking Integration*. London: Routledge.

McCabe, Ian, 1991. *A Diplomatic History of Ireland, 1948–49: The Republic, the Commonwealth, and NATO*. Dublin: Irish Academic Press.

NESC (National Economic and Social Council), 1989. *Ireland in the European Community: Performance, Prospects and Strategy*. Dublin: National Economic and Social Council, Report No. 88.

Nugent, Neill, 2003. *The Government and Politics of the European Community*, 5th edn. London: Macmillan.

O'Mahony, Jane, 2001. ' "Not so Nice": the Treaty of Nice, the International Criminal Court, the abolition of the death penalty – the 2001 referendum experience', *Irish Political Studies* 16: 201–13.

Salmon, Trevor, 1989. *Unneutral Ireland: An Ambivalent and Unique Security Policy*. Oxford: Oxford University Press.

Sinnott, Richard, 2001. *Attitudes and Behaviour of the Irish Electorate in the Referendum on the Treaty of Nice*. Dublin: European Commission Representation in Ireland; also available http://www.ucd.ie/dempart/workingpapers/nice1.pdf [accessed 28 February 2004].

Skelly, Joseph Morrison, 1997. *Irish Diplomacy at the United Nations, 1945–65: National Interests and the International Order*. Dublin: Irish Academic Press.

Tonra, Ben, 2001a. 'Irish foreign policy', in William Crotty and David Schmitt (eds), *Ireland on the World Stage*, London: Pearson Education/Longman, pp. 24–45.

Tonra, Ben, 2001b. *Europeanisation of National Foreign Policy: Dutch, Danish and Irish Foreign Policies in CFSP*. Aldershot: Ashgate.

Tonra, Ben, and Eilís Ward (eds), 2002. *Ireland in International Affairs: Interests, Institutions and Identities*. Dublin: Institute for Public Administration.

Websites

www.europa.eu.int/index_en.htm (link: institutions)   European Union central site, with links to institutions and governments.

www.foreignaffairs.gov.ie   Department of Foreign Affairs site, with valuable links.

Appendices

John Coakley

Note
The data in these appendices refer to the territory of the Republic of Ireland, except where otherwise stated.

Appendix 1 Demographic data

1a Population and social indicators, 1841–2002

Year	Population Total	Urban (%)	Dublin (%)	Makes in agriculture (%)	Religion RC (%)	Religion Other (%)	Irish-speakers (%)	Birthplace Other county	Birthplace Other country
1841	6,528,799	16.7	3.7	74.3	–	–	–	*5.0*	0.8
1851	5,111,557	22.0	5.8	68.8	–	–	29.1	*8.8*	1.5
1861	4,402,111	22.2	6.7	64.6	89.3	10.7	24.5	*8.1*	2.1
1871	4,053,187	22.8	7.4	63.1	89.2	10.8	19.8	*9.3*	2.8
1881	3,870,020	23.9	8.4	62.6	89.5	10.5	23.9	*10.2*	3.0
1891	3,468,694	25.3	9.6	61.4	89.3	10.7	19.2	*11.2*	3.4
1901	3,221,823	28.0	11.2	61.7	89.3	10.7	19.2	*12.7*	3.7
1911	3,139,688	29.7	12.3	59.5	89.6	10.4	17.6	*13.4*	4.3
1926	2,971,992	31.8	13.7	58.9	92.6	7.4	19.3	*13.4*	3.4
1936	2,968,420	35.5	15.9	55.9	93.4	6.6	23.7	*14.5*	3.4
1946	2,955,107	39.3	17.1	54.1	94.3	5.7	21.2	16.1	3.3
1961	2,818,341	46.4	19.1	43.1	94.9	4.9	27.2	14.1	3.5
1971	2,978,248	52.2	26.9	31.9	93.9	4.3	28.3	14.8	4.6
1981	3,443,405	55.6	29.1	21.7	93.1	3.7	31.6	17.6	6.7
1991	3,525,719	57.0	29.1	19.1	91.6	4.2	32.5	18.1	6.5
1996	3,626,087	58.1	29.2	15.1	–	–	43.5	18.9	7.5
2002	3,917,203	59.6	28.7	8.4	88.4	6.1	42.8	19.7	10.4

Source: Calculated from *Census of Ireland*, *Statistical Abstract of Ireland* and *Statistical Yearbook of Ireland*, various dates, and from David Fitzpatrick, 'The disappearance of the Irish agricultural labourer, 1841–1912', *Irish Economic and Social History* 7, 1980: 66–92.

Notes

All data refer to the present area of the Republic of Ireland except where otherwise stated. Urban areas are defined as those with a population of 1,500 or more, but figures for these and for Dublin are difficult to compare over time due to changes in boundary definition criteria; in 1971, Dublin is defined as including Dun Laoghaire; and from 1981 it has been taken as including all of Dublin county. The data on involvement in agriculture are also difficult to compare over time due to varying classification criteria, and it has been possible to compute comparable data for men only. Data on religion are expressed as percentages of the total population (which includes those refusing to give information on this matter). Data on Irish speakers from 1926 onwards refer to the population aged over three years, but the form of the question changed in 1996, so the data for this and subsequent years are not strictly comparable with the earlier ones. In all cases, knowledge of the language is self-assessed. 'Birthplace other county' refers to those born in Irish counties other than that in which they were resident at the date of the census (for the 1841–1911 period these percentages, which are italicised, refer to the whole island); 'birthplace other country' refers to those born outside the 26 counties.

1b Emigration and immigration, 1841–2002

Period	Total emigration	Annual average
1841–51	*1,132,000*	*108,000*
1852–60	791,648	87,961
1861–70	697,704	69,740
1871–80	446,326	44,633
1881–90	616,894	61,689
1891–1900	377,017	37,702
1901–10	266,311	26,631
	Net emigration	
1911–26	405,029	27,002
1926–36	166,751	16,675
1936–46	187,111	18,711
1946–61	531,255	35,417
1961–71	134,511	13,451
1971–81	−103,889	−10,389
1981–91	206,053	20,605
1991–96	−8,302	−1,660
1996–2002	−153,881	−25,647

Sources: Computed from W. E. Vaughan and A. J. Fitzpatrick (eds), *Irish Historical Statistics: Population, 1821–1971* (Dublin: Royal Irish Academy, 1989); *Commission on Emigration and Other Population Problems 1948–1954, Reports* (Dublin: Stationery Office, [1956]); and *Census 2002*, Vol. 4, *Usual Residence, Migration, Birthplace and Nationalities* (Dublin: Stationery Office, 2003).

Notes
The data for 1841–51 (italicised) are estimates based on the assumption that the proportion of Irish emigrants coming from the present territory of the Republic was the same as in the 1852–60 period (the data begin in mid-year 1841). Net emigration refers to out-migration less in-migration, and the negative values in 1971–81 and since 1991 indicate a surplus of immigrants over emigrants in these periods.

Appendix 2 Electoral data

2a Distribution of parliamentary seats by party, 1801–1918

Year	Southern Ireland					All Ireland				
	Tory/ Unionist	Whig/ Liberal	Nat. etc.	Others	Total	Tory/ Unionist	Whig/ Liberal	Nat. etc.	Others	Total
1801	23	16	–	39	78	34	16	–	50	100
1802	27	26	–	25	78	43	28	–	29	100
1806	34	34	–	10	78	50	36	–	14	100
1807	37	32	–	9	78	54	33	–	13	100
1812	43	28	–	7	78	59	30	–	11	100
1818	41	32	–	5	78	61	34	–	5	100
1820	44	29	–	5	78	63	32	–	5	100
1826	38	37	–	3	78	56	41	–	3	100
1830	34	41	–	3	78	49	48	–	3	100
1831	26	48	–	4	78	40	56	–	4	100
1832	14	26	42	–	82	30	33	42	–	105
1835	22	26	34	–	82	37	34	34	–	105
1837	14	38	30	–	82	32	43	30	–	105
1841	23	39	20	–	82	43	42	20	–	105
1847	20	21	36	5	82	31	25	36	13	105
1852	21	11	48	2	82	40	15	48	2	105
1857	26	43	13	–	82	44	48	13	–	105
1859	33	49	–	0	82	55	50	–	0	105
1865	24	58	–	0	82	47	58	–	0	105
1868	19	63	–	0	82	39	66	–	0	105
1874	16	4	60	–	80	33	10	60	–	103
1880	7	10	63	–	80	25	15	63	–	103
1885	2	–	76	–	78	18	–	85	–	103
1886	2	–	76	–	78	19	–	84	–	103
1892	4	–	74	–	78	23	–	80	–	103
1895	4	–	74	–	78	21	1	81	–	103
1900	3	–	75	–	78	21	1	81	–	103
1906	3	–	75	–	78	20	1	82	–	103
1910–1	3	–	75	–	78	21	1	81	–	103
1910–2	2	–	76	–	78	19	1	83	–	103
1918	3	–	2	70	75	26	–	6	73	105

Sources: Calculated from Henry Stooks Smith, *The Parliaments of England from 1715 to 1847*, 2nd edn, edited by F. W. S. Craig (Chichester: Political Reference Publications, 1973) and Brian M. Walker, *Parliamentary Election Results in Ireland, 1801–1922* (Dublin: Royal Irish Academy, 1978).

Notes
'Southern Ireland' refers to the present territory of the Republic of Ireland. Before 1832 party affiliations are approximate only. 'Tory/Unionist' includes Liberal Unionists; 'Nationalist, etc.' includes the Repeal Party (1832–47), the Independent Irish Party (1852–57) and the Home Rule or Nationalist Party, including breakaway factions and independent nationalists (1874–1918); 'Others' includes nonaligned MPs (1801–32), Peelites (1847–52) and two Irish Confederates in the South (1847); in 1918 it refers to Sinn Féin MPs.

2*b* Distribution of first preference votes in Dáil elections by party, 1922–2002 (%)

Year	Fianna Fáil	Fine Gael	Labour Party	Farmers' parties	Republican parties	Others	Turnout
1922	21.7	38.5	21.3	7.8	–	10.6	45.5
1923	27.4	39.0	10.6	12.1	–	10.9	61.2
1927–1	26.1	27.5	12.6	8.9	3.6	21.4	68.1
1927–2	35.2	38.7	9.1	6.4	–	10.7	69.0
1932	44.5	35.3	7.7	3.1	–	9.4	76.5
1933	49.7	30.5	5.7	9.2	–	5.0	81.3
1937	45.2	34.8	10.3	–	–	9.7	76.2
1938	51.9	33.3	10.0	–	–	4.7	76.7
1943	41.9	23.1	15.7	11.3	0.3	7.7	74.2
1944	48.9	20.5	8.8	11.6	–	10.2	67.7
1948	41.9	19.8	8.7	5.5	13.2	10.9	74.2
1951	46.3	25.8	11.4	2.9	4.1	9.6	75.3
1954	43.4	32.0	12.1	3.1	3.9	5.6	76.4
1957	48.3	26.6	9.1	2.4	7.0	6.6	71.3
1961	43.8	32.0	11.6	1.5	4.2	6.8	70.6
1965	47.7	34.1	15.4	–	0.8	2.1	75.1
1969	45.7	34.1	17.0	–	–	3.2	76.9
1973	46.2	35.1	13.7	–	2.0	3.0	76.6
1977	50.6	30.5	11.6	–	1.8	5.5	76.3
1981	45.3	36.5	9.9	–	2.5	5.9	76.2
				Prog. Dems	*Sinn Féin*		
1982–1	47.3	37.3	9.1	–	1.0	5.3	73.8
1982–2	45.2	39.2	9.4	–	–	6.3	72.9
1987	44.1	27.1	6.4	11.8	1.9	8.7	73.3
1989	44.1	29.3	9.5	5.5	1.2	10.4	68.5
1992	39.1	24.5	19.3	4.7	1.6	10.9	68.5
1997	39.3	27.9	10.4	4.7	2.6	15.1	65.9
2002	41.5	22.5	10.8	4.0	6.5	14.7	62.6

Sources: Michael Gallagher (ed.), *Irish Elections 1922–44: Results and Analysis* (Limerick: PSAI Press, 1993); Brian M. Walker (ed.), *Parliamentary Election Results in Ireland 1918–92* (Dublin: Royal Irish Academy and Belfast: Institute of Irish Studies, 1992); *28th Dáil General Election June 1997: Election Results and Transfer of Votes* (Dublin: Stationery Office, 1998); Ibid. [29th Dáil, May 2002] (Dublin: Stationery Office, 2003).

Notes
Fianna Fáil includes Anti-Treaty Sinn Féin (1922–3). Fine Gael includes Pro-Treaty Sinn Féin (1922) and Cumann na nGaedheal (1923–33). 'Farmers' parties' includes the Farmers' Party (1922–32), the National Centre Party (1933) and Clann na Talmhan (1943–61). 'Republican parties' refers to Sinn Féin, including the original party before 1970 (1927–1, 3.6%; 1954, 0.1%; 1957, 5.3%; 1961, 3.1%), 'Official' Sinn Féin in the 1970s (1973, 1.1%; 1977, 1.7%) and the following parties: Córas na Poblachta (1943, 0.3%), Clann na Poblachta (1948, 13.2%; 1951, 4.1%; 1954, 3.8%; 1957, 1.7%; 1961, 1.1%; 1965, 0.8%), Aontacht Éireann (1973, 0.9%), the Irish Republican Socialist Party (1977, 0.1%; 1982–1, 0.2%) and the National H-Block Committee (1981, 2.5%). 'Others' includes the National League (1927–1, 7.3%; 1927–2, 1.6%), National Labour (1944, 2.7%; 1948, 2.6%), the National Progressive Democrats (1961, 1.0%) and the Green Party (1987, 0.4%; 1989, 1.5%; 1992, 1.4%; 1997, 2.8%; 2002, 3.8%), as well as smaller groups and independents. From 1981, Sinn Féin the Workers' Party and its successor, the Workers' Party, have been grouped with 'others' (1981, 1.7%; 1982–1, 2.2%; 1982–2, 3.1%; 1987, 3.8%; 1989, 5.0%; 1992, 0.7%; 1997, 0.4%; 2002, 0.2%), as has Democratic Left (1992, 2.8%; 1997, 2.5%).
The first Dáil was convened on the basis of the UK general election of 1918; at this election all seats in the north were contested, but only two-thirds of those in the south (50); in the remaining 25, Sinn Féin candidates were returned unopposed, so vote totals do not give an accurate picture of party strengths. The second Dáil was convened on the basis of the elections in 1921 to the proposed Houses of Commons of Southern Ireland and Northern Ireland; at this, all seats were contested in the north, but none was in the south.

2c Distribution of seats in Dáil by party, 1922–2002

Year	Fianna Fáil	Fine Gael	Labour Party	Farmers' parties	Republican parties	Others	Total
1922	36	58	17	7	–	10	128
1923	44	63	14	15	–	17	153
1927–1	44	47	22	11	5	24	153
1927–2	57	62	13	6	–	15	153
1932	72	57	7	4	–	13	153
1933	77	48	8	11	–	9	153
1937	69	48	13	–	–	8	138
1938	77	45	9	–	–	7	138
1943	67	32	17	14	–	8	138
1944	76	30	8	11	–	13	138
1948	68	31	14	7	10	17	147
1951	69	40	16	6	2	14	147
1954	65	50	19	5	3	5	147
1957	78	40	12	3	5	9	147
1961	70	47	16	2	1	8	144
1965	72	47	22	–	1	2	144
1969	75	50	18	–	–	1	144
1973	69	54	19	–	–	2	144
1977	84	43	17	–	–	4	148
1981	78	65	15	–	2	6	166
				Prog. Dems	Sinn Féin		
1982–1	81	63	15	–	–	7	166
1982–2	75	70	16	–	–	5	166
1987	81	51	12	14	–	8	166
1989	77	55	15	6	–	13	166
1992	68	45	33	10	–	10	166
1997	77	54	17	4	1	13	166
2002	81	31	21	8	5	20	166

Sources: As for Appendix 2b.

Notes

Fianna Fáil includes Anti-Treaty Sinn Féin (1922–3). Fine Gael includes Pro-Treaty Sinn Féin (1922) and Cumann na nGaedheal (1923–33). 'Farmers' parties' includes the Farmers' Party (1922–32), the National Centre Party (1933) and Clann na Talmhan (1943–61). 'Republican parties' refers mainly to Clann na Poblachta (1948–65) but includes also Sinn Féin (1927–1, 5 TDs; 1957, 4 TDs) and the National H-Block Committee (1981, 2 TDs). 'Others' includes the National League (1927–1, 8 TDs; 1927–2, 2 TDs), National Labour (1944, 4 TDs; 1948, 5 TDs), the National Progressive Democrats (1961, 2 TDs), Sinn Féin the Workers' Party and its successor, the Workers' Party (1981, 1 TD; 1982–1, 3 TDs; 1982–2, 2 TDs; 1987, 4 TDs; 1989, 7 TDs), the Green Party (1989 and 1992, 1 TD; 1997, 2 TDs; 2002, 6 TDs) and Democratic Left (1992 and 1997, 4 TDs), as well as smaller groups and independents.

The first Dáil was convened on the basis of the British general election of 1918; at this election Sinn Féin won 73 seats (all except three of these in the south; two of the northern seats were won by candidates who were also successful in the south and one candidate was returned for two constituencies in the south, leaving Sinn Féin with 70 MPs), the Unionists 26 (all except three in the north) and the Nationalists won six (four in the north and two in the south). The second Dáil was convened on the basis of the elections in 1921 to the proposed Houses of Commons of Southern Ireland and Northern Ireland; at this, Sinn Féin won 130 seats (all except six of these in the south; five of the northern seats were won by candidates who were also successful in the south, leaving Sinn Féin with 125 MPs), the Unionists 40 (all in the north), the Nationalists six (all in the north) and independents won four (all in the south).

2d Distribution of men and women in the Oireachtas, 1922–2002

Dáil Éireann				Seanad Éireann			
Year	Men	Women	Total	Year	Men	Women	Total
1922	126	2	128	–	–	–	–
1923	148	5	153	1922	56	4	60
1927–1	149	4	153	1925	56	4	60
1927–2	152	1	153	1928	55	5	60
1932	151	2	153	1931	55	5	60
1933	150	3	153	1934	57	3	60
1937	136	2	138	1938–1	56	4	60
1938	135	3	138	1938–2	57	3	60
1943	135	3	138	1943	57	3	60
1944	134	4	138	1944	57	3	60
1948	142	5	147	1948	57	3	60
1951	142	5	147	1951	57	3	60
1954	142	5	147	1954	57	3	60
1957	142	5	147	1957	56	4	60
1961	141	3	144	1961	57	3	60
1965	139	5	144	1965	56	4	60
1969	141	3	144	1969	55	5	60
1973	140	4	144	1973	56	4	60
1977	142	6	148	1977	54	6	60
1981	155	11	166	1981	51	9	60
1982–1	158	8	166	1982	52	8	60
1982–2	152	14	166	1983	54	6	60
1987	152	14	166	1987	55	5	60
1989	153	13	166	1989	54	6	60
1992	146	20	166	1993	52	8	60
1997	146	20	166	1997	49	11	60
2002	144	22	166	2002	50	10	60

Notes

The data refer to the position immediately after general elections to Dáil Éireann (1922–2002) and Seanad Éireann (1938–2002). The earlier data on Seanad Éireann refer to the position immediately after the initial installation of the first Seanad under the Free State constitution (1922) and after the triennial elections which renewed a portion of its membership (1925–34).

Only one woman was returned from the 105 Irish seats in the British general election of 1918; of the 73 Sinn Féin seats, 72 were occupied by men (since three of these seats were double returns, the full potential membership of the first Dáil was 69 men and one woman). Eight women were returned from the 180 seats to the Houses of Commons of Southern Ireland and Northern Ireland in 1921, two Unionists in the north and six Sinn Féin members in the south (since the 130 Sinn Féin seats were occupied by only 125 people due to double returns, the full potential membership of the second Dáil was 119 men and six women).

2e Distribution of first preference votes in European Parliament elections, 1979–2004 (%)

Year	Fianna Fáil	Fine Gael	Labour Party	Workers' Party	Sinn Féin	Green Party	Others	Turnout
1979	34.7	33.1	14.5	3.3	–	–	14.4	63.6
1984	39.2	32.2	8.4	4.3	4.9	–	11.0	47.6
1989	31.5	21.6	9.5	7.5	2.3	3.7	23.9	68.3
1994	35.0	24.3	11.0	1.9	3.0	7.9	16.9	44.0
1999	38.6	24.6	8.7	–	6.3	6.7	15.0	50.2
2004	29.5	27.8	10.6	–	11.1	4.3	16.7	58.8

Notes
'Workers' Party' includes Sinn Féin the Workers' Party; 'Others' includes Democratic Left (1994, 3.5%) and the Progressive Democrats (1989, 11.9%; 1994, 6.5%).

2f Distribution of first preference votes in local elections, 1967–2004 (%)

Year	Fianna Fáil	Fine Gael	Labour Party	Workers' Party	Sinn Féin	Green Party	Others	Turnout
1967	40.2	32.5	14.8	–	–	–	12.5	69.0
1974	40.1	33.7	12.8	1.5	–	–	11.9	61.1
1979	39.2	34.9	11.8	2.3	2.2	–	9.6	63.6
1985	45.5	29.8	7.7	3.0	3.3	–	10.7	58.2
1991	37.9	26.4	10.6	3.7	1.7	2.0	17.7	55.1
1999	38.9	28.1	10.7	0.5	3.5	2.5	15.8	50.3
2004	31.8	27.6	11.4	–	8.1	3.9	17.2	59.6

Notes
These figures relate to the results in county and county borough elections only. 'Workers' Party' includes Sinn Féin (1974) and Sinn Féin the Workers' Party (1979); 'Others' includes Progressive Democrats (1991, 5.0%; 1999, 2.9%; 2004, 3.9%). 2004 turnout figure provisional.

2g Distribution of votes in presidential elections, 1945–97

Year	Candidate	Count 1		Count 2			Comment
		No.	(%)	Transfers	Result	(%)	
1945	McCartan, Patrick	212,834	(19.6)				Ó Ceallaigh elected
	MacEoin, Seán	335,539	(30.9)	+117,886	453,425	(44.5)	turnout: 63.0%
	Ó Ceallaigh, Seán T.	537,965	(49.5)	+27,200	565,165	(55.5)	non-transferable: 67,748
1959	de Valera, Eamon	538,003	(56.3)				de Valera elected
	MacEoin, Seán	417,536	(43.7)				turnout: 58.4%
1966	de Valera, Eamon	558,861	(50.5)				de Valera elected
	O'Higgins, Thomas F.	548,144	(49.5)				turnout: 65.4%
1973	Childers, Erskine	635,867	(52.0)				Childers elected
	O'Higgins, Thomas F.	587,771	(48.0)				turnout: 62.2%
1990	Currie, Austin	267,902	(17.0)				Robinson elected
	Lenihan, Brian	694,484	(44.1)	+36,789	731,273	(47.2)	turnout: 64.1%
	Robinson, Mary	612,265	(38.9)	+205,565	817,830	(52.8)	non-transferable: 25,548
1997	Banotti, Mary	372,002	(29.3)	+125,514	497,516	(41.3)	McAleese elected
	McAleese, Mary	574,424	(45.2)	+131,835	706,259	(58.7)	turnout: 46.8%
	Nally, Derek	59,529	(4.7)				non-transferable: 66,061
	Roche, Adi	88,423	(7.0)				
	Scallon, Rosemary	175,458	(13.8)				

Note
In 1938, 1952, 1974, 1976 and 1983 no contests took place as only one candidate was nominated.

2h Referendum results, 1937–2004 (%)

Date	Subject (article altered)	For	Against	Turnout	Spoiled
1.7.37	Approve new constitution	56.5	43.5	75.8	10.0
17.6.59	Replace proportional representation by plurality system (*3rd amdt; 16*)	48.2	51.8	58.4	4.0
16.10.68	Permit flexibility in deputy–population ratio (*3rd amdt; 16*)	39.2	60.8	65.8	4.3
16.10.68	Replace proportional representation by plurality system (*4th amdt; 16*)	39.2	60.8	65.8	4.3
10.5.72	Permit EC membership (3rd amdt; 29)	83.1	16.9	70.9	0.8
7.12.72	Lower voting age to 18 (4th amdt; 16)	84.6	15.4	50.7	5.2
7.12.72	Remove 'special position' of Catholic Church (5th amdt; 44)	84.4	15.6	50.7	5.5
5.7.79	Protect adoption system (6th amdt; 37)	99.0	1.0	28.6	2.5
5.7.79	Permit alteration of university representation in Senate (7th amdt; 18)	92.4	7.6	28.6	3.9
7.9.83	Prohibit legalisation of abortion (8th amdt; 40)	66.9	33.1	53.7	0.7
14.6.84	Permit extension of voting rights to non-citizens (9th amdt; 16)	75.4	24.6	47.5	3.5
26.6.86	Permit legalisation of divorce (*10th amdt; 41*)	36.5	63.5	60.5	0.6
26.5.87	Permit signing of Single European Act (10th amdt; 29)	69.9	30.1	43.9	0.5
18.6.92	Permit ratification of Maastricht Treaty on European union (11th amdt; 29)	69.1	30.9	57.3	0.5
25.11.92	Restrict availability of abortion (*12th amdt; 40*)	34.6	65.4	68.2	4.7
25.11.92	Guarantee right to travel (13th amdt; 40)	62.4	37.6	68.2	4.3
25.11.92	Guarantee right to information (14th amdt; 40)	59.9	40.1	68.1	4.3
24.11.95	Permit legalisation of divorce (15th amdt; 41)	50.3	49.7	62.2	0.3
25.11.96	Permit refusal of bail (16th amdt; 40)	74.8	25.2	29.2	0.4
30.10.97	Guarantee cabinet confidentiality (17th amdt; 28)	52.5	47.5	47.2	5.2
22.5.98	Permit ratification of Amsterdam Treaty (18th amdt; 29)	61.7	38.3	56.2	2.2
22.5.98	Permit changes agreed in Good Friday Agreement (19th amdt; 29 (and 2, 3))	94.4	5.6	56.3	1.1
11.6.99	Require local elections at least every five years (20th amdt; 28)	77.8	22.2	51.1	7.6
7.6.01	Prohibit legislation allowing for death penalty (21st amdt; 13, 15, 28, 40)	62.1	37.9	34.8	1.5
7.6.01	Permit ratification of International Criminal Court statute (23rd amdt; 29)	64.2	35.8	34.8	1.8
7.6.01	Permit ratification of Nice Treaty (*24th amdt; 29*)	46.1	53.9	34.8	1.5
6.3.02	Restrict right to abortion (*25th amdt; 46*)	49.6	50.4	42.9	0.5
20.10.02	Permit ratification of Nice Treaty (26th amdt; 29)	62.9	37.1	48.5	0.4
11.6.04	Permit citizenship change (27th amdt; 9)	79.2	20.8	59.9	1.1

Sources: Referendums in Ireland 1937–1999 (Dublin: Stationery Office, 2000) and information supplied by the Department of the Environment.

Notes
Amendment numbers in italics refer to constitutional amendment bills rejected at a referendum. The first amendment bill (state of emergency, affecting Article 28) and the second amendment bill (emergency provisions and various matters, affecting Articles 11–15, 18, 20, 24–8, 34, 40, 47 and 56) were passed by the Oireachtas without a referendum in 1939 and 1941 respectively (see Chapter 3). The 22nd amendment bill (dealing with impeachment of judges) lapsed in the Dáil (see p. 89 above).

2i Opinion poll support for parties by social group, 1969–2002

Party	Year	All	Middle class	Working class	Large farmers	Small farmers
Fianna Fáil	1969	43	45	42	38	53
	1977	49	46	50	48	48
	1981	44	39	43	42	53
	1985	42	37	45	41	46
	1989	38	35	38	39	47
	1993	36	35	34	40	44
	1997	36	32	37	40	40
	2002	47	47	47	41	61
Fine Gael	1969	25	28	16	46	26
	1977	28	30	21	42	38
	1981	32	41	28	43	32
	1985	28	37	21	38	23
	1989	23	25	17	43	21
	1993	16	14	15	29	15
	1997	23	22	19	36	35
	2002	18	18	15	42	17
Labour Party	1969	18	14	28	2	5
	1977	9	7	15	1	5
	1981	10	4	14	1	4
	1985	5	6	5	0	2
	1989	6	5	9	3	2
	1993	15	16	18	3	8
	1997	9	9	12	1	7
	2002	10	10	11	2	5

Notes
The figures relate to the percentage of each occupational group that expressed an intention to vote for the party in question. The occupational groups are defined as follows: middle class, ABC1 (professional, managerial and clerical); working class, C2DE (skilled and unskilled manual workers); large farmers, F1 (farmers with 50 acres or more, except in 1969, when the cutoff was 30 acres); small farmers, F2 (farmers with less than 50 acres, except in 1969, when the cutoff was 30 acres). Poll dates were April 1969 (Gallup), May–June 1977 (IMS), May 1981 (IMS), February 1985 (MRBI), June 1989 (MRBI), July 1993 (MRBI), 28 May 1997 (MRBI) and February 2002 (TNS-MRBI). Percentages for a given occupational group will not necessarily total 100 across parties due to the omission of supporters of other parties or of none. Comparable data are not available for 1973–4.

Appendix 3 Political office-holders

3a Heads of state, 1922–2004

Dates of office	Name
	King
6.12.22–20.1.36	George V
20.1.36–11.12.36	Edward VIII
11.12.36–18.4.49	George VI
	Governor-General
6.12.22–1.2.28	Timothy Healy
1.2.28–1.11.32	James MacNeill
26.11.32–12.12.36	Dónal Ó Buachalla
	President
25.6.38–25.6.45	Douglas Hyde
25.6.45–25.6.59	Seán T. Ó Ceallaigh
25.6.59–25.6.73	Eamon de Valera
25.6.73–17.11.74	Erskine Childers
19.12.74–22.10.76	Cearbhall Ó Dálaigh
3.12.76–3.12.90	Patrick Hillery
3.12.90–12.9.97	Mary Robinson
11.11.97–	Mary McAleese

Note
The King continued to represent the state in external affairs until 1949. The President's role was exclusively domestic until then. The President's functions were filled by the Presidential Commission (the Chief Justice, the Ceann Comhairle and the Cathaoirleach of the Seanad) during those periods when the office was vacant.

3b Heads and deputy heads of government, 1922–2004

Date	Head of government	Deputy head of government
	President of the Executive Council	*Vice President of the Executive Council*
6.12.22	William T. Cosgrave	Kevin O'Higgins
		Ernest Blythe (10.7.27)
9.3.32	Eamon de Valera	Seán T. Ó Ceallaigh
	Taoiseach	*Tánaiste*
29.12.37	Eamon de Valera	Seán T. Ó Ceallaigh
		Seán Lemass (14.6.45)
18.2.48	John A. Costello	William Norton
13.6.51	Eamon de Valera	Seán Lemass
2.6.54	John A. Costello	William Norton
20.3.57	Eamon de Valera	Seán Lemass
23.6.59	Seán Lemass	Seán MacEntee
		Frank Aiken (21.4.65)
10.11.66	Jack Lynch	Frank Aiken
		Erskine Childers (2.7.69)
14.3.73	Liam Cosgrave	Brendan Corish
5.7.77	Jack Lynch	George Colley
11.12.79	Charles Haughey	George Colley
20.6.81	Garret FitzGerald	Michael O'Leary
9.3.82	Charles Haughey	Ray MacSharry
14.12.82	Garret FitzGerald	Dick Spring
		Peter Barry (20.1.87)
10.3.87	Charles Haughey	Brian Lenihan
		John Wilson (13.11.90)
11.2.92	Albert Reynolds	John Wilson
		Dick Spring (12.1.93)
15.12.94	John Bruton	Dick Spring
26.6.97	Bertie Ahern	Mary Harney

3c Composition of governments, 1922–2004

Date	Government	Initial composition					Dáil support
		Fianna Fáil	Fine Gael	Labour	Other	Total	
14.1.22	Collins	–	8	–	–	8	*49.0*
22.8.22	Cosgrave 1	–	9	–	–	9	*49.0*
9.9.22	Cosgrave 2	–	11	–	–	11	45.3
6.12.22	Cosgrave 3	–	10	–	–	10	45.3
19.9.23	Cosgrave 4	–	11	–	–	11	41.2
23.6.27	Cosgrave 5	–	10	–	–	10	30.7
11.10.27	Cosgrave 6	–	9	–	–	9	40.5
2.4.30	Cosgrave 7	–	9	–	–	9	40.5
9.3.32	de Valera 1	10	–	–	–	10	47.1
8.2.33	de Valera 2	10	–	–	–	10	50.3
21.7.37	de Valera 3	10	–	–	–	10	50.0
30.6.38	de Valera 4	10	–	–	–	10	55.8
1.7.43	de Valera 5	11	–	–	–	11	48.5
9.6.44	de Valera 6	11	–	–	–	11	55.1
18.2.48	Costello 1	–	6	2	5	13	45.6
13.6.51	de Valera 7	12	–	–	–	12	46.9
2.6.54	Costello 2	–	8	4	1	13	50.3
20.3.57	de Valera 8	12	–	–	–	12	53.1
23.6.59	Lemass 1	13	–	–	–	13	53.1
11.10.61	Lemass 2	14	–	–	–	14	48.6
21.4.65	Lemass 3	14	–	–	–	14	50.0
10.11.66	Lynch 1	14	–	–	–	14	50.0
2.7.69	Lynch 2	14	–	–	–	14	52.1
14.3.73	Cosgrave	–	10	5	–	15	50.7
5.7.77	Lynch 3	15	–	–	–	15	56.8
12.12.79	Haughey 1	15	–	–	–	15	56.8
30.6.81	FitzGerald 1	–	11	4	–	15	48.2
9.3.82	Haughey 2	15	–	–	–	15	48.8
14.12.82	FitzGerald 2	–	11	4	–	15	51.8
10.3.87	Haughey 3	15	–	–	–	15	48.8
12.7.89	Haughey 4	13	–	–	2	15	50.0
11.2.92	Reynolds 1	13	–	–	2	15	50.0
12.1.93	Reynolds 2	9	–	6	–	15	60.8
15.12.94	Bruton	–	8	6	1	15	50.6
26.6.97	Ahern 1	14	–	–	1	15	48.8
6.6.02	Ahern 2	13	–	–	2	15	53.6

Notes

The first three governments were provisional governments. 'Fine Gael' includes also the Pro-Treaty party or Cumann na nGaedheal (1922–33). 'Others' include two Clann na Poblachta, one Clann na Talmhan, one National Labour and one independent in 1948, one Clann na Talmhan in 1954, two Progressive Democrats in 1989, 1992 and 2002 and one in 1997, and one Democratic Left in 1994. 'Dáil support' refers to Dáil seats held by parties participating in government as percentage of total Dáil membership immediately after the formation of the government; independent deputies committed to supporting the government are not included (even though one of these was actually a member of the government in 1948); the first two figures in this column are estimates.

3d Ceann Comhairle of Dáil and Cathaoirleach of Seanad, 1922–2004

Date	*Ceann Comhairle*	*Date*	*Cathaoirleach*
9.9.22	Michael Hayes (CnG)	12.12.22	Lord Glenavy (Ind)
9.3.32	Frank Fahy (FF)	12.12.28	Thomas Westropp Bennett (CnG)
		27.4.38	Seán Gibbons (FF)
		8.9.43	Seán Goulding (FF)
		21.4.48	T. J. O'Donovan (FG)
13.6.51	Patrick Hogan (Lab)	14.8.51	Liam Ó Buachalla (FF)
		22.7.54	Patrick Baxter (FG)
		22.5.57	Liam Ó Buachalla (FF)
7.11.67	Cormac Breslin (FF)	5.11.69	Michael Yeats (FF)
		3.1.73	Mícheál Cranitch (FF)
14.3.73	Seán Treacy (Lab)	1.6.73	James Dooge (FG)
5.7.77	Joseph Brennan (FF)	27.10.77	Séamus Dolan (FF)
16.10.80	Pádraig Faulkner (FF)	8.10.81	Charlie McDonald (FG)
30.6.81	John O'Connell (Ind)	13.5.82	Tras Honan (FF)
14.12.82	Tom Fitzpatrick (FG)	23.2.83	Pat Joe Reynolds (FG)
10.3.87	Seán Treacy (Ind)	25.4.87	Tras Honan (FF)
		1.11.89	Seán Doherty (FF)
		23.1.92	Seán Fallon (FF)
		12.7.95	Liam Naughten (FG)
		27.11.96	Liam T. Cosgrave (FG)
26.6.97	Séamus Pattison (Lab)	17.9.97	Brian Mullooly (FF)
6.6.02	Rory O'Hanlon (FF)	12.9.02	Rory Kiely (FF)

3e Leaders of political parties, 1922–2004

Fianna Fáil	*Fine Gael*	*Labour Party*
Eamon de Valera (1926–59)	Eoin O'Duffy (1933–4)	Thomas Johnson (1918–27)
Seán Lemass (1959–66)	William T. Cosgrave (1935–44)	T. J. O'Connell (1927–32)
Jack Lynch (1966–79)		William Norton (1932–60)
Charles Haughey (1979–92)	Richard Mulcahy (1944–59)	Brendan Corish (1960–77)
Albert Reynolds (1992–4)		Frank Cluskey (1977–81)
Bertie Ahern (1994–)	James Dillon (1959–65)	Michael O'Leary (1981–2)
	Liam Cosgrave (1965–77)	Dick Spring (1982–97)
	Garret FitzGerald (1977–87)	Ruairí Quinn (1997–2002)
	Alan Dukes (1987–90)	Pat Rabbitte (2002–)
	John Bruton (1990–2001)	
	Michael Noonan (2001–2)	
	Enda Kenny (2002–)	

Progressive Democrats	*Cumann na nGaedheal*
Desmond O'Malley (1985–93)	William T. Cosgrave (1922–33)
Mary Harney (1993–)	

Appendix 4 Government departments, 1924–2004

The organisation of Irish government departments was laid out by the Ministers and Secretaries Act (No. 16 of 1924), and modified by subsequent legislation. The Ministers and Secretaries (Amendment) Act (No. 36 of 1939) authorised the government to alter the name of any department, or to transfer functions between departments. By the end of 2002, 181 orders of this kind had been made, and other orders and legislation also had effect in this area. The following is a list of departments as they have existed since 1924 (with current names in bold, and departments that have disappeared in italics). It should be noted that functions may have been transferred between departments without name changes, and that in some cases 'shells' of departments that remained after the loss of all staff and functions were later given entirely new identities.

1 Department of the President of the Executive Council
Established by the Ministers and Secretaries Act, 1924; renamed **Department of the Taoiseach**, 1937, following adoption of new constitution.

2 Department of Finance
Established by the Ministers and Secretaries Act, 1924.

3 Department of Justice
Established by the Ministers and Secretaries Act, 1924; renamed **Department of Justice, Equality and Law Reform**, 1997.

4 Department of Local Government and Public Health
Established by the Ministers and Secretaries Act, 1924; renamed Department of Local Government, 1947 on loss of functions to new Department of Health and Department of Social Welfare; renamed Department of the Environment, 1977; renamed Department of the Environment and Local Government, 1997; renamed **Department of Environment, Heritage and Local Government**, 2003.

5 Department of Education
Established by the Ministers and Secretaries Act, 1924; renamed **Department of Education and Science**, 1997.

6 Department of Lands and Agriculture
Established by the Ministers and Secretaries Act, 1924; renamed Department of Agriculture in 1928 on transfer of Land Commission to Department of Fisheries; renamed Department of Agriculture and Fisheries, 1965; renamed Department of Agriculture, 1977; renamed Department of Agriculture and Food, 1987; renamed Department of Agriculture, Food and Forestry, 1993; renamed Department of Agriculture and Food, 1997; renamed Department of Agriculture, Food and Rural Development, 1999; renamed **Department of Agriculture and Food**, 2002.

7 Department of Industry and Commerce
Established by the Ministers and Secretaries Act, 1924; renamed Department of Industry, Commerce and Energy, 1977; renamed Department of Industry, Commerce and Tourism, 1980; renamed Department of Trade, Commerce and Tourism, 1981; renamed Department of Industry, Trade, Commerce and Tourism, 1983; renamed Department of Industry and Commerce, 1986; renamed Department of Enterprise and Employment, 1993; renamed **Department of Enterprise, Trade and Employment**, 1997.

8 Department of Fisheries
Established by the Ministers and Secretaries Act, 1924; renamed Department of Lands and Fisheries, 1928, on transfer of Land Commission from Department of Lands and Agriculture; renamed Department of Lands in 1934; renamed Department of Fisheries, 1977; renamed Department of Fisheries and Forestry, 1978; renamed Department of Tourism, Fisheries and Forestry, 1986; renamed Department of the Marine, 1987; renamed Department of the Marine and Natural Resources, 1997; renamed **Department of Communications, Marine and Natural Resources**, 2002.

9 Department of Posts and Telegraphs
Established by the Ministers and Secretaries Act, 1924; abolished by the Ministers and Secretaries (Amendment) Act, 1983.

10 Department of Defence
Established by the Ministers and Secretaries Act, 1924.

11 Department of External Affairs
Established by the Ministers and Secretaries Act, 1924; renamed **Department of Foreign Affairs**, 1971.

12 Department of Supplies
Established by the Ministers and Secretaries (Amendment) Act, 1939; abolished in 1945 and functions transferred to Department of Industry and Commerce by the Minister for Supplies (Transfer of Functions) Act, 1945.

13 Department of Health
Established by the Ministers and Secretaries (Amendment) Act, 1946; renamed **Department of Health and Children**, 1997.

14 Department of Social Welfare
Established by the Ministers and Secretaries (Amendment) Act, 1946; renamed Department of Social, Community and Family Affairs, 1997; renamed **Department of Social and Family Affairs**, 2002.

15 Department of the Gaeltacht
Established by the Ministers and Secretaries (Amendment) Act, 1956; renamed Department of Arts, Culture and the Gaeltacht, 1993; renamed Department of Arts, Heritage, Gaeltacht and the Islands, 1997; renamed **Department of Community, Rural and Gaeltacht Affairs**, 2002.

16 Department of Transport and Power
*Established by the Ministers and Secretaries (Amendment) Act, 1959; renamed **Department of Tourism and Transport**, 1977; renamed **Department of Transport**, 1980; abolished by the Ministers and Secretaries (Amendment) Act, 1983.*

17 Department of Labour
Established by the Ministers and Secretaries (Amendment) Act, 1966; renamed Department of Equality and Law Reform, 1993; functions transferred to Department of Justice, Equality and Law Reform in 1997 (this department still exists in theory as a 'shell' without any staff or functions).

18 Department of the Public Service
Established by the Ministers and Secretaries (Amendment) Act, 1973; functions transferred to Department of Finance, 1987; renamed Department of Tourism and Transport, 1987; renamed Department of Communications, 1991; renamed Depart-

ment of Tourism, Transport and Communications; renamed Department of Transport, Energy and Communications, 1993; renamed Department of Public Enterprise, 1997; renamed **Department of Transport**, 2002.

19 Department of Economic Planning

Established by the Ministers and Secretaries (Amendment) Act, 1977; functions transferred to Department of Finance, 1980; renamed Department of Energy, 1980; renamed Department of Industry and Energy, 1981; renamed Department of Energy, 1983; renamed Department of Tourism and Trade, 1993; renamed Department of Tourism, Sport and Recreation, 1997; renamed **Department of Arts, Sport and Tourism**, 2002.

20 Department of Communications

Established by the Ministers and Secretaries (Amendment) Act, 1983; functions transferred to Department of Marine and Department of Tourism and Transport, 1987 (this department still exists in theory as a 'shell' without any staff or functions).

Appendix 5 Biographical notes on major political figures

The following notes give basic information on all those who have held the post of Governor-General, President, President of the Executive Council, Taoiseach, Vice President of the Executive Council or Tánaiste. For further information on most of these, see Louis McRedmond (ed.), *Modern Irish Lives: Dictionary of 20th-Century Biography* (Dublin: Gill and Macmillan, 1996), Henry Boylan, *A Dictionary of Irish Biography*, 2nd edn (Dublin: Gill and Macmillan, 1988), Ted Nealon's *Guides* to the Dáil and Seanad, various years, and *Who's Who, What's What and Where in Ireland* (London: Geoffrey Chapman, in association with the *Irish Times*, 1973).

Ahern, Bertie. Born Dublin, 12 September 1951; educated Christian Brothers, Whitehall, Dublin, and College of Commerce, Rathmines; worked as an accountant; Fianna Fáil TD since 1977; leader of Fianna Fáil since 1994; minister of state, 1982; government minister, 1987–94; Taoiseach since 1997. A very popular deputy and committed constituency worker, he also developed an outstanding reputation as a negotiator and compromise broker; although he has also been accused of vacillation and indecisiveness, his skills and commitment were displayed particularly impressively during the negotiation of the Good Friday Agreement of 1998 and of the EU constitution in 2004.

Aiken, Frank. Born Camlough, Co. Armagh, 13 February 1898; educated Christian Brothers, Newry; worked as a farmer; active in Gaelic League and in Irish Volunteers; leading figure in IRA during war of independence and civil war; anti-Treaty Sinn Féin and Fianna Fáil TD, 1923–73; government minister, 1932–48, 1951–4 and 1957–69; Tánaiste, 1959–69; died 18 May 1983. One of the last IRA divisional commanders to take sides in the civil war, was associated with the pursuit of neutrality also in international affairs; as Minister for External Affairs, guided Ireland along an independent line in the United Nations.

Barry, Peter. Born Cork, 6 August 1928; educated Christian Brothers, Cork; worked as a tea importer and wholesaler; Fine Gael TD, 1969–97; government minister, 1973–7, 1981–2 and 1982–7; Tánaiste, 1987. A popular and respected elder statesman in Fine Gael, built up a positive image as foreign minister; nevertheless, did not succeed to the party leadership in a 1987 contest where youth appeared to take precedence over experience; Tánaiste only for a few weeks after the collapse of the Fine Gael–Labour coalition in 1987.

Blythe, Ernest. Born Lisburn, Co. Antrim, 13 April 1889; educated locally; worked as a clerk in the Department of Agriculture; active in the Gaelic League, IRB and Irish Volunteers; Sinn Féin MP/TD, 1918–22; pro-Treaty Sinn Féin and Cumann na nGaedheal TD, 1922–33; lost his seat, 1933; minister in Dáil government, 1919–22; government minister, 1922–32; Vice President of the Executive Council, 1927–32; died 23 February 1975. A northern Protestant, was strongly associated with the Irish language movement and with Irish cultural activities, going on after his retirement from politics to become managing director of the Abbey Theatre; as Minister for Finance, won notoriety for reducing the old age pension from ten to nine shillings (from 63 cent to 57 cent!).

Bruton, John. Born Dublin, 8 May 1947; educated St Dominic's College, Dublin, Clongowes Wood College, Co. Kildare, University College Dublin, and King's Inns; qualified as a barrister; Fine Gael TD since 1969; leader of Fine Gael, 1990–2001; parliamentary secretary, 1973–7; government minister, 1981–2 and 1982–7;

Taoiseach, 1994–7. Noted as a sincere, hard-working politician with an abiding interest in parliamentary reform; his distinctive perspective on Northern Ireland politics placed him close to the unionist position, and made him an object of some suspicion to nationalists; his political skills were challenged when his first budget was defeated in the Dáil in 1982, precipitating a general election; showed considerable flexibility and skill in heading a 'rainbow coalition' that took over following the collapse of the Reynolds government in 1994; ousted as party leader, 2001.

Childers, Erskine. Born London, 11 December 1905; educated Norfolk and Cambridge University; worked in Paris for an American travel organisation; advertising manager, Irish Press; Fianna Fáil TD, 1938–73; government minister 1951–4 and 1957–73; Tánaiste, 1969–73; President of Ireland, 1973–4; died 17 November 1974. Was a son of Robert Erskine Childers (1870–1922), a Clerk in the House of Commons who had Irish connections, became involved in the Irish nationalist movement, took the anti-Treaty side during the civil war and was executed in 1922.

Colley, George. Born Dublin, 18 October 1925; educated Christian Brothers, Dublin, and University College Dublin; worked as a solicitor; Fianna Fáil TD, 1961–83; parliamentary secretary, 1964–5; government minister, 1965–73 and 1977–81; Tánaiste, 1977–81; died 17 September 1983. Contested the leadership of Fianna Fáil against Jack Lynch in 1966 and against his long-time rival and former school classmate, Charles Haughey, in 1979; intensely suspicious of Haughey since the arms crisis of 1970, insisted during Haughey's first government on being given a veto on appointments to the security ministries (Defence and Justice).

Collins, Michael. Born Clonakilty, Co. Cork, 16 October 1890; educated local national school; worked in London as a clerk in the post office and for a firm of stockbrokers; participated in 1916 rising as IRB member; Sinn Féin TD/MP, 1918–22; minister in Dáil government, 1919–22; Chairman of Provisional Government and Commander-in-Chief of the new national army, 1922; killed in an ambush at Béal na mBláth, Co. Cork, by anti-Treaty forces during the civil war on 22 August 1922. Was a charismatic leader during the Anglo-Irish war of 1919–21 and a very effective director of intelligence for the IRA; his influence helped to swing the IRB (of whose Supreme Council he was President) and many members of the IRA into support for the Anglo-Irish Treaty, which he had negotiated as one of the representatives of the Irish side.

Corish, Brendan. Born Wexford, 19 November 1918; educated Christian Brothers, Wexford; worked as a local government official; Labour TD, 1945–82; leader of the Labour Party, 1960–77; parliamentary secretary, 1948–51; government minister, 1954–7; Tánaiste, 1973–7; died 17 February 1990. Though a popular party leader, was relatively unassertive in his later years and allowed strong-willed colleagues considerable latitude when the party was in government, 1973–7.

Cosgrave, Liam. Born Dublin, 13 April 1920; educated Christian Brothers, Castleknock College and King's Inns; called to bar, 1943; Fine Gael TD, 1943–81; leader of Fine Gael, 1965–77; parliamentary secretary, 1948–51; government minister, 1954–7; Taoiseach, 1973–7. A son of William T. Cosgrave; his period as Taoiseach was marked by a strong emphasis on the maintenance of law and order.

Cosgrave, William T. Born Dublin, 6 June 1880; educated Christian Brothers, Dublin; joined the early Sinn Féin movement and the Irish Volunteers and participated in 1916 rising; Sinn Féin MP/TD, 1917–22; pro-Treaty Sinn Féin, Cumann na nGaedheal and Fine Gael TD, 1922–44; leader of Cumann na nGaedheal, 1923–33 and of Fine Gael, 1935–44; minister in Dáil government, 1919–22; President of Executive Council, 1922–32; died 16 November 1965. Despite his background as a revolutionary in 1916, was associated with conservative policies during the first decade of the new state.

Costello, John A. Born Dublin, 20 June 1891; educated University College Dublin; called to bar, 1914; worked in Attorney General's office, 1922–6; Attorney General, 1926–32; Cumann na nGaedheal and Fine Gael TD, 1933–43, 1944–69; head of first and second Inter-Party governments and Taoiseach, 1948–51 and 1954–7; died 5 January 1976. Associated with a striking about-face in Fine Gael when he moved in 1948 to sever Ireland's links with the Commonwealth and declare the state a republic; did not support his Minister for Health, Noel Browne, whose 'Mother and Child' health care proposals in 1950 were strongly opposed by the Catholic Church and led ultimately to the collapse of Costello's first government.

de Valera, Eamon. Born New York city, 14 October 1882; brought up Bruree, Co. Limerick; educated Christian Brothers, Charleville, Blackrock College, Dublin, and Royal University; teacher of mathematics; involved in early Gaelic League and Irish Volunteers and participated in 1916 rising; senior surviving commandant of rising; leader of Sinn Féin, 1917–22, of anti-Treaty Sinn Féin, 1922–6 and of Fianna Fáil, which he founded, 1926–59; Sinn Féin TD/MP, 1917–22; anti-Treaty Sinn Féin and Fianna Fáil TD, 1922–59; President of Dáil government, 1919–22, President of Executive Council, 1932–7, Taoiseach, 1937–48, 1951–4 and 1957–9; President of Ireland, 1959–73; died 29 August 1975. An enigmatic figure who played a leading role in Irish politics from 1916 to 1973, and a controversial one at certain times, such as 1921–3 and 1926–7; was largely responsible for leading the bulk of the anti-Treaty side into operating within a constitutional framework in the 1920s; though committed to Irish unity and the Irish language, made little progress on the former and saw the latter weaken further; was more successful in the area of foreign relations, where he succeeded in greatly enhancing the state's independence.

FitzGerald, Garret. Born Dublin, 9 February 1926; educated Belvedere College, University College Dublin and King's Inns; worked as a research and schedules manager in Aer Lingus and later as lecturer in Political Economy, University College, Dublin; Fine Gael senator, 1965–9 and TD, 1969–92; leader of Fine Gael, 1977–87; government minister, 1973–7; Taoiseach, 1981–2 and 1982–7. Led his party to its largest ever share of electoral support in 1982; his liberal agenda was undermined by conservative outcomes in referendums on abortion (1983) and divorce (1986), but his Northern Ireland policy was significantly advanced by the signing of the Anglo-Irish Agreement (1985).

Griffith, Arthur. Born Dublin, 31 March 1871; educated Christian Brothers, Dublin; worked as a printer and then as a journalist; editor of a number of nationalist periodicals and pamphlets; founder of Sinn Féin party and member of Irish Volunteers, but did not participate in 1916 rising; Sinn Féin MP/TD, 1918–22; minister in Dáil government, 1919–22; President of Dáil government, 1922; died 12 August 1922. Was responsible for popularising the Sinn Féin policy of economic self-reliance after 1905; this also envisaged following the Hungarian model of 1867, by which an independent Irish state would be established as part of a dual monarchy, linked to Britain only by the crown.

Harney, Mary. Born Ballinasloe, Co. Galway, 11 March 1953; educated Convent of Mercy, Goldenbridge, Dublin, Coláiste Bhríde, Dublin, and Trinity College, Dublin;

employed as research worker; Fianna Fáil senator, 1977–81; Fianna Fáil TD, 1981–5; Progressive Democrat TD since 1985; leader of the Progressive Democrats since 1993; minister of state, 1989–92; Tánaiste since 1997. The youngest ever member of the Seanad, the first woman leader of a political party and the first woman Tánaiste, she has fought hard to maintain the identity of the Progressive Democrats (of which she was a founding member) in unfavourable circumstances.

Haughey, Charles J. Born Castlebar, Co. Mayo, 16 September 1925; educated Christian Brothers, Dublin, University College Dublin, and King's Inns; worked as an accountant; Fianna Fáil TD, 1957–92; leader of Fianna Fáil, 1979–92; parliamentary secretary, 1960–1; government minister, 1961–70 and 1977–9; Taoiseach, 1979–81, 1982 and 1987–92. A son-in-law of Seán Lemass; was dismissed as Minister for Finance by Jack Lynch in 1970 in the course of the 'Arms Crisis', but was acquitted in court of all charges; fought his way back to emerge as party leader in 1979 with the support of the party's backbenchers; led his party into its first ever coalition government in 1989; following his retirement his financial affairs were subjected to rigorous examination by tribunals established to enquire into allegations of irregularities during his time as Taoiseach.

Healy, Timothy. Born Bantry, Co. Cork, 17 May 1855; educated local Christian Brothers; worked in England as a railway clerk and later as a nationalist journalist; Nationalist MP, 1880–6, 1887–1910 and 1911–18 (anti-Parnellite, 1890–1900, then an independent Nationalist); Governor-General, 1922–8; died 26 March 1931. Noted as a lively and witty debater, but divisive as a political figure.

Hillery, Patrick. Born Miltown Malbay, Co. Clare, 2 May 1923; educated Rockwell College and University College, Dublin; practised as a medical doctor; Fianna Fáil TD, 1951–72; government minister, 1959–72; Irish member of EC Commission, 1973–6; President of Ireland, 1976–90, a post for which he was an unopposed nominee. As Minister for External Affairs, was responsible for handling Irish foreign policy in the difficult period coinciding with the outbreak of the Northern Ireland troubles and with the negotiation of EC membership.

Hyde, Douglas. Born Castlerea, Co. Roscommon, 17 January 1860; educated Trinity College, Dublin; collector of Irish folklore, of which he published many volumes; professor of Modern Irish, University College Dublin; founder member of Gaelic League, of which he was first president (1893–1915); maintained a non-political role, and resigned as president of the League when it began to follow a more political path; independent member in Senate of Irish Free State, 1925, but failed to secure election in 1925 Senate general election; senator (Taoiseach's nominee), 1938; President of Ireland, 1938–45, a post for which he was an all-party choice; died 12 July 1949. Son of a Protestant rector in Co. Roscommon, was much loved by language revivalists for his work for their movement, and was the author of the first play in Irish ever to appear on a professional stage (1901).

Lemass, Seán. Born Dublin, 15 July 1899; educated Christian Brothers; worked in his father's drapery shop; joined Irish Volunteers and participated in 1916 rising; active in IRA, 1919–23; anti-Treaty Sinn Féin and Fianna Fáil TD, 1924–69; government minister, 1932–48, 1951–4 and 1957–9; Tánaiste, 1945–8, 1951–4 and 1957–9; Taoiseach, 1959–66; died 11 May 1971. Associated with the shift in Fianna Fáil, of which he was a founder member, from traditional nationalist policies to support for rapid economic development, especially in the 1960s, and with normalisation of relations with Britain and Northern Ireland.

Lenihan, Brian. Born Dundalk, Co. Louth, 17 November 1930; educated Marist Brothers, Athlone, University College Dublin and King's Inns; worked as a barrister; Fianna Fáil TD, 1961–73 and 1977–95; lost his seat, 1973; Fianna Fáil senator, 1973–7; parliamentary secretary, 1961–4; government minister, 1964–73, 1977–81, 1982 and 1987–90; Tánaiste, 1987–90; died 1 November 1995. An enormously popular politician, was a casualty of an incident during the 1990 presidential election campaign in which he appeared to be giving contradictory versions of an event in 1982 involving an alleged attempt to bring undue pressure to bear on the President; though he sought to explain the incident away in terms of his medical condition (he was seriously ill at the time and under heavy medication), it is believed to have cost him the presidency and it brought about his dismissal as Tánaiste.

Lynch, John (Jack). Born Cork, 15 August 1917; educated Christian Brothers, Cork, University College Cork, King's Inns; worked in civil service and later as a barrister; Fianna Fáil TD, 1948–81; parliamentary secretary, 1951–4; government minister, 1957–66; Taoiseach, 1966–73 and 1977–9; died 20 October 1999. His sporting background (in Gaelic football and hurling) and personable character won him immense popularity; his qualities as a leader were severely tested in the early years of the Northern Ireland troubles (1969–70), as his party sought to come to terms with the state's impotence in the face of attacks on nationalists in the North; in 1977, led his party to its greatest ever size in the Dáil and largest share of the vote since 1938, but ironically was forced to step down as leader two years later.

McAleese, Mary. Born Belfast, 27 June 1951, as **Mary Leneghan**; educated Falls Rd convent secondary school, Belfast, and Queen's University, Belfast; Reid Professor of Law at Trinity College, Dublin, 1974–9 and 1981–7; journalist and television presenter, 1979–81; Director, Institute of Professional and Legal Studies, Queen's University, Belfast, 1987–97, and Pro Vice-Chancellor, Queen's University, Belfast, 1994–7; President of Ireland since 1997. Though associated with Fianna Fáil, was seen as an outsider within the party; during her election campaign her Northern origins and links were used against her, apparently counter-productively; despite a lukewarm relationship with the media at the beginning of her presidency, her popularity improved following a number of very successful visits abroad.

MacEntee, Seán. Born Belfast, 22 August 1889; educated St Malachy's College, Belfast, and Belfast Municipal College of Technology; worked as a consulting electrical engineer and registered patent agent; active in Irish Volunteers; participated in 1916 rising, sentenced to death but reprieved; active in IRA; Sinn Féin MP/TD, 1918–22; Fianna Fáil TD, 1927–69; government minister, 1932–48, 1951–4, 1957–65; Tánaiste, 1959–65; died 10 January 1984. Noted as a poet in his early life, later devoted himself fully to politics.

MacNeill, James. Born Glenarm, Co. Antrim, 27 or 29 March 1869; educated Belvedere College, Dublin, and Cambridge University; worked in Indian civil service; on early retirement joined Sinn Féin; Irish high commissioner in London, 1923–8; Governor-General, 1928–32; died 12 December 1938. Though with a less political past than his elder brother, Eoin (Professor of History at University College Dublin, leader of the Irish Volunteers and government minister, 1922–5), became fully immersed in political conflict in 1932 following the change of government; de Valera forced his resignation as Governor-General within a few months.

MacSharry, Ray. Born Sligo, 29 April 1938; educated locally and Summerhill College, Sligo; worked as a haulier, auctioneer and farm owner; Fianna Fáil TD,

1969–89; minister of state, 1977–79; government minister, 1979–81, 1982, 1987–89; Tánaiste, 1982. Rated very highly as minister for finance; went on to become an extremely successful EC commissioner for agriculture, a position from which he retired in 1992.

Norton, William. Born Dublin, 1900; educated locally; worked in the post office and as a trade union official; Labour TD, 1926–7 and 1932–63; lost his seat, 1927; leader of the Labour Party, 1932–60; Tánaiste, 1948–51 and 1954–7; died 4 December 1963. Though he built up the support base of his party until 1943 and led it into government for the first time ever in 1948, in his later years was more preoccupied with trade union affairs and with his own constituency than with the leadership of the party.

Ó Buachalla, Dónal (also known by the English form of his name, **Daniel Buckley**). Born Maynooth, Co. Kildare, 3 February 1866; educated Belvedere College and Catholic University School, Dublin; owner of a shop in Maynooth; member of the Gaelic League and IRB; participated in 1916 rising; Sinn Féin MP/ TD 1918–22; Fianna Fáil TD, 1927–32 (lost his seat in 1922 and again in 1932); Governor-General, 1932–6; died 31 October 1963. Achieved early prominence when prosecuted for painting his name in Irish on his cart; as Governor-General avoided meeting the King, never left the state and resided in a house in Dun Laoghaire rather than in the Viceregal Lodge in the Phoenix Park.

Ó Ceallaigh, Seán T. (also known by the English form of his name, **Seán T. O'Kelly**). Born Dublin, 25 August 1882; educated Christian Brothers; active in Gaelic League, Celtic Literary Society, IRB and Sinn Féin; participated in 1916 rising; Sinn Féin MP/TD, 1918–22; anti-Treaty Sinn Féin and Fianna Fáil TD, 1922–45; Ceann Comhairle of first Dáil; government minister, 1932–45; Vice President of Executive Council, 1932–7; Tánaiste, 1937–45; President of Ireland, 1945–59; died 23 November 1966. Though personally popular, was in effect 'pushed upstairs' to the presidency in 1945, making way for Seán Lemass, 17 years his junior, to take over as Tánaiste and heir apparent to de Valera.

Ó Dálaigh, Cearbhall. Born Bray, Co. Wicklow, 12 February 1911; educated Christian Brothers and University College Dublin; called to bar, 1944; active in Fianna Fáil; Attorney General 1946–8 and 1951–3; Supreme Court judge, 1953; Chief Justice, 1961; Irish member of European Court of Justice, 1972; President of Ireland, 1974–6, a post for which he was an unopposed nominee; died 21 March 1978. A lover of the Irish language; his resignation from the presidency was precipitated by a chain of events that began when the Minister for Defence, speaking at a military function, described him as 'a thundering disgrace' for referring an Emergency Powers Bill to the Supreme Court to test its constitutionality.

O'Higgins, Kevin. Born Stradbally, Co. Laois, 7 June 1892; educated Clongowes Wood and University College Dublin; early member of Sinn Féin; Sinn Féin MP/ TD, 1918–22; pro-Treaty Sinn Féin and Cumann na nGaedheal TD, 1922–7; government minister, 1922–7; Vice President of the Executive Council, 1923–7; assassinated on 10 July 1927 while walking to mass by a group of anti-Treaty IRA members of the 1922–3 period who came upon him by accident. As Minister for Home Affairs during the civil war, was associated with the strong measures taken by the government to ensure victory, including the execution of 77 of the anti-Treaty side.

O'Leary, Michael. Born Cork, 8 May 1936; educated Presentation College, Cork and University College Cork; worked as a trade union official; Labour TD, 1965–82; Fine Gael TD, 1982–7; leader of the Labour Party, 1981–2; government minister, 1973–7 and 1981–2; Tánaiste, 1981–2. Associated with his party's move to the left in the late 1960s and initially an opponent of coalition, his switch of allegiance to Fine Gael in 1982 was one of the more spectacular somersaults in Irish politics.

Reynolds, Albert. Born Rooskey, Co. Roscommon, 3 November 1932; educated Summerhill College, Sligo; worked as director of his own petfood company; Fianna Fáil TD, 1977–2002; government minister, 1979–81, 1982 and 1987–92; Taoiseach, 1992–4. Though regarded as one of the more conservative members of his party, negotiated a coalition agreement with Labour following his defeat in the 1992 general election; noted as a risk-taker, he played a crucial role in paving the way for the Good Friday Agreement, 1998, by facilitating Sinn Féin's entry into negotiations.

Robinson, Mary. Born Ballina, Co. Mayo, 21 May 1944, as **Mary Bourke**; educated Mount Anville, Paris, Trinity College, Dublin, and Harvard University; Reid Professor of Constitutional and Criminal Law, Trinity College, Dublin; independent senator, 1969–76 and 1985–9; Labour party senator, 1976–85; President of Ireland, 1990–7. Resigned the Labour whip in 1985 over the party's support for the Anglo-Irish Agreement, but was nominated and supported by Labour in her successful presidential election campaign in 1990; an extremely popular and assertive President, she played a subtle but significant political role; she resigned shortly before the expiry of her term of office to assume the position of United Nations High Commissioner for Human Rights, a post she held until 2002.

Spring, Dick. Born Tralee, Co. Kerry, 29 August 1950; educated Christian Brothers, Tralee, St Joseph's, Roscrea, Trinity College, Dublin and King's Inns; worked as a barrister; Labour TD, 1981–2002; leader of the Labour Party since 1982; Tánaiste, 1982–7 and 1993–7. Enjoying an enormously high rating with the voters as leader of his party, his victory in 1992 placed him in a much stronger position than any previous Labour leader in hammering out a coalition deal and in giving Labour a more powerful position in cabinet than ever previously; resigned following the defeat of Adi Roche, the candidate sponsored by his party in the 1997 presidential election.

Wilson, John. Born Kilcogy, Co. Cavan, 8 July 1923; educated St Mel's College, Longford, University of London and University College Dublin; worked as a teacher and university lecturer; Fianna Fáil TD, 1973–92; government minister, 1977–81, 1982 and 1987–92; Tánaiste, 1990–2; headed the southern Victims' Commission after the Good Friday Agreement, 1998–9. One of the more popular elder statesmen within Fianna Fáil, took over as Tánaiste when the politically wounded Brian Lenihan was dismissed during the presidential election campaign; a witty contributor in the Dáil, and a Latin scholar.

Appendix 6 Chronology of main political events

The following lists a selection of the main events in Irish political history. For further information, see *A Chronology of Irish History to 1976: A Companion to Irish History Part 1*, Volume 8 of *A New History of Ireland* (Oxford: Clarendon Press, for the Royal Irish Academy, 1982); J. E. Doherty and D. J. Hickey, *A Chronology of Irish History since 1500* (Dublin: Gill and Macmillan, 1989); Jim O'Donnell (ed.), *Ireland: The Past Twenty Years: An Illustrated Chronology* (Dublin: Institute of Public Administration, 1986); and the annual chronology appearing in *Irish Political Studies*, beginning in Volume 8 (1993).

1169, May	Norman invasion of Ireland begins; most of Ireland subsequently subdued.
1264, 18 June	First Irish parliament meets at Casteldermot, Co. Kildare.
1541, 18 June	King of England declared also to be King of Ireland.
1607, 4 September	'Flight of the earls': Earl of Tyrone (Hugh O'Neill), Earl of Tyrconnell (Rory O'Donnell) and others sail from Co. Donegal for continental Europe, symbolising the end of the Gaelic social and political order and the near completion of the English conquest.
1608, 19 July	Initiation of 'survey' of ownership of six counties of Ulster (followed by the 'plantation' of these counties with English and Scottish settlers).
1641, 22 October	Beginning of rebellion of Catholics (who subsequently organised as the 'Confederation of Kilkenny', but whose rebellion had been largely crushed by Oliver Cromwell by 1650).
1688, 5 November	William of Orange lands in Devon to become King of England (war between William and the deposed James II follows in Ireland, 1689–91, with the Irish defeat at the Siege of Derry, which ended on 31 July 1689, the Battle of the Boyne, 1 July 1690 [12 July, old calendar] and the Treaty of Limerick, 3 October 1691, as its most noted events).
1798, 23 May	Beginning of 'United Irish' rebellion, which was defeated within a few weeks.
1800, 1 August	Act of Union passed; came into effect 1 January 1801.
1845, 9 September	First report of arrival of potato blight, which led to famine in Ireland over the next four years, with deaths reaching a peak in 1847.
1848, 29 July	'Battle of Widow McCormack's cabbage-patch': principal event in short-lived 'rebellion' of the Young Ireland movement.
1858, 17 March	Foundation of Irish Republic Brotherhood (IRB) in Dublin (popularly known as the Fenians, it was the principal republican organisation until 1916, and continued to exist for some years after 1922).
1867, 12 February	Beginning of Fenian rebellion; skirmishes took place over the following month.
1884, 6 December	Representation of the People Act passed; this greatly extended the franchise, permitting the development of mass electoral politics.
1886, 8 April	First Home Rule Bill introduced in parliament; defeated in the House of Commons on 8 June.

1893, 13 February	Second Home Rule Bill introduced in parliament; passed in House of Commons on 2 September, defeated in House of Lords on 9 September.
1905, 28 November	First use of term 'Sinn Féin' by radical nationalists; the Sinn Féin League was formed on 21 April 1907 through an amalgamation of existing organisations.
1912, 11 April	Third Home Rule Bill introduced in parliament; passed in House of Commons on 16 January 1913; defeated in House of Lords on 30 January 1913; passed in House of Commons a third time, thus overriding the Lords' veto, 25 May 1914; implementation suspended.
1913, 31 January	Foundation of Ulster Volunteers.
1913, 25 November	Foundation of Irish Volunteers.
1916, 24 April	'Easter rising' (IRB-led rebellion in Dublin that ended on 29 April).
1918, 14 December	General election, at which Sinn Féin won 73 of the 105 Irish seats, going on to call a meeting of the 'First Dáil' for 21 January 1919.
1919, 21 January	Opening shots in war of independence, which lasted until a truce on 9 July 1921.
1920, 25 February	Government of Ireland Bill introduced in parliament; passed 23 December; House of Commons of Northern Ireland meets, 7 June 1921, giving effect to partition; Act largely ineffective in south.
1921, 6 December	Signing of Anglo-Irish Treaty by representatives of Dáil and of British government; approved by Dáil, 7 January 1922; formal transfer of power to provisional government on 16 January 1922.
1922, 16 June	General election for Dáil; pro-Treaty parties win substantial majority.
1922, 28 June	Provisional government attack on Four Courts marks beginning of civil war, which lasted until 27 April 1923.
1922, 25 October	Constitution of Irish Free State approved by Dáil; approved by British parliament, 5 December 1922; comes into effect 6 December 1922.
1926, 11 March	Split in Sinn Féin at *ard-fheis*; de Valera withdraws; Fianna Fáil founded on 16 May.
1927, 10 July	Assassination of Kevin O'Higgins, Minister for Justice; government responds with a legislative package that has the effect of forcing Fianna Fáil deputies to take their seats in the Dáil on 11 August.
1932, 9 February	Formation of Army Comrades Association; renamed National Guard on 20 July 1933; popularly known as the Blueshirts.
1932, 9 March	Fianna Fáil forms government after becoming largest party in general election.
1933, 2 September	Foundation of United Ireland Party through merger of Cumann na nGaedheal, the National Centre Party and the National Guard; in later years the party became known as Fine Gael.
1936, 29 May	Senate abolished by constitutional amendment.

1936, 11 December	Abdication of Edward VIII; constitutional amendment to remove remaining references to King and Governor-General; King allowed to retain external functions.
1937, 1 July	Referendum approves new constitution; comes into effect 29 December.
1938, 25 April	Anglo-Irish agreements covering 'treaty ports', financial relations and trade.
1948, 4 February	Fianna Fáil loses power in general election; replaced 18 February by 'Inter-Party' government.
1948, 7 September	Taoiseach John A. Costello announces that Ireland is to become a republic; Republic of Ireland Act passed, 21 December; in effect, 18 April 1949.
1958, 11 November	Programme for Economic Expansion published; formed basis for shift from Sinn Féin protectionist policies to more open policy on industrial development and trade.
1965, 14 December	Anglo-Irish free trade agreement signed; in effect, 1 July 1966.
1968, 15 October	Clash between civil rights marchers and police in Derry marks escalation of civil unrest in Northern Ireland.
1970, 11 January	Split in Sinn Féin, with secession of supporters of 'Provisional' IRA (who had seceded from the 'Official' IRA in December 1969).
1970, 6 May	Dismissal of Charles Haughey and Neil Blaney from government in connection with alleged illegal importation of arms for supply to Northern Ireland; resignation of Kevin Boland.
1972, 10 May	Referendum on Ireland's membership of EEC; in effect, 31 December.
1973, 14 March	Coalition government takes office after 16 years of Fianna Fáil rule.
1979, 13 March	Republic joins European monetary system; break in parity of Irish currency with sterling follows.
1983, 30 May	First meeting of New Ireland Forum, representing Fianna Fáil, Fine Gael, Labour and the SDLP; reports on 2 May 1984 endorsing Irish unity as a solution to the Northern Ireland problem.
1985, 15 November	Anglo-Irish Agreement on government of Northern Ireland signed.
1985, 21 December	Foundation of Progressive Democratic Party.
1987, 26 May	Referendum on Single European Act.
1989, 12 July	Fianna Fáil enters coalition government for the first time, with the Progressive Democrats.
1992, 22 February	Resignation of six of the seven Workers' Party TDs; formed party named New Agenda, 3 March; name changed to Democratic Left, 29 March.
1992, 18 June	Referendum on Maastricht Agreement on European unity.
1993, 12 January	Fianna Fáil and Labour Party form coalition government, changing nature of interparty relations in Ireland.
1993, 15 December	Downing Street Declaration by British and Irish prime ministers lays down parameters for a Northern Ireland settlement.
1994, 17 November	Resignation of Albert Reynolds as Taoiseach following withdrawal of Labour from government; 'rainbow' coalition of Fine Gael, Labour and Democratic Left takes office under John Bruton without an election, 15 December.

1998, 10 April   Good Friday Agreement signed in Belfast; approved by referendums North and South, 22 May.

1998, 12 December   Democratic Left agrees to merge with Labour Party; merger in effect, 24 January 1999.

1999, 2 December   Good Friday Agreement comes into effect, with devolution to new Belfast institutions; first meetings of North–South Ministerial Council (13 December) and British–Irish Council (17 December) follow.

2001, 7 June   Electorate rejects Nice treaty; treaty passed in new referendum, 20 October 2002.

Index

Politics in the Republic of Ireland

Politics in the Republic of Ireland is now available in a fully revised fourth edition. Building on the success of the previous three editions, it continues to provide an authoritative introduction to all aspects of politics in the Republic of Ireland. Written by some of the foremost experts on Irish politics, it explains, analyses and interprets the background to Irish government and contemporary political processes. Crucially, it brings the student up to date with the very latest developments.

Ireland enters the twenty-first century as a country of cultural vitality, economic dynamism and rapid social change, and its politics reflects this new air of liveliness. New patterns of government formation, challenges to the established political parties, ever-deepening, if sometimes ambivalent, involvement in the process of European integration, a growing role in the politics of Northern Ireland and sustained discussion of gender issues are among these developments – along with evidence, revealed by several tribunals of enquiry, that Irish politics is not as free of corruption as many had assumed.

Politics in the Republic of Ireland combines real substance with a highly readable style. It is aimed particularly at undergraduates studying Irish politics, but will meet the needs of all those who are interested in knowing how politics and government operate in Ireland.

John Coakley is Associate Professor in the Department of Politics at University College Dublin. He is a vice president of the International Social Science Council and former secretary general of the International Political Science Association. **Michael Gallagher** is Associate Professor in the Department of Political Science at Trinity College, University of Dublin, where he teaches Irish politics and comparative politics. He has also been a visiting professor at New York University and at the City University of Hong Kong.